Dear James _x_

london

Hope this comes in handy.

Come to London and meet more british People! ▽ ▽

Thanks for everything,
Happy 21st Birthday
Love Becky _x_

FODOR'S TRAVEL PUBLICATIONS
NEW YORK • TORONTO • LONDON • SYDNEY • AUCKLAND

WWW.FODORS.COM

Contents

KEY TO SYMBOLS

✚ Map reference
✉ Address
☎ Telephone number
🕐 Opening times
✋ Admission prices
Ⓤ Underground station
🚌 Bus number
🚉 Train station
⛴ Ferry/boat
🚩 Tours
📖 Guidebook
🍴 Restaurant
☕ Café
🏪 Shop
🚻 Toilets
🛏 Number of rooms
🅿 Parking
🚭 No smoking
🏊 Swimming pool
🏋 Gym
EH English Heritage
NT National Trust

UNDERSTANDING LONDON

London is one of the world's most exciting and rewarding cities to visit. Two thousand years have left the capital of the United Kingdom with more than 19,000 buildings officially listed as having special architectural or historic interest. The city has grown largely unplanned, which makes for a piquant unpredictability as the scene and atmosphere change from one corner to the next. With its royal palaces and pageantry, its stylish shops, its theatres, music and art, it is also a dynamic financial and business hub. London is crowded and noisy and can be hard to get about in—and now and again it rains—but it is vigorously alive.

THE GEOGRAPHY

London lies in the southeast of England, some 40 miles (64km) inland from the North Sea, and the rest of Britain has always complained that London and the southeast take up too much attention and too many resources. Greater London is an area of more than 600sq miles (1,550sq km), roughly oval in shape. Inside it is the smaller oval of Inner London, covering about 100sq miles (260sq km), and at the heart of that are the two principal areas from the point of view of both Londoners and visitors—the West End and the City. Both lie on the north side of the River Thames, which winds its way through London from west to east before disappearing towards the North Sea.

WEST AND EAST

When Londoners speak of 'the City', they do not mean London as a whole. They mean the City of London itself, the area of just over 1sq mile (2.5sq km) where London's history began. The City is the financial district, crowded with office workers during the week but almost empty at weekends, with a resident population of only about 7,000. Its principal points of interest for visitors are the Tower of London, St. Paul's Cathedral, the Museum of London and the Barbican cultural complex, and there's some extraordinary post-modern architecture.

Lying either side of the City are the West End, which was always smart, and the East End, which was not. The East End is the world of the docks and working-class London, of cockneys and rhyming slang (see page 7) and Jack the Ripper. It took a battering in World War II and in the last 50 years the area has been substantially rebuilt.

The West End is smart, elegant London, the London of Buckingham Palace, Covent Garden and the National Gallery, Hyde Park, Piccadilly Circus and Trafalgar Square. It is where theatres cluster, along with most of the top shops and restaurants, nightclubs and hotels.

TWO IN ONE

London contains two cities, not one, and the West End is set in the second—the City of Westminster. Its nucleus is the area round Westminster Abbey, Big Ben, the Houses of Parliament and Whitehall, from which a quarter of the world's population was ruled in the days of the British Empire. Also in Westminster are Mayfair, St. James's and Soho, neighbourhoods only vaguely defined geographically, but each with a character of its own.

Mayfair, lying west of Hyde Park, is the smartest and most expensive of all London districts to live in, shop in and eat in. It has the chic Bond Street dress shops, jewellers and art dealers, Park Lane

Camden and Regent's Park In north London, home of the famous Madame Tussaud's and the London Zoo

Chelsea and Belgravia Smart, leafy streets just north of the Thames with the King's Road and Sloane Square for shopping

The City The original settlement, and now the financial heart of the capital with the major attractions of the Tower of London, Tower Bridge and St. Paul's Cathedral

Clerkenwell and Islington On the periphery of the City, heading northward: traditional heartland of radical politics, now very trendy with expensive cafés and craft shops

Docklands A happy blend of old and modern architecture–shops, offices and apartments–stretching downstream from the City

Kensington Well-established and well-heeled swathe west of Hyde Park focused on Kensington Palace and Kensington Gardens

HMS Belfast *and Tower Bridge on the Thames (left). Georgian architecture in Bedford Square (centre). The Houses of Parliament and Big Ben beyond Westminster Bridge (right)*

Knightsbridge High-profile shopping streets south of Hyde Park, with Harrods and Harvey Nichols leading the way

Mayfair Relatively quiet, wealthy residential area just west of Hyde Park, sandwiched between Oxford Street and Piccadilly

Notting Hill and Holland Park Fashionable quarters associated with celebrities, northwest of Hyde Park: home of Portobello Road market and the Notting Hill Carnival

Piccadilly and St. James's Elegant and expensive: right at the heart of the city, encompassing Green Park and St. James's, two royal parks, and Buckingham Palace

Soho and Covent Garden Lively, very central areas northeast of Trafalgar Square packed with individual shops, restaurants and nightlife

South Kensington and Earl's Court Mansion houses and serious museums southwest of central London

South Bank Revamped riverside strip from Westminster to London Bridge, now dominated by the London Eye

Westminster amd Whitehall Seat of government, with key riverside landmarks Westminster Abbey and the Houses of Parliament

and Berkeley Square, Savile Row, Claridge's, the Royal Academy and the Burlington Arcade. Immediately to the south, on the other side of Piccadilly, the St. James's area is known for gentlemen's clubs and gentlemen's tailoring, Fortnum's, the Ritz Hotel and feeding the ducks in St. James's Park.

In contrast Soho, east of Mayfair, is known for its strippers and sex shows and a cosmopolitan mix of restaurants, as well as Liberty department store, Carnaby Street and Chinatown.

STYLE, ART AND INTELLECT

South of Hyde Park, Belgravia is an aristocratic district with street after street of gleaming white neoclassical houses and a showcase of exclusive grandeur in Eaton Square. Knightsbridge, Kensington and Chelsea were country villages until London engulfed them. Today Knightsbridge is best known for Harrods and the smart shops

in Sloane Avenue and Beauchamp Place, on the way to the museum district of South Kensington. Here you will find the Victoria & Albert Museum, the Natural History Museum and the Science Museum.

Kensington is expensive residential territory, known for the Royal Albert Hall, Kensington Gardens and Kensington Palace, where Princess Diana lived. Lying along the river, the pretty streets of Chelsea make another quarter with an artistic and intellectual reputation, spiced with the upmarket boutiques around Sloane Square and the King's Road.

North of Oxford Street, Bloomsbury has a high-brow and arty reputation, partly because of the British Museum, London University and the Slade School of Art, an echo of the Bloomsbury Group of writers and artists, which formed around novelist Virginia Woolf and biographer Lytton Strachey before World War I.

To the east, Holborn (pronounced 'Hoe-bun') has a quirky mixture of lawyers' offices in Lincoln's Inn and Gray's Inn, diamond-dealers in Hatton Garden and Smithfield's meat market. Out to the northeast Hoxton, which was, within living memory, one of London's worst slums, has turned into a trendy Brit Art area with galleries and the hippest London pop music scene.

SOUTH OF THE RIVER

The southern bank of the Thames has been the poor relation of the north bank ever since Roman times, when the borough of Southwark (pronounced 'Suthuck') began to evolve at the wrong

financial centres in the world. It handles almost a third of the entire global foreign exchange market, nearly twice that of Wall Street. Manufacturing, by contrast, is no longer one of London's strengths. Before World War II London's factories made beer and sweets, textiles and furniture, and soon moved on to electronics and pharmaceuticals, but there was a dramatic decline in the 1960s and '70s as business firms found themselves newer premises and a cheaper workforce elsewhere.

The same period saw the collapse of the London docks as, after 1960, ships and containers increased in size beyond their capabilities. The East India Dock was closed in 1967 and the

Hampstead, north London. The Lloyds Building, in the City. Borough Market, south of London Bridge

end of London Bridge. Today, however, it is home to the South Bank cultural complex, Tate Modern, the London Eye, the Globe Theatre and the Saatchi Gallery, not to mention the unspeakable horrors of the London Dungeon.

OUTER SUBURBS

Farther out from the heart of London, more country villages that were swallowed up by the remorselessly expanding city in the 19th century retain a distinctive character. In the west, Richmond has Georgian streets and a highly regarded theatre, Kew has the sumptuous botanical gardens and Wimbledon has the tennis championships.

North, on the range of hills called the Northern Heights, Hampstead is known for its village atmosphere and its concentration of high-minded intellectuals, supporting London's largest percentage of psychiatrists per head of population. Highgate, next door, has a Georgian high street and London's most evocative cemetery.

Away to the east, Greenwich is famous for the National Maritime Museum, the *Cutty Sark* and Greenwich Mean Time (see the Royal Observatory, pages 156–157).

MAKING MONEY

A massive share of London's economy is taken up by the financial and business services sector, whose contribution to the city's Gross Domestic Product is nearly 40 per cent—more than double the ratio in the United Kingdom as a whole. The City of London is one of the most successful

Mail Order
Greater London is divided up by postal areas, which can be confusing for outsiders. Since World War I a combination of letters and numbers has been used, W standing for west, WC for west central, EC for east central, N for north, SW for southwest, and so on. The higher the number, the farther out from the centre the location is.

others followed over the next 15 years. St. Katharine's Dock, near the Tower of London, was turned into a classy yacht marina and its warehouses were transformed into flats, shops and restaurants. Similar developments occurred farther down the river. From the 1980s the Isle of Dogs was redeveloped as a business and residential district, with the Canary Wharf tower, the London Arena, the new Docklands Light Railway and some of the country's most striking post-modern architecture.

While manufacturing and the docks were in decline, London was profiting from an upsurge in the service sector, which brought a noticeable increase in the quantity of office accommodation in the capital. At the same time the tourist industry boomed on cheap air travel and the city's 1960s reputation as 'swinging London'. Visitor numbers swelled from 1 million to 3 million a year between 1960 and 1965, and by 1977 had topped 8 million. The influx of visitors gave shops, restaurants and visitor attractions a powerful boost. By 2000 the number of visitors was getting on for 15 million a year, or five visitors for each inhabitant of Inner London.

GETTING ABOUT

London, like every heavily populated city in the world, has its problems. Litter is one of them; getting around is another. The average Inner Londoner travels more than 4,000 miles (6,450km) a year inside the city—to get to work and back, on business, for shopping, to take the children to school, to go visiting—by some combination of car, taxi, motorcycle, bus, tube, bicycle or foot. The average Inner Londoner walks about 250 miles (400km) a year altogether and cycles only about 30 miles (48km), while spending on transport fares is higher in London than in any other region of the United Kingdom. This is despite the fact that approximately half London's households own a car (10 per cent of London households have two or more cars). The speed of London's motorized traffic is notoriously slow; today's cars and buses move no faster than the horse-drawn traffic of the 1880s. The average daytime speed in central London is

POPULATION

The 2001 census produced population figures of 2.8 million for Inner London and 4.4 million for Outer London. The city has always drawn people from the rest of the country and the rest of the world like a magnet, and today ethnic minorities account for 30 per cent of the population of Inner London (in Greater London as a whole the figure is 25 per cent). The 1980s saw the downward trend in London's population—which had been above 8 million in 1951—beginning to reverse. The city stopped losing more people every year to emigration (mainly to the rest of the country) than it gained from immigration.

Canary Wharf above Rotherhithe docks. The Gates of Chinatown. Bilingual street names in the East End

currently about 10mph (16kph), but the introduction of congestion charging in the city centre in 2003 was estimated to have cut the number of vehicles clogging the streets by a fifth in the first four months.

RICH AND POOR

There has always been a gulf between London's rich and poor. The contrast was particularly glaring in Victorian days and the response was slum clearance. A start was made in the 1840s on demolishing the appalling St. Giles 'rookery' (see page 33) around the eastern end of Oxford Street. Today's theatre-lined Shaftesbury Avenue was carved through an area previously occupied by squalid slums in the 1870s and '80s.

Although the divide is now less extreme, five of England's ten most deprived local authority areas are in London. Homelessness is a persistent problem and begging, in the street and the Underground, has re-emerged since the 1980s. As big cities go, and provided you behave sensibly, London is not a dangerous place. So just relax and enjoy it!

London's immigrants have all added to the city's vibrant mix, bringing their languages, traditions and food. As a result there's a vast choice of ethnic establishments ranging from African crafts emporia to Arab bookshops, Austrian sausage parlours, Caribbean fishmongers, Chinese brocade galleries, Greek jewellers, Israeli crafts outlets, Lebanese butchers and Polish patisseries. Besides the main European, Indian, Chinese and Thai cuisines, you can find restaurants serving food from Brazil, Burma, Cuba, Egypt, Ethiopia, Jamaica, Japan, Mexico, Morocco, Peru, Poland, Russia, Scandinavia, Syria, Vietnam and elsewhere.

The great majority of Londoners speak English, but more than 300 languages from every corner of the globe may be heard on the street.

The majority of incomers to London are aged between 16 and 44. This helps to explain why London's death rate is 6 per cent lower than that of the country as a whole, while the birth-rate is higher. The number of people above retirement age, on the other hand, is lower than outside. About 45 per cent of all London dwellings are apartments, compared with 25 per cent nationally.

Better Adam 'n' Eve It

Cockney rhyming slang's origins are unknown, but some say it was developed to thwart the newly formed police force in the early 19th century. This was when expressions such as 'Would you Adam 'n' Eve [believe] it?' and 'Get up them apples and pears [stairs]' emerged among east Londoners. Some had a particularly sardonic note, as in 'trouble and strife' for wife or 'artful dodger' for lodger. The slang still peppers many Londoners' speech. Anyone lacking cash is 'borassic' (from boracic lint, rhyming with skint); a face is a 'boat' (from Boat Race) and a hat is a 'titfer' (from tit for tat). Lies are 'porkies' (from pork pies), taking a look is having a 'butcher's' (from butcher's hook) and 'Brahms and Liszt' means intoxicated. Celebrities can also end up as part of the vocabulary. American jockey Todd Sloane provided the expression 'on your Todd (own)', and a Gregory (Peck) is a cheque.

THE BEST OF LONDON

BEST PLACES TO SHOP

Fortnum and Mason (see page 180)—famous food emporium

Hamleys (see page 177)—Britain's biggest toy shop

Harrods (see page 178)—legendary department store selling practically anything you can think of

Heal's (see page 181)—stylish things for the home

Liberty (see page 179)—classic clothing and expensive luxuries in a beautiful building

Portobello Road (see page 183)—fascinating street market selling everything from antiques to vegetables

Harrods of Knightsbridge

BEST MUSEUMS

British Museum (see pages 80–85)—a vast array of antiquities from around the world

Museum of London (see page 103)—come here to discover the history of London

Natural History Museum (see pages 112–113)—dinosaurs to lichens: millions of specimens from the natural world

Science Museum (see pages 124–25)—innovative hands-on museum that brings science to life

Sir John Soane's Museum (see pages 128–29)—one man's taste: an unusual house packed with unusual curiosities

Victoria & Albert Museum (see pages 144–49)—a dazzling collection of decorative arts

The British Museum's Great Court

BEST ART GALLERIES

Courtauld Gallery (see pages 130–131)—a superb collection in the grand rooms of Somerset House

National Gallery (see pages 104–109)—European masterpieces from the 13th to 19th centuries

National Portrait Gallery (see pages 110–111)—pictures of royalty, the rich and the famous

Tate Modern (see pages 134–35)—superb modern art in a dynamic setting

Wallace Collection (see page 150)—exceptional private art collection housed in a palatial mansion

Carvings on the front of the National Portrait Gallery depict famous figures

Tate Modern's logo

BEST PLACES TO SEE THE PERFORMING ARTS

Aldwych Theatre (see page 198)—the Royal Shakespeare Company's base, with drama and dance

Odeon Leicester Square (see page 193)—giant West End cinema showing new release blockbusters

Ronnie Scott's (see page 197)—renowned jazz venue with top artists

Royal Festival Hall (see page 195)—concert hall with classical and contemporary music, dance and events

Theatre Royal Drury Lane (see page 201)—venue of countless hit musicals in Covent Garden

Lovers of opera and classical music are well catered for in London

Alastair Little in Frith Street

BEST RESTAURANTS

Alastair Little Soho (see page 252)—top chef Alastair Little's Soho restaurant

Blues Bistro & Bar (see page 254)—lively informal eatery in the heart of Soho

The Cinnamon Club (see page 256)—traditional Indian cookery in the unlikely setting of a former library

Hakkasan (see page 258)—exotic Chinese restaurant serving some of the best food of its kind in the city

Kensington Place (see page 259)—retro furniture and a buzzy atmosphere near fashionable Nottting Hill

Moro (see page 260)—busy Spanish restaurant with meals based on a wood-fired oven

Orrery (see page 261)—a Marylebone stalwart serving fine French food

St. John (see page 263)—traditional British food (for carnivores only) in Clerkenwell

Smiths of Smithfield (see page 263)—organic food in a former warehouse near the City

BEST PUBS

The Bleeding Heart Tavern (see page 266)—rustic tavern dating from the mid-18th century serving good restaurant food

Cittie of York (see page 267)—sandwiches and simple dishes in one of London's oldest pubs

The Eagle (see page 268)—one of London's first gastro-pubs, on the edge of Clerkenwell

The Grapes (see page 269)—riverside pub with separate restaurant once frequented by novelist Charles Dickens

The Peasant (see page 270)—pub with Victorian interior, serving rustic-style food

Swag and Tails (see page 271)—cottagey pub restaurant in a Knightsbridge backwater

Pie, chips and peas with a pint of beer—traditional pub food

BEST PLACES TO STAY

The Bonnington in Bloomsbury (see page 280)—smart, well-situated mid-range hotel in Bloomsbury

Delmere (see page 282)—small, privately owned hotel on the edge of Hyde Park

The Halkin Hotel (see page 284)—elegant, contemporary hotel with an excellent Thai restaurant

The Landmark London (see page 285)—one of the city's top hotels providing every luxury

Lincoln House Hotel (see page 286)—good value bed and breakfast in a Georgian townhouse near Oxford Street

Raffles Brown's (see page 289)—very comfortable, traditional hotel in Mayfair

The Willett (see page 291)—quiet bed and breakfast in a Chelsea townhouse

Lincoln House Hotel

Formal afternoon tea at Raffles Brown's in Mayfair

Cross the river Stroll across the Millennium Bridge or Westminster Bridge, preferably at sunset, for classic London river views

Antiques and bric à brac in Portobello Road

Browse the markets Hunt for bargains and enjoy the atmosphere at a street market such as Portobello Road (see page 183) or Petticoat Lane (see page 182)

Hop on a bus View the city from the top deck of a bus to get your bearings

Go to Harrods Even if you don't want to buy anything, it's worth visiting this huge, luxurious store

Shop at Covent Garden Find unusual items in the specialist shops in the area

Ride on the London Eye The huge millennium wheel gives unrivalled views of London

Take tea Skip lunch and go to Fortnum and Mason, or the Ritz, for a full afternoon tea

Enjoy the parks and squares Take a picnic to one of the city's many green spaces

See a live performance Whatever your taste, you'll find it in London: The choice of entertainment is huge

Watch Changing the Guard Witness British tradition in action: daily ceremony outside Buckingham Palace

Go on the river Take a boat trip on the Thames for a different perspective of the city (see page 234)

The London Eye

Drink in a local Have a pint in a traditional London pub (see pages 266–271), one that has changed little since Dickens's day

Get out of town Leave the city centre for a day and visit at least one of the following: Hampstead, Greenwich, Hampton Court, Kew Gardens (see pages 156, 158, 159, 163)

Wander off the beaten track Take a street map and explore areas such as Bloomsbury and the City on foot

Lunch in style Try at least a couple of the city's superb restaurants (see pages 252–265): at lunchtime, prices are usually very reasonable

Catch a traditional festival or event Look out for the events large and small that take place year round (see pages 222–224)

One of Covent Garden's many attractive pubs

The biggest street carnival in Europe (left) takes place each year in Notting Hill during the last weekend of August

Guardsman (above left) at the Changing the Guard ceremony

Living London

'If you want to know the way, ask a policeman.' London's bobbies are ready to help

The 325m (1,066ft) Millennium Bridge links the City of London and St. Paul's with the Tate Modern on Bankside

Outdoor café culture in London (above), weather permitting! Essential fashion item—the mobile phone (right)

London's **People**

Oxford Street (above) is always seething with shoppers. A less than serious figure (right) in the Lord Mayor's Show Parade, which takes place every November

There's no simple way of defining a Londoner. The city has a population of about 7 million, swollen every day by a million commuters coming in to work by train, mainly from southeast England. More than 270 nationalities make up the fabric of the city itself, and ethnic minorities add up to roughly a quarter of all Londoners. Many have family roots in Africa and India, formerly governed by the British Empire. In the 1950s, a huge number of West Indians arrived.

Within the city, the Thames provides another means of identification, dividing north London from south; some people never cross the river. Cockneys are east Londoners born 'within the sound of Bow Bells'—the bells of the church of St.-Mary-le-Bow, east of the City.

This is a city with a fascinating mix of tradition and change. You'll find the same types—the wealthy City worker, the lawyer in 18th-century wig and gown, the talkative London cabbie—but today they are men and women from a wide range of ethnic and social groups. The typical Londoner doesn't exist, and probably never did.

Londoners Alone

One third of Londoners, about 2.5 million people, live alone. Many of them are single young people, with good jobs and money. They're at the forefront of a changing society with a 50 per cent divorce rate, serial marriages and jobs that are part-time or freelance. Many of these people will not marry, or live with a partner, until they are 30. Their income is 15 per cent higher than the rest of the country and this pushes up prices, especially for London property, where increases of 25 per cent a year are common. They shop on the Internet, eat out and network with their friends, who provide them with the stability once offered by the family group.

Elegantly attired participant at the Spitalfields Japanese Festival

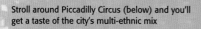

A taste of India (left). Let the black cab take the strain (right)

Madonna, arguably Kensington's most famous, if only part-time, resident

Bollywood is Here

The Asian community in London is more than 200 years old and enjoys a thriving cultural and commercial life. There are 200 Indian millionaires; Meena Pathak of Pathak Spices, for example, has created one of the most famous brands in the country. You can enjoy some of the best Indian food in the world at Veeraswamy's in Regent Street, the oldest of hundreds of restaurants in the capital; see a film in Hindi, released direct from Bombay, in Upton Park; check out the saris and jewellery in Southall, centre of the Asian community, and take in the hit West End musical, *Bombay Dreams*, a celebration of the extraordinary phenomenon of Bollywood, as India's film industry is called.

Speaker's Corner

Speaker's Corner is at the northeast tip of Hyde Park, overlooking Marble Arch. Once the site of the Tyburn gallows (see page 33), where public executions drew massive crowds, it's now a place devoted to free speech. Anyone can stand up, usually on a step-ladder, and say anything they like—except, that is, about the Queen, as this is a royal park. Russian revolutionary Lenin (1870–1924) spoke here, as did novelist George Orwell (1903–50) and the Pankhurst family of suffragettes. Most speakers give vent to extreme views on religion, politics and diet at great and tedious length. Meanwhile the heckler plays an equally time-honoured part, shouting jokes or insults, which the best speakers answer back. In the age of e-mails and TV, Speaker's Corner still provides that oldest form of communication, the shouting match.

London Cabbies

There are 20,000 black cabs in London, and an average of 31,000 people looking for a ride, so cabbies have to move fast. Since 1851 they've taken an exam, set up by the Public Carriage Office, to test them on the best routes round 25,000 streets. It's called the Knowledge, and it takes three years to prepare for. Scientists have found that parts of the brain used for navigation are actually larger in a cabbie—but this brainpower is now under threat. The PCO wants to computerize the exam, and some companies are actually introducing computerized navigation systems in their cabs. Cabbies don't like it. Computers can't tell if a route is traffic-jammed, they say—and how do they know where the best restaurants are?

Madonna in Kensington

Everyone knows that Madonna, the working-class pop icon born and bred in America's heartland, loves London. She's got a British husband, a London house and a mansion in the country. She even likes to go shooting dressed in traditional tweeds. The British are clever, she says, and the social life is good; celebrity friends such as Gwyneth Paltrow think so, too, and have started to arrive. 'I'm in awe of the architecture of the city,' Madonna has said. Living in a £7 million house in fashionable Kensington, she would think that.

Oxford (above) and Cambridge University teams take part in the Boat Race every spring

In British pubs, beer and lager are still served in pint (0.568L) and half-pint glasses

England all-rounder Craig White batting against India (above)

Shopping is one of Londoners' preferred pastimes

Sport and Leisure

London is the focal point of the three main English sports: football (soccer), rugby and cricket. Until 2000, Wembley Stadium hosted the Football Association Cup Final in May, the climax of the football year. The main ground for rugby, invented in 1823 by an English schoolboy tired of kicking the ball, is in the south London suburb of Twickenham (see page 213), and cricket has had its headquarters in north London since the 1830s, when the Marylebone Cricket Club moved there (see page 210).

About 80 per cent of Londoners take part in some form of physical activity, mainly walking, swimming and keeping fit. Some of this energy is expended on good causes. The Marathon Company, which runs the annual London Marathon (see page 17), also organizes the Flora Light Women's Challenge and other events, whose profits go towards facilities in London boroughs.

Londoners' favourite form of leisure, though—closely connected to sport by tradition—is drinking. There are 5,000 pubs in the city, but they are no longer the preserve of men and beer. Now you can buy wine, tea or coffee and often excellent food.

Arsenal vs Tottenham

The feud between these two great football teams began in 1913. Arsenal moved from southeast London to Highbury, near the north London home of Tottenham Hotspur, White Hart Lane. Arsenal needed more fans, and soon the community was split. The teams are very different. Arsenal (whose manager Herbert Chapman invented numbered shirts in the 1920s) is solid and defensive; Tottenham is free-flowing and exciting. One of their famous clashes was the 1991 Football Association Cup Semi-Final. The streets of north London were deserted. After a great match Spurs won 3-1. Such passionate rivalries ensure the game's popularity across the country, despite its recent financial difficulties.

Pub Crawl Protocol

One of the best ways to get to know London and see a cross-section of the capital's population is to go on a pub crawl— an afternoon and/or evening spent visiting one pub after another. There's a pub on almost every corner, so areas such as Mayfair or Fleet Street can be studied at close quarters in an enjoyable way. Until 2003 Britain's licensing laws were a source of amazement and annoyance to visitors as they meant that pubs had to close at 11pm, but local authorities can now decide what time individual pubs and clubs shut their doors. Whereas nightowls and visitors welcome the change, it remains to be seen whether residents do as well.

Lloyd Scott took more than five days to walk the London Marathon for charity dressed in a diving suit

The new Wembley Stadium, venue for football matches and pop concerts, will have a futuristic look

The Five-Day Marathon

The British love to do mad or strange things to raise money for charity. More than 30,000 people take part in the London Marathon in April and most finish in a few hours, but one year Lloyd Scott took over five days. He was wearing an antique diving suit weighing 55kg (120lb). In 1987 Lloyd had been diagnosed with leukemia. Having beaten the disease, he decided to raise money for research. He could walk only 400m (1,300ft) in his suit before stopping to recover his strength. A nurse and two soldiers walked with him to help, and he joined his wife and children every night in a caravan. It was all worth it: Lloyd raised more than £100,000.

A New Stadium

Londoners have a special affection for Wembley Stadium. Its famous two white towers have been part of the skyline since 1924. The great athletic, football and rugby events are played at Wembley, and the biggest rock stars in the world have played there. In 1996 a replacement stadium to hold 90,000 people—the world's most expensive, at £715 million—was announced. Then the problems started. The government gave £120 million, but banks refused to lend the rest, demanding to know who was in charge of the project—the government or the Football Association? When demolition of the old towers finally began they proved more stubborn than expected, and work was slow. It's hoped that the new stadium will be ready in 2006, giving London a sporting landmark fit for the third millennium.

Sales Mania

The January sales in London promise some great bargains after the Christmas spree, and Harrods (see page 178) does it bigger and better than the rest. On the first day a high-profile film star draws up in a horse-drawn carriage, to the accompaniment of bagpipes, to open the doors. Then, if they have any sense, they run. The daily average of 30,000 visitors swells to a scary 300,000, and staff sometimes have to shut the doors on a packed store. To be first in line shoppers arrive the previous day and sleep on the pavement. Seasoned bargain-hunters know the exact route to their chosen goods and make for them at top speed. With discounts of 50 or 60 per cent, who can blame them?

Harrods, decked out in Christmas lights. On the first day of the January sale, lines of people wait to get the best bargains

Tottenham's Robbie Keane celebrates

'IT' girl Tara Palmer-Tomkinson, one of London's high-society party people

A regimental band of Guards parades down the Mall

The Household Cavalry has been guarding the life of the sovereign since the time of Charles II

Royalty and Fame

Brian May at the Queen's Golden Jubilee celebrations at Buckingham Palace

London's royal pageantry is unique. Members of the royal family, who have been through good times and bad, still star in a regular series of splendid parades and processions. The Trooping the Colour in June and the State Opening of Parliament in November, for instance, feature hundreds of soldiers, golden carriages, music and the Queen dressed in diamonds. There are less showy traditions, too: At the New Year's Honours and the Birthday Honours in June the Queen hands medals and awards to hundreds of people from all walks of life. Her official role as Head of State is reflected in meetings with the Prime Minister every Tuesday to discuss government business. As the head of a very public and expensive monarchy, she attracts both criticism and huge affection—as shown in the months of tours, parties and displays celebrating her Golden Jubilee in 2002.

This heady combination of privilege and wealth has always intrigued and attracted visitors. Film stars and billion-aires still like to be seen mingling with the royals, and the spectacle does its bit to pull in the 13 million tourists who spend about £7 billion every year.

Buckingham Palace Rocks

On Monday, 3 June 2002, at the height of the Queen's Golden Jubilee celebrations, rock guitarist Brian May stood on the roof of Buckingham Palace, hair flying in the wind, and played his own version of *God Save the Queen* on an electric guitar amplified for the 250,000 fans below. Then the Queen's garden exploded into a rock concert performed by the likes of Eric Clapton, Paul McCartney and Ozzy Osbourne. While Prince William rocked along, the Queen wore bright yellow ear plugs. She must have taken them out at some point, because when former Beatle Paul McCartney asked whether they could do it all again next year, she replied: 'Not on my lawn'.

Polo, a game brought back from India by army officers, has royal devotees

Princes William and Harry at one of the Golden Jubilee events (above). Lucian Freud's portrait of the Queen (below)

Stylish, often outlandish, headwear (right) is de rigueur on Ladies Day at Ascot races. Blue Plaques mark the homes of the famous (left)

LCC
CHARLES DICKENS
1812-1870
Novelist
Lived Here

Homes of the Famous

Would Jimi Hendrix (1942–70) and George Frederick Handel (1685–1759) have got along, swapping notes on chords, tough crowds and the setting alight of instruments? Perhaps; they were neighbours, after all—albeit separated by 270 years, as well as a brick wall. Jimi stayed at No. 23 Brook Street in Mayfair from 1968 to 1969, entertaining, among others, the Beatles. George Frederick lived next door in No. 25 (see page 90) for much of his life, making his name as a composer. Today this cosmic twist of fate is commemorated by a Blue Plaque, one of nearly 800 dished out in London by English Heritage to mark the homes of notable residents. Look hard enough and you'll spot one on virtually every corner, particularly in the Royal Borough of Kensington and Chelsea. The scheme has been gradually extended across the country.

Royal Warrants

Keep your eyes open and you'll spot royal warrants everywhere in London. Companies and individuals appointed to provide goods and services to the royal family can display a royal coat of arms for five years. The practice, which started in the 15th century, gives an interesting insight into the royal lifestyle. There is a royal mole controller and a chimney sweep. No fewer than six champagne houses have royal warrants, and several chocolatiers—Cadbury's for the staff, Prestat/Bendicks for the royals. This sporty family has providers of riding breeches and fishing tackle, four official gunmakers and a busy royal taxidermist. Warrants can be as easily removed as granted: Mohammed al Fayed, owner of Harrods, lost his royal custom by rashly accusing Prince Philip, the Duke of Edinburgh, of plotting to murder Diana, Princess of Wales.

The Season Hamper

Once upon a time Britain's social elite laid out rugs and picnics at the summer race meets and open-air operas that make up The Season. Today you're more likely to find corporate hospitality tents, but it's still worth making the effort to impress with the perfect picnic hamper. Smoked salmon for example, should be wild, not farmed; strawberries should be English rather than Spanish. Scots may prefer to include some specialities from north of the border, such as cullen skink soup or oatcakes. There are simple rules for drinks: Cans must be avoided. Pimms, a sweet, deceptively alcoholic drink first created in the 1840s, is traditional, but chilled champagne is preferable.

The Great and the Good

In 2002 a portrait of the Queen by Lucian Freud—celebrated as Britain's greatest contemporary painter—was revealed. Although monarchists considered it unflattering, it testifies to the importance of the portrait in British history as a record of who's who. It's difficult to go around a stately home or an established art gallery without being watched by likenesses of the great and the good. The art of portraiture was given a boost by two factors: the fashion for genealogy among the aristocracy, and the Protestant Reformation, when artists sought an alternative market to religious imagery. The best place to see portraits is the National Portrait Gallery (see pages 110–111).

Henry Moore sculpture at the Tate Modern (right)

Poster outside the National Film Theatre (right)

Nicole Kidman won a BAFTA award in 2003 for her role in *The Hours*

The Royal Ballet Company performing *Four Schumann Pieces* at the Royal Opera House, Covent Garden

Arts and Media

London has some of the best theatre in the world. There are two government-subsidized companies—the Royal National Theatre and the Royal Shakespeare Company, and Shaftesbury Avenue forms the heart of commercial theatre in the West End. Movie stars such as Nicole Kidman and Kevin Spacey have come to soak up some of its prestige, Spacey taking up the role of artistic director of the Old Vic (see page 200). BAFTA (British Academy of Film and Television Arts) has moved its awards ceremony to February, to avoid being overshadowed by the Oscars, and attracts many Hollywood stars. While they're here they have to face the toughest paparazzi in the world, as well a voracious tabloid press.

Art and style are part of the London experience. The Tate Modern gallery (see pages 134–135), one of London's most exciting spaces, is so popular that it stays open until 10pm on Fridays and Saturdays. And the artists of the catwalk, London's fashion designers, are at the peak of their creativity, developing the city's quirky street fashion and producing radicals such as John Galliano, who heads Christian Dior, to revolutionize haute couture.

The Lottery in London

Since it started in 1994 the National Lottery has raised hundreds of millions of pounds for big London institutions such as the Royal Opera House. But smaller amounts, which don't attract the headlines, are also distributed across the city to places such as Kentish Town's City Farm (see page 221), a popular scheme for youngsters who might never have seen animals or the countryside. When the Lottery awarded the farm £47,000 for its drama and arts programme, it set up workshops for young asylum-seekers in the area to create their own stories and attend art classes. Debate about the Lottery's administration and aims continues to rage, but there's no denying that some of its contributions make a real difference.

Tate Modern has exhibits to shock and surprise (above)

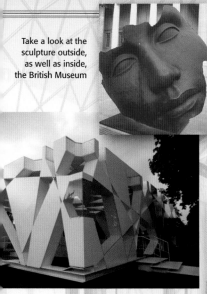

Take a look at the sculpture outside, as well as inside, the British Museum

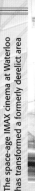

The space-age IMAX cinema at Waterloo has transformed a formerly derelict area

Have lunch inside a contemporary sculpture at the Serpentine Gallery's café in Kensington Gardens

The bullet-shaped profile of the Swiss-Re headquarters in the City of London

The People's Art

The Royal Academy Summer Exhibition is held between June and mid-August at the Royal Academy (see page 115) in Piccadilly. First held in 1769, it remains open to every artist in the country from the humblest amateur to the greatest professional. Anything can be submitted: drawings, prints, models, sculpture, cosily traditional or severely abstract, and everything is viewed. Around a thousand works are chosen to go on display, every one for sale. There was a time when artists queued all day with their submissions until an Academician shouted aloud—and very public—acceptance or rejection. The selection process is more civilized these days, and for those whose work is accepted, there's always a chance of seeing their local landscape hanging next to a David Hockney.

Theatre for All

Chicken Shed is one of the largest theatre companies in the UK, and has a substantial theatre with a recording and dance studio in Southgate. Jo Collins and Mary Ward founded it in 1974 with the simple aim of including anyone with a love of theatre, including children. One of their most famous performances was *Anansi*, based on African tales, in which 1,000 London children took part. After seeing it Princess Diana became the company's patron, and when she died in 1997 Chicken Shed recorded a tribute single, 'I Am in Love With the World', that reached No. 14 in the charts. Chicken Shed projects have spread across the country, proving again that the simplest ideas are often the best.

Architectural Supremo

How far do you have to go to escape Norman Foster's work? Not Bilbao, where the top British architect has redesigned much of the metro system. Not Berlin, where his renovation of the Reichstag won the Prtizker architecture prize. Nor Hong Kong, if you pass through Chek Lap Kok international airport, built on a man-made island. And certainly not London: Canary Wharf's transcendental tube station, the Great Court in the British Museum (see pages 80–85) and the Greater London Authority's new home, City Hall, are some of the most distinctive buildings in Britain, all designed by Foster and Partners. The newest addition to London's skyline, the 40-floor Swiss-Re headquarters (aka the Gherkin), embodies environmentally friendly architecture with layers of 'lightwells' inside and a largely self-ventilating structure.

Rags to Riches

From London's East End to the fashion houses of Paris via Savile Row, the Alexander McQueen story crosses the capital and then the English Channel. McQueen was born in 1969, the son of an East End taxi driver, and left school at 16. More interested in couture than cab-driving, he served his apprenticeship on Savile Row, London's tailoring heart, before taking an MA at St. Martin's School of Art. After a celebrated final collection, fashion's *enfant terrible* left London for Paris, working for Givenchy and then Gucci. By 2001 the three-time British Designer of the Year had made his fortune and a reputation for being brilliant but awkward, once turning down an invitation from the Queen. Every year, during London Fashion Week, alumni of Britain's art colleges aspire to follow in his footsteps.

Ritual still prevails in the House of Lords, and the Lord Chancellor's Procession to the House is a daily routine

The Lords (right) and the Commons sit in the Palace of Westminster (above)

Tony Blair led New Labour to landslide victories in 1997 and 2000

Money and Power

There are several layers of government in London. The British Parliament, made up of the House of Commons and the House of Lords, sits in the Houses of Parliament (see page 92). Just up the road is Whitehall and the major offices of government, including the Prime Minister's home at No. 10 Downing Street. At the top of Whitehall, the Mall leads down to Buckingham Palace, official home of the Queen, the constitutional Head of State.

Then comes the government of London itself—and this gets even more confusing. The City of London, known as 'the square mile', is its historic heart and financial centre, and still guards its medieval privileges. Since 1189 the Lord Mayor has been head of the fiercely independent Corporation of London, the first local authority in England.

The modern city, encompassing its sprawl of suburbs, is known as Greater London and, in 2000, elected its first mayor, Ken Livingstone. His powers are limited but he is responsible for services such as transport. The Mayor and the Greater London Authority have to co-ordinate the work of 32 London boroughs and have a budget of £4 billion.

Politician-Authors

As if being part of the world's oldest parliamentary democracy didn't keep them busy enough, dozens of members of parliament (MPs) supplement their £56,000-plus salaries with second jobs. Many are directors of companies or highly paid consultants, some pulling in huge annual salaries. But the most intriguing moonlighters are the novelists. In the 1990s Tory MP Edwina Currie began writing racy novels in her spare time (eg *A Parliamentary Affair*). Fellow Tory Ann Widdecombe, known for her uncompromising views, was advanced £100,000 for two rather more restrained novels. Interestingly, one Labour MP's analysis in 2002 of MPs' voting records revealed that those who have second jobs turn up to 30 per cent fewer votes than those who don't.

House of Lords

Historically, the most reliable way of gaining a seat on the red leather benches of Parliament's upper chamber was to inherit it. But in 1999 the Labour government reforms threw all but 92 of the aristocrats out. So how do you get a life peerage today? You should be British: Newspaper owner Lord Black renounced his Canadian citizenship for the purpose. Senior figures in the military and the judiciary have an advantage, and Britain's 25 bishops are guaranteed a spot. Ex-politicians and business people aren't uncommon. And you needn't be old: Media mogul Lord Waheed Alli is in his 30s. You can even be nominated as one of 15 People's Peers—but with brain specialist Professor Susan Greenfield among them, they are hardly average, either.

Property prices in fashionable areas of London, such as Chelsea, are unbelievably high

There has been a Lord Mayor of London since 1189. Elected annually by the City's aldermen, he plays a largely ceremonial role

10 Downing Street, the Prime Minister's official residence

Who Owns London?

After the Queen and the Church, Gerald Grosvenor, 6th Duke of Westminster, is the greatest landowner in London. His ancestor, Mary Davies, married Sir Thomas Grosvenor in 1677. Mary owned 100ha (247 acres) of damp farmland. Today this is Mayfair and Belgravia, some of the most expensive land in the world. The Duke's rents and freeholds have created a fortune worth at least £5 billion. He owns more land elsewhere in the UK, and in Canada, Australia and the USA. The present Duke lives simply, but his forebears spent on an imperial scale, splashing out on Old Masters and jewellery by Fabergé. The 4th Duke was a suitor of Paris fashion designer Coco Chanel, and, on finding that the mail was too slow for his liking, set up a private postal system just for her.

House Prices Rising and Rising

Sixty per cent of Londoners own their homes, but houses don't come cheap. London has the highest property prices in the world. A small three-bedroom house in Chelsea will cost more than £1 million; a one-bedroom flat in an average area is £200,000—and prices are doubling every five years. For those who can afford it, even a small London property is a great investment, but anyone earning less than £30,000 a year is in trouble. Teachers, social workers, nurses, firemen and policemen, all vital to the capital, are unable to afford their own homes, and renting is not easy. It's not all bad, though: Elderly people who bought their houses decades ago now find themselves sitting on a small fortune.

London's Highest Earners

At the other end of the scale, some of the City's financial stars earn the kind of money to make your head spin. Philip Green, a chain-store entrepreneur who commutes to London by jet from his Monaco home, once earned £157 million from his business dealings in the City. The previous year, Bernie Ecclestone, king of Formula One motor racing, made £788 million. As for the run-of-the-mill City employees, they work for a system based on encouragement and reward, which can lead to mind-boggling prizes. The director of the City branch of the Tokai Bank, for example, takes home a cool £22 million a year.

Mayor Ken Livingstone introduced traffic congestion charges (see page 61) in 2003

Chancellor Gordon Brown

Red deer still roam in Richmond Park, created as a hunting ground by Charles I in 1637

Not a common sight in London, but hawks are used to control the pigeons

Feeding pigeons in Trafalgar Square is now being discouraged because the birds are becoming pests

Grey squirrels can be seen in most of London's parks

Foxes find the pickings easy on the city's outer limits

Urban Wildlife

Along with millions of people, London is home to a surprising amount of wildlife. Within 20 miles (30km) of St. Paul's, 2,000 species of flora and fauna thrive in parks, squares, churchyards, ponds and gardens. Flora include the London plane tree and the pink-flowered saxifrage called London pride. Fauna ranges from deer, foxes, badgers and rabbits to grey squirrels, the ubiquitous pigeons and stealthy armies of rats and mice. Voles do so well that in 2001 London appointed its first vole officer. The endangered stag beetle finds sanctuary in private gardens, and fish have returned to the once polluted Thames.

Pigeons under Fire

The British have an odd relationship with the pigeon; the Royal Pigeon Racing Association has around 46,000 members, and a prize bird can sell for over £100,000. Meanwhile, the famous pigeons of Trafalgar Square (see page 136), all 30,000 of them, are on the Mayor of London's wanted list. These 'rats with wings' carry disease and leave a mess behind them, in his opinion, so pigeons are on a diet—hopefully they will go away. Tourists cannot feed them, and Rayner's Stall, which sold pigeon feed, is closed. Hawks also go flapping overhead every morning to scare them off. These methods may not work, but they make more sense than Switzerland's efforts to put pigeons on the pill.

Planes versus Pollution

As well as being beautiful, trees play a vital anti-pollution role. The Trees for London charity, which plants ten thousand of them a year, is campaigning for a million more by 2010 'to help London breathe'. A characteristic feature of the capital's streets and gardens, the London plane tree (*Platanus x hispanica*) which periodically sheds its dirt-absorbing bark, is a hybrid of the oriental plane, introduced in 1562, and the western plane, which was imported from Virginia in 1636. The oldest surviving examples in garden squares are the huge ones in Berkeley Square (see page 226), planted in 1789. William Wordsworth wrote a poem about the ancient plane tree at the corner of Cheapside and Wood Street in the City, which is still there.

Foxes on the Run

Foxes like big cities because it is easy to find food. There are about 20,000 in London. Some people like foxes and encourage them into their gardens, but others are scared and dislike their piercing shrieks at night. The government officially recommends trapping the foxes and releasing them into the wild, which usually means they just come back, but one area of London has taken the drastic step of employing a hunter to kill the foxes. He traps the foxes and then shoots them. Animal rights activists oppose this and the man has to work anonymously. However, the major cause of fox death is far less dramatic. Eighty per cent of them die before the age of two, squashed beneath the wheels of the urban car.

The Story of London

The Beginnings of London

London is where it is because of a decision made by the Roman army commanders after their invasion of England in AD43. A site for a base was chosen on the north bank of the Thames at the highest point of the tide accessible to ships from the European Continent. A bridge was built across the river and quays along the bank, and the military base developed into a town, a busy commercial and administrative district that became the hub of the Roman road network and succeeded Colchester as the capital of Roman Britain. The civic centre was where Leadenhall Market (see page 232) is now. Besides barracks, houses and shops, there were temples, public baths and an amphitheatre, and from around AD200 the whole town was surrounded by a wall.

After the Roman army withdrew from Britain, the Anglo-Saxons established their own town outside the wall on the west, in today's Aldwych area, but attacks by Vikings drove the inhabitants back inside the Roman wall in the 9th century. In the 11th century, King Edward the Confessor founded Westminster Abbey (see pages 152–153) a mile (1.6km) or so to the west, built a palace there and created a second London, the centre of the royal government, alongside the first.

The Peopling of Roman London

All through its history London has grown by attracting settlers from elsewhere. The early population included many Celts from various parts of Britain, but London also imported people from all over the Roman Empire, from across the English Channel in Gaul (France)—such as Julius Classicianus, the first Londoner whose name is known—to Greece and the eastern Mediterranean. Soldiers, officials, doctors, shopkeepers, entertainers, craftsmen, clerks, cooks, slaves—some with their families—brought their gods and goddesses, languages, costumes, habits and traditions with them to create a cosmopolitan mix. Roman London probably resembled a frontier town in the Wild West—crowded, noisy, smelly, and often dangerous.

Head of the Roman god Mithras (2nd to 3rd century) from the Temple of Mithras, now in the Museum of London

Statues of two legendary giants, Gog and Magog (right), stand in the Guildhall

AD43

Statue of warrior-queen Boadicea (Boudica) on the Victoria Embankment (right). Danish Vikings sailed to Britain in longships (below) and in 872 made London their headquarters

Boadicea's Revolt

Queen Boadicea (or Boudica; the name means 'victory'), ruler of the Celtic Iceni people of East Anglia in AD60, was an ally of the Romans until enraged by their arrogance and mistreatment. After Roman soldiers had flogged her and raped her daughters, she led her tribespeople to sack Colchester and then descended on London in her war chariot, seeking vengeance. She plundered the fledgling town, burned it to the ground and slaughtered those inhabitants who had not fled. The Roman army quickly regrouped and defeated the Iceni in battle somewhere to the north, and Boadicea killed herself rather than be captured. London was quickly rebuilt, but archaeologists have found clear traces of extensive fire damage deep below the current ground level.

In the Arena

One of the pleasures of life in Roman London was going to the amphitheatre, near the area now occupied by the Guildhall (see page 90). Oval in shape, with high earth banks supporting wooden benches for some 5,000 spectators, it was used for entertainments (including executions) and could be hired for private functions. Wild animals were butchered in the arena for the audience's delight, but gladiatorial combats were the star attraction. These might involve a heavily armed fighter against one more lightly armed and more agile, or a contest between a *retiarius* (gladiator equipped with a net and trident) against an opponent with sword and shield. All the gladiators paraded round the arena together before fighting each other—usually to the death.

Death and Bay Leaves

A lavish sarcophagus discovered in the Spitalfields area of the City in 1999 was expected to be that of a powerful citizen of Roman London. When the lead casket inside was opened, however, it was found to contain the skeleton of a young woman. Buried around AD350 and in her 20s when she died, she clearly came from an extremely rich family. The sarcophagus was decorated with scallop shells, symbols of life after death. She had been wrapped in expensive garments of silk and wool, some shot through with gold thread. Also interred with her were glass and jet objects and, touchingly, her head had been put gently to rest on a pillow of fresh, sweet-smelling bay leaves.

The Royal Saint

Edward the Confessor (1042–66) was the only English king ever canonized. A deeply religious man, he gave his patronage to a Benedictine monastery on Thorney Island in the Thames marshes west of London, paying for its church to be rebuilt in the Romanesque style which was fashionable in Normandy, and establishing a royal palace near the site. The monastery relics included fragments of the True Cross, blood from Christ's wounded side, some of the Virgin Mary's milk and one of St. Paul's fingers. When Edward died in 1066, leaving his kingdom without an heir and his throne in dispute, he was laid to rest there— behind the high altar of Westminster Abbey (see pages 152–153).

Edward the Confessor, son of Ethelred the Unready, was the last king of the Old English royal line

Harold II succeeded Edward the Confessor. He died at the Battle of Hastings in 1066, having been shot through the eye with an arrow

1066

King Alfred the Great recaptured London from the Vikings in 886

Medieval and Tudor London

London's importance was underlined when William I, 'the Conqueror' (1027–87), built the Tower of London to keep the city under control after the Norman conquest. Over the following centuries streets were paved for the first time, hospitals and prisons were built, and church spires studded the skyline. Rich merchant guilds took over the government of the city, which had its own mayor and aldermen. Merchants and financiers came to London from Germany, Denmark, France and Italy; until its expulsion in 1290 there was a flourishing Jewish community. Westminster, meanwhile, became a regular meeting place of Parliament, and magnates built houses along the river between the city and Westminster.

In 1500 London had a population of perhaps 50,000, which was quadrupled by immigration in the Tudor period. City merchants virtually monopolized England's foreign trade, with ships leaving the Port of London for the Mediterranean and the East, America and Africa. Bricks were used in more buildings and the most expensive houses had pumped water. Constables and marshals were employed to deal with crime and vagrancy. Disease was rife, but life was longer on average in London than elsewhere.

Old London Bridge

London's only bridge in the Middle Ages was a remarkable sight. People lived on it in houses along each side, from three to seven floors high. These were not finally removed until 1762. There were shops on the ground floors—more than a hundred of them—and at the core a two-storey chapel dedicated to St. Thomas Becket. Below, the bridge's 19 arches created dangerous rapids. In 1390 the bridge was turfed over for a great tournament between English and Scottish champions. It had more gruesome uses too. The heads of executed traitors were parboiled in the gatehouse, dipped in tar and stuck on the gateway. One visitor of 1598 counted more than 30 on display.

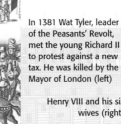

In 1381 Wat Tyler, leader of the Peasants' Revolt, met the young Richard II to protest against a new tax. He was killed by the Mayor of London (left)

Henry VIII and his six wives (right)

1066

William, Duke of Normandy and cousin of Edward the Confessor, defeated Harold II at Hastings in 1066 and was crowned King William I on Christmas Day

The Zoo in the Tower

Until the 1830s the Tower of London (see pages 138–143) housed a royal collection of wild animals. Henry III (1207–72) had a polar bear which liked to fish in the Thames, three leopards sent by the Holy Roman Emperor and an elephant, a gift from France, which caused great excitement when it arrived but survived for only two years. An official Keeper of the King's Lions and Leopards was appointed, and lions still lived in the Tower in the time of James I (1566–25), who liked to set mastiffs on them. Around 1750 the zoo had lions, tigers, leopards, bears, monkeys, eagles, vultures and an ostrich.

The Killing of Wat Tyler

In 1381 thousands of rebels objecting to a poll tax journeyed from Kent and Essex to London. The followers of the Peasants' Revolt—whose demands included the redistribution of church wealth—killed several government officials before the 13-year-old king, Richard II (1367–1400), agreed to meet them at Smithfield. After some initial dialogue there was a scuffle, as the Mayor of London, William Walworth, tried to arrest Wat Tyler, the rebel leader. Tyler struck at him with a dagger but Walworth, saved by the mail shirt under his clothes, ran Tyler through with his sword. Richard rode towards the rebels, proclaiming himself their true leader and the crowd fled. Poll taxes were rarely imposed again—and never without resistance.

Queen Elizabeth at Tilbury

When the Spanish Armada sailed for an invasion of England in 1588, Elizabeth I (1533–1603) insisted on visiting her troops at Tilbury. Accompanied by her courtiers, she arrived riding a white horse and wearing a steel corselet over her white velvet dress. Having dismounted, she walked through the ranks before delivering a stirring address. The Queen was a superb orator and her defiant speech is one of the most famous in English history. 'I know I have but the body of a weak and feeble woman,' she announced, 'but I have the heart and stomach of a king, and of a king of England too.' Elizabeth was still at Tilbury when news arrived of the Spanish Armada's defeat.

Shakespeare and the Globe

Bankside in the time of William Shakespeare (1564–1616) was London's most notorious entertainment area, known for its drinking dens and 'stews' (brothels), its bull- and bear-baiting pits and its theatres. A new theatre called the Globe (see page 126)—polygonal, thatched and built of wood—opened there in 1599 and staged many of Shakespeare's plays, including *Macbeth*, *Othello* and probably *Henry V* (with its veiled reference to the theatre as 'this wooden O'). Bottled ale sold well to the audiences, and buckets served as emergency lavatories. When the theatre was destroyed by fire in 1613 the only person hurt was a man whose breeches were set alight, but he resourcefully quenched the flames with a bottle of beer.

Explorer Sir Walter Raleigh (1552–1603) named the US colony of Virginia after Elizabeth I

Elizabeth I ruled for 45 years. England's confidence and prosperity grew during her reign, and the arts flourished

Seaman Sir Francis Drake (c1540–96) fought the Spanish Armada in 1588

1600

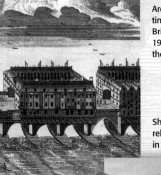

Around 1200, stone replaced timber as the fabric of London Bridge (left). It was supported by 19 arches, and houses occupied the bridge until the 18th century

The Beefeaters of the Tower of London were formed in 1485 as Henry VII's bodyguard (right)

Shakespeare's Globe Theatre, rebuilt in authentic style, reopened in 1997 (below)

Stuart London

When James VI of Scotland (1566–1625) arrived in London to be crowned James I of England in 1603 the city was 10 times the size of any other in the kingdom. The first horse-drawn cabs appeared on the streets in the 1620s, annoying the Thames watermen, who ran London's earliest taxi service, and the development of the West End as a fashionable quarter started in Covent Garden (see page 88). The city guarded its privileges jealously. When Charles I (1600–49) interfered with them he met with fierce opposition, which was to be a major factor of his defeat in the Civil War. The 11-year Commonwealth government brought further encroachments, and London rejoiced when Charles II (1630–85) rode through the streets to reclaim the throne in 1660.

Smart neighbourhoods developed, such as St. James's and Bloomsbury, but most of the medieval city was devoured by the Great Fire. Sir Christopher Wren (1632–1723) rebuilt St. Paul's Cathedral (see pages 118–123) and the city churches, but his plan for new streets was rejected. The old layout was restored, though the new buildings were in brick. The city soon recovered its dominance and in 1694 the Bank of England (see page 76) was founded.

The West View of St. Paul's Cathedral before the Fire of London

Unrecognizable today, this is St. Paul's Cathedral before it was destroyed in the Great Fire of London, 1666 (left). Oliver Cromwell (right) signed Charles I's death warrant and ruled the Commonwealth of England, Ireland and Scotland until his death in 1658

Gunpowder, Treason and Plot

A group of conspirators intent on a coup to restore Roman Catholicism in England found a Yorkshire soldier of fortune named Guy Fawkes, who was ready to blow up Parliament, killing James I and the government ministers gathered for the State opening ceremony in 1605.

After renting a cellar that ran beneath the House of Lords, they filled it with 36 barrels of gunpowder and a quantity of iron bars, concealed under masses of rubbish. Word of the plot leaked out, however; the building was searched and Fawkes was found lurking there with a length of slow-match, tinder and a watch. After interrogation under torture in the Tower of London, he was hanged, drawn and quartered, as were his fellow plotters.

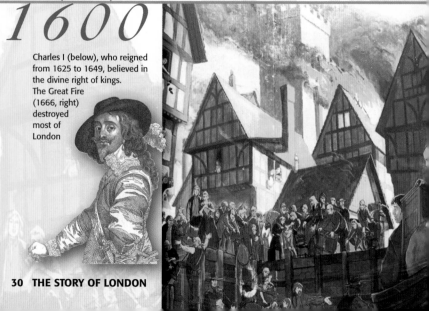

1600

Charles I (below), who reigned from 1625 to 1649, believed in the divine right of kings. The Great Fire (1666, right) destroyed most of London

The Execution of Charles I

Civil War was at an end, and Charles I had been convicted of waging war against his own people. On a cold January afternoon in 1649 he donned an extra shirt—in case his shivers were mistaken for fear—and stepped through a window of the Banqueting House (see page 77) in Whitehall on to a specially built scaffold, watched by a large crowd. The King pushed his hair up under his cap and knelt awkwardly at the block, which was only 26cm (10in) high. In complete silence he stretched out his arms as a signal to the executioner, who brought the axe down and severed the King's head with one stroke. A groan went up from the crowd, and one or two spectators passed out.

The Great Plague

An epidemic of bubonic plague in 1664–65 killed around 100,000 people in London, or one in three of the population. People who could get out of town did so, though many doctors and clergy stayed to fulfil their duties. The disease was transmitted by fleas and spread by flea-ridden rats, but this was not understood at the time, and misguided remedies included a cull of dogs and cats. Every plague-stricken house had a cross daubed on its door, and the inhabitants were locked inside for 40 days' quarantine. To the cry of 'Bring out your dead', carts clattered through the streets collecting corpses, which were thrown into 'plague pits' and covered with a layer of quicklime.

The Great Fire

A catastrophic fire started in a bakery in Pudding Lane near London Bridge in the early hours of a September morning in 1666. Fanned by a strong wind and fuelled by wooden houses, it destroyed 80 per cent of the city's buildings and made 100,000 people homeless. Charles II sent diarist Samuel Pepys (1633–1703) to the scene to order the construction of fire breaks and the next day the King and his brother, the future James II, took charge of operations. Flames raged up to 91m (300ft) high and threw out a rain of sparks. The navy was called in and houses were pulled down or blown up. Finally the wind dropped and after four days the fire burned itself out.

Blood and the Crown Jewels

Colonel Thomas Blood was an adventurous Irishman who had his estates confiscated after supporting Parliament against Charles I. In 1671 he made an audacious attempt to steal the Crown Jewels, which were put on display in the Martin Tower of the Tower of London by the Keeper of Regalia, Talbot Edwards. Disguised as a clergyman, Blood befriended the Keeper and won his trust, returning later with three accomplices to steal the crown, orb and sceptre. They overpowered the Keeper and were making off with their booty when he recovered and raised the alarm. All three were caught, Blood with the crown under his parson's cloak. Charles II, apparently amused by the escapade, pardoned Blood and restored his Irish estate.

Sir Christopher Wren designed the new St. Paul's (below) after the Great Fire. His tomb is inside the cathedral

In the 1660s diarist Samuel Pepys recorded such historic events as the Great Plague and the Great Fire, as well as his own extra-marital affairs

1700

Guy Fawkes, hanged for conspiracy in the Gunpowder Plot in 1606

Georgian London

London's population grew towards the million mark as people from all parts of the country flocked in to seek their fortunes in the heart of England's political, commercial and artistic life. London covered more than twice as much ground in 1800 as in 1700. The villages of Knightsbridge, Kensington and Chelsea became extensions of the West End. Elegant squares and streets went up in Mayfair to house wealthy families with their servants. There were fashionable shops in Bond Street, Oxford Street and the Strand, smart coffee-houses and the Vauxhall and Ranelagh pleasure gardens to enjoy. The British Museum (see pages 80–85) and the Royal Academy (see page 115) opened their doors, Handel's oratorios were premiered at Covent Garden (see page 88) and exotic plants from around the world were grown at Kew Gardens (see page 163).

It was also a London of smoke and stench, open sewers, high infant mortality rates and appalling slum 'rookeries'. Disease, drunkenness, prostitution and thieving were rife. Highwaymen, notably Dick Turpin, preyed on travellers into and out of London. There was no organized police force or fire brigade. Areas such as Seven Dials were avoided altogether by respectable citizens, who hired linkmen with torches to light them through the dark.

At the Cheshire Cheese

The Cheshire Cheese pub in Fleet Street has a list of famous past patrons. Lexicographer Dr. Samuel Johnson (1709–84) lived round the corner and came here or to the Turk's Head in Gerrard Street to gossip with his friends, writer James Boswell, painter Sir Joshua Reynolds, author Oliver Goldsmith and actor David Garrick. Johnson's memory has been saluted at the Cheshire Cheese by many later literary figures. Writer G. K. Chesterton once took his part at a Johnsonian dinner, and Irish poet W. B. Yeats and his contemporaries conducted a regular literary circle there in the 1890s.

The Cheshire Cheese pub was a meeting place for artists and writers in the 18th century

The Georgian period was one of architectural elegance, with simple, classical styles. Parks and gardens were laid out, with tea houses and water features, for the wealthy to enjoy

Ye Olde Cheshire Cheese REBUILT 1667

1700

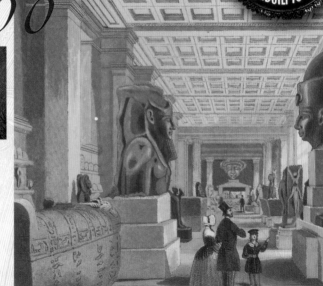

Sir Hans Sloane (above). The Egyptian room of the British Museum (right)

The St. Giles Rookery

In about the middle of the 18th century the area round the church of St. Giles in the Fields was one of London's worst slums. Its narrow streets, alleys and yards were synonymous with squalor, beggars, prostitution, crime and drink, with up to 50 people crammed into each ramshackle little house. Notorious taverns and gin-shops in the area included the Maidenhead Inn, in Dyott Street, and the Rat's Castle. When the nearby brewery's giant vat burst in 1814 and beer flooded the streets, the slum's inhabitants rushed out with jugs and cups. Even the children brought spoons, and some unfortunate people trying to lap beer from the gutters fell in and were drowned.

Collectors All in a Row

Sir Hans Sloane (see page 85) left his vast cornucopia of antiquities, art works, manuscripts, natural history specimens and weird curiosities to the nation. The British Museum (see pages 80–85) was founded to house them and other treasures such as the Harleian Collection of manuscripts, assembled by the Earls of Oxford, and the Cotton family's books and antiquities. Money was raised by public lottery to pay for the building in Great Russell Street and the museum opened in 1759. In due course many more collections were purchased or donated, including Sir William Hamilton's antique vases, Egyptian antiquities, classical sculptures, the marble friezes removed from the Parthenon in Athens by Lord Elgin, and King George III's library.

Tyburn Tree

Marble Arch (see page 100) stands on the site once occupied by the Tyburn gallows. Convicts were brought here to be hanged, travelling from Newgate prison three to a cart, sitting on their own coffins. On the way they were allowed to stop at taverns for free drinks and many, mercifully, arrived drunk. The hangman was sometimes in a similar condition. Huge crowds gathered to watch as the noose was fastened round the prisoner's neck, the horse was whipped up and the cart moved on, leaving the rope to drop. Friends would rush to tug on the dangling victim's legs and shorten the ordeal. From 1783 executions were conducted in Newgate, ending some 600 years of Tyburn hangings, which had claimed more than 50,000 souls.

The London Mob

In 1780 Member of Parliament Lord George Gordon (1751–93) led a huge demonstration to the Houses of Parliament (see page 92) to protest against the relaxation of penalties on Roman Catholics. Some members of the crowd went on the rampage; Irish people and Roman Catholics were assaulted and their houses destroyed, and Roman Catholic chapels were looted to screams of 'No Popery'. Toughs poured out of the slums to drink, rape, kill and steal. Prisons were stormed and the prisoners released, and a mob armed with muskets attacked the Bank of England. After a week of mayhem the government called out the troops. In the ensuing suppression 285 people were killed. Gordon himself was acquitted of high treason, but 25 of the rioters were hanged.

In the reign of George III the American colonies won their independence

A dissolute prince and king, George IV secretly wed his mistress, Mrs. Fitzherbert

Aged 24, William Pitt the Younger was Britain's youngest-ever prime minister

1800

This terrace in Bedford Square shows the symmetry and classical lines of Georgian architecture

A successful society portrait painter, Joshua Reynolds became the first president of the Royal Academy

The Great Wen

In the first half of the 19th century 'the great wen' (growth), as journalist William Cobbett called London, continued to expand. It was now the financial capital of the world and improved roads turned villages such as Hampstead and Highgate, Camberwell and Dulwich into suburbs for commuting businessmen. Meanwhile, as the docks expanded down the Thames, cheap housing spread through Whitechapel, Stepney and Bethnal Green in the East End. Architect John Nash (1752–1835) designed Regent's Park, Belgravia was laid out in style, Lord's cricket ground opened and London University was founded. London Zoo (see page 160) opened and the National Gallery (see pages 104-109) and Nelson's Column were new landmarks in Trafalgar Square (see page 136). Gas lighting made streets seem safer and in the 1820s and 1830s London acquired a police force and a fire brigade. The first horse-drawn omnibuses ran in 1829, and the railways arrived soon afterwards.

In stark contrast to such progress were the pressing problems of overcrowding and poverty, which spurred on the advocates of sweeping political and social reform.

Stained-glass window of Charles Dickens (left). Elizabeth Fry, prison reformer (right)

Lord Nelson's Funeral

Admiral Lord Horatio Nelson (1758–1805) died in action against the Napoleonic fleet at the Battle of Trafalgar. He was brought home in his flagship, HMS *Victory*, and his coffin taken by boat to Greenwich (see pages 156–157) and up the river. At the Admiralty in Whitehall it was placed on a funeral car made to resemble *Victory*, with a winged figure of Fame at the prow. The Royal Scots Greys led the procession to St. Paul's. Bells tolled, guns boomed and fifes and drums played as the cortege moved through streets lined with people. A dozen sailors from *Victory* bore the coffin. Darkness was gathering before the service was over and Nelson was lowered into a place of honour directly beneath the cathedral dome (see page 121).

1800

Dickens lived in this house in Doughty Street from1837 to 1840 and wrote *Oliver Twist* and *Nicholas Nickleby* here

Sir George Gilbert Scott designed the hotel that fronts St. Pancras Station (1868–74) in Victorian Gothic style, using red brick, granite and stone

The Peelers

As Home Secretary in 1829, Sir Robert Peel (1788–1850) introduced London's first effective police force. Called 'peelers' or 'bobbies' after their creator, the officers—many of them ex-soldiers—stepped on to the streets in blue uniforms and top hats, and made their Whitehall headquarters off Scotland Yard. At first the constables were regarded with suspicion and hostility by Londoners, who prized their freedom. 'Blue devils' was another popular nickname. Policemen were often attacked and when one was killed by rioters in 1831 the coroner's jury brought in a verdict of justifiable homicide. Gradually, under their Irish chief, Richard 'King' Mayne, who ran the force until his death in 1868, they acquired a reputation for discipline and restraint.

Madame Tussaud and the Waxworks

Marie Tussaud (1760–1850) arrived in England from her native France in 1802 with her two sons—having abandoned their father—and toured her waxworks show around the country until settling in London in 1835. In Paris, during the Terror that followed the French Revolution, she had been forced to make wax models of the severed heads of prominent victims of the guillotine, some of whom she had known personally. After fleeing the country she attracted wide attention for her display of lifesized likenesses of famous figures. Madame Tussaud's sons continued the business after her death and moved it to the present Baker Street site in 1884 (see page 101).

Newgate's Dreadful Walls

Newgate prison was the most famous and dreaded in the country, originally established in the city's west gatehouse in the 12th century. Charles Dickens wrote of 'Those dreadful walls of Newgate, which have hidden so much misery and such unspeakable anguish.' New arrivals were liable to be robbed of everything they had, including clothes, and were bullied by both seasoned inmates and prison officials. Occasionally rich prisoners could buy special treatment and live quite comfortably in an airy room, playing skittles or tennis and drinking in one of the taverns inside the walls. Most prisoners, however, endured grim cells, dirt, lice and vermin, an appalling stench and dreadful food. The prison was demolished in 1902.

The Mudlarks

Mudlarks were poor scavengers who lived by scouring the Thames shore after the tide had gone down to pick up any articles they could sell. Sometimes up to their waists in the thick, greasy mud, they ranged from small children to bent old women in clothes so tattered and filthy they could scarcely even be called rags. Most of them lived near the river and would come out soon after high tide and wait for the chance to scrabble about among barges and boats on the shore. They gathered pieces of coal, wood, rope or iron, bones, tools and copper nails, which were particularly valuable. Coal would be sold to their neighbours and other finds to the local rag-and-bone shops.

 Admiral Horatio Nelson, hero of the Battle of Trafalgar

 Michael Faraday, the self-taught son of a blacksmith, first produced an electric current in 1831

 A successful soldier, the Duke of Wellington later became prime minister

1850

The bustling thoroughfare of Fleet Street in 1848 (above). Sign for Madame Tussaud's waxworks (above left)

An early 'peeler', one of the Metropolitan Police force founded in 1829

The World's
Largest City

As the Great Exhibition of 1851 in Hyde Park displayed Britain to the world in the world's largest city, vigorous reform was under way. From the 1860s the Peabody Trust built new housing for the poor; in the 1870s slums were cleared to make way for Shaftesbury Avenue and Charing Cross Road, philanthropist Thomas Barnardo (1845–1905) opened his first homes for destitute children and the London School Board set out to give every London child an elementary education.

The population rose steeply, hitting 4 million by the end of the century. In the City and central districts, however, numbers fell as cheap transport allowed people to live farther from their places of work. With the introduction of underground trains and trams London spread over yet more of the surrounding country, swallowing Hammersmith, Putney, Clapham, Stratford, Tottenham and Hornsey. The London County Council was founded in 1888 to run an area of well over 100 sq miles (256sq km). By the end of the century electricity lit the streets and new department stores were attracting custom, including Harrods (see page 178) and Liberty (see page 179).

The Great Stink

The Thames in 1858 was an open sewer for all the filth of London. That year's hot summer created a stench so horrific that it was dubbed the Great Stink. Noxious fumes penetrated the Houses of Parliament—and consequently something was done. Sir Joseph Bazalgette (1819–91), chief engineer of the new Metropolitan Board of Works, built 500 miles (800km) of main sewers and 13,000 miles (21,000km) of lesser drains, superbly constructed in brick and still working today. The Victoria Embankment (see page 150) was built along the north bank of the river with a massive sewer inside as well as a tunnel for the new underground trains. On top were gardens and a new road to relieve London's traffic congestion. It was an engineering feat of genius and earned Bazalgette a knighthood.

Queen Victoria's husband, Prince Albert (left), planned the Great Exhibition of 1851 (below), which showcased industrial enterprise worldwide

1850

Florence Nightingale, 'The Lady of the Lamp', nursed the wounded during the Crimean War (1853–56)

Big Ben

Edmund Beckett Denison, later Lord Grimthorpe (1816–1905), was one of the top barristers of his day. Savagely aggressive and sarcastic, he also knew more about clockmaking than anyone in the country. It was Denison who designed the 5-tonne/ton timepiece in the new clock tower of the Houses of Parliament (see page 92), equipped with its own revolutionary gravity escapement and a giant bell weighing more than 13 tonnes/ton and nicknamed Big Ben. The clock began operation in 1859. Denison was a difficult character and engaged in prolonged controversy with the architect of the Houses of Parliament, Sir Charles Barry (1795–1860), but his clock keeps excellent time to this day, and its chime is one of London's most familiar and evocative sounds.

On the First Tube

The world's first underground trains began running in 1863 on a line nicknamed 'the Drain', 4 miles (6km) long, between Paddington, Euston, King's Cross and Farringdon Street stations. The steam-powered trains caught on at once. Despite the smoke, grime and smell, Victorian gentlemen in stove-pipe hats rode them with perfect equanimity. The dark green carriages were well lit, trains ran every 10 minutes at peak times and tickets cost from three pence to six pence, depending on class of travel rather than on distance. Almost 10 million journeys were made in the railway's first year. More lines soon opened and in 1890 electric trains appeared in the City, on the first line to be called 'the tube' (see page 49).

Jack the Ripper

To this day no one knows the identity of the killer who stalked the cobbled, gas-lit alleys of Whitechapel in 1888, killing prostitutes. The dead body of Mary Anne Nicholls, the first undoubted victim of the Whitechapel Murderer—as he was known at first—was discovered in Durward Street, with her throat cut, and horribly mutilated. Four more victims were found over the following weeks. The murders caused a sensation in the press, especially when mocking letters signed 'Jack the Ripper' were sent to the police. Suspects have ranged from a deranged policeman to a Russian spy, Dr. Thomas Barnardo, the Royal Physician, and even an heir to the throne, the Duke of Clarence.

The Diamond Jubilee

Queen Victoria's 60 years on the throne were honoured in 1897 in a spectacular celebration of the British Empire. The little figure in black widow's weeds was cheered by huge crowds lining the streets to see her driven in her state landau to a brief thanksgiving service on the steps of St. Paul's Cathedral. The sun blazed down on soldiers in glittering array from every corner of the globe—cavalry from India and Australia, Gurkhas and Sikhs, Africans, Chinese, Dyaks from Borneo. Prime ministers of the colonies had a prominent place and there were many foreign royalties and statesmen, but the main plaudits were for 'the Widow at Windsor', who could not restrain her tears.

Sir Joseph Bazalgette, engineer of London's sewage system

Liberal prime minister, William Gladstone

Benjamin Disraeli, Tory prime minister in 1868 and 1874–80

1900

The clock tower Big Ben takes its name from the huge bell that chimes the hour (above). Dense horse-drawn transport near St. Paul's in the 1890s (right)

20th-Century London

The London of 1900 was the capital of the largest empire the world had ever known. Suburban sprawl continued and by 1939 the population was 9 million. The Greater London Council was responsible for an area of 600 square miles (1,550sq km) from 1965 until its abolition in 1986, which left no central London authority. Motor cars and buses replaced horses and hansom cabs, though the average speed of travel in London in 1999 was no faster than in 1899. Damage in World War I was slight, but in World War II the winter Blitz of 1940–41 killed 20,000 people. Many more casualties were later inflicted by flying bombs and rockets. Some underground stations served as air-raid shelters, where Londoners bedded down on the platforms.

The war was followed by exhaustion, austerity and the collapse of the London docks. Immigration was encouraged to fill the shortage of workers, and new arrivals from the West Indies, Pakistan and Bangladesh added to London's cultural mix. With recovering affluence in the 1960s came the youth culture of coffee bars, boutiques and 'swinging London'. Skyscrapers changed the skyline, while planners and architects replaced houses with concrete tower blocks.

The One and Only

Queen of the Edwardian music halls Marie Lloyd (1870–1922), was a Cockney born and bred, who started life as Matilda Wood in Hoxton, where her father made artificial flowers. She went 'on the halls' in the 1880s and sang a series of popular hits, including 'My Old Man Said Follow the Van' and 'One of the Ruins That Cromwell Knocked About A Bit'. Engaging and saucy, she seemed to take effortless command of her audiences. During her career she toured the United States, Australia and South Africa and married three times. The stage was her first love, and she was working until a few days before her death. She was buried in Hampstead Cemetery.

Suffragettes chained themselves to railings to win women the right to vote

Two 20th-century prime ministers: James Ramsay MacDonald (left) and Winston Churchill (right)

1900

Bomb damage during the Blitz (right). An awards ceremony at the 1948 London Olympics (below)

The Unknown Soldier

Garlanded with red poppies and set in the floor near Westminster Abbey's (see pages 152–153) west door is the grave of the unknown soldier. It contains the remains of a soldier selected at random from among those killed but never identified on the Western Front in World War I. He was reburied in the abbey on Armistice Day in 1920 as a memorial to a lost generation, lying in a coffin of British oak and interred in earth brought from France under a slab of marble from Belgium. The ceremony took place in the presence of King George V and many heads of state and military leaders, with a guard of honour formed by 100 holders of the Victoria Cross. Nearby is the Congressional Medal of Honour, conferred by the United States.

The Café de Paris Bomb

The Café de Paris in Coventry Street was a well-known nightclub in the heart of the West End. One March night in 1941 customers were dining and dancing in the basement, advertised as 'the safest place to dance in town', when there was a blinding flash as two high explosive bombs fell on the cinema above. The West Indian band leader Ken 'Snakehips' Johnson and some of his musicians were killed, as were entire parties seated at some tables. Survivors staggered up into the night, in shock, bleeding and covered with dust. Some of the first on the scene were looters, stealing wallets and wrenching rings off dead and dying fingers. In all, 34 bodies were eventually brought out.

The Festival of Britain

A century after the Great Exhibition of 1851, the Festival of Britain was held to boost national morale after the war. In London it centred on a site on the South Bank, where 11ha (27 acres) of bomb-blasted Victorian buildings were cleared. The story of Britain's past was told, but the emphasis was on science, technology and the future. In the five months it lasted, 8.5 million people went to admire the futuristic Skylon sculpture and investigate the Dome of Discovery, the Design Review Pavilion, the 3-D polaroid cinema, the crazy Emmet railway, and the new Royal Festival Hall (see page 127), as well as Battersea Park (see page 154). The festival's permanent legacy was the South Bank complex (see page 127).

A Cleaner City

The 1956 Clean Air Act, which prohibited coal fires in central London, finally put an end to the city's famous fogs, which would cloak the whole town in thick, impenetrable, clammy mist. On the streets in a fearsome four-day 'pea-souper' smog in December 1952 it was hardly possible to see beyond the end of one's outstretched arm. Traffic was brought to a virtual standstill and several people died of aggravated chest and lung complaints. In 1957 there were no fish in the Thames between Richmond and Tilbury. A campaign began to clean up the river, and was so effective that to general astonishment a salmon was caught in the Thames in 1974.

In 1936 Edward VIII abdicated to marry divorced American socialite Wallis Simpson

Inventor of the mini-skirt and hot pants, Mary Quant epitomized 1960s fashion

1999

Prince Charles and Lady Diana Spencer were married in St. Paul's Cathedral in 1981, an event watched by millions (right)

Baroness Margaret Thatcher (left) was Britain's first woman prime minister. A Conservative, she held office from 1979 until 1990

In the 1960s you could eat in the revolving restaurant on BT Telecom's Tower (right)

London's
Millennium

London greeted the 21st century with its first elected mayor, the construction of a vast, tent-like exhibition hall known as the Millennium Dome, a giant Ferris wheel called the London Eye (see page 99), the new Tate Modern art gallery (see pages 134–135) and a wobbling bridge (see below). Two years after the celebration of a new millennium, the death of Elizabeth, the Queen Mother, marked the end of an era.

The Farewell

Half a million people waited for up to 12 hours to file past the Queen Mother's coffin in Westminster Hall before her funeral on 9 April, 2002, when Westminster Abbey's great tenor bell tolled 101 times, once for each year of her life. An estimated 300 million watched on television as a gun-carriage bore the coffin to the abbey, followed by the royal family, to the lament of massed bagpipes and drums. The abbey and Chapel Royal choirs took part in the service, at the end of which the coffin was taken out of the west door on its final journey to Windsor (see pages 236–237).

New Bridges

When the first pedestrians crossed the new Millennium Bridge (see page 100), formally opened by the Queen in 2000, it swayed so badly that some of them felt seasick. After a day or two the bridge had to be closed as dangerous. Fixed at a cost of £5 million, it reopened unobtrusively in 2002. Later that year came the less heralded new Hungerford Bridge, either side of the railway from Charing Cross. Designed with a gossamer elegance of white masts and steel cables by the Lifschutz Davidson partnership, it was inspired by Isambard Kingdom Brunel's original plan of 140 years before.

Greeting the Millennium

An estimated 3 million people turned out to line the Thames as fireworks blazed for New Year's Eve 2000, but a much-heralded 'river of fire' designed to sweep up the Thames did not seem to materialize. In Trafalgar Square (see page 136) 2,000 police were fielded to cope with a crowd of 65,000, but there were fewer arrests than usual and only 114 people were injured, of whom 21 had to be hospitalized. At Greenwich, meanwhile, the Queen and the Prime Minister arrived for the opening of the Millennium Dome. When the orchestra struck up Gustav Holst's *Jupiter* at 11pm many of the invited guests were still waiting for security checks at the tube stations, but those who did get to their seats on time enjoyed a spectacular show.

2000

Queen Elizabeth joined Prime Minister Tony Blair for New Year celebrations at the Millennium Dome in Greenwich (below and left). Many people turned out to mourn the death of the Queen Mother in April 2002 (above)

On the Move

ARRIVING

BY AIR

This is how most visitors enter the UK. London has air connections to all major world cities. If you are coming from another continent you will almost certainly arrive at either Heathrow, London's biggest and the world's busiest airport, or Gatwick, the next in size. London's three other airports, Stansted, Luton and London City, serve mainly short-haul destinations.

All five airports have information desks, shops, banks, restaurants, car rental firms, hotel reservation desks and left luggage facilities. For security reasons there are no luggage lockers at any of the airports.

London Heathrow (LHR), 12 miles (19km) to the west of central London, can be overwhelming.

There are four terminals: Terminals 1, 2 and 3 are located

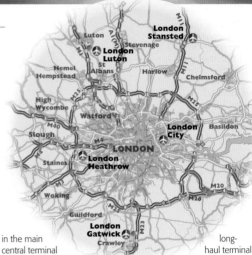

in the main central terminal complex; Terminal 4 is on the south side of the airport. **Terminal 1** serves all domestic flights, most UK departures to Europe and El Al and South African Airways flights. **Terminal 2** serves non-UK carriers' flights to Europe and some long-haul destinations. **Terminal 3** is the

long-haul terminal for the United States, South American, Asian and Asia Pacific airlines, plus most African carriers. **Terminal 4** serves British Airways (BA) long-haul flights and BA flights to Amsterdam, Athens, Paris, Moscow and Tel Aviv. KLM and Qantas also use Terminal 4.

GETTING TO CENTRAL LONDON FROM THE AIRPORT		
AIRPORT (CODE)	**HEATHROW (LHR)**	**GATWICK (LGW)**
TAXI	£45 1 hour	£75 1–1 hour 15 min
OVERLAND TRAINS	Heathrow Express to Paddington. Every 15 min 5.10am–11.40pm 365 days a year. £23 return. Save ⅛ on advanced bookings. Journey time: 15–20 min.	Gatwick Express to Victoria. Every 15 min 5.20am–1.35am and hourly 1.35am–4.30am. £21.50 return (under 16s £11). Journey time: 30 min. Thameslink service to King's Cross, Farringdon, City, Blackfriars and London Bridge. Tickets from £9.80 one way. Journey time: 40 min. Connex trains to Charing Cross via London Bridge. Every 15–30 min, once an hour 1am–4am. £8.20 one way. Journey time: 45 min.
TUBE (Underground)	Piccadilly Line from Terminals 1, 2 and 3 or Terminal 4. £3.60 adult/£1.50 child. Runs 5.30am–11.45pm daily. Tickets available in all baggage reclaim areas. Journey time: 1 hour.	N/A
BUS	National Express No. 412, 032 or 035 to Victoria Coach Station. Every 30 min. £15 return. Journey time: 40 min. A2 Airbus to King's Cross station. Every 30 min. £12 return. Journey time: 1 hour 30 min.	National Express No. 025 from North and South Terminals to Victoria Coach Station. £10 return. Every hour. Journey time: 1 hour 20 min.
CAR	Terminals 1, 2 and 3: junction 4, M4. Terminal 4: junction 3, M4. Travel eastbound along M4.	Junction 9, M23. Travel northbound along M23.

All four terminals are linked to the London Underground (one station serves Terminals 1, 2 and 3, another serves Terminal 4), reached by well-signposted moving walkways and elevators. American Airlines, BA and United Airlines now have check-in facilities at Paddington station. Passengers with connecting flights should follow the signs.

London Gatwick (LGW), Heathrow's smaller cousin, is 30 miles (48km) to the south of central London. It has two terminals, North and South, linked by the Gatwick Transit, an efficient and free monorail. Trains run every three to four minutes from each terminal, with a journey time of just under two minutes. The South Terminal handles the bulk of Gatwick's traffic, serving domestic, international and charter flights. BA and American Airlines passengers can check luggage in at Victoria station, central London.

London Stansted (LST), third in size, is 35 miles (56km) northeast of London, in Essex. The passenger terminal occupies a modern glass and steel building (1991) designed by British architect Norman Foster. Driverless rapid transit trains shuttle between this and the airport's other two buildings. Stansted is London's fastest-growing airport.

London Luton (LTN) occupies an ugly array of buildings 32 miles (52km) north of central London. A new passenger terminal opened in 1999, along with Luton Parkway railway station, from which there are frequent trains to King's Cross. It serves mainly low-cost charter flights, but some scheduled services operate from here.

London City Airport (LCA) is the capital's smallest airport, 6 miles (10km) from central London. Much used by business travellers, the airport has facilities

ON THE MOVE

TIPS
● When departing from Heathrow or Gatwick, check which terminal you will need.
● Ensure that departure tax is included in your airline ticket price. All domestic flights and those to destinations within the EU carry a £10 departure tax. For flights to other cities the charge is £20.
● Note that there are no black taxi cabs at Stansted.

such as meeting rooms and full secretarial services. Flights operate to 21 European destinations and 8 British airports. Check-in time is only 20 minutes before departure.

On arrival, you have several choices of transport to central London. The table below compares the methods of transport from each of the airports, with costs, journey times and frequency.

STANSTED (LST)	LUTON (LTN)	CITY (LCA)
£80 1–2 hours	£50–55 1 hour 45 min	£30 20–30 min
Stansted Express to Liverpool Street (Central line). Change at Tottenham Hale for the Victoria line. Runs 5.30am–12.30am. Every 15–30 min. No service on Sun. £23 return (child £12.50). Journey time: 45 min.	Free shuttle bus from terminal to Luton airport parkway station (8 min). Thameslink service to King's Cross, Farringdon, City, Blackfriars and London Bridge. Every 5–15 min 7am–10pm. £10 one way. Journey time: 35 min.	N/A
N/A	N/A	Green Shuttle to Canning Town. Every 10 min 6am–10.20pm. £2.50 one way. Journey time: 5 min. Blue Shuttle to Liverpool Street via Canary Wharf. Every 10–15 min 6.05am–10pm.. £12 return Liverpool Street,. £6 return Canary Wharf. Journey time: 25 min from Liverpool Street, 10 min from Canary Wharf. Reduced service Sat and Sun.
A6 Airbus to Victoria Coach Station. Every 30 min. £15 return (child £7.50). Journey time: 1hour 30 min.	Greenline Bus No. 757 to Victoria Coach Station. Every 30 min peak, every hour off peak. £11.50 return (child £8). Journey time: 1hour 30 min.	N/A
Junction 8, M11. Travel southbound along M11.	2 miles (3km) from junction 10, M1. Travel southbound along M1.	N/A

BY RAIL

Eurostar, the company that operates the Channel Tunnel rail service, links France (Paris and Lille) and Belgium (Brussels) directly to London in less than three hours. Eurostar's high-speed trains arrive in south London at Waterloo International station, which is served by the Underground as well as suburban and national rail.

Passports are required for travel and you must check in at least 30 minutes before the train is due to depart. One item of hand luggage and two suitcases are allowed per person.

On arrival you must clear passport control and customs. The Underground and buses are clearly marked or you can take a taxi from the rank immediately outside the station on the left.

National trains arrive from other parts of Britain into one of London's 11 main railway stations (see page 59). All stations have Underground links.

BY CAR

Eurotunnel operates the train service for cars, caravans and motorcycles through the Channel Tunnel. The journey between Calais and Folkestone takes 20 minutes, during which time drivers and passengers remain in their vehicles.

Upon arrival at Folkestone in the UK leave the terminal on the M20 northbound, joining at junction 11a. Traffic permitting, the drive to London takes just over one hour.

BY FERRY

Eurostar and Eurotunnel have taken a lot of traffic away from the ferries, but it is still a cheaper way of crossing the Channel. Various ferry companies operate services between British ports and ports on the European continent. Connex trains run from ports on the south coast—Dover, Folkestone, Ramsgate and Newhaven—to London Victoria. Great Eastern Railways and Anglia Railways operate a service from Harwich to Liverpool Street. Along with regular ferry services, certain ports (such as Calais) operate faster Seacat and Superseacat vessels.

BY COACH

If you travel to London by long-distance coach you will probably arrive at Victoria Coach Station (VCS) on Buckingham Palace Road, near Victoria main railway station. The coach station is a few minutes' walk from the Underground station, which is on the Victoria, District and Circle lines. Alternatively, there is a taxi rank immediately outside VCS.

USEFUL TELEPHONE NUMBERS AND WEBSITES

AIRPORTS

HEATHROW: tel 0870 0000123, www.baa.co.uk/heathrow
- Lost Property: tel 0870 0000123
- Left Luggage: Terminal 1 tel 020 8745 5301. Terminals 2, 3 and 4 tel 020 8759 3344.
  Offices can forward luggage
- Trains: Heathrow Express tel 0845 600 1515, www.heathrowexpress.co.uk
- Bus: tel 08705 747 777, www.nationalexpress.com
- Taxi: Terminal 1 tel 020 8745 7484. Terminal 2 tel 020 8745 5408. Terminal 3 tel 020 8745 4655. Terminal 4 tel 020 8745 7302

GATWICK: tel 0870 000 2468, www.baa.co.uk/gatwick
- Lost Property: tel 01293 503162
- Left Luggage: South Terminal tel 01293 502014, 24 hours. North Terminal tel 01293 502013.
- Trains: The Gatwick Express tel 0845 850 1530, www.gatwickexpress.co.uk. South Eastern Trains tel 0845 748 4950, www.setrains.co.uk. Thameslink tel 0845 748 4950, www.thameslink.co.uk
- Bus: tel 08705 747 777, www.nationalexpress.com
- Taxi: Checker Cars tel 1293 568 800

STANSTED: tel 0870 0000303, www.baa.co.uk/stansted
- Lost Property: Items lost in the airport tel 01279 663293
- Left Luggage: tel 0870 0000303.
- Trains: The Stansted Express tel 0845 850 0150, www.stanstedexpress.co.uk
- Bus: Airbus A6 tel 08705 747777, www.nationalexpress.com
- Taxi: Stansted Airport Cars tel 01279 662444

LUTON: tel 01582 405100, www.london-luton.co.uk
- Lost Property: tel 01582 395728
- Left Luggage: tel 01582 405100
- Trains: Thameslink tel 0845 7484950, www.thameslink.co.uk
- Bus: Greenline tel 08706 087261, www.greenline.co.uk
- Taxi: Cabco tel 01582 736666. Dial-a-cab tel 01582 595555. Taxirank outside terminal building

LONDON CITY: tel 020 7646 0088, www.londoncityairport.com
- Lost Property: tel 0207 646 0088
- Left Luggage: tel 0207 646 0088
- Trains: tel 0207 646 0088
- Bus: Shuttlebus tel 0207 646 0088, www.londoncityairport.com/shuttlebus
- Taxi: Taxirank outside terminal building

GENERAL AIRPORT INFORMATION:
- www.worldairportguide.com

COACH AND TRAIN
- Coach Tourism Council: www.coachtourismcouncil.co.uk
- Eurolines: tel 01582 404511
- Eurostar: UK tel 08705 186186. France tel 0033 089235353. Belgium tel 0032 25282828, www.eurostar.com
- Eurotunnel: tel 08705 35 35 35, www.eurotunnel.com
- National Express: tel 08705 808080, www.nationalexpress.com
- National Rail enquiries: tel 08457 484950
- Train timetables: www.railtrack.co.uk
- Victoria Coach Station: tel 020 7730 3466

GETTING AROUND
London Transport

London is a large city and at some stage you are bound to need to use its extensive public transport system, run by London Regional Transport (LRT). The Underground (tube), buses and overground trains principally make up the network, with the Docklands Light Railway (DLR), riverboats and Tramlink as additional options.

Electronic boards give minute-by-minute information about train arrivals and departures

Of the two main choices, Underground or bus, the Underground is certainly the quickest way to get around, but it is sometimes far from satisfactory and you will have to be patient at least once during your visit as a train is delayed or grinds to a halt for no apparent reason. It can also be very uncomfortable, hot and claustrophobic, involving long walks and several escalators and staircases. Buses, on the other hand, offer views and a chance to get to grips with the geography of London.

Taxis are useful for short distances, but longer journeys are expensive.

See pages 58–60 for train travel and coach (long-distance bus) information.

TRAVEL INFORMATION
● The main London Transport Information Centre, at Piccadilly Circus Underground station, is open daily 9 to 6 and supplies free route maps and schedules as well as information brochures in several languages.

You can also phone for around the clock information *(tel 020 7222 1234)*.

● Other travel information offices can be found at Heathrow Airport (Terminals 1, 2 and 3), Euston, King's Cross, Oxford Circus, St. James's Park, and Liverpool Street Underground stations, and Victoria train station.

CHILDREN AND PUBLIC TRANSPORT
● Accompanied children under the age of five are entitled to travel free on all Underground and DLR services.
● Up to two accompanied children under the age of five can travel free on the buses and Tramlink (see page 56).
● Pushchairs may need to be folded and placed in the storage areas on buses.
● Child fares apply to children aged 5 to 15.
● Children aged 14 or 15 need a child photocard to buy and use any child fare ticket or travel card. These are available from all Underground stations or London Transport Information Centres.
● Children travel on all bus routes for 40 pence, except after 10pm, when they must pay full adult fare on all buses.

DISCOUNTS
● Various youth and student reductions are available on weekly and monthly travelcards.
● Reductions for people over the age of 60 are available to London residents only.

TICKETS
● You can buy tickets for all forms of public transport at most Underground stations, London Travel Information Centres and national rail stations, and at 2,500 local ticket outlets, including many newsagents.

● If you know where you want to travel use the ticket machines. Change is given. Touch-screen ticket machines at Underground stations also accept Electron and Solo cards.
● Ticket offices at Underground stations do close occasionally.
● One-day tickets can be bought four days in advance; try to order and collect tickets outside morning or evening rush hour.
● Underground stations and London Travel Information Centres accept personal cheques, supported by a cheque guarantee card, and credit cards.
● Monthly travelcards are available through Ticketline *(www.ticket-on-line.co.uk or www.ticket-on-line.com if you are buying tickets outside the UK)*.
● For further information on London fares, see the individual transport entries below or pick up a copy of the 'Fares and Tickets' leaflet from Underground stations and London Travel Information Centres.

TIPS
● If possible avoid travelling during the rush hour (weekdays 7.30 to 9.30am and 4 to 7pm). The Underground in particular gets extremely crowded and many buses are so full that waiting passengers are unable to board.
● Buy a travelcard (see page 48), which is valid for the entire transport network.
● Use common sense when travelling alone at night, but there is no need to be unduly concerned.
● Do not smoke on any public transport—it is banned.

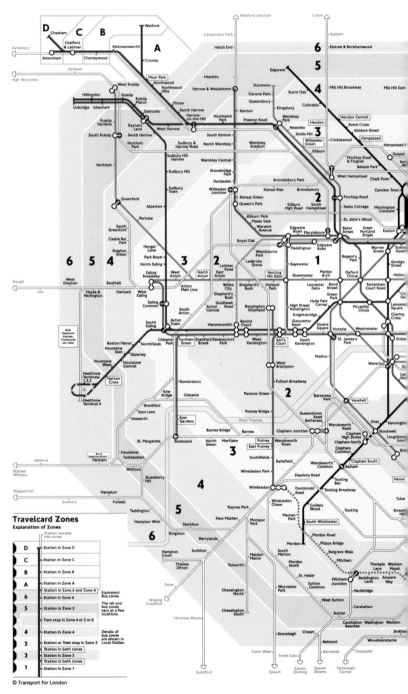

Travelcard Zones
Explanation of Zones

		Station outside the zones
D		Station in Zone D
C		Station in Zone C
B		Station in Zone B
A		Station in Zone A
6		Station in Zone 6 and Zone A	Equivalent bus zones
6		Station in Zone 6	The rail and bus zones vary at a few locations.
5		Station in Zone 5	
4		Station in Zone 4	Details of bus zones are shown in Local Guides.
3		Station or Tram stop in Zone 3	
2		Station in both zones	
2		Station in Zone 2	
1		Station in both zones	
1		Station in Zone 1	

© Transport for London

London Transport Zones Map

TRAVELCARDS AND ZONES

- Travelcards are valid for the entire transport network in selected zones, including buses, Underground (tube), Docklands Light Railway (DLR), Croydon Tramlink and Suburban national rail services within the London area (excluding Heathrow Express).
- Travelcards give you unlimited travel within the zone area paid for, as well as one-third off most riverboat services. They are available from Underground stations, London Travel Information Centres, national rail stations (in the London area) and many newsagents across the capital. You can buy a travelcard up to four days before you intend to use it.
- For the purposes of transport pricing the London area is divided into zones, central London occupying Zone 1 with Zones 2–6 following in progressively wider concentric rings (see pages 46–47).
- The concept is simple. The more zones you want to travel in, the more you have to pay. Ensure that your travelcard or ticket is valid for the zones that you travel in or through, or you may find yourself paying a £10 on-the-spot fine.

TRAVELCARDS	VALID	ZONES AND PRICES	NOTES
1 Day Travelcard (Peak)	1am–4.30am the following day, Mon–Fri (except public holidays).	Zones 1 and 2: £5.10 adult, £2.50 child. Zones 1–6: £10.70 adult, £5.30 child.	For Underground, bus, Tramlink and DLR services, it is cheaper to buy a one-day LT card.
1 Day Travelcard (Off-Peak)	From 9.30am Mon–Fri and 1am on Sat, Sun and public holidays until 4.30am the following day.	Zones 1 and 2: £4.10 adult, £2 child (children must buy a Zone 1–6 ticket). Zones 1–6: £5.10 adult, £2 child.	If you are using only Underground, bus, Tramlink and DLR services, it is cheaper to buy a one-day LT card.
1 Day LT Cards	Every day of the week, 1am–4.30am the following day. Selected zones on Underground, Tramlink, DLR and bus services except certain special services.	Zones 1–6: £8 adult, £3.50 child. Seven-day, monthly and yearly LT cards are available. If you are travelling within Zones 1–4 only, a peak or off-peak day travelcard will be cheaper.	Not valid for travel on national rail services, or stations on the Bakerloo line between Kenton and Harrow & Wealdstone.
Weekend Travelcard	Sat and Sun or any two consecutive days during public holidays. From 1am on the first day until 4.30am on the final day.	Zones 1 and 2: £6.10 adult, £3 child (children must buy a Zone 1–6). Zones 1–6: £7.60 adult, £3 child.	25 per cent cheaper than two separate off-peak day travelcards. Not available from DLR and Tramlink ticket machines.
Carnet	Book of 10 single tickets for the Underground within Zone 1 for up to 12 months from date of purchase.	Zone 1: £11.50 adult (£1.15 per journey), £5 child (50p per journey).	
Weekly Travelcard	Valid, with a photocard only, for seven consecutive days and can be used at any time. For travel on Underground, buses, Tramlink, DLR and most national rail services in the London area.	Zones 1 and 2: £19.60 adult, £8 child. Zones 1–6: £37.20 adult, £15.90 child.	
Visitor Travelcard	All-zone visitor travelcards are available for varying periods of time from two to seven consecutive days.	All zones. Prices vary depending on agents where you purchase your ticket. You can also buy online at www.ticket-on-line.com.	Can be purchased only overseas through a travel agent (not for sale in the UK). Redeem voucher at any Underground ticket office or London Travel Information Centre. Vouchers issued saving up to £25 on attractions and restaurants.

London Underground

London's Underground system is also known as the tube. The earliest lines, dating from the mid-19th century, were constructed close to the surface using a technique known as 'cut and cover'; builders dug a trench, laid the tracks, then roofed over the trench and replaced the earth. The later, deeper lines were constructed using tunnel boring machines. These lines were called 'tubes', and the name stuck.

ON THE MOVE

Every Underground station is well signposted

The London Underground system is the oldest and most extensive network of its kind in the world, with more than 500 trains and over 260 stations, and maintenance is an on-going challenge. Much of the track is old and subject to repairs, leading to breakdowns and delays. That said, the Jubilee line was extended and opened in 1999 to provide a state-of-the-art metro system between central and eastern London. It was Europe's biggest engineering project and the new stations built along the line are an attraction in their own right. Prominent architects were chosen to design the stations. Canary Wharf, for example, hailed as an 'underground cathedral', was designed by Norman Foster.

Twelve lines make up the Greater London Underground system and each has its own name and is colour-coded on the Underground map (see inside back cover). Stations with interchanges with other lines and with suburban rail are marked with a white circle on the map.

Trains run from approximately 5.30am Monday to Saturday (7am Sunday) to approximately midnight Monday to Saturday (11pm Sunday).

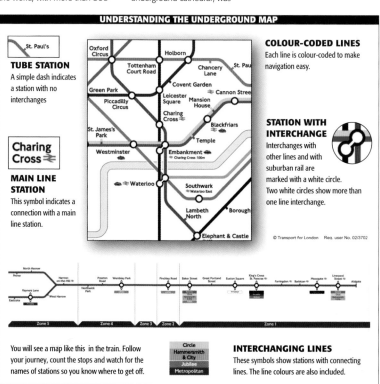

UNDERSTANDING THE UNDERGROUND MAP

TUBE STATION
A simple dash indicates a station with no interchanges

MAIN LINE STATION
This symbol indicates a connection with a main line station.

COLOUR-CODED LINES
Each line is colour-coded to make navigation easy.

STATION WITH INTERCHANGE
Interchanges with other lines and with suburban rail are marked with a white circle. Two white circles show more than one line interchange.

© Transport for London Req. user No. 02/3702

You will see a map like this in the train. Follow your journey, count the stops and watch for the names of stations so you know where to get off.

INTERCHANGING LINES
These symbols show stations with connecting lines. The line colours are also included.

HOW TO SURVIVE THE UNDERGROUND

- Stand on the right on escalators so that people in a hurry can walk on the left (see figure 1).
- Be aware that if you cannot produce a valid ticket you will be given an on-the-spot fine of £10.
- Watch out for keys, security passes and some handbag clasps; they may cause magnetic interference and damage your ticket.
- If you are travelling with bulky items, pushchairs or folding bicycles, use the special wide gates provided. Ask a member of staff to let you through.
- Stand clear of the train's closing doors. Obstructing them slows trains down and causes delays (see figure 2).
- Mind the gap between the platform and the train (see figure 3).
- Let passengers off the train first before embarking (see figure 4).
- Stand behind the yellow line on the platform when waiting for a train (see figure 5).
- Avoid taking too much luggage on the Underground. Storage space is limited, and there are no porters.
- Be prepared for heat in summer. There is no air-conditioning, and delays are not uncommon.
- Mobile phones are permitted, but don't expect to get a signal underground.
- Report threats and violent behaviour to members of staff.
- Watch out for pickpockets. Keep your bags securely fastened and don't carry valuables in back pockets or rucksacks (see figure 6).

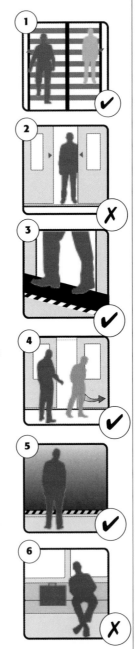

You can estimate your journey time by allowing three minutes between each station

TIPS

- Check the service update section of www.thetube.com/content/visit in German, Spanish, French, Italian or Portuguese to see if trains are running smoothly. A journey planner on the site helps you plan how to get from A to B in the easiest way.
- Also see www.thetube.com or tel 020 7222 1234 for up-to-date news and information.
- To avoid ending up at the wrong destination, be sure to check the indicator display on the platform and the front of the train displaying the final destination station.
- Buy a pocket-size London Underground map, sold at most Underground stations.
- Travel after 9.30am and at weekends for cheaper tickets.
- Buy tickets at the machines, or at a sales booth.
- Note there are two types of machine. One has a few buttons for the most common fares (one destination, single or return ticket and travel cards), the other has lots of buttons, one for every station and ticket type.
- You will need your ticket to get out of the station, so don't throw it away.

A TYPICAL JOURNEY ON THE UNDERGROUND

From South Ealing to Oxford Circus.

SOUTH EALING

Journey time: 42 min
Zones used: 1, 2, 3
Single fare: adult £2.30, child £1

Find a map and identify the colours of the lines you will need.

Buy a ticket for all the zones you will be travelling through.

Insert your ticket face upwards in the front of the machine at the gates. When it emerges from the top slot, take it out and the gates will open.

Follow signs for the PICCADILLY LINE, going down stairs or escalators where necessary.

Check the board between the two platforms and choose the platform for the train heading towards Green Park.

Wait for the PICCADILLY LINE train on the platform. The electronic display on the platform tells you when the train is due to arrive and where it terminates.

Get on the train heading for COCKFOSTERS, ARNOS GROVE, OAKWOOD or KING'S CROSS ST. PANCRAS. This information will be displayed on the electronic platform displays as the train arrives and on the front of the train.

Board the train quickly and carefully.

Track the number of stops until you need to change on the route map above the window in the train. On arrival at stations, announcements inform you of the connections available at each one. Stations are easily identified by the large Underground signs mounted on platforms and visible from inside the train. (34 min)

GREEN PARK

Leave the train at GREEN PARK.
Change on to the VICTORIA LINE. Follow signs. (2 min)

Wait for the VICTORIA LINE train on the platform. (3 min)

Get on the train heading for WALTHAMSTOW CENTRAL, SEVEN SISTERS or KING'S CROSS ST. PANCRAS. (3 min)

OXFORD CIRCUS

Leave the train at OXFORD CIRCUS. When you complete your journey, your ticket will be retained in the machine at the exit..

Follow signs to the relevant exit for the street you want.

ON THE MOVE

FARES

Fares for the Underground depend on the zones you wish to travel in. If you are travelling through many zones several times a day, consider purchasing a travelcard or taking advantage of discounted fares (see page 48). Child fares apply to children 5 to 15; children age 14 or 15 require a photocard.

Zones	Adult (£)	Child (£)
One Zone (at a time)		
Zone 1	1.60	60p
Zones 2–6	1.00	40p
Two Zones		
Zones 1–2	2.00	80p
Zones 2–3, 3–4, 4–5, 5–6	1.30	60p
Three Zones		
Zones 1–3	2.30	1.00
Zones 2–4, 3–5, 4–6	1.70	80p
Four Zones		
Zones 1–4	2.80	1.20
Zones 2–5, 3–6	2.10	1.00
Five Zones		
Zones 1–5	3.40	1.40
Zones 2–6	2.30	1.10
Six Zones		
Zones 1–6	3.70	1.50

COLOURS OF UNDERGROUND LINES

BAKERLOO
CENTRAL
CIRCLE
DISTRICT
EAST LONDON
HAMMERSMITH & CITY
JUBILEE
METROPOLITAN
NORTHERN
PICCADILLY
VICTORIA
WATERLOO & CITY
DOCKLANDS LIGHT RAILWAY

Buses

London's bright red double-decker buses, along with the black cabs (see page 57), have become a London icon. You cannot fail to notice them as you walk around the capital. Increasingly you will see other types of buses travelling around London, as well as the more traditional red buses. A London bus route runs along most main roads in central London. For short journeys and if you are not in a hurry the buses can be a pleasant way of getting around. On longer journeys they are slower than trains or the Underground but they are usually less expensive and quite comfortable.

ON THE MOVE

- Daytime buses in London run Monday to Saturday from around 6am to midnight and Sunday from 7.30am to 11.30pm. In theory, buses run at least once every 10 to 15 minutes in each direction along the route, and much more frequently on heavily used routes. In practice, because of the traffic conditions, you can wait 30 minutes for a bus to arrive, and then three are likely to come along at once.
- Buses come in two styles, so-called Routemaster buses, with a conductor, and driver-only buses.
- Routemaster buses are older and have an open platform at the back where you get on and off; the conductor will sell you a ticket or check your pass.
- Driver-only buses have two doors: one at the front, where you board, and one midway, where you get off. Pay the driver when you board. You need to have change ready.
- Drivers and conductors prefer the exact money, but they will give change.

- On both types of bus you have to let the driver know you want to get off at a particular stop. Press the red button on a driver-only bus, or pull the cord at the side of the cabin on a Routemaster.
- If you do not have a travelcard (see page 48), simply tell the driver or conductor where you want to go and he or she will tell you the fare.
- Hold on to your ticket until the end of the journey, because inspectors regularly board the buses to check tickets and catch fare-dodgers.

TICKET OPTIONS
- For single adult cash bus fares the whole of the London bus network is divided into two separate areas: Zone 1 (£1) and any journey in the rest of London not passing through Zone 1 (70p).
- For child single cash fares, a flat ticket price of 40p applies on all journeys.
- Remember that return fares are not available on London bus services.
- Alternatively you can purchase a 'saver' ticket. This is a book of six single tickets costing £3.90, which works out at 65p per journey. A book of six child tickets costs £2.10 and works out at 35p per journey.
- On certain marked routes, cash single fares are not available on the buses. If you do not hold a bus pass, a book of tickets or a travelcard, you must buy a cash single ticket or a one-day bus pass before boarding. Roadside ticket machines are located at all bus stops on routes where this system applies.

UNDERSTANDING BUS STOPS

BUS NUMBERS
Each route is marked by a number on the front and the back of the bus corresponding to the numbers on the bus stops. The final destination of the bus is often displayed on the bus along with a brief list of the areas of London on the route.

TIMETABLES
Timetables can be found at bus stops either posted inside bus shelters or attached to individual bus stops. They show the first and last buses on the route you want and allow you to work out the frequency of the service, the times the bus will arrive at your stop and when it will reach the destination you require. The stop that you are standing at will be marked in bold on the timetable.

BUS STOP

Marble Arch

towards
Oxford Circus

6	12	15
23	94	159
N3	N6	N12
N15	N16	N36
	N23	N98

BUS STOP TYPES
- Bus stops are marked by a London Transport circular BUS STOP sign which has a line through the middle with either a white or red background.

- At main bus stops (signs show a red circle on a white background) you will find information on bus routes, route numbers and times. The bus will stop here automatically.

- At request stops (white circle on a red background) you must hail the bus.

- At night treat all stops as request stops.

- As on the Underground, you can purchase day passes, priced at £2 for adults and £1 for children, or week passes at £8.50 for adults, £4 for children.
- However, if you are going to use the Underground as well during the day you are better off buying an Underground travelcard, as these are valid on buses, but not vice versa.

NIGHT BUSES
- Night buses (the number is preceded by 'N') run between 11pm and 6am on main routes through London; the majority pass through Trafalgar Square.
- A leaflet called 'Buses for Night Owls' detailing the routes and times is available from London Travel Information Centres.
- Night buses stop only at bus stops if requested, and fares are the same as daytime fares, except for children, who pay adult fares after 10pm.

TIP
- To find out how to get around by bus, call London Transport (*tel 020 7222 1234 or visit www.transportforlondon. gov.uk*).

Buses run 24 hours a day throughout central London

ON THE MOVE

BUS BUSTER CHART

Use this chart to find out which buses you'll need to travel from one destination to another. Follow the rows of squares horizontally and vertically from the names of the destinations until they meet. This square contains the number(s) of the bus(es) you'll need to catch. Only the most frequent buses have been included.

Bus numbers on white squares are direct.

Numbers in coloured squares show that you have to change buses. Start out on the first bus listed, then change to the second bus. Look at the key to find out where you must change.

Routes change regularly. Check an up-to-date timetable or bus map before setting out.

CHANGE AT:
- The Aldwych
- Hyde Park Corner
- Trafalgar Square
- Piccadilly Circus
- Tottenham Court Road
- Warren Street

MAIN VISITOR BUS ROUTES

Certain routes link key attractions or provide interesting views. Below are seven routes of particular interest.

8

St. Paul's Cathedral
The City
Buckingham Palace, Westminster Abbey
Petticoat Lane Market
Wellington Arch
British Museum
Mayfair

Victoria Station · Hyde Park Corner · Green Park Station · Berkeley Square · Oxford Circus · Tottenham Court Rd Station · Holborn Station · Chancery Lane Station · Holborn Circus · Holborn Viaduct · St. Paul's Station · Bank · Liverpool Street Station · Shoreditch · Bethnal Green · Roman Road · Old Ford · Bow Church

Older-style Routemaster buses have an open platform at the back and a conductor

Newer, driver-only buses have two sets of automated doors and passengers pay the driver on entry

11

Houses of Parliament, Westminster Abbey, Cabinet War Rooms, Whitehall
Buckingham Palace
National Gallery, National Portrait Gallery
Covent Garden
The City

Fulham Broadway · King's Road · Chelsea · Sloane Square · Victoria coach Station · Victoria Station · Westminster · Trafalgar Square · Strand · Aldwych · St. Paul's Cathedral · Ludgate Circus · St. Paul's Cathedral · Mansion House Station · Bank · Liverpool Street Station

14

The Natural History, Science, V&A museums
Buckingham Palace, Wellington Arch
Royal Academy, Shaftesbury Avenue theatres
Harrods
British Museum

Putney Heath · Putney Station · Putney Bridge · Fulham Road · Fulham Broadway · Fulham Road · Fulham Road · South Kensington Station · Knightsbridge Station · Hyde Park Corner · Green Park Station · Piccadilly Circus · Tottenham Court Road Station

15

Mansion House
National Gallery, National Portrait Gallery
Petticoat Lane Market · Tower of London
Selfridge's
Monument
Covent Garden

Blackwall Station (day) or East Ham (eve) · Poplar · Limehouse · Limehouse Station · Commercial Road · Aldgate Station · Tower Hill · Monument Station · Cannon Street · Mansion House Station · St. Paul's Cathedral · Ludgate Circus · Aldwych · Strand · Trafalgar Square · Piccadilly Circus · Oxford Circus · Bond Street Station · Oxford Street · Marble Arch · Edgeware Rd · Padd

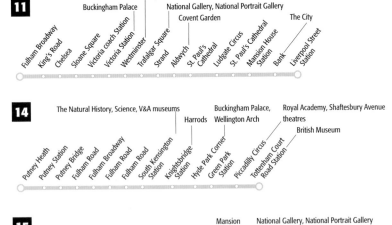

MAIN VISITOR BUS ROUTES

74

Madame Tussaud's & London Planetarium
Buckingham Palace
Selfridge's — Harrods, Hyde Park — Natural History, Science, V& A museums

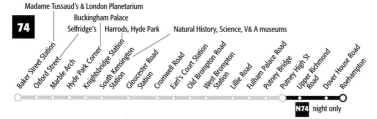

Baker Street Station · Oxford Street · Marble Arch · Hyde Park Corner · Knightsbridge Station · South Kensington Station · Gloucester Road Station · Cromwell Road · Earl's Court Station · Old Brompton Road · West Brompton Station · Lillie Road · Fulham Palace Road · Putney Bridge · Putney High St. · Upper Richmond Road · Dover House Road · Roehampton

N74 night only

188

National Maritime Museum, *Cutty Sark*   Covent Garden

North Greenwich Station · Greenwich District Hospital · Greenwich · Creek Road · Deptford · Surrey Quays Station · Surrey Quays Shopping Centre · Canada Water Station · Bermondsey Station · Tower Bridge Road · Bermondsey Square · Bricklayers Arms · Elephant & Castle · Waterloo Station · Aldwych · Holborn Station · Russell Square

NEW RV1 ROUTE

A bus service of particular interest to visitors is Riverside 1, which links the South Bank to the West End and the City. The route, aimed at boosting tourism, employment and accessibility for local communities, brings together more than 30 arts and visitor attractions, five Underground stations, three national rail stations and five river piers. The service runs from Tower Gateway past London Bridge station, Bankside and Waterloo station up to Covent Garden.

The buses, sporting the traditional red livery of London buses, carry a Riverside bus logo and a series of icons identifying key destinations on the route. In addition, special information

screens on the bus alert passengers to approaching destinations and their attractions.

RV1 buses run daily every 10 minutes between 6am and midnight. On board, you can pick up a guide to local attractions.

For details visit www.southbank london.com/ riverside.

The RV1 route is useful as it links many of the city's main visitor attractions

RV1   London Bridge City Pier   London Eye, Waterloo, Millennium Pier   OXO Tower   Festival Pier

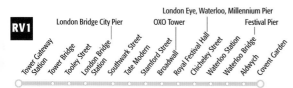

Tower Gateway Station · Tower Bridge · Tooley Street · London Bridge Station · Southwark Street · Tate Modern · Stamford Street · Broadwall · Royal Festival Hall · Chicheley Street · Waterloo Station · Waterloo Bridge · Aldwych · Covent Garden

DLR and River Boats

The Docklands Light Railway (DLR) and London's river transport network complement London's Underground and buses to provide an integrated public transport system.

The efficient Docklands Light Railway covers eastern areas of London

River cruises go past the Thames Barrier, installed to prevent flooding in the city

DOCKLANDS LIGHT RAILWAY

● The computerized and driverless trains of the Docklands Light Railway (DLR) serve the Docklands area to the east of the City. For the most part they run on an elevated track, allowing panoramic views.
● The DLR is part of the Underground system, so travelcards (see page 48) may be used.
● From Bank or Tower Gateway station (near Tower Hill Underground), the system runs south through the Isle of Dogs and Greenwich to Lewisham, north to Stratford, or east to Beckton.
● Mechanical and engineering faults have dogged the DLR, but it can usually be counted upon to run Monday to Friday 5.30am to 12.30pm with a more limited weekend service.
● There is a 10 per cent discount for group single, return, One-Day Shuttle and Flyer tickets. They must be booked at least seven days in advance by calling DLR Customer Services (tel 020 7363 9700).
● For more information on the DLR contact DLR Customer Services or visit www.dlr.co.uk.

LONDON RAIL AND RIVER ROVER TICKETS

● These allow you one full day unlimited hop-on hop-off travel on City Cruises River Boats and the Docklands Light Railway. It is possible to go by boat from Westminster to Greenwich, for example, and return on the DLR to Tower Hill.
● Tickets can be bought at all DLR stations except Bank and Canning Town: £8.30 for adults, £4.20 for children and £22 for a family. Group and family tickets can be bought seven days in advance.
● For more information visit www.dlr.co.uk or tel 020 7363 9700.

RIVERBOATS

● Travelcard holders (see page 48) receive a third-off discount on most riverboat services. Most services start and end at Westminster Pier, which is the midway point along the Thames.
● Boats operate from 6.30am to 10pm but vary slightly according to the route. The network extends from Hampton Court Palace (see page 159) in the west to the Thames Barrier (see page 164) in the east.
● You can travel on the river with a single, return or DLR River Rover ticket.
● There are ticket offices on the piers or on the boats themselves in some cases.
● Upriver, you can go from Westminster Millennium Pier to Hampton Court Pier via Kew and Richmond piers. This service operates, subject to tides, at 10.30am, 11.15am, noon and 2pm (Kew only) March to October. A round trip to Hampton Court can take between seven and eight hours. The last boat from Hampton Court is at 5pm. A single ticket is £12 and a return is £18. Children travel half price. For more information contact Westminster Passenger Services (tel 020 7930 2062).
● Downriver, you can go from Embankment Pier to Greenwich Pier via Waterloo Millennium Pier, Bankside Pier and Tower Pier. These services depart from Embankment every 45 minutes from 10.30am until 4pm. The last boat returns from Greenwich at 5.45pm. A return ticket costs between £4 and £8. Children (5–16) travel half price; under 5s free. Hopper passes cost £9 for adults, £4.50 for children. For more information contact Catamaran Cruisers (tel 020 7987 1185).

TRAMLINK

● Tramlink, the south London tram network, comprises three routes that run between the Wimbledon, Croydon and New Addington areas.
● Tickets must be bought before boarding at the automatic ticket machines at all Tramlink stops. Failure to do so will result in a £25 fine.
● See Travelcards and Zones on page 48 for more ticket information.

Taxis and Minicabs

There are two types of taxi in London: black cabs and minicabs.

BLACK CABS

Like the buses, London's black cabs are world-famous. The black cabs' design remains distinctive despite the fact that cabs now have advertising and come in colours other than the traditional black. You can rely on a London cabbie (driver) to know where he's going. Drivers must be licensed and have to pass extensive exams, dubbed 'the Knowledge' (see page 15), to demonstrate that they know the city well enough to take passengers anywhere in London following the most direct route.

● Cabs operate 24 hours a day, 365 days a year, but you will be hard pushed to find one on New Year's Eve, when the England football team is playing, or in a downpour when West End theatres and cinemas empty.

The ubiquitous black cab

● Drivers must accept a fare of up to 12 miles (19km) in London, 20 miles (32km) if the journey is from Heathrow Airport, and journeys of up to one hour in Metropolitan and City districts. Although they may be willing, taxi drivers are not obliged to accept journeys outside this range. If they do accept, and the journey is wholly within the London area, the fare payable is as shown on the meter.

● For more information on London taxis and charges, visit www.transportforlondon.gov.uk.

Cabs can be hailed in the street when the light is on

TIPS
To get a cab:
● Hail one in the street. Only those with an illuminated TAXI sign are vacant and will stop.
● Go to a designated taxi rank, usually found outside railway stations and large hotels.
● Ring Black Cab London *(tel 0800 169 5296)*, for airport journeys and sightseeing; reservation only.

CHARGES
● The cost of a cab journey is regulated through a metering system and is displayed inside the cab, at the front.
● Tariffs are calculated according to the distance you have travelled, unless the taxi speed drops below 10mph (16kph), when it is calculated per minute.
● Extra charges are made for telephone booking, travel during the Christmas and New Year period, and for additional luggage.
● It is common practice to tip 10–15 per cent of the total fare. Although this is not compulsory, drivers expect it.

Monday to Friday 6am to 8pm
£2 up to: 361m or 77.6 seconds. Then: additional 20p every 180.5m/38.8 seconds (up to £12.40)
Thereafter: additional 20p every 125.9m/27.7 seconds

Saturday & Sunday 6am to 8pm
£2 up to: 296.6m or 63.8 seconds. Then: additional 20p every 148.3m/31.9 seconds (up to £14.80)
Thereafter: additional 20p every 128.9m/27.7 seconds

Every night and all times on public holidays 8pm to 6am
£2 up to: 238.2m or 501.2 seconds. Then: additional 20p every 119.1m/25.6 seconds (up to £18)
Thereafter: additional 20p every 128.9m/27.7 seconds

MINICABS
● These are saloon cars and must be booked by phone or from a minicab firm office. Do not hail a minicab in the streets, as drivers may be untrained or uninsured.
● Avoid taxi touts who operate at airports and stations as they overcharge and are even more likely to be unlicensed or uninsured. Take licensed black cabs from taxi ranks at airports and stations or ring a recommended minicab firm in advance to arrange for someone to pick you up.

TAXI FIRMS
Airport taxi: tel 020 7486 4400
Computer Cab: tel 020 7286 0286
Dial-A-Cab: tel 020 7253 5000
Lady Cabs: tel 020 7254 3501
London Taxi: tel 0700 596 3532
Radio Taxi Cabs: tel 020 7272 0272

LEAVING LONDON

BY TRAIN

London has 11 mainline rail stations, each serving a different region of the country as well as providing cross-city services (see opposite). Most parts of the UK can be reached in a day from London: Intercity trains on major routes travel at 140mph (225kph), so journey times from one end of the country to the other can take just a few hours. Conversely, some trains stop at every station so travelling a relatively short distance can seem interminable.

Several different companies now operate the railway network, which can lead to some curious price anomalies as each company determines its own fare structure. It is worth checking whether another company serving the same region can offer an alternative route or price.

There are two classes of train travel: first and second. First is more expensive but does guarantee you a seat on crowded trains as well as complementary drinks and newspapers. Otherwise second class (standard) is perfectly acceptable and you can reserve a seat if you book in advance.

Sleeping compartments can be booked with Scotrail on some overnight services to and from Scotland *(tel 08457 550033)*.

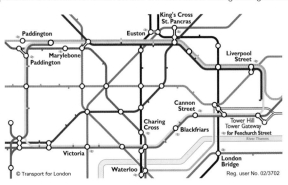

LONDON'S MAINLINE RAILWAY STATIONS

Map shows distribution of main line stations and the interconnecting Underground lines.

King's Cross St. Pancras
Paddington
Euston
Marylebone
Paddington
Liverpool Street
Cannon Street
Charing Cross
Blackfriars
Tower Hill
Tower Gateway
for Fenchurch Street
River Thames
Victoria
Waterloo
London Bridge
© Transport for London
Reg. user No. 02/3702

On Board

● Because many different train operators run services on the national network, the services and conditions on board trains vary depending on the service you use.

● All trains have toilet facilities, and longer routes tend to have some form of catering service on board, usually a refreshments trolley.

● Ask the train operator about any lost property.

● No smoking. It is banned on most train services except where smoking carriages are provided.

● In some carriages, the use of mobile phones is prohibited.

Stations

● All but very small local stations have toilet and refreshment facilities.

● Few stations have left-luggage facilities for security reasons, but King's Cross station provides a good if expensive facility.

● Larger stations have information desks where you can report lost property.

● If you are changing trains, check information screens when you arrive to find the right platform for your connection. The destination of a train should be marked on screens on the platform or on the train.

Tickets

● You can get a ticket for any company or any destination from any rail station, either from the ticket office or from auto-mated machines. Most Underground stations sell rail tickets, too, as do travel agents. Tickets can also be booked and paid for over the phone.

● Many different ticket options are available, so it pays to do some homework in advance, particularly as the cheapest options require buying tickets a week or more in advance.

● For a day trip, cheap-day return tickets are the best buy, but they can be purchased and used only after 9.30am.

● If you intend to leave London by train on several occasions, it may pay to buy a national rail-card, valid for a year. It costs £20, for which you get a 33 per cent discount on fares to sta-tions in southeast England for up to four people.

MAINLINE STATIONS AND MAJOR DESTINATIONS				
STATION	**REGIONS**	**MAJOR TRAIN OPERATORS**	**UNDERGROUND CONNECTIONS**	**MAJOR DESTINATIONS**
Euston	Midlands, North West, Scotland	Virgin, Scotrail, Silverlink	Northern, Victoria, Hammersmith and City, Metropolitan	Glasgow Manchester
St. Pancras	Midlands	Midland Mainline, Thameslink	Northern, Victoria, Piccadilly, Hammersmith and City, Circle, Metropolitan	Edinburgh Manchester
King's Cross	East Midlands, Yorkshire, North East, Scotland	GNER, Hull trains, Thameslink	Northern, Victoria, Piccadilly, Hammersmith and City, Cirlce, Metropolitan	Cambridge Edinburgh York
Liverpool Street	East Anglia, Essex	Stansted Express, WAGN, Anglia Trains, First Great Eastern	Hammersmith and City, Circle, Metropolitan, Central	Cambridge Norwich
Fenchurch Street	Thames Estuary, Essex	C2C	Circle, District	Southend
London Bridge	South East	Thameslink, South Central	Jubilee, Northern	
Charing Cross	South East	South Central, South Eastern Trains	Northern, Bakerloo,	Dover
Waterloo	South West, Wales	South West Trains, Wales & Borders, Eurostar	Northern, Bakerloo, Jubilee, Waterloo and City	Cardiff Exeter, Salisbury Winchester, Windsor
Victoria	Southern England	Gatwick Express, South Central	Victoria, District, Circle	Brighton, Canterbury
Paddington	South and West Midlands, West Country, Wales	First Great Western, Thames Trains, Heathrow Express	District, Circle, Hammersmith and City, Bakerloo	Bath, Bristol, Oxford Stratford-upon-Avon Windsor (change at Slough)
Marylebone	Midlands	Chiltern Railways	Bakerloo	Birmingham

● A young person's railcard (for those aged 16 to 25 and mature students in full-time education) costs £18 and gives a third off rail travel across the country (*www.youngpersons-railcard.co.uk*).
● Senior citizens railcards cost £20 and give a third off fares.
● To buy railcards, you need a passport-size photo.
● Children under five travel free and 5- to 15-year-olds pay half price for most tickets—but check, as there are exceptions.

SUBURBAN TRAINS
The national rail network offers another way of getting across London and to the edges of the city. This service is particularly useful in south and southeast London, where the Underground system is less extensive. Travelcards (see page 48) are valid on trains for journeys within the zone system (see pages 46–47).

Scotrail
● Scotrail runs the City Flyer service from Bedford, north of

TIPS
● If you want to be sure of a seat, avoid rush hour (weekdays 7 to 9.30am and 4 to 7pm). Thousands of London commuters use the services daily at that time.
● Telephone 08457 484950 for prices and timetables for all UK trains and destinations, or visit www.railtrack.com for timetables.

London, through London. This stops at five main London stations (King's Cross Thameslink, Farringdon, City Thameslink, Blackfriars and London Bridge) and continues down to Brighton.

● The Thameslink City Flyer service also connects London with Luton Airport and Gatwick Airport (see page 43).

● Thameslink also operates a city metro service, linking the City with the West End.

Silverlink Train Services

● Silverlink operates a county rail service connecting London and Birmingham, stopping at Milton Keynes, Northampton, Hemel Hempstead and Watford. It also runs a metro suburban route covering west, north and east London.

COACH

● Coaches (long-distance buses) run from London to all parts of the country, leaving from Victoria Coach Station (VCS), 164 Buckingham Palace Road SW1W 9TP. They provide a much cheaper but slower alternative to rail travel (see below).

● VCS has a travel counter, open 8 to 7 Monday to Friday, 8 to 4.30 Saturday and 8 to 3 Sunday. Here you can buy or book airport coach tickets, tours and excursions, London travelcards, theatre and concert tickets, rail tickets, ferry and hovercraft tickets and travel insurance, and arrange Western Union money transfer.

National Express

● The largest bus company is National Express (tel 08705 808080), which operates to all regions of the UK.

● It is best to book your seat in advance. You can do so online at www.nationalexpress.com, or visit the ticket hall at Victoria

Coach Station, open 6am to 11.30pm daily. Telephone sales (tel 020 7730 3499) are open 8.30 to 7 Monday to Friday, 8.30 to 4 on Saturday; all major credit and debit cards are accepted.

● You can get advance purchase coach tickets until two hours before departure. It is cheaper to book in advance and travel mid-week.

Other Coach Services

● Citylink coaches run to and from Oxford (tel 0865 785400, www.oxfordbus.co.uk).

● Airbuses run to Heathrow, Stansted and Luton airports (tel 08705 80 80 80, www.airbus.co.uk).

● Greenline coaches connect local cities and airports to the capital (tel 0870 608 7261 or visit Green Line Travel Office, 4a Fountain Square, 123–151 Buckingham Palace Road SW1 W0SR).

COACH VERSUS TRAIN

All prices are based on day-return tickets. Significant savings can be made on train and bus tickets if they are purchased in advance. To ensure availability, bookings should be made at least 24 hours in advance.

See page 59 for the relevant mainline stations. All coaches leave from Victoria.

BATH
Train 1 hour 25 min. £39.50
Coach 3 hours 15 min. £15

BRIGHTON
Train 50 min. £15.10
Coach 2 hours. £9

CAMBRIDGE
Train 45 min. £15.60
Coach 2 hours. £9

CANTERBURY
Train 1 hour 25 min. £16.50
Coach 1 hour 50 min. £10.50

NORWICH
Train 1 hour 40 min. £31.30
Coach 3 hours. £14

OXFORD
Train: 1 hour 30 min. £16
Coach: 1 hour 40 min. £11

STRATFORD-ON-AVON
Train 2 hours 10 min. £23
Coach 3 hours 30 min. £14

WINDSOR
Train (from Waterloo) 50 min. £6.50 (from Paddington change at Slough) 35min. £6.50
Coach 1 hour 10 min. £6.80

YORK
Train 2 hours. £63.90
Coach 5 hours. £27.50

YORK 212 MILES (342KM)

CAMBRIDGE 60 MILES (90KM)

NORWICH 115 MILES (185KM)

STRATFORD-ON-AVON 102 MILES (164KM)

OXFORD 57 MILES (92KM)

WINDSOR 25 MILES (40KM)

LONDON

BATH 116 MILES (187KM)

CANTERBURY 62 MILES (100KM)

BRIGHTON 60 MILES (97KM)

ON THE MOVE

DRIVING IN LONDON

A car can be a liability in London, and the best advice for anyone contemplating driving in the capital is simple: don't. Getting around will take you longer than travelling on public transport and parking is scarce and expensive. However, a car is one of the best ways of seeing the surrounding area and travelling farther afield. On the whole, motorists drive safely, roads are good and signposting very efficient.

THE LAW
● Traffic in the UK drives on the left.
● Seat belts are obligatory, including those in the back if fitted.
● Motorcyclists must wear helmets at all times.
● The speed limit in built-up areas is 30mph (48kph); 60mph (97kph) on single carriageways, and 70mph (113kph) on dual carriageways (two-lane highways) and motorways, unless a sign indicates otherwise.
● Currently you are permitted a blood alcohol level of 80mg/100ml, but the advice is not to drink at all if you are driving.
● Red routes are priority routes controlled by the city police where no stopping is allowed at any time. On the carriageway they are marked with red lines.
● Private cars are banned from bus lanes—watch out for signs.
● Give way to your right at roundabouts (see diagram below).

FUEL
● All large garages are self-service. They sell higher octane unleaded fuel, unleaded 95 octane and diesel fuel.

● Prices vary slightly across the country.
● There are 24-hour fuel stations in central London at 83 Park Lane, 71 King's Cross Road and 104 Bayswater Road.

CONGESTION CHARGING
● A congestion charge was introduced in central London in February 2003. See pages 316–331 for the area concerned.
● Every private car must pay £5 to drive into the congestion area between 7am and 6.30 pm Monday to Friday, excluding public holidays.
● You can pay online (www.cclondon.com), by phone 24 hours a day (tel 0845 900 1234), in person at various outlets throughout the UK, including fuel stations and shops, or by credit or debit card at self-service machines at car parks inside the congestion area and other selected locations. You will need your vehicle details.
● You can pay before midnight on the day or up to 90 days before your journey into the congestion zone. The charge rises to £10 if you pay after 10pm on the day of travel.
● Fixed and mobile digital cameras check number plates and those in breach of

regulations are fined £80 (£40 if paid within 14 days).

TIPS
● Know your route.
● Plan parking in advance.
● Avoid driving in the rush hour (weekdays 7.30 to 9.30am and 4.30 to 7pm).

PARKING
● Street parking in London is limited. Check signs for any restrictions.

Never Park
● If you cannot comply with or don't understand the regulations.
● On a pedestrian crossing or area marked with zigzags.
● At the side of a road that has a central double white line.
● On a clearway (main road not allowing vehicles to stop).
● On a cycle or bus lane or a tramway.
● In bays reserved for doctors, ambulances, disabled drivers or others.

Meters
● Meter parking in central London is £3 per hour (20p and £1 coins accepted).
● The maximum stay is 2 hours.

MAKING IT EASY AT ROUNDABOUTS

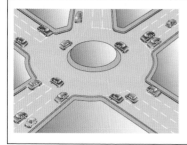

When reaching a roundabout give priority to traffic on your right, unless directed otherwise by signs, road markings or traffic lights. Look forward before moving off to make sure traffic in front has moved. Watch out for vehicles already on the roundabout; be aware they may not be signalling correctly or at all.

Approach mini roundabouts in the same way. Vehicles MUST pass round the central markings.

You can pay for a particular bay once only and cannot return within an hour.

• Generally, meter parking is free after 6.30pm Monday to Friday and from 1.30pm on Saturday and all day Sunday, but there are exceptions, so check meters.

On-Street Pay and Display

• If you park in a 'pay and display' area you must buy a ticket from one of the machines located in the parking zone.

• Some machines require you to type in the first three numbers of your vehicle registration plate; you can then buy time as you require, within designated limits.

• Display the ticket clearly inside your vehicle.

Parking Restrictions

• Yellow lines on the road and curb and yellow plates on lamp-posts indicate on-street parking restrictions.

• A single line indicates that parking restrictions apply; notices explain exactly what these are.

• A double line means that no parking is allowed at any time.

• A broken line indicates limited restrictions.

• A single red line indicates that no stopping is permitted.

• Many streets are reserved for permit-holders only.

Car Parks

• The biggest car park operator in London is National Car Parks (NCP); car parks are recognizable by black-on-yellow signs with 'NCP' displayed prominently. Be aware that rates are very expensive. Further information from NCP (tel 0870 606 7050, www.ncp.co.uk).

• NCP parks include: Arlington House, Arlington Street SWIA 1RJ (tel 020 7499 3312), 21 Bryanston Street W1H 7AB (tel 020 7499 0313) and 2 Lexington Street W1F 0LA (tel 020 7734 9497).

• Masterpark (tel 0800 243 348, www.masterpark.org.uk) also operates car parks in central London.

• There are several 24-hour parking garages in central London. Park Lane, below Marble Arch roundabout, is the biggest; there are usually spaces here even when all other car parks are full. Other 24-hour garages are at Brewer Street W1, Newport Place WC1 and Upper St. Martin's Lane WC1.

TRAFFIC WARDENS/FINES

• Metropolitan Police traffic wardens patrol London's streets. The current Fixed Penalty Notice for parking offences is £60.

If You Get a Parking Ticket

• Don't ignore it. Many parking fines carry a 50 per cent discount if you pay within 14 days. The payment address is on the back.

• Appeal if you think the ticket is unfair. Write to the address on the back, giving as much tangible evidence as possible. Take notes and photographs at the scene.

STOPPING

• You may pick up and drop off passengers in restricted areas but not on clearways (eg red routes in London).

• Continuous loading/unloading is permitted except where curb markings indicate a loading ban, or on clearways.

• Check for notices on posts or walls to see when restricted hours apply.

CLAMPING AND TOWING AWAY

• If your car is parked illegally it may be immobilized by a wheel clamp; the notice posted on your windscreen explains how to get it released.

• Vehicles are usually released within one hour of payment (£38 plus the parking fine).

• If your vehicle is towed away, it will cost at least £125 to get it back. Vehicles must be collected in person and you must produce at least one form of identification such as your driver's licence.

CAR BREAKDOWN AND ACCIDENTS

• Several organizations in the UK can assist in the event of breakdown. Check whether membership in your home country entitles you to reciprocal help from a British organization.

At the Scene of an Accident

• If, as a driver, you are involved in a road-traffic accident, stop and remain at the scene for a reasonable period and give your vehicle registration number, your name and address, and that of the vehicle owner (if different), to anyone entitled to ask.

• If you do not exchange those details at the scene you must report the accident at a police station or to a police constable within 24 hours.

BREAKDOWN ORGANIZATIONS

The Automobile Association (AA)
119–21 Cannon Street EC4. Tel 0870 600 0371 (information), tel 0800 444999 (new members). Open 24 hours daily. You can become a member on the spot but it will cost you more than if you join beforehand.

The AA website (www.theaa.com) provides advice on what to do in the event of breakdown; a 'Route Planner', with maps and directions; traffic news and online road status reports. AA Roadwatch (tel 0870 600 0371) has the latest on traffic jams. Calls cost up to 75p per minute from landlines. Mobile costs may vary.

The Environmental Transport Association (ETA)
Freepost, KT4021, Weybridge, Surrey KT13 8RS. Tel 01932 828882. Open Mon–Fri 8–6, Sat 9–4, closed Sun. Breakdown number supplied on joining, which can be done around the clock at www.eta.co.uk.

The Royal Automobile Club (RAC)
RAC House, 1 Forest Road, Feltham TW13 7RR. Tel 08705 722722 (membership enquiries). Open Mon–Fri 8am–9pm, Sat 9–5, Sun 10–4. Breakdown number (tel 0800 828282 24 hours, www.rac.co.uk).

ROAD SIGNS AND DRIVING TIPS

Circles order and prohibit
Plates below signs qualify their message

No stopping
(clearway)

No entry for
vehicular traffic

No overtaking

40

Maximum
speed

Give priority to
vehicles from
opposite direction

Mini roundabout
(roundabout
circulation)

Triangles warn

Dual carriageway
ends

Cycle route
ahead

Roundabout

Waiting restrictions

 At any time

8 am - 6 pm

No waiting at
any time

No waiting during
times shown on sign

Rectangles provide information

 One-way travel

URBAN
CLEARWAY
Monday to Friday

am	pm
8.00 - 9.30	4.30 - 6.30

No stopping during times shown
except for as long as necessary to set
down or pick up passengers

Other road markings

Box junction.
You must not
enter the box
until your exit
road or lane is
clear

Warning of 'Give
Way' just ahead

CYCLING IN LONDON

Cycling is a good alternative to often time-consuming and frustrating travel on the Underground or bus, but be prepared for the heavy traffic. Some roads and parks have designated cycle routes and it is possible to cycle along parts of the Thames Path and canal towpaths. A series of 19 free cycling maps covers all of London *(tel 0207 222 1234, www.transportforlondon.gov.uk)*.

BICYCLES ON TRAINS
● You can take your bicycle on the surface lines of the Underground network—District, Circle, East London, Hammersmith and City, and Metropolitan lines—but not on the deeper lines that have elevators and escalators. A map available from any Underground station shows which parts of the network you can use.
● Folding bicycles can be taken on all lines.
● Many mainline train services allow bicycles. For long-distance services it is often necessary to book before you travel.

● National rail information *(tel 08457 484950)*.

BICYCLE TOURS
The London Bicycle Tour Company, based in Gabriel's Wharf on the South Bank *(www.londonbicycle.com)*, operates three guided tours of London. A bicycle is included.
● The Royal West Tour: Sundays, 9 miles (14km), 3.5 hours, £14.95.
● The East Tour: Saturdays, 9 miles (14km), 3.5 hours, £14.95.
● Middle London Tour: Weekdays, 6 miles (10km), 3 hours, £14.95 (on request).

SAFE CYCLING
● Wear bright, colourful clothing. Use lights and wear fluorescent clothing at night.
● Make other road-users aware of your movements.
● Watch out for doors opening in stopped or parked cars.
● Don't cycle down the inside of traffic when there is a left-turning junction ahead.
● Wear helmets for extra safety, although they are not compulsory. Face masks filter out traffic pollution.
● Always lock your bicycle to a fixed object.

ON THE MOVE WITH A DISABILITY

ON THE MOVE

Transport staff in London are aware of the needs of passengers with disabilities and generally go out of their way to help. It is best to phone in advance if you need special help or services.

AIR

Most airlines have a department dedicated to making arrangements for passengers with special requirements; some budget airlines may charge.

Designated disabled spaces are available in all BAA-run airports (tel 0800 844844).

Heathrow

All Airbus (tel 020 7222 1234) vehicles and Heathrow Express (tel 0845 600 1515) trains are wheelchair-accessible. The Disabled Living Foundation, which has a Travelcare service at Heathrow (tel 020 8745 7495, minicom 0208745 7565), produces a special needs leaflet, which includes practical advice.

Gatwick

Only certain train services are wheelchair-accessible. Information (tel 0845 123 7770).

Stansted

The Stansted Express train is wheelchair-accessible. Buses from Stansted to other airports and central London are not. Recorded information tel 08700 000303. Coach/bus information, Airport Travel Line (tel 08705 747777).

Luton

The shuttle bus to Luton Airport Parkway station is wheelchair-accessible and there are elevators at the station. Information (tel 01582 405 100).

London City

Wheelchair-accessible shuttle buses run from the airport to Liverpool Street station. Information (tel 020 7646 0000).

BUS

● The Stationlink bus service that operates between major rail stations features low entrance ramps, low floors and spaces for wheelchairs.
● Low-floor buses are being introduced and currently run on more than 35 routes across London (tel 020 7222 1234).

COACH

● Coaches tend to have high steep steps that may be difficult to negotiate. People who are sufficiently mobile may use coach services, but staff are not permitted to help passengers with boarding.
● Manual wheelchairs can be carried, but only if folded and if there is room. Powered vehicles or wheelchairs are not permitted on coach services.

DRIVING

Parking

The City of London Information Centre (tel 020 7332 1456) produces a leaflet for people with disabilities.

Breakdown

The Automobile Association (AA) has a disability helpline for members with disabilities (tel 0800 262 050).

EUROTUNNEL

The Shuttle has been designed with passengers with disabilities in mind. There is no need to get out of your car during the journey, but Eurotunnel does require prior notice of visitors with disabilities. Amenities in the passenger terminal buildings are wheelchair-accessible.

DOCKLANDS LIGHT RAILWAY

● The DLR was constructed much more recently than the main Underground system, so is generally easier to use.
● Most stations are accessible by elevator or ramp. Call the DLR Customer Services

(tel 0207 7363 9700) during office hours to check details.
● There are elevators, escalators and/or ramps on every station platform. All platforms are level with the trains for easy access. There is a designated wheelchair bay on every train.
● Platforms have tactile edges for visually impaired passengers and passenger information displays show train information.

FERRY

Recently improvements have been made to UK ports to cater for passengers with disabilities, but it is still advisable to contact the port in advance.

RAIL

● Portable ramps are available at most stations and some trains carry lightweight versions for use at unmanned stations.
● Increasingly, accessible lavatories are available on long-distance trains and many regional services.
● Eurostar trains are wheelchair-accessible (as is the arrival point at Waterloo International) with space for a maximum of two chairs per train. Reservations and information (tel 08705 186 186).

TAXI

● All taxis are wheelchair-accessible.

UNDERGROUND

● The new Jubilee line trains are wheelchair-accessible from all the new stations between Westminster and Stratford.
● Check the operation of elevators (tel 020 7941 4600 in office hours) or (tel 020 7222 1234 evenings and weekends). An 'accessibility tube map' is available from www.thetube.com.
● Guide dogs are permitted on all forms of public transport in London.

This section is divided into three parts: Sightseeing Areas, consisting of six areas (shown on the map inside the front cover) highlighting what to see; A–Z of Sights, an alphabetical listing of places to visit in central London, all located on the maps on pages 66–69; and Farther Afield, which describes attractions outside the city centre (see map on pages 8–9).

The Sights

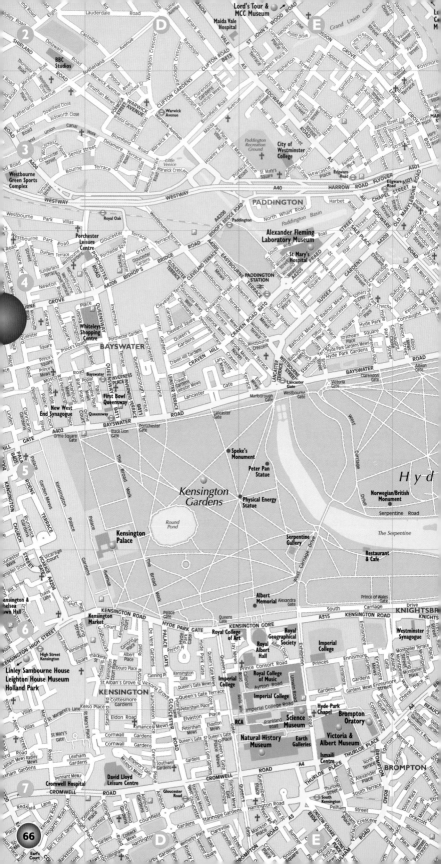

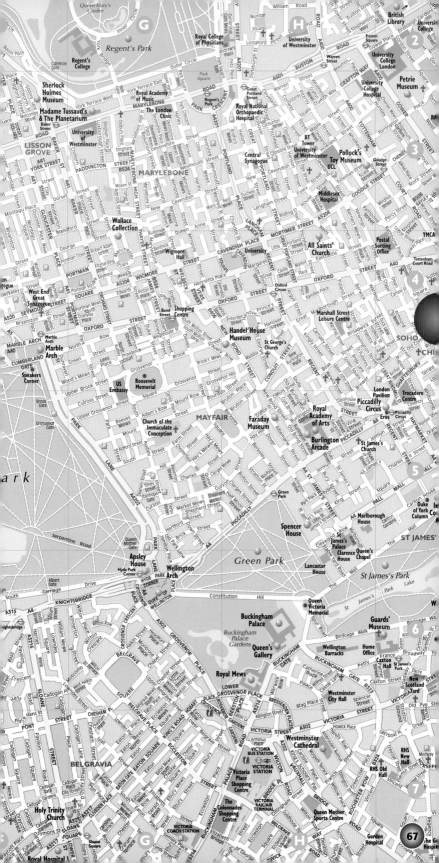

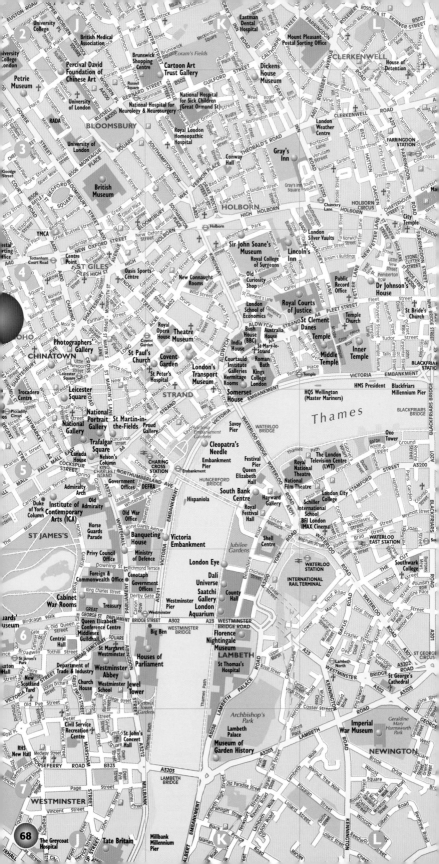

Kensington

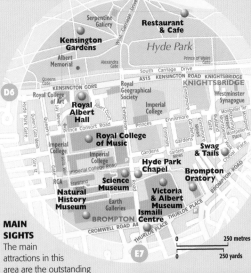

HOW TO GET THERE

The Museums
🚇 South Kensington
🚌 C1, 14, 74

Kensington Gardens (south side)
🚇 High Street Kensington
🚌 9, 10, 49, 52

Hyde Park (see page 93) and Kensington Gardens separate the West End from Kensington, which maintains an air of being apart from the rest of central London.

Now an area of immaculate stucco houses set in leafy avenues, Kensington was once a small rural village. Today many of the fine houses have been converted into apartments. West of Kensington Gore the High Street, once a country lane, is now a wide thoroughfare lined with shops.

To the south of Kensington Gardens is the huge, domed

The Royal Albert Hall is home to the BBC Promenade Concerts from July to September each year

Royal Albert Hall (see page 194) and other grandiose buildings built with money raised from the 1851 Great Exhibition. Housed in the Crystal Palace in Hyde Park, this was a spectacular public showcase of British Imperial goods and inventions. Its profits funded a new museum complex, a pet project of Prince Albert, which aimed to bring culture to the masses. The Victoria & Albert Museum, the Science Museum and the Natural History Museum were constructed over the former market gardens of South Kensington.

MAIN SIGHTS

The main attractions in this area are the outstanding museums off Exhibition Road. As it would be impossible to visit all three in a day and do them justice, combine one or two with a visit to Kensington Gardens or the Brompton Oratory.

Brompton Oratory
Splendid baroque church. See page 78.

Kensington Gardens
Lovely formal gardens with statuary and sculpture. See page 94.

Natural History Museum
Examples of practically every known creature, rock or mineral. See pages 112–113.

Science Museum
One of the city's most exciting hands-on museums; very good for children. See pages124–125.

Victoria & Albert Museum
Decorative arts from around the world. See pages 144–149.

OTHER PLACES OF INTEREST
Royal College of Music
Gabled redbrick building, with a museum of musical instruments.

Hyde Park Chapel
The first Mormon chapel to be built in London (1961), in Exhibition Road.

Ismaili Centre
Modern religious and cultural centre for Ismailis in Cromwell Road, built in 1984.

WHERE TO EAT

The Victoria & Albert Museum, Science Museum and Natural History Museum all have excellent cafés and restaurants.

Skeleton of a triceratops in the Natural History Museum

Swag and Tails
Pub near the Brompton Oratory. See page 271.

In Kensington Gardens you can choose between the **Serpentine Restaurant and Café** *(tel 020 7402 6075)* or have a picnic.

On the western edge of the park is **The Orangery**, attached to Kensington Palace. See page 95.

TIP

● Remember that you can go to any museum shop or café without visiting the museum.

St. James's

HOW TO GET THERE

🚇 Victoria, Green Park, Hyde Park Corner

🚌 11, 211, 139, C1, C10

As Westminster is the centre of government, nearby St. James's is the formal seat of royalty.

Buckingham Palace, the Queen's official London residence, sits at one end of The Mall. This wide avenue, laid out in 1660, forms the ceremonial route taken by the royal family on great state occasions, such as Trooping the Colour (see page 222) and the State Opening of Parliament (see page 224).

Not far away is the much older St. James's Palace, surrounded by buildings of aristocratic elegance that house such institutions as the Royal Society, the Royal Fine Art Commission and the Institute of Directors. Gentlemen's clubs, such as the

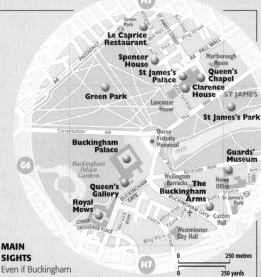

Guards of the Blues and Royals parade past Buckingham Palace

Athenaeum and the Reform, dominate Pall Mall and St. James's Street, and the exclusive tone of the whole district is confirmed by Jermyn Street's long-established specialist stores.

Some shops have been trading here since the 1760s and several retain their 18th-century frontages and fittings. In general, they cater to traditional, upscale tastes of wealthy men, but you can also find women's clothes, food, antiques and jewellery.

Outside Bates the Hatter, look out for Blinks, the shop cat, stuffed in 1926; he is wearing a smart black topper.

MAIN SIGHTS

Even if Buckingham Palace is not open, it's worth strolling past the gates in time to see the Changing the Guard (see page 224). From the palace, walk across Green Park to Spencer House, or across St. James's to the Guards Museum and Queen's Gallery.

Buckingham Palace
The Queen's official residence. See page 79.

Green Park
Informal royal park. See page 90.

Guards' Museum
Regimental memorabilia. See page 90.

Queen's Gallery
Treasures from the Royal Collection. See page 114.

Royal Mews
Working stables of Buckingham Palace. See page 116.

St. James's Park
Royal park with lake. See page 116.

Spencer House
Aristocratic home. See page 127.

OTHER PLACES OF INTEREST

Although neither is open to the public, you can walk past St. James's Palace (see page 116, and Clarence House (see page 116), former home of the Queen Mother and now the home of Prince Charles.

WHERE TO EAT

Take a picnic to **St. James's Park**, with enough to feed the ducks.

The Buckingham Arms
Pub near Buckingham Palace in

St. James's Park is always a good place to feed the ducks or, in this case, a pelican

Petty France. See page 266.

Le Caprice
Glamorous, pricey restaurant. See page 255.

Fortnum and Mason
Take afternoon tea in one of the three restaurants in this venerable food emporium in Piccadilly, founded in 1707 *(tel 020 7734 8040)*. See page 180.

TIP

● Note that Buckingham Palace is only open during August and September.

Westminster

HOW TO GET THERE

Left bank of the river
🚇 St. James's Park, Westminster
🚌 11, 12, 24, 159, 453

Right bank of the river
🚇 Waterloo, Embankment,
Charing Cross
🚌 77, RV1

Gossip and intrigue—
political, royal and religious—
have filled the streets and
buildings of Westminster
since it first developed
5 miles (8km) southwest of
the City of London.

It was Edward the Confessor
who began the original
Westminster Abbey after moving
the royal court out of the City in
1042, triggering London's west-
ward expansion. Since then
Westminster has been synonymous with government. Its major
buildings house the Treasury and
the Foreign and Commonwealth

*The Houses of Parliament and
Big Ben, from the Embankment*

Office. At its heart stand
Westminster Abbey, the Houses
of Parliament, Parliament Square
and Whitehall.

Across the river County Hall,
Ralph Knott's palatial riverside
building completed in 1933 as
the headquarters of London's
administrative body, the Greater
London Council (abolished in
1986), is now home to the Dalí
Universe, the London Aquarium
and the Saatchi Gallery.

Westminster Pier, which
extends alongside Westminster
Bridge on Victoria Embankment,
is the central departure point for
boat trips up and down the River
Thames (see pages 234–235).

MAIN SIGHTS

In contrast to
the pomp and cere-
mony of Westminster are the
attractions in County Hall and the
hugely popular London Eye, all
across Westminster Bridge on the
south bank.

Cabinet War Rooms
Powerhouse of World War II in
the underground rooms near
Whitehall. See page 86.

Dalí Universe
Weird and wonderful art from the
Spanish master of surrealism.
See page 87.

Florence Nightingale Museum
Small museum dedicated to the
pioneering nurse. See page 89.

Houses of Parliament
Seat of Britain's government and,
together with Big Ben, a famous
riverside landmark. See page 92.

London Aquarium
Underwater wonders great and
small. See page 98.

London Eye
State-of-the-art Ferris wheel built
for the millennium. See page 99.

Saatchi Gallery
London's latest museum of
modern art. See page 116.

Victoria Embankment
Gardens by the river, opened in
1870. See page 150.

Westminster Abbey
Magnificent church where
English monarchs have been

crowned for hundreds of years.
See pages 152–153.

Whitehall
All the major government depart-

*The choir stalls lead to the gilt
altar of Westminster Abbey*

ments are on or near this long,
broad street. See page 151.

OTHER PLACES OF INTEREST
St. Margaret Westminster
The 16th-century church in
Parliament Square. A tablet near
the altar marks the spot where
Sir Walter Raleigh, the explorer
and writer, who was beheaded
for treason, is said to be buried.

WHERE TO EAT
The Dalí Universe and London
Aquarium both have cafés.

TIP
● Take a map on the Eye to
identify London's landmarks.

Trafalgar Square and Covent Garden

HOW TO GET THERE

🚇 Charing Cross, Leicester Square

🚌 9, 11 24, 29

Trafalgar Square (see page 136) is literally the centre of the city—a plaque in the pavement behind Charles I's statue marks the spot.

Until the 1970s Soho, to the north, was a byword for sex clubs and sleaze, and Covent Garden (see page 88) was the run-down patch for vegetable- and flower-traders. Now Covent Garden is a buzzing, trendy area in the heart of London. The central Piazza and its side streets are pedestrian zones, and the many shops and market stalls are small, each selling its individual range of products, from buttons and bows to books and works of art.

Soho too has been cleaned up, and the large Chinatown

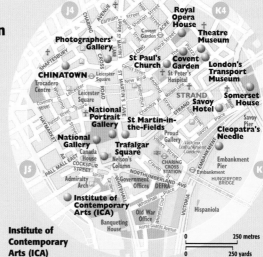

Trafalgar Square's fountains invite a cooling dip on a hot day

quarter (see page 86) at its heart is now a pedestrian district. Today Soho is again the hub of London nightlife, where people meet in bars, eat in the many restaurants, dance the night away in clubs and, in summer, just promenade.

MAIN SIGHTS

Choose from one of the three major art galleries on or near Trafalgar Square before wandering around the shops and stalls of Covent Garden.

Cleopatra's Needle

Obelisk (see page 86) on the Embankment (see page 150).

Institute of Contemporary Arts (ICA)

Cutting-edge arts centre. See page 93.

London's Transport Museum

Vehicles and exhibits recalling the history of London's transport. See page 100.

National Gallery

Seven centuries of Western art. See pages 104–109.

National Portrait Gallery

Portraits down the ages. See pages 110–111.

Photographers' Gallery

Contemporary shows. See page 114.

St. Paul's Church

Covent Garden's church. See page 117.

St. Martin-in-the-Fields

Imposing church, with concerts. See page 117.

Somerset House

Three art collections in handsome riverside buildings. See pages 130–131.

Theatre Museum

A tribute to all things theatrical. See page 136.

OTHER PLACES OF INTEREST

Royal Opera House
Spectacularly restored. Backstage tours available. See page 195.

London buses at London's Transport Museum

WHERE TO EAT

The Portrait Restaurant
The National Gallery's chic restaurant. See page 262.

The Admiralty Restaurant
In Somerset House. See page 252.

The Savoy
Tea served Mon–Fri 2.30–5, Sat and Sun 2 and 4; booking advised. See page 291.

TIPS

● Visit Covent Garden on a Monday to catch the antiques and collectables market.

● For a glimpse of grand early 20th-century architecture look into the marble foyer of Australia House (Melbourne Place) and at the façade of Bush House (Aldwych), home of the BBC World Service.

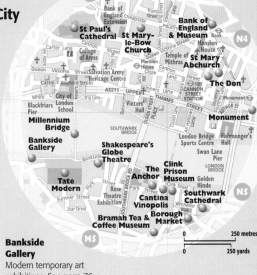

Bankside and the City

HOW TO GET THERE

Ⓤ Bank, Blackfriars, Monument, Mansion House

🚌 15, 17, 25, 521, 381, 705, RV1

THE SIGHTS

The City still covers roughly the area of the trading city founded by the Romans in AD43, when Emperor Claudius needed a Thames crossing between his ports in Kent and the capital of the new Roman province, Camulodunum (Colchester).

Here, almost 2,000 years later, the City remains the compact financial heart of Britain. Soaring modern buildings loom over medieval lanes and Wren churches; and international financiers are subject to the rules of the Corporation of London.

Although St. Paul's Cathedral escaped major damage in the Blitz, the surrounding area was flattened and redeveloped in the 1960s with a series of dreary,

Shakespeare's Globe Theatre, rebuilt close to the original site

windswept buildings. These are gradually being replaced with more dynamic (though controversial) architecture.

South of the river is Bankside. In Shakespeare's day, theatres, bear pits and brothels were banned from the City, so the actors moved south to this area, out of the City's jurisdiction.

MAIN SIGHTS

The Millennium Bridge links two of London's oldest areas, the City and Bankside.

Bank of England Museum
Displays relating to the Bank of England. See page 76.

Bankside Gallery
Modern temporary art exhibitions. See page 76.

Bramah Tea and Coffee Museum
Traces the history of tea and coffee. See page 77.

Clink Prison Museum
Grisly reminders of the penal system of old. See page 86.

Millennium Bridge
Elegant 21st-century pedestrian bridge. See page 100.

Monument
Column commemorating the Great Fire of 1666. See page 102.

St. Paul's Cathedral
Britain's only domed cathedral, built by Sir Christopher Wren. See pages 118–123.

Shakespeare's Globe
Reconstruction of the Elizabethan theatre. See page 126.

Southwark Cathedral
Handsome cathedral on an ancient site. See page 127.

Tate Modern
Modern art in a former power station. See pages 134–135.

OTHER PLACES OF INTEREST
Borough Market
Excellent food market open 12–6 Fri, 9–4 Sat.

St. Mary Abchurch
A Wren church with woodcarving by Grinling Gibbons.

St. Mary-le-Bow Church
Church of the famous 'Bow Bells' See page 232.

The Millennium Bridge brings you to the City

WHERE TO EAT

The Anchor
Historic pub, associated with Dr. Samuel Johnson. See page 266.

Cantina Vinopolis
Bankside restaurant with a difference. Explores the history of the grape with interactive exhibits and tastings. See page 254.

The Don
Smart, modern, City restaurant. See page 256.

TIP

● Many City pubs and restaurants close on Saturday and Sunday.

London Bridge City

HOW TO GET THERE

🚇 Tower Hill, London Bridge
🚌 15, 25, 47, 381, RV1

The redeveloped strip of waterfront on the south bank of the Thames, stretching from London Bridge eastwards to Tower Bridge and beyond, into Shad Thames, is known as London Bridge City.

Modern, sleek towers of glass stand hard by survivors from docks days, including giant warehouses now transformed into airy loft apartments.

From Hay's Galleria you can follow the riverside east along St. Martin's Walk up to Tower Bridge. On the east side of the bridge is Shad Thames, land once owned by the Knights Templar (its name is a corruption of St. John at Thames). Here, warehouse walls rise up, linked high above by a network of metal gangway

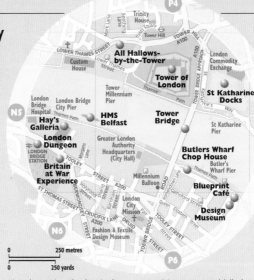

Historic vessels mingle with privately owned boats at St. Katharine's Dock

bridges formerly used by warehouse workers to move loads to and from the interconnecting buildings.

The area between Shad Thames and the river is known as Butler's Wharf, a huge development (1987–89) combining revitalization with conservation to preserve the historical spirit of the spice warehouses.

Opposite, the Tower of London symbolizes London's history and origins, its architectural style echoed by Tower Bridge.

Nestled against the Tower is St. Katharine's Dock, built in 1824–28 by Thomas Telford.

Since becoming obsolete in the late 1960s, the warehouses have been converted to luxury flats for boat lovers, whose yachts are moored in the two main basins.

MAIN SIGHTS

The Tower of London is one of London's must-see sights, but a handful of other places close by are well worth a visit, too.

Britain at War Experience

Life during World War II. See page 78.

Design Museum

Museum devoted to the design of everyday items. See page 87.

HMS *Belfast*

Huge warship, now a floating museum. See page 91.

London Dungeon

Vignettes of torture and horror. See page 98.

Tower Bridge

Mock-gothic bridge which opens for river traffic. See page 137.

Tower of London

Fortress representing the history of London from earliest times. See pages 138–143.

OTHER PLACES OF INTEREST

Hay's Galleria

A stylish shopping complex built on the site of a former dock and comprising a courtyard full of cafés and gift stalls, sheltered by a glass atrium supported on iron columns.

All-Hallows-by-the-Tower

This church just west of the

You can get panoramic views of London from the footbridge of Tower Bridge

Tower has a Roman floor in the crypt and a small museum tracing the history of the church. Samuel Pepys is said to have watched the Great Fire of 1666 from the tower.

WHERE TO EAT

Blueprint Café
Stylish restaurant in the Design Museum. See page 254.

Butlers Wharf Chop House
Traditional English food by Tower Bridge. See page 254.

TIP

● Try and time a visit to see the opening of Tower Bridge.

THE SIGHTS

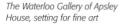
The Waterloo Gallery of Apsley House, setting for fine art

Uniformed doorkeepers (right) can usually be seen standing at the doors of the Bank of England (above) during banking hours

ALEXANDER FLEMING LABORATORY MUSEUM

🟦 66 E4 • St. Mary's Hospital, Praed Street W2 1NY ☎ 020 7886 6528
🕐 Mon–Thu 1–5, Fri 10–5 by appointment 🎟 Adult £2, child £1
🚇 Paddington 🚌 7, 15, 27, 36
www.st-marys.org.uk

In 1928 Scottish bacteriologist Alexander Fleming (1881–1955) discovered penicillin while working in St. Mary's Hospital, next to Paddington station. In the hospital's small museum, you can see the cramped laboratory where he cultivated the naturally antibiotic mould that revolutionized medicine. Museum volunteers are on hand to relate their personal experiences of the impact of antibiotics, and displays and a video tell Fleming's story and trace the role of penicillin in the fight against disease.

ALL SAINTS' CHURCH

🟦 67 H4 • 7 Margaret Street W1W 8JQ
☎ 020 7636 1788 🕐 Daily 7–7
🎟 Free 🚇 Oxford Circus
🚌 7, 8, 10, 98, 176

All Saints' soars up from its crowded site north of Oxford Street. Designed by William Butterfield (1814–1900) in 13th-century Gothic style, its lofty architecture and lavish interior of granite, marble and polychrome tiles make it one of the most impressive Victorian churches in London. At 69m (227ft), the cross-banded spire is the second highest in the city. Visit after dark if possible, as the church looks its best in candlelight.

APSLEY HOUSE

🟦 67 G6 • Hyde Park Corner W1J 7NT
☎ 020 7499 5676 🕐 Tue–Sun 11–5
🎟 Adult £4.50, child (under 18) free.
Free entry on Waterloo Day (18 Jun)
🚇 Hyde Park Corner 🚌 8, 10, 22, 52, 74
www.apsleyhouse.org.uk

Designed by Robert Adam in 1771, this aristocratic town house at the western end of Piccadilly, between Hyde Park and Green Park, became the London home of war hero and future prime minister Arthur Wellesley, 1st Duke of Wellington, in 1817.

Known as 'No. 1 London', because it was the first house within the city toll gates on the western approach, it houses the Duke's outstanding collection of paintings, porcelain, silver, sculpture, furniture, medals and memorabilia—now including his own death mask. The Waterloo Gallery, 27m long (90ft), contains the Duke's magnificent art collection, with works by Goya, Rubens and Murillo. Between 1992 and 1995 the interior of the house was restored to its early 19th-century appearance.

Although the 7th Duke gave the house and its contents to the nation in 1947, several apartments were retained for use as the family home.

Don't miss the Sèvres 'Egyptian' dessert service, a divorce present from Emperor Napoleon to Josephine, who rejected it.

BANK OF ENGLAND MUSEUM

🟦 69 N4 • Bank of England, Threadneedle Street EC2R 8 AH ☎ 020 7601 5545 🕐 Mon–Fri and day of Lord Mayor's Show (see page 224) 10–5
🎟 Free 🚇 Bank 🚌 8, 11, 25, 43, 76
🏧
www.bankofengland.co.uk

The Old Lady of Threadneedle Street, the nation's central bank, occupies a massive, undistinguished, seven-storey office building designed and erected by English architect Sir Herbert Baker between 1925 and 1939. Sculptures on its façade of Britannia are by sculptor Sir Charles Wheeler (1892–1974),

and inside there's a museum (entrance on Bartholomew Lane) tracing the history of the nation's finances from the bank's foundation in 1694 to today's high-tech environment. On display are a faithful restoration of the 1790s bank stock office, a late 18th-century banking hall by Sir John Soane (see pages 128–129) and chronological displays of minted coins, bank notes, gold bars from ancient times to the modern market bar, plus unexpected items such as pikes and muskets used to defend the bank. There are also documents relating to such famous customers as Horatio Nelson and George Washington.

Two interactive displays give you a peek behind the doors and reveal the intricacies of bank note design and production. A computerized simulation allows you to play at wheeling and dealing on the stock market.

Don't miss the £1-million note, used for accounting purposes only.

BANKSIDE GALLERY

🟦 69 M5 • 48 Hopton Street SE1 9JH
☎ 020 7928 7521 🕐 Tue–Fri 10–5, Sat–Sun 11–5 🎟 Free 🚇 Blackfriars, Southwark 🚌 45, 63, 100 🚢 Bankside Pier 🏧
www.banksidegallery.com

Two historic art societies have their homes in this south bank gallery, near Tate Modern (see pages 134–135): the Royal Watercolour Society, the world's first institution to specialize in watercolours, and the Royal Society of Painter Printmakers, founded in 1880 to seek recognition for artists working in etching, engraving and mezzotint. Housed in the converted ground floor of a 1970s block of flats, the gallery showcases the activities of both societies with a mix of one-person shows and

In 1634 Flemish artist Peter Paul Rubens was commissioned by Charles I to paint the entire ceiling of the Banqueting House

The Bramah Museum's giant Bramah Teapot

themed exhibitions of water-colours and prints.

BANQUETING HOUSE

✚ 68 J5 • Whitehall SW1A 2ER
☎ 0870 751 5178 🕙 Mon–Sat 10–5. May close at short notice for state functions 💷 Adult £4, child (5–16) £2.60, under 5s free 🚇 Westminster, Embankment 🚌 11, 24, 53, 88, 159 💷
www.hrp.org.uk

The Banqueting House is all that remains of Whitehall Palace, the sovereign's main residence from 1530 until its destruction by fire in 1698. English architect Inigo Jones (1573–1652) amazed the public with his Palladian design of three central bays and Ionic columns, giving London (and Britain) its first glimpse of neo-classical architecture. State occasions, plays and masques were held in the magnificent main hall in which the painted ceiling by Peter Paul Rubens allegorically glorifies the reign of James I, and a less propitious period for the monarchy was marked when Charles I stepped out of the first-floor balcony to face his execution in 1649.

The undercroft, designed as a drinking den for James I, now houses a small exhibition and video on the history and use of the building.

THE BARBICAN

✚ 69 M3 • Silk Street EC2Y 8DS
☎ 020 7638 8891 🕙 Mon–Sat 9am–11pm, Sun noon–11pm. Box office daily 9–8 💷 Free; separate charges for productions and exhibitions in Level 3 gallery 🚇 Barbican 🚌 4, 56, 153 🍴 💷 🗓
www.barbican.org.uk

This area of the city was once a maze of small streets and warehouses, before its devastation by bombs in December 1940. Today's Barbican complex, 14ha

(35 acres) of concrete buildings, was built over the site between 1971 and 1982. It incorporates flats, an arts centre and premises for the Guildhall School of Music and Drama. At its heart is the D-shaped arts centre, Europe's largest multi-arts and conference venue and home of the London Symphony Orchestra. A wide range of innovative exhibitions of 20th-century and current art and design is staged in the gallery on Level 3 and in The Curve (ground floor). There's also a lively programme of jazz, classical, contemporary and world music, and two cinemas showing independent, art-house and mainstream films. Stage productions take place in the Barbican Theatre or the smaller Pit.

BETHNAL GREEN MUSEUM

✚ 69 P2 • Cambridge Heath Road E2 9PA ☎ 020 8980 2415 🕙 Sat–Thu 10–5.50 💷 Free 🚇 Bethnal Green 🚌 8, 106, 253, 309, 388 💷
www.museumofchildhood.org.uk

With nearly 6,000 exhibits spanning 400 years of childhood, this is one of the biggest and oldest collections of its kind in the world. Housed in a 19th-century building decorated with murals depicting the arts, sciences and agriculture, the museum opened in 1872 as the east London branch of what would eventually become the Victoria & Albert Museum (see pages 144–149). Exhibits include swaddling bands (cloth used to wrap babies) from the 16th century, dolls from the 17th, games from the 18th, toy theatres from the 19th, model trains from the 20th

and construction kits from the 21st. Children can play with items such as coin-operated mechanical toys and the rocking horse, and there's a collection of children's costumes and a display of nursery and baby equipment. Children's events and activities take place at weekends and during school holidays. **Don't miss** the Nuremberg Dolls' House, made in 1673—the only example of its type outside Germany.

BRAMAH TEA AND COFFEE MUSEUM

✚ 69 M5 • 40 Southwark Street SE1 1UN ☎ 020 7403 5650 🕙 Daily 10–6 💷 Adult £4, child (under 14) £3, family £10 🚇 London Bridge 🚌 RV1, 381, 705 💷 🗓
www.bramahmuseum.co.uk

The stories of two of the world's most important commodities, tea and coffee, and their effect on our daily lives from the 17th century to the present day are told in this fascinating museum. Having spent a lifetime in the trade, Edward Bramah started the museum in 1992 with his own collection of teapots.

One section of the museum explains with prints, posters, maps and photographs how Britain developed into the world's largest tea-importing nation. It explores the history of tea, beginning with the East India Company (formed in 1600) and continuing through early 18th-century London tea gardens to smuggling, tea auctions, the Boston Tea Party, clipper ships and tea-growing in India and Sri Lanka.

The coffee story is traced from its first recorded use by a 9th-century Arab physician via

Wooden dolls from the Bethnal Green Museum

St. Paul's Cathedral during the Blitz in December 1940

Isaac Newton's statue in the forecourt of the British Library

The Brompton Oratory's Italianate interior

the 19th-century espresso machine to instant coffee and automatic filters.

On show are tea and coffee sets, tea caddies, teaspoons, strainers and sugar tongs, kettles, giant tea urns and early Italian espresso machines. There are different types of tea to sniff and coffee beans to handle, and notes on such themes as the Japanese tea ceremony, tea bricks, tea dances and the 1950s London coffee bar phenomenon.

BRITAIN AT WAR EXPERIENCE

⊞ 69 N5 • Churchill House, 64–66 Tooley Street SE1 2TF ☎ 020 7403 3171 ◷ Daily 10–5.30, Apr–Sep; 10–4.30, Oct–Mar ⓥ Adult £7, child (5–15) £4, under 5s free, family £16 ⓠ London Bridge ⊟ 21, 35, 40, 43, 133, 381 ⊞ www.britainatwar.co.uk

Here you can learn what it was like to be on Britain's Home Front during World War II, the most turbulent period in the nation's 20th-century history. The Britain at War Experience is not a war museum devoted to the instruments of destruction but a tribute to ordinary people who lived their lives against the backdrop of air raids, the blackout, rationing and evacuation.

Begin your journey by taking an elevator down into the converted railway arches beneath London Bridge train station, where a mock-up of an underground air-raid shelter serves as a prelude to a huge collection of evocative photographs and assorted items ranging from rolls of toilet paper, ration books, gas masks and bombs to a complete Anderson Shelter.

You can also see re-creations of a 1940s shopping arcade, a BBC radio studio, a theatre dressing room and a club for GIs.

Special effects re-create the

sights, sounds, even smells of a London street during the Blitz, and you can walk through the shattered remains of a bombed department store, a cinema, a pub and homes.

BRITISH LIBRARY

⊞ 67 J2 • 96 Euston Road NW1 2DB ☎ 020 7412 7000 ◷ Public areas, exhibition galleries and bookshop: Mon, Wed–Fri 9.30–6, Tue 9.30–8, Sat 9.30–5, Sun 11–5. Reading rooms open to readers only ⓥ Public areas, exhibition galleries, bookshop free ⓠ King's Cross, St. Pancras, Euston, Euston Square ⊟ 10, 30, 73, 91 ▯ ⊞ www.bl.uk

Britain's national library, formerly housed in the British Museum (see pages 80–85), gained its own purpose-built complex in 1998—the UK's biggest 20th-century public building. This stunning new package consists of a spacious piazza, three public galleries, new public art works, two restaurants, a shop and plenty of activities and tours. Eight of its fourteen floors are above ground, six below; beneath these are basements extending to a depth of 25m (82ft).

Before entering the galleries, go up the steps by the information desk and walk around the floor-to-ceiling central glass shaft to enjoy some of the beautiful bindings of the King's Library, George III's 60,000 volumes donated by his son George IV in 1823. The outer walls store the British Library's stamp collection—the world's finest—and you can pull out the vertical trays of stamps to examine specimens.

The Exhibition Galleries display more of the library's treasures, including various editions of the Magna Carta (the 13th-century charter of public liberties) and the only surviving manuscript in Shakespeare's own hand. You can listen to recordings of rare

bird song or a speech by Sir Winston Churchill.

The Workshop of Words, Sounds and Images explains how books and newspapers are created and printed and how sound is recorded. Finally, the Pearson Gallery interprets the library's great collections and stages special exhibitions.

The reading rooms are accessible only to pass-holders, who can consult any work from the collection, including every book printed since 1911. There are currently about 150 million items in more than 400 languages; some 8,000 titles are added each working day.

Don't miss Leonardo da Vinci's notebook.

BRITISH MUSEUM
(see pages 80–85)

BROMPTON ORATORY

⊞ 66 E7 • Brompton Road SW7 2RP ☎ 020 7808 0900 ◷ Daily 6.30–8 ⓥ Free ⓠ South Kensington ⊟ C1, 74, 14 www.brompton-oratory.org.uk

Standing next door to the V&A (see pages 144–149) is the flamboyant Brompton Oratory (London Oratory of St. Philip Neri), an Italian baroque church designed by Herbert Gribble in 1876. This was the first new Roman Catholic church to be built in London after Henry VIII broke away from papal authority. Its design imitates Gesù Church in Rome, with nave and side chapels instead of aisles, and sumptuous statuary and decoration. Dominating the nave are Giuseppe Mazzuoli's gigantic 17th-century marble statues of the Apostles, originally from Siena Cathedral.

On a more intimate scale is the Chapel of St. Wilfrid, with a triptych by English artist Rex Whistler (1905–44).

BUCKINGHAM PALACE

A world-famous symbol of monarchy and focus for ceremonial and public occasions.

The palace so familiar to millions from newsreels and postcards took shape comparatively recently, after centuries of piecemeal architectural changes. Originally plain Buckingham House, it was built as the Duke of Buckingham's country mansion at the western end of St. James's Park and Green Park. George III snapped it up as a private residence in 1761 and work began on embellishments and additions to the shell of the Duke's old home. When Queen Victoria and Albert moved into the palace in 1837 a whole new wing was added to accommodate their fast-growing family.

THE STATE ROOMS

You enter the palace through the Ambassadors' Court, in the south wing, and go through John Nash's dramatic Grand Hall to climb the curving Carrara marble stairs of the Grand Staircase to the first-floor State Rooms. Beyond the small Guard Room, hung with Gobelin tapestries, is the Green Drawing Room, an antechamber to the Throne Room, where official visitors gather before being presented to the Queen. Ahead is the Throne Room, a theatrical space leading up to the Chairs of State under a baroque proscenium arch.

From here you go into the Picture Gallery, 47m long (155ft), hung with works by Rubens, Rembrandt, Canaletto and Van Dyck. The Silk Tapestry Room, with its monumental French pedestal clock, links the Picture Gallery with the East Gallery, part of Queen Victoria's new block, leading into the Ball Supper Room and the vast Ballroom, now used for investiture ceremonies and state banquets.

More Gobelin tapestries are displayed in the smaller West Gallery, which leads to the State Dining Room, vividly decorated in white and gold with deep-red walls and carpet. Next comes the sumptuous Blue Drawing Room, with a dazzling ceiling by John Nash and huge Corinthian columns; and the opulent decoration continues in the Music Room, with its vaulted, domed ceiling and columns of lapis lazuli scagliola (imitation stone, made of glue and plaster).

A blaze of white and gold greets you in the White Drawing Room, where there are more pieces of wonderful French furniture. The intricately designed Minister's Staircase leads back to the ground floor and the Marble Hall, displaying statues of nymphs and portraits of Victoria's relations. From the Bow Room tours exit into the garden.

Other attractions are the Queen's Gallery (see page 114) and the nearby Royal Mews (see page 116).

Changing the Guard outside Buckingham Palace (main picture). Queen Victoria's memorial (inset top), outside the palace. The palace Throne Room (inset bottom)

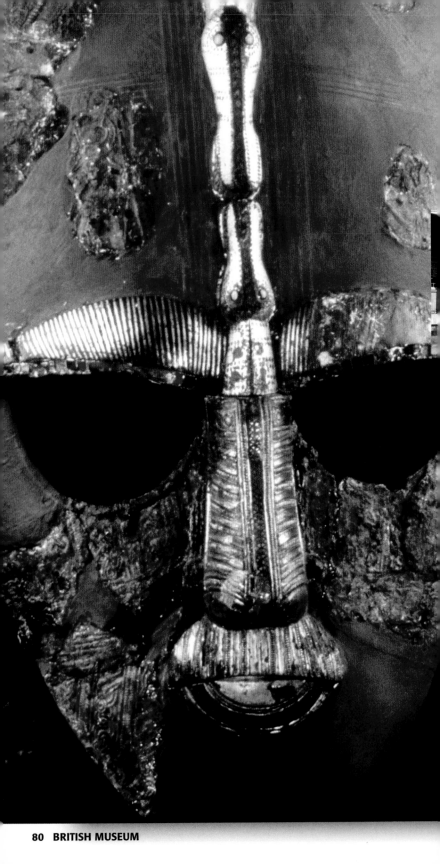

British Museum

Britain's largest museum, covering 33ha (81.5 acres), with 4 million-plus objects on display in more than 90 galleries.
Unrivalled for the variety and quality of its treasures.
The result of 200 years of collecting, excavation and unashamed looting.

Smirke's colonnaded façade, inspired by Greek architecture

Sir Hans Soane, founder of the museum

Norman Foster's glass-covered Great Court, opened in 2000

SEEING THE BRITISH MUSEUM

There are two entrances to the museum: one (the main entrance) on Great Russell Street (south) and the other on Montague Place (north). Both lead into the covered Great Court, which is the hub of the museum, forming the crossroads between all the galleries. It also serves as the main information centre and the location of the shops and eateries.

The museum's collections are arranged by geography, culture and theme, but having said that, the layout and sheer size of the place can be bewildering. Note that collections from the same culture are not necessarily on the same floor (see page 83). The best way to tackle the museum is to focus on the highlights or on one or two collections.

HIGHLIGHTS

GREAT COURT AND READING ROOM

Entering Sir Robert Smirke's imposing, neoclassical building has become a pleasure in itself since the addition in 2000 of Norman Foster's glorious, curved glass canopy over the central Great Court, turning the previously dark and confusing area cluttered with store-rooms into a huge, light space—now Europe's largest covered square. It's worth lingering here to enjoy the sculpture displays set around the Great Concourse Gallery (such as the Easter Island statue and a reconstructed chariot) while deciding which galleries to visit.

In the middle of the court is the circular Reading Room, completed in 1857 to the design of Smirke's brother, Sydney. Karl Marx and other intellectuals once beavered here. From a viewing area at the front, you can enjoy the domed ceiling, restored to its original colour scheme of blue, cream and gold, the low-lit desks and the floor-to-ceiling bookcases. There's an information desk near the entrance.

MAIN FLOOR

Rosetta Stone (Room 4)
Though not particularly impressive to look at, the Rosetta Stone was instrumental in solving many of the puzzles of the ancient Egyptian world. The slab of black basalt, discovered by Napoleon's army in the

RATINGS	
Good for kids	●●
Historic interest	●●●●●
Specialist shopping	●●●●

TIPS

● Get your bearings in the Great Court, where you can pick up plans and information.

● Don't expect to see everything in a day; focus on what interests you and make for one or two galleries.

● Make a trip here in the evening on Thursday to Saturday, when the Great Court's restaurants and shops remain open. On Thursdays and Fridays the major galleries stay open late.

Helmet (left) retrieved from the ship burial at Sutton Hoo, dating from the 7th century

✚ 68 J3 • Great Russell Street WC1B 3DG

☎ 020 7323 8299

🕐 Sat–Wed 10–5.30, Thu–Fri 10–8.30. Great Court Sun–Wed 9–6, Thu–Sat 9am–11pm. Check times for temporary exhibitions. Late views: selected galleries only; check ahead

💵 Free; charges for some temporary exhibitions

🚇 Holborn, Tottenham Court Road, Russell Square, Goodge Street

🚌 7, 38, 10, 91, 188

📷 'Highlights' 90-minute tours: daily 10.30, 1, 3, adult £8. For foreign language tours call 020 7323 8656. 'eyeOpener' 50-minute introductory tours; choose from ancient Egypt, the Classical world, prehistoric/Roman Britain, the world of Asia, treasures of the Islamic world, the Americas, Europe: medieval/modern, the ancient Near East, the arts and cultures of Africa. Daily every half hour 11–noon, 1–3.30, free. Various audiotours in several languages, £3.50

📖 A good selection for adults and children from £4 to £16.99. Available in English, French, German, Italian, Spanish, Korean, Chinese, Japanese

🍽 Court restaurant on upper floor of Great Court serves hot and cold meals, morning coffee, afternoon tea, evening dinner. Open Sun–Wed 11–5 (last orders), Thu–Sat 11–9. Reservations, 020 7323 8990

☕ Court café (east and west) serving hot drinks, light meals. Open Sun–Wed 9–5.30, Thu–Sat 9–9. Gallery café, next to Room 12, serving hot and cold light meals, morning coffee and afternoon tea. Open daily 10–5

📕 Bookshop on north side of Great Court concourse, selling art, history, archaeology etc titles. Children's shop on east side of Great Court. Souvenir and guide shop on west side of Great Court concourse. Grenville shop on east side of Weston Great hall, selling replica sculpture, jewellery, silk scarves and ties
🛍

www.thebritishmuseum.ac.uk
Good level of practical information and educational links; layout of the collections a bit confusing but once you find what you're looking for there's plenty of background and attractive illustrations.

Nile Delta in 1799, reproduces the same (not very exciting) text in three languages: Greek, Demotic and Egyptian. This offered the first opportunity for modern scholars to crack the code of Egyptian hieroglyphics by comparing them with known scripts.

Elgin Marbles (Room 18)
The question of where they should be—in Greece or in Britain—still causes passionate debate. In fact, such is the controversy raging around them that the marbles' quality can be overlooked. These frieze reliefs, taken from the Parthenon, the temple to Athena on the Acropolis at Athens, are some of the finest sculptures of antiquity. Displayed in a vast room, they are best viewed as a kind of cartoon strip depicting a festival to commemorate Athena's birthday.

Following a visit to Athens in 1800 Lord Elgin, then British

Monumental figures in the Egyptian Sculpture Gallery largely honour the kings and deities of the ancient Egyptian civilization

ambassador in Constantinople, obtained a licence from the Turkish Sultan to remove the stones, which had suffered severe damage during a skirmish between the Turks and a Venetian fleet in 1687. Arguing that the marbles would not survive if they remained in Greece, Elgin had them transported to Britain. The eventful journey involved a shipwreck and Elgin's detention in France.

UPPER FLOORS
Portland Vase (Room 70)
This ancient cameo-glass vase was probably made in Rome between AD5 and 25. Nothing is known about it prior to its appearance in the description of a cardinal's art collection in 1601. After passing to a series of buyers, it eventually reached the hands of the 3rd Duke of Portland in 1786. He lent it to potter Josiah Wedgwood, who copied its cameo design and made it world-famous.

Love and marriage are the themes of its decoration, with a mythological slant, and one theory is that it was made as a wedding gift, at a time when glass-blowing was a relatively new technique.

Sutton Hoo Ship Burial (Room 41)
This comprises the collection of treasures from an Anglo-Saxon royal burial ship that survived intact in Suffolk and was excavated in 1939. The ship was probably a monument to Raedwald, the last great pagan king of East Anglia, who died in about 625. Besides fine gold jewels, the boat contained a sceptre, a gold purse, silver bowls and plates, mounted silver drinking horns, bronze cauldrons and silver and gold ship fittings. Among a number of weapons were a shield, a sword with jewelled gold hilt, and an iron helmet with bronze and silver fittings and 'eyebrows' edged in garnets.

Lewis Chessmen (Room 42)
Carved from the tusks of walruses, these squat, sometimes comical-looking little figures were discovered on the island of Lewis in the Outer Hebrides of Scotland in 1831 by a crofter while working his land. Scandinavian in origin, they depict the figures used on a chess board and are believed to date from the mid-12th century. There are 80 pieces in all.

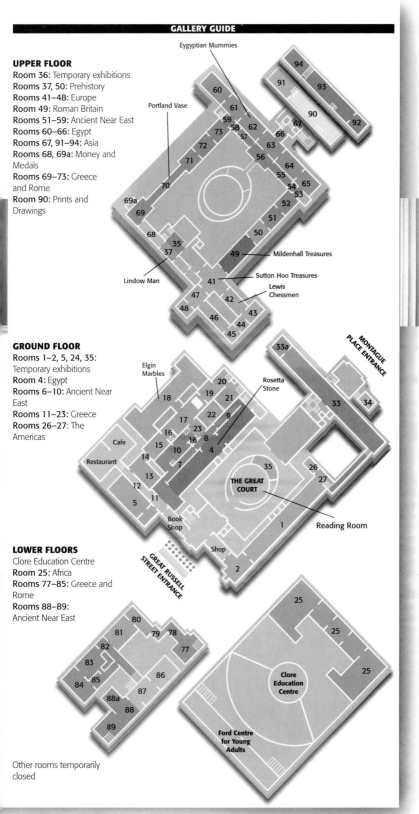

Eygyptian Mummies

UPPER FLOOR
Room 36: Temporary exhibitions
Rooms 37, 50: Prehistory
Rooms 41–48: Europe
Room 49: Roman Britain
Rooms 51–59: Ancient Near East
Rooms 60–66: Egypt
Rooms 67, 91–94: Asia
Rooms 68, 69a: Money and Medals
Rooms 69–73: Greece and Rome
Room 90: Prints and Drawings

Portland Vase

Mildenhall Treasures
Sutton Hoo Treasures
Lewis Chessmen
Lindow Man

GROUND FLOOR
Rooms 1–2, 5, 24, 35: Temporary exhibitions
Room 4: Egypt
Rooms 6–10: Ancient Near East
Rooms 11–23: Greece
Rooms 26–27: The Americas

Elgin Marbles
Rosetta Stone
Cafe
Restaurant
THE GREAT COURT
Reading Room
Book Shop
Shop
MONTAGUE PLACE ENTRANCE
GREAT RUSSELL STREET ENTRANCE

LOWER FLOORS
Clore Education Centre
Room 25: Africa
Rooms 77–85: Greece and Rome
Rooms 88–89: Ancient Near East

Clore Education Centre
Ford Centre for Young Adults

Other rooms temporarily closed

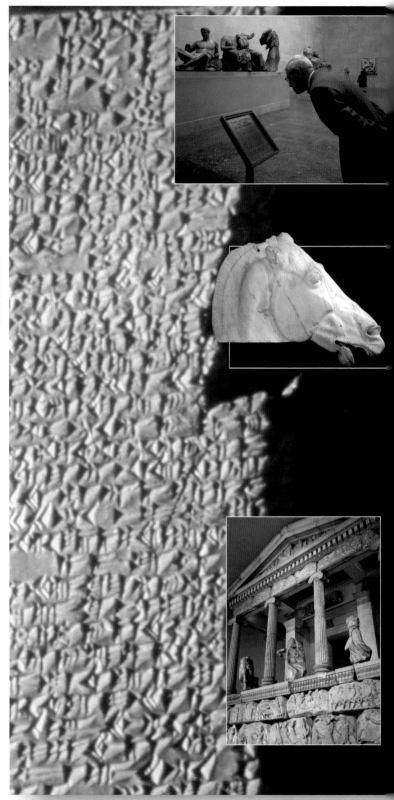

Mildenhall Treasure (Room 49)

A farmer ploughing his field near Mildenhall in Suffolk in 1942 unearthed an entire set of late-Roman silver tableware. There were no coins, so it was not easy to date, but the collection's design suggests it was used during the 4th century AD, by someone of high standing. The level of decoration on the platters, ladles and spoons, bowls and dishes is superb, and includes handles shaped like dolphins and depictions of Bacchus, god of wine—a fashionable touch in silver dining sets throughout the Roman period.

Egyptian Mummies (Rooms 61–66)

One of the most popular displays in the British Museum is that of Egyptian mummies and sarcophagi. Row after row of preserved bodies, wrapped in bandages and surrounded by their prized possessions and favourite food, exercise a gruesome fascination, especially for children. Most disturbing of all is the preserved body of 'Ginger,' a Predynastic Egyptian from 3400BC in a reconstructed grave pit. The craftsmanship and elegance of the items surrounding and celebrating the dead is superb—such as the intricately painted wooden coffin of Passenhor, its body busy with figures and texts, its head painted to represent a serene, young face framed by a headdress. Discovered in Thebes, it was created in about 700BC.

Lindow Man (Room 37)

Nicknamed 'Pete Marsh' by the archaeologists who found him in a waterlogged peat bog in Cheshire, the Lindow Man is an almost perfectly preserved—albeit somewhat leathery—2,000-year-old corpse. Among the current theories is one that he was sacrificed during a Druid ceremony, in which he was beaten to death. There are signs of a blow to his head and a wound to his throat, and mistletoe grains were found in his gut, suggesting that he was fed a hallucinatory meal before being knocked out, strangled and drowned.

The Flood Tablet (main picture opposite) is a cuneiform (early form of writing) tablet from Iraq that tells a story from the Epic of Gilgamesh, a legendary ruler of Uruk
The famous Elgin Marbles (inset top and centre)
A reconstruction of the Nereid Monument (inset bottom) from Xanthos in Asia Minor
Marble dogs (below), found near Lanuvio in Italy

LOWER FLOORS

Assyrian Reliefs

Vivid carved figures carrying pots and weapons, taking part in daily activities or military campaigns, were cut into panels for the Assyrian kings' palaces and temples, and have survived since about 880–612BC. Originally set on the buildings' mud-brick walls—some to a height of 2.6m (8.5ft), they were coloured with paint, traces of which can sometimes still be seen. Like comic strips, they relate their stories from one end of a wall to the other. Some of the most striking friezes come from the great palace—known as the Southwest Palace—of King Sennacherib, who came to the throne of Assyria in 704BC and moved his capital from Dur-Sharrukin (modern Khorsabad) to the ancient city of Nineveh, which he rebuilt in magnificent style. The palace was his great showpiece, many of its rooms covered with alabaster wall reliefs.

BACKGROUND

Wealthy physician Sir Hans Sloane (1660–1753) spent his life collecting assorted coins, books and natural history specimens, which by his death amounted to some 80,000 items. The government bought this collection and it was first put on display as the British Museum in 1759, at Montague House, which occupied the museum's present site. However, augmented by donations from benefactors, travellers, historians and archaeologists, the museum soon outgrew its home and Sir Robert Smirke's classical building (1823–47) was built to replace Montague House. As the museum continued to grow, more galleries were added, but space was still a major problem and by the late 20th century it became clear that a more radical solution had to be found. So in 1998 the British Library (see page 78), which had occupied the Reading Room, was moved to St. Pancras and the Great Court was given a complete overhaul.

SIR HANS SLOANE

Having developed a keen interest in nature as a child in Ireland, Hans Sloane studied chemistry and botany in London, and medicine in France. A three-month voyage to Jamaica as physician to the new governor, the 2nd Duke of Albermarle, gave him the chance to observe the local fauna and flora, customs and natural phenomena such as earthquakes, and to collect plants, molluscs, insects and fish. He was intrigued by a popular local drink, cocoa, and concocted a variation adding milk to reduce its bitterness. On his return to England Sloane's version was sold as a medicine before passing to Messrs. Cadbury, who turned it into their famous drinking chocolate. Sloane continued his career as a distinguished physician while collecting curiosities and publishing works on his travels and studies. By the time of his death at the age of 93, his precious collection took up a large part of his house, and was looked after by a full-time curator.

Luxury goods tempt passersby in the covered Burlington Arcade

The Cabinet War Rooms Map Room, pivotal to World War II

Carved Egyptian figure at the base of Cleopatra's Needle

BURLINGTON ARCADE

✚ 67 H5 • Piccadilly W1 ◷ Mon–Sat 9–6 🎫 Free Ⓜ Green Park, Piccadilly Circus 🚌 8, 9, 14, 19 38 ♿
www.burlington-arcade.co.uk
Tourist Information Office
Britain Visitor Centre, 1 Lower Regent Street SW1Y 4XT (no telephone)

Leather goods, bespoke shoes, antique and contemporary jewellery, cashmere garments, perfumery and unusual gifts can all be found behind the Regency-style mahogany shop-fronts of this Piccadilly arcade. Built in 1819 with a central, timberframe glass canopy, its original purpose was to prevent passersby tossing rubbish into the garden of Burlington House (see Royal Academy of Arts, page 115). Former soldiers of the regiment of the 10th Hussars were recruited to keep order. 'Beadles' in Edwardian frock coats and top hats still enforce the original Regency laws of courtesy and decorum, which forbid whistling, singing, hurrying and carrying large packages.

CABINET WAR ROOMS

✚ 68 J6 • Clive Steps, King Charles Street SW1A 2AQ ☎ 020 7930 6961 ◷ Daily 9.30–6, Apr–Sep; 10–6, Oct–Mar 🎫 Adult £7, child (under 16) free Ⓜ Westminster, St. James's Park 🚌 11, 12, 24, 88 🎁 ♿
www.iwm.org.uk

Nowhere is the personal experience of war and the sense of crisis more keenly felt than in these cramped underground rooms in Whitehall, where the most senior figures of Britain's government and armed forces worked and slept during World War II. Most interesting of those rooms open to the public are the Map Room, its walls covered in pinhole-riddled maps as the progress of the war was tracked; the Cabinet Room, where the work of

government carried on during bombing raids; the Transatlantic Telephone Room, which had direct communication with Washington's White House; and the Prime Minister's Room, where Sir Winston Churchill broadcast to the nation.

An audio-guide navigates you through corridors that reverberate to the sound of sirens and the voices of guards as bombs explode and fires rage outside.

CARTOON ART TRUST GALLERY

✚ 68 K3 • 7–13 Brunswick Centre, Bernard Street WC1N 1AF ☎ 020 7278 7172 ◷ Tue–Sat 10–5 🎫 Free Ⓜ Russell Square 🚌 59, 68, 91, 168 www.cartooncentre.com

Set in a terraced concrete-and-glass block, which also houses shops, flats and leisure facilities, the gallery is run by a charity dedicated to collecting and conserving the best of British cartoons, caricatures, comics and animation. Regular exhibitions are held, plus lectures and workshops for adults and children. The Trust is dedicated to founding a National Museum of Cartoon Art.

CHINATOWN

✚ 68 J4 ◷ Open access 🎫 Free Ⓜ Leicester Square, Tottenham Court Road 🚌 14, 19, 38 🍴 🎁 ♿
Tourist Information Office
Britain Visitor Centre, 1 Lower Regent Street SW1Y 4XT (no telephone)

North of Leicester Square, this vibrant enclave centred on pedestrianized Gerrard Street is crammed with dozens of Asian food shops, eateries and book, video and record/CD shops. Since the 1950s Chinese immigrants have made the area their own and the community congregates here to shop and socialize. Ornate gateways stand at either

end of the pedestrian area, and even the phone boxes have pagoda-style roofs. At Chinese New Year celebrations (late January/early February, see page 222), huge papier-mâché lions dance through the streets against a background of firecrackers and exuberant street events.

CLEOPATRA'S NEEDLE

✚ 68 K5 ◷ Open access 🎫 Free Ⓜ Embankment 🚌 176, 188, RV1 ⛴ Embankment Pier
Tourist Information Office
Britain Visitor Centre, 1 Lower Regent Street SW1Y 4XT (no telephone)

This pink granite obelisk was constructed for the Egyptian Pharaoh Tuthmose III in about 1500BC, and its elaborately carved hieroglyphics and inscriptions were added to mark the victories of Rameses II. Its association with Cleopatra began when it was moved to Alexandria. In the 19th century, it was given to the British by the Egyptian viceroy, but its weight made shipment impossible for several decades.

Plaques mounted round the base of the obelisk give a brief history of the needle and commemorate the men who died during its transportation. It was placed here beside the Thames, in 1879, flanked by two Victorian bronze sphinxes. Nearby benches are also decorated with an Egyptian motif of winged sphinxes.

CLINK PRISON MUSEUM

✚ 69 N5 • 1 Clink Street SE1 9DG ☎ 020 7378 1558 ◷ Daily 10–6 🎫 Adult £4, child (in full-time education) £3, family £9 Ⓜ London Bridge 🚌 35, 43, 705. RV1 ♿
www.clink.co.uk

A skeleton hanging in a cage marks the entrance to the gloomy basement housing the museum—a taste of what's to

Works from Dalí's Sensuality and Feminity exhibition

Chinese-style gates mark the entrance to Chinatown

A 1950s warehouse is now home to the Design Museum

come. From the 12th century until 1780, when the building was burned down during the Gordon Riots (see page 33), this was the site of the notorious Clink Prison, where clerics, heretics, debtors, prostitutes and an assortment of Bankside lowlife were imprisoned in appalling conditions. Its name is said to derive from the 'clinch' irons that were used to pin prisoners down, and 'the clink' has become a slang term for any prison. The museum covers the history of the prison using archive material, tableaux of torture scenes and displays of gruesome instruments.

COVENT GARDEN (see page 88)

DALÍ UNIVERSE

✚ 68 K6 • Riverside Building, County Hall, Westminster Bridge Road SE1 7PB ☎ Information line: 020 7620 2720; ticket sales line: 0870 060 2319 ⏰ Daily 10–5.30 🎟 Adult £8.50, child (3–9) £1, (10–16) £4.95, under 3s free Ⓜ Waterloo, Westminster 🚌 11, 24, 76, 159

🚢 Westminster Millennium Pier, Waterloo Millennium Pier 📅 www.daliuniverse.com

Laid out as a labyrinth of galleries at County Hall (the former headquarters of the Greater London Council on the South Bank), this stylish exhibition is dedicated to Spanish self-publicist and surrealist artist Salvador Dalí (1904–89). It has more than 500 of his works on loan from various European collectors, including sculpture, drawings, lithographs and gold and glass objects. Reflecting the major influences in his life and work, the exhibits are grouped into three themes: Sensuality and Femininity (where you'll find the famous bright red Mae West Lips sofa), Religion and Mythology and Dreams and Fantasy.
Don't miss *Spellbound,* an oil painting created for the set of Sir Alfred Hitchcock's Hollywood movie (1945) of the same name.

DESIGN MUSEUM

✚ 69 P6 • 28 Shad Thames SE1 2YD ☎ 020 7403 6933 ⏰ Sat–Thu 10–5.45, Fri 10–9 🎟 Adult £6, child (6–16) £4, under 5s free, family £16 Ⓜ London Bridge, Tower Hill (or Tower Gateway for DLR) 🚌 42, 47, 78, 188 🚢 St. Katharine's Pier 📷 📅 www.designmuseum.org

In 1989 a 1950s warehouse on Butlers Wharf was converted into the modernist Design Museum, the first in the world to be dedicated to 20th- and 21st-century design. One of London's most inspiring cultural attractions, it promises to be more than a conventional museum, with a mission 'to excite everyone about design'. An evolving, permanent collection presents mass-produced design classics including cars, cameras, furniture, domestic appliances and office equipment, while temporary exhibitions range from retrospectives about great designers to thematic shows.

The first-floor Review Gallery showcases the most innovative contemporary designs and technologies from around the world.

DICKENS HOUSE MUSEUM

✚ 68 K3 • 48 Doughty Street WC1N 2LX ☎ 020 7405 2127 ⏰ Mon–Sat 10–5, Sun 11–5 🎟 Adult £4, child (under 16) £2, family £10 Ⓜ Russell Square, King's Cross, Chancery Lane (closed Sun) 🚌 19, 38, 45, 55 📅 www.dickensmuseum.com

Charles Dickens (1812–70), the prolific novelist and commentator on Victorian society, lived at no fewer than 15 addresses during his life. This Georgian terraced house in Bloomsbury, where he lived from 1837 to 1839, is the only one still standing. Now a museum of his life and work, it houses original manuscripts, first editions, personal effects, memorabilia, furniture and 19th-century paintings, and includes the study where Dickens completed his first full-length novel, *The Pickwick Papers,* and later *Oliver Twist* and *Nicholas Nickleby.*

The cluttered drawing room where the novelist entertained has been restored to its original Regency style, while reconstructions in the basement washhouse and wine cellar convey a little more of the atmosphere of Dickensian London.
Don't miss the Dickens Family Tree, in the morning room.

Sculpture from the collection of surrealist work displayed at the Dalí Universe

87

COVENT GARDEN

Fashionable area of shops, eateries, museums and performance, ranged around London's first formal square and focusing on the 19th-century market halls.

RATINGS

Good for kids	● ● ● ●
Historic interest	● ●
Photostops	● ● ●
Specialist shopping	● ● ● ● ●

BASICS

✚ 68 K4 ⊙ Open access 🎟 Free
Ⓒ Covent Garden 🚌 6, 9, 13, 23, 77A, RV1 🎫 💻 ⊞

www.coventgardenmarket.co.uk
Gives a list of shops and what they sell; partly aimed at shopkeepers and stallholders.

Tourist Information Office
The Management Office, 41 The Market, Covent Garden WC2E 8RF ☎ 020 7836

The converted cellar area (main picture), where the Punch and Judy pub (inset) can be found. In former days, flower-sellers (below) were a familiar sight

Covent Garden Piazza was London's first residential square, laid out in the 1630s by architect Inigo Jones and the model for one of the city's most distinctive features. It later became a thriving fruit and vegetable market, renowned for its flower-sellers and for the costermongers (a term originally meaning 'apple-sellers'), who effortlessly balanced towering stacks of baskets on their heads. When the traders moved out to Vauxhall, south London, in the 1970s, the market area was transformed into the Piazza, a mix of specialist shops, stalls and eating places, with street entertainers to amuse the crowds. The central halls, still covered with their 1870s iron roofs and fronted at the eastern end, the original entrance, by grand stone columns, form the heart of this buzzing area.

Steps lead down to the converted cellar area of the halls, now housing more shops and the Punch and Judy pub. Shoppers sitting at the outdoor tables or leaning on the balcony above are entertained by street performers who must prove their worth by audition before being let loose on the public.

Retailers too are carefully chosen for their suitability to the Covent Garden spirit, so the Piazza's shops all have a certain character—such as Culpeper the Herbalist, or The Doll's House Company, selling miniature furniture.

There's still a daily market here (10.30–7.30), set up in the North Hall and collectively known as the Apple Market. More than 200 stall-holders are registered to trade in it, and because most exhibit only once or twice a week, there is always an enormous variety of crafts, jewellery, clothing and accessories (Tue–Sun). On Mondays, the market is turned over exclusively to stalls selling antiques and collectables.

AROUND AND BEYOND THE PIAZZA

On the northeast corner of the Piazza is the magnificently refurbished Royal Opera House (see page 195). Its design incorporates the original iron framework of the market's Floral Hall. Across the Piazza is the former Flower Market, now the site of London's Transport Museum (see page 100). The Theatre Museum (see page 136) is to the east, on Russell Street, and nearby are two of the area's famous theatres, the elegant Theatre Royal Drury Lane (see page 201) and the Lyceum (see page 199), on Wellington Street.

The area known as Covent Garden spreads well beyond the Underground station and into the narrow streets leading off the Piazza, themselves full of arty specialist shops.

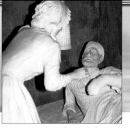

The study where Charles Dickens wrote prodigiously

A stained-glass portrait of Johnson, in his London home

Reconstruction of nurse Florence Nightingale at work

DR. JOHNSON'S HOUSE

68 L4 • 17 Gough Square EC4A 3DE
020 7353 3745 Mon–Sat
11–5.30, May–Sep; Mon–Sat 11–5,
Oct–Apr Adult £4, child (10–16) £1,
under 10s free, family £9 Blackfriars,
Temple, Holborn, Chancery Lane
(closed Sun) 11, 26, 76, 172
www.drjh.dircon.co.uk

This large, dark-brick house buried in a maze of courtyards and passages is one of the few residential 18th-century buildings surviving in the City of London. It was the home and workplace of journalist, poet and lexicographer Dr. Samuel Johnson (1709–84) from 1748 to 1759, and it was here that Johnson compiled the first comprehensive English dictionary, published in 1755.

Restored to its original condition, with panelled rooms and a pine staircase, the house contains a collection of period furniture, prints and portraits, as well as first editions of the dictionary. While Johnson worked on his entries for the dictionary in his own corner of the house, six copyists stood in the garret to transcribe them.

FARADAY MUSEUM

67 H5 • The Royal Institution of Great Britain, 21 Albemarle Street W1S 4BS 020 7409 2992 Mon–Fri 9.30–5 Adult £1 Green Park, Piccadilly Circus 8, 14, 19, 38
www.rigb.org/heritage/faradaypage.html

Two rooms in the basement of the 18th-century Royal Institution building just north of Piccadilly house a small museum devoted to scientist Michael Faraday (1791–1867), discoverer of electro-magnetic induction, electro-magnetic rotations, the magneto-optical effect and much else besides. His original laboratory shows reconstructions of experimental set-ups and historical equipment, including his first electric generator and magneto-spark apparatus.

The Royal Institution was founded in 1799 to promote and popularize scientific research, and is the oldest independent research body in the world.

FLORENCE NIGHTINGALE MUSEUM

68 K6 • 2 Lambeth Palace Road SE1 7EW 020 7620 0374 Mon–Fri 10–5, Sat, Sun 11.30–4.30 Adult £4.80, child (5–18) £3.80, under 5s free, family £12 Westminster, Waterloo 12, 159, 211, 507 Westminster Millennium Pier
www.florence-nightingale.co.uk

Set in a modern annexe of St. Thomas's Hospital, where Florence Nightingale (1820–1910) established the first-ever nurses' training school in 1860, the museum covers her career and contribution to public health. Her work nursing soldiers during the Crimean War, which earned her the title 'the lady with the lamp', and her contribution to public health, are evoked with personal mementoes, clothing, furniture, books, letters, portraits and nursing equipment, plus audiovisuals and realistic reconstructions.

GEFFRYE MUSEUM

69 P2 • Kingsland Road, Shoreditch E2 8EA 020 7739 9893 Tue–Sat 10–5, Sun noon–5. Garden open Apr–Oct during museum opening hours Free Old Street, Liverpool Street 67, 149, 242, 243
www.geffrye-museum.org.uk

A series of rooms decorated and furnished in period style takes you through 400 years of domestic life, starting with an oak-panelled, 17th-century room and passing through Georgian restraint and elaborate Victorian decor to reach a 20th-century converted warehouse space.

A 1998 extension brings displays up to the present, and includes modern furniture and interiors, as well as a temporary exhibition gallery and design centre. Changes in horticultural style are reflected in the gardens, arranged as outdoor rooms and including a walled herb garden.

The Geffrye Almshouses—14 houses and a chapel—were converted to house the museum, which opened in 1914. They were originally built for elderly and impoverished ironmongers and their widows in 1715 on land bequeathed by Sir Robert Geffrye, a former Lord Mayor of London.

GOLDEN HINDE

69 N5 • St. Mary Overie Dock, Cathedral Street SE1 9DE 0870 0118 700 Daily from around 10am to dusk, but hours vary Adult £2.75, child (4–18) £2.25, under 4s free, family £8. Guided tour (must be pre-booked): adult £3.50, child £2.50 London Bridge 17, 35, 43, 47 London Bridge City Pier, Bankside Pier
www.goldenhinde.co.uk

Nestling in a small dock on Bankside is an exact full-scale replica of the galleon in which Sir Francis Drake (c1543–96) circumnavigated the globe between 1577 and 1580. The ship's cramped interior would have been home to more than 80 sailors. Its five decks include a gun deck that holds 22 cannons. As there are no information panels, it's best to take one of the tours led by well-versed guides dressed in Elizabethan costume.

For those wanting to find out just what it was like to sleep aboard ship, it is possible to stay overnight as part of an educational visit.

DR. JOHNSON'S HOUSE–*GOLDEN HINDE* 89

The Canada Memorial in Green Park, a water feature made out of rose granite from Nova Scotia, was unveiled in 1994 by the Queen

The rehearsal room at 25 Brook Street, Handel's former home

THE SIGHTS

GRAY'S INN

➕ 68 K3 • The Honourable Society of Gray's Inn, 8 South Square, Gray's Inn WC1R 5ET ☎ 020 7458 7800 🕐 Public access to gardens Mon–Fri noon–2.30 💷 Free Ⓜ Chancery Lane (closed Sun), Holborn, Farringdon 🚌 8, 17, 45, 46 www.graysinn.org.uk

Gray's Inn is one of the four Inns of Court (along with Lincoln's Inn, see page 97, and Inner and Middle Temple, see page 136) established in the 14th century to provide accommodation for lawyers and their trainees. Toether they now serve as the home of London's legal profession.

Although wartime bombing destroyed much of Gray's Inn, the most important buildings have been well restored. These include the 17th-century gateway on High Holborn, which gives access to the gardens, the only part open to the public. Known as the Walks, the gardens were first laid out in 1606 by English philosopher and statesman Sir Francis Bacon (1561–1626) when he was treasurer here.

Paths lead through quadrangles of varying character: Redbrick Georgian buildings line South Square, a quiet precinct with lawns and a statue of Bacon; late 17th-century houses and a chapel are found in Gray's Inn Square; and 18th-century houses distinguish Field Court.

GREEN PARK

➕ 67 H6 🕐 Open access 💷 Free Ⓜ Green Park, Hyde Park Corner 🚌 8, 14, 19, 82 www.royalparks.gov.uk

Tourist Information Office
The Store Yard, Horse Guards Approach, St. James's Park SW1A 2BJ ☎ 020 7298 2000

Henry VIII bought this swathe of land for hunting, along with Hyde Park (see page 93) to the west and St. James's Park (see pages 116–117), on the other side of the long street called The Mall. Famous for its mature trees and tree-lined avenues, Green Park's 16ha (40 acres) are less formal than London's other royal parks.

In the southwest corner is the Wellington Arch (see pages 150–151).

GUARDS' MUSEUM

➕ 67 J6 • Wellington Barracks, Birdcage Walk SW1E 6HQ ☎ 020 7414 3271 🕐 Daily 10–4. Closed on ceremonial days; call ahead to check 💷 Adult £2, under 16s free Ⓜ St. James's Park 🚌 11, 24, 148, 211 ♿ www.army.mod.uk

The Guards are the monarch's personal bodyguard, made up of soldiers from the Grenadier, Coldstream, Scots, Irish and Welsh Guards. Their 350-year regimental history is explored using more than 30 displays of uniforms, weapons and tableaux depicting famous battles from the 17th-century English Civil War to the present day.

All this is found under the parade ground at the east end of Wellington Barracks, whose classical façade overlooks St. James's Park (see pages 116–117).

GUILDHALL

➕ 69 M4 • Aldermanbury EC2P 2EJ ☎ 020 7606 3030 🕐 Daily 10–5, May–Sep; Mon–Sat 10–5, Oct–Apr. Closed during ceremonies/events. Art gallery Mon–Sat 10–5, Sun noon–4. For clock museum check ahead ☎ 020 7332 1868/1870 💷 Guildhall and clock museum free; art gallery £2.50, child (under 16) free; free all day Fri and from 3.30pm Mon–Thu, Sat Ⓜ Bank, St. Paul's, Mansion House, Moorgate 🚌 8, 11, 15, 76 www.cityoflondon.gov.uk

England's third-largest civic hall, begun in 1411, is the City's only secular stone structure to have survived the Great Fire of 1666 (see page 31). The Corporation of London, which governs the City, still has its home here.

Beyond the unusual entrance, designed in 1788 with Gothic and Indian influences, is a medieval great hall with stained-glass windows and monuments to national heroes such as Lord Nelson, the Duke of Wellington and Sir Winston Churchill. Beneath are medieval crypts.

The Guildhall library contains prints, drawings and books about the history of London, as well as the Clock Museum, which has some 600 watches, 30 clocks and 15 marine timekeepers dating from the 15th to the 20th century.

Since the 17th century the Corporation has collected works of art, mostly portraits, and paintings of naval battles and views of historic London; a changing selection is displayed in the Guildhall art gallery.

HANDEL HOUSE MUSEUM

➕ 67 H4 • 25 Brook Street W1K 4HB ☎ 020 7495 1685 🕐 Tue, Wed, Fri, Sat 10–6, Thu 10–8, Sun noon–6. During busy periods, tickets may be timed 💷 Adult £4.50, child (6–15) £2, under 6s free Ⓜ Bond Street, Oxford Circus 🚌 8, 3, 25, 53, 55, 176 ♿ www.handelhouse.org

No. 25 Brook Street was the Mayfair home of German-English composer George Friedrich Handel (1685–1759) from 1723 until his death. It was here that he composed some of his best-loved works, including the *Messiah*, *Zadok the Priest* and the *Fireworks Music*. Portraits of Handel and his contemporaries, scores, prints and sculpture form the collection on display.

Part of No. 23, next door (see page 19), provides space for exhibitions and live music.

HMS *BELFAST*

The only surviving example of the armoured warships built for the Royal Navy in the first half of the 20th century.

Launched in March 1938, this huge warship had an active career during World War II and played a leading part both in the destruction of the German battle cruiser *Scharnhorst* at the Battle of North Cape and in the Normandy landings. She now floats off the south bank of the Thames near Tower Bridge, an awesome sight with her heavy armour and massive gun turrets.

TOURING THE DECKS

A self-guided tour starts on the quarterdeck, where officers and guests of honour were piped aboard and guards and bands paraded, and leads to the top of the bridge, with its four Bofors gun mountings, three of which can be aimed by hand (anyone can have a go). The tour then takes you down through nine decks to see the triple 6-inch gun turrets, the shell rooms and magazines and the cramped mess-decks, officers' cabins, galley and sick bay. Life-size models represent members of the crew going about their business—a surprisingly realistic and disconcerting touch.

The operations room is manned by models, re-enacting the ship's part in the Battle of North Cape on 26 December 1943. It's a simple gimmick but an effective one, enhanced by photographs and memorabilia that emphasize the human cost of the conflict.

The ship's company galley dates from the period after HMS *Belfast*'s modernization in the 1950s, when meals were prepared by properly trained and qualified staff and served from the counter; more figures are shown dishing up and following the precise rules posted up around the galley. In the sickbay, a well-equipped operating room reflects the need for every kind of health care on a cruiser designed to spend long periods at sea.

The tour ends with a visit to the boiler and engine rooms, where massive boilers produced superheated steam at high pressure to be piped to the turbine engines, which in turn drove the propeller shafts. It took about four hours to raise sufficient steam for the ship to get under way.

Videos trace the history of each zone on the tour, and officers are on hand to answer questions and keep crowds flowing.

Don't miss the signatures of 36 survivors from a crew of 1,963 on the *Scharnhorst*, on display in the exhibition room.

RATINGS	
Good for kids	● ● ● ●
Historic interest	● ●
Photostops	● ● ●

BASICS

✚ 69 N5 • Morgan's Lane, Tooley Street SE1 2JH ☎ 020 7940 6300
🕐 Daily 10–6, Mar–Oct; 10–5, Nov–Feb 🎫 Adult, £6, child (under 16—must be accompanied by adult) free 🚇 London Bridge, Tower Hill
🚌 36, 705, RV1 ⛴ London Bridge City Pier, Tower Millennium Pier
🎧 Visits take form of self-guided tours
📖 £3.25, in English, French, German
☕ Walrus Café in zone 3
🎁 Gifts, models and books with general war/armed forces theme 🛍

www.iwm.org.uk/belfast
Detailed notes on the ship's main areas, with comprehensive visitor information.

TIP

● If you are claustrophobic, you may not like the deeper regions, and the tour involves climbing down steep ladders without much headroom.

Bristling with guns, the Belfast *gives a comprehensive insight into the lives and work of her crew (main picture). The ship's silver bell (inset) was presented by the people of Belfast in October 1948*

RATINGS

Good for kids	●●
Historic interest	●●●●

BASICS

🚇 68 K6 • Parliament Square SW1A
0AA ☎ House of Commons 020 7219
4272, House of Lords 020 7219 3107,
tickets for summer tours 0870 906 3773
🕐 Tour during summer recess, Mon,
Tue, Fri, Sat 9.15–4.30, Wed–Thu
1.15–4.30, Jul–Aug; Mon, Fri, Sat
9.15–4.30, Tue–Thu 1.15–4.30, Sep–Oct;
Clock Tower Mon–Fri 10.30, 11.30, 2.30
🎟 Strangers' Gallery and Clock Tower
free; for tours see below
🚇 Westminster 🚌 3, 12, 77A
🚢 Westminster Millennium Pier
🎫 Tour during summer recess: adult
£7, child (4–16) £5, under 4s free, fam-
ily £22. Surcharge of £2 for tours in
French, Spanish, German or Italian
📖 Free 'Brief Guides' in several lan-
guages. Various souvenir guidebooks
📚 Gift shop in Westminster Hall
☕ Jubilee Café in Westminster Hall
♿

www.parliament.uk
Details of current debates and Bills, with
facilities for watching sessions; panora-
mas of various parts of Westminster.

*The Lords' Chamber (main
picture). The famous clock tower
(inset right) housing Big Ben
(see page 37) was completed in
1858. View of the buildings from
the London Eye (inset left)*

HOUSES OF PARLIAMENT

**The headquarters of State power for more than 700 years.
A magnificent building with a story to tell at every turn.**

Despite their Gothic appearance, the present Houses of Parliament
are quite recent. The medieval Palace of Westminster was virtually
destroyed by fire in 1834, and a competition was held to design a
replacement in the Elizabethan style. It was won by architect Charles
Barry (1795–1860) and his assistant, Augustus Pugin (1812–52).

TOURING PARLIAMENT
At the State Opening of Parliament (see page 224) the Queen
processes through the building on a route that can be followed on a
public tour during the summer recess, when Members of Parliament
take their annual break. After passing through the Norman porch,
tours enter the Queen's Robing Room, a dazzle of gold and crimson.
The Royal Gallery comes next, hung with portraits of monarchs. Huge
Victorian portraits of the Tudors decorate the Prince's Chamber. From
here you enter the Lords' chamber, where the Queen addresses
Parliament and the Lord Chancellor takes up position on the
Woolsack, a wool-stuffed cushion representing British prosperity.

This is the end of the Queen's journey, but visitors continue through
the Peers' Lobby to the Central Lobby, between the two Chambers.
This is where members of the public can come face to face with their
political representatives to plead their particular cause—that is, to
lobby. From here a corridor leads into the Commons Lobby, with a
red line marking the boundary between Government and Opposition
members—traditionally seated at just over two swords' lengths apart,
for safety's sake. Next comes St. Stephen's Hall, on the site of the
original chapel, and finally the 11th-century Westminster Hall, now
used only occasionally for ceremonial occasions.

You can attend debates in the House of Commons or the House of
Lords. Wait outside St. Stephen's Entrance, but note that queues can
be long for the most interesting debates or for Prime Minister's
Questions. If you're visiting from overseas, you must apply to your
embassy or high commission in the UK for a card of introduction,
which permits entry during the early afternoon. Each embassy may
issue only four cards per day so book well in advance. To arrange a
tour of the Big Ben clock tower, UK residents can contact their MP;
overseas visitors should write, at least three months in advance, to
Clock Tower Tours, Parliamentary Works Services Directorate, 1 Canon
Row, London SW1A 2JN.

Holy Trinity Church's huge east window, depicting saints

Riders from the local riding school regularly use Rotten Row in Hyde Park, the bridleway running along the south side of the Serpentine

HOLLAND PARK

⊞ 66 off C6 ◷ Open dawn to dusk
💷 Free ⊕ Holland Park, High Street
Kensington, Kensington Olympia
🚌 9, 94, 148 🅿️
www.rbkc.gov.uk
Tourist Information Office
The Stable Yard, Holland Park, Ilchester
Place W8 6LU, tel 020 7471 9813

Thanks to World War II bombing, little remains of Holland House, the Jacobean mansion that stood in wooded parkland here. What's left is now used as a youth hostel, and the park itself is a busy public area with playgrounds, tennis courts, a football pitch, a netball court, cricket nets, a golf bunker, a cafeteria and an ecology centre, as well as formal and informal gardens. An outdoor theatre on the terrace of the house stages a 10-week summer season of opera and ballet.
Don't miss the Japanese Kyoto Garden on the west side of the park, created for the 1991 London Festival of Japan.

HOLY TRINITY CHURCH

⊞ 67 F7 • Sloane Street SW1X 9DF
☎ 020 7730 7270 ◷ Mon–Sat
9.30–5.30 💷 Free ⊕ Sloane Square,
Knightsbridge 🚌 19, 22, 137, C1
www.holytrinitysloanestreet.org

Built between 1888 and 1890 to a design by John Dando Sedding, Chelsea's Holy Trinity is regarded as one of London's best examples of the Arts and Crafts style, which grew up in the late 19th century as part of a reaction against mass-produced goods. Sir John Betjeman (1906–84), poet and writer, described the church as a 'cathedral of the Arts and Crafts movement', particularly admiring the ornate wrought-iron chancel gates. Artist Edward Burne-Jones and designer William Morris produced the huge east window with 48 panels depicting saints.

HOUSES OF PARLIAMENT
(see opposite)

HYDE PARK

⊞ 66 F5 ◷ Open 5am–midnight
💷 Free ⊕ Hyde Park Corner, Marble
Arch, Knightsbridge 🚌 9, 14, 16, 19,74
🅿️🍴
www.royalparks.gov.uk
Tourist Information Office
Ranger's Lodge, Hyde Park W2 2UH
☎ 020 7298 2000, 020 7262 5484

Together with Kensington Gardens (see page 94), Hyde Park forms a wide sweep of green to the southwest of Marble Arch. Henry VIII originally claimed it as hunting ground, but it was opened to the public by James I at the beginning of the 17th century. In the 1730s Queen Caroline, George II's wife, created the artificial lake known as the Serpentine for boating and bathing. Today the park is still used as a recreation area and gathering place, with rowing boats and pedal boats for hire on the lake in summer, bandstand music at lunchtime in June, July and August, and occasional fairs, concerts and rallies.

Speakers' Corner (see page 15), near Marble Arch, has for centuries provided an open-air forum where anyone and everyone can air their views.

Rotten Row—a linguistic corruption of *route du roi* (king's road)—was built to link rural Kensington Palace (see page 95) to Piccadilly and St. James's Palace. Members of the Household Cavalry Brigade, among others, now exercise their horses along it, and at around 10.30am (9.30am on Sunday) and noon you can see them riding to and from the Changing the Guard ceremonies at Buckingham Palace (see page 79).

IMPERIAL WAR MUSEUM
(see page 96)

INSTITUTE OF CONTEMPORARY ARTS (ICA)

⊞ 68 J5 • The Mall SW1Y 5AH ☎ 020
7930 3647 ◷ Mon noon–10.30,
Tue–Sat noon–1am, Sun noon–11.
Gallery daily noon–7.30 (during exhibitions); New Media Centre Wed–Fri 4–8,
Sat 2–6 💷 Day membership £1.50
weekdays, £2.50 weekends; check
ahead for individual events/exhibitions
🚇 Charing Cross, Piccadilly Circus
🚌 9, 11, 13, 19, 88 🅿️🍴
www.ica.org.uk

English art critic and historian Sir Herbert Read (1893–1968) established the ICA soon after World War II. Originally housed in Dover Street, it was moved in 1968 to Carlton House Terrace, a long and elegant white-stone building fronted by neoclassical columns and designed by John Nash (1752–1835). Behind its formal façade the Institute presents contemporary films, exhibitions of avant-garde art, talks and dance productions.

JEWEL TOWER

⊞ 68 J6 • Abingdon Street SW1P 3JY
☎ 020 7222 2219 ◷ Daily 10–6,
Apr–Sep; 10–5, Oct; 10–4, Nov–Mar
💷 EH. Adult £2, child (5–16) £1.50,
under 5s free ⊕ Westminster 🚌 3, 12,
77A 🅿️
www.english-heritage.org.uk

The three-storey red-brick Jewel Tower was built in about 1365 as part of the original Palace of Westminster and used to store Edward III's treasures. A moat surrounded it at that time.

On the first floor an exhibition records the history of Parliament from 1066 to the present day, and on the second floor a 50-minute video explains the workings of government, and a virtual tour takes you round the Houses of Parliament.
Don't miss the Saxon sword discovered on the site.

KENSINGTON GARDENS

**Peaceful gardens extending over 111ha (274 acres).
Designed for royalty and laid out on an elegant plan.**

*Kensington Gardens (main
picture). Painters, composers,
poets and architects are
portrayed around the Albert
Memorial (inset), and its corners
illustrate the peoples of Asia,
America, Europe and Africa.
Allegorical figures represent
Albert's interests: Commerce,
Manufacturing, Engineering and
Agriculture*

London's greenery extends westwards from Hyde Park (see page 93)
into Kensington Gardens, but the two parks have quite different characters. Unlike the former hunting ground of Hyde Park, which still has
an open informality, Kensington Gardens were created to a formal
plan as the grounds of Kensington Palace, which sits at their western
boundary. Much of the layout dates from work carried out for Queen
Caroline, wife of George II, in the early 18th century, when the upper
reach of Hyde Park's artificial lake, the Serpentine, was claimed and
re-named the Long Water. At its northern end is a paved garden with
a pavilion and four fountains.

The Serpentine Gallery, in the park's southern section, hosts changing exhibitions of contemporary art *(tel 020 7402 6075/7298 1515,
open daily 10–6 during exhibitions, free)*. It was built in 1908 and
formerly served as a fashionable tea pavilion.

North of here are two sculptures: *Physical Energy* (1904), an
equestrian bronze by George Frederick Watts (1817–1904), and
Peter Pan (1912) by Sir George Frampton (1860–1928), commemorating the hero of J. M. Barrie's play, written in 1904. Nearby is the
Diana, Princess of Wales Memorial Playground (see page 219).

AROUND THE ALBERT MEMORIAL

Kensington Gardens entered a new phase of their history when they
were opened to the public in 1841, during Queen Victoria's reign. The
Queen's beloved husband, Prince Albert, is commemorated in a flamboyant monument by Sir George Gilbert Scott (1811–78), southwest
of the Serpentine Gallery. At its centre is Albert himself, holding the
catalogue for the 1851 Great Exhibition, which he organized (see
page 36). Across Kensington Gore Road is another monument to the
Prince—the domed Royal Albert Hall (see page 194).

Behind the Albert Memorial the Flower Walk runs east to meet the
Broad Walk, which runs north between Kensington Palace and the
Round Pond, west of the Serpentine Gallery. Created in 1728, the
pond is where children and adults traditionally come to sail model
boats. There's a bandstand to its south, where music is sometimes
performed on summer days.

Don't miss the arch (1979) sculpted from Roman Travertine by
Henry Moore, on the east bank of the Long Water.

KENSINGTON PALACE

A royal home for more than three centuries, providing a private retreat for kings and queens.

In 1689 the asthmatic William III set up home in Kensington Palace to escape from the damp and smoke of riverside Whitehall Palace. He bought the existing 1605 house and had it enlarged by Sir Christopher Wren (1632–1723); George I had further extensions added in the 1720s.

The palace has been home to many members of the royal family, but is most famously where Diana, Princess of Wales, lived until her death in 1997; it was her marital home before her marriage to Prince Charles ended.

DRESS COLLECTION AND STATE APARTMENTS

On the ground floor the Royal Ceremonial Dress Collection presents a superb array of finery from the 18th to the 20th century, including a permanent collection of dresses belonging to Diana, Princess of Wales. You're taken through the elaborate process of dressing for court, from a replica of a shop where materials are chosen to a visit to the seamstress for a final fitting.

First of the State Apartments, upstairs, are the Queen's Apartments, the largest of which is the 26m (84ft) Queen Mary's Gallery, a panelled room hung with royal portraits. Several smaller rooms are decorated with 17th-century furnishings and pictures, including the State Bed, in Queen Mary's Bedchamber, with its original hangings.

By contrast, the King's Apartments are very opulent. Italianate in style, the rooms have magnificent ceiling paintings by William Kent (c1685–1748). Most impressive is the Cupola Room, with its pillars, figures of Greek and Roman deities, and busts of Roman emperors and ancient philosophers. Queen Victoria was baptized here.

Courtiers and visitors would have used the King's Grand Staircase, designed by Wren, with its scrolled wrought-ironwork by Jean Tijou and walls and ceiling coated in Venetian-style paintings by Kent. The *trompe-l'oeil* wall painting of a gallery crowded with figures includes many contemporary portraits of George I's courtiers and servants.

Don't miss the pretty sunken garden, made in 1909, with lime trees trained to form a hedge on three sides and flower beds framing the central lily pond (to which there is no public access), or the wind-direction dial, set above the fireplace in the King's Gallery and connected to the weather vane outside.

RATINGS

Good for kids	●
Historic interest	●●●●
Value for money	●●

BASICS

✚ 66 D5 • Kensington Palace State Apartments, Kensington Gardens W8 4PX ☎ 0870 751 5170
🕐 Daily 10–6, Mar–Oct; 10–5, Nov–Feb 💷 Adult £10.20, child (5–15) £6.60, under 5s free, family £31
🚇 High Street Kensington, Queensway
🚌 9, 10, 12 52, C1
📟 Sound guide included in entry; guidebook £3.95, in English and German 🍴 Orangery Restaurant
🛍 The Shop ♿

www.kensington-palace.org.uk
Limited information as part of the Historic Royal Palaces site.

TIP

● Look for access to the palace from the Broad Walk in Kensington Gardens.

When Diana, Princess of Wales died, the ornate black and gold wrought-iron gates (detail, main picture) outside Kensington Palace (inset) were piled high with flowers for weeks on end

IMPERIAL WAR MUSEUM

The country's most impressive military museum, examining much more than the weaponry of war.

An imposing pair of naval guns guards the entrance to the Imperial War Museum—just a taster of the museum's diverse collection, which covers wars involving Britain or the Commonwealth since 1914. This includes not only World Wars I and II, but many other international conflicts, from Korea and Vietnam to Suez and the Arabian Gulf.

THE EXHIBITS

You're first confronted by a confusing array of military equipment in the airy Large Exhibits Gallery: Tanks, artillery, fighter planes, trucks and submarines are haphazardly parked—or suspended—in the domed space. Take time to wander among the vehicles, many of which have stories of bravery attached. There's the wooden dinghy *Tamzine*, for instance, the smallest surviving boat to have taken part in the evacuation of 200,000 troops from Dunkirk in 1940. Sometimes it's simply the sense of scale that impresses, in exhibits such as the colossal V2 rocket or the cramped World War II fighter cockpit.

On the lower ground floor are well-conceived re-creations of the 1940–41 Blitz and World War I trench warfare, complete with sound effects and smells. The section about the British Home Front is fascinating, and includes evocative touches such as posters exhorting the women of Britain to 'come into the factories', or 'dig for victory'.

Elsewhere on the labyrinthine lower floor collections can easily be overlooked. World War II receives the fullest coverage, with detailed sections on the eastern front and war in northwest Europe and the Far East. Tucked away in the maze of displays is the bronze eagle from the German Reich's Chancellory, given to the British by a Russian officer.

Move up to the first floor for the absorbing Secret War exhibition. Items on show include bottles of invisible ink used by German spies and one of the few remaining German Enigma machines used to encode messages.

The art galleries on the second floor are a popular section of the museum, with work by Paul Nash, Henry Moore and Stanley Spencer. On the third floor is the distressing counterpoint to the martial display below. The Holocaust Exhibition examines the Nazi persecution of Europe's Jewish communities and other groups, such as gypsies and homosexuals, between 1933 and 1945. Exhibits include shoes collected from prisoners at Majdanek concentration camp in Poland.

RATINGS

Good for kids	●●●○
Historic interest	●●●●○
Specialist shopping	●●○

BASICS

✚ 68 L7 • Lambeth Road SE1 6HZ
☎ 020 7416 5000 🕐 Daily 10–6
🎫 Free (except for some special exhibitions) Ⓜ Lambeth North, Elephant and Castle, Southwark, Waterloo
🚌 3, 12, 344, C10 🎧 Audio tours available 📱 £3.25, in English only
🍴 On ground floor, 10–5.30; children's lunchbox £2.45 🎁 Gifts with relevant themes 👥

www.iwm.org.uk
Comprehensive visitor information and details of current exhibitions.

TIP

● Note that curators don't recommend the Holocaust Exhibition for children under 14.

World War I biplanes to modern missiles (main picture). British naval guns outside the museum (inset top). Take Off (inset) by Dame Laura Knight, painted during World War II, on show in the art galleries

Street artists in Leicester Square vary in standard: choose carefully

Pre-Raphaelite paintings decorate Leighton House

Chancery Lane, one of the four Inns of Court

LEICESTER SQUARE

⊞ 68 J5 • Leicester Square WC2H 7NJ
🕘 Open access to the square. Cut-price ticket booth: Mon–Sat 10–7, Sun noon–3.30 (for matinées only) 🎟 Free
🚇 Leicester Square 🚌 24. 29. 176
🍴 🖥 🏛
www.officiallondontheatre.co.uk
for cut-price tickets

By night, particularly on a Friday or Saturday, this pedestrianized central London square is one of the most crowded places in the city, teeming with people on their way to or from cinemas, night-clubs, restaurants, fast-food out-lets and bars. By day its tiny central garden is a favourite lunchtime resting place. In the middle of the garden is the marble Shakespeare Memorial Fountain (1874) by Giovanni Fontana, facing a bronze statue of Charlie Chaplin (1981) by John Doubleday. Around the perimeter are busts of the square's former local residents—Sir Joshua Reynolds, Sir Isaac Newton, William Hogarth and John Hunter.

A cut-price ticket booth in the clock tower building on the south side of the square is the best way to buy discount theatre tickets (see page 198).

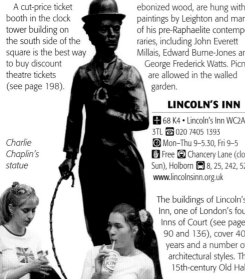

Charlie Chaplin's statue

LEIGHTON HOUSE MUSEUM

⊞ 66 off C6 • 12 Holland Park Road W14 8LZ ☎ 020 7602 3316
🕘 Wed–Mon 11–5.30. Garden Apr–end Sep 🎟 Free; donations welcome 🚇 High Street Kensington 🚌 9, 10, 27, 28, 33
www.rbkc.gov.uk

Victorian artist Frederic, Lord Leighton (1830–96) had this three-storey, red-brick studio-house built to his own design on the edge of Holland Park. The result was a private palace devoted to art, equipped with only one bedroom as he didn't want to be bothered with house guests. Every room has been restored in period style; the most remarkable is the Arab Room, complete with pool and marble pillars and based on a Moorish banqueting hall in Palermo, Sicily. Islamic tiles collected by Leighton on his travels through Damascus, Cairo and Rhodes cover the walls and floor.

Other rooms, less exotically finished with red walls and ebonized wood, are hung with paintings by Leighton and many of his pre-Raphaelite contempo-raries, including John Everett Millais, Edward Burne-Jones and George Frederick Watts. Picnics are allowed in the walled garden.

LINCOLN'S INN

⊞ 68 K4 • Lincoln's Inn WC2A 3TL ☎ 020 7405 1393
🕘 Mon–Thu 9–5.30, Fri 9–5
🎟 Free 🚇 Chancery Lane (closed Sun), Holborn 🚌 8, 25, 242, 521
www.lincolnsinn.org.uk

The buildings of Lincoln's Inn, one of London's four Inns of Court (see pages 90 and 136), cover 400 years and a number of architectural styles. The 15th-century Old Hall,

where the Court of Chancery sat between 1733 and 1873, is the setting for the protracted Jarndyce v Jarndyce case in Charles Dickens' novel *Bleak House*. A 17th-century chapel built above a beautiful open undercroft has massive pillars and dramatic vaulting, and gas lamps still light the 17th-century houses in New Square. The mock-Tudor Great Hall, with its red brick and black frame, is a 19th-century addition.

An archway at the northwest corner of New Square leads to Lincoln's Inn Fields, at 5ha (12 acres) the largest square in London and once a popular venue for duels. Today lawyers battle it out on the tennis courts here in their lunch hour. On the north side is Sir John Soane's Museum (see pages 128–129).

LINLEY SAMBOURNE HOUSE

⊞ 66 C6 • 18 Stafford Terrace W8 7BH ☎ 020 7602 3316 🕘 Sat–Sun guided tours at 10, 11.15, 1, 2.15, 3.30. Mon–Fri open for group bookings only 🎟 Adult £6, under 18s £1 🚇 High Street Kensington 🚌 9, 10, 27, 28, 49, 52, 70
www.rbkc.gov.uk

A mass of paintings, cartoons and photographs covers the walls in the Victorian house occupied by political cartoonist and illustrator Edward Linley Sambourne (1844–1910) from 1874 until his death.

The family continued to use the house until 1980, when it was opened as a museum, having remained almost totally unaltered during the intervening years, preserving its over-furnished, late 19th-century appearance. The rooms still have their original William Morris wall-papers, and Asian rugs, stained-glass windows and heavy, Gothic-inspired furniture complete the look.

THE SIGHTS

A clownfish—colourful resident of the London Aquarium

Geometric patterning of the London Central Mosque ceiling

A typically theatrical tableau in the London Dungeon

THE SIGHTS

LONDON AQUARIUM

✚ 68 K6 • County Hall, Westminster Bridge Road SE1 7PB ☎ 020 7967 8000 🕐 Daily 10–6 💷 Adult £8.75, child (3–14) £5.25, family £25 🚇 Waterloo, Westminster, Embankment 🚌 12, 53, 159, 211, 381 ♿ ⌨
www.londonaquarium.co.uk

More than 3,000 forms of marine life can be found swimming around under the former offices of the Greater London Council in County Hall, one of Europe's largest aquariums. Laid out across three floors, it displays its residents in tanks representing a variety of environments, from ponds to rivers to oceans.

The focal point is the three-floors-high Atlantic and Pacific exhibit, where large sharks and stingrays glide silently between giant, submerged Easter Island-style heads. There are countless gaudy fish to enjoy in the Reef and Corals and Indian Ocean exhibitions, and children get a real thrill from stroking a stingray on the 'beach'. It takes some 2 million litres (440,000 gallons) of Thames water and tons of imported salt to fill the tanks.

The aquarium is committed to conservation and as a way of raising money for research you're invited to adopt one of 30 species of fish. Not surprisingly, the sharks, piranhas and rays are the most popular choices.

LONDON CENTRAL MOSQUE

✚ 66 F2 • 146 Park Road NW8 7RG ☎ 020 7724 3363 🕐 Mon–Fri 9.30–5 💷 Free 🚇 Baker Street, Marylebone 🚌 13, 82, 113, 274 ⌨
www.islamicculturalcentre.co.uk

The showpiece Islamic Culture Centre and mosque, opened in 1978 on the eastern side of Regent's Park, provides a focus for London's Muslim communities, with lecture and conference facilities, a bookshop and a library. About 4,000 worshippers can be accommodated in the mosque, which has marble floors and intricate mosaics. Sir Frederick Gibberd (1908–84) designed the building with its splendid golden dome, 25m (82ft) high, and white minaret.

LONDON DUNGEON

✚ 69 N5 • 28–34 Tooley Street SE1 2SZ ☎ 020 7403 7221, 0870 8460666 🕐 Daily 10–7.30, mid-Jul–Sep; 10–5.30 Apr–Jun, early Sep–Oct; 10.30–5, Nov–Mar 💷 Adult £12.95, child (5–14), £8.25, under 5s free 🚇 London Bridge 🚌 43, 47, RV1 ♿ ⌨
www.thedungeons.com

Hidden away in the vaults beneath London Bridge railway station is a grisly parade of life-size tableaux, complete with disturbing sound and special effects. Along with scenes of death from disease, early surgery, murder and various methods of torture and execution, the museum presents re-enactments of some of the most horrific events in British history.

The Great Fire of London is a £1-million re-creation of the fire-ravaged streets of London in 1666; Judgement Day is an 18th-century courtroom drama followed by a trip on an executioner's barge through Traitors' Gate at the Tower of London to the block. Jack the Ripper takes you back to 1888 for a terrifying tour through the district of Whitechapel, following the bloody footsteps of the most infamous serial killer of his time. Wicked Women concentrates on *femmes fatales* from history, with a special show featuring the exploits of 17th-century highwaywoman Lady Katherine Ferriers.

One of the most spectacular and ambitious exhibitions is the one about the Great Plague, which opened in 2003; it will certainly challenge the squeamish as it vividly and realistically re-creates the horrors of the plague that claimed more than 100,000 lives in 1665. Expect to see black rats (they carried the disease) running around, and to walk through a tunnel piled up with the ravaged corpses of plague victims.

Throughout the museum, actors in period costume help sustain the menacing mood and keep you constantly on guard.

LONDON EYE (see opposite)

LONDON FIRE BRIGADE MUSEUM

✚ 69 M6 • Winchester House, 94A Southwark Bridge Road SE1 0EG ☎ 020 7587 2894 🕐 Visit by guided tour only (Mon–Fri 10.30 and 2) by prior arrangement 💷 Adult £3, child (7–14) £1.50, under 7s free 🚇 Borough, Southwark, Elephant and Castle 🚌 344 ⌨
www.london-fire.gov.uk

The Great Fire of 1666 marks the starting point for this journey through the history of firefighting in London. Exhibits housed in two buildings of the London Fire Brigade's Training Centre include original fire engines, pumps, helmets, uniforms and various types of uncomfortable-looking breathing apparatus.

Among the museum's possessions are the personal belongings of Captain Eyre Massey Shaw. He was in charge of the brigade from 1861 and is credited as the father of the modern fire service. His silver helmet and KCB decoration are on display.

A collection of paintings by World War II firefighters shows telling scenes of the Blitz as they experienced it.

98 LONDON AQUARIUM–LONDON FIRE BRIGADE MUSEUM

Survey London from the comfort of a stable pod on the Eye

LONDON EYE

**Spectacular views across the city in every direction.
London's most visible icon, soaring 135m (443ft) above
the River Thames.**

The world's largest observation wheel is four times wider than the
dome of St. Paul's and more than 200 times larger than the wheel of
an average racing bicycle, and it offers a ride that's enthralling even for
those who hate heights.

RIDING HIGH

Passengers ride in one of 32 podlike capsules that rotate smoothly in
a slow-moving, 30-minute flight. Each capsule is fully enclosed and
comfortably holds 25 people. Because the capsules are secured on
the outside of the wheel (rather than hung from it, as they would be
on a Ferris wheel), views through the large glass windows are totally
unobstructed. And because the capsules are kept level by a motorized motion stability system, you can walk around inside them quite
safely—although seating is provided. For additional safety, each capsule is in touch with the ground via camera and radio links. Note,
however, that flights may be cancelled at the last minute owing to
weather conditions. You can ask for a flight attendant to accompany
you, to point out major landmarks. The wheel is in constant motion,
revolving continuously at a quarter of the average walking speed and
enabling you to walk straight on and off the moving capsules.

After dark, the trees lining the approach to the London Eye are
bathed in green lights, and the boarding platform appears to float on
a cloud of blue light. Sunset and after-dark flights are also available.

BACKGROUND

The British Airways London Eye was conceived by David Marks and
Julia Barfield to celebrate the millennium, using a design that represents the turning of the century. It took seven years and the expertise
of hundreds of people from five European countries to realize their
vision, and over a week to lift the Eye upright from a horizontal position across the Thames—a procedure previously attempted only in
oil-rigging operations. Although originally intended as a temporary
structure, the Eye is so popular that it is unlikely that it will
disappear from the skyline.

RATINGS	
Good for kids	●●●●●
Photostops	●●●●●
Value for money	●●●●

BASICS

✚ 68 K6 • British Airways London Eye,
Riverside Building, County Hall
Westminster Bridge Road SE1 7PB
☎ Bookings: 0870 5000 600 (24-hour
automated booking line) ⏱ Times vary
with season; call ahead to check
💷 Adult £11, child (5–15) £5.50, under
5s free 🚇 Waterloo, Westminster,
Embankment, Charing Cross
🚌 77, 139, RV1 🚢 Waterloo
Millennium Pier 📖 *Essential Eye
Souvenir Book* and in-flight mini guide
available from the ticket hall or shop £5,
in English, French, German, braille
🍴 In the Flight Zone in County Hall
and outside in Jubilee Gardens 🎁 In
Jubilee Gardens, selling souvenirs and
gifts, including Eye-inspired jewellery

www.ba-londoneye.com
Includes an on-line booking facility.

TIPS

● Book ahead. Although not
essential, it is recommended.

● Flying times may vary; arrive
30 minutes before your flight.

● To gain free admission for
under 5s, pre-book a ticket.

Trams and trolleybuses at London's Transport Museum

This window was unveiled in the Lord's Museum in 1993

Marble Arch, built as a grand entrance to Buckingham Palace

THE SIGHTS

LONDON PLANETARIUM
(see opposite)

LONDON'S TRANSPORT MUSEUM

✚ 68 K4 • Covent Garden Piazza, Covent Garden WC2E 7BB ☎ 020 7379 6344 or 020 7565 7299 (24-hour recorded information) ◷ Sat–Thu 10–6, Fri 11–6 🎫 Adult £5.95, under 16s accompanied by an adult free ⊖ Covent Garden, Leicester Square, Holborn, Charing Cross 🚌 6, 9, 13, 23, 77A, RV1 ▢ 🏛
www.ltmuseum.co.uk

Covent Garden's former Flower Market (see page 88) now houses London's Transport Museum, which tells the story of the city's transport since the early 1800s and explores its impact on the lives of Londoners.

The museum's permanent displays consist of more than 350,000 items—the most comprehensive collection of historic urban transport in the world. Fulfil your childhood fantasies by clambering into the driving seat of a bus or operating a simulated tube train, and admire the handsomely designed horse-drawn and electric trams. Alternatively, you can have a go at being a station announcer.

In addition to the vehicles themselves, there are posters, photographs, drawings, maps, films, models, uniforms, signs and other equipment. Touch screens provide more information, and there are many working models and hands-on exhibits.

One video tells the story of the people who have kept London on the move for the last two centuries, from stablehands to the men and women (known as fluffers) who cleaned the tunnels of dirt, paper and hair on the Underground system.

Children can follow the 15 interactive KidZones, stamping a souvenir ticket as they go, and under fives can run riot in the Funbus play area.

MADAME TUSSAUD'S
(see opposite)

LORD'S TOUR AND MCC MUSEUM

✚ 66 E2 • Lord's Cricket Ground, St. John's Wood NW8 8QN ☎ 020 7616 8595 ◷ Tours daily 10, noon, 2, Apr–Sep; noon, 2, Oct–Mar. No tours during major matches or on preparation days. On other match days, only the 10am tour enters the Pavilion. MCC Museum included in tours 🎫 Adult £6.50, child (5–16) £4.50, under 5s free, family £20 ⊖ Marylebone, St. John's Wood 🚌 139, 189 ▢ 🏛
www.lords.org

Cricket divides the British nation between devoted fans on the one hand and those who find it baffling and boring on the other. Lord's historic cricket ground has a wider appeal, however, and tours of the Marylebone Cricket Club (MCC) give an intriguing behind-the-scenes glimpse of a sporting venue which has been in use since the 18th century.

In the Long Room, the cricket-watching room at the heart of the Pavilion, an art gallery contains portraits of the game's celebrities. You can also take a look in the players' dressing rooms and visit the MCC Museum, where paintings, photographs and mementoes trace 400 years of cricketing history.

Don't miss the tiny, delicate Ashes urn in the museum or the footage of matches shown in the Brian Johnston Memorial Theatre.

MARBLE ARCH

✚ 67 F4 ◷ Open access 🎫 Free ⊖ Hyde Park Corner, Marble Arch, Bond Street, Green Park 🚌 10, 36, 74, 137, 274

Tourist Information Office
Britain Visitor Centre, 1 Lower Regent Street SW1Y 4XT (no telephone)

John Nash designed this elegant monument of white Carrara marble in 1828 as the main entrance to Buckingham Palace (see page 79), but it was moved to its current site next to Speakers' Corner in Hyde Park (see page 93) when the palace was extended in 1851. At the time it was intended to form the park's principal entrance, but it now stands isolated on a grassy traffic island.

The triple-arched design was inspired by the Constantine Arch in Rome and is carved with intricate reliefs of winged, wreathed Victories, a Roman warrior and Justice, Peace and Plenty, plus representations of England, Scotland and Ireland.

MILLENNIUM BRIDGE

✚ 69 M5 ◷ Open access 🎫 Free ⊖ Blackfriars, St. Paul's, Southwark 🚌 344, 11, 15, 17, RV1 ⛴ Blackfriars Millennium Pier, Bankside Pier
Tourist Information Offices
Britain Visitor Centre, 1 Lower Regent Street SW1Y 4XT (no telephone); City Information Centre, St. Paul's Church Yard EC4M 8AD ☎ 020 7332 1456

Two of London's famous landmarks—St. Paul's Cathedral (see pages 118–123) in the City and the Tate Modern gallery (see pages 134–135) at Bankside—are connected by this bridge built in 2000, the first pedestrian crossing to be built over the Thames in more than a century.

Architect Norman Foster and engineer Ove Arup designed it to give the impression of a single sweeping 'blade of light', illuminated from deck level with an innovative light pipe system. The steel structure is 325m (1,066ft) high and carries 3,000 tonnes/tons of horizontal force. See also page 40.

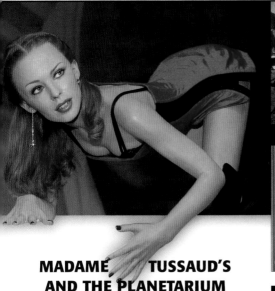

MADAME TUSSAUD'S AND THE PLANETARIUM

**Come face to face with anybody who is anybody.
Have your photograph taken with celebrities old and new.**

Madame Tussaud's waxworks collection, a quirky eccentricity just beyond the southeast corner of Regent's Park, is one of London's most popular attractions. More than 2 million visitors come here every year to spot the likenesses of famous figures and pose beside heroes of sports and entertainment. The collection changes all the time: Celebrities know they've made it when their waxwork appears here, and they know they've had their day when their likeness is melted down to be turned into another rising star. Unlike fame, however, the techniques used to make the models are timeless and have barely changed since Madame Tussaud started her business 200 years ago. The hair used is real and the wax is similar to candlewax, which would melt in the heat of sunlight—thus explaining why the displays are kept in darkened rooms.

The first tableau is the Garden Party, where waxwork images of leading TV, film and sport stars mingle at an informal gathering. Upstairs, in the Grand Hall. royalty, politicians and world leaders rub shoulders with artists and musicians. But the highlight of a visit for many visitors is the ghoulish Chamber of Horrors. Exhibits here include Vlad the Impaler (the real life Count Dracula); Joan of Arc, burning at the stake; Guy Fawkes, hanged, drawn and quartered; objects from London's brutal Newgate Prison (see page 35); Jack the Ripper; and a scene that would have been familiar to Madame T.—execution by guillotine.

Tours end with a Spirit of London time-travel trip in a taxicab (complete with sounds and smells) from Elizabethan times through the Plague and Great Fire to the Swinging Sixties.

LONDON PLANETARIUM

Occupying the green dome of the building is the London Planetarium—the first in Britain, completed in 1958, and still one of the largest in the world. On the way into the theatre you'll pass wax figures of astronauts and personalities such as Albert Einstein and Galileo, plus hands-on stations about the planets.

The show Wonders of the Universe is an enjoyable romp through space; 3-D simulator action enlivens some of the more educational aspects of the accompanying commentary on the cosmos.

Don't miss the oldest figure on display, *Sleeping Beauty*, made in 1765 and based on Louis XV's mistress, Madame du Barry, or the 'anonymous' tourists, sitting on benches or standing around chatting. You'll find yourself caught out more than once.

RATINGS	
Good for kids	●●●●●
Historic interest	●●
Photostops	●●●●●
Value for money	●●●

BASICS

✚ 67 G3 • Marylebone Road NW1 5LR
☎ 0870 400 3000 (booking only; fee applies) ◐ Daily 10–5.30. Planetarium shows run every 20 mins Mon–Fri 12.30–5, Sat, Sun 10.30–5
💷 Includes entry to Planetarium. Non-timed tickets: adult £14.95, under 16s £11.50. Planetarium show only: adult £2, under 16s £1.50 ◉ Baker Street
🚌 13, 27, 74, 82, 139 🎧 £4, in English, French, German, Italian, Spanish
☕ Costa Coffeeshop on site, offering large, milky coffees and expensive snacks 🎁 Souvenirs and gifts ♿

www.madame-tussauds.com
Site currently inoperable.
www.london-planetarium.com
Limited background information but useful for booking tickets.

TIP

● Queues for Madame Tussaud's can be very long. To avoid them, book a timed ticket in advance.

Life-size models of the famous and the infamous include Kylie Minogue (main picture), the Beatles (inset top) and Elizabeth Taylor (inset bottom)

A cage was built around the Monument's gallery in 1842

The Pedlar's Window in the Church of St. Mary-at-Lambeth

Justice, 3.5m (12ft) tall, stands on top of the Old Bailey

THE SIGHTS

MONUMENT

✠ 69 N5 • Monument Street EC3R 8AH ☎ 020 7626 2717 ◉ Daily 10–6 💺 Adult £2, child (5–16) £1, under 5s free. Joint ticket with Tower Bridge (see page 137) £5 🚇 Monument 🚌 15, 21, 25 ⛴ London Bridge City Pier
www.cityoflondon.gov.uk

The devastating Great Fire of 1666 (see page 31) wiped out the medieval heart of London. The Monument commemorates this event and the later rebuilding. Built between 1671 and 1677 to a design by Sir Christopher Wren, chief architect of the new city, it stands on the northern bank of the Thames, east of London Bridge. The fluted column of Portland stone is 62m (202ft) high, which equals the distance from the start of the fire in Pudding Lane. At the top a flaming urn of copper symbolizes the fire.

The 311 steps of a steep internal spiral stairway lead to the viewing platform, 41m (133ft) above the ground.

MUSEUM OF GARDEN HISTORY

✠ 68 K7 • Lambeth Palace Road SE1 7LB ☎ 020 7401 8865 ◉ Daily 10.30–5, Feb–Dec 💺 Suggested donation £3 🚇 Lambeth North, Westminster 🚌 C10, 3, 344, 77, 507 📷 ♿
www.museumgardenhistory.org

The redundant parish church of St. Mary-at-Lambeth provides the setting for this collection of gardening tools and machinery, including everything from spades to cloches and mowers. Outside, in the church courtyard, a knot garden uses plants popular in the 17th century, including fragrant old roses.

Two major figures in the development of English gardening, John Tradescant the elder

(1570–1638) and his son, John, gardeners to Charles I and II, are laid to rest here, A window in the church commemorates them.

MUSEUM OF LONDON
(see opposite)

NATIONAL GALLERY
(see pages 104–109)

NATIONAL PORTRAIT GALLERY
(see pages 110–111)

NATURAL HISTORY MUSEUM
(see pages 112–113)

OLD BAILEY (CENTRAL CRIMINAL COURT)

✠ 69 M4 • Central Criminal Court, Old Bailey EC4M 7EH ☎ 020 7248 3277 ◉ Mon–Fri 10–1, 2–5 (approx); reduced court sitting Aug. No admission for children under 14 💺 Free 🚇 St. Paul's 🚌 8, 25, 56, 242
www.cityoflondon.gov.uk

Its correct title is the Central Criminal Court, but everyone knows the courthouse as the Old Bailey, a name borrowed from the nearby street. Major criminal trials from all over England and Wales are heard in this baroque building, erected in 1907 on the site of the notorious Newgate prison (see page 35).

A bronze, gilded figure of

Barristers wearing traditional wigs and gowns

Justice carrying her sword and scales (but not blindfolded) crowns the green copper dome, echoing the design of nearby St. Paul's Cathedral.

Public galleries are open for viewing of trials in session.

PERCIVAL DAVID FOUNDATION OF CHINESE ART

✠ 68 J3 • School of Oriental and African Studies, 53 Gordon Square WC1H 0PD ☎ 020 7387 3909 ◉ Mon–Fri 10.30–5 💺 Free; tours £4 per head 🚇 Russell Square, Euston Square, Euston, Goodge Street 🚌 8, 10, 19, 24, 188
www.soas.ac.uk

In an elegant Georgian townhouse not far from the British Museum you'll find the finest collection of Chinese ceramics outside China, plus a library of East Asian and Western books relating to Chinese art and culture. Both were presented to the University of London in 1950 by scholar Sir Percival David.

In all there are about 1,700 Chinese ceramics, reflecting court taste and dating mainly from the 10th to the 18th century. Items range from bowls, teapots, cups and vases to incense burners and perfume baskets, spittoons, garden seats, flower- holders, lamp stands and candleholders, animal figurines and figures of Buddhas and deities.

Highlights include a collection of stoneware from the Song (960–1279) and Yuan (1279–1368) dynasties, as well as blue and white, polychrome and monochrome porcelains.

MUSEUM OF LONDON

Trace the city's development from prehistoric times to the 20th century.

Laid out in a striking, modern building near the Barbican (see page 77), the Museum of London uses exhibits, film sequences, voice commentary and interactive tools to bring the city's past to life. The displays are organized over two floors around a central courtyard. You start on the upper floor and descend a series of ramps to explore nine exhibitions, leading through London's history up until 1914.

A £33 million redevelopment, due for completion in 2005, will almost double the available gallery space.

ENTRANCE LEVEL

The London Before London gallery looks at the lives of prehistoric settlers in the area. Finds include a 9,000-year-old antler mattock (an agricultural pickaxe) recovered near the present-day site of the New Scotland Yard police headquarters, and a stone axehead, probably imported 2,500 years ago from continental Europe. Objects found along the banks of the Thames—a vital resource for the prehistoric community—are displayed in the centre.

Most impressive is the Roman London gallery, which explains the founding of *Londinium* in about AD50 and traces its development until AD410, when the Roman army left Britain. Large models show the city's growth, and a huge array of ordinary items shows how people lived and worked. These range from leather shoes to a hoard of gold coins, each one representing a month's pay for a Roman soldier.

Anglo-Saxon settlers and Viking raiders have their place in Dark Age and Saxon London, while Medieval London takes a look at the role of traders' guilds and religious and secular architecture.

LOWER LEVEL

London underwent rapid changes during the late 17th and 18th centuries, from the rebuilding after the Great Fire to a trading and commercial boom and great leaps forward in medicine and technology—all of which are examined here. The World City galleries cover the period from the French Revolution to the outbreak of World War I (1789–1914). Every aspect of city life is covered, including education, travel, the Great Exhibition and entertainment. More than 3,000 exhibits range from Queen Victoria's parliamentary robes to models of narrow winding streets lined with original Victorian shop-fronts and workshops, representing trades from engraving to pawnbroking.

RATINGS

Good for kids	● ● ●
Historic interest	● ● ● ●
Specialist shopping	● ● ●

BASICS

✚ 69 M3 • London Wall EC2Y 5HN

☎ 0870 444 3852 ◉ Mon–Sat 10–5.50, Sun noon–5.50 🌀 Free

◉ Moorgate, Barbican, St. Paul's, Bank

🚌 56, 100 📖 £7.95, in English, German, French, Italian, Japanese, Spanish ☕ Café on lower level

🏛 Small shop with good selection of books on London 🚻

www.museumoflondon.org.uk
Well-organized site with good information on temporary exhibition galleries and future plans.

The Lord Mayor's coach (main picture) displayed on the lower level near the lift and the Roman god Mithras (inset)

National Gallery

Home of the nation's permanent collection of Western European art. A superb and accessible guide to Western paintings from about 1250 to 1900, including work by most of the greatest artists. Established for the benefit of all.

The modern Sainsbury Wing (above left) showcases early Renaissance work. The columns from Carlton House, demolished to make way for the museum, were saved for the central portico (centre and right)

SEEING THE NATIONAL GALLERY

The collection is clearly arranged by period in four wings on the main floor, with other works in the collection shown in the lower floor galleries A to G (lower gallery A is always open on Wednesday afternoons). All the paintings in the collection are on display, except those on loan and those being reframed or repaired, and it would take several long visits to see them all.

The Tate Modern (see pages 134–135) tells the story of art from the 20th century—and a visit there is all the more fascinating after exploring the preceding centuries in the National Gallery.

TIP

● Visit on a Wednesday if your schedule is tight. There's an extra tour at 6.30pm and late opening to 9pm.

HIGHLIGHTS

THE SAINSBURY WING
The Wilton Diptych
The grey stone arches and plain walls of the Sainsbury Wing are a perfect backdrop for the vivid golds and blue lapis lazuli of this medieval painting on two hinged panels, created in about 1395–99. On one panel Richard II is shown dedicating his kingdom to the Virgin Mary and kneeling to receive her blessing, accompanied by John the Baptist, King Edmund and Edward the Confessor. On the other panel we see Mary and the Christ child surrounded by the heavenly host. The work glitters with gold leaf, all finely punched; Christ's halo, for instance, is decorated with a design of thorns, foreshadowing the crown of thorns that he will eventually wear.

Jan van Eyck (c1389–1441), *Arnolfini Portrait*
One of the secular works in the Sainsbury Wing's collection is the famous *Arnolfini Portrait* by Van Eyck, sometimes misleadingly called *The Arnolfini Wedding*. His depiction of an affluent Italian merchant and his wife in the Netherlands was painted in the mid-15th century and shows the couple surrounded by the ordinary furnishings of a domestic life: the bed, a few oranges on a side-table, discarded wooden sandals and a little dog. Every texture, including the velvets, silks and furs of their clothes is immaculately conveyed, and a round mirror at the back of the room repeats it all in tiny, convex reflection, above which the artist has declared 'Jan van Eyck was here, 1434'.

Jan van Eyck's Arnolfini Portrait. *His wife is not pregnant, as is sometimes thought, but holding up her voluminous dress in the fashion of the time*

The refurbished Victorian North Wing (opposite)

68 J5 • Trafalgar Square WC2N 5DN

☎ 020 7747 2885

🕐 Daily 10–6, Wed till 9pm. Temporary exhibitions may have extended opening hours

💷 Free; donations box provided

🚌 19, 24, 6, 9, 11, 13

🚇 Charing Cross, Leicester Square

📖 Several guides from £1 to £9.95, some in several languages

🎧 Free guided tours daily 11.30am and 2.30pm; extra tour Wed 6.30pm. Tours leave from the Sainsbury Wing Information Desk.
Free family talks Sat 11.30am and 2.30pm. Check meeting place on arrival. Audio-guides with themed tours, each looking at about 20 paintings. Portable CD-ROM audio-guide with information on over 1,000 paintings (a label next to a picture displays a number that calls up the appropriate commentary). *Highlights* tour in six languages: English, French, German, Spanish, Italian, Japanese. Security or deposit requested. Payment by voluntary contribution

🍴 Crivelli's Garden restaurant and Italian bar (named after Paula Rego's mural) on the Sainsbury Wing's first floor, with spectacular views over Trafalgar Square and Nelson's Column. Open daily 10–5, last orders 7.45pm Wed. Reservations: 020 7747 2869

☕ Self-service café on ground floor of main building. Open daily 10–5.45, until 8.45pm Wed

🏪 Main shop selling National Gallery publications, art books, gifts, cards, CDs. Room 3 shop selling gifts, posters, cards. Orange Street shop in the National Gallery Education Centre, designed for children and teachers. Exhibition shop, in the Sainsbury Wing basement, supports temporary exhibitions

♿

www.nationalgallery.org.uk
Excellent site with full coverage of collection and easily accessible information, including news on current exhibitions and talks.

Sandro Botticelli (*c*1445–1510), *Venus and Mars*
Created in Florence in 1485, Botticelli's beautifully composed image of the gods of love and war shows them lying on the grass, Mars exhausted by love and Venus ready for more. Between them three child-satyrs, one wearing Mars' helmet, try in vain to wake Venus' lover. The crisp colours and Venus' contemporary dress give this scene from classical mythology an irresistible freshness, and the gentle humour of the theme suggests that it might have been painted as a gift for a newly married couple. The wasps (*vespe* in Italian) may be a pun on Vespucci, the name of a family who sometimes commissioned Botticelli, or it may be a reference to the stings of love.

Venus and Mars by Botticelli, possibly intended as a bedhead or to decorate a chest or bench

THE WEST WING
Hans Holbein (1497–1543), *The Ambassadors*
Painted in 1533, this enormous panel shows full-length portraits of two Frenchmen, Jean de Dinteville, ambassador to England, and Georges de Selve, bishop of Lavaur. The two men lean on each side of a table cluttered with objects, each one symbolizing their life and interests—a globe, a compass, a musical score, a book. There's a more profound theme, however, than worldly interests. The transience of life and its occupations is represented by a lute with a broken string and, strangest of all, a distorted shape between the men's feet, which turns out to be a skull. In the top left corner, a barely visible crucifix symbolizes the eternal life beyond death.

THE NORTH WING
Pieter de Hooch (1629–84), *The Courtyard of a House in Delft*
This domestic scene dating from 1658 is a masterpiece of composition and light, showing a woman and child in the brick courtyard, a passage along the side of a burgher's house and another woman looking out towards the canal and the neighbour's house. The contrasts of light and colour in the red and yellow brick, the tiled passage floor and the daylight beyond are a perfect illustration of a Dutch master at his best. A stone plaque is set over the arched entrance to the passage; its inscription, which starts 'This is in St. Jerome's vale', is a clue to the real tablet, which originally hung over the entrance to the Hieronymusdale cloister in Delft, Holland.

THE EAST WING
Joseph Wright of Derby (1734–97), *An Experiment on a Bird in the Air Pump*
Joseph Wright was a painter of the new industrial age, using dramatic lighting techniques inspired by artists such as Caravaggio to show blacksmiths at work, cotton mills and furnaces and, as in this work, scientists. The gruesome experiment taking place by the candlelight involves placing a bird in a vacuum; everyone in the small group gathered to watch reacts in a different way—including a couple (representing Mary Barlow and Thomas Coltman, friends of Wright) who are interested only in each other.

Joseph Turner (1775–1851), *The Fighting Temeraire*
In his depiction of the old warship (which saw action at the Battle of

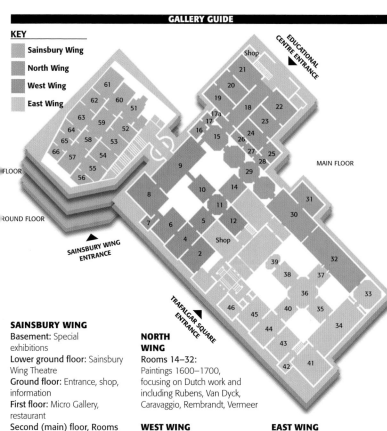

KEY

■ Sainsbury Wing

■ North Wing

■ West Wing

■ East Wing

EDUCATIONAL CENTRE ENTRANCE

Shop

MAIN FLOOR

FLOOR

ROUND FLOOR

SAINSBURY WING ENTRANCE

TRAFALGAR SQUARE ENTRANCE

Shop

SAINSBURY WING
Basement: Special exhibitions
Lower ground floor: Sainsbury Wing Theatre
Ground floor: Entrance, shop, information
First floor: Micro Gallery, restaurant
Second (main) floor, Rooms 51–66: Early Renaissance work, 1250–1500, including Van Eyck, Masaccio, Duccio, Piero della Francesca, Botticelli, Leonardo da Vinci, Raphael

NORTH WING
Rooms 14–32:
Paintings 1600–1700, focusing on Dutch work and including Rubens, Van Dyck, Caravaggio, Rembrandt, Vermeer

WEST WING
Rooms 2, 4–12: Paintings 1500–1600, including Titian, Cranach, Michelangelo, Bronzino

EAST WING
Rooms 33–46: Paintings 1700–1900, including the Impressionists, Gainsborough, Constable and Van Gogh

THE SIGHTS

The Central Hall was designed in the 1880s by Sir John Taylor, a distinguished architect of royal palaces

Trafalgar in 1805) being towed to a ship-breaking yard in 1838, Turner makes the most of his innovative treatment of light and colour, which foreshadowed the new optical techniques of the Impressionists. Pale and spectral, the old ship—redundant in the age of steam—sails to its end against a blazing sunset, reflected in the shimmering surface of the water.

Vincent Van Gogh's Sunflowers, *1888 (right), was one of many pictures of the same subject painted to decorate his yellow house in Provence*

The main entrance hall off Trafalgar Square, where a model of the National Gallery is used as a collecting box for donations to the gallery

Vincent Van Gogh (1853–90), Room 45

A fine collection of paintings by Vincent Van Gogh includes such works as *Sunflowers* (1888), in rich shades of gold and yellow, and *Chair* (1888), a still life that illustrated his belief in the direct relationship of art to nature and daily life. *A Wheatfield, with Cypresses,* painted in 1889, when Van Gogh was in the St.-Rémy mental asylum, conveys the movement of clouds and wind with bold, swirling brush strokes. Seen together, Van Gogh's paintings are a perfect illustration of the bright colours and apparently spontaneous strokes that revolutionized art in the late 19th century.

BACKGROUND

In April 1824 the House of Commons paid £57,000 for 38 pictures from the collection of banker John Julius Angerstein; seven years later Parliament agreed to construct a building to house them at Trafalgar Square. The spot, at the crossroads of the city, could be easily reached by the rich in the west and the poor in the east. William Wilkins' neoclassical design attracted much criticism, but plans to replace it altogether were shelved. A new wing built in 1876 added seven new exhibition rooms at the east end, including the impressive dome.

In 1907 barracks behind the Gallery were cleared and work began on five new galleries. Between 1928 and 1933 the National Gallery commissioned Boris Anrep to lay three mosaics in the Vestibule of the Main Hall to illustrate the Labours of Life and the Pleasures of Life; another, laid in 1952, depicts Modern Virtues. The Northern Extension opened in 1975, and the Sainsbury Wing, funded by Lord Sainsbury, was opened in 1991.

The Beach at Trouville (opposite) was painted by Monet in the summer of 1870. The grains of sand visible in the thick oil paint suggest that the work, at least in part, was executed on the beach

Joseph Turner's The Fighting Temeraire *(1838). It is believed that the painting may have meant to symbolize Britain's declining naval power*

ART THROUGH THE AGES

The gallery's chronological display reveals how artists' methods and materials developed over the centuries. Most of the earliest works—in the Sainsbury Wing—are painted on wood, using either tempera (pigments in egg yolk) or slow-drying oils applied to a chalk or gesso background. Some also use gold leaf, which was beaten from coins into wafer-thin sheets. By 1510, when the West Wing's collection starts, oils were the main medium, painted onto sail-cloth, or canvas, which could be rolled up and shipped off to international patrons. In the 17th century, subjects tended to be secular and domestic, and painters such as Caravaggio perfected techniques of realistic light and shadow. New synthetic paints had a huge influence on art after 1800, and the fact that they were stored in flexible metal tubes and sold via merchants (rather than made up by the artists themselves) made it possible to leave the workshop and work alone, virtually anywhere that inspiration struck.

National Portrait Gallery

**The most comprehensive portrait collection in the world.
A role call of politicians, royals, writers, artists, scientists and other public
figures ranging from the Tudor age to the present day.**

*Thomas Macaulay (1800–59),
on the façade of the building*

RATINGS

Good for kids	◕
Historic interest	◕ ◕ ◕ ◕
Specialist shopping	◕ ◕ ◕

BASICS

✚ 68 J5 • St. Martin's Place WC2H OHE ☎ 020 7306 0055 ◷ Sat–Wed 10–5.50, Thu–Fri 10–8.50 💷 Free. Charge for some special exhibitions Ⓞ Leicester Square, Charing Cross ⊟ 24, 29, 176 ⬛ National Portrait Gallery Sound Guides 📖 *Visitor's Guide* £5, *Illustrated Guide* £17.50, *Architectural History* £40, in English only ⬛ The Portrait Café in the basement 🍴 The Portrait Restaurant on the top floor (see page 262): tea from 3pm 🎟 Art-themed books, posters, cards, jewellery, frames, stationery, book shop (basement), selling titles on British history, art, portraiture, photography, costume, literature and biography. Exhibition shop outside Wolfson Gallery 🏛

www.npg.org.uk
Full virtual tour of the collection, though some images have not yet been transferred on to the web.

TIP

● Rent the CD guide in the ground floor entrance hall to hear contemporary sitters talking about their portraits.

SEEING THE NATIONAL PORTRAIT GALLERY

The gallery entrance is a surprisingly modest doorway tucked away at the back of the National Gallery (see pages 104–109). Exhibits are arranged chronologically, but a little confusingly, over three floors, with the selection beginning on the second floor and ending on the ground floor.

To reach the start of the collection, take the escalator up from the main hall to the Tudor Galleries, the Stuart Rooms and work from the 18th century, which follows themes such as the Kit-cat Club, the arts, and science and industry. The Victorians, their art and their achievements occupy most of the first-floor rooms, including daguerreotypes (early photographs). Rooms 30–33 cover the period from World War I to 1990 and include a collection of portraits of the royal family. The Balcony Gallery, also on the first floor, covers 1960–90 with photographs, busts and figurines, and back on the ground floor Britain since 1990 is represented in a constantly changing exhibition of contemporary portraits, with new acquisitions also displayed here.

HIGHLIGHTS

SECOND FLOOR
The Tudor Galleries
A magnificent series of royal, aristocratic and family portraits makes this whole, compact section of the gallery a must-see. Among the most stunning works is the dazzling Ditchley Portrait of Elizabeth I by Marcus Gheeraerts the Younger (1592), a tour de force of political propaganda. Gheeraerts shows the Queen triumphantly standing on a map of Britain with storm clouds behind her to the right, intended to represent the defeated Spanish Armada, and bright skies to the left, signalling a glorious future under the Virgin Queen's reign. Look out too for the huge ink-and-watercolour cartoon of Henry VIII by Hans Holbein—a preparatory work for the mural showing Henry, his parents and his third wife, Jane Seymour, which hung in Whitehall Palace until its destruction by fire in 1698; Rowland Lockey's group portrait of Sir Thomas More and his household and five generations of descendants; the full-length portrait of Catherine Parr by Master John; and a fiery-cheeked Sir Francis Drake, by an unknown artist.

George Villiers, Duke of Buckingham (Stuart Rooms)
William Larkin's sumptuous full-length portrait of James I's handsome favourite was painted in 1616, when its subject was 24 years old. Villiers is almost upstaged by the lush red velvet of his cape and the bronze folds of silk drapery above him. These curtains were, in fact, green until 1985, when experts found traces of the original paint and removed the top layer to reveal the artist's rich shades, now displayed as he had intended.

FIRST FLOOR
The Brontë Sisters (Victorian Rooms)
Branwell Brontë (1817–48) painted this portrait of his sisters Anne

GALLERY GUIDE

GROUND FLOOR
Rooms 34–41: Britain since 1990; new acquisitions

FIRST FLOOR
Rooms 21–29: The Victorians. Introduction: Queen Victoria, Statesmen's Gallery, Expansion and Empire, Early Victorian Arts, Portraits and Politics, Portraits by G. F. Watts, Science and Technology, Late Victorian Arts, Turn of the Century

The Tudor portraits (background picture) are displayed in spacious and environmentally controlled galleries. Actress Ellen Terry (above) was briefly married to G. F. Watts, who painted this portrait

(1820–49), Emily (1818–48) and Charlotte (1816–55) in about 1834. Growing up in a remote North Yorkshire parsonage, the siblings shared a vivid imaginary world, and the three young women went on to produce passionate and dark works including *The Tenant of Wildfell Hall* (Anne), *Wuthering Heights* (Emily) and *Jane Eyre* (Charlotte). Branwell failed in his attempts to make his name as a writer and as an artist, and succumbed to drink and opium. A poignant outline, clearly seen between Emily and Charlotte, shows where he has painted out the self-portrait that originally completed the group. Technically the painting may not be impressive but the image of three remarkable 19th-century novelists is fascinating.

Zandra Rhodes (Balcony Gallery)
Andrew Logan's sculpture of the larger-than-life fashion designer is one of several late 20th- and early 21st-century pieces in the National Portrait Gallery using unconventional materials and forms to bring out the personalities of their subjects. Logan has opted for resin and bright, theatrical colours to express Rhodes' extrovert character and flamboyant style. It makes a striking contrast to the gallery's earlier sculptures, mainly in marble or bronze, as well as to contemporary works such as the cool ceramic figure of Coco Chanel.

BACKGROUND

The gallery was founded in 1856 by the 5th Earl Stanhope, historian, politician and trustee of the British Museum, to collect the likenesses of famous British men and women. After 40 years of being moved around London to a succession of unsuitable homes it was finally given a permanent new gallery on St. Martin's Place. After several appeals for permission to increase the gallery space it was agreed in 1928 that a new wing could be built along Orange Street, and in the 1990s there was further expansion into the old Royal Dental School (now home to the Heinz Archive and the reference library).

In 2000 the Queen opened the Ondaatje Wing, named after benefactor Christopher Ondaatje.

Rooms 30–31: Early 20th Century. World War I, The Armistice to the New Elizabethans
Room 32 (Balcony Gallery): Late 20th Century. Britain 1960–90

FIRST-FLOOR LANDING
Room 33: The Royal Family

Rooms 1–3: Tudor Galleries. The Early Tudors, The Elizabethan Age, Miniatures Gallery
Rooms 4–8: 17th Century. The Jacobean Court, Charles I and the Civil War, Science and the Arts in the 17th century, Charles II: the Restoration of the Monarchy, The Later Stuarts
Rooms 9–14: 18th Century. The Kit-cat Club, The Arts in the Early 18th Century, Britain in the Early 18th Century, The Arts in the Later 18th Century, Science and Industry in the 18th Century, Britain becomes a World Power, Landing, William Hazlitt's Spirit of the Age
Rooms 17–20: The Regency Weldon Galleries. Royal Celebrity and Scandal; Art, Invention and Thought: The Romantics; Art, Invention and Thought: Making the Modern World; The Road to Reform

Natural History Museum

**Home to the country's biggest collection of dinosaur remains.
More than 67 million items, ranging from whales to insects to meteorites.
One of the worlds' leading scientific research centres.**

The museum's twin-towered main entrance

RATINGS

Good for kids	● ● ● ● ●
Historic interest	● ● ● ●
Specialist shopping	● ●

BASICS

✚ 66 E7 • Cromwell Road SW7 5BD
☎ 020 7942 5000 🕐 Mon–Sat
10–5.50, Sun 11–5.50. Wildlife Garden
daily 12–5, May–Sep 🎫 Free. Special
exhibitions around £5, child (5–16)
🚇 South Kensington 🚌 14, 49, 70, 74,
C1 🎟 Regular Highlight tours: adult £3,
child (5–16) £1.50 🎧 £3.50, in English
only. Free floorplans and map
🍽 Waterhouse Café 🍴 Life Galleries
Restaurant: self-service meals and
snacks 📖 Bookshop and two gift shops
🚻

www.nhm.ac.uk
Features topical natural history links,
museum news and online booking facility, as well as thorough exploration of
the collection.

TIP

● If the queues at the main
entrance are very long, make
for the side entrance on
Exhibition Road.

SEEING THE NATURAL HISTORY MUSEUM

The main entrance, approached via a grand flight of stone
steps from Cromwell Road, leads straight into the huge and
richly decorated Central Hall, which has been likened to the
nave of a cathedral. This also forms Gallery 10 of the Life
Galleries, which has exhibitions on dinosaurs, mammals,
creepy crawlies (including a robotic scorpion), fish and other
marine life, plants and minerals, meteorites and the story of
evolution. The Life Galleries continue onto the first floor; rooms
are numbered but don't always follow a clear sequence.

The museum's side entrance leads into the Earth Galleries,
opened in 1996 and housed in rooms on the ground, mezza-
nine, first and second floors, linked by a central escalator which
travels through a huge globe. State-of-the-art displays tell the
story of the Earth's formation, with sections on volcanoes and
earthquakes, hands-on stations demonstrating the forces of
wind, water and heat, and galleries focusing on the Earth's
natural geological treasury of gemstones and discussing ways of
protecting our world for the future.

Outside the museum, the Wildlife Garden, planted in 1993 on
the west lawn, provides both peace and quiet and the chance to
study some of Britain's habitats, from oak woodland to reedbeds,
and their associated plants and animals.

HIGHLIGHTS

LIFE GALLERIES

Dinosaurs (Room 21)
This is one of the most popular galleries, with a high-level walkway
bringing you eye to eye with some of the ancient monsters. The lighting is low and atmospheric, and there is an animatronic re-creation of
the creatures in action, including one of the world's most advanced
models of its kind, a terrifying 4m-high (13ft) *Tyrannosaurus rex*, now
the subject of debate as to whether it was a hunter or a scavenger.
Soaring staircases provide a views of the hall's detailed decoration
(note the monkeys scrambling up and down the arches) and look
down on the plaster-cast skeleton of *Diplodocus carnegii* (which
comes from Wyoming), 150 million years old, 26m (86ft) long, and
one of the largest animals ever to have roamed the earth.

The Blue Whale (Room 24)
Suspended from the ceiling in the Mammals section is another giant—
a life-size model of a blue whale almost 28m (93ft) in length and
dwarfing the African elephant, the largest land mammal.

Ant Colony (Room 33)
The museum has its very own labour force of leafcutter ants, and
you can watch as members of the thousands-strong colony grow and
tend the fungus that provides its food, cut up the leaves collected
from their feeding area and are guarded as they work by the soldier
ants with vicious-looking jaws. The colony can also be watched online via AntCast, which uses an infra-red camera to provide video and
static pictures.

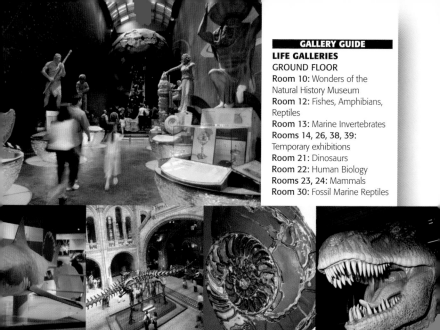

The Visions of Earth gallery (top). Exhibits from the plant, animal and mineral kingdoms are displayed in the Life Galleries (above)

Giant Sequoia (Room 201)

One of the most intriguing exhibits is a passage cut through this enormous tree (*Sequoiadendron giganteum*) displayed on the stairs to the first floor. This particular specimen was cut down in 1892, by which time it was 84m (276ft) tall and measured 15m (49ft) around the girth. A tree ring count indicates that it was 1,335 years old when felled, having started its life in California in AD557.

EARTH GALLERIES

The Power Within/Earthquake (Room 61)

This unnerving series of displays has become one of the museum's top attractions. The exhibition explores the powerful forces of heat and pressure that are constantly on the move between the ground that we inhabit and the centre of the Earth. A simulator gives you some idea of how it feels to be in an earthquake; film footage of the Kobe earthquake in Japan in 1995 shows the terrors of the real thing, as a supermarket is shaken to its foundations. Volcano eruptions are re-created, and you can keep an update of the most recent earthquake occurrences around the world.

BACKGROUND

Built on land purchased by Prince Albert from money raised at the Great Exhibition of 1851 (see page 36), the huge French Romanesque Natural History Museum was designed by Alfred Waterhouse (1830–1905) to house the British Museum's natural history collection, and opened to the public in 1881. Relief panels in terracotta showing animals, fossils, plants and insects run the whole length of the façade; living species of the time are shown to the left of the entrance, extinct ones to the right.

Thousands of animal, plant and mineral specimens were bequeathed by Sir Hans Sloane (see page 85), including more than 10,000 animal specimens and 338 volumes of pressed plants. Sir Joseph Banks, who accompanied Captain Cook on his first voyage around the world in the 1760s, was another important benefactor. Today the museum owns more than 65 million specimens and more than a million books and manuscripts.

A new home is planned for the Petrie Museum's collection

Neon billboards first appeared around Piccadilly Circus in 1910

Pollock designed his theatres so they could be made by children

THE SIGHTS

PETRIE MUSEUM

✚ 67 J3 • University College London, Malet Place WC1E 6BT ☎ 020 7679 2884 🕒 Tue–Fri 1–5, Sat 10–1 🎟 Free. Donations welcome 🚇 Euston, Euston Square, Warren Street, Russell Square 🚌 18, 24, 29, 73, 176 www.petrie.ucl.ac.uk

This collection, kept in the University of London's Institute of Archaeology building, consists of about 80,000 Egyptian and Sudanese items. It was started by Victorian enthusiast Amelia Edwards and expanded by Professor William Flinders Petrie (1853–1942), who excavated dozens of major sites. Treasures include finds from the Roman cemeteries at Hawara, famous for its beautiful mummy portraits, Amarna, the city of king Akhenaten, and the first true pyramid, at Meydum.

PHOTOGRAPHERS' GALLERY

✚ 68 J4 • 5 and 8 Great Newport Street WC2H 7HY ☎ 020 7831 1772 🕒 Galleries: Mon–Sat 11–6, Sun noon–6. Print Sales Gallery: Tue–Sat 11–6 🎟 Free 🚇 Leicester Square 🚌 24, 29, 176 www.photonet.org.uk

Britain's first independent photographic gallery, founded in 1971, is now a leading venue for contemporary shows with a full schedule of exhibitions and educational events. Temporary exhibitions aim to throw new light on the history of photography. (Sir Joshua Reynolds lived here in the 18th century.) Two buildings refurbished in 1993 accommodate the three galleries, a bookshop and a café, off Charing Cross Road.

PICCADILLY CIRCUS

✚ 67 J5 🕒 Open access 🎟 Free 🚇 Piccadilly Circus 🚌 9, 12, 15, 19, 139 🚻 ♿

Tourist Information Office
Britain Visitor Centre, 1 Lower Regent Street, Piccadilly Circus SW1Y 4XT (no telephone)

One of the world's busiest traffic circles, formed by the junction of five streets in the West End, the Circus has become a byword for urban clamour and crowds. It was creatd by John Nash as part of scheme to link St. James's with Regent's Park. Neon advertisements flash above the constant flow—or crawl—of traffic and the tourists, workers and shoppers who throng the area at all hours.

Its focal point is the aluminium statue known as Eros, above a bronze fountain erected in 1892 as a memorial to the philanthropic 7th Earl of Shaftesbury. Sir Alfred Gilbert, the designer, intended it as an angel of Christian charity rather than the Greek god of love, and was so dismayed by changes to his design that he refused to attend the unveiling.

Piccadilly is believed to take its name from a 16th-century frilly collar called a pikadil. A dressmaker who made his fortune selling these fashion items built his house nearby.

The Duke of Westminster unveiled the controversial statue of Eros in 1893. It was London's first aluminium statue

POLLOCK'S TOY MUSEUM

✚ 67 H3 • 1 Scala Street W1T 2HL; entrance on 41 Whitfield Street ☎ 020 7636 3452 🕒 Mon–Sat 10–5 🎟 Adult £3, child (3–18) £1.50, under 3s free 🚇 Goodge Street 🚌 10, 24, 29, 73 ♿ www.tao2000.net/pollocks

An eclectic assortment of toys, puppets, dolls, bears, games, scraps, cards and all manner of curiosities is crammed into three floors of a pair of small 18th- and 19th-century townhouses. A toy shop sells games, toys, dolls and the toy theatres made from sheets of card for which Pollock's is renowned.

Other exhibits include board games, optical, mechanical and constructional toys, English tin toys and puppets, wax and composition dolls, teddy bears, lead miniatures, dolls' houses, folk toys from Europe, India, Africa, China and Japan and tableaux, including a 1900 girl's nursery and a 19th-century toy theatre workshop.

QUEEN'S GALLERY

✚ 67 H6 • Buckingham Palace Road SW1A 1AA ☎ 020 7766 730 (booking line) 🕒 Daily 10–5.30 (timed ticketing) 🎟 Adult £6.50, child (5–17) £5, family £16 🚇 Victoria, Green Park, Hyde Park Corner 🚌 11, 139, 211, C1, www.royal.gov.uk

In the course of 500 years or so British royalty has amassed a huge collection of fabulous art and treasures. Items from that collection, held in trust for the nation by the Queen, are on show at this gallery in Buckingham Palace (see page 79). The changing selection includes paintings by Canaletto, Frans Hals and Leonardo de Vinci; French, English and Asian porcelain, including Sèvres china; a dazzling

Regent's Park has become one of the city's principal recreation areas, with formal gardens, a boating lake and playgrounds

The Royal Academy summer festival draws huge crowds

THE SIGHTS

array of snuff boxes; exquisite Fabergé eggs and flowers; furniture; and personal pieces selected from the collection of Queen Elizabeth, the Queen Mother (1900–2002).

The gallery itself was built in the 1960s from the ruins of the private chapel on the west front of Buckingham Palace, damaged by bombs during World War II. After massive redevelopment, it was reopened by the Queen in her golden jubilee year, 2002.

REGENT'S PARK

⊞ 67 G2 ◐ Open access 🎫 Free 🚇 Baker Street, Marylebone, Regent's Park, Great Portland Street, Camden Town 🚌 27, 82, 113, 274, C2 **www.royalparks.gov.uk**
Tourist Information Office
Storeyard (Inner Circle), Regent's Park NW1 4NR ☎ 020 7486 7905

Originally part of Henry VIII's royal hunting grounds, Regent's Park came into its own during the reign of the Prince Regent, later George IV, who gave the park its name. The original, grandiose plans, devised by John Nash, were to include a palace to the south in St. James's and a triumphal route up to the pleasure gardens. The park itself was to be girded by grand, stuccoed houses. Money ran out before the plans could be fully realized, but the park, some of the terracing and the first part of the triumphal route—Regent's Street—were completed before work came to a halt.

The York Gate entrance, near the Baker Street Underground station, lies just beyond Madame Tussaud's and the Planetarium (see page 101). As you walk up to the park you'll notice, on the right, the Royal Academy of Music, founded in 1822, where some of the world's finest musicians, singers and composers have trained.

On York Bridge, look back to see St. Mary's Church, on Marylebone High Street. When Nash laid out Regent's Park he deliberately aligned the York Gate axis to take in a view of the church, with its majestic Corinthian portico and circular tower. York Bridge continues past Regent's College, on the left, now a centre for European studies. Beyond lies Queen Mary's Garden. Here, Nash had intended a temple dedicated to the memory of all who had contributed to British history and culture. Instead, the 6.8ha (17-acre) circle contains London's finest rose garden, planted to honour George V's wife, Queen Mary, and the Open-Air Theatre (see page 200), founded in 1932.

To the west is the Y-shaped boating lake, and a walk around the upper part of the lake brings you to Hanover Gate, where the park's newer buildings are found. The London Central Mosque (see page 98) is to the north, and to the south, fronting the Outer Circle, are Quinlan Terry's neo-Nash villas of 1992.

ROYAL ACADEMY OF ARTS

⊞ 67 H5 • Burlington House, Piccadilly W1J 0BD ☎ 020 7300 5760 (recorded information) ◐ Sat–Thu 10–6, Fri 10–10 🎫 Prices vary according to exhibitions; currently adult £5–£7, child (12–18) £3, (9–11) £2, under 9s free. Tours free 🚇 Green Park, Piccadilly Circus 🚌 9, 14, 19, 22, 38 🚻 🛍 ♿ **www.**royalacademy.org.uk
Limited number of exhibition tickets available online

Burlington House, on Piccadilly, was built as a Palladian palazzo (mansion) for the Earl of Burlington around 1720. Since 1768 it has been the home of the Royal Academy of Arts, the country's first formal art school. English portrait-painter Sir

Joshua Reynolds (1723–92) was the first president and painters John Constable (1776–1837) and Joseph Turner (1775–1851) were among the first students.

Major international exhibitions on loan from collections around the world fill two suites of galleries and draw huge crowds. The top floor of the building (the Sackler Wing, reached by glass lift or steps) was remodelled by Norman Foster, himself an Academician, in 1991, and is used for smaller exhibitions, including shows by living artists.

The Royal Academy Summer Exhibition (*Jun–mid-Aug*) is a hugely popular show of work by amateurs and professionals (see page 21), any of whom can submit pieces for consideration. **Don't miss** Michelangelo's marble tondo (circular relief) of the Madonna and Child with the infant St. John (outside the Sackler Wing), carved between 1504 and 1505.

ROYAL COURTS OF JUSTICE (LAW COURTS)

⊞ 68 K4 • Strand WC2 2LL ☎ 020 7947 6000 ◐ Mon–Fri 9.30–4.30. Cases start around 10am and break for lunch at 1pm 🎫 Free 🚇 Chancery Lane, Temple 🚌 4, 11, 15, 76

Crowds, cameramen and reporters eager for a verdict often congregate outside the Royal Courts of Justice, at the end of the Strand. The country's most important and high-profile civil cases are tried in this elaborate neo-Gothic building, designed by George Edmund Street in the 1870s. A concoction of spires and pinnacles, it houses 50-odd courtrooms. Public galleries are open to anyone, but security is very tight and to enter you'll have to undergo stringent checks.

On reaching the Main Hall ask

Elaborate detailing on the Royal Courts of Justice

A Chelsea Pensioner in full dress uniform, worn at ceremonies

Gates to the Royal Mews, which were built in 1824

for a plan and guide to the complex at the information desk. Cases being heard that day are posted here. An exhibition in the minstrels' gallery traces the history of lawcourt dress.

ROYAL HOSPITAL

✚ 67 F7 • Royal Hospital Road SW3 4SL ☎ 020 7730 0161 ⊙ Mon–Sat 10–noon, 2–4, Sun 2–4 🎫 Free 🚇 Sloane Square 🚌 11, 137, 211, 239

At the behest of Charles II, Chelsea's Royal Hospital was built by Sir Christopher Wren in the late 17th century as almshouses for veteran soldiers. It still serves that purpose today, and the Chelsea Pensioners, as the residents are known, are a familiar sight in the area. Their dress uniform is the scarlet tunic of the Duke of Marlborough, worn with blue trousers and a tricorn hat; at other times you may see them in blue tunics. To catch them in their ceremonial garb, come here on Oak Apple Day (29 May), when they commemorate the Battle of Worcester—from which Charles II escaped by hiding in an oak tree in 1651—by festooning his statue in the central courtyard with oak leaves.

In the small museum you can see the pensioners' uniforms and medals, the barrel-vaulted chapel and the panelled Great Hall. Outside, you can wander in the south grounds, site of the annual Chelsea Flower Show (see page 222) since 1913, and Ranelagh Gardens, to the east of the main complex.

ROYAL MEWS

✚ 67 H6 • Buckingham Palace Road SW1A 1AA ☎ 020 7321 2233 ⊙ Daily 11–4, Apr–Oct 🎫 Adult £5, child (5–17) £2.50, under 5s free, family £12.50 🚇 Victoria, Green Park 🚌 11, 139, 211, C1, C10 www.royal.gov.uk

Run as a working stables, the Royal Mews gives a fascinating glimpse of daily life in one of Buckingham Palace's royal household departments. The royal family's state vehicles are on permanent display, including the fairytale gold state carriage, commissioned by George III in 1762. Gilded in 22-carat leaf and weighing in at 4 tonnes/tons, this ornate colossus needs eight horses to draw it and is apparently a most uncomfortable ride.

You can also usually see the 30 or so carriage horses stabled here for much of the year. Most are Cleveland Bays, the only British breed of carriage horse, and Windsor greys, which, by tradition, draw the Queen's carriage.

SAATCHI GALLERY

✚ 68 K6 • County Hall, Southbank SE1 7PB ☎ 020 7823 2363 ⊙ Sun–Thu 10–6, Fri–Sat 10–10 🎫 Adult £8.50 🚇 Waterloo 🚌 12, 53, 159, 211 www.saatchi-gallery.co.uk

The focus of Charles Saatchi's art gallery, opened in April 2003, is contemporary art by unseen young artists and work by artists of international repute that has either not been exhibited, or exhibited very little, in the UK. Oak panelling in most of the rooms recalls the building's former use as governmental offices.

ST. CLEMENT DANES

✚ 68 K4 • Strand WC2R 1DH ☎ 020 7242 8282 ⊙ Mon–Fri 9–4, Sat–Sun 9–3; Sun service 11am 🎫 Free 🚇 Temple (closed Sun), Charing Cross, Blackfriars 🚌 4, 11, 15, 76

This small and elegant building surrounded by traffic in the middle of the Strand is the latest in a succession of churches on the site. The 11th-century church was first rebuilt by William the Conqueror, then again in the 14th century, demolished and rebuilt by Wren in 1680–82 and virtually destroyed by bombs in 1941, leaving only the steeple (1719) and walls. The interior was rebuilt and dedicated to the Royal Air Force in 1958, and daily prayers and memorial services are held here for its members. **Don't miss** the black Welsh slate badges of units of the RAF set into the church floor.

ST. JAMES'S PARK

✚ 67 J6 ⊙ Open access 🎫 Free 🚇 St. James's Park, Green Park 🚌 11, 12, 53, 88, 211 www.royalparks.gov.uk
Tourist Information Office
Park Office, The Store Yard, Horse Guards Approach, St. James's Park SW1A 2BJ ☎ 020 7930 1793

St. James's Park is the most attractive of all London's green spaces. From the footbridge that crosses the lake at its heart there are uninterrupted views westwards to the façade of Buckingham Palace, while to the east is the rear of Sir George Gilbert Scott's classical government offices, and the turrets and onion domes of the National Liberal Club.

Three palaces surround the park: The oldest, Westminster, is now the Houses of Parliament (see page 92); St. James's Palace, across The Mall, remains the official court, and since 1837 the monarch has lived at the third, Buckingham Palace (see page 79), at the southern end. Clarence House, on the park's northwestern edge, was the home of Queen Elizabeth, the Queen Mother, and is now the home of Prince Charles; Admiralty Arch, at the northern tip of the park, marks the other end of The Mall.

But St. James's isn't just a map of institutional landmarks; it's also a place of daily relaxation. The central feature is the lake,

THE SIGHTS

Choir stalls in St. Clement Danes, church of the RAF

In summer, brass bands play free concerts in St. James's Park

St. Martin-in-the-Fields, modelled on a classical temple

created by John Nash from the canal originally excavated from the marshy land for Charles II. Charles was responsible for introducing the geese, pelicans and waterfowl whose descendants still live here. Duck Island is their sanctuary, maintained as a wildlife reserve; for information on guided tours of the island contact the park office.

On the west side of the island are the park's resident pelicans, a gift to Charles II from a Russian ambassador. It's since become something of a tradition for ambassadors to offer a pelican to the park.

The Cake House has a restaurant with a landscaped roof with a seating area and a timbered promenade.

Don't miss watching the resident pelicans being fed every day at 3pm near Duck Island Cottage.

ST. JOHN'S GATE

🔢 68 L3 • St. John's Lane EC1M 4DA ☎ 020 7324 4070 🕐 Mon–Fri 10–5, Sat 10–4; tours Tue, Fri, Sat 11am, 2.30pm 🎟 Free. Donations requested for tours: adult £5 (St. John Ambulance members free) 🚇 Farringdon 🚌 63, 143, 221 🏛
www.sja.org.uk

Clerkenwell's medieval priory of St. John was the base of the Knights Hospitallers, who sent men, money and supplies to hospitals on the great pilgrim routes in Europe. Today all that remain of the buildings are the crypt of the Norman church and the Tudor gatehouse, part of which houses a museum of the history of the Order of St. John, with exhibits such as Crusader coins and Turkish Ottoman mail armour.

Victorian pioneers began the St. John Ambulance voluntary first-aid movement here. Its service continues today, and an interactive gallery relates its history.

ST. MARTIN-IN-THE-FIELDS

🔢 68 J5 • Trafalgar Square WC2N 4JJ ☎ 020 7766 1100 🕐 Mon–Sat 8–6.30, Sun 8–7.30; brass-rubbing Mon–Sat 10–6, Sun 12–6 🎟 Free; brass-rubbing from £2.90, child (under 12) £1 off fee 🚇 Charing Cross, Leicester Square 🚌 6, 9, 11, 13, 15, 24, 2 🍴 🏛
www.stmartin-in-the-fields.org

Steps lead up to the magnificent Corinthian portico of the church of St. Martin-in-the-Fields, at the northeastern corner of Trafalgar Square. Scottish architect James Gibbs (1682–1754) designed it in the 1720s, and the lavish interior is decorated with ornate Italian plasterwork on the barrel-vaulted ceilings. Officially the parish church of Buckingham Palace, St. Martin's has strong royal connections—George I was a warden here, and there's a royal box to the left of the high altar. It's also well known for its work with the homeless, which began shortly after World War I as a way to help ex-soldiers of the parish, and continues today with soup kitchens for the West End's homeless.

Classical concerts are held regularly (see page 195). At the Costermongers' Harvest Festival (see page 224), Cockney market stallholders converge, dressed, for charity, in the outfits of Pearly Kings and Queens.

Downstairs, the crypt incorporates a gallery and brass-rubbing centre (see page 214).

ST. PAUL'S CATHEDRAL
(see pages 118–123)

ST. PAUL'S CHURCH

🔢 68 K4 • Bedford Street WC2E 9ED ☎ 020 7836 5221 🕐 Daily 8.30–4.30 🎟 Free 🚇 Covent Garden, Leicester Square 🚌 24, 29, 176

St. Paul's was conceived as an integral feature of Inigo Jones's 17th-century Italianate piazza, Covent Garden (see page 88), and its Tuscan pillars and columns still dominate the west side of the square. However, this portico was never used as the church's main entrance is on Bedford Street.

With the Theatre Royal Drury Lane (see page 201) and the Royal Opera House (see page 195) nearby, St. Paul's has always been associated with the theatre and is consequently known as the actors' church. Dozens of plaques commemorate distinguished figures of the thespian world, such as London-born film actor and director Charlie Chaplin (1889–1977). Other memorials in the church include those for artist Joseph Turner, baptized here in 1775, and woodcarver Grinling Gibbons, buried here in 1721.

A statue of St. Peter stands outside St. Paul's Church

St. Paul's Cathedral

Britain's only domed cathedral, with one of the world's largest domes,
second only to that of St. Peter's in Rome.
Sir Christopher Wren's masterpiece, a unique fusion of Classical and Gothic styles.

Despite towering office blocks, the great cathedral dome remains one of the skyline's most distinctive outlines

Lord Nelson was brought here after dying in battle

SEEING ST. PAUL'S CATHEDRAL

A wide flight of steps leads up to the west front entrance, flanked by two clock towers. Wren's original Classical design, using a Greek cross with the dome over the central intersection, was modified to provide an impressive processional space for the clergy, and the first view on entering is of the three-bay-long nave provided for this purpose. To the left are All Souls' Chapel and the bell tower, then St. Dunstan's Chapel. To the right is the Chapel of St. Michael and St. George. Farther down, in one of the nave arches, is the Wellington memorial, and ahead is the massive dome. Nelson's memorial is to the right, in the south transept, and beyond it is the entrance to the crypt and shop. The choir stalls and the organ case are ahead, and behind the high altar is the American Memorial Chapel. Stairs at the southwest corner of the crossing lead up to the dome and its galleries.

HIGHLIGHTS

THE DOME AND GALLERIES

Eight pillars support this huge structure, over 111m (364ft) high and weighing about 66,000 tonnes (65,000 tons). It's a stiff climb up 259 steps to the Whispering Gallery, which runs around the dome's interior. Here, acoustics are such that someone standing on the opposite side of the gallery can hear your whispers quite clearly after several seconds' delay—though only early visitors have the peace to test the theory properly. There are fine views down to the nave below and up to the frescoes of the dome above, where scenes from the life of St. Paul were painted by Sir James Thornhill between 1716 and 1719.

Another 119 steps lead to the Stone Gallery, which encircles the exterior of the dome's base, 53m (173ft) up. Climbing higher still you pass through the timberwork that rests on the inner dome, supporting the wooden skin of the outer, lead-covered dome. Between these two domes is a third: the brick cone supporting the elegant lantern that crowns the whole structure. This can be viewed from the Golden Gallery, the smallest of the galleries, which runs around the highest point of the outer dome, 85m (280ft) and 530 steps from ground-level. A hole in the floor gives a dizzying view straight down to the

RATINGS

Good for kids	●●
Historic interest	●●●●●
Value for money	●●●●●

TIPS

● The cathedral sometimes closes for special events so it's wise to check before a visit.

● Buy guide books at the west end of the cathedral or from the shop in the crypt, or online.

● If you come to one of the free organ recitals at 5pm every Sunday, bring some loose change for the collection at the end.

The nave (opposite), a dramatic combination of vast space and elaborate decoration

cathedral floor. Above are the ball and cross at the very top, originally added in 1708 and replaced in 1821. For safety reasons visitors are not allowed into the interior of the ball.

THE CHANCEL

This part of the cathedral, near the choir and altar, is a riot of Byzantine-style gilding, with mosaics of birds, fish and animals, dating from the late 19th century. In the north choir aisle is a marble sculpture by Henry Moore (1898–1986), *Mother and Child*. French master metalworker Jean Tijou (*fl*1689–*c*1711) designed the wrought-iron gates—along with most of the cathedral's decorative metalwork.

A statue of the Virgin and Child, originally part of the Victorian altar screen, which was damaged by a bomb during World War II, stands in the south choir aisle. Also here is a marble effigy of poet John Donne

The Duke of Wellington's tomb under the crossing

Detailed woodcarving on the choir stalls by Grinling Gibbons

The Whispering Gallery lives up to its name—crowds permitting

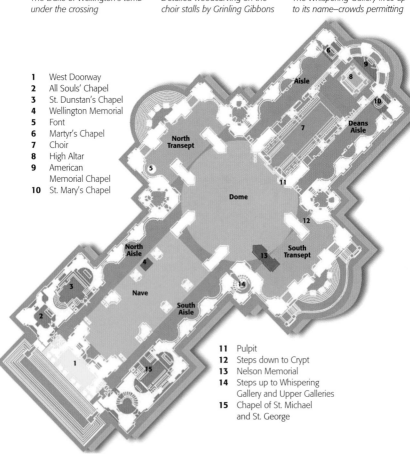

1   West Doorway
2   All Souls' Chapel
3   St. Dunstan's Chapel
4   Wellington Memorial
5   Font
6   Martyr's Chapel
7   Choir
8   High Altar
9   American Memorial Chapel
10 St. Mary's Chapel

11 Pulpit
12 Steps down to Crypt
13 Nelson Memorial
14 Steps up to Whispering Gallery and Upper Galleries
15 Chapel of St. Michael and St. George

(1572–1631), who was dean of the cathedral. This is one of few effigies to have survived the Great Fire of London in 1666, and you can still make out the scorch marks on its base.

The organ is the third largest in Britain, with 7,189 pipes, 5 keyboards and 138 organ stops. Its case was carved by Grinling Gibbons (1648–1721), as were the choir stalls. The high altar, made of marble and carved and gilded oak and incorporating a canopy based on a sketch by Wren, replaced its bomb-damaged predecessor in 1958.

WELLINGTON'S TOMB
The Duke of Wellington (1769–1852), military hero of the Napoleonic Wars and prime minister from 1828 to 1830, lies in a simple, Cornish granite casket under the crossing. Designed in 1858 by F. C. Penrose, it has echoes of the style of Napoleon's tomb in Les Invalides in Paris. Banners made for Wellington's funeral procession hang around the tomb, but the Prussian flag that originally hung there was removed during World War I and has never been reinstated.

NELSON'S TOMB
Admiral Nelson (1758–1805), who died in action against Napoleon at the Battle of Trafalgar, lies in the middle of the crypt, one of around 200 tombs contained in this huge space, which was part of the medieval cathedral. Nelson's coffin—carved from the mast of a defeated French ship—went with him into battle and was kept handy behind his desk. After his death, Nelson was preserved in French brandy for the journey home, and at Gibraltar the coffin was placed into a lead-lined casket and steeped in distilled wine. Finally, his remains were encased in two more coffins before being buried in the crypt under Cardinal Wolsey's 16th-century sarcophagus, which had remained empty since its confiscation by Henry VIII. The monument to Nelson shows two naval cadets being introduced to their hero by Britannia. It was sculpted by John Flaxman (1755–1826), an internationally famous artist in his time.

THE TREASURY
In the southwest section of the crypt, just before the entrance to the shop and restaurant, is the cathedral's collection of gold, silver and other precious objects. Much of the original treasury of gold and silver

BASICS
✚ 69 M4 • St. Paul's Churchyard EC4
☎ 020 7246 8348
🕐 Mon–Sat 8.30–4.30. Daily for services. Timed tickets: for Triforium (Library, West End Gallery, Trophy Room and Wren's Great Model) tours only (advance booking required, tel 020 7246 8319, Mon and Thu 11.30 and 2.30)
🚇 St. Paul's, Blackfriars
🚌 4, 11, 15, 17
🚆 Blackfriars
🎫 Cathedral, Crypt and Galleries: adult £6, child (6–16) £3, under 6s free
💷 £3.25, in English, French, German, Italian, Japanese, Spanish
📷 Mon–Sat 11am, 11.30am, 1.30pm and 2pm. Adult £2.50, under 10s £1 Audiotours: £3.50. English, French, German, Italian and Spanish
🍽 Crypt Café. Light and airy with good snacks and light lunches; licensed
🏪 CDs of psalms, organ and choral music; guidebooks; religious merchandise; Christmas decorations
♿

www.stpauls.co.uk
Virtual tour of the cathedral. Good to look at, but gives only a fairly basic level of background information.

Looking up at the dome's painted ceiling (above)

St. Paul's choir first appears in the records in 1127, when the Bishop of London, Richard de Belmeis, founded a choir school. To celebrate the opening of Wren's cathedral the choir sang an anthem composed by its leader, John Blow, and was accompanied by the new organ, described by diarist John Evelyn as the best in Europe. After 1860, when the screen that originally supported the organ was

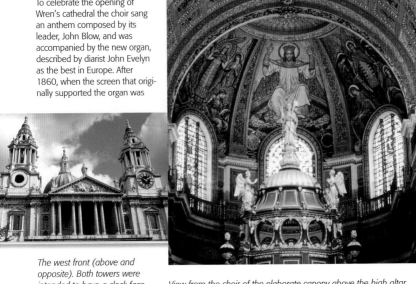

The west front (above and opposite). Both towers were intended to have a clock face

View from the choir of the elaborate canopy above the high altar

taken away, a bigger choir was needed as well as a new organ, to fill the now much larger space. The organ was built in 1872 and the choir increased to a total of 58 voices, which enabled it to establish a wider repertoire of works. Today the choir consists of 30 choristers (boy trebles), eight probationers (who will become choristers) and 18 adults—all chosen by audition. It still follows the monastic tradition of singing services: daily evensong and matins, eucharist and evensong on Sundays. It also has a busy schedule of concerts, broadcasts and recordings. The choirboys are given a normal schooling along with their musical training, which involves learning the piano and another instrument and attending two daily choral rehearsals.

Memorial to pioneer nurse Florence Nightingale, see page 89

was stolen during a robbery in 1810, and more than 200 of the ceremonial vessels and accessories in the current display are actually on loan from other London churches. One of St. Paul's own possessions is the 1977 Jubilee Cope, made for a thanksgiving service in honour of the 25th anniversary of Queen Elizabeth II's accession and worn by Gerald Ellison, the Bishop of London. Its ornate decoration depicts 73 embroidered London church spires. Other interesting exhibits are two effigies dating from before the Great Fire. Though they look like wood, these are stone effigies, originally painted in vivid colours. The heat of the fire fused the paint to the surface and turned them the colour of polished oak.

SIR CHRISTOPHER WREN'S MEMORIAL

A plain black slab gives tribute to the cathedral's architect, with the exhortation *'circumspice si monumentum requiris'* ('if you require a memorial, look about you'). It was inserted in the late 18th century by the surveyor of St. Paul's, Robert Mylne, after a heated debate about a suitable monument; a grand statue had also been proposed. It was Wren's son who provided the memorial's telling phrase. Other architects are commemorated nearby, along with artists including William Blake (1757–1827) and Joseph Turner (1775–1851).

BACKGROUND

The first St. Paul's was built in 604. Rebuilt three centuries later after a Viking attack, the structure was replaced by a Norman cathedral, now known as Old St. Paul's, in 1087. By the 17th century this had a dubious reputation as the home of several obscure cults and the site of horse fairs and secular entertainments. After the Civil War its nave was used as a cavalry barracks, and shops were set up in its portico.

Following its destruction in the Great Fire of 1666 Sir Christopher Wren (1632–1723) was commissioned to build a new version. His first design was rejected and the second was abandoned; the final version was an uneasy compromise between the architect and the clergy.

Science Museum

Celebrates and explains humankind's greatest inventions and scientific, engineering and technical achievements.
More than 300,000 items covering 3ha (8 acres) of floor space.

Hands-on science for children

RATINGS

Good for kids	●●●●●
Historic interest	●●●●
Specialist shopping	●●●

BASICS

✚ 66 E7 • Exhibition Road SW7 2DD
☎ 0870 870 4868 (recorded information), 020 7942 4455 ◷ Daily 10–6
💷 Main museum free; IMAX adult £7.10, child (under 16) £4, family £19.95; Simex Simulator adult £3.50; charges for some special exhibitions
Ⓢ South Kensington 🚌 9, 10, 14, 74, C1 📖 Science Museum Guide £2.95, in English, French, German, Italian, Japanese, Spanish; children's trail guides ☕ Deep Blue Café in the Wellcome Wing; Museum Café; Eat Drink Shop; Gallery Café 📚 Ottakars Bookshop; Science Museum Store selling educational toys, games, stationery 🎁

www.sciencemuseum.org.uk
Inventive and active site with features such as Sciencemuseumintouch, for visitors who create their own web pages at the museum, and games and surveys built around current exhibitions.

SEEING THE SCIENCE MUSEUM

The museum is arranged over seven floors of the main building and in the new four-storey Wellcome Wing, which is connected to the old building at each level. Look out for the touch-screen computers that guide you from section to section.

The basement houses a popular hands-on gallery exploring the basic concepts of science, with separate interactive exhibitions for younger children (3–6) and 7- to 11-year-olds. There's also an exhibition explaining the technology behind ordinary domestic gadgets.

On the ground floor are displays on power and space, with three main exhibition areas: the East Hall is filled with engines of all kinds, and the rest of the floor traces the history of rockets and landmark scientific and technological inventions. Exhibitions on the first floor cover pretty much every material known to man, plus a series of themed displays on aspects of communications, fuel and industry. A variety of exhibits on the second and third floors look at more areas of the appliance of science in daily life plus the exploration of sea and air, and a sound studio explains the mechanics behind radio. Galleries on the fourth and fifth floors tell the story of medicine and veterinary history with objects including an Egyptian mummy, leech jars and Louis Pasteur's microscope.

The Wellcome Wing has three floors of high-tech, interactive exhibitions about current science.

HIGHLIGHTS

GROUND FLOOR
Apollo 10 (Space)
One of the museum's main attractions is the full-size replica of the Apollo 10 command module. This was the Command Module that took astronauts Tom Stafford, John Young and Gene Cernan around the moon and returned them to Earth in May 1969, as a rehearsal for the first manned lunar landing two months later. Its outer surface was scorched during re-entry of the Earth's atmosphere. Visitors who are inspired by the module can even have a go at designing a spacecraft; a computer display will show whether the end result takes to the skies or comes down to earth with a bump.

Stephenson's *Rocket* (Making of the Modern World)
This pioneering rail locomotive was Robert Stephenson's winning design in trials held at Rainhill in 1829 to decide how to power the Liverpool & Manchester Railway. Despite being a breakthrough in railway engine design, the *Rocket* was substantially rebuilt within 18 months to keep up with fast-developing technology and laid aside within 10 years. Nevertheless it made history as the prototype for all future steam locomotives.

THE SIGHTS

Close-up of a Boeing engine (main picture) in the Flight Lab. The suspension bridge in Launch Pad (inset left). Touch screens (inset right) all over the museum educate and entertain

FIRST FLOOR
Cooke and Wheatstone's Telegraph (Telecommunications)
Patented in 1837 by William Cooke (1806–79) and Charles Wheatstone (1802–75), this five-needle telegraph was the first successful electric telecommunication device. It was put to use on the new railways and within a year was sending public telegrams and railway messages between London and West Drayton, 21km (13 miles) to the west. In 1845 the needle telegraph relayed a description of a murderer, who was arrested as he left the train.

SECOND FLOOR
Babbage's Calculating Engines (Computing)
Charles Babbage was designing computers in the early 19th century, creating his Difference Engine No. 1, the first successful automatic calculator, in 1832. One section remains (the rest was melted for scrap), consisting of 2,000 parts and still in working order. His Difference Engine No. 2 was built here in 1991 to his original designs.

THIRD FLOOR
Alcock and Brown's Vickers Vimy (Flight)
Pilot and navigator John Alcock and Arthur Whitten Brown made the first non-stop flight across the Atlantic in this aircraft in June 1919. The Vimy was made of wood and fabric, based on a British World War I bomber and driven by Rolls-Royce engines. Its journey from Newfoundland, Canada to Clifden, Ireland took 16 hours.

BACKGROUND
The Science Museum grew out of the early scientific acquisitions of what would eventually become the V&A (see pages 144–149), which included ship models from the Admiralty, scientific instruments and a science library, plus important British Industrial Revolution inventions. In 1909 the science collection was hived off on its own. The main building of 1913 was designed by Sir Richard Allison as a combination of office block (outside) and department store (inside).

TIP
● Head for the higher, quieter floors to escape the crowds.

GALLERY GUIDE
BASEMENT
Children's science sections and domestic gadgets

GROUND FLOOR
Spacecraft, engines, important inventions. Wellcome Wing: IMAX cinema, Simex Simulator, science and technology news

FIRST FLOOR
Telecommunications, materials, agriculture, surveying, weather, time. Wellcome Wing: genetics and psychology

SECOND FLOOR
Weighing and measuring, lighting, printing, physics, chemistry, mathematics, computing and technology, ships. Wellcome Wing: digital technology

THIRD FLOOR
Optics, 18th-century science, photography, health, temperature, geophysics and oceanography, night skies, recording studio, flight. Wellcome Wing: future developments

FOURTH AND FIFTH FLOORS
Medical and Veterinary History

RATINGS

Good for kids	●●●●
Historic interest	●●●●
Value for money	●●●●

BASICS

⊞ 69 M5 • 21 New Globe Walk SE1 9DT ☎ 020 7902 1400. Box office: 020 7401 9919 ◎ Daily 9–noon (theatre tour and exhibition), 12.30–4 (exhibition and virtual theatre tour), May–Sep; daily 10–5 (theatre tour and exhibition), Oct–Apr. Performances most afternoons and evenings daily, May–Sep
◉ Exhibition and theatre tour: adult £8, child (5–15) £5.50, under 5s free, family £24. Performance: £13–£29, plus £5 (standing); advance booking recommended ◉ Blackfriars, Cannon Street, London Bridge, Mansion House, St. Paul's, Southwark ◉ 15, 45, 63, RV1
☛ Theatre tour daily 9–noon, May–Sep; 10–5, Oct–Apr
📖 *Shakespeare's Globe: The Guidebook*, £5, in English, French, German ⑪ Shakespeare's Globe Restaurant for pre- and post-performance meals ◉ Shakespeare's Globe Café, on the Piazza level
⊞ Shakespeare- and Globe-related gifts and books ⑪

www.shakespeares-globe.org
Information on performances and events, publications, the theatre itself and the exhibition.

The reconstructed Elizabethan theatre inside (main picture) and out (inset)

SHAKESPEARE'S GLOBE

A faithful reconstruction of the Elizabethan playhouse where many of William Shakespeare's plays were first performed.

Bankside's original Globe was one of England's first true playhouses, built in 1599 by a company that included William Shakespeare. Before this, acting companies would tour the country, often performing in the courtyards of inns. Unfortunately, the Globe didn't last long—it was destroyed by fire during a production of *Hamlet* in 1613. A replacement was built, with a tiled roof, a year later but was demolished by the Puritans in 1642, and for the next three centuries the site remained empty.

After visiting Bankside in 1949, American film actor and director Sam Wanamaker (1919–93) was determined to create an accurate, functioning reconstruction of the Globe, built as near as possible to the original site and using materials, tools and craft techniques closely matching those of Elizabethan times. Although the project began in 1969, reconstruction wasn't started until 1987, and it was another 10 years before the new Globe's completion in 1997.

Small by modern standards, the Globe is an O-shaped, white-plastered building constructed with unseasoned oak and held together with 6,000 oak pegs. It's crowned with the first thatched roof to be built in the city since the Great Fire in 1666; the modern version plays it safe with a sprinkler system. In the middle, an elevated stage and a yard are surrounded on three sides by tiers of benches.

In the interests of authenticity, productions are held during the afternoon, much as in Shakespeare's day, without artificial lighting, and only in fine weather. As with the original, there is standing room in front of the stage, where groundlings (the term used in Shakespearean times for standing members of the audience) can heckle the actors in Elizabethan fashion.

UNDERGLOBE

Beneath the theatre, the huge space called the UnderGlobe houses the Shakespeare's Globe exhibition, All the World's a Stage. Here the roles of actor, musician and audience are brought to life through text, film, music and multimedia. You can learn about the techniques used to design and make the costumes in the Theatre Workroom, and in Special Effects you discover what was used for blood and how the sound of thunder in *Macbeth* was created.

Don't miss editing *Hamlet*—create your own version of a scene and print the result on a computer.

Holmes's trademarks: deerstalker, pipe and magnifying glass

The Royal National Theatre, part of the South Bank Centre

Most of Southwark Cathedral was restored by the Victorians

SHERLOCK HOLMES MUSEUM

✚ 67 F3 • 221b (239 postal address) Baker Street NW1 6XE ☎ 0207 935-8866 🕐 Daily 9.30–6 💷 Adult £6, under 16s £4 🚇 Baker Street, Marylebone 🚌 13, 82, 113, 274 💻 ww.sherlock-holmes.co.uk

Fictional detective Sherlock Holmes, created by Sir Arthur Conan Doyle (1859–1930), 'lived' at 221b Baker Street with his friend and colleague Dr. Watson. The 1815 house, used as lodgings in Victorian times and now the Sherlock Homes Museum, is actually 239 Baker Street, but 221b is the number on the door. Dedicated to the life and times of Holmes, the house has been furnished to reflect descriptions in Conan Doyle's stories, with Holmes's study overlooking Baker Street on the first floor, Dr. Watson's bedroom on the second floor and the room occupied by their housekeeper, Mrs Hudson, at the front.

'Personal' belongings include the detective's deerstalker hat, magnifying glass, violin and chemistry equipment, and papers include a variety of exhibits from Holmes's cases, and the 'diary' of Dr. Watson. The third-floor exhibition rooms house wax models of characters and scenes from the stories. **Don't miss** posing for photos in Holmes's armchair by the fireside.

SIR JOHN SOANE'S MUSEUM
(see pages 128–129)

SOMERSET HOUSE
(see pages 130–131)

SOUTH BANK CENTRE

✚ 68 K5 • Belvedere Road SE1 8XX ☎ 020 7960 4242 (box office) 🕐 Foyer daily 10am–10.30pm 💷 Performances only 🚇 Waterloo, Embankment 🚌 77, RV1 **www.sbc.org.uk**

London's premier centre for the performing arts sits on the south side of the river between the Hungerford and Waterloo bridges. It includes the Royal Festival Hall (see page 195), a major concert venue; the National Film Theatre (see page 192), with cinemas, a café and shop; the Queen Elizabeth Hall (see page 194) and adjoining Purcell Room (see page 194), staging smaller concerts and chamber music respectively, along with a clutch of high-profile theatre spaces.

This was the site of the 1951 South Bank Exhibition, part of the Festival of Britain, held as a morale-booster during the post-war years of austerity. The only building to survive from that time is the Royal Festival Hall, where exhibitions and events are held in the huge open-plan foyer, and high-profile music and ballet productions take place in the auditorium above.

To the east is the Hayward Gallery *(tel 020 7960 5226, Thu–Mon 10–6, Tue, Wed 10–8, adult £7, under 16s and members free, www.hayward.org.uk)*, a grim concrete bunker built in 1968, which hosts major contemporary art exhibitions, with the emphasis on British artists.

SOUTHWARK CATHEDRAL

✚ 69 N5 • Montague Close SE1 9DA ☎ 020 7367 6700 🕐 Mon–Fri 8–6, Sat 9–5, Sun 12.30–5 and for services 💷 Free, but donations requested; exhibition adult £3, child (5–15) £1.50, family £12.50 🚇 London Bridge 🚌 344, 381, 705, RV1 🍴 💻 **www.dswark.org/cathedral**

This stone building, originally built between 1220 and 1420 as part of a medieval priory, is tucked away near London Bridge on the south bank of the Thames. Prior to 1905, when it was given cathedral status, it was the parish church of St. Saviour. Inside, it's worth seeking out many of the tombs and memorials, including that of Shakespeare's brother, Edmund, who died in 1607. A monument to the playwright himself depicts characters from his plays.

Next door a new visitor centre houses an exhibition called The Long View of London, which uses impressive multimedia gadgetry in a presentation on the cathedral and Southwark, including touch-screen computers, panoramic views from the top of the tower by way of installed cameras, and a 24-hour record of Southwark speeded up to just six minutes.

SPENCER HOUSE

✚ 67 H5 • 27 St. James's Place SW1A 1NR ☎ 020 7499 8620 🕐 By guided tour only: Sun 10.30–5.45; closed Jan, Aug. Times vary, so phone ahead 💷 Adult £6. Gardens only £3.50. No admission to under 10s 🚇 Green Park 🚌 9, 14, 19, 22, 38 **www.spencerhouse.co.uk**

Best known now as the ancestral home of Diana, Princess of Wales, Spencer House is a mid-18th-century Palladian mansion.

To see the interior you must take a guided tour, which leads into half a dozen state rooms restored to their original style by the current owners, the Rothschilds. Company executives occupy the rest of the building.

Interior décor is lavish, to say the least, from the ornate green and gold ceiling in the Great Room to the classical murals in the Painted Room. A highlight is the Palm Room, where gilded columns and painted fronds stretch out like palm trees.

During spring and summer the magnificent 18th-century gardens are also open occasionally.

Sir John Soane's Museum

●

**A fascinating and bizarre collection of objects displayed in a house of curious but brilliant design.
One of London's secret treasures.**

The picture room uses hinged screens to provide more space

SEEING SIR JOHN SOANE'S MUSEUM

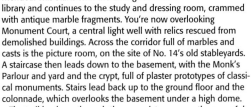

From the moment you arrive it's apparent that this is a museum unlike any other. The entrance is through the front door of No. 12; don't be disconcerted if it's shut—just climb the steps and knock for admission. This is one of three townhouses containing the vast collection of sculptures, paintings, carvings and curios amassed by Sir John Soane (1753–1837).

It's possible to wander at will, but a floorplan suggests the route Soane himself recommended. This starts with the dining room and library and continues to the study and dressing room, crammed with antique marble fragments. You're now overlooking Monument Court, a central light well with relics rescued from demolished buildings. Across the corridor full of marbles and casts is the picture room, on the site of No. 14's old stableyards. A staircase then leads down to the basement, with the Monk's Parlour and yard and the crypt, full of plaster prototypes of classical monuments. Stairs lead back up to the ground floor and the colonnade, which overlooks the basement under a high dome.

The trail leads on through the new picture room; the peaceful breakfast parlour; a dining room housing changing exhibitions as the Soane Gallery; another breakfast parlour, and up the curved staircase to the spacious first-floor drawing rooms, where you can see a pencil sketch of Mrs. Soane and portraits of Soane and of his sons, John and George.

HIGHLIGHTS

Soane's cluttered study

The Picture Room

This small room is crowded with paintings, most prominently William Hogarth's two series of satirical fables, *A Rake's Progress* (1733) and *An Election* (1754)—the original paintings on which his popular engravings were based. By using hinged screens instead of walls Soane managed to fit more than a hundred works into this room; the screens are opened regularly to show the paintings on the other sides. Three works by Canaletto, the pride of Soane's collection, are displayed in the New Picture Room, upstairs.

Sarcophagus of Pharaoh Seti I

Taking pride of place in the atmospheric crypt is this huge stone coffin, covered in delicate hieroglyphics and bought by Soane in 1824. The sarcophagus dates from around 1370BC and was considered an extremely important archaeological find—one of the finest items of its kind outside Egypt, in fact. Nevertheless, the British Museum turned down the opportunity to add the sarcophagus to its collection before Soane put in his bid.

Timepieces

Among the items in the museum is an important collection of clocks and timepieces, going back to the 17th century. Included are a

calendar watch presented to Sir Christopher Wren by Queen Anne in the 1690s; one of five astronomical clocks made by Raingo of Paris for the Prince Regent and his brothers; clocks by Benjamin Lewis Vulliamy and Thwaites and Reed in cases designed by Soane himself; and a late 18th-century eight-day marine chronometer designed by Thomas Mudge for the Duke of Marlborough. This last item was No. 10 of a series of 15 chronometers made to Mudge's design by his son, and regarded as the finest in existence.

Cast Collection

Soane's collection of casts made from sculptures and other pieces, mainly kept in the crypt, is an invaluable guide to the methods of cast-manufacturing in the early 19th century. This busy trade involved casting work from private and public collections, and Soane provided a useful archive by recording the makers in his journals and ledgers. Included in his extensive collection are rare life-masks of the artist Thomas Banks and actress Sarah Siddons, but one of the most noteworthy sections is the group of 91 casts made by the workshop of sculptor Antonio Canova (1757–1822) in Rome. These include items from temples, churches and from the sculpture collection of Polish Prince Poniatowsky. Soane obtained the collection in 1834.

BACKGROUND

Soane was Professor of Architecture at the Royal Academy (see page 115) and made his collection of curios, casts and models available to his students and to enthusiastic amateurs. For that purpose he demolished and rebuilt three houses in succession on the north side of Lincoln's Inn Fields between 1792 and 1824, keeping 12 Lincoln's Inn Fields as a family home and office and using 13 and 14 as his museum. The house was open to visitors the day before and the day after each of his lectures, and by 1827 was already known as the Academy of Architecture.

BASICS

🏠 68 K4 • 13 Lincoln's Inn Fields WC2A 3BP ☎ 020 7405 2107
🕐 Tue–Sat 10–5; first Tue each month also 6–9pm 💷 Free; donations box provided 🚇 Chancery Lane (closed Sun), Holborn 🚌 8, 25, 521
🎫 Public lecture tour for first 25 visitors Sat 2.30pm, includes Model Room, normally open only on request, £3
📖 £1, in English only (includes floor plan) 🏛 Salespoints selling books on art and architecture, cards 🛍

www.soane.org
Many items described, plus good general information.

Busts, urns, architectural fragments (main picture)—the museum's eclectic collection has been gathered from several continents
Convex mirrors are cleverly used to extend views (inset)

Somerset House

**Three outstanding collections of art in one place.
Handsome Georgian architecture and spectacular views across the
River Thames from the terrace.**

THE SIGHTS

TIPS

● To save money, get a joint ticket to the Gilbert Collection and Courtauld Gallery.

● Check the schedule of events, which includes guided tours, events and lectures for each collection and workshops for all ages.

GALLERY GUIDE
COURTAULD GALLERY
GROUND FLOOR
Gallery 1: Early medieval art and objects

FIRST FLOOR
Gallery 2: Early Renaissance art
Gallery 3: High Renaissance and Mannerism
Gallery 4: 16th-century northern European art
Gallery 5: Rubens collection
Gallery 6: 17th-century portraits
Gallery 7: 18th-century portraits

SECOND FLOOR
Gallery 8: Early Impressionists
Gallery 9: Impressionists and Post-Impressionists
Galleries 10 and 11: Early 20th-century art

GILBERT COLLECTION
GROUND FLOOR
Pietre dure furniture and art; Asian furniture

FIRST FLOOR
Main Gallery: Silver, silver gilt and gold objects; snuff boxes; micromosaics; portrait miniatures

SEEING SOMERSET HOUSE

This great riverside landmark south of the Strand has been given a new lease of life as a combination of art galleries, exhibitions and public leisure areas. You can enter through one of two entrances. The Great Arch on Victoria Embankment gives access to the Gilbert Collection; the Strand Block entrance leads to the Courtauld Institute of Art's collection. The third major collection, the Hermitage Rooms, is on the ground floor of the South Building (Embankment entrance) and reached through the Seamen's Waiting Hall, which itself houses models of ships and portraits of naval heroes. In the Hermitage Rooms there's a regularly changing display of objects on loan from St. Petersburg's State Hermitage Museum. The first exhibition alone had more than 500 works of art—paintings, jewellery, metalwork and antiques—that related to the time of Empress Catherine the Great (1729–96). Since exhibitions are temporary and attract big crowds, timed tickets are often sold in advance.

Other spaces accessible from the river side are the Introductory Gallery, explaining the evolution of the site, and the King's Barge House, where you can see a gilded 18th-century barge. At the heart of the complex is a granite-paved courtyard, occupied by fountains and café tables in summer and an ice rink in the winter.

HIGHLIGHTS
COURTAULD GALLERY
The Courtauld Gallery contains six private collections, featuring Old Masters, Impressionist and post-Impressionist paintings, sculpture and applied arts, and was started in 1931 by textile magnate Samuel Courtauld (1876–1947). The first floor's grand rooms house European art from the early Italian Renaissance to 18th-century British portraiture and include a room full of sumptuous paintings by Rubens, including a portrait of his family. Farther up the spiral staircase, a suite of softly top-lit rooms contains a stunning array of Impressionist and post-Impressionist paintings, including eight Cézanne canvases and several by Van Gogh and Gauguin. Other rooms display British 20th-century pictures.

Adam and Eve (1526)
Lucas Cranach (1472–1553) created strikingly original religious works, portraying the subjects with detailed intensity and working the background into the whole, instead of using it as a scenic backdrop. Here he depicts a very real and human couple struggling with uncertainty and temptation.

Self-Portrait with Bandaged Ear (1889)
Vincent Van Gogh (1853–90) painted this portrait of himself after

cutting off a piece of his right ear following a quarrel with fellow artist Paul Gauguin when both were living in Arles. Later in the same year he was admitted into an asylum at St. Rémy.

GILBERT COLLECTION

The Gilbert Collection is the most recent addition to Somerset House, donated by Sir Arthur Gilbert (1913–2001), who made his fortune in the clothing trade. Made up of more than 800 works of art, it's one of the most important collections ever donated to a British gallery, and focuses mainly on mosaic work—large, bold pieces on the ground floor; the main collection of pietre dure (hard stone), a technique using an inlay of semiprecious stones, and, upstairs, examples of a technique known as micromosaic.

Micromosaics

Mosaic techniques are taken to their ultimate refinement in pieces such as these, created in Rome during the 18th century to sell as souvenirs. They use tiny glass threads, barely visible to the naked eye; as many as 5,000 individual components, or tesserae, might be used in 6.5sq cm (1sq in) of a picture.

Snuff Boxes

There are no fewer than 200 tiny and exquisitely decorated snuff boxes in the collection, including curiosities such as the half-dozen 18th-century boxes that contained snuff for Frederick the Great.

BACKGROUND

Somerset House was built between 1776 and 1786 on the site of the Duke of Somerset's Tudor palace. It housed offices of state such as the Navy Office and the Exchequer, and later became a warren of civil servants' offices. The Strand Block was set aside for 'useful learning and polite arts', and taken over by institutions such as The Royal Academy of Arts, the Royal Society and the Society of Antiquaries.

Following the exit of several government departments from the complex in the 20th century, Somerset House was given a major overhaul. The water jets that now play in the courtyard are the first major public fountains to be commissioned in London since those made for Trafalgar Square in 1845.

The Courtauld Gallery's elegant Nelson Staircase (inset left)
The Bridge at Courbevoie by Georges Pierre Seurat (inset centre)
Jets of water spout from the courtyard (main picture and inset right) in summer

BASICS

✚ 68 K4 • Strand WC2R 0RN ☎ 020 7845 4600 (recorded information) ◷ Daily 10–6; extended hours apply to Courtyard, River Terrace and restaurant ◰ Somerset House: free. Courtauld Gallery, Gilbert Collection: adult £5, under 18s £3. Hermitage Rooms: adult £6, under 16s free. Free admission to Courtauld Gallery Mon 10–2 except public holidays; free admission to Gilbert Collection daily after 4.30 ◰ Temple (closed Sun), Covent Garden, Holborn ◰ 9, 11, 15, 23, 91 ⛴ Embankment Pier ◰ Free schedule at shop and information desks ◰ Gifts and gallery merchandise in Courtauld Gallery, Hermitage Gallery and Gilbert Collection; Somerset House shop next to Navy Office entrance ◰ Admiralty restaurant ◻ River Terrace summer café; café in Introductory Gallery; take-away food/courtyard lunches at deli-catessen near Seamen's Hall ◰

www.somerset-house.org.uk
Excellent site with information on all the collections and Somerset House itself, including a virtual tour, details of temporary exhibitions and an image library.

Tate Britain

The world's largest collection of British art from 1500 to the present day, with more than 3,500 paintings, plus prints, drawings, sketches and sculptures.

New and refurbished galleries lie behind the Victorian façade

RATINGS

Good for kids	◐ ◐
Historic interest	◐ ◐ ◐ ◐
Specialist shopping	◐ ◐ ◐ ◐

BASICS

✚ 68 J7 • Millbank SW1P 4RG
☎ 020 7887 8000, 020 7887 8008 (recorded information)
🕐 Daily 10–5.50 💷 Free but donations welcome Ⓟ Pimlico, Vauxhall, Westminster 🚌 3, C10, 36, 77A, 88
🚆 Daily 11, noon, 2, 3, free. Audiotours £1, in English, French, German, Italian, Spanish 📖 Catalogues to specific collections available in the shop for £20–£30 🍴 Tate Britain Restaurant
☕ Tate Café 📚 Excellent selection of art books, plus related souvenirs 🛍

www.tate.org.uk
Online shop and database of 50,000 works plus links to Tate Modern (see pages 134–135) and branches in St. Ives, Cornwall and Liverpool.

SEEING TATE BRITAIN

Since the transfer of its international collection to Tate Modern (see pages 134–135) in 2000, the Tate's British collection has been able to spread out in its Millbank premises. Despite this, the gallery still owns far more than it can display at once, and the pictures on show are changed regularly every year. Generally, the art is displayed chronologically, with rooms devoted to specific artists or themes, but because of the annual rehangs it's impossible to say with any certainty what can be seen where.

There are three entrances to the gallery. The Manton Entrance, on Atterbury Street (left of the main steps) leads to special exhibitions on Level One; the Clore Gallery Entrance leads through the sculpture garden (right) and up to rooms 35–45 on Levels Two and Three (the Clore Galleries), devoted to works by Joseph Turner (1775–1851) and his contemporaries. The Millbank Entrance provides the main access, up the riverside steps, taking you into the main part of the collection, on Level Two.

Rooms are set out chronologically, starting with 16th-century works in Room 1 at the top of the Manton Staircase.

HIGHLIGHTS

LEVEL TWO

The Cholmondeley Ladies (Room 2)
This intriguing and touching portrait painted by an unknown artist some time between 1600 and 1610 shows two straight-backed young women sitting up in bed side by side, dressed in intricate white dresses with large collars and headdresses, each holding a baby wrapped in rich red christening robes. At first glance mothers and children seem exactly alike, but you could spend hours exploring the subtle differences: in eye colour, jewellery and even in the minute detail of the lace edging on their clothes.

The Great Day of His Wrath by John Martin (Room 14)
Swirling black clouds and fiery red light are used in one of a triptych of 'judgement pictures' painted in 1851–53 by John Martin (1789–1854), inspired by the Book of Revelation in the New Testament. Martin developed Turner's ideas about the power of nature to the full, using dramatic scenes like this to convey the weakness of humanity. Here he gives a faithful depiction of the Bible's account of the Last Judgement: 'there was a great earthquake and the sun became black as sackcloth of hair and the moon became as blood. And the heaven departed as a scroll…and every mountain and island were moved out of their places.'

Recumbent Figure by Henry Moore (Room 21)
This powerful, abstract figure of a woman lying on her side was sculpted by Moore (1898–1986) from Hornton stone in 1938. The stone, which is formed in shallow beds, had to be laminated together in three pieces to make the block. It was commissioned by architect Serge Chermayeff and kept on his garden terrace in the Sussex Downs, creating a link between the rolling countryside and his

modern house. Moore and his contemporaries were particularly keen on using local materials and making their work a part of the landscape, in the way of prehistoric figures and monuments.

The Golden Stairs by Sir Edward Coley Burne-Jones (Room 15)
Burne-Jones (1833–98) produced this beautifully composed scene of 18 women in white descending a staircase in 1880. The theme of the painting is something of a mystery, as were many of his works, whose medieval and mythical escapism was particularly popular in the late Victorian industrial age. The late 19th century, with its dizzying technological progress and industrialization, produced a reaction in artists such as Burne-Jones and the Pre-Raphaelite Brotherhood (formed in 1848), who romanticized the Middle Ages as a time when objects and pictures were individually produced by craftsmen and imbued with the value of their involvement and labour.

BACKGROUND

The story of the Tate begins with Henry Tate (1819–99), the sugar millionaire, who was determined that London should have a showcase for British art. He offered his own collection of Victorian paintings to get it going (including Millais' *Ophelia*), together with funds for a gallery. Finally, the government took up his idea and Sidney Smith's building was constructed in 1812–21 on the north bank of the Thames, a short way south of the Houses of Parliament.

Piecemeal additions and donations followed, including the central cupola and sculpture galleries given by art dealer Joseph Duveen and his son, Lord Duveen, in 1937, and the restaurant, with its landscape murals (*The Pursuit of Rare Meats*, 1920s) by Rex Whistler, in 1983. A northwestern extension was built in the 1970s, and in 1987 the Clore Galleries, designed by Sir James Stirling, were opened.

The grim Millbank Penitentiary prison once occupied the site; across the Embankment steps lead down to the Thames, where convicts condemned to transportation boarded ships bound for Australia. The prison was closed and demolished in the 1890s.

Flatford Mill *by John Constable (main picture)*
Turner's Norham Castle *(inset)*
Jacob and the Angel *by Sir Jacob Epstein (below left) is one of a group of monumental carvings with religious themes*

GALLERY GUIDE

LEVEL ONE
Sculpture Garden
Special exhibitions

LEVEL TWO
Rooms 1–17: British art from 1500 to 1900 covering Tudor and Stuart portraiture, works by William Hogarth, George Stubbs, John Constable and William Blake, plus Victorian paintings

Rooms 18–31: British art from 1900 to the present day, including bronze casting, sculpture and works by Ronald Moody, Graham Sutherland and Paul Neagu, plus new exhibits

CLORE GALLERIES
LEVELS TWO and THREE
Rooms 35–45: Works by Joseph

TIPS

● Pick up a gallery plan from the information desks to see what's on show where.

● To be sure of seeing a particular work, check with the gallery that it is on display.

Tate Modern

**A superb collection of international modern art from 1900 to the present day.
Housed in the spectacularly restored Bankside Power Station.
One of London's newest and most dynamic attractions.**

View from the restaurant

BASICS

✚ 331 M5 • Bankside SE1 9TG ☎ 020
7887 8000; recorded information 020
7887 8008 ⏰ Sun–Thu 10–6, Fri–Sat
10–10 (galleries open daily at 10.15)
💷 Free, donations welcome. Charge
(variable) for special exhibitions
🚇 Southwark, Blackfriars, St. Paul's
🚌 45, 63, 100, 344, RV1
🚢 Bankside Pier 🎧 Choice of audiotours covering permanent collection,
architecture, children's trail, tour for the
visually impaired. Available from near
the Turbine Hall information point and
Level 3, £1, in English, French, German,
Italian, Spanish 📖 Official guide £4.99,
in English French, German, Italian,
Spanish, catalogue £16.99
🍴 Restaurant on Level 7 with exceptional views ☕ Cafés on Levels 2 and
7; kiosk by the north entrance; bar on
Level 4 🎫 Large shop on Level 1 with
comprehensive range of art books,
posters, prints, stationery and postcards
🚻

www.tate.org.uk
Tate Modern link with information on
current exhibitions and brief account of
site's development.

SEEING TATE MODERN

Towering over the Millennium Bridge on the
south bank of the Thames, Tate Modern
opened in 2000 as one of the world's leading
museums of modern art, and it's been pulling
in huge crowds ever since.

You can use entrances on the western or the
northern side of the former power station. On
the west side there are two; the main entrance
takes you down an access ramp into the enormous, airy Turbine Hall, which acts as a dramatic interior plaza for temporary installations.
Another entrance on this side of the building
gives level access to the second floor. The main shop and information point are on Level One (the basement) and escalators
take you up to the galleries on the upper levels.

The collection is divided into four broad themes: Still
Life/Object/Real Life; Landscape/Matter/Environment;
History/Memory/Society; and Nude/Action/Body. Each has combinations of film media, installations, painting, photography and
sculpture, linking historic works with contemporary. Every year
there are three additional special loan exhibitions and several
shows focusing on a single artist, theme or period.

HIGHLIGHTS

Tate Modern continues the story of art where the National Gallery
(see pages 104–109) leaves off. Its displays are changed regularly, to
show the widest possible range of exhibits, but they always include
works by the most influential artists of the 20th century, such as
Picasso, Matisse, Dalí, Moore, Bacon, Gabo, Giacometti and Warhol.

LEVEL 3
Still Life/Object/Real Life
The Inattentive Reader by Henri Matisse (Art of the Everyday)
Matisse (1869–1954) painted this work in 1919, while staying in a
hotel in Nice in the south of France. He was hugely influential in his
use of bold forms and bright slabs of colour, and this is an excellent
example of his mastery of everyday subjects, showing the model in a
relaxed pose in front of a mirror reflecting flowers in a vase.

Mandora by Georges Braque (Modern Life)
Braque (1882–1963) was a leading light among the Cubists, whose
experiments in form and perception revolutionized the art world.
Braque collected early musical instruments and in this image of a
mandora, a small lute, he uses his fragmented style to suggest
rhythm and sound—a very active kind of still-life painting.

LEVEL 5
History/Memory/Society
Unique Forms of Continuity in Space by Umberto Boccioni (Across
History)
The Futurist movement was founded by writers and artists such as

As part of the power station's redevelopment, the roof of the Turbine Hall (main picture) was removed, along with that of the old Boiler House
Six escalators (inset far left) take visitors between the different levels of the gallery
Works of art (inset centre and right) change regularly

Umberto Boccioni (1882–1916) in the early 20th century, when industrialization was engulfing Italy and innovations such as cars and electricity seemed to promise a dynamic and thrusting age ahead. This 1913 sculpture shows the air in the wake of the moving figure, giving a vivid sense of speed and progress.

Nude/Action/Body

Venice Woman IX by Alberto Giacometti (Alberto Giacometti Room) Giacometti (1901–66) began to sculpt his series of emaciated human figures in the 1940s, providing a sober answer to the 'super-man' philosophy of the pre-war Futurists. The fragility and dignity of this bronze piece, with all its resonance of human suffering, under-lines Giacometti's own view that his thin sculptures were truer to humanity than larger works.

Girl in a Chemise by Pablo Picasso (Naked and Nude) During his 'blue period' Picasso (1881–1973) produced several por-traits of people from society's margins. This study of a melancholy, thin young girl is included in the Naked and Nude collection in con-trast to the idealized nude. It's a poignant work, which goes beyond the depiction of a model and into the realms of social commentary.

BACKGROUND

By the early 1990s the Tate Gallery, now called Tate Britain (see pages 132–133), needed more space. Its international modern art collection had nearly doubled in 40 years, and the decision was made to divide the collection between British and other works of art. A major new gallery was planned to house the international work, and the venue chosen was a decommissioned power sta-tion, a huge 1950s brick and steel-frame building designed by Sir Giles Gilbert Scott (1880–1960). A competition was mounted for the best plan to transform the site, and the winners, out of 148 entrants, were Swiss architects Herzog & de Meron. Renovation began in 1995 and the gallery opened on 12 May 2000.

The height of the central chimney was limited to 99m (325ft) in order to be lower than the dome of St. Paul's Cathedral

Effigies of Knights Templar supporters in Temple Church

Exhibit from the stage musical Cats, by Andrew Lloyd Webber

The fountains in Trafalgar Square–irresistible in summer

TEMPLE, INNER AND MIDDLE

✚ 68 L4 • Inner Temple EC4Y 7HL; Middle Temple EC4Y 9BT ☎ Inner Temple 020 7797 8250; Middle Temple 020 7427 4830 🕐 Inner Temple Gardens Mon–Fri 12.30–3. Middle Temple Hall Mon–Fri 10–noon, 3–4, 1 Mar–1 Dec. Middle Temple Gardens Mon–Fri noon–3, May–Jul, Sep. Church Wed–Sat 11–4, plus services (☎ 020 7353 3470) 🎟 Free 🚇 Temple (closed Sun), Blackfriars, Holborn, Chancery Lane (closed Sun) 🚌 11, 15, 23 🚢 Savoy Pier
www.innertemple.org.uk
www.middletemple.org.uk

Two Inns of Court (see pages 90 and 97) make up the Temple, named after the crusading Knights Templar, who acquired the land in 1160. The 12th-century circular Temple Church still stands at the heart of this network of gardens and courtyards.

In addition to the church, you can visit the Inner and Middle Temple gardens and the 16th-century Middle Temple Hall, where the first recorded performance of Shakespeare's *Twelfth Night* took place. It has an impressive hammerbeam roof and screen, Elizabethan tables and royal portraits. The other buildings can be admired only from the outside.

THEATRE MUSEUM

✚ 68 K4 • 1e Tavistock Street WC2E 7PR. Entrance is on Russell Street ☎ 020 7943 4700 🕐 Tue–Sun 10–6 🎟 Free 🚇 Covent Garden, Leicester Square, Embankment 🚌 6, 9, 13, 23, 77A, RV1 🎫
www.theatremuseum.org

At the heart of theatreland, in Covent Garden's Victorian Flower Market (see page 88), this offshoot of the Victoria & Albert Museum opened in 1987 and focuses on performing arts from Shakespeare's day to the present.

If you're at all stage-struck you'll be fascinated by the model theatres, sets, props, costumes, photographs, programmes, posters, tickets and souvenirs.

Famous actors' voices can be heard, and personal possessions include the boots in which Sarah Siddons trod the boards, Noël Coward's dressing gown, and even a Mick Jagger jumpsuit.

Museum guides, mostly actors, entertain as well as enlighten. A series of hands-on demonstrations reveals the secrets of stage make-up and costume.

TOWER BRIDGE
(see opposite)

TOWER OF LONDON
(see pages 138–143)

TRAFALGAR SQUARE

✚ 68 J5 🕐 Open access 🎟 Free 🚇 Charing Cross, Leicester Square 🚌 11, 12, 24, 88
Tourist Information Office
Britain Visitor Centre, 1 Lower Regent Street, Piccadilly Circus SW1Y 4XT (no telephone)

One of the world's most famous squares sits at the northern end of Whitehall (see page 151), where it was laid out to John Nash's design between 1829 and 1841, as a commemoration of Admiral Lord Nelson's victory against the French at the 1805 Battle of Trafalgar.

Feeding the pigeons in Trafalgar Square, once a must for any visitor to London, is now forbidden (see page 24).

STATUARY
Nelson towers on his 56m (185ft) column at the centre of the square. The statue itself, though 5m (17ft) high, can be seen only from strategic viewpoints such as the National Portrait Gallery's top floor restaurant (see page 262), but the four huge bronze lions that guard him, sculpted in the 1860s by Sir Edwin Landseer, are clearly on view, as well as the reliefs around the base of the column, showing Nelson's naval victories. A 17th-century equestrian monument commemorating Charles I, by Hubert Le Sueur (1633), stands on a traffic island.

At the square's corners are four great plinths. Three support more statuary: George IV, again on horseback, by Chantrey and T. Earle (1834), originally meant for Marble Arch; Sir Henry Havelock, by William Behnes (1861), and Sir Charles Napier, by G. G. Adams (1855)—both celebrating military heroes of their time. The fourth, the northwestern plinth, is empty. An inspired scheme has made it the setting for a series of modern sculptures, and its future occupant is still the cause of heated debate.

The famous fountains, decorated with sculptings of mermaids and men, sharks and dolphins, were installed in the 19th century and embellished by Sir Edwin Lutyens in 1939.

Leaping into the water during New Year celebrations is another tradition that has now been ruled out on grounds of safety. However, the water still plays in the fountains from 10am daily.

Don't miss the view across the square towards Big Ben from the northern side.

Nelson's Column. The statue of Lord Nelson on top of the granite column is three times life size

TOWER BRIDGE

Stupendous views across London from the high-level walkway, 43m (140ft) above the Thames. A close-up view of one of the world's most recognizable bridges and its workings.

London's best-known bridge, linking the Tower of London (see pages 138–143) and the south bank promenade, has been a tourist attraction since 1982, with access to the upper walkways and engine rooms and a Tower Bridge Experience exhibition tracing its history. The hydraulically operated bascules (from the French for 'see-saw') are the main attraction. Originally designed (in the late 19th century) to allow tall ships to sail through, they are still lifted more than 900 times a year for cruise liners and other large river craft.

The famous neo-Gothic towers, with their mock-medieval turrets, are an attraction in themselves. DVD shows and graphic display panels in the towers and on the walkways give an idea of the debates and controversies that led to the construction of the bridge, discussed since 1800 but not officially planned until 1876. Some of the designs submitted over the following seven years included a futuristic-looking structure with sliding roadways, a rolling bridge and a sub-riveran arcade. The winning design, submitted by Sir Horace Jones and adapted by engineer John Wolfe Barry, took eight years to build.

From the south tower, follow the blue guideline to the engine rooms, which house the beautifully crafted Victorian machinery used to power the bridge between 1894 and 1976.

PLANNING THE BRIDGE

Between 1750 and 1850 10 new bridges had been built along the Thames to cope with the increasing trade and traffic of a booming city. East of London Bridge, where the population had expanded to over a million by the late 19th century, there was no river crossing. Plans were delayed and disrupted by wharfingers and shipping traders, who feared the decline of river business, and by the need for 43m (140ft) of clearance for tall-masted ships. A competition was finally opened for a new design. The winning architect, Sir Horace Jones, died in 1887 before the foundations were complete, and the task was passed on to his assistant, George Daniel Stevenson, who had an even greater passion for the Victorian Gothic style.

Don't miss the interactive computer displays, which help pick out the most famous buildings on the skyline.

RATINGS

Good for kids	● ● ● ● ●
Historic interest	● ● ● ●
Photostops	● ● ● ● ●
Value for money	● ● ● ●

BASICS

✚ 69 P5 • Tower Bridge SE1 2UP
☎ 020 7403 3761 ◉ Daily 9.30–6
Adult £4.50, child (5–15) £3, under 5s free, family discounts from £9.50. Joint ticket with Monument £5 (child as above) ◉ Tower Hill, London Bridge
🚌 15, 42,78, 100, RV1 Tower Millennium Pier Available for pre-booked groups (minimum 10) only
£2.50, in English, French, German, Dutch, Japanese Tower Café under north tower; indoor and outdoor seating Small kiosk in engine rooms selling limited range of souvenirs

www.towerbridge.org.uk
Plenty of information on different tours and prices; not much background detail on the bridge itself.

TIP

● Try and time a visit to coincide with the bridge opening. A list of the times is posted in the entrance kiosk to the exhibition daily. Vessels pass through with a minimum of 24 hours' notice.

The bridge (above) was given a royal opening in 1894, with a gun salute from the Tower of London to greet the first raising of the bascules

Tower of London

**Symbolizes nearly 1,000 years of Britain's royal history.
Home to the English Crown Jewels and the largest diamond in the world.
Yeoman Warders, or Beefeaters, in their Tudor costumes, treat groups of sightseers
to their own brand of guided tour, an entertaining mix of history and myth.**

The towers of Tower Bridge were designed to emulate those of the Tower of London

Forty Yeomen Warders have office at the Tower; one, the Ravenmaster, cares for the eight resident ravens

SEEING THE TOWER OF LONDON

The Tower's layout illustrates its development from William the Conqueror's White Tower to the complex of defences completed by Edward I and Henry III and essentially unchanged today.

Entry to the Tower is through the Middle Tower in the southwest corner of the site. Once inside, you can wander at will. At the heart of the complex is the White Tower, 36m (118ft) across and 27m (90ft) high, with weather vanes topping the corner turrets. It is surrounded by 13th-century outer and inner walls, the latter punctuated by 12 towers.

A complex of later buildings within the inner wall includes the New Armouries, Waterloo Barracks and the Fusiliers' Museum.

HIGHLIGHTS

WHITE TOWER

At the heart of the Tower is its oldest medieval building, thought to date from 1078 and probably marking a site of political significance for many centuries before that. It earned its name in the 13th century, when Henry III had the exterior whitewashed, but the original stone, brought over from Caen in Normandy, has mainly been replaced over the years with Portland stone from Dorset. The windows and doors are also replacements, added in the 17th and 18th centuries, and the turret roofs were a 16th-century feature.

The White Tower was built to serve as a fortress, armoury and a royal residence, and is split inside into three floors and a basement, where the 11th-century well still holds fresh water. On the ground floor is an exhibition about small arms, from the Royal Armouries collection; spiral stairs lead to the first floor, with the gloriously simple Chapel of St. John the Evangelist, a double-height room original to the building. Used as chapel throughout the Middle Ages, from the 16th to the 19th centuries it stored state records. The adjacent large room may have been used for banquets and royal ceremonies.

Temporary exhibitions are held on the top floors and stairs lead to the turrets above, where Charles II's astronomer, John Flamsteed, observed the stars until a new observatory was built at Greenwich (see pages 156–157).

(see pages 156–157).

RATINGS				
Good for kids	●	●	●	● ●
Historic interest	●	●	●	● ●
Photo stops			●	● ●
Value for money		●	●	● ●

TIPS

● Crowds can be a problem in the summer. To save lining up, buy tickets in advance by calling 0870 756 7070 or online at www.hrp.org.uk.

● It's possible to walk along a section of the defensive walls between the Salt Tower and Martin's Tower, where there's a display on the making of the Crown Jewels.

● Check at the main entrance near the Middle Tower for times of free daily guided tours by Yeoman Warders.

The arms and armour (opposite) on display in the White Tower represent only a fraction of the Royal Armouries' collection

THE SIGHTS

BASICS

🔲 69 P5 • London EC3N 4AB ☎ 0870
756 6060; tickets: 0870 756 7070
🕐 Mon–Sat 9–6, Sun 10–6, Mar–Oct;
Tue–Sat 9–5, Sun–Mon 10–5, Nov–Feb.
All buildings inside the gates close
30 min after last admission; Tower
closes 1 hour after last admission. To
watch the nightly Ceremony of Keys
apply in advance: tel 0870 756 7070
💷 Adult £13.50, child (5–16) £9, under
5s free, family £37.50
Ⓠ Tower Hill
🚌 15, 42, 78, 100, RV1
⛴ Tower Millennium Pier
📖 £3.95, in English, French, Russian,
Japanese, Spanish, Italian, German
🎧 Prisoners of the Tower sound guide,
£3, in English, French, German, Italian,
Spanish, Japanese, Russian
🍴 New Armouries restaurant
☕ Tower Café and kiosk on wharf
🛍 West Gate Shop at main entrance in
the Salvin Pumphouse; Jewel House
Shop in Lower Martin Tower; White
Tower Shop, in basement of White
Tower; Medieval Palace Shop; Beefeater
Shop, in Water Lane
🚻

www.hrp.org.uk
Straightforward site (part of the historic
royal palaces website) with good links,
historical background and full visitor
information.

The White Tower, which replaced an earlier wooden building

*The familiar and much loved Beefeaters wear a dark blue and red uniform for every day; scarlet (right) for ceremonies
The Tower was built close to the river (above) so enemies approaching could be sighted immediately*

GUIDE TO THE TOWER

1 Middle Tower
2 Byward Tower
3 Bell Tower
4 Traitors' Gate
5 St. Thomas's Tower
6 Bloody Tower
7 Wakefield Tower
8 White Tower
9 Chapel of St. John the Evangelist
10 Queen's House
11 Gaoler's House
12 Tower Green
13 Scaffold Site
14 Beauchamp Tower
15 Royal Chapel of St. Peter ad Vincula
16 Waterloo Barracks with Crown Jewels
17 Devereux Tower
18 Flint Tower
19 Bowyer Tower
20 Brick Tower
21 Martin Tower
22 Fusiliers' Museum
23 Former Hospital
24 Workshop
25 Constable Tower
26 Broad Arrow Tower

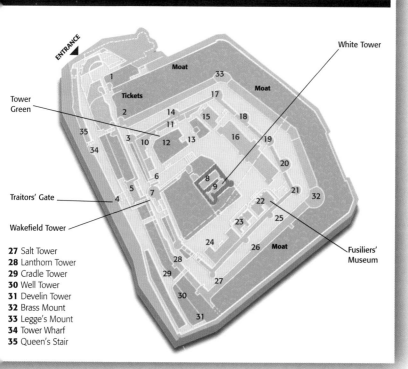

ENTRANCE

White Tower

Moat

Moat

1

33

Tickets

17

Tower Green

2

14

15

18

35

11

3 10 12 13 16 19

34

6

8 20

5 9

Traitors' Gate 4 7 21 32

22

Wakefield Tower 25

23

24 26 Moat

Fusiliers' Museum

28

29

27

30

31

27 Salt Tower
28 Lanthorn Tower
29 Cradle Tower
30 Well Tower
31 Develin Tower
32 Brass Mount
33 Legge's Mount
34 Tower Wharf
35 Queen's Stair

JEWEL HOUSE

First stop for many visitors is the Jewel House (in the Waterloo Barracks), north of the White Tower. Here you pass through a series of displays giving a history of the Coronation Regalia (Crown Jewels) before reaching the treasury, where the collection is kept. An excellent visual story of the jewels entertains those waiting to view the exhibits, and it is possible to repeat the circuit round the actual jewels immediately for a second look at no extra cost.

The jewels mainly date from the restoration of the monarchy in 1660; the older regalia were melted down on Oliver Cromwell's orders, and only three swords and a coronation spoon survive. The sovereign's orb and sceptre (topped with a dove), made for Charles II in 1661, have been used in every coronation since, but there are also many later additions, such as the new sets made for

'Off with his head!' Execution axe from the Armoury

Anne Boleyn was one who took her final journey through Traitors' Gate

Small arms from the Armouries collection

BEHEADED

The Scaffold Site in front of the Chapel of St. Peter ad Vincula saw the executions of the only five women to be beheaded for treason—four of them during Henry VIII's reign. First on the block was Anne Boleyn in 1536; she and the next victim, wife No. 5, Catherine Howard, were both accused of adultery. Catherine's lady-in-waiting Jane, Viscountess Rochford, met her fate along with her mistress. In 1541, 70-year-old Margaret Pole, Countess of Salisbury, was executed for her Catholic and Yorkist loyalties. Henry's daughter Mary I continued the family tradition by dispatching the fifth woman, Lady Jane Grey, proclaimed queen in 1553 in an attempt to secure a Protestant succession.

James II's wife, as queen consort, and for Mary II, crowned with William III but queen in her own right. Among the priceless stones used in the regalia are the world's biggest cut diamond, the 530-carat First Star of Africa, set in the head of the sceptre. The 317-carat Second Star of Africa diamond is part of the Imperial State Crown, made for the coronation of George VI in 1937 and set with no fewer than 2,868 diamonds, as well as 17 sapphires, 11 emeralds, 5 rubies and 273 pearls.

TOWER GREEN

Endlessly fascinating to visitors are the Tower's famous prisoners and their grisly deaths. Tower Green, west of the White Tower, is the main focus for stories of suffering and heroics: some of the tower's best-known prisoners were held in the buildings around this area of garden, including Sir Walter Ralegh, whose stay in the Bloody Tower led to the addition of a new floor to provide room for him and his family. The tower's name dates from the supposed murder of the two princes, Edward and Richard, sons of Edward IV and allegedly the victims of their ambitious uncle, Richard III.

The Queen's House, a black-and-white, half-timber building next to the Bloody Tower, was the scene of Guy Fawkes' interrogation in 1605 (see page 30) and of a daring escape when the Earl of Nithsdale, imprisoned after the 1715 Jacobite rebellion, dressed as a woman and made his getaway. Particularly high-ranking prisoners were kept in the 13th-century Beauchamp Tower. In the upper chamber you can still see inscriptions carved by the prisoners, some with amazing skill and intricacy.

TRAITORS' GATE

Just beyond the entrance to the medieval palace, opposite the gateway of the Bloody Tower, is a great stone archway. Above it is Tudor timber framing and below the wooden watergates that gave direct access from the river. Its name derives from the number of prisoners accused of treason who were brought by boat through this entrance. Until the 1860s there was an engine in the pool behind the gate that used water-power or horse-power to raise water to a tank on the roof of the White Tower.

The Chapel of St. John the Evangelist, in the White Tower

During the 19th century, the Armouries in the White Tower became a series of displays instead of a working arsenal

WAKEFIELD TOWER

Next in size to the White Tower, this was built in the 13th century to house King Henry III's main private room and included a private river entrance, still visible in Water Lane. Its impressive upper chamber was the king's bedroom, and has been decked out according to accounts written in his son Edward I's reign, when it served as a throne room. The current throne is a copy of the Coronation Chair in Westminster Abbey, and sits flanked by candelabra under the magnificent vaulted ceiling. A painted timber screen divides the main room from the chapel, reputed to be the site of Henry VI's murder while at prayer, though like many of the Tower's legends this is probably more convenient than true (see side panel).

FUSILIERS' MUSEUM

King James II established the Royal Regiment of Fusiliers in 1685 to guard the Tower's arsenal. They took their name from the 'fusil', a then-state-of-the-art musket which they were the first to use. The museum and the regiment headquarters occupy a 19th-century building which was initially the officers' mess. Inside is a display tracing the Fusiliers' service in the American War of Independence, the Crimean War, World War I and World War II, among many other campaigns. Some of the quirkier exhibits include a metal boot worn by a soldier who had avoided action for more than three years during the Napoleonic Wars by putting a corrosive lotion on his leg to create an open sore. His leg was cured within days of the boot being fitted.

BACKGROUND

The White Tower was built in the 11th century on a site, commanding the Thames, that probably had earlier royal significance. Between 1190 and 1285 it was encircled by two towered curtain walls and a moat, and in the 14th century the wharf was added. Further additions included the Chapel Royal and Queen's House, built in Henry VIII's reign, and the 17th-century New Armouries. In the 19th century Waterloo Barracks and the Fusiliers' Museum were added in the Inner Ward. In 1988 the Tower of London was designated a World Heritage Site.

TRADITIONS

The Tower has many ancient traditions. One is the nightly Ceremony of the Keys (see page 224), when the Chief Yeoman Warder locks the main gates of the Tower at 9.53pm, after which a bugler sounds the Last Post. This ceremony has scarcely changed in more than 700 years, except that it now takes place under floodlights with an audience.

Eight ravens live in the gardens, well cared for by the official Ravenmaster; legend has it that the Tower will collapse if they fly away, but in fact their wings are clipped so this will never happen.

On 21 May members of Eton College and King's College, Cambridge put white roses and lilies in Wakefield Tower in memory of Henry VI, who founded both institutions and who was murdered here in 1471.

Victoria & Albert Museum

One of the world's biggest and most highly regarded collections of decorative arts ranging across European, American, Asian and African cultures. A freshness and diversity that adds to the excitement of personal discoveries.

TIPS

● Colour-coded signs and banners, corresponding to key areas of the museum, help you find your way around.

● Take advantage of the late-night opening until 10pm every Wednesday.

The grand façade of the V&A (above left) includes contributions by several sculptors and art students of the day: Queen Victoria (above centre) is one of the figures The Italian Cast Court (above right) displays plaster casts of celebrated examples of European sculpture The Three Graces (opposite), by Antonio Canova, sculpted in marble beween 1814 and 1817, can be seen in the Britain 1714–1837 galleries

SEEING THE V&A

Contemporary glass sculptor Dale Chihuly's extraordinary chandelier in twisted, colourful blown glass dominates the V&A's entrance hall and provides a sense of what's ahead—displays of tens of thousands of items, including fashion and textiles, furniture and paintings, jewellery, ceramics, glass, silver and ironwork.

The main entrance on Cromwell Road is on Level 1, but the galleries start (numerically) one level down (Level 0) with the European collection. On Level 1 are sculpture, plaster casts and photography; Islamic and Asian collections; the Raphael Gallery, and the dress collection.

The museum's 15 British Galleries begin on Level 2 and continue on Level 4. Level 3 features the 20th-century gallery, ironwork, tapestry and silver; glass objects are on show on Level 4 and ceramics on the museum's top floor, Level 5.

HIGHLIGHTS

EUROPEAN COLLECTION
The Becket Casket
Part of the medieval treasury, this gilt copper and blue enamel reliquary was made in about 1180. It is the oldest and largest of about 50 items associated with Thomas à Becket's martyrdom that survive from the workshops of the Limoges enamellers—experts at making beautiful goods with hard-wearing and cheap materials. The murder of Becket, the Archbishop of Canterbury who incurred Henry II's wrath and was assassinated at the cathedral altar, is pictured on the front; one of the knights can be seen hacking off the martyr's head. The lid of the casket shows Becket's funeral.

The Burghley Nef
This dazzling salt-holder is one of the boat-shaped objects (known as nefs) that were all the rage on well-stocked dinner tables in 16th-century France. It was made in Paris in about 1527, with a rare nautilus shell serving as the salt bowl and set into the 'hold' of an elaborate silver sailing ship, resting on an elegant golden-haired mermaid. The intricately worked details on the ship include two minute figures playing chess—representing Tristan and Iseult, the legendary ill-fated lovers associated with the tales of King Arthur and Camelot.

BASICS

🗺 66 E7 • Cromwell Road SW7 2RL

☎ 020 7942 2000

🕐 Mon, Tue, Thu–Sun 10–5.45, Wed, last Fri of month 10–10

💷 Free, except for some exhibitions and events

📖 *V&A: A Hundred Highlights* £4.95, in English, French, German, Japanese; *The British Galleries at the V&A* £4.95, in English only

🎧 Free introductory tours daily (1 hour) 10.30–3.30; also 4.30 and 7.30 on Wed; meet in the Grand Entrance

Ⓜ South Kensington

🚌 C1, 14, 74

☕ Café on Level 1 of the Henry Cole Wing; open daily 10–5.30 (Wed until 9.45)

🏪 Shop on Level 1 selling gifts and books inspired by objects in the museum; small shop selling postcards and children's items next to the café

♿

www.vam.ac.uk
Includes a round-up of all galleries but without much in-depth information on the collections.

Exhibits in the Italian Cast Court (above) Portrait of Margaret Laton (right), believed to be by Marcus Gheeraerts the younger (1561–1636)

ASIAN AND ISLAMIC COLLECTION

Chinese Pagoda

The centrepiece of the Gerard Godfrey Gallery of Chinese Export Art (Room 28) is a brightly coloured 2.7m (9ft) porcelain model of a 17-tier Chinese pagoda, one of only 10 of its kind believed to have survived. Each of the progressively smaller tiers is decorated with exquisitely delicate blues and golds and shows a tiny figure looking through an open window, shaded by green and silver canopies. At the time of its creation—between 1800 and 1815—trade was booming between Europe and China, and mass production of souvenirs for European buyers was at a peak. This pagoda was specially made to an individual order, rather than put together on an assembly line, and is based on the 15th-century pagoda of Nanking, (destroyed in 1853).

Tippoo's Tiger

One of the V&A's best-known objects is kept in the Nehru Gallery of Indian Art (Room 48). The 18th-century model of a tiger savaging a man, complete with mechanically produced growls and screams, was made for Tipu Sultan, son of Haidar Ali Khan, ruler of the state of Mysore. Known as the Tiger of Mysore, Tipu had the tiger emblem worked into many of his surroundings and possessions, but this example, with its sound-effects organ built into the brightly coloured tiger's side, is unique. It may represent the actual fate of the son of General Sir Hector Munro in Bengal. Tipu suffered defeat at the hands of the British at Seringapatam in 1799, and his tiger was brought back as booty to be put on show in the East India Company Museum, later to be transferred to the Victoria & Albert.

BRITISH GALLERIES

Writing Box

Henry VIII owned this portable stationery set, made in 1525 and elaborately decorated. Inside the lid of the box, the gilded leather lining shows the coat of arms of the king and Catherine of Aragon, cherubs and copies of a German woodcut of Venus and Mars; other parts of the box are illustrated with miniature profiles and intricate motifs and designs. Drawers and compartments are built into the design, which incorporates a Latin inscription wishing Henry triumph over his adversaries.

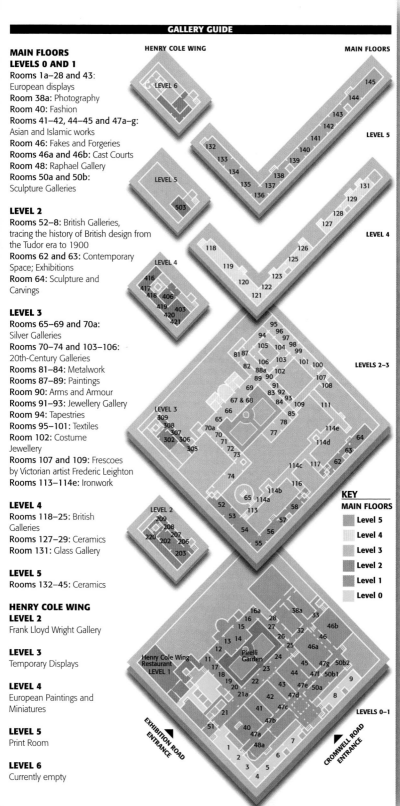

MAIN FLOORS
LEVELS 0 AND 1

Rooms 1a–28 and 43:
European displays
Room 38a: Photography
Room 40: Fashion
Rooms 41–42, 44–45 and 47a–g:
Asian and Islamic works
Room 46: Fakes and Forgeries
Rooms 46a and 46b: Cast Courts
Room 48: Raphael Gallery
Rooms 50a and 50b:
Sculpture Galleries

LEVEL 2

Rooms 52–8: British Galleries,
tracing the history of British design from
the Tudor era to 1900
Rooms 62 and 63: Contemporary
Space; Exhibitions
Room 64: Sculpture and
Carvings

LEVEL 3

Rooms 65–69 and 70a:
Silver Galleries
Rooms 70–74 and 103–106:
20th-Century Galleries
Rooms 81–84: Metalwork
Rooms 87–89: Paintings
Room 90: Arms and Armour
Rooms 91–93: Jewellery Gallery
Room 94: Tapestries
Rooms 95–101: Textiles
Room 102: Costume
Jewellery
Rooms 107 and 109: Frescoes
by Victorian artist Frederic Leighton
Rooms 113–114e: Ironwork

LEVEL 4

Rooms 118–25: British
Galleries
Rooms 127–29: Ceramics
Room 131: Glass Gallery

LEVEL 5

Rooms 132–45: Ceramics

HENRY COLE WING
LEVEL 2
Frank Lloyd Wright Gallery

LEVEL 3
Temporary Displays

LEVEL 4
European Paintings and
Miniatures

LEVEL 5
Print Room

LEVEL 6
Currently empty

HENRY COLE WING

MAIN FLOORS

LEVEL 6

LEVEL 5

LEVEL 5

LEVEL 4

LEVEL 5

LEVEL 4

LEVEL 4

LEVELS 2–3

LEVEL 3

LEVEL 2

KEY
MAIN FLOORS
Level 5
Level 4
Level 3
Level 2
Level 1
Level 0

Henry Cole Wing
Restaurant
LEVEL 1

Pirelli
Garden

LEVELS 0–1

EXHIBITION ROAD ENTRANCE

CROMWELL ROAD ENTRANCE

THE SIGHTS

VICTORIA & ALBERT MUSEUM 147

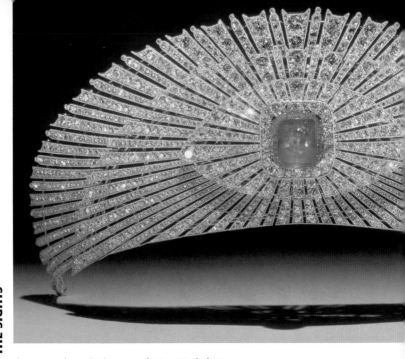

The museum has a dazzling collection of jewellery, including this Cartier tiara (above) The coat (below) worn by James II at his wedding in 1673

The Great Bed of Ware

Celebrated in literature and lore, the Great Bed of Ware was made between 1590 and 1600 for an inn in Ware, Hertfordshire, as a kind of marketing ploy, enticing travellers with its unusually large dimensions and ornamental carving—which would originally have been picked out in vivid colours. To modern eyes, the bed itself may not seem remarkably large, but the frame is certainly massive. It includes panels made by German immigrant craftsmen and Dutch-influenced marquetry. The bed had fulfilled its promotional function by 1601, when it warranted a mention in Shakespeare's play *Twelfth Night.*

Strawberry Thief by William Morris (1834–96)

In reaction against the dehumanizing processes of 19th-century mass industry, William Morris and his contemporaries in the Arts and Crafts movement sought to revive the craftsmanship of the Middle Ages. *Strawberry Thief,* a repeated design of thrushes stealing fruit among leaves and flowers used on fabric and wallpaper, is an example of Morris's attempt to bring individualism and beauty into middle-class homes. He produced it using an ancient indigo-discharge printing technique; for the first time, with this pattern, he used red and yellow along with blue and white, a long and difficult process that made this one of his firm's costliest cottons. Despite the high price, this design was to be one of the most popular and successful produced by Morris & Company.

THE DRESS COLLECTION
Sack-Back Gown

A finely worked satin gown made in France in the 1770s illustrates the way fashion developed in high society, incorporating casual dress (which sack-back gowns originally were) and combining old and new. The bodice, with its front fastening, is the height of contemporary style, while the square, wide 'saddle-bag' hoops and elbow-length, ruffled sleeves harked back 20 years or so. Delicate blue padded satin and chenille lace are used to decorate the ivory-coloured gown and petticoat, along with embroidered floral sprigs and gathered ribbon.

A replica of Trajan's Column in Rome dominates the Italian Cast Court (above)
Robert Adam designed the ceiling taken from the London home of David Garrick (left)

PHOTOGRAPHY AT THE V&A

Only four years after the opening of the V&A, when photography was still in its infancy and regarded as strictly inferior to other art media, the museum began a collection of photographic work. One of its first exhibitions was a display of life studies by Clementina, Lady Hawarden (1822–65), who took many photographs of her daughters in their home at South Kensington in London. Her experiments with light, shade and reflection give added interest to these early examples of photography as an art form.

The V&A has now amassed more than 300,000 works in its photographic collection, which has its own exhibition space in the Canon Photography Gallery, opened in 1998.

Bar Suit, Christian Dior (1905–57)

Dior's New Look designs hit the fashion shows in 1947 and created an immediate sensation among women accustomed to the pared-down, austere styles of wartime Europe. The bar suit has a cream silk jacket nipped in to show off a 46cm (18in) waist; a full black wool crêpe skirt flares out beneath it, with a hem measuring 7.3m (24ft) in circumference. Topping the ensemble is a low-brimmed hat, adding the finishing touch to an overall image of elegant chic.

BACKGROUND

The V&A was founded in 1852 with profits from the Great Exhibition of 1851. Its aim was to give the working classes access to great art and to inspire British manufacturers and designers. Originally housed in Marlborough House, near Buckingham Palace, it was moved to the present site in 1857 as the South Kensington Museum. It was given its current name in 1899, when Queen Victoria laid the foundation stone of a new building that was later opened in 1909.

WALLACE COLLECTION

One of London's best collections of art, and one of the least known.

The Great Gallery, hung with 17th- and 18th-century paintings

➕ 67 G4 • Hertford House, Manchester Square W1U 3BN
☎ 020 7563 9500 🕐 Mon–Sat 10–5, Sun noon–5 💷 Free
Ⓜ Bond Street, Baker Street 🚌 2, 10, 13, 74, 82 🎧 Free guided tours weekdays 1pm, also Wed, Sat 11.30am, Sun 3pm 🎧 £7, in English only 🍴 Café Bagatelle during the museum's opening hours 🎁 Gifts and books, many exclusive to the collection

RATINGS	
Good for kids	◐
Historic interest	●●◐
Specialist shopping	●●◐

www.wallace-collection.org.uk
Chatty site with illustrations of collection, news about restoration etc, plus information on history, daily events and exhibitions.

Four generations of the Hertford family amassed this world-class collection of art, on show in Hertford House, a beautiful 18th-century mansion. It was started when the 4th Marquess of Hertford, living as a recluse in Paris with his illegitimate son, Richard Wallace, during the French Revolution, bought French 18th-century paintings, porcelain and furniture to add to his inheritance of Sèvres porcelain and paintings by Canaletto and Gainsborough. Richard inherited the collection in 1870 and brought it to England, escaping the unstable political situation in France. He in turn added many fine examples of Renaissance ceramics, bronzes, armour and jewellery, and his widow left the collection to the nation in 1897, on condition that it remained intact and was never removed from central London.

The rooms are packed with all sorts of beautiful objects, from paintings, furnishings and fittings originally made for the palaces of Fontainebleau and Versailles to 18th-century saucepans.

About 70 paintings from the 17th and 18th centuries hang in the Great Gallery. Most famously, these include *The Laughing Cavalier* by Frans Hals (1624), a portrait of an unknown young man (although he is neither a cavalier nor laughing), and a touching portrait by Rembrandt of his son Titus (c1657).

There's also a superb display of European arms and armour, much of it made by specialist metal-workers and embellished with fine inlay decoration. Seek out the late 15th-century set of armour for a man and his horse, made in Germany.

Don't miss the marvellous portrait of King George IV by Sir Thomas Lawrence (1769–1830) in the Great Gallery.

Dolphins on the lampposts along the Victoria Embankment

VICTORIA EMBANKMENT

➕ 68 K5 🕐 Open access 💷 Free
Ⓜ Embankment, Charing Cross
🚌 9, 11, 15, 24, 88
Tourist Information Office
Britain Visitor Centre, 1 Lower Regent Street, Piccadilly Circus SW1Y 4XT (no telephone)

The Victoria Embankment, built in the late 1860s to 1870s, was a massive engineering project, reclaiming land from the north bank of the River Thames. In addition to creating a buffer against flooding, it relieved congestion on the busy Strand; improved the sewage system (see page 36); and provided space to extend the Underground network—you can still hear trains clattering underneath the gardens here. A more immediately visible benefit was the addition of well-groomed lawns and flowerbeds, which still provide relief from the city.

The wide promenade across Victoria Embankment road was part of the original design, but is less attractive than it was because of the constant traffic. This is where you'll find Cleopatra's Needle (see page 86), the city's oldest monument.

WELLINGTON ARCH

➕ 67 G6• Hyde Park Corner W1J 7JZ
☎ 020 7973 2726 🕐 Wed–Sun 10–5.30, Apr–Sep; Wed–Sun 10–5, Oct; 10–4, Nov–Mar 💷 EH. Adult £2.50, child (5–16) £1.50, under 5s free
Ⓜ Hyde Park Corner 🚌 2, 8, 9, 10, 14, 16, 19
www.english-heritage.org.uk

England's answer to the Arc de Triomphe in Paris is a neoclassical arch erected in 1826 to celebrate the Duke of Wellington's victories in the Napoleonic Wars. A huge equestrian statue of the Duke was added 20 years later. Originally the arch served as the northern

THE SIGHTS

Decimus Burton designed the Wellington Arch at the age of 28

The canopy above the High Altar in Westminster Cathedral

A daily guard is mounted outside Banqueting House

gate into the grounds of Buckingham Palace (see page 79), but it was moved to its present position at the southeast corner of Hyde Park, opposite Apsley House (see page 76), as part of a new 19th-century city planning scheme.

The bronze group quadriga (horse-drawn chariot), by Adrian Jones, was placed on top of the arch just before the start of World War I. A boy pulls at the reins of the four horses while an enormous figure of the Angel of Peace descends from heaven.

At one time the rooms inside the arch housed a police station; now there's a permanent exhibition on the statues and memorials of London, and you can enjoy the views from the platform beneath the sculpture.

WESTMINSTER ABBEY
(see pages 152–153)

WESTMINSTER CATHEDRAL

67 H7 • Victoria Street SW1P 1QW 020 7798 9055 Mon–Fri 7–7, Sat 8–7, Sun 7am–7.45pm; campanile daily 9–5, Apr–Nov; Thu–Sun 9–5, Dec–Mar Free; lift to campanile adult £2, under 18s £1, family £5 Victoria 11, 24, 211 **www.**westminstercathedral.org.uk

Britain's premier Roman Catholic church is a striking Westminster landmark with its 83m (273ft) campanile (bell-tower) and striped patterning of red brick and white Portland stone. Designed in Byzantine style by Victorian architect John Francis Bentley (1839–1902), it echoes the Basilica of St. Mark in Venice. Bentley's brief was that the church should have an extra wide nave that could accommodate large congregations, and that it should bear no resemblance to the nearby Protestant Westminster Abbey.

The foundation stone was laid in 1895 and the fabric of the building was completed eight years later, but funds for the interior decoration ran out, leaving the upper walls in bare brick—a striking contrast to the lavish marble and coloured mosaics below. Sculptor Eric Gill (1882–1940) carved the 14 Stations of the Cross on the nave pillars. The cross on top of the campanile is one of the repositories of a relic of the True Cross.

Don't miss going to the top of the campanile (there's a lift) for views of Big Ben, Buckingham Palace and Nelson's Column.

WHITECHAPEL ART GALLERY

69 P4 • 80–82 Whitechapel High Street E1 7QX Recorded info: 020 7522 7878, other enquiries: 020 7522 7888 During exhibitions Tue–Sun 11–6, Thu 11–9 Free except one paying show per year; Tue free all year Aldgate East 15, 25, 67, 253 Liverpool Street **www.**whitechapel.org

Founded in 1901 to 'bring great art to the people of the East End of London', the gallery shows a changing programme of contemporary and 20th-century art, featuring new and acknowledged artists in solo shows, group exhibitions and commissions. Media range from painting and sculpture to video and photography.

The Arts and Crafts building, designed by Charles Harrison Townsend in 1901, provides over 2,230sq m (24,000sq ft) of gallery space, and was the first purpose-built British gallery to host changing exhibitions.

WHITEHALL

68 J5 Open access Free Charing Cross, Westminster 11, 12, 24, 88, 159
Tourist Information Office
Britain Visitor Centre, 1 Lower Regent Street, Piccadilly Circus SW1Y 4XT (no telephone)

Whitehall is the broad avenue connecting Trafalgar Square (see page 136) with Parliament Square—and the heart of the British government—to the south. Heading south, the first building on the right, the Admiralty, is fronted by Robert Adam's stone screen (1759), adorned with two sea horses. The country's naval affairs were run from this building when the British fleet was considered to be the most powerful in the world.

Next comes Horse Guards, where two members of the Household Cavalry mount guard on horseback daily between 10 and 4—a tradition that persists even though all that remains of the former royal palace is the Banqueting House (see page 77), opposite. The soldiers keep to their stations without moving or making eye contact with passersby, despite visitors trying to distract them!

Beyond Horse Guards is the gated entrance to Downing Street. This has been the official residence of the Prime Minister (No. 10) since 1731 when Sir Robert Walpole was in office. No. 11 is the home of the Chancellor of the Exchequer.

Farther along Whitehall, directly outside the Foreign and Commonwealth Office, Sir George Gilbert Scott's Italianate building of 1873, is the Portland-stone Cenotaph, designed by Sir Edwin Lutyens and unveiled in 1920 to commemorate the victims of World War I. This provides the focus of the Remembrance Day celebrations held annually on the Sunday nearest 11 November since 1918 (see page 224).

To reach the Cabinet War Rooms (see page 86), turn right down King Charles Street.

Westminster Abbey

●

**London's largest surviving medieval church.
The setting for all royal coronations since 1066.
A mausoleum of famous historical figures, commemorating 3,300 people in all.**

SEEING WESTMINSTER ABBEY

The abbey (the Collegiate Church of St. Peter in Westminster) forms the south side of Parliament Square. You enter by the north transept, through one of three great doorways beneath the large rose window, whose pattern is repeated in the floor tiles of the chapter house. Inside, turn left to take a one-way, clockwise tour of the church and cloisters, passing a succession of chapels with a bewildering throng of tombs and monuments, before leaving by the west door.

HIGHLIGHTS

LADY CHAPEL

North of the sanctuary is the Lady Chapel, where you can view the white-marble effigy of Elizabeth I (died 1603), who shares a tomb with her half sister, Mary I (died 1558). From the aisle you enter the main part of the chapel, with its exquisite fan-vaulted ceiling. It makes an impressive setting for the royal tombs arranged around the altar and aisles. Among the finest of these is the tomb of Henry VII, in front of the altar, and of his mother, Lady Margaret Beaufort, near the south aisle altar. They died in the same year (1509), and their tombs are the work of the Florentine sculptor Pietro Torrigiano (1472–1528), who, as a boy, was often involved in fights with Michelangelo. Note the carvings on the stall misericords (1512): Subjects include mermaids, monsters and a wife beating her husband.

The towers of the west front were added in the 18th century

RATINGS	
Good for kids	●
Historic interest	● ● ● ● ●
Value for money	● ● ● ●

TIPS

● Attend a service and hear the choirboys, accompanied by the abbey organ on which composer Henry Purcell (1659–95) once played.

● Note that the cloisters are free, entered through Dean's Yard.

POETS' CORNER

The south transept, also known as Poets' Corner, is where, since the 16th century, great poets, authors, artists and actors have been honoured with memorials (not all are buried here). Here are the remains of poet Geoffrey Chaucer (c1345–1400), who lived in the abbey precincts while a royal clerk of the works (or buildings inspector). William Shakespeare's monument is here too, though his statue and assumed likeness dates from 1740, over a century after his death. Among the best monuments are the busts of 17th-century poets John Dryden, Ben Jonson and John Milton, and poet and artist William Blake (1757–1827)—the last sculpted in bronze by Sir Jacob Epstein in 1957.

THE QUIRE AND SANCTUARY

This is the ceremonial heart of the church, where services and royal coronations take place. In front of the high altar is the Cosmati Pavement, a mosaic made of glass and precious stones and laid by Italian craftsmen in 1268.

CHAPTER HOUSE, PYX CHAMBER AND ABBEY MUSEUM

A door in the south quire aisle leads to the cloister, with its flowing tracery and superb views of the flying buttresses supporting the nave. The chapter house is an octagonal building of 1253, whose floor is still covered in its

Shakespeare's monument in Poets' Corner

WILLIAM SHAKESPEARE 1564 - 1616
BURIED AT STRATFORD-ON-AVON

Sir Winston Churchill's tomb (inset far left)
Superb vaulting (main picture) above the nave
Henry VII's (or Lady) Chapel (below)

original tiles. The Norman undercroft, which survives from Edward the Confessor's original church (see page 27), houses the abbey museum, where you can see macabre wax effigies, including those of Queen Elizabeth I, Charles II and Lord Nelson, made using their death masks and real clothes. Some effigies were made to lie in state in place of the body.

The Pyx Chamber, also part of the original abbey, contains the building's oldest altar, dated at around 1240. It's now home to original pyxes (money chests) and the abbey's church plate.

THE NAVE

Here you can enjoy the majestic nave roof, 32m (105ft) high. The complex patterning carries the eye eastwards; only by looking up can you appreciate the enormous length of the building, since at ground level the view is blocked by the 19th-century choir screen, where Sir Isaac Newton and other scientists are remembered. The Tomb of the Unknown Soldier (see page 39) and St. George's Chapel are near the west door. Just outside the chapel is a portrait of Richard II (1377–99)—the oldest known true portrait of an English monarch.

BACKGROUND

The church that gave its name to Westminster was standing here by the 8th century, but Edward the Confessor began the present building around 1050. Having died a week after its consecration, on 6 January 1066, he was the first monarch to be buried here. Almost a year later, William the Conqueror was crowned here, confirming the royal status of the church, which has seen the coronation of every subsequent English monarch with the exception of Edward V and Edward VIII.

Edward the Confessor was later canonized, and Henry III embarked on large-scale rebuilding in 1245 to make a shrine fit for the veneration of the sainted king. Today's church, greatly influenced by the French Gothic cathedrals of Amiens and Reims, was the result. In 1503 the Lady Chapel at the east end was replaced by the Henry VII Chapel, architectural high point of the church. The west front was not completed until 1745, when the two towers were built to Nicholas Hawksmoor's design.

BASICS

✚ 68 J6 • Parliament Square SW1P 3PA ☎ 020 7222 5152 🕐 Mon–Fri 9.30–4.45 (last admission 3.45), Wed also 6–7pm, Sat 9.30–2.45 (last admission 1.45). Sun worship only. Chapter House daily 9.30–5, Mar–Sep; daily 10–5, Oct; daily 10–4, Nov–Mar. Abbey museum daily 10.30–4. Cloisters daily 8–6 subject to availability, closed during special events. College Garden Tue–Thu 10–6, Apr–Sep; Tue–Thu 10–4, Oct–Mar. Free lunchtime band concerts Thu 12.30–2pm, Jul–Aug 💷 Adult £6, child (12–16) £4, under 11s (max of 2 children per paying adult) free, family £12. Services free. Museum £1 (free with abbey church ticket). Cloisters, college garden free, donations welcome for upkeep of garden 🚇 St. James's Park, Westminster 🚌 11, 12, 24, 159, 211 🎧 90-min tours, £3 per person. For bookings and further details ☎ 020 7222 7110. Audioguides £2 📖 £3, in English, French, German, Spanish, Italian, Russian, Japanese, £8, in English only 🛒 Stall in north cloister and outside west towers; hot and cold drinks, light snacks, sandwiches 🏪 Outside west door exit; souvenirs, postcards, gifts, history, religious books 📖

www.westminster-abbey.org
Excellent site with lots of good background information.

Take to the water on the boating lake in Battersea Park

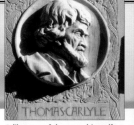
A likeness of the man himself on this plaque on Carlyle's House

Gate detail of the god Apollo, at the Chelsea Physic Garden

FARTHER AFIELD

The sights listed in the following pages are outside central London, but all can be reached easily by public transport within an hour or so. They are located on pages 8–9.

THE SIGHTS

BATTERSEA PARK

3 miles (5km) SW of Trafalgar Square
✉ Battersea Park SW11 4NJ ☎ 020 8871 7534 🕐 Open 8am–dusk 🎫 Free 🚇 Sloane Square, then bus 🚌 East of park (Queenstown Road) 137; west of park (Battersea Bridge Road) 19, 49; south of park (Battersea Park Road) 344 🚢 Cadogan Pier 🚉 Battersea Park, Queenstown Road ♿

Tourist Information Office
Britain Visitor Centre, 1 Lower Regent Street, Piccadilly Circus SW1Y 4XT (no telephone)
www.wandsworth.gov.uk

Officially opened in 1858 by Queen Victoria, this riverside park was created on marshy common land known as Battersea Fields, partly to rid it of a reputation for illegal racing, drinking and gambling.

It has since become one of London's most popular parks, with three million visitors a year. Attractions include the original Victorian carriage drives, sports facilities, an art gallery, two playgrounds, a boating lake, sculptures by Henry Moore and Barbara Hepworth and a Japanese Peace Pagoda, given to London in 1985 by the Buddhist Order as a symbol of peace. Cycling has been a popular pastime here since 1896.

A £10.3 million revamp is underway to re-emphasize the Victorian layout, construct a riverside promenade to original designs and restore the 1951 Festival Gardens area.
Don't miss the contemporary art exhibition in the Pump House art gallery (*free*).

CARLYLE'S HOUSE

3 miles (5km) SW of Trafalgar Square
✉ 24 Cheyne Row SW3 5HL ☎ 020 7352 7087 🕐 Wed–Fri 2–5, Sat, Sun 11–5, Apr–Oct 🎫 NT. Adult £3.70, child (5–16) £1.80, under 5s free 🚇 Sloane Square, South Kensington 🚌 11, 19, 22 🚢 Cadogan Pier
www.nationaltrust.org.uk

Scottish historian and essayist Thomas Carlyle (1795–1881) lived in this Queen Anne house off the Chelsea Embankment from 1834 until his death. Inside you'll find Victorian furniture, pictures, portraits and books as they were during Carlyle's lifetime. He wrote many of his scholarly and historical works in the top-floor garret study, built specially for him in 1853.

Other literary figures of the day met at the house, including novelist Charles Dickens and poet Robert Browning.

CHELSEA PHYSIC GARDEN

3 miles (5km) SW of Trafalgar Square
✉ 66 Royal Hospital Road SW3 4HS ☎ 020 7352 5646
🕐 Wed noon–5, Sun 2–6, early Apr–late Oct. Also for snowdrops: first and second Sun in Feb, 11–3; Chelsea Flower Show: Mon–Fri noon–5, mid-May; Chelsea Festival: Mon–Fri noon–5, mid-Jun 🎫 Adult £5, child (5–15) £3, under 5s free 🚇 Sloane Square 🚌 11, 19, 22, 211, 239 🅿 ♿
www.chelseaphysicgarden.co.uk

Founded in 1673 by the Society of Apothecaries of London to study plants for medicinal purposes, this is Britain's second-oldest botanical garden after Oxford's, which predates it by 52 years. It is still used for medical and botanical research.

The walled plot (2ha/3.5 acres) holds around 5,000 species and many rare trees. A rock garden was created in 1773 with basaltic lava brought back from Iceland by English botanist Sir Joseph Banks (1743–1820), who accompanied Captain James Cook on his 1768 expedition around the world in *Endeavour*.

Flowering shrubs and rare peonies grow in a wilder area of the garden, and other displays include culinary herbs, edible flowers, poisonous plants and those that are used to make dyes and fibres.
Don't miss the largest fruiting olive tree growing outdoors in Britain.

CHISWICK HOUSE

6 miles (10km) W of Tralfagar Square
✉ Burlington Lane W4 2RP ☎ 020 8995 0508 🕐 Sun–Fri 10–6, Sat 10–2, Apr–Sep; Sun–Fri 10–5, Sat 10–2, Oct; Wed–Fri, Sun 10–4, Sat 10–2, Nov–Mar. Closed 1–16 Jan 🎫 EH. Adult £3.50, child (6–18) £3, under 6s free 🚇 Turnham Green 🚌 27, 190, 391 🚉 Turnham Green 🚢 Daily summer, weekends winter 🈺
www.english-heritage.org.uk

This superb example of Palladian architecture is the work of Richard Boyle, 3rd Earl of Burlington (1694–1753), who made it his mission to promote the style in Britain. The perfectly symmetrical exterior, with its octagonal central dome and classical portico with six

The Classical façade and dome of 18th-century Chiswick House

Dulwich Picture Gallery was England's first public art gallery

Part of the Meissen collection on display in Fenton House

Corinthian columns, gives no clue to the sumptuously decorated rooms inside. The classical Italianate gardens were laid out to complement the architecture.

Don't miss the gilding in the Blue Velvet Room or the domed saloon, lit from the drum windows, which were derived from the Roman baths of Diocletian.

DULWICH PICTURE GALLERY

7 miles (11km) SE of Trafalgar Square ✉ Gallery Road, Dulwich Village SE21 7AD ☎ 020 8693 5254 🕐 10–5 Tue–Fri, 11–5 Sat and Sun. Free tours Sat–Sun 3pm (normal admission charge) 💳 Adult £4, under 16s £3. May be additional charge for temporary exhibitions 🚌 P4 from opposite Brixton tube or Lewisham bus station; 3 to West Dulwich station; 37 to North Dulwich station 🚉 West Dulwich, North Dulwich 🅿 ♿ www.dulwichpicturegallery.org.uk

More than 300 masterpieces make up this fine collection, most painted in the 17th and 18th centuries and including works such as Van Dyck's *Madonna and Child*, Poussin's *Return of the Holy Family from Egypt* and Rembrandt's portrait of Jacob III de Gheyn, stolen several times from the gallery but recovered on each occasion. The

Poussin's Rinaldo and Armeida *in the Dulwich Picture Gallery*

neoclassical building, designed by Sir John Soane in 1811, was England's first purpose-built art gallery. A striking addition by Rick Mather, opened in 2000, provides more exhibition space, an education centre for children and adults, and a café overlooking the large garden.

The gallery also serves as a mausoleum: At the rear of the building are the tombs of Noel Desenfans, who was responsible for putting the collection together in the 1790s, and Sir Francis Bourgeois, who bequeathed it to Dulwich College in 1811.

ELTHAM PALACE

12 miles (19km) SE of Trafalgar Square ✉ Off Court Road, Eltham SE9 5QE ☎ 020 8294 2548 🕐 Wed–Fri, Sun 10–6, Apr–Sep; Wed–Fri, Sun 10–5, Oct; Wed–Fri, Sun 10–4, Nov–Mar. Palace and grounds closed 23 Dec–31 Jan 💳 EH. House and gardens: adult £6.50, child (5–16) £3.50, under 5s free; gardens only: adult £3.60, child £1.80 🚌 132, 161, 162, 233, 286, 314 to Eltham station 🚉 Eltham 🅿 ♿ www.english-heritage.org.uk

Moated parkland surrounds the remains of one of England's largest but least known royal medieval palaces and the flamboyant house built next door by film director Stephen Courtauld in the 1930s and furnished in art deco style. Inside it's fitted out with the modern conveniences of the day, including an electrically operated central vacuum cleaner, loudspeakers relaying jazz to the ground floor, and an internal phone system. The grounds include a rose garden and colour-themed planting. **Don't miss** Virginia Courtauld's exotic bathroom lined with onyx and gold mosaic and featuring a bust of Psyche, and the centrally heated cage once occupied by the Courtaulds' pet lemur.

FENTON HOUSE

5 miles (8km) NW of Trafalgar Square ✉ Windmill Hill NW3 6RT (Entrance on Hampstead Grove) ☎ 020 7435 3471, general information 01494 755563 🕐 Sat, Sun 2–5, Mar; Sat, Sun 11–5 and Wed–Fri 2–5, Apr–Oct 💳 NT. Adult £4.60, child (5–16) £2.30, under 5s free, family £11.50 🚉 Hampstead 🚌 46, 268 🚉 Hampstead Heath www.nationaltrust.org.uk

This redbrick house built in 1695 is one of the best of its kind surviving in London. Period furnishings are complemented by a fine collection of ceramics, Georgian furniture and 17th-century needlework. The Benton Fletcher Collection of keyboard instruments from the 17th and 18th centuries is regularly put to use for concerts given in the house. Roses grow in the charming walled garden, and there's an orchard and vegetable garden as well.

FREUD'S HOUSE AND MUSEUM

5 miles (8km) NW of Trafalgar Square ✉ 20 Maresfield Gardens NW3 5SX ☎ 020 7435 2002/7435 5167 🕐 Wed–Sun 12–5 💳 Adult £5, under 12s free 🚉 Finchley Road 🚌 13, 82, 113 🚉 Finchley Road and Frognal, Hampstead Heath ♿ www.freud.org.uk

Sigmund Freud (1856–1939), Austrian neurologist and founder of psychoanalysis, lived at 20 Maresfield Gardens in south Hampstead from 1938 (when he escaped from Nazi-occupied Vienna). His youngest daughter, Anna, herself a psychoanalyst, continued to live there until her death in 1982. The house is now a museum devoted to Freud's life and work and contains his famous couch, along with his books, letters, diaries and other personal mementoes.

THE SIGHTS

Greenwich

**Home to some of London's finest buildings, set against a backdrop of beautiful parkland, and the largest maritime museum in the world.
A lively riverside town with a weekly market, specialist shops and good places to eat.**

Meridian line information plaque

The best way to reach Greenwich is by river, as the view from the riverside is one of the finest in London. Most people come here to admire the assembly of historic buildings—the former Royal Naval College, the National Maritime Museum in the Queen's House and the Old Royal Observatory, in Greenwich Park. It's also worth browsing the craft stalls at the covered weekend market and sampling some of the many good pubs and restaurants.

An off-beat place worth visiting is the Fan Museum at 12 Croom's Hill (*Tue–Sat 11–5, Sun 12–5*), dedicated to the ancient art of fan-making. There are some 4,000 fans in the collection, dating from the 11th century onwards, on show in changing, themed exhibitions and in permanent displays.

The west wing of the Old Royal Naval College

VERDICT	
Good for kids	● ● ● ●
Historic interest	● ● ● ●
Specialist shopping	● ●
Value for money	● ● ●

BASICS

7 miles (11km) SE of Trafalgar Square on the south bank, downstream from London Bridge

✉ *Cutty Sark*: King William Walk SE10 9HT. Old Royal Naval College: entrance from King William Walk. National Maritime Museum: Greenwich Park, SE10 9NF. Ranger's House: Chesterfield Walk, Blackheath, SE10 8QX ☎ *Cutty Sark*: 020 8858 3445. Old Royal Naval College: 020 8269 4747. National Maritime Museum: 020 8858 4422, recorded information 020 8312 6565. Ranger's House: 020 8853 0035

🕐 *Cutty Sark*: daily 10–5. Old Royal Naval College: daily 10–5, grounds 8–6. National Maritime Museum: daily 10–5, Sep–Jun; 10–6, Jul–Aug. Ranger's House: Wed–Sun 10–6, mid-Mar–Sep; 10–5, Oct; 10–4 Nov–late Dec; closed Jan–early Mar 💷 *Cutty Sark*: adult £3.95, child (5–16) £2.95, under 5s free, family £9.80. Old Royal Naval College: free; guided tours £5. National Maritime Museum: free, charge for special exhibitions. Ranger's House: EH. Adult £4.50, child (5–15) £2.50, under 5s free

🚉 Greenwich 🚌 188 ⛴ River boat from Westminster Millennium Pier (1hr 10 min) 🚈 DLR to Island Gardens,
(continued on page 157)

HIGHLIGHTS

CUTTY SARK

This sleek tea clipper anchored by Greenwich Pier was built in 1869 to carry cargoes between Britain and the Orient. In 1871 she broke the world record for sailing between London and China, completing the trip in only 107 days. You can climb aboard to get some idea of the cramped living conditions endured by the 28-man crew, and to see an exhibition of ships' figureheads below deck.

Nearby is *Gipsy Moth IV*, the tiny yacht in which Sir Francis Chichester (1901–72) made the first single-handed circumnavigation of the globe in 1967 (you cannot baord the boat).

OLD ROYAL NAVAL COLLEGE

This monumental group of buildings was laid out by Sir Christopher Wren in 1664 as a hospital for infirm and aged seamen. After the hospital closed in 1869, the complex was taken over by the Royal Naval College, training officers from all over the world, and it's now used by the University of Greenwich and the Trinity College of Music.

Two areas are open to the public: the Painted Hall and the chapel. The Painted Hall, created by Sir James Thornhill in 1707–17, has some of the finest baroque paintings anywhere in England, showing joint monarchs William (1650–1702) and Mary (1662–94) surrounded by allegorical figures symbolizing the triumph of virtue over vice. The chapel (1718–25), restored by James Stuart after a fire in 1779, is in neo-Grecian style. The vast altar painting, *St. Paul Shaking Off the Viper*, is by American artist Benjamin West (1738–1820).

NATIONAL MARITIME MUSEUM

A suite of stunning new galleries centred on the glass-roofed Neptune Court has given the museum more space to tell the story of Britain's maritime history from the failed 16th-century invasion of the Spanish Armada to the 19th century, focusing on exploration, trade and

The Ranger's House has a new role as a home for art treasures

empire and exploring themes such as luxury liners and naval heroes. Among the huge collection of ships (including hundreds of models), paintings, navigational instruments and the relics of sailors and explorers, seek out the luxurious state barge made for Frederick, Prince of Wales, in 1732, and the jacket Nelson was wearing when he was fatally wounded at the Battle of Trafalgar in 1805.

The museum's central building, the Queen's House, was England's first example of the neoclassical Palladian style, brought from Italy by Inigo Jones (1573–1652). Begun in 1616 as a palace for James I's wife, Anne of Denmark, it was not completed until 1635 in the reign of Charles I for his queen, Henrietta Maria. Inside, the best feature is the Tulip Stair, named after the pattern on its balustrade.

Also in the care of the National Maritime Museum is the Old Royal Observatory, founded by Charles II in 1675 to tackle the problem of finding longitude at sea. The original building, Flamsteed House, was designed by Wren for John Flamsteed, the first Astronomer Royal. Early telescopes and time-measuring instruments are on display, and there's a modern astronomy gallery. The large red ball on top of one of the building's two turrets still drops down its mast at 1pm each day, enabling Thames navigators to set their chronometers.

The large Gate Clock measures Greenwich Mean Time, the standard by which time is set all round the world. In the courtyard you can straddle the eastern and western hemispheres by standing astride the simple brass strip that marks the Greenwich Meridian.

RANGER'S HOUSE

At the southern end of Greenwich Park is the 17th-century Ranger's House, now a showcase for the Wernher Collection, formerly at Luton Hoo in Bedfordshire, which belonged to diamond and gold merchant Sir Julius Wernher. There are more than 700 works of art including paintings, tapestries, furniture, ceramics, ivories and jewels from the 16th and 17th centuries.

Get a taste of 19th-century seafaring life on the Cutty Sark

then walk through the tunnel 🖼 Time and Tide shop, Level 1 of National Maritime Museum 🍴 Regatta Café and Upper Deck Coffee Bar, Level 2 of National Maritime Museum 🚻

www.cuttysark.org.uk
www.greenwichfoundation.org.uk
www.nmm.ac.uk
www.english-heritage.org.uk

TIP
● Buy a computer printout recording the precise time you stand astride the meridian line (0° longitude).

The 24-hour Gate Clock at the Royal Observatory shows Greenwich Mean Time

Seventeenth-century style in the Great Hall at Ham House

Take a tour of Victorian funerary statues in Highgate Cemetery

The garden at Hogarth's House, a summer retreat for the artist

THE SIGHTS

HAM HOUSE

11 miles (18km) SW of Trafalgar Square

✉ Ham Street, Richmond-upon-Thames, Surrey TW10 7RS ☎ 0208 940 1950 ◷ Sat–Wed 1–5, Apr–Oct; gardens daily 11–6 or dusk if earlier ✦ NT. Adult £7, child (5–16) £3.50, under 5s free, family £17.50. Garden only: adult £3, child £1.50, family £7.50 ⬢ Richmond, then bus 371 or taxi ⬛ 65 Ealing Broadway–Kingston, 371 Richmond–Kingston ⬛ Richmond Landing Stage ⬛ Richmond ⬛ ⬛ ⬛ www.nationaltrust.org.uk

Ham House is one of the most beautiful and well-preserved Stuart period houses in Britain. Built in 1610, it was the home of the Tollemache family, who were deeply involved in the Civil War and Restoration court politics. Their story is told throughout the house, which is filled with rare furniture, paintings and textiles. It also has wonderful formal gardens and the occasional ghost.

HAMPSTEAD HEATH

5 miles (8km) NW of Trafalgar Square

✉ Hampstead Heath Information Centre, Parliament Hill Lido ☎ 020 7482 7073 ◷ Open access ✦ Free ⬢ Hampstead ⬛ 24, 46, 168, C11, C12 ⬛ Hampstead Heath www.cityoflondon.gov.uk/openspaces

Hampstead Heath is a wonderfully diverse public open space of 320ha (790 acres), with areas of ancient woodlands, bogs, hedgerows and natural grassland. Londoners come to walk, jog, ride horses, enjoy picnics, fly kites, play petanque and swim in the three ponds. Just east of the ponds is Parliament Hill, offering views over London. Local legend claims that Queen Boadicea (Boudica), who led her Iceni people against the Roman occupiers (see page 27), lies buried here.

At the northern end of the heath is Kenwood House *(Mon, Tue, Thu, Sat, Sun 10–5.30, Wed, Fri 10.30–5.30, Apr–Sep; closes 5pm in Oct and 4pm Nov–Mar)*, built in 1616 and remodelled by Robert Adam in 1764–79 for the Earl of Mansfield. It was left to the nation in 1927 by the 1st Earl of Iveagh, along with its outstanding collection of paintings. Here you will find Rembrandt's *Portrait of the Artist* (c1665), Vermeer's *The Guitar Player* (c1676) and Gainsborough's fine portrait of *Mary, Countess Howe* (c1764), among other important works by English and Dutch masters.

Open-air lakeside concerts are held in the grounds in June, July and August, with fireworks as a spectacular finale to some performances.

HIGHGATE CEMETERY

5 miles (8km) N of Trafalgar Square

✉ Friends of Highgate Cemetery, Swain's Lane, N6 6PJ ☎ 020 8340 1834 ◷ Eastern Cemetery: Mon–Fri 10–4.30, Sat–Sun 11–4.30, Apr–Oct; Mon–Fri 10–3.30pm, Sat–Sun 11–3.30, Nov–Mar. Closed during funerals. Western Cemetery: Admission by tour only. Mon–Fri 2pm, Sat–Sun 11, noon, 1, 2, 3, 4, Apr–Oct, last tour 3pm, Nov–Mar. No weekday tours Dec, Jan, Feb; special tours can be arranged by request. No children under 8 ✦ Eastern Cemetery £2, camera permit £1 (no video cameras). Western Cemetery standard tour £3, camera permit £1 for personal use only (no video cameras or tripods) ⬢ Archway ⬛ 143, 210, 271 to Lauderdale House ⬛ Upper Holloway ⬛ www.highgate-cemetery.org

During the 19th century everyone who was anyone in London was laid to rest in Highgate Cemetery. When it fell out of use, the main buildings became dilapidated and the landscape choked with brambles and

sycamores. In the 1980s volunteers rescued and restored the grounds, clearing the tombs and graves but leaving enough greenery to create a romantic air.

The cemetery is divided in two by Swain's Lane: the original West Cemetery, Victorian Gothic in style, and the newer East Cemetery, peaceful, leafy and less visited. You can visit the West Cemetery by guided tour only. The exceptional collection of Victorian funerary architecture here includes the graves of about 850 famous figures, including German political theorist Karl Marx (1818–83), novelist George Eliot (1819–80) and chemist Michael Faraday (1791–1867, see page 89), plus 18 Royal Academicians, six Lord Mayors of London and 48 Fellows of the Royal Society. The surroundings are laid out as a mixed woodland of hornbeam, exotic limes, oak, hazel, sweet chestnut, tulip and field maple. **Don't miss** the Egyptian Avenue and Terrace Catacombs in the West Cemetery.

HOGARTH'S HOUSE

6 miles (10km) W of Trafalgar Square

✉ Hogarth Lane, Great West Road, Chiswick W4 2QN ☎ 020 8994 6757 ◷ Tue–Fri 1–5, Sat, Sun 1–6, Apr–Oct; Tue–Fri 1–4, Sat, Sun 1–5, Oct–Mar (closed Jan) ✦ Free; donation welcomed ⬢ Turnham Green ⬛ 27, 190, 391 ⬛ Turnham Green

Today, Hogarth's House stands close to a busy roundabout, but when the 'little country box by the Thames' was used as a summer home by artist and satirical engraver William Hogarth (1697–1764), it was set in open fields. The simple rooms are hung with copies of his work, including the moral tales *Marriage à la Mode* (1745) and *A Rake's Progress* (1735).

HAMPTON COURT PALACE

One of the oldest and most interesting of London's royal palaces, with beautiful riverside gardens.

Cardinal Thomas Wolsey, Archbishop of York and chancellor to Henry VIII, built Hampton Court in 1514 as a country residence. In 1528 he made an unsuccessful bid to retain the king's favour by handing over his new home. Henry extended it, turning it into a royal palace. The layout remained unchanged until the 1690s, when William and Mary employed Sir Christopher Wren to make further changes and additions. The result was a striking mix of Tudor and classical styles.

AROUND THE PALACE

You approach the palace through the Trophy Gates, with the Tudor Great Gatehouse ahead. Terracotta roundels, originally painted and gilded, depict Roman emperors in the two side turrets. Carved on the opposite gateway are the intertwined initials 'H' and 'A'—Henry and Anne. Henry finally gained his divorce in order to marry Anne, but the marriage lasted only four years before Boleyn was beheaded at the Tower of London (see pages 138–143).

Clock Court comes next, named after the huge astronomical clock (1540) on the gateway's inner side. On the left is Henry VIII's Great Hall, with its oriel window, minstrels' gallery and hammerbeam roof. Nearby, in the Tudor kitchens, more than 200 staff cooked for 600 people at a time. Opposite, through Wren's elegant colonnade, you enter the State Apartments (1689–94), decorated with paintings, furnishings and tapestries. Jean Tijou (fl1689–c1711), a French blacksmith, made the ironwork balustrades of the staircases, Grinling Gibbons (1648–1721) carved the woodwork and Antonio Verrio (c1639–1707) painted many of the ceilings. The smaller Queen's Apartments look over Wren's Fountain Court, and the public rooms look out on to avenues, canals and fountains.

THE GARDENS

Today's formal landscaping of avenues and lakes originated in William and Mary's time. To the south, the Privy Garden was for the use of the royal family and was separated from the river by Tijou's wrought-iron screen. Nearby are Henry VIII's Pond Garden and an Elizabethan Knot Garden of aromatic herbs. The Great Vine, planted in 1768 by Capability Brown, still produces black Hamburgh grapes.

North of the palace are the Rose Gardens, formerly the tiltyards, where jousting took place, and the Wilderness, 4ha (9 acres) of natural woodland. The Maze, planted in 1690, is in the top corner.

RATING	
Good for kids	● ● ● ● ●
Historic interest	● ● ● ● ●
Value for money	● ● ● ●

BASICS

13 miles (21 km) SW of Trafalgar Square

✉ East Molesey, Surrey KT8 9AU

☎ Recorded information: 0870 752 7777; Ticket sales: 0870 753 7777

🕐 Mon 10.15–6, Tue–Sun 9.30–6, end Mar–late Oct; Mon 10.15–4.30, Tue–Sun 9.30–4.30, late Oct–end Mar; Maze and Privy Gardens: daily 10–5.45 summer, 10–4 winter 💷 Adult £11.50, child (5–15) £ 7.50, under 5s free, family £34

🚉 Hampton Court 🚌 111, 411, 416, 513, R68 🚤 Summer services from Westminster Pier 🚉 Hampton Court

🎧 Tours, audio-guides, exhibitions

📖 £3.95 ☕ Privy Kitchen Coffee Shop; Tiltyard Tea-room, palace gardens

🏬 Barrack Block Shop in former palace barracks; Garden Shop; Base Court Shop, between Base Court and Clock Court; Tudor Kitchens Shop, next to Tudor Wine Cellar 🚻

www.hrp.org.uk

Efficient information from the historic royal places site.

TIPS

● Take a free introductory tour from one of the guides.

● Buy a combined train and palace entry ticket—it gives 10 per cent off admission.

Life mask of poet John Keats, on display at Keats House

Check the daily schedule of events and talks at London Zoo

The Museum of Rugby is a must for all fans of the sport

JEWISH MUSEUM

3 miles (5km) N of Trafalgar Square
✉ Raymond Burton House, 129–131 Albert Street NW1 7NB ☎ 020 7284 1997 🕑 Mon–Thu 10–4, Sun 10–5 💷 Adult £3.50, under 15s £1.50, family £8 🚇 Camden Town 🚌 31, 274, C2 ♿
www.jewishmuseum.org.uk

The long history of Britain's Jewish community is examined here through exhibits and an audiovisual presentation. An outstanding collection of ceremonial objects dates mostly from the mid-17th century, when Lord Protector Oliver Cromwell abolished prohibitive laws on Jewish settlement. There are earlier objects, too, including the 13th-century bankers' tallies and 16th-century handwritten scrolls. Another branch of the museum is at the Sternberg Centre, 80 East End Road, in north London *(tel 020 8349 1143).*
Don't miss the medieval notched wooden tax receipts in the history gallery.

KEATS HOUSE

5 miles (8km) NW of Trafalgar Square
✉ Keats Grove, Hampstead NW3 2RR ☎ 020 7435 2062 🕑 Tue–Sun 12–5, mid-Apr–Oct, 12–4 Nov–Mar (phone to confirm dates). Guided tours Sat, Sun 3pm, no booking necessary 💷 Adult £3, under 16s and entry to garden free 🚇 Belsize Park, Hampstead 🚌 24, 46, 168, C11, C12 🚇 Hampstead Heath
www.keatshouse.org.uk

Poet John Keats (1795–1821) came to live here in 1818, fell in love with the girl next door, Fanny Brawne, and became engaged to her in 1819. In 1820 he left for Italy for health reasons; it was there that he died in 1821. During his brief time in this house he wrote some of his best-loved poems, including *Ode to a Nightingale;* the plum tree under which he wrote it has

gone, but a replacement in the garden marks the spot. The rest of the house displays letters, manuscripts and furnishings in period style.

LONDON CANAL MUSEUM

3 miles (5km) N of Trafalgar Square
✉ 12–13 New Wharf Road, King's Cross N1 9RT ☎ 0207 713 0836 🕑 Tue–Sun 10–4.30 💷 Adult £2.50, child (8–15) £1.25, under 8s free 🚇 King's Cross 🚌 10, 46, 73, 205 🚇 King's Cross
www.canalmuseum.org.uk

Here on Regent's Canal, within striking distance of one of the city's busiest areas, you can see inside a narrowboat cabin, trace the history of London's canals and learn about the cargoes they carried, the people who lived and worked on the waterways when they formed the nation's commercial arteries, and the horses that pulled their boats. The museum is housed in a former warehouse built for famous ice-cream-maker Carlo Gatti, and also explores the history of the ice trade and ice cream.
Don't miss looking down into the Victorian ice well.

LONDON WETLAND CENTRE

6 miles (10km) SW of Trafalgar Square
✉ Queen Elizabeth's Walk, Barnes SW13 9WT ☎ 0208 409 4400 🕑 Summer daily 9.30–6, winter 9.30–5 💷 Adult £6.75, child (4–16) £4, under 4s free, family £17.50 🚌 Hammersmith 🚌 283 Duck Bus from Hammersmith Underground to Wetland Centre; 209, 72, 33 to Red Lion pub 🚇 Barnes ♿
www.wetlandcentre.org.uk

The world's first wetland habitat created within a capital city sprawls over 42ha (105 acres) on the site of the former Barnes

Elms reservoirs. Among the cleverly designed attractions are 14 different wetland environments, such as New Zealand whitewater, African floodplains, northern Tundra and Hawaiian lavaflow, and a Pond Zone; you will also find sustainable gardens, a trail and, of course, plenty of wildlife, including frogs, newts, damselflies and dragonflies. At the Peter Scott Visitor Centre you can see a film about the environment called *Planet Water.*

LONDON ZOO

3 miles (5km) NW of Trafalgar Square
✉ Outer Circle, Regent's Park NW1 4RY ☎ 020 7722 3333 🕑 Daily 10–5.30, early Mar–late Oct; 10–4, late Oct–early Mar 💷 Adult £12, child (3–15) £9, under 3s free, family £38 🚇 Camden Town 🚌 274, C2 🚢 London Waterbus Company (☎ 020 7482 2660) runs scheduled services from Camden Lock and Little Venice: daily 10–5, Apr–Sep ♿ ♿
www.londonzoo.co.uk

Occupying 15ha (36 acres) of the northeast corner of Regent's Park (see page 115) and straddling the Regent's Canal, the London Zoological Gardens opened in 1828. It was the world's first institution dedicated to the study and display of animals. Today the zoo's focus has changed: Its Web of Life, opened in 1999, is a conservation and preservation institution where 65 live animal exhibits and interactive displays show the world's biological diversity and interdependence.

Before you start your tour, look at the daily events schedule and try to be in the right place for feeding times and Animals in Action presentations.

Across the road from the main entrance in Albert Road are the Cotton Terraces, where giraffes, zebras, okapi, oryx and other African grazers live. Behind the

Henrietta Howard, mistress of George II, entertained writers and artists in the Great Room (above right) at Marble Hill House

Orleans House Gallery was opened to the public in 1972

walk-through Snowdon Aviary, designed by Lord Snowdon in 1964. Next door, small nocturnal animals scurry about in the Moonlight World house.

Back on the main site, near the entrance, you'll find the noisy primates, the silent world of the aquarium and the reptile house. The Mappin Terrace (with sloth bears, monkey-like langurs and muntjac deer) was designed by radical architects John Belcher (1841–1913) and J. J. Joass (1868–1952) in 1931; Joass had also designed a new aquarium for the zoo in 1924. The modernist Penguin Pool, always crowded at feeding time, was designed by Berthold Lubetkin (1901–90) in 1931.

MARBLE HILL HOUSE

10 miles (16km) SW of Trafalgar Square
✉ Richmond Road, Twickenham TW1 2NL ☎ 020 8892 5115, 0870 333 1181 for concerts ◷ Daily 10–6, Apr–Sep; 10–5, Oct ⚑ EH. Adult £3.50, child (5–16) £2, under 5s free ◷ Richmond ⬛ 65, 371 ⬛ St. Margarets ⬛ 🏛
www.english-heritage.org.uk

Built to make the most of the views over the river towards Richmond Hill, Marble Hill House is an exemplary Palladian villa. It was designed as a rural retreat for Henrietta Howard, mistress of the Prince of Wales, the future George II, in 1729; later it was given to another royal consort, Mrs Fitzherbert, who was secretly married to the future George IV in 1785 but had to give way to Caroline of Brunswick.

As with all Palladian villas, the main rooms are on the second floor. The Great Room is a perfect cube, in keeping with the Palladian love of geometry. It is furnished as it would have been in Henrietta Howard's time, when regular visitors included the writers John Gay, Horace

Walpole and Alexander Pope, who advised on the layout of the garden, with its groves of statuesque trees and manicured lawns. Today the grounds provide an atmospheric riverside backdrop for a series of outdoor concerts.

MUSEUM OF RUGBY

11 miles (18km) SW of Trafalgar Square
✉ Twickenham and Twickenham Stadium Tours, Rugby Road, Twickenham TW1 1DZ ☎ 020 8892 8877 ◷ Tue–Sat 10–5, Sun 11–5. Closed Sun after match days
⚑ Museum and stadium tour: adult £8, family £25; museum only (match days only): £3 ◷ Richmond, then R68, R70 to Twickenham centre; Hounslow East, then 281 ⬛ 33, 110, 267, 280, 281, 290, 490, H22, R28, R70 ⬛ Twickenham
www.rfu.com

Rugby Union fans will love this collection of memorabilia dating back to the 1800s. You can see the Calcutta Cup, the oldest jersey in existence and use the interactive touch-screen computers to learn about the history of the game. Or test your strength on the scrum machine, re-live the greatest-ever tries, and witness the highs and lows of the world's most prestigious competitions in the audiovisual theatre.

NATIONAL ARCHIVES

9 miles (15km) W of Trafalgar Square
✉ Ruskin Avenue, Kew TW9 4DU ☎ 020 8392 5323, 020 8876 3444 or 5202 (events) 9198 (minicom) ◷ Mon, Wed, Fri 9–5, Tue, 10–7, Thu 9–7, Sat 9.30–5 ⚑ Free ◷ Kew Gardens ⬛ 65, 237, 267, 391, 964 ⬛ Kew Pier ⬛ Kew Gardens 🍴 🏛
www.nationalarchives.gov.uk

All central government records, from the Norman Conquest in

1066 to the present day, are stored here, as well as all law court records, stacked away on 104 miles (167km) of shelving. There's a public display of some of the most significant pieces, such as the Domesday Book, the great land survey of 1086, plus curiosities such as letters from murderer Jack the Ripper, the last telegram sent from *Titanic* before it sank and pop star Elton John's change of name (from Reginald Dwight) by deed poll.

NATIONAL ARMY MUSEUM

3 miles (5 km) SW of Trafalgar Square
✉ Royal Hospital Road, Chelsea SW3 4HT ☎ 020 7730 0717 ◷ Daily 10–5.30 ⚑ Free ◷ Sloane Square ⬛ 11, 19, 22; 239 (Mon–Sat) to museum ⬛ Cadogan Pier ⬛ 🏛
www.national-army-museum.ac.uk

The British army's story is traced from the Middle Ages and the 1415 Battle of Agincourt to modern conflicts including the Falklands War and the Gulf War. Although wartime experience is naturally to the fore, space is also given to peacetime military life.

In addition to describing campaigns and battles, the museum focuses on the lives of ordinary soldiers, using paintings, photographs, uniforms and equipment along with reconstructions and life-size models.

Star attractions include the skeleton of Napoleon's beloved war horse, Marengo, and a huge model of the Battle of Waterloo at a critical moment, 7.15pm on Sunday 18 June 1815.

Weekend special events follow a different theme every month, with uniformed interpreters, specialist lectures and children's workshops.
Don't miss the Tudor cannon, 5m (16ft) long, and Florence Nightingale's lamp (see page 89).

Ceiling detail from the Tapestry Room in Osterley House

Fallow deer coexist with walkers and cyclists in Richmond Park

Statue of Apollo in the apse of the Great Hall of Syon House

THE SIGHTS

ORLEANS HOUSE GALLERY

11 miles (18km) SW of Trafalgar Square
✉ Riverside TW1 3DJ ☎ 020 8892 0221 🕐 Tue–Sat 1–4.30, Sun 2–4.30, Oct–Mar; Tue–Sat 1–5.30, Sun 2–5.30, Apr–Sep 🅿 Free 🚌 33, H22, R68, R70, 290, 490 🚉 Twickenham 🚇
www.visitrichmond.co.uk

All that remains now of 18th-century Orleans House is the Octagon, a garden room built in 1720. The building, together with modern extensions at the back, houses a public gallery, workshops and temporary exhibitions. **Don't miss** the medallion portraits of George II and Queen Caroline.

OSTERLEY PARK

12 miles (19km) W of Trafalgar Square
✉ Jersey Road, Isleworth TW7 4RB ☎ 020 8232 5050; infoline 01494 755566 🕐 House, Jersey Galleries: Sat, Sun 1–4.30, Mar; Wed–Sun 1–4.30 Apr–Oct (daily in Aug). Closed Good Fri. Grand Stables: Sun afternoons during open season. Park and pleasure grounds: daily 9–7.30 or sunset if earlier; park closes early before major events 🅿 NT. Adult £4.50, child (5–16) £2.25, under 5s free, family £11.20. 🚇 Osterley 🚌 H28, H91 🚉 Syon Lane 🚏 🚇
www.nationaltrust.org.uk/osterley

One of London's largest surviving estate parks, with an elegant neoclassical villa at its heart, Osterley feels a thousand miles from the bustle of central London. The original Elizabethan villa was built by Thomas Gresham in 1576 and remodelled by Robert Adam in the late 18th century for the descendants of Francis Child, who had made his money in the gold trade.

The house is surrounded by pleasure gardens, ornamental lakes and parkland, and the 16th-century stables are now a café. **Don't miss** the Eating Room, with its elaborately decorated plaster ceiling, statues and paintings, and the Gobelin tapestries in the Tapestry Room.

RICHMOND PARK

9 miles (15km) W of Trafalgar Square
✉ Park Office, Holly Lodge, Richmond Park, Richmond, Surrey TW10 5HS ☎ 020 8948 3209 🕐 Open access during daylight hours 🅿 Free 🚇 Richmond, then bus 371 to Lass of Richmond Hill stop 🚌 72, 74, 85, 371 🚉 Richmond, then bus 371 to Lass of Richmond Hill stop 🍴
www.royalparks.gov.uk

Originally enclosed as a hunting ground by Charles I in 1637, Richmond Park is, at 1011ha (2,500 acres), London's largest open space. Its diverse landscape takes in grassland, areas of bog and bracken, wetland, woodland and ancient parkland trees, and herds of fallow (350) and red (300) deer still graze here—but in safety, nowadays. In spring, when camellias, magnolias, azaleas and rhododendrons come into flower, the Isabella Plantation is a treat to visit.

SOUTH LONDON GALLERY

4 miles (6km) SE of Trafalgar Square
✉ 65 Peckham Road SE5 8UH ☎ 020 7703 6120 🕐 Tue, Wed, Fri 11–6, Thu 11–7, Sat–Sun 2–6 🅿 Free; admission charge to individual events 🚇 Elephant and Castle, then bus; Oval then bus 🚌 12, 36, 171 🚉 Peckham Rye
www.southlondongallery.org

This is one of London's foremost contemporary art galleries, showing work by local, national and international artists. Acclaimed artists who have exhibited here to date include Tracey Emin, Barbara Kruger, Christian Boltanski and Keith Tyson. A permanent collection of nearly 2,000 works, ranging from the 1880s to contemporary artists, can be viewed by appointment.

SYON HOUSE AND PARK

9 miles (15km) W of Trafalgar Square
✉ Syon Park, Brentford, Middlesex TW8 8JF ☎ 020 8560 0881 🕐 House: Wed, Thu, Sun 11–5, Mar–Nov; gardens daily 10.30–5.30 or dusk if earlier; miniature steam railway Apr–Oct weekends 🅿 House, gardens, Great Conservatory, rose garden: adult £6.95, under 16s £5.95, family £15; gardens, Great Conservatory: adult £3.50, child £2.50, family £8 🚇 Gunnersbury, then bus 🚌 237, 267 to Brentlea Gate 🚉 Kew Bridge or Gunnersbury, then bus 🚏 🚇
www.syonpark.co.uk

Outside, this historic seat of the Dukes of Northumberland looks forbidding, but the battlemented mid-16th-century building contains some of the most elegantly decorated rooms in England. Robert Adam (1728–92) remodelled the interior between 1761 and 1768 using marble, gilded statues and plasterwork to create a magnificent palace.

Among the duke's private rooms, now on view, are the Drawing Room with its splendid Adam fireplace, rescued from Northumberland House in the Strand when it was demolished in 1874. Upstairs is the suite of rooms furnished for the young Princess Victoria, to whom the 3rd Duchess of Northumberland was governess before she became queen.

Capability Brown landscaped the grounds of Syon House between 1767 and 1773 by creating an idyllic version of the countryside, with lakes, lawns and fine specimen trees. The centrepiece, linking lake and garden, is the Great Conservatory, built between *(continued on page 164)*

(continued on page 164)

Giant water lilies, up to 2m (6ft) across, are grown annually from seed. The Palm House (right) and the Chinese Pagoda (below)

ROYAL BOTANICAL GARDENS, KEW

A royal palace, magnificent glasshouses, mature trees and 120ha (300 acres) of spectacular gardens.

Given World Heritage Site status in July 2003, the Royal Botanic Gardens have renovated and updated their magnificent glasshouses to make them more accessible for today's visitors.

The gardens were created by combining two royal estates in 1772. Under the patronage of George III they developed into one of the world's foremost centres of horticultural research, largely thanks to botanist Sir Joseph Banks (see page 113), who became the King's adviser in 1773 after his voyage around the world with Captain Cook. The early botanic garden occupied just a small area; the rest was landscaped by Capability Brown (his lake and Rhododendron Dell remain) and dotted with fanciful buildings to amuse courtly visitors.

AROUND THE GARDENS

The oldest building is the 10-storey pagoda, built in 1761–62 to the designs of William Chambers. Kew began to change after 1841, when the gardens were handed over to the State, and several greenhouses were added. The Palm House, designed by Decimus Burton, opened in 1848. It was thoroughly refurbished in 1985.

Next was the Temperate House, also by Decimus Burton, begun in 1859. On completion, 40 years later, it was the world's largest greenhouse. From its elevated gallery you get a good view of the plants, including the Chilean wine palm, planted in 1846 and now claimed to be the largest greenhouse plant in existence.

The Princess of Wales Conservatory opened in 1987. Much of it is below ground level (for insulation) and is lit by a series of low, tentlike glass roofs. You pass through different climate zones, from arid desert at one end to orchid-filled tropics at the other.

British native wildflowers are the theme at Queen Charlotte's Cottage and Gardens on the southwestern fringes of the site, named after George III's queen. This is now a woodland nature reserve, as requested by Queen Victoria.

VERDICT	
Good for kids	● ●
Historic interest	● ● ●
Specialist shopping	● ● ●
Value for money	● ● ● ● ●

BASICS

8 miles (13km) W of Trafalgar Square
✉ Kew, Richmond, Surrey TW9 3AB
☎ 020 8332 5655 ⏱ Mon–Fri 9.30–6.30, Sat, Sun 9.30–7.30, Apr–Aug; daily 9.30–6 Sep, Oct;. 9.30–4.15 Nov–mid-Feb; 9.30–5.30 mid-Feb–Mar 💷 Adult £7.50, under 16s free 🚇 Kew Gardens 🚌 65, 237, 391 🚉 Kew Bridge, Kew Gardens 📖 £4.95, in English only 🍴 Cafés on site 🍽 Restaurant in the Orangery 🎁 At Victoria Gate and White Peaks ♿

www.kew.org
In-depth site with lots of background information and detail about the gardens and their work.

TIP

● Take the Kew Explorer, a train that tours all the key sites in 40 minutes. Tickets are £3, available from the main entrance.

Stuart royal portraits in the Red Drawing Room of Syon House

Before the Thames Barrier was built (1974–84), London was prone to flooding. Try and visit when the barrier gates are being tested

1820 and 1827 by Charles Fowler, the architect of Covent Garden market (see page 88). Several different planting environments are housed here, ranging from damp fernery to the hot, dry cactus beds.

The rose garden, between the house and the river, was replanted in 1995 with moe than 8,000 roses. Farther off, a stroll around the lakes takes in many moisture-loving plants, flowering shrubs and unusual trees.

In the London Butterfly House hundreds of species fly freely in a jungle-like setting, and there's a display of giant spiders, scorpions and other creepy-crawlies. In the Aquatic Experience fish, reptiles, amphibians and birds are kept in near-natural habitats. Within the grounds there is also a giant indoor adventure playground, and studios for art, needlecraft and gardening.

Don't miss Cipriani's 239 painted ceiling medallions in the Red Drawing Room.

THAMES BARRIER

10 miles (16km) E of Trafalgar Square
✉ Unity Way, SE18 5NJ ☎ 020 8305 4188 ⏰ Daily 11–3.30, Oct–Mar; 10.30–4.30, Apr–Sep 👆 Adult £1, under 16s 50p 🚇 Greenwich 🚌 180 🚢 Charlton Barrier Pier 🅿 ♿
www.environment-agency.gov.uk

In 1953, 300 people died when the Thames broke its banks and flooded London. Since then the river has risen by another 50cm (20in)—and it will continue to rise by about 1m (3ft) every hundred years. The Thames Barrier was opened in 1984 to prevent further flooding, and its spetacular stainless steel gates, 61m (200ft) wide, are now a familiar landmark. Electrically powered hydraulic power packs, housed immediately below the stainless steel roofs, rotate the gates, which are regularly closed

and reopened for experiments and inspection. Other exhibits explain river tides, anti-pollution strategies and the return of river wildlife.

Don't miss the working model of the barrier and the re-creation of the great Victorian stench in the information office.

WILLIAM MORRIS GALLERY

9 miles (15km) NE of Trafalgar Square
✉ Lloyd Park, Forest Road, E17 4PP ☎ 020 8527 3782 ⏰ Tue–Sat, 1st Sun of month 10–1, 2–5 👆 Free; donations welcome 🚇 Walthamstow Central 🚌 34, 97, 12,3 215, 275, 357, 505 to Bell Corner 🚇 Walthamstow Central ♿
www.lbwf.gov.uk/wmg

This is the only public museum devoted to the designer, craftsman, writer and socialist William Morris (1834–96). Along with his contemporaries in the Arts and Crafts movement, he reintroduced craftsmanship into everyday domestic objects as a reaction against industrialization. Their work and Morris's life and influence are illustrated with displays of their fabrics, rugs, carpets, wallpapers, furniture, stained glass and painted tiles. There are also examples of Arts and Crafts furniture, textiles, ceramics and glass from the 1880s to the 1920s.

Don't miss *Beauty and the Beast* and *Labours of the Months* tile panels.

2 WILLOW ROAD

5 miles (8km) NW of Trafalgar Square
✉ 2 Willow Road, Hampstead NW3 1TH ☎ 020 7435 6166 ⏰ 🚃 Sat 12–5 Mar, Nov; Thu–Sat 12–5, Apr–Oct; timed ticket, guided tour only (1hr), noon, 1, 2; unrestricted access 3–5 👆 NT. Adult £4.50, child (5–16) £2.25, under 5s free, family £11. Joint ticket with Fenton House (see page 155)

£6.30 🚇 Hampstead, Belsize Park 🚌 46, 268 🚉 Hampstead Heath www.nationaltrust.org.uk

London's only modernist house open to the public was designed in the 1930s by Ernö Goldfinger, who lived here with his family until his death in 1987. It is the heart of a terrace of three houses and holds a collection of British and European works by 20th-century artists, such as Max Ernst and Henry Moore.

WIMBLEDON COMMON

8 miles (13km) SW of Trafalgar Square
✉ The Ranger's Office, Windmill Road, Wimbledon Common SW19 5NR ☎ 020 8788 7655 ⏰ Open access 👆 Free 🚇 Putney Bridge, Southfields, Wimbledon 🚌 93 🚉 Wimbledon 🅿 www.wpcc.org.uk

Together with Putney Lower Common, this slice of greenery covers about 461ha (1,140 acres). Among the areas of woodland, scrubland, heathland and recreation parks are a nature trail, an 18-hole golf course, cricket pitches, 16 miles (26km) of bridle paths, soccer and rugby pitches and athletics facilities.

A restored 1817 windmill now houses a museum (*Sat 2–5, Sun 11–5, Apr–Oct*) with models, flour-grinding machinery and a collection of woodworking tools.

East of the common, on Church Road, is the All England Lawn Tennis Club, venue for the annual Wimbledon championships. The displays in the Tennis Museum provide a chronicle of the game of tennis from its origins in the 1860s to the present day (*daily 10.30–5; closed middle Sun of championships, Mon after championships*).

Don't miss the footage of championship matches in the museum.

This chapter gives information on things to do in London other than sightseeing.

Shops and performance venues are located on the maps at the beginning of each section.

What to Do

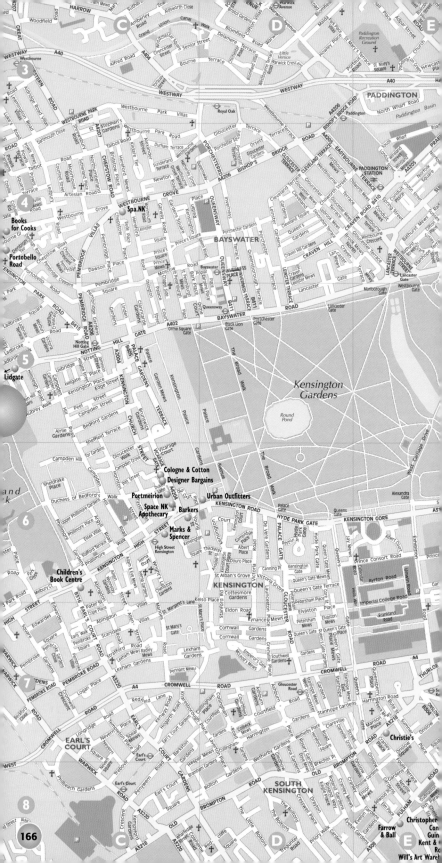

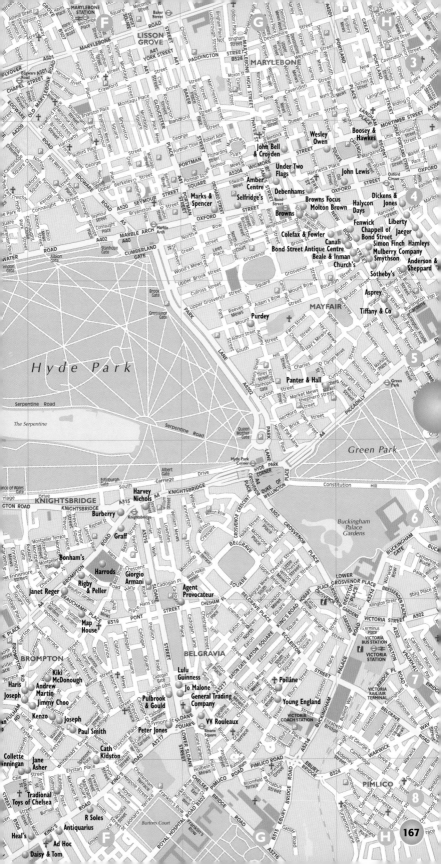

SHOPPING

London offers shoppers a vast range, from smart department stores and speciality shops to market stalls and bargain basements. Many people come to London just to shop. Oxford Street and Regent Street can be crammed to bursting point in summer and during the Christmas shopping season—which starts in November. Particularly long queues can be expected at the most popular stores such as Hamleys, the world-famous toy shop, but there are quieter areas too.

Shops have adopted increasingly flexible opening hours and it is difficult to generalise. Late opening, until 9 or 10, is common in the busiest areas and many shops also open on Sundays at varying times.

Shopping has become a major leisure pursuit throughout Britain

SALE TIME
Twice a year, London stores slash their prices in order to sell off the previous season's remaining stock. The best bargains are at the January sales, starting immediately after Christmas—sometimes before—and continuing well into February. Determined bargain-hunters camp out in the streets for several days in advance to be first in line when the sales open at Harrods (see page 178) or Selfridge's (see page 178). Summer sales begin in June or July and last to the end of August.

Strict rules govern the way that sales operate in Britain, and the fact that you buy an item in a sale does not affect your statutory rights as a consumer. You are, for example, entitled to a full refund if the goods prove faulty (unless they were sold as damaged goods)—but you must retain your receipt as proof of purchase.

TAX-FREE SHOPPING
If the goods you buy are going to be exported to a non-European Union country, you are exempt from Value Added Tax (VAT, a sales tax of 17.5 per cent levied on a great many goods, with the exceptions of food, children's clothes and books). This can amount to a considerable saving, but you have to spend a minimum amount, and this varies from shop to shop. Most leading stores have details of the tax-free shopping policy and can help with your claims.

PAYING
Most shops accept the major credit cards, but there are exceptions. Travellers' cheques may be accepted, but you will need to show your passport. Personal cheques must be drawn from a UK bank account. Street markets are the main exception to these rules.

STREET SELLERS
With the exception of market traders, who pay to maintain regular spots at established markets, it's smart to beware of street sellers anywhere in London. The products they sell may not be what they're claimed to be.

MARKETS
Markets come in all shapes and sizes in London, from the stylish to the basic. For wonderful atmosphere, cheeky traders' patter and piled-high goods ranging from leather jackets to second-hand records, visit Petticoat Lane in Liverpool Street (see page 182) or Brick Lane *(Sun 8am–1pm)*, both in the East End and reached from

Flower stalls on street corners are common all over the city

the Liverpool Street or Aldgate East Underground station. At Camden Lock, reached from Camden Town Underground station *(daily 10–6)*, students and antique-hunters flock to the stalls of bric-à-brac and trendy clothes. Berwick Street market (see page 182) sells produce and a huge assortment of household goods.

SHOPPING AREAS
Pages 171–175 highlight five very different areas (see inside front cover map) in central London that are particularly good for a half- or full-day shopping trip.

Kensington

🚇 High Street Kensington
🚌 9, 10, 27, 28, 49

This is a great destination for typical UK shops (see chain store guide, pages 184–185) and will appeal to many different ages of shopper. However, there are also plenty of individual shops to discover, a selection of which can be found on the following route.

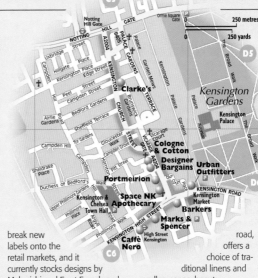

KENSINGTON HIGH STREET

From the Underground station turn right and go past **Marks & Spencer** to **Barkers** (No. 63), an art deco department store originally built in 1870 and now part of the extensive House of Fraser chain. Men's fashions are for sale in the basement, accessories and cosmetics on the ground floor, and women's fashions on the floors above as well as house-

Beautiful linens and toiletries in Cologne and Cotton

wares, TV, audio and other electrical goods. The second-floor restaurant, run by celebrated chef Albert Roux, is a good place to stop for lunch. Like all the major department stores, Barkers provides a free personal shopper on request.

Farther east along the street, on the other side of the road, is **Urban Outfitters** (Nos. 36–38) a must for trend-conscious teenagers. Laid out within a large, raw space, it houses an ever-changing selection of clothing (for both sexes) and home accessories, plus 'indie' and club music. First developed on US university campuses, it aims to

break new labels onto the retail markets, and it currently stocks designs by Maharishi and Frost French and a good selection of 'vintage' clothing. Madonna, Britney Spears and Prince Harry come here to work up a new look.

Turn right back up the High Street and take the first major road on the right-hand side—Kensington Church Street. This winds its way north up to Notting Hill and is lined with several small, independent shops well worth a visit.

KENSINGTON CHURCH STREET

First is **Space.NK.Apothecary** (No. 3), which stocks a tempting selection of beauty and grooming products from small, independent manufacturers, as well as its own label. There are 15 branches in London; this is one of the biggest, but it is still calm and relaxed. Cutting edge labels, often recommended in glossy journals, include Eve Lom, Laura Mercier and Era (spray-on foundation).

Continue along the same side of the road to reach **Portmeirion** (No. 13), which stocks the distinctive floral pottery made in the Italianate village of Portmeirion, in Wales.

It's worth browsing in **Designer Bargains** (No. 29), which stocks a wide variety of second-hand vintage clothes for women, with labels such as Chanel, Versace and Jimmy Choo—all in very good condition and at a fraction of their original price.

Cologne and Cotton (No. 39), on the same side of the

road, offers a choice of traditional linens and candles, soaps, beauty products and perfumery.

Farther along the street you'll find several interesting antiques shops (some are open by appointment only), second-hand bookshops and picture galleries.

Kensington Church Street is a good place to look for antiques

CAFFÈ NERO
1 Wright's Lane W8 5RY
Tel 020 7937 1605
www.caffenero.com
Ideal for a quick cup of coffee.
🕐 Mon–Fri 7am–8pm, Sat 8am–9pm, Sun 8–8

CLARKE'S
122 and 124 Kensington Church Street W8 4BH
Tel 020 7221 9225 (restaurant),
020 7229 2190 (café)
www.sallyclarke.com
All pastries, biscuits and jams made here and sold next door.
🕐 Restaurant: 12.30–2, 7–10, Sat brunch 11–2. Café: Fri 8–8, Sat 9–4

King's Road

HOW TO GET THERE
🚇 Sloane Square
🚌 11, 19, 22, 211, C1

Since the 1960s, the King's Road, Chelsea, has been a byword for off-the-wall fashions, attracting new generations to its punk and New Romantic boutiques. There are still avant-garde shops among the mainstream stores, while higher-priced labels can be coveted on smart Sloane Street, nearby.

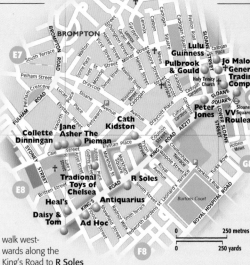

AROUND SLOANE SQUARE

From the Underground station turn to your right, then right again after Oriel (a French-style brasserie). The small parade of shops you will soon see are worth a look. **V V Rouleaux** (*No. 54*), the most interesting. has a fantastic selection of ribbons, silk flowers, elaborate trimmings and

Elegant packaging for Jo Malone's luxury beauty products

other intriguing items of haberdashery—a fashionista's dressing-up box, often recommended in the British edition of *Vogue*.

From here, turn left into Sloane Square and continue to the right into Sloane Street. After a minute's walk, on the right, you'll come across the flagship store of **Jo Malone** (see page 186). Back on Sloane Square, Peter Jones (see page 178), one of a chain of John Lewis department stores, is at the bottom of King's Road.

KING'S ROAD

Cowboy enthusiasts should head for a shop about three minutes'

walk westwards along the King's Road to **R Soles** (*No. 109a*), which since 1974 has been selling cowboy boots in every conceivable hue, size and decoration. There's a funky, irreverent atmosphere to the shop, which gets praise from the fashion press whenever cowboy chic makes a come-back.

Continue in the same direction to Markham Street on the right. Walk along here to Chelsea Green, where there are several more good shops. You'll find novelty party cakes in the **Jane Asher** shop; beautiful wooden toys for children are sold in **Traditional Toys** (see page 177) and dreamy dresses at **Collette Dinnigan** (*No. 26 Cale Street*). **Cath Kidston** (see page 181) sells 1950s-style fabrics, wallpapers and accessories—florals in pinks, yellows and greens.

Back on the King's Road is **Ad Hoc** (*No. 153*); teenagers love its hats, costume jewellery, wigs, fancy hosiery and other highly unsuitable garments!

For younger family members, **Daisy & Tom** (see page 177), a short distance farther along the King's Road, just after Chelsea Town Hall, sells designer togs, toys and furniture.

Beyond this point are lots of great shops including **Designers Guild** (*No. 267*), selling interiors, fabrics and wallpapers; **Osborne & Little** (*No. 304*) for fabrics and more wallpapers; **Mimi** (*No. 309*), a designer boutique; **Brora** and **Rococo** (see pages 179 and 180).

Another half a mile (1km) or so (take the No. 22 bus to save

time) brings you to a strip of shops offering antiques, lighting, architectural ironmongery and bedroom furniture. From here you're about 10 minutes' walk from Chelsea Harbour (see page 181), an interior design centre.

Ribbons galore in V V Rouleaux, plus much more

WHERE TO EAT
THE PIEMAN
16 Cale Street SW3 3QU
Tel 020 7225 0587
Delicious sandwiches in the Chelsea Green area, behind the King's Road.
🕐 Mon–Fri 9–6, Sat 9–3

THE CHELSEA BUN
9a Lamont Road SW10 0HP
Tel 020 7352 3635
Light fare by day and tasty English and Italian dinners in the evening towards the western end of the King's Road, on a road running parallel off Limerston Street.
🕐 Mon–Sat 7am–midnight, Sun 9–7

WHAT TO DO

Knightsbridge

HOW TO GET THERE

🚇 Knightsbridge

🚌 9, 10, 14, 74, C1

London's smartest and most expensive real estate conurbation, with shops and price tags to match. If you have money to spend and a need for some exhilarating retail therapy, Knightsbridge is for you.

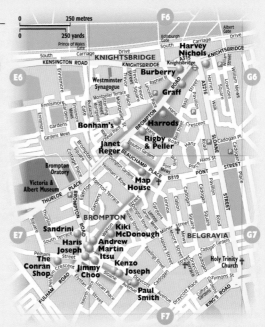

BROMPTON ROAD

As you leave the Underground station you'll see **Harvey Nichols** (see page 178), now London's most fashionable department store—although Selfridges's (see page 178) is catching up.

On emerging from Harvey Nichols, head back towards the Underground station and continue along Brompton Road. Opposite is a huge **Burberry** store *(No. 2)*, known for its distinctive tan-and-grey check on

Harvey Nichols department store in Brompton Road

scarves, bags and raincoats. On the left as you walk towards the canopied shopfront of **Harrods** (see page 178) is **Graff** *(No. 55)*, with breathtaking window displays of diamond jewellery.

Leave Harrods by the Hans Road exit and you'll see **Rigby & Peller** (see page 182), across the street.

Return to Brompton Road and turn left to reach Beauchamp (pronounced 'beecham') Place on the left. On the right is the **Map House** *(No. 54)*, with precious maps and engravings dating back several centuries. At the top of Beauchamp Place, turn right into Walton Street.

WALTON STREET AND DRAYCOTT AVENUE

Along both sides of Walton Street are shops selling a good selection of jewellery: Try **Kiki McDonough** *(No. 77c)* for contemporary pieces made with gratifyingly large semi-precious stones. **Andrew Martin** *(No. 200)* is irresistible for understated furniture.

At the southern end of the street turn left into Draycott Avenue to find **Jimmy Choo** (see page 179). At these prices, you may only be trying them on, but you won't find more glamorous shoes anywhere in the world.

ON AND OFF SLOANE AVENUE

Head back up Draycott Avenue and turn left round **Joseph** *(No. 77 Fulham Road)* and **Kenzo** *(No. 70 Sloane Avenue)*, both selling beautiful women's clothes. If you have time, try Kenzo's famously flattering trousers—not much use, though, if you're average size or larger. Soon you'll reach Sloane Avenue. On the right is the glorious **Conran Shop** *(No. 81 Fulham Road)*, an emporium filled with super-stylish household items for fans of modern interiors,

including a few classics. Turning right out of the shop you'll find a number of men's high fashion

Extreme elegance from Jimmy Choo—at a price

stores, including **Paul Smith** *(Nos. 84–86 Sloane Avenue)* and the men's collection by **Joseph** *(No. 74)*.

WHERE TO EAT

HARVEY NICHOLS
Restaurants and café-bars on the 4th and 5th floors, and a conveyor-belt sushi bar on the 5th (see page 257).

SANDRINI
260 Brompton Road SW3 2AS
Tel 020 7584 1724
An authentic Italian trattoria with friendly waiters and a warm welcome for children.
🕐 Daily 12–3, 7–12.30

WHAT TO DO

Oxford Street, Bond Street and Regent Street

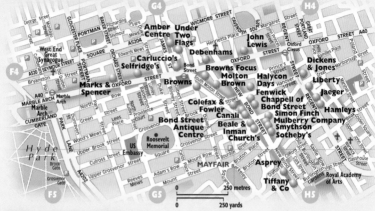

HOW TO GET THERE

🚇 Marble Arch

🚌 10, 12, 74, 159, 274

If Knightsbridge is where the money is, Oxford Street is where the crowds are; on Bond Street, the prices are higher and crowds thinner.

Beauty products in Selfridge's The Lab department

OXFORD STREET

From Marble Arch turn eastwards along Oxford Street and head for the flagship store of that stalwart of British clothing retailing, **Marks & Spencer** (No. 458). Open since 1930, it stocks all M&S lines and has a popular food section in the basement. Across Orchard Street is **Selfridge's** (see page 178).

As a contrast to these giant stores, try St. Christopher's Place, a narrow alley on the left. Take a look in the **Amber Centre** (No. 24) for unusual jewellery, or step into a different world at **Under Two Flags** (see page 181).

Return to Oxford Street to visit another good department store—**Debenhams** (Nos. 334–348), with moderately priced clothes, jewellery and handbags, plus much more.

SOUTH MOLTON STREET

Cross Oxford Street and go down South Molton Street. Expensive new labels targeted at twenty-somethings are sold at **Browns Focus** (Nos. 38–39), with some stunningly beautiful designer clothing at **Browns** (see page 179). At the bottom of this short street is **Colefax & Fowler** (No. 39 Brook Street), with ornaments as well as designer wallpaper and fabric for sale.

BOND STREET

Bond Street, divided into New and Old, crosses over Brook Street at the traffic lights. As well as fabulous designer clothes, the street has a reputation for top quality classic menswear—try **Canali** (No. 122), **Beale & Inman** (No. 131) or **Church's** (No. 133) for shoes.

Bond Street is also famous for serious jewellery, with the **Bond Street Antique Centre** (No. 124), the royal jeweller, **Asprey** (No. 169), and **Tiffany & Co** (No. 25). Walk back up New Bond Street towards Oxford Street and turn right.

REGENT STREET

From Oxford Circus head south down Regent Street to **Dickens & Jones** (Nos. 224–244), a spacious House of Fraser department store. On the opposite corner is the half-timbered **Liberty** (see page 179) façade,

with **Jaeger** (Nos. 200–206), on the left, offering mid-priced classic tailored wear for men and women. Next to Jaeger, narrow lanes head off in the direction of Carnaby Street, once a hotbed of fashion and grooviness. Although it's since lost that edge, it's still good for browsing.

Expensive clothes and jewellery shops line Bond Street

Back on Regent Street, Hamleys toy shop (see page 177) is just a few doors down.

WHERE TO EAT

CARLUCCIO'S
St. Christopher's Place W1U 1AY
Tel 020 7935 5927
www.carluccios.com
Stylish but inexpensive Italian.
🕐 Mon–Fri 8am–11pm, Sat 10am–11pm, Sun 11–10

ARTHUR'S RESTAURANT, IN LIBERTY
Breakfasts, lunches, and afternoon tea served from 3pm.
🕐 Mon–Wed 10–6.30, Thu 10–8, Fri, Sat 10–7, Sun noon–6

Covent Garden

HOW TO GET THERE

🚇 Covent Garden

🚌 9, 11, 13, 15, RV1

Covent Garden is a compact shopping area and is easily covered in a morning or afternoon. Don't come here if you're in search of major chain stores or mainstream shops. The Piazza, which forms the main focus of Covent Garden, is full of quirky specialist shops as well as street entertainers of all kinds.

As you leave the Underground station turn right and walk the short distance to the Piazza and its central halls. Under the Victorian roof there are now chic shops such as **Culpeper the Herbalist** (see page 186), selling sweet-scented aromatherapy, herbal medicines and culinary products. The North Hall houses a daily market known as the **Apple Market** (see page 88), selling antiques and collectables every Monday and crafts, jewellery, clothes and accessories

The distinctive blue of Neal's Yard toiletries

the rest of the week.

Among the shops surrounding the Piazza, outside the halls, is the **Dr Martens Department Store** (Nos. 1–4 King Street), selling the famous boots that never quite go out of fashion.

NEAL STREET

From the market walk back towards the Underground station, cross over Long Acre and venture into Neal Street. Teenagers and twentysomethings will love the mix of trendy clothes shops and music outlets, but everyone will enjoy **The Kite Store** (see page 181). If you believe in seeing the future

through the stars, try **The Astrology Shop** (No. 78), where you can get a personalized horoscope in five minutes.

Turning back towards the Underground station, look for signs to Neal's Yard, a tiny courtyard on the west side of Neal Street. Tucked in here is a collection of small cafés serving fruit smoothies and food from around the world. There's also a great shop stocked with delicious herbal tinctures, lotions and bathing treats—**Neal's Yard Remedies** (No. 15 Neal's Yard).

SHELTON STREET TO BEDFORD STREET

From Neal's Yard turn left, then right into Shelton Street. Along here is the **London Graphic Centre** (see page 186), which has a huge range of artists' materials—papers, canvases, paints, pens, brushes, easels.

Turn back along Shelton Street and into Langley Court to reach a huge **Ted Baker** shop (Nos. 1–2 Langley Court), selling fashions for men and women; then turn left into Floral Street to visit the **Paul Smith** (Nos. 40–44) collection of clothes for men and women by the London-based designer.

Turn right into Bedford Street and head south for a short distance, keeping a look-out for

Paul (No. 29 Bedford Street), an old-fashioned French boulangerie and pâtisserie selling delicious breads and cakes. There's a small restaurant at the back—an ideal place to stop and reflect on your shopping endeavours.

Ted Baker's fashionable designs, aimed at younger men and women

WHERE TO EAT

PONTI'S

4–5 The Piazza, Covent Garden
WC2E 8RA

Tel 020 7836 0272

A straightforward café serving snacks, sandwiches and drinks.

🕐 Daily 8am–11.30pm

PUNCH & JUDY

40 The Market WC2E 8RF

Tel 020 7379 0923

Try a pint of beer and a traditional plate of fish and chips in this pub in the heart of the market.

🕐 Mon–Sat 10am–11pm, Sun noon–10.30

WHAT TO DO

Shopping Directory

The selection below represents some of the best individual and specialist shops in the capital, but it is just the tip of the iceberg. See maps on pages 188–191.
Clothes size chart see page 296.
Chain stores see pages 184–185.

See maps on pages 188–191.
Clothes size chart see page 296.
Chain stores see pages 184–185.

ART AND ANTIQUES

ANTIQUARIUS
Map 167 F8
131–141 King's Road SW3 5PW
Tel 020 7351 5353
This large building houses around 100 individual dealers specializing in jewellery, art nouveau, art deco, militaria, chinoiserie, lamps, bronzes, porcelain and more. Huge variety of prices. Great fun for browsing on rainy days.
Mon–Sat 10–6 Sloane Square
11, 19, 22, 211, C1

GUINEVERE
Map 167 E8
574–580 King's Road SW6 2DY
Tel 020 7736 2917
www.guinevere.co.uk
The original antiques emporium on this now famous strip of the King's Road, and probably the best. The 10 rooms give a vastly eclectic selection of fine antiques, ranging as much in price as in age and origin.
Mon–Fri 9.30–6, Sat 10–5.30
Fulham Broadway 11, 14, 22

PANTER & HALL
Map 167 G5
9 Shepherd Market W1J 7PF
Tel 020 7399 9999
www.panterandhall.co.uk
Tiffany and Matthew opened this small gallery specializing in Scottish contemporary art, notable for fresh, clear colours and traditional work, in 2000 and have established a relaxed and informal contrast to some of the more intimidating galleries close by in Albemarle, Bond and Dover streets.
Mon–Fri 10–6, Sat by appointment
Green Park 8, 9, 14, 19, 22

WILL'S ART WAREHOUSE
Map 167 E8
Unit 3, Heathman's Road SW6 4TJ
Tel 020 7371 8787
www.wills-art.com
Informal, approachable art at its best. This big warehouse in a small

industrial park just off Parsons Green is jam-packed with modern art priced at between £35 and £3,000. Exhibitions change every four to eight weeks.
Daily 10.30–6 (later by appointment)
Parsons Green 14, 22, 28

AUCTION HOUSES

BONHAM'S
Map 167 F6
Montpelier Street SW7 1HH
Tel 020 7393 3900
www.bonhams.com
Operating since 1793, this international auction house deals in a wide variety of interesting lots—including football and cricket memorabilia. British and Continental art, fine art, furniture, carpets and silver and plate are among their auction themes.
Knightsbridge 9, 10, 14, 74, C1

CHRISTIE'S
Map 166 E7
85 Old Brompton Road SW7 3LD
Tel 020 7930 6074
www.christies.com
James Christie conducted his first sale in 1766 and went on to hold the greatest auctions of his time. Christie's salerooms are world famous, auctioning major works such as Rembrandt's *Portrait of a Lady*—sold in 2000 for more than £19 million. Most auctions are free and public; book tickets for those that require one.
South Kensington 14, 70, 74, 414, C1

SOTHEBY'S
Map 167 H4
34–35 New Bond Street W1A 2AA
Tel 020 7293 5000
www.sothebys.com

Since its beginnings in 1744, when Samuel Baker sold several hundred rare books, Sotheby's has branched out to every aspect of fine and decorative art, dealing in everything from Old Masters and Impressionists to contemporary art.
Bond Street 8, 10, 14, 19

BOOKS

BLACKWELL'S
Map 168 J4
100 Charing Cross Road WC2H 0JG
Tel 020 7292 5100
www.blackwell.co.uk
Set on a corner of the book-lover's paradise, Charing Cross Road, Blackwell's is part of an Oxford-based chain that stocks academic titles as well as fiction and general interest. This outlet is particularly strong in history, philosophy, fiction, medical and computing titles.
Mon–Sat 9.30–8, Sun 12–6 Leicester Square 14, 19 24, 29, 176

BOOKS FOR COOKS
Map 166 off C4
4 Blenheim Crescent W11 1NN

Tel 020 7221 1992
www.booksforcooks.com
You can sample different recipes every day in this hugely popular shop for foodies. More than just a fabulous cookbook bookshop, it hosts a variety of demonstrations and short courses run by proprietor Eric Treuille and other food writers and chefs.
🕐 Tue–Sat 10–6 🚇 Ladbroke Grove
🚌 7, 23, 52, 70

FOYLES
Map 168 J4
113–119 Charing Cross Road WC2H 0EB
Tel 020 7437 5660
www.foyles.co.uk
This enormous and confusing bookshop stocks a massive 1.4 million titles—and a promise that you're more likely to find that elusive title here than in any other bookshop. It has an active schedule of literary luncheons, a big music section, a snazzy jazz café and a section of books for, by and about women.
🕐 Mon–Sat 9.30–8, Sun 12–6
🚇 Tottenham Court Road 🚌 14, 19, 24, 29, 176

SIMON FINCH
Map 167 H4
53 Maddox Street W1S 2PN
Tel 020 7499 0974
www.simonfinch.com
This leading UK dealer of rare books, specializing in medieval texts and 16th-century science books, with prices ranging from £100 to £500,000, promises to obtain any rare book on sale worldwide. Knowledgeable and helpful staff.
🕐 Mon–Fri 10–6 🚇 Bond Street
🚌 8, 10, 14, 19

HATCHARDS
Map 168 H5
187 Piccadilly W1J 9LE
Tel 020 7439 9921
www.hatchards.co.uk
John Hatchard started his bookshop in 1797 and moved it to the current site in 1801. Hatchards will find you any book in print in Britain. Stocked categories include art and architecture, food and wine, military, performing arts, science, philosophy and sports.
🕐 9.30–6.30, Tue 10–6 🚇 Piccadilly Circus
🚌 9, 14, 19, 22

WATERSTONE'S
Map 168 H5
203–206 Piccadilly W1V 1LE
Tel 020 7851 2400
www.waterstones.co.uk
This flagship branch of the major chain (see pages 184–185) is Europe's biggest bookshop, with specialist floors focusing on fiction, academic titles, children's books and other subjects. Refreshments on the fifth floor.
🕐 Mon–Sat 10–10, Sun 12–6 🚇 Piccadilly Circus 🚌 9, 14, 19, 22

WESLEY OWEN
Map 167 G4
3–9 Wigmore Street W1U 1AD
Tel 020 7493 1851
www.wesleyowen.com
The UK's largest stockist of Christian books and music has three floors over 372sq m (4,000sq ft) and bibles in 20 languages—many more by order.
🕐 Mon–Fri 9.30–6, Sat 9.30–5.30 🚇 Bond Street 🚌 13, 74, 82, 274

CHILDREN

BENJAMIN POLLOCK'S TOY SHOP
Map 168 K4
44 The Market, Covent Garden WC2E 8RF
Tel 020 7379 7866
www.pollocks-coventgarden.co.uk
Benjamin Pollock started selling theatrical sheets—a penny plain, twopence coloured—to children in the 19th century, and this extraordinary shop carries on the tradition of selling beautifully made toy theatres, as well as old-fashioned, hand-crafted items such as Punch and Judy puppets, dolls, miniatures, paper gifts and every imaginable unusual toy.
🕐 Mon–Sat 10.30–6, Sun 11–4 🚇 Covent Garden 🚌 6, 9, 13, 23, RV1

DAISY & TOM
Map 167 E8
181 King's Road SW3 5EB
Tel 020 7352 5000
www.daisyandtom.com
Smart shop for Chelsea tots, stocking children's books, toys, nursery furniture and, upstairs, beautiful designer clothes. Worth a visit for the puppet shows (*Peter and the Wolf*) peformed several times daily. The hair salon specializes in fast haircuts, with videos to distract.
🕐 9.30–6, Thu, Sat 9.30–7, Sun 11–5
🚇 Sloane Square 🚌 11, 19, 22, C1

SPECIAL

HAMLEYS
Map 167 H4
188–196 Regent Street W1B 5BT
Tel 0870 333 2455
www.hamleys.co.uk
The World's Finest Toyshop and great fun for all ages. Five large

floors full of the latest playthings—soft toys, dolls, dressing up, computer games, train sets, kites, LEGO and much more. Staff demonstrate the latest gadgets.
🕐 Mon–Sat 10–8, Sun 12–6 🚇 Oxford Circus 🚌 8, 10, 12, 13

KENT & CAREY
Map 167 E8
154 Wandsworth Bridge Road SW6 2UH
Tel 020 7736 5554
www.kentandcarey.co.uk
Enjoy browsing through this collection of children's clothes, which includes classic pinafores, woollen coats and pyjamas. There are also beautiful corduroy trousers and checked shirts for little boys.
🕐 Mon–Sat 9.30–5.30 🚇 Parsons Green 🚌 14, 22, 28

TRADITIONAL TOYS OF CHELSEA
Map 167 F8
53 Godfrey Street SW3 3SX
Tel 020 7352 1718
As the name suggests, this is the place to come for traditional wooden toys. Also soft toys, dressing up costumes for children, fairytale dolls and puppets—but definitely no computer games!
🕐 Mon–Fri 10–5.30, Sat 10–6, Sun 11–4.30 🚇 South Kensington, Sloane Square 🚌 11, 19, 22, 211

WHAT TO DO

YOUNG ENGLAND

Map 167 G7
47 Elizabeth Street SW1W 9PP
Tel 020 7259 9003
www.youngengland.com

Traditional, classic children's clothing including pinafore dresses, kilts, romper suits and velvet-trimmed woollen coats.
Mon–Fri 10–5.30, Sat 10–3 Sloane Square, Victoria 11 19, 22, 211, C1

DEPARTMENT STORES

BARKERS

See page 171

FENWICK

Map 167 H4
63 New Bond Street W1A 3BS
Tel 020 7629 9161
www.fenwick.co.uk
Unintimidating department store with five floors of fashions and accessories, lingerie and housewares. Personal shopping suite.
Mon–Sat 10–6.30, Thu 10–8 Bond Street 8, 10, 14, 19

HARVEY NICHOLS

Map 167 F6
67 Brompton Road SW1X 7RJ
Tel 020 7235 5000 (recorded information)
www.harveynichols.com
Chic department store with marvellous window displays and an ultra-trendy beauty bar that can even sell you 10 minutes of fresh air! Six floors of clothing, housewares and a food market on the fifth floor. Stylish café, restaurant (see page 257) and sushi bar.
Mon, Tue, Sat 10–7, Wed, Thu, Fri 10–8, Sun 12–6 Knightsbridge 9, 10 14, 74, C1

SPECIAL

HARRODS

Map 167 F6
87–135 Brompton Road SW1X 7XL
Tel 020 7730 1234
www.harrods.com
Harrods is a miniature kingdom. Its vast, terracotta building occupies 6ha (15 acres)—a far cry from its origins as a small grocer's shop in 1849. Its Latin motto is *omnia, omnibus, ubique*—'everything for everyone,

everywhere'. Pick up the Store Guide at the entrance for details of exhibitions and demonstrations.
For many, the first-floor food halls are the highlight, partly for the range of good foods on display, but also for W. J. Neatley's tiled ceilings (1902).
Equally lavish art-deco ceramics decorate both the men's hairdressing rooms and the women's lavatories. The elaborate central escalator is inspired by the art of Ancient Egypt.
Mon–Sat 10–7 Knightsbridge 9, 10 14, 74, C1

JOHN LEWIS

Map 167 H4
Oxford Street W1A 1EX
Tel 020 7629 7711
www.johnlewis.co.uk
Largest by far of this chain of department stores, this is the place to shop for household goods, from batteries and towels to furniture and entire kitchens. Very good quality, clearly and logically set out and 'never knowingly undersold'. Also sells beauty products and conservatively priced clothing.
Mon–Sat 9.30–7, Thu 9.30–8 Oxford Circus, Bond Street 8, 10, 12, 23, 73

PETER JONES

Map 167 F7
Sloane Square SW1W 8EL
Tel 020 7730 3434
www.peterjones.co.uk
While the branch in Oxford Street is the largest John Lewis store (see below), PJ (as it's affectionately known) is a more personal part of the chain. Remains one of the best shops in London for housewares and middle-market clothing.
Mon–Sat 9.30–7 Sloane Square 11, 19, 22, 211, C1

SELFRIDGE'S

Map 167 G4
400 Oxford Street W1A 1AB
Tel 0870 8377 377
www.selfridges.com

A Victorian façade hides this popular store, now a modern emporium filled with designer clothes, accessories and a huge beauty hall. Also has a food hall with eclectic foodstuffs from around the globe.
Mon–Fri 10–8, Sat 9.30–8, Sun 12–6 Marble Arch, Bond Street 6, 7, 10, 12, 13, 15, 23, 73, 94, 98, 113, 137, 139, 159

DISCOUNTERS

CONRAN 2

Map 167 E8
Bluebird, 350 King's Road SW3 5UU
Tel 020 7559 1140
Formerly known as the Conran Sale Shop, this outlet in the Bluebird complex sells end-of-line products from The Conran Shop such as vases, lamps and crockery by the British designer's team. A frequent turnover of stock. The Cook Shop offers a great selection of simple, well-made products.
Mon–Sat 10–6, Wed 10–8, Sun 11–5.30 Sloane Square 11, 19, 22, 211, 328

WHAT TO DO

LIBERTY

Map 167 H4
210–220 Regent Street W1B 5AH
Tel 020 7734 1234
www.liberty.co.uk

Mock-Tudor building, complete with creaky timber staircase and sloping ceilings, actually built in the 1920s. The interior contains an eclectic stock ranging from ornaments and rugs that seem to have been gathered on some explorer's travels to designer apparel. Menswear boutique with shirts and ties of every colour imaginable.

⏰ Mon, Tue, Wed 10–6.30, Thu 10–8, Fri, Sat 10–7, Sun 12–6 🚇 Oxford Circus, Piccadilly Circus 🚌 8, 10, 12, 13, 23

DESIGNER BARGAINS

Map 166 C6
29 Kensington Church Street W8 4LL
Tel 020 7795 6777
A wide selection of designer clothing, mainly for women, but has a particularly good Chanel section. You need to search to find something good, but that's half the fun. Also sells good designer shoes, including some by Jimmy Choo and Manolo Blahnik.

⏰ Mon–Sat 10–6 🚇 Kensington High Street 🚌 9, 10, 27, 52

ANDERSON & SHEPPARD

Map 167 H4
30 Savile Row W1S 3PT
Tel 020 7734 1420
Established in 1906, Anderson's is very traditional, with wooden counters and tape measures. Superlative classic English gentlemen's suits are hand-crafted here by expert tailors at a cost of nearly £2,000 per suit. Also sells blazers and overcoats.

⏰ Mon–Fri 8.30–5 🚇 Piccadilly Circus, Oxford Circus 🚌 12, 13, 15, 23, 139

GIORGIO ARMANI

Map 167 F6
37–42 Sloane Street SW1X 9LP
Tel 020 7235 6232
www.giorgioarmani.com
Comparatively understated fashion. This shop is one of a number of showcases of big Italian names along this street, also including Alberta Ferretti at No. 205 and Prada at No. 43.

⏰ Mon–Sat 10–6, Wed 10–7 🚇 Knightsbridge 🚌 19, 22, 137, C1

BRORA

Map 167 E8
344 King's Road SW3 5UR
Tel 020 7352 3697
www.brora.co.uk
Cashmere heaven. Beautiful, soft classics for men, women and children in sometimes startling hues, as well as blankets and tweedy bags and slippers. Not cheap but great quality.

⏰ Mon–Sat 10–6 🚇 South Kensington, Sloane Square 🚌 11, 19, 22, 211, 328

BROWNS

Map 167 G4
23–27 South Molton Street W1K 5RD
Tel 020 7514 0000
www.brownsfashion.com
The latest and funkiest labels for women makes this smart boutique look intimidating, and it isn't cheap, but the people here know what's in vogue. See Browns Focus (No. 38) across the road for younger lines and Browns Labels for Less (No. 49) along the street for sale items. Small men's selection.

⏰ Mon–Sat 10–6.30, Thu 10–7 🚇 Bond Street 🚌 8, 10, 12, 73, 139

JIMMY CHOO

Map 167 F7
169 Draycott Avenue SW3 3AJ
Tel 020 7584 6111
www.jimmychoo.com
The best place to find sexy high-heeled shoes in the Western hemisphere, this is in Brompton Cross, the playground of the beautiful rich. Your wallet could be stretched by these fabulous items, but trying them on costs nothing and they make you feel like a superstar.

⏰ Mon–Sat 10–6, Wed 10–7, Sun 1–6 🚇 South Kensington 🚌 14, 49, 360

TURNBULL & ASSER

Map 168 H5
71–72 Jermyn Street SW1Y 6PF
Tel 020 7808 3000
www.turnbullandasser.com

The place to buy men's shirts off the peg or bespoke is set among other similar shops. Turnbull & Asser makes Prince Charles's shirts and used to make them for Edward VIII when he was Prince of Wales. Opened in 1885, the shop occupies a fine old building with a wood-panelled interior.

⏰ Mon–Fri 9–6, Sat 9.30–6 🚇 Green Park, Piccadilly Circus 🚌 9, 14, 19, 22, 38

BERRY BROS & RUDD

Map 168 H5
3 St. James's Street SW1A 1EG
Tel 020 7396 9600
www.bbr.com
Holding two royal warrants, this is perhaps the oldest wine merchant in the world, established in 1698. The firm offers a huge variety of wines and can supply 2,500 different types, maintaining perfect climate control in its warehouse in Hampshire. The St. James's Street shop is a beautiful, very old building with sloping floors.

⏰ Mon–Fri 10–6, Sat 10–4 🚇 Green Park, Piccadilly Circus 🚌 9, 14, 19, 22, 38

FORTNUM AND MASON

See page 180

HARRODS FOOD HALL

See page 178

LIDGATE

Map 166 off C5
110 Holland Park Avenue W11 4UA
Tel 020 7727 8243

Famous traditional butcher's shop in Holland Park. Established in 1850, it sets the standard in the trade. Also makes its own meat pies (steak and kidney, turkey and bacon and the like) and stocks many British cheeses.

🕐 Mon–Fri 7–6, Sat 7–5 🚇 Holland Park 🚌 94, 148

NEAL'S YARD DAIRY

Map 168 J4
17 Shorts Gardens
WC2H 9AT
Tel 020 7240 5700

The queen of cheese shops in Covent Garden concentrates on cheese made by small-scale makers in the British Isles. Owners Randolph Hodgson and Jane Scotter buy direct from farms and sell around 60 to 70 varieties in the dairy, a wonderful place displaying vast round cheeses, where you can sample the wares.

🕐 Mon–Thu 11–6.30, Fri, Sat 10–6.30 🚇 Covent Garden 🚌 6, 9, 13, 23, 77A

POILÂNE

Map 167 G7
46 Elizabeth Street SW1W 9PA
Tel 020 7808 4910
www.poilane.com

An English outpost of a truly Parisian bread and pâtisserie bakery. Poilâne uses an enormous wood-fired oven to bake 80 loaves of its delicious and famously expensive sourdough bread every two hours. Have a look at the extraordinary bread chandelier, the original of which was made by artist Salvador Dalí in payment for his daily loaf.

🕐 Mon–Fri 7.30–7.30, Sat 7.30–6 🚇 Sloane Square 🚌 11, 19, 22, 211, C1

ROCOCO

Map 167 E8
321 King's Road SW3 5EP
Tel 020 7352 5857
www.rococochocolates.com

Incredible chocolates, mostly handmade on the premises. Choose from hundreds of different varieties including quails' eggs (pralines), marzipans, violet creams and great big bars. Situated on a pleasant row of shops about 20 minutes' walk from Sloane Square.

🕐 Mon–Sat 10–6.30, Sun 12–5 🚇 South Kensington, Sloane Square 🚌 11, 19, 22, 211, 319

R TWINING & CO

Map 168 L4
216 Strand, Covent Garden WC2R 1AP
Tel 020 7353 3511
www.twinings.com

One of London's oldest firms, trading in tea for about 300 years, this shop—still on its original site—sells a wide range of teas, as well as fruit and herb infusions plus teapots, cups, mugs and biscuits. A small museum at the back traces the family's history and displays oddities from the tea-trading world.

🕐 Mon–Fri 9.30–4.45 🚇 Temple, Charing Cross 🚌 9, 11, 13, 15, RV1

HALCYON DAYS

Map 167 H4
14 Brook Street W1S 1BD
Tel 020 7629 8811
www.halcyondays.co.uk

Look no further if you want small enamel boxes, clocks and precious trinkets—ideal gifts for christenings, birthdays and

FORTNUM AND MASON

Map 168 H5
Piccadilly W1A 1ER
Tel 020 7734 8040
www.fortnumandmason.co.uk

Founded in 1707 as a grocery, this famous store is wood-panelled and lit with chandeliers. The ground-floor food hall is particularly good. Treat yourself to a snack in the Fountain Restaurant or try the Salmon & Champagne Bar. Outside, the clock chimes the hour and Mr. Fortnum and Mr. Mason emerge and bow.

🕐 Mon–Sat 10–6.30, Sun (Food Hall and Patio Restaurant only) 12–6 🚇 Green Park, Piccadilly Circus 🚌 9, 14, 19, 22, 38

weddings—to order. The 18th-century craft of enamelling was revived when this shop opened in the 1960s. It holds all current royal warrants for *objets d'art*.

🕐 Mon–Fri 9.30–6, Sat 10–6 🚇 Bond Street 🚌 8, 10, 14, 19

JAMES SMITH & SONS

Map 168 J4
53 New Oxford Street WC1A 1BL
Tel 020 7836 4731
www.james-smith.co.uk

This very traditional old London shop, established in 1830, manufactures umbrellas by hand—a real craft. You'll also find shooting sticks, parasols and walking sticks in which you can keep dice—or a dram of whisky.

🕐 Mon–Fri 9.30–5.20, Sat 10–5.20
🚇 Tottenham Court Road 🚌 8, 14, 98

LULU GUINNESS
Map 167 F7
3 Ellis Street SW1X 9AL
Tel 020 7823 4828
www.luluguinness.com
Opened in 1996, this sleek, modern shop sells quirky 1950s handbags, hats and shoes. Lulu studied art in Paris and decided to push the boundaries of the bag— hence the handbags in the shape of flower baskets, spiders' webs and even castles—and her creativity has made her famous.

🕐 Mon–Fri 10–6, Sat 11–6 🚇 Sloane Square 🚌 11, 19, 22, 211, C1

PULBROOK & GOULD
Map 167 F7
Liscartan House, 127 Sloane Street SW1X 9AS
Tel 020 7730 0030
In a bright, modern conservatory-style shop scented with rare orchids, you will find some of the most stylish flower arrangements in London. Most are classic with a twist (berries or herbs, perhaps mixing with the blooms). Also offers short courses in flower-arranging and social etiquette.

🕐 Mon–Fri 9–5.30, Sat 10–2 🚇 Sloane Square 🚌 11, 19, 22, 211, C1

THE KITE STORE
Map 168 J4
48 Neal Street WC2H 9PA
Tel 020 7836 1666
You'll find every kite you can imagine here, from very simple models for £1 to huge stunt kites for £650. Open since 1976, the store also sells materials for making your own kite as well as kite-surfing kits for the beach.

🕐 Mon–Fri 10–6, Thu 10–7, Sat 10.30–6 🚇 Covent Garden 🚌 1, 9, 11, 13, 15

PLAYIN' GAMES
Map 168 J3
33 Museum Street WC1A 1JR
Tel 020 7323 3080
www.playingames.co.uk

Central London's only indoor games specialist. Set a stone's throw from the British Museum and among a number of bookshops and print galleries (which themselves are worth a visit). The store offers board games, classic, family and role-playing games.

🕐 Mon–Sat 10–6, Thu 10–7, Sun 12–6
🚇 Tottenham Court Road 🚌 7, 188

UNDER TWO FLAGS
Map 167 G4
4 St. Christopher's Place W1U 1LZ
Tel 020 7935 6934
www.undertwoflags.com
This little shop on atmospheric St. Christopher's Place sells toy and model soldiers as well as books to educate you on the subject. You can spend £50 for a set of toy soldiers or up to £600 for a single handmade model soldier.

🕐 Tue–Sat 10.30–5 🚇 Bond Street
🚌 8, 10, 12, 23, 73

CATH KIDSTON
Map 167 F8
8 Elystan Street SW3 3NS
Tel 020 7584 3232
www.cathkidston.co.uk
Cath Kidston's pretty and now famous floral designs, inspired by 1950s patterns, are available on fabrics, wallpapers, bed linen, table linen, vintage jewellery and ornaments in this charming Chelsea Green shop. The original store is in Clarendon Cross, Holland Park, and there is also one in Fulham Road.

🕐 Mon–Sat 10–6 🚇 Sloane Square, South Kensington 🚌 11, 19, 22, 211, 319

CHELSEA HARBOUR DESIGN CENTRE
Off map
Chelsea Harbour, Lots Road SW10 0XF
Tel 020 7225 9100
www.chdc.co.uk
This huge, conservatory-style building houses approximately 80 design showrooms, including Colefax & Fowler, Mary Fox Linton and Zimmer & Rohde. The most sumptuous choice of fabrics and wallpapers—some papers go for hundreds of pounds per roll. A good place to spot trends.

🕐 Mon–Fri 10–5 🚇 Fulham Broadway
🚌 14, 28, 211, 424

HEAL'S
Map 167 F8
234 King's Road SW3 5UA
Tel 020 7349 8411
www.heals.co.uk
A top destination for contemporary interior design and furnishings for the past two centuries, with striking, high-quality furniture, rugs, beds, furnishing fabrics, bed linen and home accessories. The main store, on Tottenham Court Road, is immense.

🕐 Mon, Tue, Wed 10–6, Thu, Fri 10–7, Sat 10–6.30, Sun 12–6 🚇 Sloane Square; Goodge Street 🚌 11, 19, 22, 211, C1

CHRISTOPHER WRAY
Map 167 E8
591–593 King's Road SW6 2YW
Tel 020 7751 8701
www.christopherwray.co.uk

The speciality in this huge lighting emporium among the King's Road antiques shops is the Tiffany-style lamp (stained-glass shade), but you will also find wall, ceiling and table lamps in every conceivable theme, shape and hue. Contemporary lamps are in a branch across the street. Not to everyone's taste but unmissable.

🕐 Mon–Sat 9.30–6 🚇 Fulham Broadway
🚌 11, 22, 211

FARROW & BALL
Map 166 E8
249 Fulham Road SW3 6HY
Tel 020 7351 0273
www.farrow-ball.com
Handmade wallpapers and subtly tinted paints—with names such as Mouse's Back and Dead Salmon— are the speciality of this traditional

WHAT TO DO

business. The style has been copied by many and demonstrated in interiors magazines, but this is the original.
🕐 Mon–Fri 9.30–6, Wed 9.30–7, Sat 10–5 🚇 South Kensington 🚌 14, 49, 144

GENERAL TRADING COMPANY
Map 167 G7
2 Symons Street SW3 2TJ
Tel 020 7730 0411
www.general-trading.co.uk
A stylish emporium—laid out to resemble a lovely home—stocking furniture, tableware and ornaments. Since 1920 it's provided stylish wedding gifts and holds all current royal warrants. You might spot a celebrity or two in the café.
🕐 Mon–Sat 10–6.30, Wed 10–7 🚇 Sloane Square 🚌 11, 19, 22, 211, C1

LEATHER GOODS
MULBERRY COMPANY
Map 167 H4
41–42 New Bond Street W1S 2RY
Tel 020 7491 3900
www.mulberry.com
Ready-to-wear fashions for men and women, plus accessories, bags, luggage and items such as camera cases, all in top-quality leather. Founder Roger Saul originally started out as a belt designer. This flagship store has three floors and is fitted out in oak, amber glass, bronze and, of course, leather.
🕐 Mon–Sat 10–6, Thu 10–7 🚇 Bond Street 🚌 8, 10, 14, 19

LINGERIE
AGENT PROVOCATEUR
Map 167 F7
16 Pont Street SW1X 9EN
Tel 020 7235 0229
www.agentprovocateur.com
This boudoir-style shop in otherwise very proper Belgravia sells seductive and even quite raunchy underwear. Sold by the son and daughter-in-law of Vivienne Westwood, who came to fame with her outrageous punk designs in the 1970s.
🕐 Mon–Sat 10–6 🚇 Knightsbridge, Sloane Square 🚌 19, 22, 137, C1

JANET REGER
Map 167 F6
2 Beauchamp Place SW3 1NG
Tel 020 7584 9360
www.janetreger.com

Beautifully made, classic women's nightwear and lingerie in lace, satin and silk. Real luxury at a high price. Janet Reger started working as a freelance designer in 1961, and her early products are now considered collectors' pieces.
🕐 Mon–Sat 10–6 🚇 Knightsbridge, South Kensington 🚌 14, 74, C1

RIGBY & PELLER
Map 167 F6
2 Hans Road SW3 1RX
Tel 020 7589 9293
www.rigbyandpeller.com

There is nothing the women at the Queen's corsetier do not know about undergarments. They can tell what size you are without a tape measure and have underwear for every size and shape of woman. There's a huge selection of swimwear and, of course, corsets. Just opposite Harrods.
🕐 Mon–Sat 9.30–6, Wed 9.30–7 🚇 Knightsbridge 🚌 14, 74, C1

MARKETS
BERWICK STREET
Map 168 F4
Berwick Street W1
This fruit and vegetable market tucked away in Soho also sells cheese, bread, herbs and spices. Loud stallholders, media and fashion folk plus a few shady characters set a lively scene. Come at lunchtime to see the market at its best. Runs between Oxford Street and Old Compton Street.
🕐 Mon–Sat 8–6 🚇 Piccadilly Circus 🚌 10, 14, 19, 25, 38

COVENT GARDEN
Map 168 K4
Manager's office: 41 The Market WC2E 8RF
Tel 020 7836 9136 (manager's office)
www.coventgardenmarket.co.uk

Well worth a visit just to see the street performers and soak up the lively atmosphere that's in full swing throughout the day. The central area, the Piazza, hosts an antiques and collectables market on Mondays and an arts and crafts market selling jewellery, clothing, silverware and pottery the rest of the week (see pages 88 and 175).
🕐 Daily 10–7 🚇 Covent Garden 🚌 9, 11, 13, 15, RV1

LEADENHALL
Map 169 N4
Whittington Avenue EC3 (Gracechurch Street to Lime Street)
www.cityoflondon.gov.uk
Probably the most chic of London's markets includes meat, fish, poultry, cheese, wine and chocolate specialists. Worth visiting for the atmospheric building in the heart of the City (see page 232), which really comes to life early lunchtime.
🕐 Mon–Fri 7–4 🚇 Monument/Bank 🚌 8, 25, 40

PETTICOAT LANE
Map 169 P4
Middlesex Street and Wentworth Street E1
Tel 020 7377 8963
www.eastlondonmarkets.com

SPECIAL

PORTOBELLO ROAD
Map 166 C4
Market Office: 72 Tavistock Road W11 1AN
Tel 020 7727 7684
www.portobelloroad.co.uk
Famous street market with hundreds of stalls selling antiques, vintage clothing, *objets d'art* and, at the northern end, fresh fruit

and vegetables, baked goods and meat. It's not cheap and there is a lot of junk, but it's fun and you might spot a bargain face or two. Runs along Portobello Road from Pembridge Road (Notting Hill Underground station) north up to Westbourne Park Road (Ladbroke Grove Underground station). Come early if you want a better chance of finding a bargain.
🕙 Mon–Wed, Sat 8–7, Thu 8–1, Fri 8–6
🚇 Notting Hill Gate 🚌 23, 52, 94

London's most famous market was named after the garments sold by French immigrants in the 1700s. Look for clothing at bargain prices —especially fabrics and leather jackets. Around 1,000 stalls.
🕙 Mon 8–2, Tue–Fri 8–4, Sun 9–2
🚇 Liverpool Street, Aldgate 🚌 8, 42, 344

ST. JAMES'S PICCADILLY
Map 168 H5
197 Piccadilly W1J 9LL
Tel 020 7734 4511
The stalls are set up in the courtyard of this charming church (see page 195). There is an antiques market on Tuesdays and a general market with arts and crafts Wednesday to Saturday.
🕙 Tue 8–6, Wed–Sat 10–6 🚇 Piccadilly Circus, Green Park 🚌 9, 14, 19, 22, 38

ST. MARTIN-IN-THE-FIELDS
Map 168 J5
6 St. Martin's Place WC2N 4JJ
Tel 020 7930 7821
Held in the courtyard behind the church (see page 117), this busy market manages to accommodate no fewer than 200 stalls, selling handmade crafts, ceramics, jewellery and clothes. It's a tight squeeze but great for browsing.
🕙 Mon–Sat 10–6 🚇 Leicester Square, Charing Cross 🚌 24, 29, 176

MUSIC

ANDY'S
Map 168 J4
27 Denmark Street WC2H 8NJ
Tel 020 7916 5080
www.andysguitarnet.com
Professional guitarists try out new instruments, and electric, acoustic, classical, rock and even 12-string guitars—new and second-hand— can be found at competitive prices at this shop, one of several similar in this short street. Also does expert repairs.
🕙 Mon, Tue, Wed 10–7, Thu, Fri, Sat 10–8.30, Sun 12.30–6.30 🚇 Tottenham Court Road 🚌 7, 188

BOOSEY & HAWKES
Map 167 H4
295 Regent Street W1B 2JH
Tel 020 7580 2060
www.boosey.com
Founded in 1930, this place stocks a huge range of musical instruments, many made by the company. Specializes in 20th-century composers and is heavily involved in music education.
🕙 Mon–Fri 9.30–6, Sat 10–5 🚇 Oxford Circus 🚌 8, 10, 12, 13, 23

CHAPPELL OF BOND STREET
Map 167 H4
50 New Bond Street, W1S 1RD
Tel 020 7491 2777
www.chappellofbondstreet.co.uk
Established in 1811 and once frequented by Beethoven, Richard Strauss and Charles Dickens, this store has the largest selection of classical and popular printed music in the UK. Also specializes in keyboards and brass/woodwind instruments.
🕙 Mon–Fri 9.30–6, Sat 9.30–5 🚇 Bond Street 🚌 8, 10, 14, 19

FOOTE'S
Map 168 H4
10 Golden Square W1S 9JA
Tel 020 7437 1811
www.footesmusic.com

Huge selection of drums, percussion, woodwind, brass and string instruments to buy new or second-hand, or just to hire, and at reasonable prices.
🕙 Mon–Fri 9–6, Sat 9–5 🚇 Piccadilly Circus 🚌 14, 19, 38

HAROLD MOORES RECORDS
Map 168 H4
2 Great Marlborough Street W1F 7HQ
Tel 020 7437 1576
www.hmrecords.co.uk
Classical music is the focus here. The shop stocks a tremendous range, which may well be England's largest and most comprehensive collection of LPs and CDs. Second-hand LPs, too.
🕙 Mon–Sat 9.30–7 🚇 Oxford Circus 🚌 8, 10, 12, 13, 23

TOWER RECORDS
Map 168 J5
1 Piccadilly Circus W1J 0TR
Tel 020 7439 2500
www.towerrecords.co.uk
This megastore sells practically every known recording, from chart hits to specialist stock, as well as computer games.
🕙 Mon–Sat 9am–11pm, Sun 12–6 🚇 Piccadilly Circus 🚌 9, 14, 19, 22

SPORTING GOODS

FARLOWS
Map 168 J5
9 Pall Mall SW1Y 5LX
Tel 020 7839 2423
www.farlows.co.uk
Established in 1840, this shop specializes in fishing tackle, shooting
continued on page 186

CHAIN STORES

With so many shops in London, it can be a time-consuming business finding those that sell exactly what you are looking for. This chart tells you what to expect in many of the stores that can be found throughout the capital. Call the head office to find your nearest branch, or look at the website. Most sell goods online.

Gap specializes in casual, comfortable clothes for men women, children and babies

WHAT TO DO

NAME	Women's clothing and/or shoes	Men's clothing and/or shoes	Children's clothing and items	Pharmacy and toiletries	Jewellery and accessories	Souvenirs and gifts	Books, music and magazines	Sports and outdoor kit	Food and drink	Household and electrical goods	HEAD OFFICE
BHS	✔	✔	✔		✔					✔	020 7262 3288
Blacks	✔	✔						✔			01604 441111
Bodyshop			✔	✔	✔						01903 731500
Boots		✔	✔	✔	✔				✔	✔	0845 070 8090
Borders							✔				020 7379 7313
Burtons		✔									020 7636 8040
Clarks	✔	✔	✔								01458 843131
Crabtree & Evelyn				✔		✔					020 7361 0499
Dixons										✔	01442 353000
Dolcis	✔	✔	✔								01582 723131
Edinburgh Woollen Mills	✔	✔	✔		✔	✔					01387 380611
Evans	✔										020 7636 8040
French Connection	✔	✔	✔		✔						020 7399 7300
Gap	✔	✔	✔								01788 818300
Goldsmiths					✔	✔					0116 232 2000
H&M	✔	✔	✔								020 7323 2211
Habitat										✔	020 7614 5500
HMV							✔				020 7432 2000
Holland & Barrett				✔					✔		02476 244400
Jessops										✔	0116 232 6000
Jigsaw	✔										020 8392 5678
JJB	✔	✔						✔			01942 221400
Jones	✔	✔	✔								01323 730532
Laura Ashley	✔		✔		✔					✔	0870 5622 116
Marks & Spencer	✔	✔	✔	✔	✔	✔			✔	✔	020 7935 4422
Monsoon	✔		✔		✔						020 7313 3000
Mothercare			✔	✔						✔	08453 304030
Next	✔	✔	✔		✔					✔	0845 456 7777
Paperchase						✔					020 7467 6200
Past Times				✔	✔	✔	✔			✔	01993 770500
Russell & Bromley	✔	✔	✔		✔						020 8460 1122
Sole Trader	✔	✔	✔								01442 241431
Thorntons						✔			✔		0800 454537
Topshop	✔		✔								020 7636 8040
Virgin Megastores							✔				020 8752 9000
Wallis	✔										020 7636 8040
Waterstone's							✔				020 8742 3800
WH Smith							✔				01793 695195
Whittard of Chelsea						✔			✔		0800 0154 394
Woolworths	✔	✔	✔	✔	✔	✔	✔	✔	✔	✔	020 7262 1222

Goods can be exchanged or returned at any store within the chain, regardless of where you made the purchase.

The Body Shop chain was started in 1976 by Anita Roddick. She concocted a few handmade products, using natural ingredients and with as little packaging as possible

DESCRIPTION	SHOP WEBSITE
Mid-range clothing plus household goods and lighting	www.bhs.co.uk
Camping and outdoor equipment	www.blacks.co.uk
Pioneering retailer of cosmetic products using natural, sustainable resources	www.thebodyshop.com
Chemists and opticians plus cosmetics, children's and baby items and homeware	www.boots.com
Books and CDs and a wide range of magazines and papers	www.borders.co.uk
Mid-range clothing for men	www.burtons.co.uk
Good-value shoes for men, women and children	www.clarks.co.uk
Herbal goods and flowery essences of every kind	www.crabtree-evelyn.co.uk
Electrical goods from TVs and refrigerators to cameras and computers	www.dixons.co.uk
Shoes for men, women and children	www.dolcis.co.uk
Woollen products of all descriptions for men and women, plus gifts and accessories	www.ewm.co.uk
Women's fashion retailer for sizes 16+	www.evans.ltd.uk
Well-established clothing store	www.frenchconnection.com
Casual clothing for men, women and children	www.gap.com
Jewellery, clocks, watches and fancy goods	www.goldsmiths.co.uk
Bargain clothing for women and children	www.hm.com
Modern furniture and household goods with emphasis on design	www.habitat.net
Huge music retailer	www.hmv.co.uk
Health foods, vitamins and alternative remedies	www.hollandandbarrett.com
Sells all kinds of photographic equipment and accessories, including digital	www.jessops.com
Smart clothes for young women	www.jigsaw-online.com
Sportswear for men and women	www.jjb.co.uk
Good-quality footwear for men, women and children	www.jonesbootmaker.com
Own brand women's and children's clothing and home furnishings	www.laura-ashley.com
Famous clothing, food and homeware store	www.marksandspencer.com
Women and children's clothing specializing in partyware	www.monsoon.co.uk
Baby and toddler clothes, toys and equipment	www.mothercare.com
Smart, practical clothing for men, women and children	www.next.co.uk
Everything made of paper plus up-to-the-minute stationery	www.paperchase.co.uk
Reproduction period home and giftware	www.past-times.co.uk
Fashionable shoes, boots and bags	www.russellandbromley.co.uk
Casual shoes for the young and trendy	www.sole-trader.co.uk
Attractively packaged, own-brand chocolate and toffees	www.thorntons.co.uk
Up-to-the-minute fashion for the young	www.topshop.co.uk
Music retailer specializing in the popular end of the market	www.virginmega.co.uk
Ladies' fashions	www.wallis-fashion.co.uk
Britain's biggest chain of book stores with superb coverage in larger branches	www.waterstones.co.uk
Large shops sell countless magazines, plus stationery, books, videos and CDs	www.whsmith.co.uk
Specialist teas and coffees plus many associated items	www.whittard.co.uk
Stores majoring in good-value clothing for children, music and homeware	www.woolworths.co.uk

and country clothing. Also waxed Barbour jackets, walking boots and Wellington boots.

🕐 Mon–Fri 9–6, Sat 10–5 🚇 Green Park, Piccadilly Circus 🚌 29, 91, 94, 139

LILLYWHITE'S

Map 168 J5
24–36 Lower Regent Street SW1Y 4QF
Tel 0870 333 9600

A department store dedicated entirely to sports, Lillywhite's can outfit you for virtually any pastime, from golf to skiing. Particularly strong on footwear.

🕐 Mon–Sat 10–9, Sun 12–6 🚇 Piccadilly Circus 🚌 9, 14, 19, 22

PURDEY

Map 167 G5
57–58 South Audley Street W1K 2ED
Tel 020 7499 1801
www.purdey.com

Founded in 1814, this glorious Victorian shop has supplied guns to every British monarch since Queen Victoria. Each shotgun and rifle is manufactured by hand.

🕐 Mon–Fri 9.30–5.30, Sat 10–5 🚇 Green Park, Marble Arch, Hyde Park Corner 🚌 10, 16, 73, 74, 137

YHA ADVENTURE SHOP

Map 169 M4
16–18 Ludgate Hill, The City EC4M 7DR
Tel 020 7329 4578
www.yhaadventure.com

The Youth Hostel Association's shop stocks everything you could possible need for walking and camping. Branches at 174 Kensington High Street W8 (*tel 020 7938 2948*), 150–152 Wardour Street W1 (*tel 020 7025 1900*), and 1 Southampton Street WC2 (*tel 020 7240 7350*).

🕐 Mon–Fri 10–6, Thu 10–7, Sat 9.30–6, Sun 11–5 🚇 St. Paul's 🚌 4, 11, 17, 23, 26,

STATIONERY

LONDON GRAPHIC CENTRE

Map 168 J4
16–18 Shelton Street WC2H 9JL
Tel 020 7759 4500
www.londongraphics.co.uk

Carved out of old Royal Opera House rehearsal and props storage rooms, this store has everything for the artist or designer—easels, canvases, oil paints, specialist pens and craft materials.

🕐 Mon–Fri 9.30–6, Thu 9.30–7, Sat 1.0.30–6 🚇 Covent Garden 🚌 6, 9, 23, RV1

PAPERCHASE

Map 168 J3
213 Tottenham Court Road W1T 9PS
Tel 020 7467 6200
www.paperchase.co.uk

The most design-led stationer in the UK carries a huge range of art papers and materials, including handmade Japanese papers. This is the vast flagship store of 34 UK stores.

🕐 Mon–Sat 9.30–7, Tue 10–7, Thu 9.30–8, Sun 12–6 🚇 Goodge Street 🚌 10, 24, 29, 73, 134

SMYTHSON

Map 167 H4
40 New Bond Street W1S 2DE
Tel 020 7629 8558
www.smythson.com

Writing paper, diaries and note books from this store established in 1887 are always elegant and beautifully made, if pricey.

🕐 Mon–Fri 9.30–6, Thu, Sat 10–6 🚇 Bond Street 🚌 8, 10, 14, 19

TOILETRIES

CULPEPER THE HERBALIST

Map 168 K4
8 The Market, Covent Garden WC2E 8RB
Tel 020 7379 6698
www.culpeper.co.uk

Herbs, oils, gifts and food in simple packaging. You can make your own cosmetics by adding essential oils to the store's face, hand, body and bath products.

🕐 Mon–Sat 10–7, Thu 10–8, Sun 10–6 🚇 Covent Garden 🚌 6, 9, 13, 23, RV1

FLORIS

Map 168 F5
89 Jermyn Street SW1Y 6JH
Tel 020 7930 2885
www.florislondon.com

This perfumery for ladies and gentlemen, established in 1730, is known for its classic perfumes, toilet waters, bath salts, scented soaps and men's shaving accessories and aftershave.

🕐 Mon–Fri 9.30–6, Sat 10–6 🚇 Green Park, Piccadilly Circus 🚌 9, 14, 19, 22, 38

JO MALONE

Map 167 F7
150 Sloane Street SW1X 9BX
Tel 020 7720 0202
www.jomalone.co.uk

A wonderful shop full of luxury face creams, scented candles and divine perfumery.

🕐 Mon, Tue, Fri, Sat 10–6, Wed, Thu 10–7 🚇 Sloane Square 🚌 19, 22, 137, C1

JOHN BELL & CROYDEN

Map 167 G4
50–54 Wigmore Street W1U 2AU
Tel 020 7935 5555
www.johnbellcroyden.co.uk

The best pharmacy in central London, this huge shop stocks everything from first-aid equipment and toothbrushes to aromatherapy items, wheelchairs and walking sticks.

🕐 Mon–Fri 9–6, Sat 9.30–6 🚇 Bond Street, Oxford Circus 🚌 8, 10, 12, 73, 176

MOLTON BROWN

Map 167 G4
58 South Molton Street W1K 5SL
Tel 020 7499 6474
www.moltonbrown.co.uk

A seductive aroma greets you as you cross the threshold to look for shampoos, bath oils, scented candles and other irresistible products. Set in a row of tempting fashion shops and cafés.

🕐 Mon–Sat 10–6.30, Thu 10–7 🚇 Bond Street 🚌 8, 10, 14, 19

TOYS

See Children

PERFORMANCE

The range and variety of performing arts and entertainment in London is enough to make you dizzy. Just wandering through the West End gives an idea of what's on offer, but it's also worth looking beyond central London and scanning the pages of *Time Out*, the city's most comprehensive guide to what's on in and around the city.

Note that almost all performance venues, other than clubs, do not permit smoking in the auditorium.

Numerous London venues stage world-class classical music concerts

CONTEMPORARY LIVE MUSIC

Live music covers everything from headliners to massive Wembley Arena gigs. Drum and bass duos perform in local pubs, and there's much in between—for example jazz at Ronnie Scott's in Soho and at the Pizza on the Park, among other venues. Free live music is available in the Royal Festival Hall and sometimes in the National Theatre foyer at lunchtime.

For folk, world music, blues, rock 'n' roll, salsa and whatever else, stray into outlying areas such as Camden, Kentish Town or Islington for lively pub-and-club scenes.

You'll find top jazz at Ronnie Scott's

CINEMA
The choice of films in London is huge. In addition to the multi-screen chain complexes that show new release blockbusters (many on and around Leicester Square) there are independent repertory cinemas that screen a range of special interest films and international fare with English subtitles. These include the ICA (see page 93) and the National Film Theatre (see pages 127 and 192), which has themed festivals and guest speakers.

CLASSICAL MUSIC, DANCE AND OPERA
A useful place to start is the South Bank Centre (see page 127), which has a full schedule of dance (staged by the English National Ballet) and concerts, either in the Royal Festival Hall or the more intimate Queen Elizabeth Hall or Purcell Room. For conventional classical music and big names,

check the Barbican, where the London Symphony Orchestra has its base. The Royal Opera House, Covent Garden, still has a reputation for high prices and stuffiness, despite its flashy new setting. Productions by the Royal Ballet company, based here, cost less than opera performances. For opera sung in English, head for the London Coliseum (see page 194) in St. Martin's Lane, home of the English National Opera.

Between July and September the Proms season (BBC Henry Wood Promenade Concerts) gets underway at the Royal Albert Hall (see page 194), with lunchtime chamber concerts as well as evening performances. If you don't mind standing, you can get in for not too much money.

Churches also host excellent recitals and concerts, particularly St. James's Piccadilly (see page 195) and St. Martin-in-the-Fields (see page 117).

THEATRE
Much of the West End's Theatreland now seems obsessed with long-running musicals, and to get tickets to these you must book several months in advance. The National Theatre stages classic and experimental work on the South Bank—cross Waterloo Bridge to see the current schedule digitally displayed on the façade.

Fringe theatre finds its place in pub rooms and other cramped or quirky venues, as well as in more conventional spaces such as The Gate in Notting Hill (see page 199), dedicated to staging work by new writers.

To book major theatrical and musical performances contact www.theonlineticketshop.com.

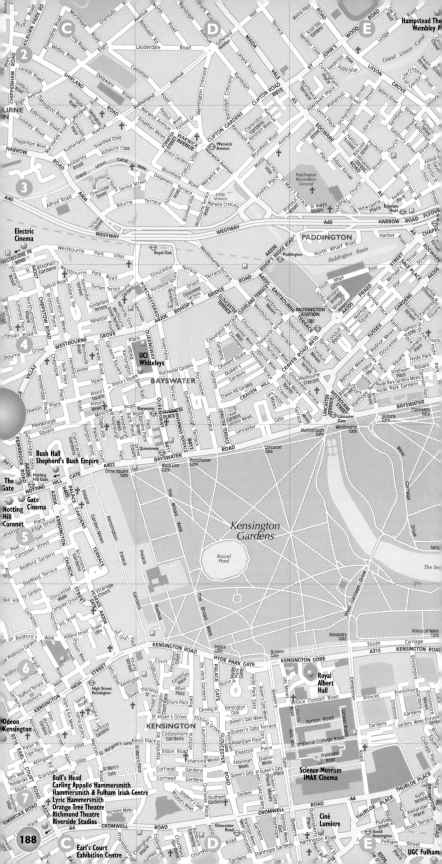

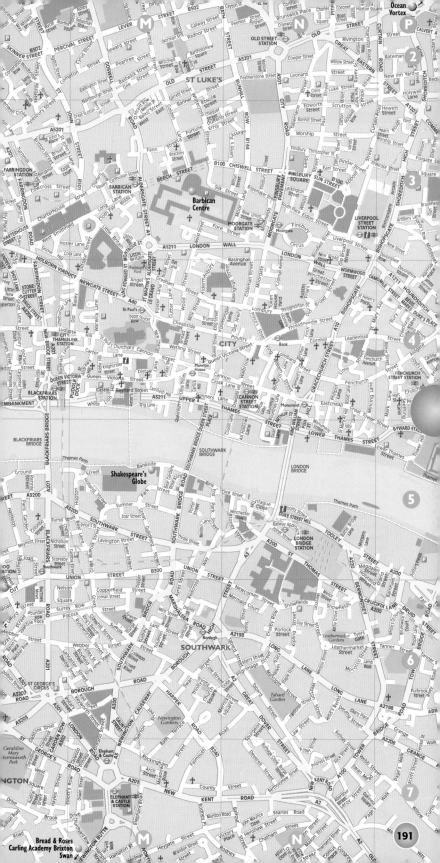

Cinemas

As a general rule, films are screened three or four times a day, starting at around midday. On Friday and Saturday nights late showings are common. It's best to book to see a big-name new release film in the West End, particularly at the weekends. Nearly all cinemas allow you to book by phone with a credit card. Tickets are often cheaper earlier in the day and on Mondays. All films have a certificate: U (universal—suitable for children of 4 or over) and PG (parental guidance advised, though the film should be suitable for children of 8 or over). The minimum age allowed for admission is denoted by a figure 18, 15 or 12A (which forbids children younger than 12 unless accompanied by an adult).

THE BARBICAN
Map 191 M4
See page 77

CURZON MAYFAIR
Map 188 G6
38 Curzon Street W1Y 7TY
Tel 020 7495 0500
www.curzon.net
Well-known art-house cinema with two screens and a bar area.
Green Park 8, 10, 14, 19

CURZON SOHO
Map 190 J5
99 Shaftesbury Avenue W1D 5DY
Tel 020 7439 4805
www.curzon.net
Three-screen cinema showing new release mainstream films and some repertory classics. Classic movies on Sundays.
Leicester Square, Piccadilly Circus 38, 19, 14

ELECTRIC CINEMA
Map 188 C4
191 Portobello Road W11 2ED
Tel 020 7908 9696
www.the-electric.co.uk
Originally opened in 1910, the Electric later turned to repertory cinema, showing old classics and independent films. Also has a brasserie.
Ladbroke Grove, Notting Hill Gate 23, 52, 94

EMPIRE
Map 190 J5
Leicester Square WC2H 7NA
Tel 0870 010 2030
www.uci-cinemas.co.uk
Large central cinema with three screens showing new releases.
Leicester Square, Piccadilly Circus 14, 24, 29

GATE CINEMA
Map 188 C6
87 Notting Hill Gate W11 3JZ
Tel 020 7727 4043
www.gatecinema.co.uk
Converted from a coffee palace in 1910; now a leading art-house venue.
Notting Hill Gate 12, 70, 94

ICA
Map 190 J6
See page 93

IMAX CINEMA
Map 190 L6
1 Charlie Chaplin Walk, South Bank
SE1 8XR
Tel 020 7902 1234
www.bfi.org.uk/imax

A 480-seat cinema in a space-age balloon, with the biggest film screen in Britain, showing exhilarating 2-D and 3-D movies.
Embankment, Waterloo 77, RV1

CINÉ LUMIÈRE
Map 188 E8
Institut Francais, 17 Queensberry Place
SW7 2DT
Tel 020 7073 1350
www.institut-francais.org.uk

Part of the French government centre of language and culture. Shows French, other European and world cinema, including premières, recent releases, classics, rare movies and visits by directors, screenwriters and actors.
South Kensington, Gloucester Road 49, 70, 74, 345

NATIONAL FILM THEATRE (NFT)
Map 190 K6
Part of the South Bank Centre (see page 127), with two cinemas showing a diverse range of British, international and old films. Focus of the annual London Film Festival (see page 224).

NOTTING HILL CORONET
Map 188 C6
103–105 Notting Hill Gate W11 3LD
Tel 020 7727 6705
A two-screen cinema showing new release mainstream films.
Notting Hill Gate 12, 70, 94

ODEON COVENT GARDEN
Map190 J5
135 Shaftesbury Avenue WC2 8AH
Tel 0870 505 0007
www.odeon.co.uk
A large single-screen cinema showing the latest feature films.
Covent Garden, Leicester Square 38, 19, 14, RV1

ODEON KENSINGTON
Map 188 C7
263 Kensington High Street W8 6NA
Tel 0870 505 0007
www.odeon.co.uk
Six screens showing the new movies from Britain and the US.
Kensington High Street 9, 10, 27, 28, 49

ODEON MARBLE ARCH
Map 189 F5
10 Edgware Road W2 2EN
Tel 0870 505 0007
www.odeon.co.uk
Five-screen multiplex.
Marble Arch 7, 10, 73

ODEON MEZZANINE
Map 190 J6
Leicester Square WC2H 7LQ
Tel 0870 505 0007
www.odeon.co.uk
Large, central, five-screen cinema showing new release mainstream films next door to its more

SPECIAL

ODEON LEICESTER SQUARE
Map 190 J6
22–24 Leicester Square WC2H 7LQ
Tel 0870 505 0007
www.odeon.co.uk

Famous central mega-cinema
and West End showpiece used
for many film premières. Six
screens show new-release blockbusters.
🚇 Leicester Square, Piccadilly Circus
🚌 24, 29, 176

---

glamorous sister, the Odeon
Leicester Square.
🚇 Leicester Square, Piccadilly Circus
🚌 24, 29, 176

ODEON PANTON STREET
Map 190 J6
11–18 Panton Street SW1Y 4DP
Tel 0870 5050 007
www.odeon.co.uk
Central four-screen multiplex
showing the lastest release main-
stream films. 🚇 Piccadilly Circus 🚌 9, 14, 19, 22

ODEON TOTTENHAM COURT ROAD
Map 190 J4
30 Tottenham Court Road W1T 1BX
Tel 0870 505 0007
www.odeon.co.uk
Tucked into a parade of shops, a
three-screen cinema showing the
latest releases.
🚇 Tottenham Court Road, Goodge Street
🚌 10, 24, 29, 73, 134

ODEON WARDOUR STREET
Map190 J5
10 Wardour Street W1D 3HG
Tel 0870 505 0007
www.odeon.co.uk

A small cinema with four screens,
dedicated to art-house and
independent films.
🚇 Leicester Square, Piccadilly Circus
🚌 14, 19, 38

ODEON WEST END
Map 190 J6
40 Leicester Square WC2H 7LP
Tel 0870 505 0007
www.odeon.co.uk
One of a group of central London
Odeon cinemas with two screens
showing mainstream releases.
🚇 Leicester Square, Piccadilly Circus
🚌 24, 29, 176

THE OTHER CINEMA
Map 190 J6
11 Rupert Street W1D 7PR
Tel 020 7437 0757
www.picturehouse-cinemas.co.uk
Comfortable, twin-screen art-
house cinema. Shows world and
art-house cinema and hosts a Latin
American Film Festival.
🚇 Leicester Square, Piccadilly Circus
🚌 14, 19, 38

PRINCE CHARLES
Map 190 J5
7 Leicester Place WC2H 7BP
Tel information 0901 2727 007, bookings
020 7494 3654
www.princecharlescinema.com
Central independent cinema offering seats at lower than usual West
End prices. Foreign-language films
shown with English subtitles.
🚇 Leicester Square, Piccadilly Circus
🚌 24, 29, 176

RENOIR
Map 190 K3
Brunswick Centre, Brunswick Square
WC1 1AU
Tel 020 7837 8402
Independent two-screen cinema
showing art-house and foreign-
language films (Engish subtitles)
and classics from the repertory.
🚇 Russell Square 🚌 7, 17, 45, 46, 188

RIVERSIDE STUDIOS
See page 194

SCIENCE MUSEUM IMAX
Map 188 E8
See page 125

SCREEN ON BAKER STREET
Map 189 G4
96–98 Baker Street W1U 6TJ

Tel 020 7486 0036, bookings 020 7935 2772
www.screencinemas.co.uk
Two-screen chain cinema showing
a mix of repertory pictures and
new-release mainstream films.
🚇 Baker Street 🚌 2, 13, 74, 82

SCREEN ON THE GREEN
Map 191 L3
83 Upper Street N1 0NP
Tel 020 7226 3520
www.screencinemas.co.uk
Opposite Islington Green, a one-
screen cinema showing
new-release mainstream films in
a dazzlingly lit building.
🚇 Angel 🚌 30, 38, 43, 73, 214

UCI WHITELEYS
Map 188 D5
2nd Floor Whiteleys Shopping Centre,
Queensway, Bayswater W2 4YL
Tel 0870 010 2030
www.uci-cinemas.co.uk
Eight-screen multiplex cinema in
a shopping complex.
🚇 Bayswater, Queensway 🚌 12, 23, 70

UGC CHELSEA
Map 188 E8
279 King's Road SW3 5EW
Tel 0870 907 0710
www.ugccinemas.co.uk
Four-screen multiplex.
🚇 Sloane Square 🚌 11, 19, 22, 211, C1

UGC HAYMARKET
Map 190 J6
63–65 Haymarket SW1Y 4RQ
Tel 0870 907 0712
www.ugccinemas.co.uk
Three-screen multiplex.
🚇 Piccadilly 🚌 14, 22, 94

UGC SHAFTESBURY AVENUE AT THE TROCADERO
Map 190 J5
13 Coventry Street W1V 7FE
Tel 0870 907 0716
www.ugccinemas.co.uk
Seven-screen multiplex.
🚇 Leicester Square, Piccadilly Circus
🚌 14, 19, 22, 38

WARNER VILLAGE WEST END
Map 190 J5
3 Cranbourn Street WC2H 7AL
Tel Bookings 08702 406020
www.warnervillage.co.uk
Nine-screen multiplex in the heart
of London's 'movieland'.
🚇 Leicester Square 🚌 24, 29, 176

Classical Music, Dance and Opera

Tickets for most productions are available by phone, online or in person direct from the staging venues. Some dance and music festivals operate a shared venue system, or sell from a centralized administrative office, or both. It's often possible to buy discounted tickets that are unclaimed or returned from main concert halls and theatres shortly before the performance—ask at the ticket desk.

THE BARBICAN
See page 77
A 2,000-seat concert hall, in the confusingly laid out arts complex. Home of the world-class London Symphony Orchestra and the English Chamber Orchestra, and visited by a stream of top-notch touring orchestras.
🎫 Tickets £6.50–£35

BUSH HALL
Map 188 C5
310 Uxbridge Road, Shepherd's Bush W12 7LJ
Tel 020 8222 6955
www.bushhallmusic.co.uk
Formerly a ballroom and a snooker hall, Bush Hall reopened in 2000 as a small concert hall staging classical concerts, recitals, jazz and rock concerts.
🎫 £5–£25 🚇 Shepherd's Bush
🚌 49, 94, 148

INSTITUTE OF CONTEMPORARY ARTS (ICA)
See page 93
A leading London modern dance venue, the ICA stages avant-garde, experimental, movement-based performances. Hosts Dance Umbrella (*www.danceumbrella. co.uk*), one of the world's top contemporary dance festivals. Seats 165 (350 standing).
🎫 £6–£9; day membership £1.50 (Mon–Fri) or £2.50 (Sat, Sun) gives equivalent discount plus admission to galleries and bar/café

KENWOOD HOUSE
See page 223

LONDON COLISEUM
Map 190 J5
St. Martin's Lane WC2N 4ES
Tel 020 7632 8300
www.eno.org
Home to the English National Opera (always sung in English) with regular visits from Welsh National Opera, Opera North and the Royal Festival Ballet. ENO aims to offer opera to the widest possible audience and is known for some innovative productions. The theatre is undergoing restoration until 2004, but performances continue.
🎫 £5–£70 🚇 Charing Cross, Leicester Square 🚌 24, 29, 176

PEACOCK THEATRE
Map 190 K4
Portugal Street WC2A 2HT
Tel 020 7863 8222
www.sadlerswells.com
The London School of Economics holds lectures here during the day. Mounts dance productions as a second stage for Sadler's Wells.
🎫 £0–£30 🚇 Holborn 🚌 1, 59, 168, 188

PURCELL ROOM
Map 190 K5
South Bank Centre SE1 8XX
Tel 020 7960 4242
www.sbc.org.uk
Smallest of the three concert auditoriums at the South Bank Centre (see page 127). An intimate space for chamber music, accompanied singers, solo singers, musicians and more.
🎫 £7–£12.50 🚇 Embankment, Waterloo 🚌 77, RV1

QUEEN ELIZABETH HALL
Map 190 K5
South Bank Centre SE1 8XX
Tel 020 7960 4242
www.sbc.org.uk

The middle-sized of the three auditoriums at the South Bank Centre hosts small orchestral concerts, groups, bands, small-scale opera and dance productions and chamber music.
🎫 £8–£20 🚇 Embankment, Waterloo 🚌 77, RV1

RIVERSIDE STUDIOS
Map 188 off C7
Crisp Road (off Queen Caroline Street) W6 9RL
Tel 020 8237 1111
www.riversidestudios.co.uk
Excellent presentations of a mix of dance, theatre and music on relatively low budgets. Former BBC television studios converted in the 1970s. Complex includes a 100-seat cinema.
🎫 £8–£25 🚇 Hammersmith 🚌 9, 190, 391

ROYAL ACADEMY OF MUSIC
Map 189 G3
Marylebone Road NW1 5HT
Tel 020 7873 7373
www.ram.ac.uk

One of London's four music colleges has free lunchtime recitals and reasonably priced evening chamber and orchestral performances. A new glass-roofed recital hall was added in 2001 and there is a small museum of musical instruments (*Mon–Fri 12.30–6, Sat, Sun 2–5.30*).
🎫 £3–£15 🚇 Regent's Park 🚌 18, 27, 30, 74

ROYAL ALBERT HALL
Map 188 E6
Kensington Gore SW7 2AP
Tel 020 7589 3203, bookings 020 7589 8212
www.royalalberthall.com
The immense domed building just south of Kensington Gardens can

seat 5,200. Venue for major concerts and the summer Proms (see page 223).
£3–£50 South Kensington
9, 10, 52, 70

ROYAL OPERA HOUSE
Map 190 K4
Bow Street WC2E 9DD
Tel 020 7304 4000
www.royaloperahouse.org
The principal venue for world-class classical music, opera and ballet was reopened in 1999 after extensive redevelopment. The building in Covent Garden hosts major operatic productions and is home to the Royal Ballet.
£3–£180 Covent Garden
24, 29, 176, RV1

SADLER'S WELLS THEATRE
Map 191 off L2
Rosebery Avenue EC1R 4TN
Tel 020 7863 8000
www.sadlerswells.com

Europe's finest dance venue offers classical ballet, modern dance and opera. The building, opened in 1998, replaces the theatre founded by Lilian Bayliss in 1931. The Lilian Bayliss Studio Theatre opened in 1988.
£8–£38 Angel 19, 38, 341

ROYAL FESTIVAL HALL
Map 190 K5
South Bank Centre SE1 8XX
Tel 020 7960 4242
www.sbc.org.uk

Part of the South Bank Centre (see page 127). Major classical music performances, with regular appearances by the Philharmonia and the London Philharmonic. Also jazz, ballet and other genres.
£6–£65 Embankment, Waterloo
77, RV1

ST. JAMES'S CHURCH PICCADILLY
Map 190 H5
197 Piccadilly W1J 9LL
Tel 020 7734 4511
www.st-james-piccadilly.org
This active church, designed by Christopher Wren and consecrated in 1684, offers popular lunchtime and evening choral and orchestral concerts in its sumptuous interior.
Phone for details Piccadilly Circus
9, 14, 19, 22

ST. JOHN'S, SMITH SQUARE
Map 190 J7
Smith Square SW1P 3HA
Tel 020 7222 1061
www.sjss.org.uk
This church is a major classical music venue, often featuring the Sainsbury Organ, one of the finest in the UK. Superb acoustics for choirs, symphony orchestras and solo recitals.
Phone for details Westminster
3, 77A, 88, 507, C10

ST. MARTIN-IN-THE-FIELDS
Map 190 J5
Trafalgar Square WC2N 4JJ
Tel 020 7766 1100
www.stmartin-in-the-fields.org

Baroque music is the focus here of the free lunchtime concerts (donations appreciated) and evening concerts, which are sometimes by candlelight.
£6–£17 Leicester Square, Charing Cross
9, 24, 176

SHAW THEATRE
Map 190 off J2
100–110 Euston Road NW1 2AJ
Tel 0207 387 6864
www.shawtheatre.com
Named after Irish playwright George Bernard Shaw, once a local councillor here. Now refurbished and associated with the next-door hotel, the Shaw Park Plaza. Stages family shows and international dance productions.
£8–£18 King's Cross, Euston
10, 30, 73, 168

SOUTH BANK CENTRE
See page 127
Map 190 K5
Arts complex comprising the Royal Festival Hall, the Queen Elizabeth Hall and the Purcell Room. See individual entries and page 127.

THE PLACE: ROBIN HOWARD DANCE THEATRE
Map 190 J2
17 Duke's Road WC1H 9PY
Tel 020 7380 1268
www.theplace.org.uk
300-seat theatre offering international contemporary dance for audiences, plus dance training at all levels in many genres. The London Contemporary Dance Theatre is based here.
£5–£15 Euston 10, 30, 73, 91

WIGMORE HALL
Map 189 G4
36 Wigmore Street W1U 2BP
Tel 020 7935 2141
www.wigmore-hall.org.uk
London's favourite intimate concert and recital venue, with acoustics of legendary perfection. Opened in 1901 as the Bechstein Hall. The architectural elegance (marble and plaster with cupola) matches the peerless quality of the great classic performances.
£8–£35 Bond Street 8, 10, 73, C2

WHAT TO DO

Contemporary Live Music

Live music in London covers every imaginable genre, and there's a range of ticket prices to match. For smaller gigs and venues you can usually expect to pay at the door; larger events generally sell direct, online or through agents such as TicketMaster *(tel 0870 534 4444, www.ticketmaster.co.uk)*, which has several offices in the city, or Stargreen Box Office *(tel 020 7734 8932, www.stargreen.com)* on Argyll Street, near Oxford Circus.

WHAT TO DO

AFRICA CENTRE
Map 190 K4
38 King Street, Covent Garden WC2E 8JT
Tel 020 7836 1973
www.africacentre.org.uk
Top African bands and others perform on Fridays at this cultural centre for African art, music, education, resources, information, news and views.
£6–£10 Covent Garden
6, 9, 13, 23, RV1

THE BARBICAN
See page 77

BORDERLINE
Map 190 J4
Orange Yard, Manette Street W1D 4JB
Tel 020 7734 5547, box office 020 7395 0777
www.borderline.co.uk
Famous small venue (capacity 275) that has seen Blur, Oasis and many other big names in its time. Music is from country to heavy metal and beyond.
£6–£16 Tottenham Court Road
8, 10, 14, 24

BREAD & ROSES
Map 191 off M7
68 Clapham Manor Street, Clapham SW4 6DZ
Tel 020 7498 1779
www.breadandrosespub.com
Spacious pub offering world music, poetry and comedy. Children's workshops on Sunday afternoon.
Free Clapham Common, Clapham North 88, 137, 345

BULL'S HEAD
Map 188 off C7
373 Lonsdale Road, Barnes SW13 9PY
Tel 020 8876 5241
www.thebullshead.com
Major home of modern, mainstream, trad jazz and blues since 1959—gigs nightly with two on Sundays. Music room for 100.
£5–£10 209, 283
Barnes Bridge

BUSH HALL
See page 194

CARLING ACADEMY BRIXTON
Map 191 off M7
211 Stockwell Road, Brixton SW9 9SL
Tel 0870 771 2000
www.brixton-academy.co.uk
Large auditorium where you can catch big name rock and pop acts on tour.
£15–£30 Brixton 133, 159

CARLING APOLLO HAMMERSMITH
Map 188 off C7
Queen Caroline Street W6 9QH
Tel 0870 606 3400
www.carlinglive.com
Huge mainstream rock and pop venue on a busy roundabout in the heart of Hammersmith. Good sound and sightlines.
£10–£40 Hammersmith
9, 190, 391

DOVER STREET WINE BAR
Map 189 H5
8–10 Dover Street W1S 4LQ
Tel 020 7629 9813
www.doverst.co.uk
This restaurant has a dance floor and a basement where live gigs cover jazz to rhythm and blues to motown.
£6–£15 Green Park 8, 9, 14

EARL'S COURT EXHIBITION CENTRE
Map 188 off C7
Warwick Road, Earl's Court SW5 9TA
Tel 020 7385 1200
www.eco.co.uk
Big enough to have its own District Line branch line and Underground station, Earl's Court mounts massive rock/pop concerts, although the sound quality is not the best.
£25–£45 Earl's Court
74, 328, C1, C3

HAMMERSMITH AND FULHAM IRISH CENTRE
Map 188 off C7
Blacks Road, Hammersmith W6 9DT
Tel 020 8563 8232
www.lbhf.gov.uk/irishcentre
Arts, cultural and education centre hosting Irish and other Celtic music ranging from traditional to contemporary folk and jazz.
£4–£10 Hammersmith 9, 27, 190, 391

INSTITUTE OF CONTEMPORARY ARTS (ICA)
See page 93

JAZZ CAFÉ
Map 189 off H2
5 Parkway NW1 7PG
Tel 020 7916 6060
www.meanfiddler.com
This slick, modern venue, a current favourite with young Londoners, buzzes nightly with live jazz, from soul, world music and R&B to hip-hop and rap—it's all here.
£10–£20 Camden Town 24, 274

LONDON ASTORIA
Map 190 J4
157 Charing Cross Road WC2H 0EL
Tel 020 7344 0044
www.meanfiddler.com
Relatively large concert hall that hosts rock and pop concerts featuring soloists such as Kylie Minogue or Donna Summer and hot bands. Hosts G-A-Y nights (see page 208).
£6–£20; G-A-Y 'pink pounder' nights £1 Tottenham Court Road
14, 19, 24, 29, 38, 176

MEAN FIDDLER
Map 190 J4
165 Charing Cross Road WC2H 0EL
Tel 020 7344 0044/020 7434 9592
www.meanfiddler.com

Established on the former premises of Astoria II (the Astoria is next door), this cult 1980s venue hosts a wide range of bands, mostly rock and blues.

🎫 £8–£18.50 🚇 Tottenham Court Road 🚌 8, 10, 14, 24

OCEAN
Map 191 off P2
270 Mare Street, Hackney E8 1HE
Tel 020 8986 5336
www.ocean.org.uk

Mid-size, modern rock venue in the East End, where you can enjoy live gigs and great sound and lighting systems.

🎫 £3–£30 🚌 26, 38, 55, 242 🚆 Hackney Central, Hackney Downs

PIZZA EXPRESS JAZZ CLUB
Map 190 J4
10 Dean Street W1D 3RW
Tel Jazz Club 020 7439 8722, restaurant 020 7437 9595
www.pizzaexpress.co.uk
All kinds of modern and contemporary jazz in a basement under the main branch of Pizza Express in Soho. Book ahead.

🎫 £15–£20 🚇 Tottenham Court Road 🚌 8, 10, 14, 24, 73

PIZZA ON THE PARK
Map 189 G6
11 Knightsbridge SW1X 7LY
Tel 020 7235 5273
See good mainstream jazz performers every night, some well-known international names, in the dining area below the main restaurant. Book ahead.

🎫 £10–£18 🚇 Hyde Park Corner 🚌 9, 10, 14, 19, 74

ROYAL ALBERT HALL
See page 194

RONNIE SCOTT'S
Map 190 J4
47 Frith Street W1D 4HT
Tel 020 7439 0747
www.ronniescotts.co.uk

Britain's top jazz venue and one of the most famous jazz clubs in the world. The best players line up to perform here.

🎫 £15–£25; more for special gigs 🚇 Tottenham Court Road 🚌 8, 10, 14, 24, 73

SHEPHERD'S BUSH EMPIRE
Map 188 off C5
Shepherd's Bush Green W12 8TT
Tel 0870 771 2000
www.shepherds-bush-empire.co.uk
This large auditorium with exceptionally good sound stages gigs by pop and rock headliners. Former TV production theatre.

🎫 £10–£30 🚇 Shepherd's Bush 🚌 49, 94

SMOLLENSKY'S ON THE STRAND
Map 190 K4
105 The Strand WC2R 0AB
Tel 020 7497 2101
www.smollenskys.co.uk
Central bar-cum-restaurant with live jazz every Sunday night, including modern, Latino and salsa. Great atmosphere and lots of variety.

🎫 £5–£7.50; jazz menu £16–£19 🚇 Charing Cross 🚌 9, 11, 13, 15, 23

SWAN
Map 191 off M7
215 Clapham Road, Stockwell SW9 9BE
Tel 020 7978 9778
www.theswanstockwell.com
Originally Irish, this loud, lively pub now draws hard-partying New

Zealanders, Australians and South Africans. Rock, indie and pop bands take the stage on Friday and Saturday nights.

🎫 Free–£6 🚇 Stockwell 🚌 2, 155, P5

VORTEX
Map 191 off P2
139–141 Church Street, Stoke Newington N16 0UH
Tel 020 7254 6516
www.vortexjazz.co.uk
Just 10–15 minutes' north of The Angel, Islington, this laid-back mainly vegetarian café is a favourite of jazz-lovers. It features live gigs—standards, modern, free-form—and even karaoke.

🎫 Free–£10 🚌 67, 73, 76, 149 🚆 Stoke Newington

WEMBLEY ARENA
Map 188 off E2
Empire Way, Wembley, Middlesex HA9 0DW
Tel 0870 739 0739
www.wembleyticket.com
Massive rock venue hosting the top names. Still has kudos but performances can be spoiled by poor views and unbalanced sound.

🎫 £15–£50 🚇 Wembley Park, Wembley Central 🚌 18

100 CLUB
Map 190 H4
100 Oxford Street W1D 1LL
Tel 020 7636 0933
www.the100club.co.uk
Billed as Europe's most famous live music venue. Music from soul, funk and jazz to R&B, swing and Latin. Opened in 1942, the 100 Club focused exclusively on jazz until the 1960s, when the Rolling Stones and The Kinks played here.

🎫 £5–£15 🚇 Tottenham Court Road 🚌 7, 8, 10, 25, 55, 73

606 CLUB
Map 189 off F7
90 Lots Road SW10 0QD
Tel 020 7352 5953
www.606club.co.uk
Popular haunt with jazz musicians who come to listen as well as play. Live jazz by local and young British artists seven nights a week. Non-members have to eat if they want to drink alcohol.

🎫 £6–£8 🚇 Fulham Broadway 🚌 11, 211, C3

Theatres

To book theatre seats either contact the venue itself or use a reliable agency such as Ticketmaster *(tel 0870 534 4444, www.ticketmaster.co.uk)* or First Call *(tel 0870 906 3700, www.firstcalltickets.com)*, but be sure to check surcharges. It's best to avoid all ticket touts. If you're desperate for specific tickets and don't mind a high surcharge, try Harrods' ticket agency *(tel 020 7225 6666)*. Some theatres (including the RNT and RSC) keep a number of tickets back for sale on the day of performance.

For half-price tickets, go to the Society of London Theatres' Half Price Ticket Booth in Leicester Square (see page 97), where tickets for some West End theatres are sold on the day of performance *(Mon–Sat noon–6.30 for matinée and evening shows, Sun noon–around 3.30 matinée only)*. The booth takes cash only and levies a small service charge. Beware of unofficial ticket booths around, but not in, Leicester Square.

ADELPHI THEATRE
Map 190 K5
Strand WC2E 7NA
Tel 020 7344 0055
Stages popular shows and musicals. Haunted by ghost of actor William Terris, stabbed to death outside in 1897. Seats 1,478.
£5–£40 Charing Cross
9, 11, 13, 15, 23

ALBERY THEATRE
Map 190 J4
St. Martin's Lane WC2N 5AU
Tel 020 7369 1740
www.theambassadors.com
Diverse productions include classical and new drama, comedies and musicals. Seats 890.
£10–£40 Leicester Square
24, 29, 176

APOLLO THEATRE
Map 190 J4
28 Shaftesbury Avenue W1D 7EZ
Tel 020 7494 5070
www.ruttheatres.com
A 1901 building with very limited provision for those with disabilities. Seats 775.
£10–£35 Piccadilly Circus
14, 19, 38

ARTS THEATRE
Map 190 J4
6–7 Great Newport Street WC2H 7JB
Tel 020 7836 3334
www.artstheatre.com
Built in 1927 as a 'theatre club', to avoid censorship laws. Now refurbished and staging a mix of drama, music and comedy. Seats 356.
£19.50–£24.50 Leicester Square
14, 19, 38

THE BARBICAN
See page 77

CAMBRIDGE THEATRE
Map 190 J4
Earlham Street WC2 9HU
Tel 020 7494 5399
www.ruttheatres.com
Musical theatre with a 1930s art-deco setting. Popular, large-scale musical productions. Seats 1,279.
£12.50–£45 Tottenham Court Road, Covent Garden 14, 19, 38

COMEDY THEATRE
Map 190 J5
Panton Street SW1Y 4DN
Tel 020 7369 1731
www.theambassadors.com
Opened in 1881. Beautifully designed building with a forest of pillars, hence several restricted view seats. High drama, small-cast productions. Seats 780.
£10–£36 Piccadilly Circus
9, 12, 13, 14

CRITERION THEATRE
Map 190 J5
Piccadilly Circus W1V 9LB
Tel 020 7413 1437
www.reducedshakespeare.co.uk
Victorian theatre built on two levels below ground. It's the UK base for the Reduced Shakespeare Company's abridged comedies. Seats 600.
£10–£32.50 Piccadilly Circus
9, 12, 13, 14

DOMINION THEATRE
Map 190 J4
Tottenham Court Road W7P 0AG
Tel 020 7413 1713

ALDWYCH THEATRE
Map 190 K4
Aldwych WC2B 4DF
Tel 020 7379 3367
www.aldwychtheatre.com
Completed in 1905, during a building boom after the demoli-

tion of London's old 'theatreland' and slums. Base of the Royal Shakespeare Company from 1960 to 1981; now stages drama, dance and musicals. Seats 1,142.
£15–£39.50 Covent Garden
6, 9, 13, 23, RV1

One of the West End's largest mainstream theatres, the Dominion was built in 1923 and used as a cinema until 1977. It now stages major musicals. Seats more than 2,500.
£25–£50 Tottenham Court Road
10, 24, 29, 73, 134

DONMAR WAREHOUSE
Map 190 J4
Earlham Street WC2H 9LX
Tel 020 7369 1732
www.donmar-warehouse.com
This small but high-profile theatre, built in 1993, rose to fame when movie director Sam Mendes, Artistic Director until November 2002, attracted big Hollywood names. Seats 250.
£15–£29 Covent Garden
14, 19, 38

DUCHESS THEATRE
Map 190 K4
Catherine Street WC2B 5LA
Tel 0870 890 1103
www.ruttheatres.com
Built in 1929 and named after the late Queen Mother when she was

Duchess of York. All 470 seats have clear views.

🎫 £17.50–£29.50 🚇 Covent Garden
🚌 6, 9, 13, 23, RV1

DUKE OF YORK'S THEATRE
Map 190 J5
St. Martin's Lane WC2N 4BG
Tel 020 7369 1791
www.theambassadors.com
Opened in 1892 and later named after the future King George V. Refurbished in 1980. Seats 650.

🎫 £8–£32.50 🚇 Leicester Square
🚌 24, 29, 176

FORTUNE THEATRE
Map 190 K4
Russell Street WC2B 5HH
Tel 020 7369 1737
www.theambassadors.com
The UK's first all-concrete public building and the first London theatre to be built after World War I, opened in 1924. Seats 430.

🎫 £12.50–£32.50 🚇 Covent Garden
🚌 6, 9, 13, 23, RV1

GARRICK THEATRE
Map 190 J5
Charing Cross Road WC2H 0HH
Tel 020 7494 5085
www.rutheatres.com

Small theatre named after the 18th-century actor and entrepreneur David Garrick (1717–79).

🎫 £15–£37.50 🚇 Leicester Square
🚌 24, 29, 176

THE GATE
Map 188 C5
11 Pembridge Road W11 3HQ
Tel 020 7229 0706
www.gatehouse.co.uk
Tiny (70–80 seats) but well established theatre above a pub. All work is translated from languages and cultures other than British.

🎫 £12 (Mon 30 'pay what you can' seats)
🚇 Notting Hill Gate 🚌 27, 28, 31, 328

GIELGUD THEATRE
Map 190 J4
33 Shaftesbury Avenue W1V 8AR
Tel 0870 890 1105
www.rutheatres.com

Named the Gielgud as a tribute to actor Sir John Gielgud (1904–2000), who frequently performed here. Seats 889.

🎫 £15–£37.50 🚇 Piccadilly Circus
🚌 14, 19, 38

GLOBE, SHAKESPEARE'S
Map 191 M5
See page 126

HAMPSTEAD THEATRE
Map 188 off E2
Eton Avenue, Swiss Cottage NW3 3EU
Tel 020 7722 9301
www.hampsteadtheatre.com
A small theatre producing new plays, which sometimes transfer to the West End. Seats up to 325.

🎫 £5–£19.50 🚇 Swiss Cottage
🚌 13, 46, 82, 113

HER MAJESTY'S
Map 190 J5
Haymarket SW1Y 4QR
Tel 020 7890 1106
www.rutheatres.com
Opened in 1879 and run by famous actor/manager Beerbohm Tree from 1897. Seats 1,160.

🎫 £20–£42.50 🚇 Piccadilly Circus
🚌 14, 19, 38

KING'S HEAD THEATRE
Map 191 off L2
115 Upper Street N1 1QN
Tel 020 7226 1916
www.kingsheadtheatre.org
A theatre in the 19th-century pub the King's Head in Islington. The schedule includes new writing, revived classics and musicals. Seats 115.

🎫 £14–£15 🚇 Angel, Highbury & Islington
🚌 4, 19, 30, 43

LONDON PALLADIUM
Map 189 H4
Argyll Street W1V 1AD
Tel 0870 890 1108
www.rutheatres.com
A colossal theatre built in 1910. Seats 2,286.

🎫 £16–£40 🚇 Oxford Circus
🚌 8, 10, 73, 453

LYCEUM THEATRE
Map 190 K4
Wellington Street WC2 E7DA
Tel 0870 243 9000

On a site occupied by David Garrick's 1771 concert hall, and where Madame Tussaud held her first waxworks exhibition (see page 101). Seats 2,015.

🎫 £17.50–£40 🚇 Charing Cross
🚌 9, 13, 23

LYRIC HAMMERSMITH
Map 188 off C7
King Street W6 0QL
Tel 0870 0500 511
www.lyric.co.uk
Modern theatre, built in 1978, showing original and touring productions. Main auditorium has 550 seats; the Studio has up to 130.

🎫 £9–£24 🚇 Hammersmith
🚌 9, 10, 27, 391

LYRIC THEATRE
Map 190 J4
Shaftesbury Avenue W1V 7HA
Tel 0870 890 1107
www.rutheatre.com
The oldest theatre on Shaftesbury Avenue, having opened with a comic opera in 1888. Seats 932.

£15–£27.50 🎭 Piccadilly Circus
🚌 14, 19, 38

NEW AMBASSADORS THEATRE
Map 190 J4
West Street WC2H 9ND
Tel 020 7369 1761
www.newambassadors.com
The West End's smallest theatre
mounts an interesting programme
of drama by contemporary artists.
Seats 400.
£15–£32.50 🎭 Leicester Square
🚌 14, 19, 38

NEW LONDON THEATRE
Map 190 K4
Drury Lane WC2B 5PW
Tel 0870 890 1110
www.rutheatres.com
In the heart of theatreland,
designed by Paul Tvrtkovic in 1973
in concrete and glass. Seats 1,102.
£20–£40 🎭 Covent Garden
🚌 6, 9, 13, 23, RV1

OLD VIC
Map 191 L6
The Cut, Waterloo Road SE1 8NB
Tel 020 7369 1722
www.oldvictheatre.com
Historic building (1818) where
Britain's National Theatre began
before transferring to the South
Bank in the 1970s. Most theatre
greats of the 20th century have
appeared here. Seats 1,051.
£10–£37.50 🎭 Waterloo, Southwark
🚌 168, 176, RV1

OPEN-AIR THEATRE
Map 189 G2
Regent's Park NW1 4NP
Tel 020 7486 2431
www.openairtheatre.org
The New Shakespeare Company
performs in this 1932 amphitheatre at the heart of Regent's Park
(Jun–Sep). There are 1,187 folding
seats plus approximately 100
spaces on grass banks. Take warm
clothing, a cushion and a picnic.
£9–£26 🎭 Baker Street, Regent's Park
🚌 18, 27, 30

ORANGE TREE THEATRE
Map 188 off C7
1 Clarence Street, Richmond TW9 2SA
Tel 020 8940 3633
www.orangetreetheatre.co.uk
New and rediscovered plays are
the focus at this theatre that began
above the Orange Tree pub across

the road in 1972. Seats 172.
£6–£16 🎭 Richmond 🚌 190, 391

PALACE THEATRE
Map 190 J4
Shaftesbury Avenue W1V 8AY
Tel 020 7434 0088
www.rutheatres.com

The successful musical production
Les Misérables, which opened in
1985, has been attracting the
crowds here ever since. Book
ahead. Seats 1,398.
£10–£42.50 🎭 Leicester Square
🚌 14, 19, 38

PHOENIX THEATRE
Map 190 J4
Charing Cross Road WC2H 0JP
Tel 020 7369 1733
www.theambassadors.com
Art deco theatre opened in 1930
to a fanfare of trumpets. Original
manager was impresario C. B.
Cochrane. Seats 1,045.
£15–£40 🎭 Leicester Square
🚌 14, 19, 176

PICCADILLY THEATRE
Map 190 H4
Denman Street W1D 7DY
Tel 020 7369 1734
www.theambassadors.com
Built in the early 1900s. The ghost
of a woman once reported in the
programme as dead is said to
appear from time to time to say
'I'm alive'. Seats 1,200.
£15–£42.50 🎭 Piccadilly Circus
🚌 14, 19, 38

PLAYHOUSE THEATRE
Map 190 K5
Northumberland Avenue WC2N 5DE
Tel 020 7369 1785
www.theambassadors.com
Opened in 1882, and a BBC
Television theatre from 1951 to

1975, it now stages classical and
contemporary drama. There are
clear sight lines from all 786 seats.
£8–£40 🎭 Embankment 🚌 3, 6, 176

PRINCE EDWARD THEATRE
Map 190 J4
Old Compton Street W1D 4HS
Tel 020 7447 5400
www.delfont-mackintosh.com
A theatre purpose-built for big
musicals and reviews in 1930.
Seats 1,619.
£22.50–£45 🎭 Leicester Square
🚌 14, 19, 38

PRINCE OF WALES THEATRE
Map 190 J5
Coventry Street W1D 6AS
Tel 020 7395 5240
www.delfont-mackintosh.com
Built in 1937 in art-deco style. Its
Stalls Bar is one of the largest in
the West End. Presents main-
stream musicals and plays. Seats
1,100.
£20–£50 🎭 Leicester Square, Piccadilly
Circus 🚌 14, 19, 38

QUEEN'S THEATRE
Map 190 J4
Shaftesbury Avenue W1V 8BA
Tel 0870 890 1101
www.rutheatres.com
Named after Queen Alexandra.
Built in 1907 as a mirror image of
the Hicks Theatre, now the Gielgud
(see page 199). Seats 990.
£10–£42.50 🎭 Leicester Square
🚌 14, 19, 38

RICHMOND THEATRE
Map 188 off C7
The Green, Richmond, Surrey TW9 1QJ
Tel 020 8940 0088
www.theambassadors.com
Built in 1899 and has a long tradition of pre-West End productions
and pantomimes. Faces onto the
leafy expanse of Richmond Park.
Seats 607.
£9–£25 🎭 Richmond 🚌 190, 391

RIVERSIDE STUDIOS
Map 188 off C7
See page 194

ROYAL COURT/JERWOOD THEATRE
Map 189 off G7
Sloane Square SW1W 8AS
Tel 020 7565 5000
www.royalcourttheatre.com

WHAT TO DO

High artistic reputation; presents only new work by leading or emerging playwrights—a bookshop sells play texts. The main theatre seats 400 and the studio 60.
£7.50–£26 Sloane Square
11, 19, 22, 211, C1

ROYAL NATIONAL THEATRE
Map 190 K5
South Bank SE1 9PX
Tel 020 7452 3000
www.nationaltheatre.org.uk
Three auditoriums: the Cottesloe, accommodating 300, with no fixed seats or staging; the 890-seat proscenium Lyttleton; and the Olivier (1,080), named after Sir Laurence Olivier, the National Theatre's first director.
£10–£34 Waterloo 77, RV1

ST. MARTIN'S THEATRE
Map 190 J4
West Street WC2H 9NZ
Tel 020 7836 1443
www.vpsmvaudsav.co.uk
St. Martin's has staged Agatha Christie's *The Mousetrap*, the world's longest-running play (opened in 1951), since it moved here in 1974. Seats 550.
£11.50–£31.50 Leicester Square
14, 19, 38

SAVOY THEATRE
Map 190 K5
Strand WC2R 0ET
Tel 020 7836 8888
www.the-savoy-group.com
Built in 1881 by Richard D'Oyly Carte to stage operettas by Gilbert and Sullivan. Redesigned in the 1920s. Seats 1,100.
£15–£37.50 Charing Cross
9, 11, 13, 23

SHAFTESBURY THEATRE
Map 190 J4

210 Shaftesbury Avenue WC2H 8DP
Tel 0870 906 3798
Independent theatre built in 1902 on the corner of Shaftesbury Avenue. Seats 1,000.
£20–£37.50 Covent Garden
14, 19, 38

STRAND THEATRE
Map 190 K4
Aldwych WC2B 4SD
Tel 020 7839 6040
www.delfont-mackintosh.com
Built as a pair with the Aldwych Theatre in 1905. Seats 1,067.
£16–£39 Covent Garden, Temple
9, 11, 13, 23

THEATRE ROYAL HAYMARKET
Map 190 J5
Haymarket SW1Y 4HT
Tel 0870 901 3356
www.trh.co.uk
Beautiful 18th-century pillared façade in white and gold. Opulent mirrors and gilding. Seats 900.
£12–£40 Piccadilly Circus
14, 19, 38

VAUDEVILLE THEATRE
Map 190 K5
Strand WC2R 4LD
Tel 0870 890 0511
Small theatre, which opened in 1870, the third theatre to occupy this site. Stages musicals and comedy. Seats 714.
£15–£37.50 Charing Cross
9, 11, 13, 23

VICTORIA PALACE
Map 189 H7
Victoria Street SW1E 5EA
Tel 020 7834 1317
Built in 1910 with a now defunct retractable roof. Musicals and hit shows. Seats 1,500.
£12–£55 Victoria 11, 24, 211, 239, C1

WHITEHALL THEATRE
Map 190 J5
Whitehall SW1A 2DY
Tel 020 7369 1745
www.theambassadors.com
Art deco-style theatre famous for the pre-war Whitehall Farces and for its post-war musical revues. Seats 648.
£12–£35 Charing Cross
11, 12, 24

SPECIAL
THEATRE ROYAL DRURY LANE
Map 190 K4
Catherine Street WC2B 5JF
Tel 0870 890 1109
www.rutheatres.com
The present theatre, built in 1812, is the fourth on this site

and stages mostly musicals. And there are ghosts—the Man in Grey walks around the Upper Circle during successful productions. Seats 2,196.
£10–£42.50 Covent Garden
6, 9, 13, 23, RV1

WYNDHAMS
Map 190 J4
Charing Cross Road WC2H 0DA
Tel 020 7369 1736
www.theambassadors.com
Built in 1899 by Charles Wyndham. Hosted long-running musicals *The Boy Friend* in the 1950s and *Godspell* in the 1970s. Another long-runner, comic drama *Art*, made its debut here in 1996. Seats 759.
£10–£40 Leicester Square
24, 29, 176

YOUNG VIC
Map 191 L6
66 The Cut, Waterloo SE1 8LZ
Tel 020 7928 6363
www.youngvic.org
Built close to its sister theatre the Old Vic (see page 200) in the 1970s, the Young Vic presents classic traditional and contemporary plays primarily by younger artists for a younger audience. Seats 350–400.
£8.50–£25 Waterloo, Southwark
1, 168, 176, 188, RV1

NIGHTLIFE

If you've got the energy and the inclination you can party 24 hours a day in London. After a period when superclubs for the young and affluent ruled the scene, there's now a genuine variety of venues and styles to cater for every taste, budget and age-range.

You name it, you'll find it in London

CLUBBING

Queues usually start to form outside favoured venues from around 11pm (when the pubs close). Some offer free admission early in the evening, relying on the price of drinks to make up the cost (and that needn't necessarily take long). Others also ratchet up their charges later at night, so check the policy if you're budgeting. Theme nights, special events, guest bands and DJs are generally advertised at the club or online.

Clubs with restaurants and/or shows sometimes offer special menu deals to keep you going through the evening. Always check your chosen venue's dress code. Some are relaxed, some insist on 'smart' dress (definitions vary wildly), and some object to specific items of clothing such as jeans and/or trainers.

Once there you will often have to pass muster with tough-looking bouncers outside. If they refuse to admit you they don't need to give a reason and there's no point arguing—they won't listen, you won't win and it may lead to trouble. Just try your luck elsewhere, but note that a sure way of invoking the bouncers' displeasure is to turn up drunk. Past the door, you may be frisked by security staff.

OTHER CLUB OPTIONS

For moderate sound volume, more space and a wider age-range, head for clubs hosting salsa or other Latin sessions or a classic cabaret-and-dinner club—not all of these charge exorbitant prices, but many require smart dress (again, definitions vary).

COMEDY

Comedy clubs boomed in the 1980s, and there's still an impressive choice of revues, sketches, double acts and stand-up comedy, from open mike novice spots to crowd-pulling big names such as Jack Dee and Eddie Izzard.

GETTING HOME

Night buses run until the early hours (see page 53), but if the venue is out on a limb or too far from the bus stop it's best to ask about taxis (there's often a rank outside). Remember that Underground trains stop running at around midnight.

Clubs and Bars

London's clubbing scene has become steadily more lively, popular and varied over the past few years, with a mind-boggling mix of music genres, themes, events and styles on offer. Soho is a clubbing hot-spot in central London, and areas farther out such as Brixton, Camden, Elephant & Castle and Clerkenwell have plenty going on.

Remember that clubs often charge way over the odds for drinks bought after 11pm; the majority take credit cards.

BAR RUMBA
36 Shaftsbury Avenue WC1D 7ER
Tel 020 7287 6933
www.barrumba.co.uk

Established basement club with great dancing and regular theme nights including a jazz-funk Monday event and salsa every Tuesday. Music includes drum and bass, house and hip-hop.
🕐 Mon–Fri 6pm–late, Sat 7pm–late, Sun 8pm–1am 💷 £3–£12; free before 9pm 🚇 Piccadilly Circus 🚌 14, 19, 38

THE BUG BAR
The Crypt, St. Matthew's Church, Brixton Hill SW2 1JF
Tel 020 7738 3366
www.bugbar.co.uk
Beneath an old church on a traffic island in central Brixton. A student-like vibe and reasonably priced drinks. Very popular so arrive early. Cool DJs and a live band on Wednesdays; lounge bar and restaurant.
🕐 Wed 7pm–2am, Thu, Sun 8pm–2am, Fri, Sat 8pm–3am 💷 £3–£6 (free before 9pm) 🚇 Brixton 🚌 45, 59, 109, 118, 189, 250

CAFÉ DE PARIS
3–4 Coventry Street W1D 6BW
Tel 020 7734 7700
www.cafedeparis.com
Elegant and original nightspot established in 1924, with velvet sash curtains and a long sweeping

staircase to the dance floor and bar. Drinks are expensive and bouncers often less than friendly. Restaurant.
🕐 Club nights Wed–Sat 6pm–4am (restaurant 6–9pm) 💷 £10–£15 🚇 Leicester Square, Piccadilly Circus 🚌 9, 12, 13, 15, 23

CARGO
83 Rivington Street, Shoreditch EC2A 3AY
Tel 020 7749 3440
www.cargo-london.com
A very cool East End bar in a cavernous building. Restaurant with huge tables that you'll have to share. Not particularly friendly, but the crowd usually enjoys the top DJs and bands.
🕐 Mon–Thu noon–1am, Fri and Sat noon–3am, Sun 12–12 💷 £5–£10 🚇 Old Street, Liverpool Street 🚌 8, 43, 55, 243

COLOSSEUM
1 Nine Elms Lane SW8 5NQ
Tel 020 7627 1283
www.clubcolosseum.com

Riverside venue with a chillout room, bar and two dance areas.
🕐 Phone for details 💷 Phone for details 🚇 Vauxhall 🚌 2, 36, 88, 77A, 344

THE DOGSTAR
389 Coldharbour Lane, Brixton SW9 8LQ
Tel 020 7733 7515
www.dogstarbar.com
One of the first cool Brixton hang-outs—a refreshing change from

West End pretensions. Late good music. Take care when leaving: pickpockets and drug dealers frequent Coldharbour Lane.
🕐 Sun–Thu noon–2am, Fri–Sat noon–4am 💷 Sun–Thu free, Fri–Sat free–£5 🚇 Brixton 🚌 3, 35, 45, 159, P5

THE END
18A West Central Street WC1A 1JJ
Tel 020 7419 9199
www.the-end.co.uk
In the minimalist vaults of a 19th-century post office, Mr. C. from band The Shamen, hosts dance, house music; also drum 'n' bass nights. Excellent sound.
🕐 Mon–Fri 6pm–3am, Sat 7pm–7am, Sun 8pm–3am 💷 £3–£15 🚇 Tottenham Court Road, Holborn 🚌 4, 8, 10, 73

FABRIC
77A Charterhouse Street EC1M 3HN
Tel 020 7336 8898
www.fabric-london.com
Fabulously cool superclub with eclectic music, an easy-going 20-something crowd and slightly more obscure DJs.
🕐 Fri 9.30pm–5am, Sat 10pm–7am 💷 £12 🚇 Farringdon 🚌 17, 45, 46, 63

FRIDGE
1 Townhall Parade, Brixton Hill SW2 1RJ
Tel 020 7326 5100
www.fridge.co.uk
A popular party place. Dance music at weekends and live nights during the week.
🕐 Mon–Thu times vary, Fri and Sat 10pm–6am 💷 £5–£20 🚇 Brixton 🚌 45, 59

LIVE AT LOCK 17
Dingwalls Middle Yard, Camden Lock, Chalk Farm Road NW1 8AB
Tel 020 7428 5929
www.dingwalls.com
Multi-tiered club mainly for seated audiences attending rock/pop gigs, featuring rock and pop to hip-hop and country. Jongleurs Comedy Club (see page 206) takes place here on Fridays and Saturdays.
🕐 Gigs: Sun–Thu doors open 7pm, 7.30pm or 8pm–2am 💷 Prices vary, check for details 🚇 Camden Town, Chalk Farm 🚌 24, 27, 31, 168

MADAME JO JO'S
8–10 Brewer Street, Soho W1F 0SP
Tel 020 7734 3040
www.madamejojos.com

Cabaret-type club hosting Deep Funk nights on Fridays, and on Saturdays a Kitsch Cabaret, followed by the Groove Sanctuary—a 'safe haven for those who are serious about their music', including deep house and nu-jazz.

🕐 Wed, Fri–Sat 10pm–3am; Cabaret Sat 7–10pm 💷 £6–£8 🚇 Leicester Square, Piccadilly Circus 🚌 9, 12, 13, 15, 23

MINISTRY OF SOUND

103 Gaunt Street SE1 6DP
Tel 020 7378 6528
www.ministryofsound.com

Perhaps the most famous club in London—its reputation stretches across The Channel—the Ministry is a huge place where you can experience every aspect of house music. Never mind the unfriendly bouncers, long queues and high admission price and party till 9am.

🕐 Fri 10pm–5am, Sat 11pm–8am
💷 £10–£15 🚇 Elephant and Castle
🚌 12, 188, 453, C10

NOTTING HILL ARTS CLUB

21 Notting Hill Gate W11 3JQ
Tel 020 7460 4459
www.nottinghillartsclub.com

Bohemian basement spot, with projected images on whitewashed

walls and fabrics. The Cuban rum and beer is great, and drinks are reasonably priced. Impressive DJs play funky tunes. Frequent live bands and special happenings.

🕐 Mon–Wed 6pm–1am, Thu–Fri 6pm–2am, Sat 4pm–2am, Sun 4pm–1am, last entry one hour before closing 💷 £5–£8
🚇 Notting Hill Gate 🚌 12, 28, 31, 52

SAND

156 Clapham Park Road SW4 7DE
Tel 020 7622 3022
www.sandbarrestaurant.co.uk

This relaxed place, with recesses for drinking and chatting, along with The White House, keeps south Clapham in the loop for cool. Good food from all over the globe.

🕐 Mon–Sat 5pm–2am, Sun 5pm–1am
💷 £5 🚇 Clapham Common
🚌 35, 88, 137, 155

THE SCALA

275 Pentonville Road N1 9NL
Tel 020 7833 2022
www.scala-london.co.uk

This former cinema turned clubbing venue with three floors and several bars hosts hip-hop and breakbeat nights. Friday is Popstarz, a gay indie night attracting many straights. Phone or check website for live music nights during the week.

🕐 Fri–Sat 10pm–5am 💷 £6–£14
🚇 King's Cross 🚌 30, 73, 214

STRINGFELLOWS

16–19 Upper St. Martin's Lane WC2H 9EF
Tel 020 7240 5534
www.stringfellows.com

Peter Stringfellow's 'cabaret of angels' has pole-dancers and explores many other means of displaying the female body (strict no-touch policy). Saturday is mixed night—when men take the floor.

🕐 Mon–Sat 8pm–3.30am 💷 £10–£20
🚇 Covent Garden, Leicester Square
🚌 24, 29, 176

TURNMILLS

63b Clerkenwell Road EC1M 5PT
Tel 020 7250 3409
www.turnmills.co.uk

One of the longest-running dance clubs in London, where house music is played. Friday and Saturday are theme nights and there's a gay evening once a month on a Saturday.

🕐 Fri 10.30pm–7.30am, Sat 10pm–late
💷 £5–£15 🚇 Farringdon 🚌 55, 63, 243

WALKABOUT@LIMELIGHT

136 Shaftesbury Avenue W1D 5EZ
Tel 020 7255 8620
www.walkabout.eu.com

One of London's more unusual clubs in a small converted chapel, where the original alcoves combine with state-of-the-art light and sound. DJs play '60s to the present day rock, pop and commercial dance music.

🕐 Mon noon–1am; Tue–Sat noon–3am; Sun noon–midnight 💷 £3–£8 🚇 Leicester Square 🚌 9, 12, 13, 15, 23

WATER RATS

328 Grays Inn Road WC1X 8BZ
Tel 020 7837 7269
www.plumpromotions.co.uk

Rock/pop wannabes play live in this stage-and-curtain function room every night except Sunday. Oasis were discovered here, and Bob Dylan played his first UK date here in the early 1960s.

🕐 Mon–Sat from 7.30pm 💷 £4–£5
🚇 King's Cross 🚌 45

WHITE HOUSE

65 Clapham Park Road SW4 7EH
Tel 020 7498 3388
www.thewhitehouselondon.co.uk

Along with Sand, this place is keeping the cool alive in south Clapham. Surprisingly serene, with low-level seating and light walls. Mediterranean and Asian food and fine cocktails.

Mon–Sat 5.30pm–2am, Sun 5.30pm–midnight 🍸 Free–£8 🚇 Clapham Common 🚌 35, 88, 137

333

333 Old Street EC1V 9LE
Tel 020 7739 5949
www.333mother.com

This city club features a mix of styles that might include breaks and beats, soul, funk, reggae, drum 'n' bass and hip-hop. Sunday is gay night.

Thu–Sat 10pm–5am, Sun 10pm–4am 🍸 £5–£10 🚇 Old Street 🚌 43, 55, 243

COMEDY CLUBS

The comedy clubs listed here have stood the test of time better than most. Bring cash—many do not accept credit cards.

AMUSED MOOSE SOHO

Moonlighting, 17 Greek Street W1D 4DR
Tel 020 8341 1341
www.amusedmoose.co.uk

Small club with alternative comedy from the newest to established names. Solo stand-up, sketches, double acts and improvisation.

Thu–Sat from 8pm 🍸 £4–£11 🚇 Piccadilly Circus 🚌 14, 19, 22, 38

CANAL CAFÉ THEATRE

Bridge House, Delamere Terrace, Little Venice W2 6ND
Tel 020 7289 6054
www.newsrevue.com

Low-budget, high-energy, fringe satirical revue that's hilariously of-the-moment; scripts change every week and the cast every six weeks. Sketches, songs, impressions.

Sat 7.30pm–8.30pm, 9.30pm–10.30pm, Sun 7pm–8pm and 9pm–10pm 🍸 £5–£10 🚇 Warwick Avenue 🚌 6, 46, 187

CHUCKLE CLUB

Three Tuns Bar, London School of Economics, Houghton Street WC2A 2AE
Tel 020 7476 1672
www.chuckleclub.com

Students bar (open to all) with cheap drinks and established comedy club, which pulls in some of the best comics in the business.

Sat 7.45pm–11pm 🍸 £8–£10 🚇 Holborn 🚌 8, 59, 168, 188

COMEDY BREWHOUSE

Camden Head, 2 Camden Walk, Camden Passage N1 8DY
Tel 020 7359 0851
www.members.lycos.co.uk/comedybrewhouse

Stand-up comedians perform above a pub built in 1899. If the jokes don't make you laugh, you can always admire the etched windows and Victorian woodwork.

Fri–Sat 9pm–11pm 🍸 £4–£5 🚇 Angel 🚌 4, 274

COMEDY CAFÉ

66 Rivington Street EC2A 3AY
Tel 020 7359 5706
www.comedycafe.co.uk

Dine and drink in comfort during shows by established stand-up acts—and a no-heckling policy. Dancing afterwards.

Wed–Sat 8.30pm–11.15pm 🍸 £5–£14, Wed free 🚇 Old Street 🚌 55, 243

COMEDY STORE

1a Oxendon Street SW1Y 4EE
Tel 0870 060 2340
www.thecomedystore.co.uk

The best in stand-up comedy features improv from the Comedy Store Players. Big British TV and radio names who cut their teeth

here include Rik Mayall, Ade Edmonson, Ben Elton, Julian Clary and Steve Coogan.

Tue–Thu, Sun 8pm–10.15pm, Fri–Sat 8pm–10.15pm, midnight–2.15am; over 18s only 🍸 £12–£15 🚇 Piccadilly Circus, Leicester Square 🚌 14, 19, 38

DOWNSTAIRS AT THE KING'S HEAD

2 Crouch End Hill, Crouch End N8 8AA
Tel 020 8340 1028

Lively North London stand-up comedy venue under a popular pub, with try-out acts as well as more established performers.

Thu, Sat–Sun from 8.30pm 🍸 £4–£8 🚇 Finsbury Park 🚌 W7

HAMPSTEAD CLINIC

Downstairs at The White Horse, 154 Fleet Road, Hampstead NW3 2QX
Tel 020 7485 2112
www.comedy-club.info

This intimate basement rather ghoulishly takes its name from the nearby Royal Free Hospital. There's stand-up comedy on Saturdays.

Sep–Jun, Sat from 9pm 🍸 £5–£7 🚇 Belsize Park 🚌 46

HEADLINERS

The George IV, 185 Chiswick High Road W4 2DR
Tel 020 8566 4067

This comedy club with tables and a cabaret stage occupies a converted warehouse behind a pub. Opened in 2002, it has a reliable line-up from the TV and alternative circuit.

Thu–Sat from 8.30pm 🍸 £2.50–£10 🚇 Turnham Green 🚌 27, 391

JONGLEURS COMEDY CLUB, BATTERSEA

Bar Risa, 49 Lavender Gardens SW11 1DJ
Tel 0870 787 0707
www.jongleurs.com

Part of a countrywide chain of comedy clubs with consistently good quality stand-up performers. This one was the first Jongleurs Club, opened in 1983. Originally a 1920s ballroom, it now has a bar, grill and late-night venue.

Thu–Sat from 8.30pm 🍸 £9–£15 🚌 77, 77A, 239, 344, 345 🚃 Clapham Junction

JONGLEURS COMEDY CLUB, BOW WHARF
221 Grove Road E3 1AA
Tel 0870 787 0707
www.jongleurs.com
Refurbished Victorian warehouse at the confluence of the Regent and Grand Union canals. Bar.
🕐 Fri–Sat from 8.30pm 💷 £13–£14
🚇 Mile End 🚌 8, 25

JONGLEURS COMEDY CLUB AT LOCK 17, CAMDEN
Middle Yard, Camden Lock, Chalk Farm Road NW1 8AB
Tel 0870 787 0707
www.jongleurs.com
A Jongleurs in the heart of Camden's market on the waterfront, with live music.
🕐 Fri–Sat from 8.15pm 💷 £15–£16
🚇 Camden Town 🚌 24, 31, 274, C2

RED ROSE COMEDY CLUB
129 Seven Sisters Road N7 7QG
Tel 020 7281 3051
www.redrosecomedy.co.uk
A working men's club with stand-up comedy acts on Saturdays. Full bar with a late licence and meals.
🕐 Sat from 9pm 💷 £7, plus £1 membership 🚇 Finsbury Park 🚌 4, 29, 153, 253

TRICYCLE THEATRE
269 Kilburn High Road NW6 7JR
Tel 020 7328 1000
www.tricycle.co.uk
Unusually, the Tricycle offers stand-up comedy performed only by black comedians in its theatre on Sunday evenings.
🕐 Sun from 7.30pm 💷 £7.50–£8.50
🚇 Kilburn 🚌 16, 98

DJ BARS

ALPHABET BAR
61–63 Beak Street W1F 3SL
Tel 020 7439 2190

Alphabet isn't the smartest or hippest bar in town, but it's great for hanging out. Large leather sofas and easy-going crowd. The basement bar is louder and fuller.
🕐 Mon–Fri noon–11pm, Sat 5pm–11pm
💷 Free 🚇 Piccadilly Circus
🚌 9, 12, 13, 23, 139

THE CANTALOUPE
35 Charlotte Road EC2A 3PD
Tel 020 7613 4411
www.cantaloupe.co.uk
A former warehouse that is now a rough and edgy mainstay of Shoreditch's bar/restaurant scene. Attracts a large crowd—mostly trendy locals—and has dancing, bars and a raised restaurant area.
🕐 Mon–Sat 11am–midnight, Sun 11am–11pm 💷 Free 🚇 Old Street
🚌 26, 55, 243

CHARLIE WRIGHT'S INTERNATIONAL BAR
45 Pitfield Street N1 6DA
Tel 020 7490 8345
DJs play Thursday to Sunday. Come for the Thai food and the beer—that's the international part —and for the diverse crowd enjoying a fun night out.
🕐 Mon–Wed noon–1am, Thu–Sun noon–2am 💷 Free (Fri, Sat £3 after 10pm)
🚇 Old Street 🚌 55, 203, 243

ELECTRICITY SHOWROOMS
39A Hoxton Square N1 6NU
Tel 020 7739 6934
A great place with atmosphere where you drink at bashed-up tables and can't fail to notice the kitsch alpine scene across one wall. Full of City boys—macho business types—on weekdays but more mellow on Saturday and Sunday.
🕐 Mon 6pm–midnight, Tue, Wed, Thu, Sun noon–midnight, Fri, Sat noon–1am
💷 Free 🚇 Old Street 🚌 55, 205, 243

FLUID
40 Charterhouse Street EC1M 6JN
Tel 020 7253 3444
www.fluidbar.com
Snacks such as *miso* soup and *sushi* set the scene in this cool Japanese-themed bar. The beer is bottled rather than draught, and there are huge leather sofas where you can soak up the atmosphere.

🕐 Mon–Wed noon–midnight, Thu–Fri noon–2am, Sat 7pm–2am 💷 Free (Fri, Sat £4 after 10pm) 🚇 Barbican, Farringdon
🚌 17, 45, 46, 63

HOME BAR
100–106 Leonard Street EC2A 4RH
Tel 020 7684 8618
In this large basement you can chill out on tatty furniture, sip drinks without interruption and enjoy laid-back grooves and upbeat tunes (retro, hip-hop). The crowd is relaxed and the atmosphere friendly.
🕐 Mon–Fri 5pm–midnight, Sat 6pm–midnight 💷 Free 🚇 Old Street 🚌 55, 205, 243

LARK IN THE PARK
60 Copenhagen Street N1 0JW
Tel 020 7278 5781
www.larkinthepark.co.uk
Tasty, well-priced food, a sociable atmosphere and events from a Battle of the Bands, where up-and-coming talent compete, to quality background music, DJs, weekend barbecues in the beer garden and occasional firewalking (over hot coals) for those who dare!
🕐 Mon–Wed noon–11pm, Thu–Sat noon–2am, Sun noon–10.30pm 💷 Free
🚇 Angel, King's Cross 🚌 17, 91, 153, 274

THE MAC BAR
102 Camden Road, Camden Town NW1 9EA
Tel 020 7485 4530
www.macbar.co.uk

The best of both worlds—a trendy London cocktail bar with a laid-back, local feel. The food, served on sticks, is priced just right to fit the venue.

🕐 Daily noon–11pm 🍸 Free 🚇 Camden Town 🚌 29, 253, 274

MARKET PLACE
11 Market Place W1W 8AH
Tel 020 7079 2020
www.marketplace-london.com
Market Place, set on two floors, is a classic London DJ bar, popular with Londoners after work, with panelled walls and very good food. Downstairs is larger, with room to dance and alcove tables.

🕐 Mon–Wed 11am–midnight, Thu–Sat 11am–1am, Sun 1pm–11pm 🍸 Free Sun–Thu, £3 Fri 9pm–11pm, £7 after 11pm, £3 Sat 8pm–11pm, £7 after 11pm 🚇 Oxford Circus
🚌 7, 8, 10, 73, 176

MASH
19–21 Great Portland Street W1W 8QB
Tel 020 7637 5555
Beers are brewed on the premises in this retro bar. Its restaurant serves modern fare at high prices. DJs four nights out of seven.

🕐 Mon–Sat noon–2am 🍸 Free
🚇 Oxford Circus 🚌 8, 453, C2

SAINT BAR
8 Great Newport Street WC2H 7JA
Tel 020 7240 1551

Drinks are reasonably priced for this part of town and the music is upbeat in this central bar with an after-work crowd of young professionals.

🕐 Mon 5pm–1am, Tue–Thu 5pm–2am, Fri 5pm–3am, Sat 7.30pm–3am 🍸 Free
🚇 Leicester Square 🚌 9, 11, 13, 15, 23

SMITHS OF SMITHFIELD
67–77 Charterhouse Street EC1M 6HJ
Tel 020 7251 7950
www.smithsofsmithfield.co.uk
This huge, chic bar spills over four floors. Bottled beers are the drink of choice on the lofty ground floor; it's champagne and cocktails on the more intimate upper floors. You can dine in style here, which is reflected in the prices.

🕐 Daily 7am–11pm 🍸 Free
🚇 Farringdon 🚌 17, 45, 46, 63

GAY CLUBS AND BARS

Gay Times and *Attitude* are available from most newsagents monthly. Both contain features, interviews and listings. Other publications include *The Pink Paper*, which is more political and campaigning; *qx*, unashamedly hedonistic; and *boyz*, which is somewhere between the two.

Local groups, campaigning groups, ethnic and cultural groups, and a vast array of organizations provide advice and support. A good starting point is the Lesbian and Gay Helpline *(tel 020 7837 3337, open daily 7.30pm–10pm)*. Also check out www.gaybritain.org

ADMIRAL DUNCAN
54 Old Compton Street W1D 4UB
Tel 020 7437 5300
This friendly, long-established pillar of gay pubbing in London attracts an older clientele. The pub was originally designed to resemble a ship's galley.

🕐 Mon–Sat noon–11pm, Sun noon–10.30pm 🍸 Free 🚇 Leicester Square, Tottenham Court Road 🚌 14, 19, 24, 29, 176

BAR CODE
3–4 Archer Street W1D 7AP
Tel 020 7734 3342
A cruisey, busy men's bar with a lively, sweaty basement dance floor, plus fruit machines and a pool table. The crowd is flirtatious and easy-going. No dress code.

🕐 Mon–Sat 4pm–1am, Sun 4pm–10.30pm 🍸 Free 🚇 Piccadilly Circus 🚌 14, 19, 38

BLACK CAP
171 Camden High Street NW1 7JY
Tel 020 7428 2721
www.theblackcap.com
There's always something happening at this famous cabaret bar, London's premier drag venue, which attracts a mixed crowd. Apart from the disco, there is Sunday lunch karaoke and Oldies and Trash nights.

🕐 Mon–Thu noon–1am, Fri–Sat noon–2am, Sun noon–12.30am 🍸 £1–£3 🚇 Camden Town 🚌 29, 253, 274, C2

THE BOX
32–34 Monmouth Street, WC2H 9HB
Tel 020 7240 5828
www.boxbar.com
Stylish bar selling good food and beer and attracting a trendy clientele. It gets very crowded on weekends and hosts a popular Comedy Camp on Tuesdays.

🕐 Mon–Sat 11am–11pm, Sun noon–10.30pm 🍸 Free 🚇 Covent Garden 🚌 14, 19, 38, RV1

CANDY BAR
4 Carlisle Street, off Dean Street W1D 3BJ
Tel 020 7494 4041
www.candybar.easynet.co.uk
This leading lesbian and bisexual bar in central London attracts a large crowd and has DJs every night and a pool table. Gay male guests are also welcome. Decidedly relaxed atmosphere, and there is no dress code.

Mon–Thu 5pm–11.30pm, Fri–Sat 5pm–2am, Sun 5pm–10.30pm 🖐 Free Sun–Thu, £5 Fri–Sat after 9pm
🚇 Tottenham Court Road 🚌 14, 19, 24, 29, 176

COMPTON'S OF SOHO

53 Old Compton Street W1D 6HJ
Tel 020 7479 7961
www.comptons-of-soho.co.uk
This is a gay London institution, legendary for being cruisey; you should stop in for a pint at least once during your visit. The club sprawls over two floors and gets very crowded.
🕐 Mon–Sat noon–11pm, Sun noon–10.30pm 🖐 Free 🚇 Leicester Square, Tottenham Court Road 🚌 14, 19, 24, 29, 176

WHAT TO DO

FRIDGE

See page 203

THE G-A-Y BAR

30 Old Compton Street W1D 4UR
Tel 020 7494 2756
Formerly Manto's, this is a new bar for the gay scene, with plasma screens and video walls plus TV-themed nights. Tickets for G-A-Y London Astoria (see below) can be purchased in advance from here to avoid a long wait.
🕐 Mon–Sat noon–midnight, Sun noon–10.30pm 🖐 Free 🚇 Leicester Square 🚌 14, 19, 24, 29, 38, 176

G-A-Y LONDON ASTORIA

157 Charing Cross Road WC2H 0EN
Tel 020 7434 9592
Trashy, cheesy G-A-Y is usually the first stop on a gay clubbing itinerary. Monday's Pink Pounder has special drink offers and themed parties; Friday is Camp Attack; bands perform on Saturday.
🕐 Mon 10.30pm–3am, Thu–Fri 11pm–3.30am, Sat 10.30pm–3.30am

🖐 £3–£12 🚇 Tottenham Court Road 🚌 14, 19, 24, 29, 38

HEAVEN

The Arches, Villiers Street WC2N 6NG
Tel 020 7930 2020
www.heaven-london.com
London's most famous gay club. Popcorn on Monday, no-attitude-party playing commercial and funky house; Wednesday is mixed party night; and on Saturday Heaven plays dance sounds for a mixed crowd into the wee hours.
🕐 Mon 10pm–3.30am, Wed 10.30pm–3am, Fri 10pm–3am, Sat 10pm–6am 🖐 £5–£12 🚇 Embankment, Charing Cross 🚌 9, 11, 13, 15, 23

POPSTARZ

275 Pentonville Road N1 9NL
Tel 020 7833 2022
www.scala-london.co.uk
Popstarz's popular gay night, in a former cinema, has a Britpop grungy feel—a rare find on the gay scene. R'n'B style in the lounge and more classic pop upstairs.
🕐 Fri 10pm–5am 🖐 £5–£8 🚇 King's Cross 🚌 30, 73, 214

RUPERT STREET

50 Rupert Street W1D 6DS
Tel 020 7292 7141

Fully glass-fronted and full of men wearing suits and flashy watches, Rupert Street is the place to be seen and to do your seeing. The drinks are expensive, and the staff less than friendly.
🕐 Mon–Sat 11–11, Sun noon–10.30pm 🖐 Free 🚇 Piccadilly Circus 🚌 14, 19, 38

TWO BREWERS

114 Clapham High Street SW4 7UJ
Tel 020 7498 4971
Two bars, a disco and nightly cabaret make this south London

venue an easy-going alternative night out, with reasonably priced drinks and an absence of attitude.
🕐 Mon–Thu 5pm–1.30am, Fri–Sat 5pm–2am, Sun 5pm–12.30am 🖐 £1–£3 🚇 Clapham Common 🚌 35, 88, 137, 155

SHADOW LOUNGE

5 Brewer Street W1F 0RF
Tel 020 7287 7988
www.theshadowlounge.co.uk
This pretentious gay club in the heart of Soho, more like an over-crowded bar, is one of the few gay venues with a straight bar-style dress code—that is, smart and fashionable.
🕐 Mon–Wed 9pm–3am, Thu–Sat 8pm–3am 🖐 £5 before 10pm, £10 after 🚇 Leicester Square 🚌 12, 13, 15, 23, 139

SUBSTATION SOUTH

9 Brighton Terrace SW9 8DJ
Tel 020 7737 2095
www.substationsouth.com
One of the original gay London haunts, it's serious but still accessible. Men only Monday to Thursday, mixed at weekends and Saturday's popular Queer Nation features New York-style house and garage.
🕐 Mon–Tue, Thu 10.30pm–2.30am, Wed 10.30pm–3am, Fri 10.30pm–5am, Sat 10.30pm–6am, Sun 10pm–2am 🖐 £5–£10 🚇 Brixton 🚌 2, 3, 45, 59, 159

VILLAGE SOHO

81 Wardour Street, Soho W1V 3TG
Tel 020 7434 2124
www.theshadowlounge.co.uk
A young, relaxed crowd enjoy this stylish, late café-bar, which fills two floors in an L-shaped building. The dance bar downstairs plays funky house and chart music.
🕐 Mon–Sat 10.30am–1am, Sun noon–2am 🖐 Free–£2 🚇 Piccadilly Circus 🚌 14, 19

THE YARD BAR

57 Rupert Street W1V 7HN
Tel 020 7437 2652
www.yardbar.co.uk
This friendly haven in the middle of frenetic Soho is a good place for a pre-club drink. The central outdoor courtyard makes a welcome change from crammed bars and there's an upstairs loft bar. Reasonable prices, good food and friendly staff.
🕐 Mon–Sat noon–11pm, Sun noon–10.30pm 🖐 Free 🚇 Piccadilly Circus 🚌 14, 19, 38

SPORTS AND ACTIVITIES

Sport is a passion for the British, despite their tendency to caricature themselves as good-humoured losers.

London is the setting for several iconic sporting venues, including historic Lord's Cricket Ground (see page 210), Wimbledon's All England Tennis Club (see page 213), where the world-famous championships are held every June–July, and Wembley stadium (see page 17), a much-loved ground for major football (soccer) and rugby matches, now demolished to make way for an up-to-the-minute replacement. Rugby's main London stadium, which hosts international contests, close to London: the Epsom Derby (see page 222) in early to mid-June, and Ascot Week (see page 223), in mid-June. The latter is attended by royalty, the rich and famous and anyone wanting to see and be seen, as well as crowds of punters there for the thrill of placing a bet—and is known as much for the women's outrageous hats as for the races themselves.

To book tickets for all major sporting events contact www.theonlineticketshop.com.

London Marathon, when everyone from top athletes to TV celebrities and charity collectors in chicken outfits pounds the course between Greenwich and The Mall (see page 17 and 222). Contact Flora London Marathon *(tel 020 7902 0189, www.london-marathon.co.uk)* or Sportstours International *(tel 0161 703 8161, www.sportstoursinternational.co.uk)* for details.

Cricket matches at Lord's and the championships at Wimbledon (inset) are highlights of the sports season

is at Twickenham (see page 213), in west London. There are countless other, small-scale venues, but the easiest way to catch a game of cricket, football or rugby is simply to turn up at a suburban municipal park or playing field and stand on the sidelines as local teams battle it out.

The football and rugby seasons run from late August to May; cricket is played between May and September.

Two of Britain's most famous horse-racing events take place

Innumerable sports centres have sprung up around the capital over the past 20 years. These range from expensive clubs, where you may be able to buy short-term membership to use gyms, saunas, swimming pools and squash courts, to municipal operations providing no-frills versions of the same kind of facilities at much lower prices.

To get the blood really moving, consider applying (well in advance) to join the thousands of participants in April's annual

London's greatest offerings for the active of all ages are its parks, greens and commons. Nothing beats walking, jogging, flying a kite or sailing a model boat on Hampstead Heath, Hyde Park, Battersea Park, Wimbledon Common or Clapham Common— each of which provides a little slice of countryside in the city.

Spectator Sport

ATHLETICS

CRYSTAL PALACE NATIONAL SPORTS CENTRE
Ledrington Road, Crystal Palace SE19 2BB
Tel 020 8778 0131
www.crystalpalace.co.uk
A venue for major athletics events, where world-class competitors do battle in the summer.
🚇 63, 322 🚊 Crystal Palace

BASKETBALL

This sport is increasingly popular. For general information, contact the English Basketball Association *(tel 0113 236 1166, www.basketballengland.org.uk)*. The British Basketball League's season starts in March or April *(tel 0121 767 9470, www.bbl.org.uk)*.

KINDER LONDON TOWERS
Crystal Palace National Sports Centre, Ledrington Road, Crystal Palace SE19 2BB
Tel 020 8778 0131
www.london-towers.co.uk
The only professional basketball team based in London competes in three domestic competitions: the British Basketball League Championship, the National Cup

(Jan–Oct) and the knockout League Trophy (mid-Mar–Oct).
🚇 63, 157, 202, 358 🚊 Crystal Palace

BOXING
Most fights are staged at the York Hall Leisure Centre, though major championship matches take place at larger arenas such as Earl's Court (see page 196), Wembley (see page 197), or the Royal Albert Hall (see page 194). For general information contact the British Boxing Board of Control *(tel 029 203 67000, www.bbbofc.com)*.

YORK HALL LEISURE CENTRE
Old Ford Road, Bethnal Green E2 9PJ
Tel 020 8980 2243
www.towerhamlets.gov.uk
Opened in 1929, this favourite is due for a major refurbishment. There are also plans for a boxing hall of fame on the premises.
🚇 Bethnal Green 🚊 8, 388

CRICKET

Marylebone Cricket Club (MCC), cricket's governing body, is based at Lord's (see opposite). Wisden, the company that publishes the annual *Cricketers' Almanack*, is a world authority on the game and its website (www.cricinfo.comnational) gives national and international cricket news.

FOSTERS OVAL
Kennington Oval, Kennington SE11 5SS
Tel 020 7582 6660
www.surreycricket.com
London's number two cricket ground—second to Lord's—hosts key matches including internationals, cup finals and important one-day internationals.
🚇 Oval 🚊 36, 185

LORD'S
St. John's Wood Road NW8 8QN
Tel MCC info 020 7289 1611,
tickets 020 7432 1000
www.lords.org.uk
Historic home of cricket, hosting internationals, one-day games, cup finals and semi-finals. The Lord's Natwest Media Centre, a modern building with boxes and facilities for commentators dominates the grounds.
🚇 St. John's Wood 🚊 13, 82, 113

FOOTBALL
Top of the football hierarchy is the Barclaycard Premier League *(www.premierleague.com)*. It is very difficult to get Premiership match tickets unless you are a member of one of the competing clubs. Tickets for the lower Nationwide League divisions are less expensive and easier to acquire; contact individual venues. The Football Association is football's governing body in England *(tel 020 7745 4776, www.thefa.com)*.

If all else fails, you'll be able to watch key games on large screens in pubs and bars all around town.

PREMIERSHIP CLUBS

ARSENAL
Arsenal Stadium, Avenell Road, Highbury N5 1BU
Tel 020 7704 4000
www.arsenal.com
Famous north London club, usually near the top of the Premiership. Known as The Gunners, a throwback to the club's connections with the former royal armaments factory.
🚇 Arsenal 🚊 4, 30

CHARLTON ATHLETIC
The Valley, Floyd Road, Charlton SE7 8BL
Tel 020 8333 4010
www.cafc.co.uk
Started as a club in 1920, Charlton Athletic became successful in the 1930s. Like many major clubs, it has an active schedule of community and junior events.
🚇 53 🚊 Charlton

CHELSEA
Stamford Bridge, Fulham Road SW6 1HS
Tel 020 7386 7799
www.chelseafc.co.uk
Very popular team founded in 1905. Chelsea won the Football

League championship 50 years later and has won many cups since. Fulham Broadway 📷 11, 414

FULHAM
Craven Cottage, Stevenage Road
SW6 6HH
Tel 0870 442 1234
www.fulhamfc.co.uk
One of the older clubs, having started as a church side for St. Andrews of West Kensington in 1878. The team joined the professional game in December 1898.
📷 White City 📷 49, 94, 148

TOTTENHAM HOTSPUR
White Hart Lane, Bill Nicholson Way, High Road, Tottenham N17 0AP
Tel 0870 420 5000
www.spurs.co.uk
Universally known as Spurs, Tottenham has played at its White Hart stadium since renting it from brewers in 1899.
📷 76, 149, 341 📷 White Hart Lane

NATIONWIDE PREMIER LEAGUE DIVISION CLUBS

DIVISION 1
CRYSTAL PALACE
Selhurst Park, Whitehorse Lane, Selhurst
SE25 6PU
Tel 020 8771 8841
www.cpfc.co.uk
The Eagles have had mixed fortunes in recent decades, with a bumpy history of relegation (going down a division) and promotion.
📷 468 📷 Thornton Heath, Selhurst

MILLWALL
Zampa Road, Bermondsey SE16 3LN
Tel 020 7231 9999
www.millwallfc.co.uk
A south London team known as the Lions; the stadium is appropriately called The Den.
📷 188, 381 📷 South Bermondsey

WEST HAM UNITED
Boleyn Ground, Green Street, Upton Park
E13 9AZ
Tel 020 8548 2700
www.whufc.com
Formed as the Thames Ironworks football club in 1895 (hence the nicknames the Irons and the Hammers). West Ham's stadium museum traces the club's past.
📷 Upton Park 📷 15, 115

WIMBLEDON
Selhurst Park, Whitehorse Lane, Selhurst
SE25 6PU
Tel 020 8771 2233
www.wimbledon-fc.co.uk
Currently sharing their stadium with Crystal Palace; planning a move to Milton Keynes at the time of writing.
📷 468 📷 Thornton Heath, Selhurst

DIVISION 2
BRENTFORD
Griffin Park, Braemar Road, Brentford,
Middlesex TW8 0NT
Tel 020 8847 2511
www.brentfordfc.co.uk
This team, which has been around for more than 100 years, has hovered between divisions two and three in the past few years.
📷 South Ealing 📷 65, 237, 267, H29, E8, E2

QUEEN'S PARK RANGERS
Loftus Road Stadium, South Africa Road, Shepherd's Bush W12 7PA
Tel 020 8740 2575
www.qpr.co.uk
Just west of the BBC Television Centre, QPR's smart stadium also plays host to the London Wasps rugby team.
📷 White City 📷 49, 94, 148

GOLF

Two top courses, Sunningdale and Wentworth, are within easy reach of central London.

For general information on golf contact the Golf Foundation (tel 01920 876200, www.golf-foundation.org).

SUNNINGDALE
Ridgemount Road, Sunningdale,
Berks SL5 9RR
Tel 01344 621681
www.sunningdale-golfclub.co.uk

Two 18-hole championship courses—Old and New (1923)—laid out on heathland and negotiating heather, gorse and pine. About 27 miles (43km) from central London.
📷 Sunningdale

WENTWORTH
Wentworth Drive, Virginia Water,
Surrey GU25 4LS
Tel 01344 842201
www.wentworthclub.com
Three 18-hole championship courses and a 9-hole course of heathland surrounded by pine, oak and birch trees. World Matchplay tournament held here in October. About 25 miles (40km) from central London.
📷 Virginia Water

GREYHOUND RACING
An evening 'at the dogs' is fun and inexpensive. The betting system is easy to understand and all tracks have restaurants and bars; book ahead if you want to watch the races from a table. For general information contact the British Greyhound Racing Board (tel 020 7292 9900, www.thedogs.co.uk).

CATFORD STADIUM
Adenmore Road, Catford SE6 4RJ
Tel 020 8690 8000
www.catfordstadium.co.uk
Race days on Thursday and Saturday evenings and Tuesday and Sunday afternoons. Restaurant and three fast-food counters.
📷 21 📷 Catford, Catford Bridge

WALTHAMSTOW STADIUM
300 Chingford Road, Chingford E4 8SJ
Tel 020 8531 4255
www.wsgreyhound.co.uk
Races on Tuesday, Thursday and Saturday evenings and on Monday

and Friday afternoons. Two restaurants, two snack bars and several tea bars.

Walthamstow Central then bus 97, 215, 357 to Walthamstow Central

WIMBLEDON STADIUM
Plough Lane, Wimbledon SW17 0BL
Tel 020 8946 8000
Races Tuesday, Friday and Saturday evenings. Silver service restaurant plus an informal restaurant and bar snacks.
Tooting Broadway, Wimbledon 155

HORSE RACING
Of the five racecourses within comfortable reach of London, Ascot and Epsom are the most prestigious. The flat racing season runs from April to September; the national hunt season (over jumps) from October to April. During the summer, meetings are held in the evenings.

ASCOT RACECOURSE
High Street, Ascot, Berkshire SL5 7JX
Tel 01344 622211
www.ascot.co.uk
The prestigious Royal Ascot Week in June is the highlight of the calendar (see page 223). About 29 miles (46km) from central London.
Ascot

EPSOM DOWNS RACECOURSE
Epsom Downs Epsom KT18 5LQ
Tel 01372 470047
www.epsomderby.co.uk

Two major flat-racing events take place here in June: the Oaks and the Derby (see page 222). About 17 miles (27km) from central London.
Epsom Town Centre or Tattenham Corner, then shuttle bus

KEMPTON PARK
Staines Road East, Sunbury-on-Thames, Middlesex TW16 5AQ
Tel 01372 470047
www.kempton.co.uk
Popular course featuring the two-day festival on 26 and 27 December, which includes the George VI Steeplechase.
Kempton Park

ROYAL WINDSOR
Maidenhead Road, Windsor, Berkshire SL4 5JJ
Tel 01753 498400
www.windsor-racecourse.co.uk
The only figure-of-eight flat course in the country hosts the three-day Royal Windsor Racing Festival late May to early June.
Windsor and Eton Riverside Riverbus service from Barry Avenue Promenade, near Eton Bridge in town centre

SANDOWN PARK
Portsmouth Road, Esher, Surrey KT10 9AJ
Tel 01372 470047
www.sandown.co.uk
Principal meetings include the Whitbread Gold Cup in April and the Coral Eclipse Stakes in July.
Esher

ICE HOCKEY

Ice hockey is gaining in popularity and matches are held between September and March. For general information contact Ice Hockey UK (tel 0115 924 1441, www.icehockeyuk.co.uk).

MOTORSPORT
Stock-car racing has an enthusiastic following. It's a noisy, tough and thrilling affair involving beaten-up and welded-together cars. For general information contact the UK's governing body, the Motor Sports Association (tel 01753 765000, www.msauk.org).

WIMBLEDON STADIUM
Plough Lane, Wimbledon SW17 0BL
Tel 020 8946 8000
www.wimbledonstadium.co.uk
Sunday evenings are a jamboree of old bangers and stock cars between mid-August and April.
Tooting Broadway, Wimbledon
Wimbledon, Earlsfield, Haydons Road

POLO
This frantic horseback game is traditionally associated with royalty and the aristocracy. The main UK season runs from May to September; indoor or arena polo is played throughout the winter. For general information, contact the Hurlingham Polo Association, the UK's governing body (tel 01367 242828, www.hpa-polo.co.uk).

GUARDS POLO CLUB
Smith's Lawn, Windsor Great Park, Egham, Surrey TW20 0HP
Tel 01784 434212
www.guardspoloclub.com
Official matches are played on Saturday and Sunday afternoons and league matches on Tuesday, Wednesday, Thursday and Friday, between mid-April and mid-September.
Egham

RUGBY
Two types of rugby are played in Britain: 15-a-side Rugby Union, and 13-a-side Rugby League. Rugby League teams play almost exclusively in the north of England, with the exception of the London Broncos. The Super League season runs from March to September. The Six Nations Championship (Jan–Mar) is the highlight of the

Rugby Union season. Contact the governing bodies, Rugby Football League *(tel 0113 232 9111, www.rfl.uk.com)* or Rugby Football Union, based at Twickenham (see below).

TWICKENHAM STADIUM
Rugby House, 21 Rugby Road, Twickenham TW1 1DS
Tel 020 8892 2000
www.rfu.com
Rugby Union's major venue has a Museum of Rugby and conducts tours of the massive stadium.
🚌 281, R62 🚇 Twickenham

RUGBY LEAGUE CLUBS

LONDON BRONCOS
Griffin Park, Braemar Road, Brentford, Middlesex TW8 0NT
Tel 0871 222 1132
www.londonbroncos.co.uk
The only team in the Tetley's Super League competition, and pioneers for the game in the south of England.
🚇 South Ealing 🚌 65, 237, 267, H29, E8, E2 🚉 Brentford

RUGBY UNION CLUBS

LONDON WASPS
Adams Park Stadium (premiership matches), Hillbottom Road Sands Industrial Estate, High Wycombe, Bucks HP12 4HJ
Tel 020 8993 8298, ticket hotline 01494 769471
www.wasps.co.uk
Formed in 1867, the Wasps followed a Victorian fashion for naming teams after birds and insects. The club enjoyed a particularly successful run in the 1990s and won both the Premiership Championship and the European Cup in 2002/3.
🚉 High Wycombe

LONDON WELSH
Old Deer Park, Kew Road, Richmond, Surrey TW9 2AZ
Tel 020 8940 2368
www.london-welsh.co.uk
This team of Welsh expatriates was established in 1885 and in recent years has performed creditably after a dip in the mid-1990s.
🚇 Richmond 🚌 65, 419, H37

NEC HARLEQUINS
Stoop Memorial Ground, Langhorn Drive, Twickenham, Middlesex TW2 7SX
Tel 020 8410 6000
www.quins.co.uk
Founded in 1866 as the Hampsteam (Hampstead) Football Club, the team was renamed in 1870 to reflect its wider membership. Harlequins was chosen from a dictionary as a way of retaining the HFC monogram.
🚌 281 🚉 Twickenham

ROSSLYN PARK
Priory Lane, Upper Richmond Road, Roehampton SW15 5JH
Tel 020 8876 6044
www.rosslynpark.co.uk
This sociable club is committed to maintaining its amateur status and offers rugby at all levels and ages. Also runs a female league team.
🚌 33, 337 🚉 Barnes

SNOOKER
Snooker has emerged from pubs and working men's clubs into the TV spotlight, making mega-rich TV stars of top players. Millions watch every ball on TV; some of it is screened from the Wembley Conference Centre (see below), where you can soak up the tension as a live spectator. World Snooker is the controlling body for international professional billiards and snooker *(tel 0117 3178200, www.worldsnooker.com)*.

WEMBLEY CONFERENCE CENTRE
Empire Way, Wembley, Middlesex HA9 0DW
Tel 0870 739 0739 (box office)
www.wembley.co.uk
The UK's first purpose-built conference centre hosts major matches on snooker's tournament circuit.
🚇 Wembley Park 🚉 18

SOCCER
See Football

TENNIS

The tennis championship held at the All England Lawn Tennis and Croquet Club during the last week in June and the first week in July is the oldest major tennis championship in the world and the only one played on grass. Most tickets are allocated to members and to those of other tennis clubs, but there is also a public lottery or ballot; to enter it apply between September and December by sending a stamped, addressed envelope to the All England Club or, alternatively, queue outside the club for a ticket on the day of the match. The Lawn Tennis Association is the governing body for tennis in the UK *(tel 020 7381 7000, www.lta.org.uk)*.

ALL ENGLAND LAWN TENNIS AND CROQUET CLUB
PO Box 98, Wimbledon SW19 5AE
Tel 020 8971 2473, recorded info 020 8946 2244
www.wimbledon.org
This private club was founded in 1868. Centre Court and the No. 1 Court are used only for the annual championships; the rest are available only to club members and LTA-sponsored players.
🚇 Southfields 🚌 39, 93

QUEENS CLUB
Palliser Road, West Kensington W14 9EQ
Tel 020 7385 3421
www.queensclub.co.uk
International tennis stars warm up for Wimbledon in the Stella Artois tournament, held here in June.
🚇 Barons Court 🚌 211, 391

Activities

BIRDWATCHING

LONDON WETLAND CENTRE
See page 160
Excellent hides and more than 130 species of birds annually. Walks, talks and workshops.

BOATING

HYDE PARK
The Ranger's Lodge, Hyde Park, W2 2UH
Tel 020 7298 2100
www.royalparks.gov.uk
The 11ha (27-acre) Serpentine has facilities for rowing, canoeing and paddle boats (see page 93).
🚇 Hyde Park Corner, Marble Arch, Knightsbridge 🚌 9 10 12, 14, 73

REGENT'S PARK LAKE
Storeyard (Inner Circle), Regent's Park NW1 4NR
Tel 020 7486 7905
www.royalparks.gov.uk
In addition to boating facilities, the lake has islands, a heronry and waterfowl (see page 115).
🚇 Baker Street, Marylebone, Regent's Park, Great Portland Street, Camden Town
🚌 27, 82, 205, 274, C2

BRASS-RUBBING

LONDON BRASS-RUBBING CENTRE
The Crypt, St. Martin-in-the-Fields, Trafalgar Square WC2N 4JJ
Tel 020 7930 9306
www.stmartin-in-the-fields.org
A collection of 90 replica church brasses shows royals, medieval and Tudor figures and Celtic designs. Tuition and materials are provided as part of the entry fee (see page 117).
🚇 Charing Cross, Leicester Square
🚌 11, 15, 24, 29, 176

CYCLING

Cycling in central London can be a hair-raising experience, but beyond the busy roads there are plenty of lanes and tracks, and an active campaign is under way to improve facilities for cyclists. For more information about options for cycling in and around the city contact the London Cyclists' Trust *(tel 020 7928 7220, www.lcc.org.uk).*

HERNE HILL VELODROME
Burbage Road, Herne Hill SE24 9HE
Tel 020 7737 4647
www.hernehillvelodrome.co.uk
Plans are in hand to expand and improve the world's oldest cycle circuit (1891), which predates local houses by nearly 30 years. Hosted the 1908 and 1948 Olympics. Regeneration proposals include adding a fitness studio, climbing walls and other facilities. Bicycle rental available (£2–£2.50 per session). About 7 miles (11km) from central London.
🚌 3, 68, 322 🚉 Herne Hill, North Dulwich

LEE VALLEY CYCLE CIRCUIT
Quartermile Lane, Stratford E10 5PD
Tel 020 8534 6085
www.leevalleypark.com

Specially built tracks offer BMX, road-racing, cyclo-cross and mountain biking summer and winter. Bring your own bicycle or rent one.
🚇 Leyton 🚌 25

GOLF

The courses listed below are within easy reach of central London and don't require membership. For more London courses contact the English Golf Union *(tel 01526 354500, www.englishgolfunion.org* or *www.thelondongolfer.com).*

BRENT VALLEY GOLF COURSE
Church Road, Hanwell W7 3BE
Tel 020 8567 1287
Good 18-hole parkland course, with lessons and trolley hire. About 12 miles (19km) from central London.
🏌 Average weekday fee £11, weekend fee £15 before noon, £12.50 after 🚇 Ealing Broadway 🚌 E3, 83, 207, 607

RICHMOND PARK GOLF COURSE
Roehampton Gate, Priory Lane, Richmond SW15 5JR
Tel 020 8876 1795
www.richmondparkgolf.co.uk
Set in 40ha (100 acres) of parkland, 7 miles (11km) from the centre of the city. Facilities include a driving range.
🏌 Weekday fee £6–£18, weekend/public hols £16–£21 🚉 Richmond 🚌 74, 170, 391

HORSEBACK-RIDING

HYDE PARK AND KENSINGTON STABLES
63 Bathurst Mews W2 2SB
Tel 020 7723 2813
www.hydeparkstables.com

This central stables offers group and individual lessons or just a ride around Hyde Park.
🐎 Group riding Tue 7.15–5, Wed–Thu 9.45–5, Fri 7.15–5, Sat–Sun 8.30–5. Phone for

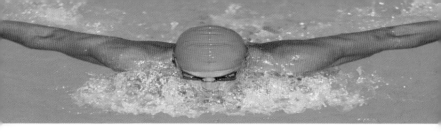

times of private riding sessions and lessons. Booking essential 🚶 Group ride £39 🚇 Lancaster Gate 🚌 12, 94, 148

WIMBLEDON VILLAGE STABLES
24 High Street, Wimbledon SW19 5DX
Tel 020 8946 8579
www.wvstables.com
These stables within easy reach of Wimbledon Common, Richmond Park and Ham Common use riding tracks through countryside and woodland, with occasional off-track riding.
🕐 Tue–Fri 9–2 winter, 9–7 summer, Sat, Sun rides at 9, 10.15, 11.30, 2 🚶 Single lesson/ride £30–£75 🚇 Wimbledon 🚌 93

ICE-SKATING

ALEXANDRA PALACE ICE RINK
Alexandra Palace Way, Wood Green N22 7AY
Tel 020 8365 2121
www.alexandrapalace.com
In a historic building (1873) with panoramic London views. Skates for rent.
🕐 Mon–Fri 11–1.30, 2–5.30, Sat, Sun 10.30–12.30, 2–4.30, plus Fri, Sat disco 8.30pm–11pm, Sun 8.30pm–11pm 🚶 Mon–Fri: adult £4.20, child (under 16) £3.50; Fri/Sat disco: everyone £5.50; Sat–Sun: adult £5.50, child (under 16) £4.50 🚇 Wood Green then W3 bus 🚌 W3 🚆 Alexandra Palace

BROADGATE ICE ARENA
Broadgate Circle, Eldon Street EC2M 2QS
Tel 020 7505 4068
www.broadgateestates.co.uk
This outdoor rink is home to the Broomball League, which plays a variation of ice hockey; matches Mon, Tue, Wed evenings (free). Skates for rent.
🕐 Mon–Fri noon–2.30, 3.30–6, Sat 11–1, 2–4, 5–8.30, Sun 11–1, 2–4, 5–7, Oct–Apr 🚶 £5 per session, child (under 16) £3, skate rental £2, child £1 🚇 Liverpool Street 🚌 8, 26, 35

SOMERSET HOUSE
See pages 130–131
In winter, the central courtyard becomes an ice rink.

STREATHAM ICE ARENA
386 Streatham High Road SW16 6HT
Tel 020 8769 7771
www.streathamicearena.co.uk
Skates for rent, lessons; disco Friday and Saturday evening.
🕐 Daily 10.30–4, plus Wed 4.30–6.30, Tue–Thu 8pm–10.30pm, Fri, Sat 6–8pm,

8.30pm–11.30pm (disco) 🚶 £4.70–£5.50, skate rental £1.50 🚌 133, 159, 319 🚆 Streatham, Streatham Common, Streatham Hill

ROLLER BLADING

A free two-hour Friday Night Skate starts at 7.30pm from the Duke of Wellington Arch, in the middle of Hyde Park Corner. To take part, you must be good at braking and turning at speed and sometimes downhill. You should also be fast enough to keep up with the group and be able to deal with varying road surfaces. Teams of volunteers (marshals) wear yellow or red vests and lead the skate. A map of the route is posted each Thursday. The skate is open to all ages and to both quad skaters (roller skaters) and inline skaters (rollerbladers), and occasionally cyclists,

skateboarders and people in wheelchairs. Friday Night Skaters are strongly advised to wear full body armour: wrist, elbow and knee pads as well as a helmet, plus bright or reflective clothing. Check the weather update at 5pm each Friday for confirmation that the skate is going ahead. The Sunday Stroll, a less taxing skate, takes place in summer only, with no marshals. Meet at 2pm on the East side of Serpentine Road, Hyde Park; expect to finish about 4pm. Further information (tel 0788 729 0179, www.citiskate.com).

The two shops below, near Hyde Park, rent skates:

CLUB BLUE ROOM
12–14 Edgware Road W2 2EN
Tel 020 7724 4884
One of London's biggest skate retailers, stocking a range of skates, equipment and accessories.
🕐 Mon–Sat 10–6.30, Sun 12–6 🚶 Rental £10 a day (£150 deposit) 🚇 Marble Arch 🚌 12, 94, 148, 705

SLICK WILLIES
41 Kensington High Street W8 5ED
Tel 020 7937 3824
Range of skates and a good helmet selection. Overnight rental after 5pm Friday to Saturday morning.
🕐 Mon–Sat 10–6.30, Sun 12–5 🚶 Rental £10 a day, £15 overnight (£100 deposit) 🚇 High Street Kensington 🚌 9, 10, 27, 28, 328

SNOOKER

CENTREPOINT SNOOKER CLUB AND GYMNASIUM
Centrepoint, New Oxford Street WC1A 1DD
Tel 020 7240 6886
All-hours club with snooker and pool tables, and a gymnasium, sauna and Jacuzzi for men only.
🕐 Daily 11am–6am 🚇 Tottenham Court Road 🚌 8, 14, 19

POOL SHACK
16 Semley House, Semley Place SW1W 9QJ
Tel 020 7823 5817
www.cuesports.uk.com/poolshack-vict.htm
Non-membership club with eight American pool tables and cable TV.
🕐 Mon–Sun 12–12 🚇 Sloane Square, Victoria 🚌 11, 705, C1

SPORTS CENTRES

CENTRAL YMCA
112 Great Russell Street WC1B 3NQ
Tel 020 7343 1700
www.centralYMCA.org.uk
The original site of the first YMCA (established 1844) houses a huge sports centre, offering almost anything you want—gym, pool, sports hall, playing fields, dance studio and more.
🕐 Mon–Fri 7am–10pm, Sat–Sun 10–8.30 🚶 Day membership £15 (use of all facilities) 🚇 Tottenham Court Road 🚌 7, 10, 24, 73

CRYSTAL PALACE NATIONAL SPORTS CENTRE
Ledrington Road, Crystal Palace SE19 2BB
Tel 020 8778 0131
www.crystalpalace.co.uk
Indoor and outdoor facilities for more than 100 activities, including athletics, swimming, football, martial arts and keep fit. Also scuba diving, canoeing, skiing and fencing.
🚌 63, 322 🚆 Crystal Palace

THE GYM COVENT GARDEN
30 The Piazza, Covent Garden WC2 8BE
Tel 020 7836 4835
www.jubileehallclubs.co.uk

SPORTS AND ACTIVITIES 215

Central, well-equipped busy gym with classes also available. Open access gym and sports centre with membership available for frequent users. Book well in advance.
🕐 Mon–Fri 7am–10pm, Sat 9–9, Sun 10–5 💷 £6.50–£8 🚇 Covent Garden 🚌 6, 9, 13, 23, RV1

OASIS SPORTS CENTRE
32 Endell Street WC2H 9AG
Tel 020 7831 1804
www.camden.gov.uk
Indoor and outdoor swimming pools, sauna, gym, massage, squash, badminton, martial arts, aerobics and fitness training.
🕐 Mon–Fri 7.30am–9pm, Sat, Sun 9.30am–5.30pm 💷 £3.10–£5.75 🚇 Covent Garden 🚌 14, 19, 38, RV1

QUEEN MOTHER SPORTS CENTRE
223 Vauxhall Bridge Road, Victoria SW1V 1EL
Tel 020 7630 5522
www.courtneys.co.uk
Badminton, swimming, martial arts, a gym and exercise studios.
🕐 Mon–Fri 6:30am–10pm, Sat, Sun 8–8 💷 Non-members £2.50 per use 🚇 Victoria 🚌 2, 36, 185

WESTWAY SPORTS CENTRE
1 Crowthorne Road, Ladbroke Grove W10 6RP
Tel 020 8969 0992
www.westway.org
One of London's finest sports centres with all-weather football pitches, indoor tennis courts, the UK's largest climbing wall and more.
🕐 Mon–Fri 8am–10pm, Sat 8–8, Sun 10–10; climbing wall Mon–Fri 10.30–10, Sat–Sun 10–8 💷 Tennis: adult from £13.50, child from £6; climbing wall from £5.50 🚇 Latimer Road 🚌 23, 52

SWIMMING
Check the *Yellow Pages* for council-run indoor pools.

SERPENTINE LIDO
Hyde Park W1J 7NT
Tel 020 7706 3422
www.serpentinelido.com
Hyde Park's lido has been in existence for more than 100 years. You can swim in the Serpentine Lake or sunbathe in a deckchair. Playground, small pool for children, changing facilities and facilities for people with disabilities.
🕐 Daily 10–5.30, Jun–mid-Sep 💷 £3.30, child (under 15) 70p, family ticket £7.50, under 3s free 🚇 Hyde Park Corner 🚌 9, 10, 14, 19, 22, 52, 74, 137

PARLIAMENT LIDO AND PONDS
Parliament Hill Lido, Gordon House Road, London NW5
Tel 020 7482 7073
www.cityoflondon.gov.uk/openspaces
There are four swimming facilities on the Heath: the lido and the Hampstead (mixed bathing), Highgate (men only) and Kenwood (women only) bathing ponds, originally clay pits dug out by brickmakers in the 19th century and earlier. The ponds are for competent swimmers only.
🕐 Lido 7–9.30am, 10am–6.30pm May–Sep; 7am–10.30am Oct–Apr. Highgate and Kenwood ponds 7am–9pm or sunset if earlier in summer; Dec–Jan 7.30–3.30, Nov, Feb 7–3, 7–sunset rest of year. Hampstead Pond 7–7, summer only 💷 Lido daily ticket £3.60, child £1.80, family ticket £10, free before 10am; ponds free 🚇 Hampstead, Highgate 🚌 43, 46, 134, 263 268

TOOTING BEC LIDO
Tooting Bec Common, Tooting Bec Road SW16 1RU
Tel 020 8871 7198
www.wandsworth.gov.uk
Open-air swimming pool, children's pool, café. Showers, toilets and changing areas and facilities for people with disabilities.
🕐 Daily 6am–7.45pm, Jun–Aug; 6–4 Sep 💷 £3.65, child (5–15) £2.50, under 5s free 🚇 Tooting Bec, Balham 🚌 155, 249, 319, 355

TENNIS
Nearly all London's public parks have hard courts that can be booked in advance. Charges are inexpensive; use of some courts is free. As a rule you have to supply your own rackets and balls.

ISLINGTON TENNIS CENTRE
Market Road, Holloway N7 9PL
Tel 020 7700 1370
www.aquaterra.org
Two outdoor courts and six indoor (at twice the price) available to non-members. Private lessons seven days a week.
🕐 Mon–Thu 7am–11pm, Fri 7am–10pm, Sat, Sun 8am–10pm 💷 Indoor £16.50, junior (4–11) £7.40, outdoor £7.40, junior £3.70 🚇 Caledonian Road 🚌 17, 91, 259, 274

TEN PIN BOWLING
For further information contact the British Ten Pin Bowling Association (*tel 020 8478 1745 www.btba.org.uk*).

ROWANS BOWL
10 Stroud Green Road, Finsbury Park N4 2DF
Tel 020 8800 1950
www.rowans.co.uk
Two-floor, air-conditioned building with 12 bowling lanes on each level. Bars, food, satellite screens and dance floors.
🕐 Sun–Thu, pub hols 10.30am–1am, Fri, Sat 10.30am–2.30am 💷 £1–£3; games £2–£3.25 each; shoe hire £1 🚇 Finsbury Park 🚌 29, 253

STREATHAM MEGABOWL
142 Streatham Hill, SW2 4RU
Tel 020 8678 6007
www.megabowl.co.uk
Bowling plus American pool, amusement area and Zapp Zone laser-gun game, bar and fast food.
🕐 Mon–Fri noon–11.30, Sat 10am–midnight, Sun 10am–11.30pm 💷 £3.75 per game, child (under 15) £2.75; shoe hire £1 🚌 45, 57, 59, 109, 118, 133, 137, 159, 201, 250, 255, 319, 333, 417 🚆 Streatham Hill

WATERSPORTS
DOCKLANDS SAILING & WATERSPORTS CENTRE
235a Westferry Road, Millwall Dock E14 3QF
Tel 020 7537 2626
www.dswc.org
Here you can enjoy everything watery from sailing and rowing to canoeing and dragonboat racing.
🕐 Daily 10–12.30, 1.30–5, 5.30–dusk May–Sep; Sun 10–12.30, 1.30–5, Tue, Thu 5.30–dusk Oct, Apr; Sun 10–12.30, 1.30–5, Nov–Mar 💷 £15 day membership for non-members 🚌 15, RV1 🚆 Docklands Light Railway, Crossharbour

Health and Beauty

Call ahead to book treatments or appointments at any of London's chic spas and salons.

BEAUTY SALONS AND SPAS

BALANCE
250 King's Road SW3 5UE
Tel 020 7565 0333
www.balancetheclinic.co.uk
Peaceful retreat offering health treatments—including nutrition advice, colonics and lymph drainage—as well as facials, massage and the like.
⏰ Mon–Wed 9–7, Thu 9–8, Fri–Sat 9–6, Sun 12–5 by appointment. Booking advisable 🖐 Manicure from £15 🚇 South Kensington, Sloane Square
🚌 11, 19, 22, 49, 211, 319

BHARTI VYAS
5 and 24 Chiltern Street W1U 7QE
Tel 020 7935 5312
www.bharti-vyas.com
Holistic beauty centre offering a range of treatments such as aromatherapy, acupressure and massage, tailor-made for individual customers.
⏰ Mon–Sat 9.30–6. Booking essential 🖐 Facial from £75 🚇 Baker Street
🚌 2, 13, 30, 74, 82, 113, 139, 189, 274

BLISSLONDON
60 Sloane Avenue SW3 3DD
Tel 020 7584 3888
www.blissworld.com

Originally opened in New York, this salon promises highly trained experts. The glass of wine and rich-chocolate brownies you're given before a treatment is surely bliss!
⏰ Mon–Fri 9.30–8, Sat 9.30–6, Sun 12–6.30. Booking essential 🖐 Manicure from £23 🚇 South Kensington
🚌 14, 49, 345

DORCHESTER SPA
The Dorchester, Park Lane W1A 2HJ
Tel 020 7495 7335
www.dorchesterhotel.com
Set in the depths of one of London's top hotels, this tranquil oasis offers gym, beauty treatments, sauna and steam rooms, a Charles Worthington hair salon and a traditional barber shop.
⏰ Daily 7am–9pm. Booking essential 🖐 Manicure from £35 🚇 Marble Arch, Hyde Park Corner 🚌 2, 10, 16, 36, 73, 74, 82, 137

ELIZABETH ARDEN RED DOOR SALON & SPA
29 Davies Street W1K 4LW
Tel 020 7629 4488
www.reddoorsalons.com
Perhaps the most famous salon of them all, this slick US-based operation offers massage, body treatments, skincare, hair design and makeup. Luxurious, modern and in the heart of smart Mayfair.
⏰ Mon 10–7, Tue 9–7, Wed–Fri 9–8, Fri–Sat 9–6, Sun 11–5 Booking advisable 🖐 Manicure from £20
🚇 Bond Street 🚌 8

JO MALONE
150 Sloane Street SW1X 9BX
Tel 020 7730 2100
www.jomalone.co.uk
Facials tailormade for each client make this calm and relaxing salon different. It uses only Jo Malone's own products. Also at 23 Brook Street (Mayfair) and 24 Royal Exchange (the City).
⏰ Mon–Tue, Fri–Sat 10–6, Wed–Thu 10–7. Booking essential 🖐 Facial (the only treatment available–90 mins) £125 🚇 Sloane Square 🚌 19, 22, 137, C1

SPA.NK
127–131 Westbourne Grove W2 4UP
Tel 020 7727 8002
www.spa-nk.com
At this sleek, modern extension of the company's shops, Nicky Kinnaird provides beauty treatments using some of her cult brands such as Eve Lom and the Spa.NK own label.
⏰ Mon, Fri 10–7, Tue–Thu 9–9, Sat 10–7,

Sun 10–5. Booking advisable 🖐 Facial from £55 🚇 Notting Hill, Ladbroke Grove 🚌 23

THE SANCTUARY
12 Floral Street WC2E 9DH
Tel 0870 770 3350
www.thesanctuary.co.uk
This famous women-only Covent Garden spa has an atrium pool (with a swing over it!) and a relaxation area with a koi carp pool.
⏰ Mon–Tue 9.30–6, Wed–Fri 9.30am–10pm, Sat–Sun 10–8 Booking essential 🖐 Day membership (use of facilities but treatments extra) £60 (£15 supplement Sat–Sun), evenings £40 🚇 Covent Garden
🚌 6, 9, 11, 13, 15, 24, 29, 77a, 91, 176

HAIRDRESSING SALONS

CHARLES WORTHINGTON
7 Percy Street W1T 1DQ
Tel 020 7631 1370
www.cwlondon.com
Award-winning but never intimidating, this chic salon in a Georgian townhouse wants to make you feel at ease and offers a drink and snacks as you sit down. Four other London salons.
⏰ Mon–Thu 8–8, Fri 10–7, Sat 9–6. Booking essential 🖐 Cut and blow dry from £45 🚇 Goodge Street, Tottenham Court Road 🚌 10, 24, 29, 73, 134

HARI'S
305 Brompton Road SW3 2DY
Tel 020 7581 5211
Hari trained alongside the big names—Trevor Sorbie and John Frieda, among others—and his sparkling salon in fashionable Brompton Cross offers great cuts and colour plus beauty treatments. Celebrity clients.
⏰ Mon–Sat 10–7. Booking essential 🖐 Cut and blow dry from £42 🚇 South Kensington 🚌 14, 74, 49, C1

NICKY CLARKE
130 Mount Street W1K 3NY
Tel 020 7491 4700
www.nickyclarke.com
Well-established Mayfair celebrity magnet. Nicky's Clarke's famously flattering feather cut is a classic here. Clarke is often seen on TV doing makeovers.
🕐 Tue–Sat 9–5. Booking advisable 💈 Cut and blow dry from £50 (£350 for cuts from salon owner Nicky Clarke; 🚇 Green Park, Bond Street 🚌 8, 14, 19

RICHARD WARD
162b Sloane Street SW1X 9BS
Tel 020 7245 6151
www.richardward.co.uk
Named salon of the year in 1999 and 2000 British Hairdressing Business Awards, this high-profile salon offers more than 80 hair and beauty treatments, plus grooming for men. Celebrity clients.
🕐 Mon–Sat 9–7. Booking essential 💈 Cut and blow dry from £50 🚇 Sloane Square 🚌 19, 22, 137, C1

VIDAL SASSOON
60 South Molton Street W1Y 1HH
Tel 020 7491 8848
www.vidalsassoon.com
The famous salon from the Swinging Sixties is now a slick modern operation with a unique three-year training school and six London salons.
🕐 Mon–Wed 10.30–6, Thu 10.30–6.45, Fri 10.30–5.15, Sat 9–5.15 Booking advisable 💈 Cut and blow dry from £42 🚇 Bond Street 🚌 8, 10, 15, 73, 139

GEO F. TRUMPER
20 Jermyn Street SW1Y 6HP
Tel 020 7734 1370
www.trumpers.com
Opened in 1875 as one of London's first barber shops and still has wood-panelled interior. You can get wet shaves and haircuts and buy handmade colognes and accoutrements. Also at 9 Curzon Street.
🕐 Mon–Fri 9–5.30, Sat 9–5. Booking essential 💈 Wet shave £26.50 (includes hot towels and moisturising) 🚇 Green Park, Piccadilly Circus 🚌 9, 14, 19, 22, 38

HEALTH AND FITNESS CLUBS
BERKELEY HOTEL & SPA
Wilton Place SW1X 7RL
Tel 020 7201 1699
www.savoy-group.co.uk

A rooftop pool with a retractable roof is the focal point of this smart, well-equipped club with Christian Dior beauty treatments.

🕐 Mon–Fri 6.30am–10pm, Sat–Sun 8–8. Booking essential 💈 Day membership £60 (£9.75 if hotel resident) 🚇 Hyde Park Corner, Knightsbridge 🚌 9, 10, 14

BROADGATE CLUB
1 Exchange Place, off Appold Street EC2M 2QT
Tel 020 7422 6400
www.broadgate-club.co.uk
This huge fitness club and spa has an enormous pool, steam, sauna, gym, Charles Worthington hair salon and a beauty spa.
🕐 Mon–Thu 6.30am–10.30pm, Fri 6.30am–10pm, Sat–Sun 10–6 💈 Day membership from £15 as member's guest, or by separate negotiation 🚇 Liverpool Street 🚌 8, 42, 78, 100

CHAMPNEYS
21a Piccadilly W1V 0BH
Tel 020 7255 8000
www.champneyspiccadilly.co.uk
An exclusive members' club in the basement of Le Meridien Hotel, with pool, gym, squash and beauty treatment rooms. A stone's throw from Piccadilly Circus.
🕐 Mon–Fri 6.30am–10.30pm, Sat–Sun 8am–9pm. Booking essential 💈 Day membership from £120 (including lunch and a massage) 🚇 Piccadilly Circus 🚌 9, 14, 19, 22, 38

HARBOUR CLUB
Watermeadow Lane SW6 2RR
Tel 020 7371 7700
www.harbourclub.com
The health club where Princess Diana was a member, this claims to be the best club in London, with two pools, 13 tennis courts and a hair and beauty salon.

🕐 Mon–Fri 6.30am–11.30pm, Sat–Sun 8am–11pm 💈 Day membership from £20 (as member's guest), or by separate negotiation 🚇 Fulham Broadway 🚌 11, 14, 28, 424, C3

THE CLUB AT COUNTY HALL
County Hall SE1 7PB
Tel 020 7928 4900
www.theclubatcountyhall.com
On the south bank of the Thames between Westminster and the London Eye, this private club within the Marriott Hotel offers a 25m (82ft) pool, steam, sauna, Jacuzzi, gym and beauty treatments.
🕐 Mon–Fri 5.30am–midnight, Sat–Sun 7am–10pm. Booking essential 💈 Day membership from £25 (as guest of member, or by separate negotiation) 🚇 Westminster, Waterloo 🚌 12, 53, 159, 211

TRIYOGA
6 Erskine Road NW3 3AJ
Tel 020 7483 3344
www.triyoga.co.uk
Europe's top spot for yoga, packed with celebrity clients, has 38 teachers running more than 100 classes weekly in a trendy, refitted factory in hip Primrose Hill. Also offers treatments such as massage, acupuncture, feng shui, shiatsu.
🕐 Mon–Fri 6.30am–10pm, Sat 8am–8.30pm, Sun 9am–9.15pm 💈 Classes from £9 🚇 Chalk Farm 🚌 31, 168, 274

NAIL SPECIALISTS
CHELSEA NAIL STUDIO
5 Pond Place SW3 6QR
Tel 020 7225 3889
Backed up by a celebrity and titled client list. Established in 1992, this elegant salon has expert staff and specializes in old-fashioned manicures and pedicures.
🕐 Mon–Fri 10–8, Sat 10–6 💈 Manicure from £22.50; pedicure from £32.50 🚇 Sloane Square 🚌 11, 19, 22, C1

NAILS INC
41 South Molton Street W1Y 1HB
Tel 020 7499 8333
One of eight New York-style nail bars established to satisfy demand for speedy, no-appointment manicures. Extensions, customized nail art, pedicures.
🕐 Mon, Wed, Fri–Sat 9–7, Tue, Thu 9–8, Sun 12–5 💈 Shape and point from £10 (10 min) 🚇 Bond Street 🚌 8, 10, 15, 73, 139

CHILDREN'S LONDON

London is particularly well equipped with attractions and museums that set out to capture young imagination, either with state-of-the-art, hands-on novelties or with good, old-fashioned activities such as games, dressing up, arts and crafts or treasure-hunt-style tours. There are children's areas—playgrounds, paddling pools in most parks—and of course there's no lack of costumed ceremonial to appeal to all ages.

Most fee-charging attractions have children's prices and discounted family tickets, though definitions of 'child' and 'family' vary considerably. Many places have free entry for children under five or six. Inevitably, the most crowded times are during school holidays—two weeks at Easter, from mid-July to the first week of September, two weeks at Christmas and week-long half-term breaks throughout the year. During those times, prices are often lower and opening hours longer.

One of the most useful sources of information on special events, shows and regular attractions alike is Capital Radio's *London for Kids* magazine (available in major bookshops). It's worth checking the children's section of *Time Out* magazine.

🕐 Tue–Fri 3.30–7, Sat, Sun 11–6 term time, daily 11–6 school holidays 🗓 Free 🚌 44, 137, 344 🚇 Battersea Park

ACTIVITIES AND SPORTS

Many of London's sports centres (pages 215–216) offer clubs and activities for children and parents.

FIRSTBOWL QUEENSWAY
17 Queensway W2 4QP
Tel 020 7229 0172
A supermodern ice rink, with 12 lanes of 10-pin bowling, hi-tech video games and amusements.
🕐 Daily 10am–10.45pm 🗓 £3.50–£6.50 per activity 🚇 Bayswater, Queensway
🚌 7, 23, 27, 70

NAMCO STATION
County Hall, Riverside Building, South Bank
SE1 7PB
Tel 020 7967 1066
www.namcostation.co.uk

Action-packed interactive entertainment on three levels, from 10-pin bowling to bumper track rides and every kind of video game and simulator imaginable, includ-

ing downhill skiing, skateboarding, Grand Prix racing, martial arts, jet-skiing, soccer, horse-racing.
🕐 Daily 10am–midnight 🗓 Free entry
🚇 Waterloo, Westminster 🚌 RV1, 77

PLAYSCAPE PRO RACING
390 Streatham High Road SW16 6HX
Tel 020 8677 8677
www.playscape.co.uk
Indoor karting raceway with state-of-the-art computer systems and fast and furious races.
🕐 Daily 10–10 🗓 From £30 an hour, £20 for 30 min 🚌 133, 159, 319 🚇 Streatham

TROCADERO
Coventry Street, Piccadilly W1V 8FE
Tel 0906 888 1100
www.troc.co.uk
Seven storeys of computer-generated fun, including games and interactive rides.
🕐 Sun–Thu 10am–midnight, Fri, Sat 10am–1am 🗓 From £5.90 🚇 Piccadilly Circus 🚌 9, 14, 19, 22, 38

ADVENTURE PLAYGROUNDS
Age restrictions often apply to play areas. Special areas for smaller children may be fenced off nearby.

BATTERSEA PARK
Sun Gate Entrance, Albert Bridge Road
SW11 4PQ
Tel 020 8871 7539
www.wandsworth.gov.uk
London's largest adventure playground has indoor and outdoor activities for 5- to 16-year-olds.

BURGESS ADVENTURE PLAYGROUND
285 Albany Road SE5 0AH
Tel 020 7277 1371
www.karrot.org.uk
Swings, slides, sandpits, a football pitch, basketball, small tennis court, table tennis, arts and crafts for children from 5 to 15 years.
🕐 Tue–Fri 3.30–7.30 term time, Mon–Fri 10.30–5 school holidays
🗓 Free 🚇 Elephant and Castle
🚌 12, 35, 40, 45

DIANA, PRINCESS OF WALES MEMORIAL PLAYGROUND
Kensington Gardens W2 2UH
Tel 020 7298 2100
www.royalparks.gov.uk
Creative fun for children up to 12. The playground has a Peter Pan theme and includes a pirate ship, crocodile, fountains and wigwams.
🕐 Daily 10am–dusk 🗓 Free
🚇 Lancaster Gate, High Street Kensington, Queensway 🚌 9, 10, 12

GLOUCESTER GREEN PLAYGROUND
Gloucester Gate entrance, Regent's Park
NW1 4RY
Tel 020 7486 7905
www.royalparks.gov.uk
Swings, slides and sandpits for children under 10 years old.
🕐 Daily 10am–dusk 🗓 Free 🚇 Camden Town 🚌 24, 27, 88, C2

HOLLAND PARK ADVENTURE PLAYGROUND
Holland Park W8 6LU
Tel 020 7471 9813
www.rbkc.gov.uk

Ropes and swings, activity games and sports, arts and crafts and adventure play. It's open to children aged 5 to 15, but there's an under-8s area available.

⏰ Daily dusk–dawn; under-8s area 12.30–4 👟 Free 🚇 Holland Park, Kensington High Street 🚌 9, 10, 94, C1

HYDE PARK PLAYGROUND
Hyde Park W2 2UH
Tel 020 7298 2100
This popular playground in the heart of Hyde Park, with slides, swings and ropes, is open to children aged 3 to 12.
⏰ Daily 5am–midnight 👟 Free 🚇 Knightsbridge 🚌 9, 10, 14, 74

KIMBER BMX/ADVENTURE PLAYGROUND
King George's Park, Kimber Road, Wandsworth SW18
Tel 020 8870 2168
Oudoor and indoor activities, for 5- to 16-year-olds (under 8s must be accompanied), with a BMX cycling track and swings bars, and (indoors), an experimental kitchen, table tennis, and arts and crafts.
⏰ Tue–Fri 3.30–7, Sat 11–6; Mon–Sat 11–6 during school holidays 👟 Free 🚇 Earlsfield 🚌 28, 44

PARLIAMENT HILL ADVENTURE PLAYPARK
Parliament Hill, Highgate Road NW5 1QR
Tel 020 7482 2116
www.cityoflondon.gov.uk/openspaces
Assault course and swings for 7- to 12-year-olds, in Hampstead Heath. Next to the playpark is a playground for younger children.
⏰ Mon–Sat 10–4.30 👟 Free 🚇 Kentish Town, Hampstead 🚌 134, 214, C2

SNAKES AND LADDERS
Syon Park, Brentford, Middlesex TW8 8JF
Tel 020 8847 0946
www.snakes-and-ladders.co.uk
An indoor playground with a huge three-tier play frame, battery-powered motorcycles, an area for 2- to 5-year-olds, a toddler's area and an outdoor adventure playground.
⏰ Daily 10–6 👟 Under 5s from £3.15, over 5s from £4.35 (2-hour sessions) 🚇 Gunnersbury then bus 237 or 267 to Brentlea Gate, Hounslow East then bus 235 or 237 🚌 235, 237, 267

CEREMONIES AND EVENTS

Pomp and ceremony are an integral part of the capital's life, and there's plenty of choice. Going to see the Christmas lights or watching the Changing the Guard are sure to please the family. So will the festivals and events (see page 222).

FILM AND THEATRE

The return of Saturday children's clubs to city and suburban cinemas (see pages 192–193) has proved a hit. There are many theatres especially for a younger audience (see below), and for the stagestruck it may also be worth checking mainstream theatres for backstage tours, workshops and other activities.

THE BARBICAN
See page 77
Children's films are shown on Saturdays.

COVENT GARDEN
See page 88
Punch and Judy shows using hand-operated puppets have been staged in a kiosk-theatre here since the 17th century. The traditional show has a familiar cast of characters and always tells the same story.

IMAX CINEMAS
See page 192

LITTLE ANGEL THEATRE
14 Dagmar Passage N1 2DN
Tel 020 7226 1787
Everything from marionettes to rod-and-glove puppets is presented at this small theatre. Most of the work is for children; age recommendations are stated for every show.

⏰ Sat, Sun 11am, 2pm (phone for times of weekday shows) 👟 £5, plus some 'pay what you can' shows 🚇 Angel, Highbury & Islington 🚌 19, 38, 43, 73

NATIONAL FILM THEATRE
See page 127
Monthly workshops for 6 to 12s, held on the South Bank, plus weekend film screenings.
👟 From £1

POLKA CHILDREN'S THEATRE
240 The Broadway SW19 1SB
Tel 020 8543 4888
www.polkatheatre.com
This theatre is specifically for children over three; with a playground and rocking horses.
⏰ Productions all year round except Sep, phone for details 👟 £5–£13 🚇 Wimbledon 🚌 57, 93, 219, 493

PUPPET THEATRE BARGE
Blomfield Road, Little Venice W9 2PF
Tel 07836 202745; 020 7249 6876
www.puppetbarge.com
Floating puppet theatre operating on a barge moored in Little Venice, suitable for children aged three and over. In summer the boat tours the Thames.
⏰ Sat 8pm, Jul–Oct 👟 £8, child (under 16) £6.50 🚇 Warwick Avenue 🚌 6, 46, 187

TRICYCLE THEATRE
269 Kilburn High Road NW6 7JR
Tel 020 7328 1000
www.tricycle.co.uk
This community theatre runs year-round activities for youngsters and children—theatre productions, films and workshops.
⏰ Children's theatre Sat 11.30, 2; Sep–Jun 👟 £4.50–£12 🚇 Kilburn 🚌 16, 31, 98, 328

UNICORN THEATRE
Information: St. Mark's Studio, Chillingworth Road N7 8QJ
Tel 020 7700 0702
www.unicorntheatre.com
Excellent productions performed for over fours since 1947. Tour various venues—phone for details.
⏰ Times vary, phone for details 👟 £5–£12

MUSEUMS AND ATTRACTIONS

Many of these attractions provide special children's events and activities.

BETHNAL GREEN MUSEUM
See page 77
This museum showcasing toys through the ages sets up a play area full of soft toys and an area for youngsters to do art projects on Saturdays and Sundays and during school holidays.

CUTTY SARK
See page 156
Sea chanty-singing and yarn-telling by costumed interpreters on summer weekends.

HAMPTON COURT MAZE
See page 159

HMS BELFAST
See page 91

LONDON AQUARIUM
See page 98

LONDON DUNGEON
See page 98

LONDON EYE
See page 99

LONDON ZOO
See page 160

MADAME TUSSAUD'S
See page 101

NATIONAL MARITIME MUSEUM
See page 156

NATURAL HISTORY MUSEUM
See pages 112–113

POLLOCK'S TOY MUSEUM
See page 114

SCIENCE MUSEUM
See pages 124–125
One of the best museums in London for children, with interactive sections aimed at specific age groups. Be sure to find out about Science Nights and sleepovers for 8- to 11-year-olds— and book ahead.
🕐 Science Nights once a month: minimum five children and one adult (tel 020 7942 4747)

TATE MODERN
See pages 134–135
Saturday workshops for over fives, with storytelling and poets. 'Start' is on Sundays (tel 020 7887 3959), with Tate-related games and puzzles.
🕐 Tate Tales one Sun (usually third) in month; 'Start' every Sun 11–5

THEATRE MUSEUM
See page 136
Stage make-up sessions where experts create horrific 'wounds' and other wonders.
🕐 Sat 11.30, 1, 2.30, 3.30, 4.30

TOWER OF LONDON
See pages 138–143

VICTORIA & ALBERT MUSEUM
See pages 144–149
Programme for 14- to 25-year olds from wide-ranging backgrounds; free drop-in activities for families.

PARKS AND CITY FARMS

CORAM'S FIELDS
93 Guilford Street WC1N 1DN
Tel 020 7837 6138
Outdoor fun for young and older children. Lawns for running, games and picnics, plus a sand pit, Astro Turf football pitch, basketball court, climbing equipment, assault course and petting zoo.
🕐 Daily 9–dusk 🖐 Free 🚇 Russell Square 🚌 17, 46, 59, 91

HAMPSTEAD HEATH
See page 158

HIGHBURY FIELDS
Highbury Crescent N5
Islington's largest open space, with tennis courts, a football pitch and a children's playground.
🕐 Open access 🖐 Free 🚇 Highbury & Islington 🚌 19, 30, 43, 271

HOLLAND PARK
See page 93

HYDE PARK
See page 93

KENSINGTON GARDENS
See page 94

KENTISH TOWN CITY FARM
1 Cressfield Close NW5 4BN
Tel 020 7916 5421
www.aapi.co.uk
Educational and recreational farm with animals, gardening space and weekend horse-riding. The first of its kind, and a model in the development of city farms.
🕐 Tue–Sun 9.30–5.30 🖐 Free; donations welcome 🚇 Kentish Town 🚌 24, 46

MUDCHUTE COMMUNITY PARK AND FARM
Pier Street, Isle of Dogs, E14 3HP
Tel 020 7515 5901/0749 (stables)
Europe's largest inner city farm, with a host of animals and an inquisitive llama as the star of the show—all set against the backdrop of Canary Wharf. Hands-on activities, horse-riding and nature trail.
🕐 Daily 9.30–4.30 🖐 Free; donations welcome 🚇 Island Gardens 🚌 D3, D6, D7,

REGENT'S PARK
See page 115

RICHMOND PARK
See page 162

ST. JAMES'S PARK
See page 116

WIMBLEDON COMMON
See page 164

FESTIVALS AND EVENTS

London has many festivals and traditions. Listed below, month by month, are the major events that take place annually. They are free unless stated otherwise.

NEW YEAR'S DAY PARADE
1 January
Parliament Square SW1A 0AA
Tel 020 8566 8586
www.londonparade.co.uk
Up to 10,000 dancers, musicians and floats gather in Parliament Square at noon and parade up Whitehall, round Trafalgar Square and along Piccadilly.

SCHRODERS LONDON INTERNATIONAL BOAT SHOW
January
Excel, London Docklands E16 1XL
Tel 0115 912 9111
www.londonboatshow.net
A must for everyone interested in boating. Small dinghies to luxury yachts, plus the gear and gizmos to go with them.
🎫 Advance tickets £10.50, child (5–15) £4, family (2+4) £26.50; on the door £12, child £5, no family tickets 🚇 Custom House for Excel

CHINESE NEW YEAR
End January/early February
Around Gerrard Street, Chinatown W1
www.chinatown-online.co.uk
Chinese dragons snake their way around Chinatown (see page 86) collecting money and gifts from surging crowds.

CHELSEA ANTIQUES FAIR
March, September (dates vary)
Chelsea Old Town Hall, King's Road SW3 5EE
Tel 0870 350 2442
www.penman-fairs.co.uk
Prestigious antiques fair held twice a year in Chelsea Old Town Hall.
🎫 £5 🚇 Sloane Square
🚌 11, 19, 22, 49, 249

OXFORD AND CAMBRIDGE BOAT RACE
March or April
On the Thames; Putney to Mortlake
www.theboatrace.org
Annual race held on the Thames, from Putney to Mortlake, between rowing eights from Oxford and Cambridge universities.
🚇 Putney Bridge, Hammersmith, Ravenscourt Park, Stamford Brook, Turnham Green 🚌 Central London–Putney 14, 22, 74; Putney Bridge 14, 220; Central London–Hammersmith 9, 10, 27, 211; Hammersmith Bridge 33, 72, 209, 283, 419; Hammersmith–Mortlake 209, 419; Chiswick Bridge 190; Hammersmith–Putney 200

FLORA LONDON MARATHON
April
Tel 020 7620 4117
www.london-marathon.co.uk

Some 35,000 runners compete on streets around London in one of the world's biggest road races (see page 17). Apply in August for the following April or see local papers for route and times so you can cheer on participants.
🚇 Start: North Greenwich. Finish: Green Park, St. James's Park 🚌 Start: 188. Finish: 11, 12, 24, 159, 453

CHELSEA FLOWER SHOW
May
Royal Hospital, Royal Hospital Road SW3 4SL
Tel 020 7649 1885
www.rhs.org.uk
Fabulous flower show at the Chelsea Royal Hospital (see page

116), attended by the Queen and huge crowds.
🎫 £13–£29 🚇 Sloane Square 🚌 239

DERBY DAY
First Saturday in June
Epsom Downs Racecourse, Epsom KT18 5LQ
Tel 01372 470047
www.epsomderby.co.uk
The premier flat race of the year, with a fairground atmosphere.
🎫 £10–£32 🚇 Epsom Town Centre or Tattenham Corner, then shuttle bus

ROYAL ACADEMY SUMMER EXHIBITION
June
See page 21

TROOPING THE COLOUR
Second Saturday in June
Horse Guards Parade, Whitehall SW1A 2AX
Tel 020 7414 2479

On the Queen's official birthday the 'colour' (flag) of one of her seven Household regiments is carried before her for inspection at a military ceremony on Horseguards Parade. Trooping began when foot regiments were officially shown their colour as a rallying point in the confusion of battle.
🚇 Westminster, Charing Cross
🚌 11, 12, 24, 159

CADOGAN OPERA HOLLAND PARK
June–early August
Holland Park, Kensington High Street W8 6LU
Tel 0845 230 9769
www.operahollandpark.com
Open-air opera, with performers and audience sheltered by a canopy.
🎫 £30–£40 🚇 High Street Kensington, Holland Park 🚌 9, 10, 27, 328, C1

SPITALFIELDS FESTIVAL
June, December
75 Brushfield Street E1 6AA
Tel 020 7377 0287; box office hotline 020 7377 1362
www.spitalfieldsfestival.org.uk
Music festival held twice a year that celebrates new and early music, works by neglected composers and new commissions, in various venues of the East End.
💷 Free–£27

ROYAL ASCOT
Mid-June
Ascot Racecourse, Ascot, Berkshire SL5 7JX
Tel 01344 876876
www.ascot.co.uk

Major society event, where the best horses compete in flat-racing events. The high point is Ladies' Day, when the Queen usually attends (see page 212).
💷 £16–£52 🚉 Ascot

CITY OF LONDON FESTIVAL
Late June–mid-July
Bishopsgate Hall, 230 Bishopsgate EC2M 4HW
Tel 020 7377 0540
www.colf.org
Dance, music, theatre, cinema and literary events, plus walks and talks, across the City of London.
💷 Wide range of prices; some free events

WIMBLEDON LAWN TENNIS CHAMPIONSHIPS
Last week June, first week July
PO Box 98, Church Road, Wimbledon SW19 5AE
Tel 020 8791 2473
www.wimbledon.org
International championships held over two weeks at the All England Lawn Tennis and Croquet Club (see page 164).
💷 Prices vary depending on day and court
🚇 Southfields, Wimbledon 🚌 39, 93

HENLEY ROYAL REGATTA
First week in July
Henley Reach, Henley-on-Thames, Oxfordshire RG9 2LY
Tel 01491 572153
www.hrr.co.uk
Major five-day society event with a spectrum of river races.
💷 Regatta Enclosure £8–£14, child (under 14) free 🚉 Henley-on-Thames

KENWOOD LAKESIDE CONCERTS
Early July–late August
Kenwood House, Hampstead Lane, Highgate NW3 7JR
Tel 020 8233 7435
www.picnicconcerts.com
Classical music's greatest hits show up at these concerts in the grounds of Kenwood House. The audience sits on wide grassy areas and many bring picnics. Fireworks nights are most spectacular.
💷 £14–£32 🚇 Golders Green, Hampstead, Highgate 🚌 210, courtesy bus on concert nights

HAMPTON COURT PALACE FLOWER SHOW
Second week in July
Hampton Court Palace, East Moseley KT8 9AU
Tel 0870 906 3791
www.rhs.org.uk
The world's largest annual flower show takes place at Hampton Court Palace (see page 159).
💷 £11–£26, child (5–15) £5 (£26 1st day), under 5s free 🚌 111, 216, 411, R68
🚉 Hampton Court 🚢 Riverboats from Westminster, Richmond, Kingston-upon-Thames

BBC HENRY WOOD PROMENADE CONCERTS
Mid-July–mid-September
Royal Albert Hall, Kensington Gore SW7 2AP
Tel 020 7589 3203
www.royalalberthall.com
The world-famous Proms feature an eclectic mix of music from world premières and startling modern music to classical standbys. The Last Night, also held in Hyde Park, draws huge crowds.
💷 £4 (standing; on the door only)–£38. Proms in the Park £18 🚇 South Kensington
🚌 9, 10, 52, 70

LONDON PRIDE PARADE
Late July
City Hall, The Queen's Walk SE1 2AA
Tel 020 7494 2225
www.prideparade.org

Themed floats and exotic costumes celebrate London's gay and lesbian community and end with a Pride in the Park event in Hyde Park.
🚇 Start: Embankment. Finish: Hyde Park
🚌 Start: 9, 11, 13. Finish: 12, 73, 74

MARBLE HILL CONCERTS
August
Marble Hill Park, Richmond Road, Twickenham, Middlesex TW1 2NL
Tel 020 8233 7435
www.picnicconcerts.com
At these concerts you can listen to mainstream classical fare while picnicking on lawns sweeping down towards 18th-century Marble Hill House (see page 161).
💷 £15–£20 🚇 Richmond then bus 33, 490, H22, R68 🚉 St. Margaret's, Richmond

GREAT BRITISH BEER FESTIVAL
First week in August
Olympia, Hammersmith Road, Kensington W14 8UX
Tel 01727 867201
www.camra.org.uk
Five days of beer- and cider-drinking plus food, music and events.
💷 £5–£6 🚇 Kensington Olympia
🚌 9, 10, 27, 28, 49

NOTTING HILL CARNIVAL
Sunday, Monday August bank holiday weekend
Notting Hill W10/W11
Tel 0870 458 4182
www.thecarnival.tv

More than a million people get together for this event—one of the biggest street parties in Europe. Fabulous costumes, steel drums and mega sound systems.
🚇 Ladbroke Grove, Holland Park, Notting Hill Gate 🚌 23, 52, 94

GREAT RIVER RACE

Early September; dates vary

On the River Thames from Ham House, Richmond, to Island Gardens, Greenwich

www.greatriverrace.co.uk

Around 300 Cornish gigs, Chinese dragonboats with drummers, cutters, longboats and other traditional boats compete to win the UK Traditional Boat Championship.

Start: Richmond. Finish: Tower Bridge

Start: 190. Finish 42, 78, RV1

PEARLY KINGS AND QUEENS HARVEST FESTIVAL

First Sunday in October

St. Martin-in-the-Fields, Trafalgar Square WC2N 4JJ

Tel 020 7766 1100

www.pearlykingsandqueens.co.uk

Victorian costermongers elected their own royalty to protect their trading interests. Today, the pearly kings and queens, who mostly devote their spare time to raising money for charity, gather in their elaborate outfits—they're covered in mother-of-pearl buttons.

Charing Cross, Leicester Square

24, 29, 176

TRAFALGAR DAY PARADE

Sunday nearest 21 October

Trafalgar Square WC2N 5DN

Tel 020 7928 8978

www.sea-cadets.org

Sea cadets commemorate Nelson's victory at the battle of Trafalgar (21 October 1805) with marching bands and music. A wreath is laid at the base of Nelson's Column.

Charing Cross, Leicester Square

24, 29, 176

LONDON FILM FESTIVAL

Two weeks late October/early November

National Film Theatre, South Bank SE1 8XT

Tel 020 7633 0274

www.lff.org.uk

The UK's biggest film festival, centred on the National Film Theatre (see page 192) and the Odeon West End. More than 150 features screened.

BONFIRE NIGHT

5 November (or nearest weekend)

Bonfires and fireworks in parks and public open spaces commemorate the Gunpowder Plot (see page 30).

STATE OPENING OF PARLIAMENT

November

House of Lords, Parliament Square, Westminster SW1A 0PW

Tel 020 7219 3107

www.parliament.uk

The Queen arrives in a State coach attended by the Household Cavalry to reopen Parliament officially following its summer recess.

Westminster 3, 77A

LORD MAYOR'S SHOW

Second Saturday in November

Streets between Mansion House and Royal Courts of Justice in the Strand

Tel 020 7332 1456, box office 0845 458 0654

www.lordmayorsshow.org

The newly elected Lord Mayor of London processes with about 140 floats to the Royal Courts of Justice, where the oath of allegiance is taken before the return journey. There are spectacular fireworks in the evening from a barge moored between Waterloo Bridge and Blackfriars Bridge.

Free along route; grandstand tickets £22

Procession: Mansion House, Temple; fireworks: Blackfriars, Embankment

Procession: 11, 15, 23; fireworks: 1, 45, 100, 168, RV1

REMEMBRANCE SUNDAY PARADE

Sunday nearest 11 November

Cenotaph, Whitehall SW1

The Queen, the Prime Minister and other dignitaries and officials lay wreaths at the Cenotaph to commemorate those who died in World Wars I and II, before a march past by veterans and servicemen.

Charing Cross 11, 12, 24, 159

VARSITY MATCH

First Tuesday after Michaelmas term (November–early December)

Rugby Road, Twickenham TW1 1DZ

Tel 020 8892 2000

www.rfu.com

The annual Oxford vs Cambridge University rugby match.

£18–£25 281, R62 Twickenham

LIGHTING OF THE CHRISTMAS TREE

Late November–early December

Trafalgar Square WC2N

A celebrity switches on the lights decorating the huge Norwegian spruce in Trafalgar Square–an annual gift from Norway since 1947 to express the nation's gratitude for British support during World War II.

Charing Cross, Leicester Square

24, 29, 176

DAILY CEREMONIES

CEREMONY OF THE KEYS

Tower of London EC3N 4AB

Tel 0870 756 7070

www.hrp.org.uk

Every evening at 9.53pm the ceremony of locking up the Tower of London begins. Apply in writing for free tickets to the Ceremony of the Keys Office, Tower of London (see pages 138–143) at least two months in advance, then assemble at the West Gate at 9.15pm.

Nightly Tower Hill

15, 42, 78, RV1

CHANGING THE GUARD

Buckingham Palace SW1A 1AA, Horse Guards SW1A 2AX, Tower of London EC3N 4AB

Tel 0207 930 4832

www.royal.gov.uk

Footguards in full dress uniform—red tunics and bearskin hats—can be seen changing shifts in a stirring display of pageantry at three locations. Arrive early for a good view.

Buckingham Palace forecourt: daily 11.30am Apr–Jun (no ceremony in very wet weather). Horse Guards Arch: Mon–Sat 11am, Sun 10am. Tower Green, Tower of London: daily 11.30am

Buckingham Palace: St. James's Park; Horse Guards: Charing Cross; Tower of London: Tower Hill

Buckingham Palace: 11, 211, 139 ,C1, Horse Guards: 11, 12, 24, 159; Tower of London: 15, 25, RV1

WHAT TO DO

London is best explored on foot and this section describes four walks that take in the most interesting parts of the city. The locations of the walks are marked on the map on the inside front cover of the book.

These pages also give suggestions for excursions outside the city.

Out and About

THROUGH MAYFAIR

Laid out in the early 18th century by courtiers and aristocrats, Mayfair was named after a fair held here annually in May. It is one of the city's most expensive and exclusive areas, with many blue plaques and shops bearing the royal crest (see page 19).

THE WALK

Length: 3 miles (5km)

Allow: 2 hours

Start at: Piccadilly Circus Underground station

End at: Oxford Circus Underground station

HOW TO GET THERE

🚇 Bakerloo or Piccadilly line to Piccadilly Circus

🚌 10, 14, 15, 453

Leave Piccadilly Circus
Underground station by Subway 3, the Piccadilly (south side) exit, and walk left along Piccadilly to St. James's Church on the left.

❶ St. James's was designed by Sir Christopher Wren and consecrated in 1684. Inside, the ceiling is decorated with ornate gold leaf. English poet and painter William Blake (1757–1827), best known for his *Songs of Innocence and Experience,* was baptized here.

Continue past Princes Arcade, Hatchards bookshop (see page 177) and Fortnum and Mason (see page 180). Cross Piccadilly to the Royal Academy of Arts (see page 115). Burlington Arcade (see page 86) is ahead; go through the arcade and turn right into Burlington Gardens, then left into Savile Row.

❷ Savile Row has become a byword for gentlemen's tailoring; Gieves and Hawkes (No. 1), the oldest outfitters, was founded in 1785.
The Beatles made their last public appearance at No. 3, on the roof of the Apple recording studio building, in 1969.

Continue along Savile Row and take the next turning left. Follow Clifford Street to New Bond Street at the far end. Turn left into a pedestrianized zone.

❸ In 1995, to mark the 50th anniversary of the end of World War II, *Allies,* a bronze sculpture of British Prime

Allies statue of Roosevelt and Churchill in New Bond Street

Minister Winston Churchill and US President Franklin Roosevelt was unveiled here.

Walk down New Bond Street into Old Bond Street. At No. 28 turn right into the Royal Arcade and pass through to Albemarle Street. Turn right. Across the street is Raffles Brown's Hotel (see page 289), where Eleanor and Franklin Roosevelt honeymooned.
At the end of the street turn left and follow Grafton Street into Dover Street. Turn right down Hay Hill and cross at the bottom into Lansdowne Row. Continue to Curzon Street, passing Geo F. Trumper (see page 218) on the right. Cross the road and go through the covered entrance into Shepherd Market.

❹ The market was built in 1735 by architect Edward Shepherd. It earned notoriety as a red-light district, but now its lanes are lined with cafés, unusual shops and eateries.

At Ye Grapes pub turn right through a pedestrianized zone. Cross cobbled Trebeck Street and continue along Shepherd Market Road. Turn right up Hertford Street to Curzon Street, turn left then right onto Chesterfield Street. Turn left into Charles Street at the top. Go right at the Red Lion onto Waverton Street and right again into Hay's Mews. Take the next right into Chesterfield Hill and at the end turn left, back into Charles Street. Follow this to Berkeley Square.

❺ Berkeley Square was laid out in the mid-18th century with long lines of houses on the east and west sides, but today only those on the west survive. In the central gardens are 30 huge plane trees (see page 24), planted in 1789.

At the northwest corner of the square, turn left into Mount Street, then left again into Mount Street Gardens, where there is an entrance to the Church of the Immaculate Conception.

❻ The church was founded by Jesuit exiles from Liege, Belgium. The altar is by Augustus Pugin (see page 92).

Go to the end of the gardens, then turn right up South Audley Street to Grosvenor Square. On the left is the US Embassy.

❼ The embassy is a huge modern block among the square's period buildings. Statues commemorate US presidents Roosevelt and Eisenhower.

Walk diagonally right across Grosvenor Square and go along Brook Street, where Handel lived (see page 90). At the next junction, turn right into New Bond Street. Turn left into Conduit Street and then immediately left into St. George Street. St. George's Church is ahead on the right.

❽ St. George's Church was, and is, a fashionable wedding venue. British Prime Minister Benjamin Disraeli, US President Theodore Roosevelt and English poet Percy Bysshe Shelley were all married here.

Continue to the end of St. George Street to reach Hanover Square. Take Princes Street from the northeast corner onto Regent Street. Turn left to reach Oxford Circus Underground station.

OUT AND ABOUT

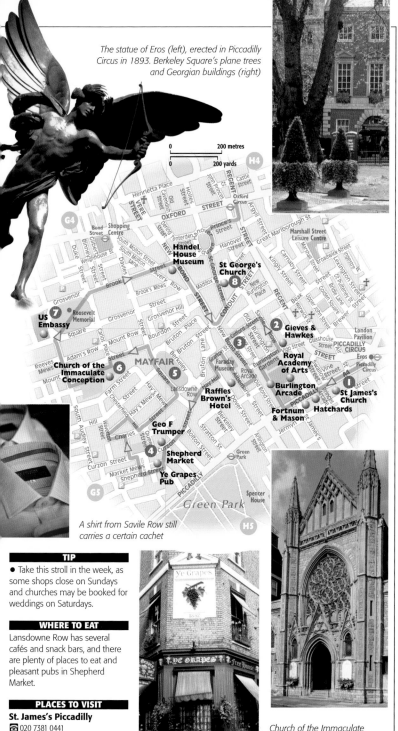

The statue of Eros (left), erected in Piccadilly Circus in 1893. Berkeley Square's plane trees and Georgian buildings (right)

A shirt from Savile Row still carries a certain cachet

H4

Map labels:
Henrietta Place · Holles Street · Gt Castle Street · Castle Street · Regent Street · John Prince's Street · Old Cavendish Street · Oxford Circus
OXFORD STREET · Prince's Street · Hanover Street · Argyll Street · Great Marlborough st · Marshall Street Leisure Centre · Carnaby Street · Broadwick Street · Marshall Street · Lexington Street · Ingestre Place
G4 · Bond Street · Shopping Centre · South Molton Street · Deering · Enterden snov · Handel House Museum · St George's Church 8 · New Burlington Place · Kingly Street · Beak Street · Upper James St · Bridle Lane · St Pulteney St · Brewer Street
Gilbert Street · Weighhouse st · South Molton Lane · Davies Street · Avery Row · Maddox Street · Conduit Street · Square · Hanover Square · Regent Street
Duke Street · Binney Street · Brook Street · Brook's Mews · New Burlington Street · Glasshouse Street · London Pavilion
US Embassy 7 · Roosevelt Memorial · Grosvenor Hill · Grosvenor Street · Bourdon Street · Gieves & Hawkes 2 · Royal Academy of Arts · PICCADILLY CIRCUS · Eros · Piccadilly Circus
Square · Carlos Place · Mount Row · Bruton Place · Bruton Lane · Burlington Gardens · Swallow St · Air St · Vine St
Reeves Mews · Adam's Row · Church of the Immaculate Conception 6 · MAYFAIR 5 · Faraday Museum · Royal Arcade · Old Bond Street · New Bond Street · Burlington Arcade · PICCADILLY · St James's Church · Hatchards
Mount Street · Farm Street · Hay's Mews · Lansdowne Row · Hay Hill · Dover Street · Burlington Arcade · Fortnum & Mason · St James's
South Audley Street · Chesterfield Hill · Hay's Mews Mews · Raffles Brown's Hotel · Stratton Street · Jermyn St
Hill Street · Waverton Street · Charles Street · Queen Street · Bolton Street · Berkeley Street
Geo F Trumper · Curzon Street · Green Park · Spencer House
G5 · Market Mews · Shepherd Street · Shepherd Market 4 · Ye Grapes Pub · PICCADILLY · Green Park · H5

0 · 200 metres
0 · 200 yards

G4 · G5 · H4 · H5

Church of the Immaculate Conception (above) in Mount Street Gardens

Ye Grapes pub (left), one of many refreshment stops in Shepherd Market

---

TIP

• Take this stroll in the week, as some shops close on Sundays and churches may be booked for weddings on Saturdays.

WHERE TO EAT

Lansdowne Row has several cafés and snack bars, and there are plenty of places to eat and pleasant pubs in Shepherd Market.

PLACES TO VISIT

St. James's Piccadilly
☎ 020 7381 0441
Free lunchtime concerts (1.10pm, donations welcomed) Mon, Wed, Fri, and evenings Thu, Fri, Sat, often with visiting choirs from around the world (prices vary; telephone for details)

A ROYAL TOUR

A walk through the original bastion of royal power in England, taking in three royal residences. You'll pass the former house of three prime ministers, skirt Whitehall and walk along Constitution Hill to see its poignant war memorial.

THE WALK

Length: 2 miles (3km)

Allow: 2 hours minimum

Start at: St. James's Park Underground station

End at: Hyde Park Corner Underground station

HOW TO GET THERE

🚇 District or Circle line to St. James's Park

🚌 11, 24, 148, 211

Start from St. James's

Underground station by turning immediately left after the ticket barriers and emerging into Petty France. Cross the road and continue ahead down Queen Anne's Gate. The huge art-deco building above St. James's Park Underground station is the London Underground headquarters. Pass through the black gates at the end of the road and cross Birdcage Walk to the entrance to St. James's Park (see page 116).

OUT AND ABOUT

❶ In the park, look for notices with a map, brief history and guide to bird life in the park. King James I is said to have housed an 'ellefant' here, plus crocodiles and other beasts, all gifts from foreign princes. The 'ellefant' was given a gallon of wine every day.

Continue straight ahead to reach the lake. Cross the bridge and turn immediately right. At the fork go left and look over to your right to see Big Ben (see page 37). Walk on to the far northeast corner of the park and exit onto the Mall.

❷ To the right of the Mall, beyond Admiralty Arch, are Trafalgar Square (see page 136) and Whitehall (see page 151). To the left is Buckingham Palace (see page 79). Royal

and parliamentary Britain come together at least once a year when the Queen leaves the palace and passes down the Mall on her way to open Parliament.

Cross the Mall to the Institute of Contemporary Arts (see page 93). With a day pass you can return later for a drink. Go around to the left of the ICA and up the steps to Waterloo Place.

❸ Statues here commemorate the Duke of York (1763–1827), second son of George III; Florence Nightingale (see page 89); Edward VII; and Robert Falcon Scott, the British Antarctic explorer who died in 1912 on an expedition to the South Pole. Scott's wife, Lady Kathleen, was the sculptor.

Leave Waterloo Place by the northern side and turn left down Pall Mall and right into St. James's Square.

❹ As you walk counterclockwise round the square, look for the former home of Nancy Astor (1879–1964), the second woman to be elected to Parliament and the first to take her seat. It's now the In-and-Out Club, one of St. James's private societies. Part of Chatham House was home to three former British prime ministers: William Pitt (1708–78), the Earl of Derby (1799–1869) and William Gladstone (1809–98). The gardens in the square are open Monday to Friday 10 to 4.30.

Continue past the East India Club and turn right into King Street. Here you'll find

Robert Falcon Scott, British Antarctic explorer

Christie's Auction House see page 176). At the end of the street, cross St. James's Street and go down towards St. James's Palace in front of you.

❺ St. James's Palace, former home of Prince Charles, is closed to the public. It was built for Henry VIII in 1532 on the site of a former lepers' hospital, and remained the principal royal residence until Queen Victoria moved to Buckingham Palace.

Take the first right into Little St. James's Street and follow the road round to Bridgewater House. In front of you across the little square is the entrance to Clarence House, former home of the late Queen Mother.

Continue round along the side of St. James's Palace into Marlborough Street, past the guard, to the Queen's Chapel.

❻ Queen's Chapel was designed by Inigo Jones in 1627 for Charles I's French wife, Henrietta Maria.

Walk past the statue of Queen Alexandra on the left and rejoin the Mall at the bottom of the street. Turn right and continue to Buckingham Palace (see page 79). If the Queen is in residence, the Union Jack will be flying.

A detour around the far side of the palace takes you to the Guards' Museum (see page 90) and the Queen's Gallery (see page 114).

Otherwise, bear right and head up Constitution Hill.

❼ At the top of Constitution Hill are the 2002 Memorial Gates, a testament to the 5 million volunteers from the Indian subcontinent, Africa and the Caribbean who died in the two world wars.

Cross over to the Wellington Arch (see page 150). The walk ends here, by Hyde Park Corner Underground station.

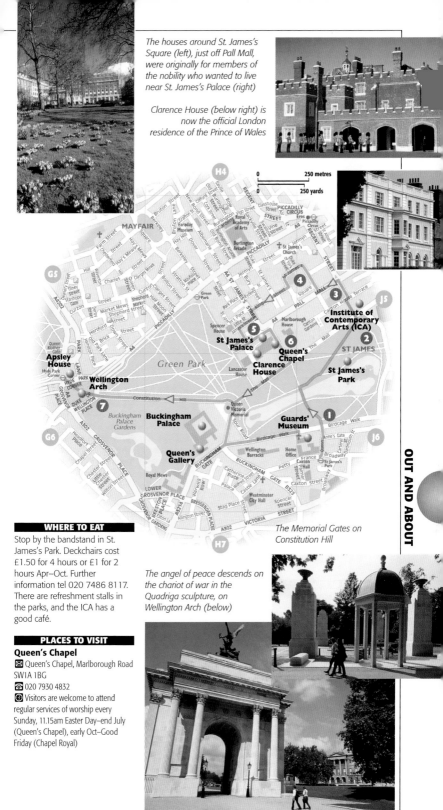

The houses around St. James's Square (left), just off Pall Mall, were originally for members of the nobility who wanted to live near St. James's Palace (right)

Clarence House (below right) is now the official London residence of the Prince of Wales

0   250 metres
0   250 yards

OUT AND ABOUT

The Memorial Gates on Constitution Hill

The angel of peace descends on the chariot of war in the Quadriga sculpture, on Wellington Arch (below)

WHERE TO EAT

Stop by the bandstand in St. James's Park. Deckchairs cost £1.50 for 4 hours or £1 for 2 hours Apr–Oct. Further information tel 020 7486 8117. There are refreshment stalls in the parks, and the ICA has a good café.

PLACES TO VISIT

Queen's Chapel
✉ Queen's Chapel, Marlborough Road SW1A 1BG
☎ 020 7930 4832
🕐 Visitors are welcome to attend regular services of worship every Sunday, 11.15am Easter Day–end July (Queen's Chapel), early Oct–Good Friday (Chapel Royal)

ALONG THE SOUTH BANK

A walk past Westminster, Britain's seat of government, and London's premier centre for the performing arts, the South Bank, with spectacular views along the Thames.

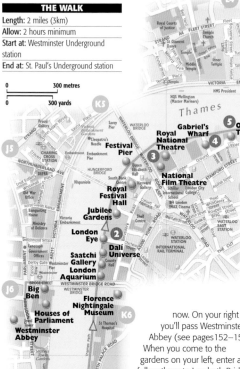

THE WALK

Length: 2 miles (3km)
Allow: 2 hours minimum
Start at: Westminster Underground station
End at: St. Paul's Underground station

HOW TO GET THERE

Jubilee, Circle or District line to Westminster

11, 12, 24, 453

Leave Westminster

Underground station by exit 1 (Pier) to reach the bank of the River Thames near Big Ben (see page 37). You can take boat trips from here up and down the river (see page 234).

Cross the road, skirt around the base of Big Ben and turn left along the Parliament Green side of the Houses of Parliament (see page 92).

At the end of the complex of buildings you can see St. Stephen's Tower—make for this now. On your right you'll pass Westminster Abbey (see pages 152–153). When you come to the gardens on your left, enter and follow them to Lambeth Bridge. Turn left across the bridge, then left along the Thames path. Across the road to your right are Lambeth Palace and the Museum of Garden History (see page 102).

❶ Since 1197 Lambeth Palace, a largely medieval complex of domestic buildings, has been the official residence of the archbishops of Canterbury. The medieval crypt and Great Hall, rebuilt in the 17th century, house the palace library (the first public library in England) and grand 19th-century reception rooms.

Continue to the edge of Westminster Bridge by St. Thomas's Hospital, where you'll find the Florence Nightingale Museum (see page 89). Cross the road and go down the steps to the former County Hall, now housing the London Aquarium

(see page 98), Dalí Universe (see page 87) and Saatchi Gallery (see page 116). Unless you want to visit either of these, continue straight on along the river path to reach the London Eye (see page 99).

❷ Behind the wheel are the Jubilee Gardens, laid out in 1977 to commemorate Queen Elizabeth's silver jubilee. The former Shell Centre, behind them, has the largest clock façade in the world. *Jubilee Oracle,* the statue on the pavement by Alexander, was completed in 1980. Street performers are often here, entertaining passers-by.

With the river on your left, continue under Hungerford Bridge and past the Royal Festival Hall (see page 195) and Festival Pier, another place where you could catch a boat along the river or over to Westminster (see page 72).

Continue under Waterloo Bridge, where there is often an open-air book fair near the entrance to the National Film Theatre (see page 192). Continue to the National Theatre (see page 201).

❸ In summer there are often live performances and stand-up comedy shows outside in Theatre Square. Notice the statue *London Pride,* by Frank Dobson (1886–1963), on the right. Street painters can

OUT AND ABOUT

sometimes be seen at work here, and on the left there is a guide to sights along the river on the North Bank.

Continue on the riverside path to Gabriel's Wharf on your right.

❹ Gabriel's Wharf is a lively collection of design and craft workshops, restaurants and bars—a great place for unusual textiles, fabrics, fashion, jewellery, ceramics, glassware and furnishings.

Continue past Bernie Spain Gardens and on to Oxo Tower Wharf.

❺ Oxo Tower, former head-quarters of the famous British cubed-beefstock company and a witty 20th-century folly with windows that spell out 'OXO', is a flagship landmark of inner-city regeneration. The tower and the building on which it stands opened to the public in 1996 as a mix of social hous-ing, retail design studios, restaurants, cafés, bars, a gallery and an exhibition.

Back outside, pass the Sea Containers House and Doggets pub and go under Blackfriars Bridge, where the subway tells the story of various historical designs for the bridge that were considered before the current version was accepted.

You'll see the Founder's Arms pub in front and then Tate Modern (see pages 134–135) to the right.

Opposite Tate Modern, turn right over the Millennium Bridge (see page 100) and continue straight ahead up Peter's Hill up the steps to St. Paul's Cathedral (see pages 118–123). The Underground station is behind the cathedral, to your right.

View across the bend in the river to St. Paul's and the City with Waterloo Bridge in the foreground (above) The Houses of Parliament (right) The London Eye and County Hall (below)

TIP

● Try to do the walk early in the day, when there are fewer crowds, and Borough Market is in full swing.

WHERE TO EAT

There are places to go for a drink all along the river. Consider EAT, behind the Oxo Tower, or outside the National Film Theatre, by the book fair.

PLACES TO VISIT

Lambeth Palace
✉ Lambeth Palace Road SE1 7JU
☎ (Library only) 020 7898 1400; (information on tours) 020 7898 1191
🕐 Apply in writing for pre-booked tours of palace and gardens (*Thu 11am, 2pm*), £5
www.archbishopofcanterbury.org, www.lambethpalacelibrary.org

Lambeth Palace (above left) The Oxo Tower (left) is now given over to housing, design studios, bars and restaurants

OUT AND ABOUT

AROUND THE CITY

The City is the financial heart of Britain, a compact area of modern buildings, medieval lanes and churches designed by Sir Christopher Wren.

THE WALK

Length: 2 miles (3km)

Allow: 2 hours minimum

Start at: Monument Underground station

End at: Bank Underground station

HOW TO GET THERE

🚇 Circle or District line to Monument

🚌 15, 35

Take the London Bridge/King William Street (south) exit from Monument Underground station. Walk straight ahead past the Monument on your left and onto London Bridge for views along the river. Tower Bridge (see page 137) is to your left, with HMS *Belfast* (see page 91) moored nearby. To the west is the Tate Modern tower (see pages 134–135).

Return towards the Underground station and turn right onto Monument Street. Follow this to the Monument (see page 102).

Climb Fish Street Hill to Eastcheap and turn right. Pudding Lane, where the Great Fire of London started in 1666, is the next road on the right. Cross Eastcheap into Philpot Lane. Lloyd's Building is ahead of you.

❶ Sir Richard Rogers (co-architect of the Pompidou Centre in Paris, France) designed this 'inside-out' building for insurance underwriters Lloyd's of London in 1978. The 14-storey glass, concrete and aluminium office block, with its exterior tangle of ventilation ducts and fire stairs, along with suspended 'boxes' (holding lavatories and service technology), attracts admiration and derision in equal measure.

At the end of Philpot Lane, cross Fenchurch Street into Lime Street and follow the cobbled street on the left, Lime Street Passage, into Leadenhall Market.

❷ Leadenhall Market (now under a wrought-iron and glass roof) has been operating as a meat and fish market since the 14th century. Today its alleys are a mix of market stalls, as well as pubs and upmarket fashion shops. Have a drink or lunch at the Lamb Tavern (closed weekends).

Take Whittington Avenue from the market and turn right into Leadenhall Street by Lloyd's. Cross the road and an open square. St. Helen's Bishopsgate is behind the tower block in the middle of the square.

❸ St. Helen's is a rare survivor of the Great Fire of London and is London's largest medieval church. It contains several fine memorials.

At the church turn left to follow Great St. Helen's to Bishopsgate. Turn left here and at the traffic lights cross into Threadneedle Street. Continue past a statue of US philanthropist George Peabody on the left, and turn right down Bartholomew Lane alongside the Bank of England (see page 76).

At the end of Bartholomew Lane turn left along Lothbury and into Gresham Street. Guildhall (see page 90) is to your right, behind St. Lawrence Jewry Church. Facing away from Guildhall, cross Gresham Street into King Street and on to Cheapside. Turn right here and head for the steeple of St. Mary-le-Bow.

❹ Sir Christopher Wren designed 51 churches in the City, of which St. Mary-le-Bow is one. Its bells once sounded the curfew for Londoners, and to be born within earshot was the definition of a Cockney.

Go round the back of the church and turn right into Bow Lane. Williamson's Tavern is on the right. Turn left into Watling Street and as you turn look right to see the dome of St. Paul's Cathedral (see pages 118–123). According to tradition, Wren conducted his business in Ye Olde Watling Pub while he was building St. Paul's.

Follow Watling Street to a major junction (intersection) and cross into Queen Victoria Street. Turn right into Bucklersbury to St. Stephen Walbrook Church.

❺ St. Stephen Walbrook is the Lord Mayor's official church, and considered to be Wren's finest City church. Its dome was probably built as a prototype (1672–79) for that of nearby St. Paul's Cathedral. Centrally placed beneath it is the altar by English sculptor Henry Moore (1987): an asymmetrical lump of stone at odds with its classical setting.

From the church turn along Walbrook and then right at the end towards the Royal Exchange building at the far side of the junction. On the right is the Mansion House (open for organized groups only).

❻ This is one of London's grandest surviving Georgian town palaces, with magnificent interiors including elaborate plasterwork and carved timber ornament. Built in the mid-18th century, it is the home of the Lord Mayor of London.

Bank Underground station is at this road junction.

Lloyd's Building (left), completed in 1986, is a high-tech structure housing one of London's most traditional institutions

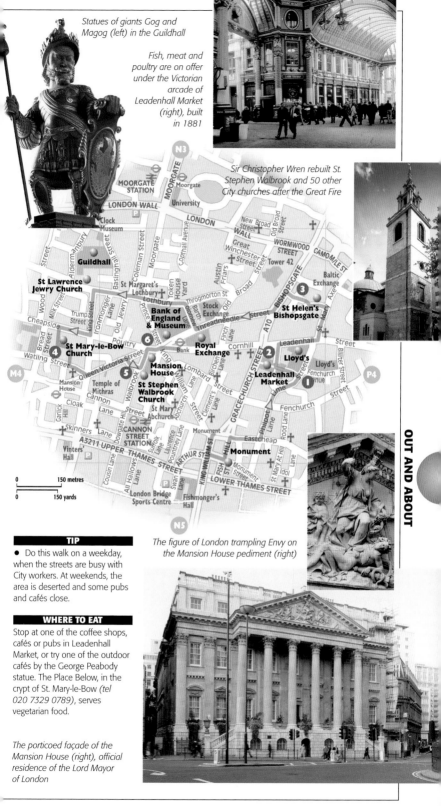

Statues of giants Gog and Magog (left) in the Guildhall

Fish, meat and poultry are on offer under the Victorian arcade of Leadenhall Market (right), built in 1881

Sir Christopher Wren rebuilt St. Stephen Walbrook and 50 other City churches after the Great Fire

OUT AND ABOUT

The figure of London trampling Envy on the Mansion House pediment (right)

TIP

● Do this walk on a weekday, when the streets are busy with City workers. At weekends, the area is deserted and some pubs and cafés close.

WHERE TO EAT

Stop at one of the coffee shops, cafés or pubs in Leadenhall Market, or try one of the outdoor cafés by the George Peabody statue. The Place Below, in the crypt of St. Mary-le-Bow *(tel 020 7329 0789)*, serves vegetarian food.

The porticoed façade of the Mansion House (right), official residence of the Lord Mayor of London

ON THE RIVER THAMES

A cruise along the Thames is a leisurely way to see the city. It gives a new perspective to its development and history, which is inextricably linked with this long and majestic river.

INFORMATION

Tourist information offices

Kingston: Market House, Market Place, Kingston upon Thames KT1 1JS
☎ 020 8547 5592

Richmond: Old Town Hall, Whittaker Avenue, Richmond TW9 1TP
☎ 020 8940 9125

Southwark: 6 Tooley Street SE1
☎ 020 7403 8299

Greenwich: Pepys House, 2 Cutty Sark Gardens, Greenwich SE10
☎ 020 8858 6376

HOW TO GET THERE

Embankment Pier
🚇 Circle, District, Bakerloo or Northern line to Embankment
🚌 9, 11, 12, 24

Westminster Pier
🚇 Circle, District or Jubilee line to Westminster
🚌 11, 12, 24, 453

The banks of the Thames have largely been opened up to walkers

As the Thames flows west to east into Greater London, on the last stages of its 215-mile (346km) journey to the sea, it loops around Hampton Court Park and the 16th-century palace of Hampton Court itself (see page 159), a reminder of the Tudor era. It's a fitting introduction to the river's course through the capital and recalls a period when the Thames was a place of regal processions, magnificent mansions and palaces, and thriving trade.

But the river's significance in the commercial and royal life of the nation goes back much further—probably to the Bronze Age and earlier—and, having turned northwards, the river flows past Kingston upon Thames, the site of many Saxon coronations.

TEDDINGTON TO KEW
Navigating the river and its ebb and flow was a problem for centuries, alleviated with the building of locks and weirs such as those at Teddington, a little farther north at the point between the non-tidal and tidal sections of the river.

During the 17th and 18th centuries the lush banks of this stretch of the river became a fashionable setting for aristocratic homes and gardens. You pass Ham House (see page 158), Strawberry Hill *(Sun 2–3.30, Apr–Sep, tours only)*, Marble Hill (see page 161) and Syon House (see page 162) as the river makes its way past the affluent town of Richmond and up through the Royal Botanic Gardens, Kew (see page 163) to the Hanoverian Kew Palace.

KEW TO BATTERSEA
From here the Thames winds through Chiswick, with its lovely Georgian riverside houses, and past Barnes, now home of the London Wetland Centre (see page 160), passing under the elaborate Victorian suspension bridge at Hammersmith. Fulham Palace *(Wed–Sun 2–5, Mar–Oct; Thu–Sun 1–4, Nov–Feb)*, private residence of the Bishops of London, is on the approach to the last southern dip of the river—where the Oxford and Cambridge Boat Race (see page 222) starts at Putney—before it flows under Battersea Bridge and between the Chelsea Embankment and Battersea Park (see page 154).

BATTERSEA TO BANKSIDE
This marks the point where the river enters central London and becomes a working highway, until recently lined with shipping, docks and warehouses. Today this is tourist London proper: The Thames flows between Lambeth Palace (see page 230) and the Houses of Parliament (see page 92) and past the London Eye (see page 99) and the South Bank complex of concert, theatre and film venues (see page 127), making a northern loop past the Victoria Embankment (see page 150) and towards the Millennium Bridge (see page 100), linking St. Paul's Cathedral (see pages 118–123) and Tate Modern (see pages 134–135).

BANKSIDE TO THE THAMES BARRIER
Beyond Shakespeare's Globe (see page 126) and Southwark Cathedral (see page 127) the river reaches London Bridge, the modern crossing that replaced the 1831 version, itself replacing its arched medieval predecessor, which was crammed with houses and shops. The next crossing is Tower Bridge (see page 137), designed to allow tall ships passage between the city and the sea. Guarding the north bank is the Tower of London (see pages 138–143), William the Conqueror's fort placed strategically to protect access to the Port of London.

From this point the river passes through an area once dominated by shipping docks and now redeveloped as smart office and residential blocks.

Seafaring is the theme from here onwards, as the Thames reaches Greenwich (see pages 156–157) before continuing its course to the Thames Barrier (see page 164) at Woolwich Reach and beyond the Greater London boundaries towards Gravesend and the sea.

OUT AND ABOUT

TIP

• Several companies run cruises and water-buses along various sections of the river. Shop around.

Get a whole new perspective on London from the water, by day (Kew Bridge, right) or in the evening (above)

RIVERBOATS

Sailing times vary with seasons and conditions.

From Embankment Pier:
Catamaran Cruisers
Tel 020 7987 1185
Regular circular/hop-on, hop-off services, Embankment–Waterloo –Bankside–Tower–Greenwich (50 minutes), 10–5 summer, 10.30–4 winter.

From Westminster Pier:
Circular Cruise Westminster
Tel 020 7936 2033
Hop-on, hop-off between Westminster and St. Katharine's Pier (1 hour), from 11am.
City Cruises Tel 020 7740 0400
Downriver Westminster to Tower Pier (25 minutes), Westminster to Greenwich (50 minutes). Sailings about every 40 minutes 10–6, winter; 8.40–6, summer.
Thames River Services
Tel 020 7930 4097 Downriver Westminster to Greenwich (50 minutes, leaves every 30 minues) or Thames Barrier (1 hour 30 minutes, leaves on the hour), 10–5 Jun–Aug.
Westminster Passenger Service Association Tel 020 7930 2062 Upriver Westminster to Hampton Court (Mar–Oct, 3 hours 30 minutes), 10.30, 11.15, noon to all destinations, 2pm to Kew Gardens only.

Taking a water taxi (above). By boat to the Thames Barrier (below)

OUT AND ABOUT

WINDSOR AND ETON

Less than an hour from London are two neighbouring towns that offer a full day out: Windsor, with the largest castle in Europe, and Eton, with one of Britain's most famous public schools.

INFORMATION

Tourist information office
24 High Street, Windsor SL4 1LH
☎ 01753 743900

HOW TO GET THERE

Windsor is 25 miles (40km) west of central London

🚇 District Line to Richmond (30 minutes from Embankment), then South West Trains to Windsor and Eton Riverside station

Train: 50 minutes from Waterloo to Windsor and Eton Riverside station or 25 minutes from Paddington to Slough, then 10 minutes from Slough to Windsor See pages 58–59

Coach (bus): daily Green Line services from Victoria Coach Station, London: 1 hour 10 minutes

Car: M4 to junction 6 or M3 to junction 3, then A322/A332 (30 minutes)

WINDSOR CASTLE

Windsor Castle *(daily)* is an unforgettable sight, towering above the town on a chalk cliff. It's the largest inhabited castle in the world and one of the principal residences of the sovereigns of England since the 12th century. Much of its present appearance dates from the 19th century, but the stone castle was built for Henry II in 1165, replacing William the Conqueror's original 11th-century fort.

There are several buildings to visit within the castle complex. **St. George's Chapel** is a masterpiece of Perpendicular Gothic architecture, begun in 1475 by Edward IV and completed in 1511. Ten monarchs are buried here. The monument in the northwest chapel to Princess Charlotte, who died in childbirth in 1817, shows her ascending to heaven with an angel carrying her stillborn child. The chapel's fan-vaulted ceiling is particularly beautiful, as are the elaborate 15th-century choir stalls covered in vignettes of animals, jesters, the Dance of Death and biblical stories, and surmounted by banners of the 26 Knights of the Garter, the highest order of knighthood, whose installation has taken place here since 1348. It was here that the Queen's youngest child, Edward, married Sophie Rhys-Jones in 1999.

The baroque **State Apartments,** restored after a devastating fire in 1992, are hung with works from the Royal Collection, one of the world's finest private art collections. Also on display is **Queen Mary's Dolls' House,** designed by Sir Edwin Lutyens for the Queen in 1924. The furnishings are designed at one-twelfth life-size, the plumbing and lighting really work, and eminent writers and artists contributed handwritten books and miniature paintings to the library.

Don't miss Prince Albert's memorial chapel at the castle,  designed by Sir George Gilbert Scott, or the Changing the Guard at Windsor Castle: Mon–Sat 11am, Apr–end Jun weather permitting; alternate days 11am (not Sun), Jul–end Mar.

WINDSOR TOWN

After visiting the castle, it's worth exploring Windsor's many shops and public buildings. The **Guildhall** on the High Street was completed in 1689 by Sir Christopher Wren. Its Tuscan columns, on the ground floor, don't quite touch the ceiling; apparently the town council insisted on having them, but Wren left the gap at the top to make the point that they were structurally superfluous.

Farther up the High Street pass the 19th-century parish church of St. John the Baptist. From here, you can continue up Park Street to the Long Walk, an avenue 3 miles (5km) long that skirts Windsor Great Park. Planted with elms, it was laid out for Charles I. The **Savill Garden** *(daily)*, 14ha (35 acres) of woodland within the park, is worth visiting at any time of the year but is especially lovely in spring when the azaleas and camellias are in bloom.

ETON

Across the river from Windsor is Eton, its appealing main street fronted by Britain's best-known public school. Eton College was founded by Henry VI in 1440 for 70 King's Scholars, also known as Collegers, who lived in the college and were educated free, and a small number of Oppidans, who lived in the town of Eton and paid for their education.

Today Eton takes about 1,280 boys between the ages of 13 and 18, all of whom are boarders. You can see the school yard, the college chapel, the cloisters and the Museum of Eton Life *(tel 01753 671177 for opening times)* throughout the summer season. Famous old Etonians include the Duke of Wellington and a number of prime ministers.

Coat of arms above the Henry VIII gate in Windsor Castle (above left)
You're never far from the Castle in Windsor town (left)

Windsor Castle's Henry VIII gate (top left). Banners of the Knights of the Garter (top right) hang in St. George's Chapel (above)

TIPS

● Ask your hotel about group tours to Windsor; many companies offer them daily and will pick you up at your hotel.

● If you want to go on your own, catch a train at Waterloo: Tickets plus admission to Windsor Castle cost £15.50 for adults, £8.25 for children (5–15).

● In Windsor town centre, look for City Sightseeing Bus tours outside Windsor Castle or outside the Riverside train

station. They run mid-March to December (times vary, phone for details). Tickets can be booked online in advance *(tel 01708 866 000, www.city-sightseeing.com)*.

● Call ahead before leaving London. Windsor Castle's State Apartments and Chapel sometimes close at short notice. St. George's Chapel is open only to worshippers on Sundays.

WHERE TO EAT

Aurora Garden Hotel ❀
Bolton Avenue, Windsor SL4 3JF
Tel 01753 868686
Water gardens set the scene for this conservatory restaurant, where you can sample such classics as baked goat's cheese with salad or roasted duck soaked in cherry brandy.

🍴 L £20, D £32, Wine from £11.95
🕐 12–2, 7–10
🚫 In dining room

Castle Hotel ❀
18 High Street, Windsor SL4 1LJ
Tel 0870400 8300
Opposite the castle, the smart restaurant of this hotel serves starters such as prawns on wilted spinach followed by pot-roasted pheasant with braised savoy cabbage.

🍴 L £17.50, D £22.90, Wine from £13.50
🕐 12–2, 7–9.45
🚫 In dining room

Sir Christopher Wren Hotel ❀ ❀
Thames Street, Windsor SL4 1PX
Tel 01753 861354
Former home of the great architect, this art-deco restaurant has good views of the Thames. Old favourites are given a modern twist–for instance, baked fillet of cod on feta cheese and chive mashed potatoes.

🍴 L £37, D £59, Wine from £16.50
🕐 12.30–2.30, 6.30–10
🚫 In dining room

Eton College School Yard

OUT AND ABOUT

WINDSOR AND ETON 237

OXFORD

Home of one of the world's oldest universities, Oxford is a vibrant city of ancient buildings and riverside walks, with excellent shopping.

INFORMATION

Tourist information office

15–16 Broad Street, Oxford OX1 3AS

☎ 01865 726871

www.oxford.gov.uk

HOW TO GET THERE

Oxford is 57 miles (92km) northwest of London

Train: from Paddington (1 hour)

Coach (bus): Victoria Coach Station: National Coach Service, X90 or Oxford Tube (90 minutes)

Car: M4 west, then M40 to junction 7 (1 hour 15 minutes)

Everywhere in this city of spires and greenery there's a sense of the long tradition of learning. There's been a university here since the arrival in 1167 of a number of English scholars expelled from the Sorbonne in Paris after a dispute between the English and French kings.

Every student is attached to one of the 39 individual colleges. They are all different in character but most have their buildings, including a chapel and a high-ceilinged dining hall, set around quadrangles (quads). Most of the central colleges have medieval origins and display an interesting mixture of architectural styles from Renaissance to Victorian.

Oxford is not huge, but its layout can be confusing. High Street, which students call the High, runs from Carfax Tower east to Magdalen Bridge over the River Cherwell, dividing the city into north and south. To get your bearings, climb the towers of St. Michael's Church, Cornmarket Street, the city's oldest building; the University Church of St. Mary the Virgin, High Street, dating from 1280 and serving the university; or the Carfax Tower, a remnant of the 14th-century St. Martin's Church, at the busy crossroads known as Carfax, the city's focal point.

Don't miss the lively covered market off the High Street, or boating on the river: Hire punts and rowing boats from Magdalen Bridge or the Cherwell Boathouse, Bardwell Road.

COLLEGES

Christ Church, St. Aldate's, founded in 1525, is the largest and most visited college and has the biggest quadrangle. Its chapel is **Christ Church Cathedral,** which predates the college and is England's smallest cathedral. **Christ Church Picture Gallery** includes works by Dürer and Michelangelo.

To the south and east spreads the bucolic **Christ Church Meadow** (entrances at St. Aldate's, Rose Lane and Merton Street), still grazed by cattle—a pocket of green countryside in the heart of the city. You can walk from the meadow or the High into the **Oxford Botanic Garden** *(daily),* the oldest botanic gardens in Britain, founded in 1621 and boasting a collection of plants from around the world.

Magdalen College (pronounced 'maudlin') is one of the richest and most spacious colleges, founded in 1458 and possessor of its own deer park. Also worth a visit are **Merton College,** its peaceful gardens partly enclosed by the old city wall; **New College,** famous for its handsome hall, cloister and gardens; the **Queen's College,** with buildings by Sir Christopher Wren (1632–1723) and Nicholas Hawksmoor (1661–1736); and, farther out in Parks Road, **Keble College,** a relative newcomer whose elaborate red-brick buildings are a Victorian tour de force. **Don't miss** the city's back lanes and alleys, particularly Merton Street/Oriel Street (sites of Merton, Corpus Christi and Oriel colleges), and Queen's Lane/New College Lane (leading past St. Edmund Hall and New College and beneath the Bridge of Sighs).

UNIVERSITY BUILDINGS

Between Broad Street and High Street is a trio of eye-catching university edifices. The **Sheldonian Theatre** (built between 1664 and 1669), the first major architectural work by Sir Christopher Wren, assumes the shape of a Roman theatre and hosts university functions and concerts. Nearby are several buildings housing the **Bodleian Library,** the world's oldest library, opened in the 14th century and now housing over 6 million books. The circular, domed **Radcliffe Camera,** completed in 1749, serves as one of the library's reading rooms; it is not open to the public.

MUSEUMS

Pick of the museums is the **Ashmolean Museum** in Beaumont Street *(Tue–Sun; closed Sun am),* Britain's oldest public museum, opened in 1683, which contains Oxford University's priceless collections from the time of early man to 20th-century paintings. The cavernous and old-fashioned **Pitt Rivers Museum** in Parks Road *(Mon–Sun pm)* has a celebrated anthropology collection of over 250,000 objects, among them masks and shrunken heads.

For a succinct survey of the city from prehistoric times to the present, from mammoths to Morris Minors, visit the **Museum of Oxford,** St. Aldate's *(Tue–Sun).* A more wacky look back at the past is provided by **The Oxford Story** at 6 Broad Street *(daily),* a ride past re-created tableaux of great events and famous faces from the past 900 years. A specialist attraction maintained by the university is the **Bate Collection of Musical Instruments,** at the Faculty of Music, St. Aldate's *(Mon–Fri 2–5, Sat 10–noon during full term only);* with 1,800 exhibits, this is the country's most comprehensive collection of its kind.

Exterior detail of Magdalen College, on the River Cherwell

OUT AND ABOUT

The Radcliffe Camera, designed by James Gibbs, now houses part of the Bodleian Library (top) Watching the punts go by on the banks of the Cherwell (left) The Bridge of Sighs (above) links the Old and the New quads of Hertford College

WHERE TO EAT

Le Petit Blanc ❀❀
71–72 Walton Street, Oxford OX2 6AG
Tel 01865 510999
Authentic provincial French cuisine from monkfish, scallop and shellfish ragout to confit of rabbit leg.
🍴 L £13.50, D £25, Wine from £11
🕐 Daily noon–3, 6–11
🚭 Except at bar

Quod Restaurant and Bar ❀
Old Bank Hotel, 92–94 High Street, Oxford OX1 4BN
Tel 01865 202505
A place that's buzzy all day long. An Italian accent marks the cold meats, pizzas, pastas and risottos; cannoli Siciliani and amaretto pannacotta are worth lingering over.
🍴 L £10, D£15, Wine £9.95
🕐 Daily noon–11pm
🚭 Section; no pipes

TIPS

● To get the real atmosphere, visit in term time.

● Use the park-and-ride on the outer ring road and take a bus into the heart of the city. The centre is pedestrianized and parking is expensive.

● Feel free to wander into many of the university and college buildings. Some charge for admission, and most have a notice indicating which areas are open and at what times.

● For an overview, join a guided walking tour of the city and colleges at the tourist information centre. Tickets are sold on a first come, first served basis.

Wren's Sheldonian Theatre was based on the design of a Roman theatre

BATH

A World Heritage Site, Britain's most complete Georgian city was built around the country's only natural hot springs—in use for about 100,000 years.

The oldest house in Bath 1482
SALLY LUNN
lived here
1680

INFORMATION

Tourist information office
Abbey Chambers, Abbey Church Yard, Bath BA1 1LY
☎ 01225 477101
www.visitbath.co.uk

HOW TO GET THERE

Bath is 80 miles (129km) west of London

Train: Paddington to Bath Spa (1 hour 25 minutes)

Coach (bus): National Express from Victoria Coach Station (3 hours 20 minutes)

Car: M4 west, exit junction 18, then A46 (2 hours)

Bath's hot springs were known long before the Roman occupation and, according to legend, were used by King Lear's father, but it was in AD44 that the Romans began to exploit their supposed healing effects by establishing the spa resort of Aquae Sulis.

Medieval Bath prospered from the wool trade, but its hot springs fell into neglect until their rediscovery in 1755, when they were made fashionable by talented dandy Beau Nash. London's high society migrated here every year to take the waters and enjoy the balls and assemblies that made the city a byword for elegance and style. Bath responded by transforming itself in the grandest manner. Its best-known examples of Georgian townscape are **The Circus,** a circular piazza (1754–70) designed by John Wood; the **Royal Crescent** (1765–75), by his son John Wood the Younger; and **Pulteney Bridge** over the River Avon, surmounted by tiny Palladian houses by Robert Adams (1769–74).

HIGHLIGHTS

The city has more than 20 museums and historic sites. In the very centre, the **Roman Baths and Pump Room** (daily) represent Bath's raison d'être. The Georgian chandelier-hung Pump Room, overlooking the cloistered King's Bath, has its own chamber trio during afternoon tea; an elaborate drinking fountain issues samples of the hot spa water. Beyond, passages lead into the Roman bath complex, set up around the water temple of the goddess Minerva, whose bust presides over the scene.

Close by, **Bath Abbey** (daily) is a crowning example of the Perpendicular style, with its ornately carved west front representing the dream of angels that inspired the abbey's reconstruction by Bishop Oliver in 1499. The impressive east window depicts 56 scenes from Christ's life.

Off the Circus, the **Assembly Rooms and Museum of Costume** (daily 10–4.30), one of the most celebrated museums of its kind, is a look back at fashion across 400 years. **No. 1 Royal Crescent** (Tue–Sun mid-Feb–Nov) displays a superb Bath townhouse interior (1767–74) with period furnishings. In Gay Street the **Jane Austen Centre** (daily) traces the life and works of the novelist, who paid two long visits to Bath in the 1700s and lived here from 1801 to 1806. The city features in two of her novels, Persuasion and Northanger Abbey.

In the elegant **Holburne Museum of Art** (Tue–Sat and Sun pm, mid-Feb–mid-Dec) at the end of Great Pulteney Street you can see the silver, paintings and porcelain collected by Sir William Holburne (1793–1874). Exquisite jade and porcelain from China is excellently displayed and captioned in the **Museum of East Asian Art** in Bennett Street (Tue–Sat and Sun pm).

To find out how Bath became the place it is, visit the **Building of Bath Museum** in the Paragon (Tue–Sun mid-Feb–Nov), where you'll find a detailed model of the city.

Museums aside, Bath is well known for its specialist shops and galleries. Other attractions include the botanical gardens in Victoria Park and the spa complex near Kingsmead Square. Consisting of new and restored Georgian buildings, it has a rooftop pool.

Don't miss Sally Lunn's Refreshment House in North Parade Passage, thought to be Bath's oldest house. The brioche bun known as 'Sally Lunn' was created here in the 17th century.

NEARBY

Just over 2 miles (3km) southeast of the city, at Claverton, the **American Museum in Britain** (Tue–Sun pm, end Mar–early Nov; daily Aug) occupies a gracious 18th-century manor house and shows re-creations of American homes from different states between the 17th and the 19th centuries, as well as folk art and exhibits on Shakers and Native Americans. There are also formal gardens and woodland walks.

A mile (1.6km) south of the city centre, **Prior Park Landscape Garden** (Wed–Mon, Feb–Nov; Fri–Sun, Dec–Jan), owned by the National Trust, is an 18th-century creation by Lancelot 'Capability' Brown (1716–83).

TIPS

● Explore on foot—the city is small enough. Free guided walks are available from the tourist information centre.

● Take an open-top bus tour (no booking required). They are available throughout the day all year round from Pulteney Weir and the abbey.

● Enjoy the River Avon on a boat trip from Pulteney Weir; daily during the summer.

OUT AND ABOUT

Figures on a detail of the Guildhall (above)
Mr. Bowler's tells the story of a small Bath firm at the Bath Industrial Heritage Centre (left)
Stone gorgon's head (right) from the Temple of Sulis Minerva, now in the museum at the Roman Baths (below)

WHERE TO EAT

Firehouse Rotisserie※
2 John Street, Bath BA1 2JL
Tel 01225 482070
Pacific Southwestern grills, gourmet pizzas and vegetarian dishes served from an open kitchen. Relaxed atmosphere.
🍴 L/D £15–£20, Wine from £11.95
🕐 Mon–Fri 12–2.30, 6–10.30, Sat 12–10.30, closed Sun D
🚭 Section

Moody Goose ※ ※
7A Kingsmead Square, Bath BA1 2AB
Tel 01225 466688
Basement restaurant in central Bath serving British and French dishes such as duck galantine and roast saddle of venison. Friendly service.
🍴 L £16–£18.50, D £25–£28.50, Wine from £13.50
🕐 Mon–Sat 12–2.30, 6–10.30
🚭 Except in lounge

No. 5
5 Argyle Street, Bath BA2 4BA
Tel 01225 444499
French bistro with simple menus. Quality and cooking of the meat are high points.
🍴 L £20, D £30, Wine from £12.50
🕐 Sun–Fri 12–2.30, 6.30–10.30, Sat 12–2.30, 6.30–11
🚭 In dining room

OUT AND ABOUT

There are many organized tours in and around London and beyond. Choices range from escorted walking tours around the streets of the city to tailormade tours in luxury chauffeur-driven limousines. River cruises, evening tours and specialist interest tours can all be found. Most tours are available in different languages and car or coach tours will pick you up from and take you back to your hotel.

For more tours, see the Around Town section of the magazine Time Out *or contact a tourist office*

OUT AND ABOUT

BICYCLE TOURS
See page 63

BUS TOURS
BIG BUS COMPANY
48 Buckingham Palace Road
SW1W 0RN
Tel 020 7233 9533
www.bigbustours.com
Tours lasting about two hours of the central London sights in open-top buses with live commentary. Board on any signed stop on three routes: Green Park–St. James's Palace; Victoria Station–London Hilton; Marble Arch–Kensington Palace.
🚌 Adult £17, child (5–15) £8, under 5s free. Tickets valid for 24 hours and interchangeable from route to route

THE ORIGINAL TOUR
Jews Row SW18 1TB
Tel 020 8877 1722
www.theoriginaltour.com
Open-top buses run by a company founded during the Festival of Britain in 1951. Commentary in several languages. Board at any signed stop (over 90).
🚌 Adult £15, child (5–15) £7.50, under 5s free

CANAL TRIPS
JASON'S TRIP
Jason's Wharf, Blomfield Road W9 2PD
Tel 020 7286 3428
www.jasons.co.uk
Ninety-minute trips in beautifully painted canal boats with live commentary. From Little Venice past Regent's Park (see page 115) and London Zoo (see page 160) to Camden Lock.
🚤 Daily 10.30, 12.30, 2.30
🚌 £5.95–£6.95, child (4–14) £4.75–£5.50, under 4s free
🚇 Warwick Avenue 🚌 6, 46, 187

LONDON WATERBUS COMPANY
West Yard, Camden Lock NW1 8AF
Tel 020 7482 2660
www.londonwaterbus.com
Travels the same route as Jason's Trip.
🚤 Daily, every hour between 10 and 5
🚌 Adult £4.80–£6.20, child (3–15) £3, under 3s free 🚇 Camden Town/Chalk Farm, Warwick Avenue 🚌 6, 46, 187

COACH TOURS
EVAN EVANS TOURS
258 Vauxhall Bridge Road SW1V 1BS
Tel 020 7950 1777
www.evanevans.co.uk
A wide range of half-day and full-day tours.

RIVER TRIPS
See pages 234–235

TAXI TOUR
BLACK TAXI TOURS OF LONDON
Tel 020 7935 9363
www.blacktaxitours.co.uk
Personalized tours in a black cab, with commentary from the cabbie. Tours usually last two hours, either by day or night. You can be picked up from and returned to your hotel. Each cab can carry a maximum of five passengers.
🚕 A two-hour guided tour around London by day between 8–6 costs £75

BLUE BADGE GUIDES
The Blue Badge is the British national standard guiding qualification. Each Blue Badge guide is selected, trained and examined by the official British tourist boards. Companies with Blue Badge guides offer a wide range of languages (up to 40) and specialist knowledge, plus punctuality and reliability.

per taxi cab; by night the cost is £85 per taxi cab. Out-of-town trips are priced on request.

TAILORMADE TOURS
TOUR GUIDES LTD
57 Duke Street W1M 5DH
Tel 020 7495 5504
www.tourguides.co.uk
Blue Badge trained guides will take you on a tour tailormade to your specification, either within London or beyond. Walking, car and coach tours are all available. Themed tours include antiques, archaeology, literature, pubs etc.
🚶 Halfday in English £89, most other languages £102. Full day in English £134, other languages £161

WALKING TOURS
Walking tours take place throughout London daily. Typically, they start and finish at Underground stations. To take part, meet the guide outside the station designated. Normally, there's no need to book unless you are in a large group.

GREAT LONDON TREASURE HUNT
123 Westminster Bridge Road SE1 7HR
Tel 020 7928 2627
www.walkingtoursinlondon.com
Organizes self-guided tours. Follow clues at your own pace.
🚶 £5

ORIGINAL LONDON WALKS
PO Box 1708 NW6 4LW
Tel 020 7624 3978
www.walks.com
One of the oldest and more established organizations operating in London. Includes many themed walks.
🚶 Adult £5, child (under 15) free

Eating

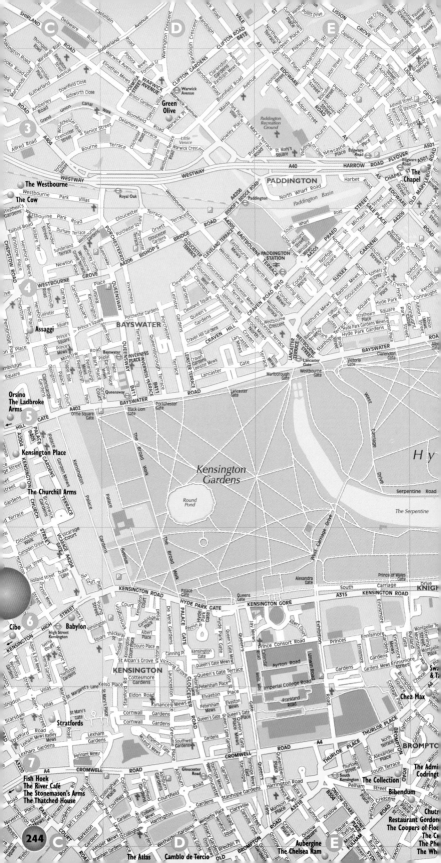

Green Olive

The Westbourne
The Cow

Assaggi

Orsino
The Ladbroke
Arms

Kensington Place

The Churchill Arms

Cibo Babylon

Stratfords

Fish Hoek
The River Café
The Stonemason's Arms
The Thatched House

The Chapel

Chez Max

Swa
& T.

The Admi
Codringt

The Collection
Bibendum

Chutn
Restaurant Gordon
The Coopers of Flo
The C
The Phe
The Wh

The Atlas   Cambio de Tercio   Aubergine   The Chelsea Ram

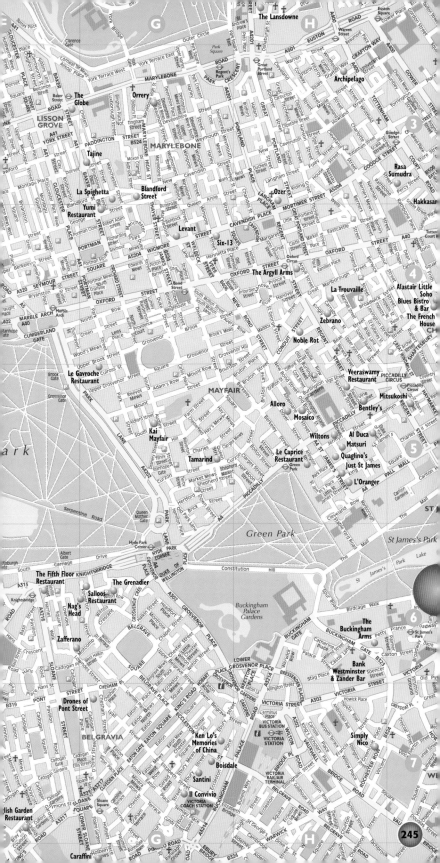

The Lansdowne

Archipelago

The Globe

Orrery

Tajine

Rasa Sumudra

La Spighetta

Blandford Street

Yumi Restaurant

Ozer

Hakkasan

Levant

Six-13

The Argyll Arms

Alastair Little Soho

La Trouvaille

Blues Bistro & Bar

The French House

Zebrano

Noble Rot

Veeraswamy Restaurant

Le Gavroche Restaurant

Mitsukoshi

Alloro

Bentley's

Kai Mayfair

Mosaico

Wiltons

Al Duca

Tamarind

Le Caprice Restaurant

Matsuri

Quaglino's

Just St James

L'Oranger

The Fifth Floor Restaurant

The Grenadier

Salloos Restaurant

Nag's Head

The Buckingham Arms

Zafferano

Bank Westminster & Zander Bar

Drones of Pont Street

Ken Lo's Memories of China

Simply Nico

Boisdale

Santini

Il Convivio

ish Garden Restaurant

Caraffini

245

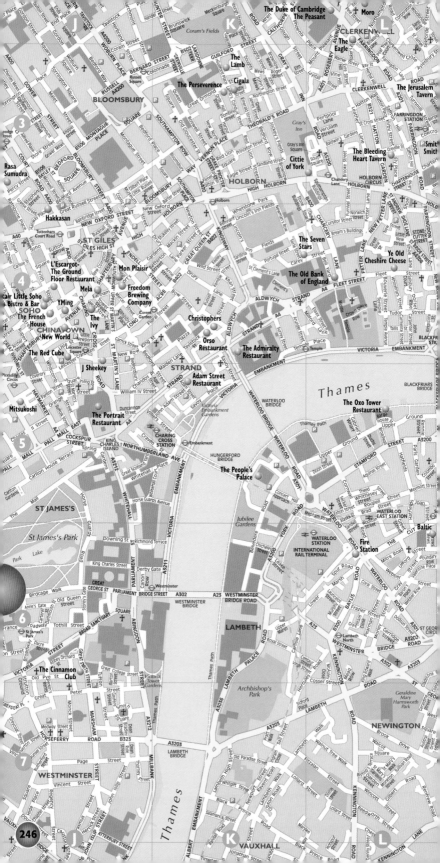

The Duke of Cambridge
The Peasant
Moro
CLERKENWELL
The Eagle
J
K
L
Coram's Fields
CALTHORPE
The Lamb
The Perseverence
Cigala
CLERKENWELL
The Jerusalem
Tavern
BLOOMSBURY
A401
Gray's
Inn
3
FARRINGDON
STATION
Smit
Smith
The Bleeding
Heart Tavern
Cittie
of York
HOLBORN
HOLBORN
HOLBORN
Rasa
Sumudra
HOLBORN CIRCUS
HIGH HOLBORN
Holborn
ST GILES
NEW OXFORD STREET
The Seven
Stars
Ye Old
Cheshire
House
Hakkasan
L'Escargot-
The Ground
Floor Restaurant
Mon Plaisir
The Old Bank
of England
FLEET STREET
4
Mela
air Little Soho
s Bistro & Bar
Freedom
Brewing
Company
ALDWYCH
YMing
Christophers
The French
House
CHINA-TOWN
New World
The
Ivy
Orso
Restaurant
The Admiralty
Restaurant
VICTORIA
EMBANKMENT
The Red Cube
J Sheekey
STRAND
Thames
BLACKFRIARS
BRIDGE
Adam Street
Restaurant
Mitsukoshi
The Oxo Tower
Restaurant
The Portrait
Restaurant
5
PALL MALL
CHARING
CROSS
STATION
Embankment
STAMFORD
A3200
HUNGERFORD
BRIDGE
The People's
Palace
ST JAMES'S
WATERLOO
EAST STATION
Baltic
St James's Park
Park Lake
WATERLOO
STATION
INTERNATIONAL
RAIL TERMINAL
Fire
Station
WATERLOO
Downing St
6
WESTMINSTER
WESTMINSTER
BRIDGE
PARLIAMENT
WESTMINSTER
BRIDGE ROAD
LAMBETH
The Cinnamon
Club
Archbishop's
Park
LAMBETH
NEWINGTON
Geraldine
Mary
Harmsworth
Park
KENNINGTON
A3203
LAMBETH
BRIDGE
7
WESTMINSTER
A3203
Thames
246
J
K
VAUXHALL
L

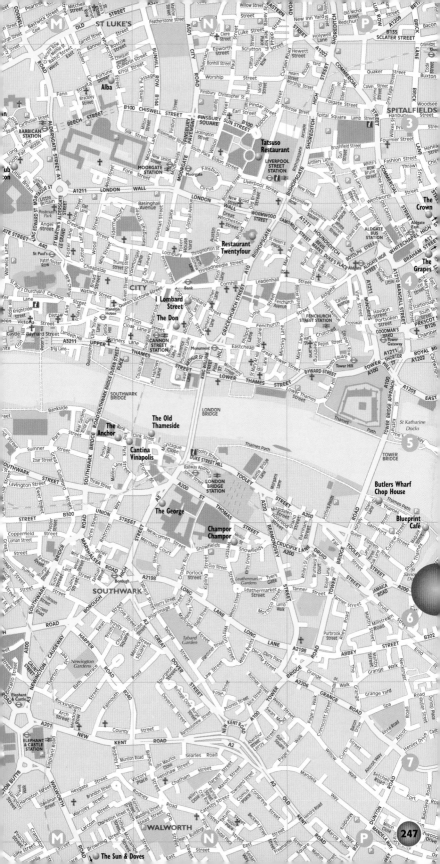

EATING IN LONDON

Britain's reputation for food has undergone a radical change in the last few years, and now ranks with the best in world. The public has become more discerning, chefs have higher profiles and the country now creates its own culinary trends. Top restaurants celebrate traditional British food, adding glamorous touches to such staples as bangers and mash, fish and chips or steak and kidney pie.

These are also standard items on most pub menus, along with adventurous dishes served in the new breed of 'gastro pubs', which provide first-class meals as well as good beer.

Britain's colonial past adds to its culinary mix: curry is said to be the nation's favourite dish. London now offers exciting modern restaurants serving truly traditional Indian, Pakistani or Bangladeshi dishes, fusions of Indian and European cooking or the very latest innovations from Bombay. Thai food is currently enjoying a boom, and Middle Eastern and North African restaurants are particularly popular in the City.

Another long-standing British favourite is Italian food. As well as the home-grown pasta and pizza chains there are innumerable Italian-run restaurants and cafés—often the best bet for a decent cup of coffee and a snack.

London is at the hub of all this gastronomic innovation and you can find pretty well anything in its streets, from cutting-edge modern cuisine through to the Middle Eastern food of Brick Lane. In some parts of the City stalls survive selling jellied eel and pie and mash—an aquired taste, but worth trying as part of London's culinary heritage.

BOOKING

In some restaurants, especially on quieter days, it's possible to walk in off the street and get a table, but if you have your heart set on dining in a particular place, it's always best to book a table in advance. Less formal establishments, especially pubs, may tell you that they do not accept bookings but work on a 'first come, first served' basis. At the other end of the spectrum, many of the UK's top restaurants are booked up for weeks or even months in advance.

It's fairly common for a table booking to last only a couple of hours, after which time guests will be expected to move on to make way for the next sitting. Many restaurants stop serving food relatively early, compared with other European countries. Don't expect to turn up at 10.30pm and be fed unless you've checked in advance.

DRESS CODE

In the past the British loved to dress for dinner and the more formal restaurants tended to have strict dress codes, especially where jackets and ties were concerned. These days things are far more flexible, though it's unwise to turn up at a pricey restaurant wearing jeans and a T-shirt. If you're in doubt, telephone in advance—it's quite acceptable.

SMOKING

Almost every establishment (barring some pubs) has a non-smoking section and in many restaurants smoking is banned throughout.

LICENSING LAWS

Britain's licensing laws have always been restrictive compared to many European countries, and though changes are afoot, the majority of pubs still stop serving at 11pm. Children aged 16 to 18 can drink alcohol only if it accompanies a meal. Some restaurants—especially those not licensed to sell alcohol—operate a 'bring your own' system, in which case it's usual for diners to pay a small corkage fee. A bottle of wine in a restaurant usually costs significantly more than in a shop.

VEGETARIAN MEALS

Most British restaurants offer meat-free dishes, but the choices are often limited and uninspired. Telephone in advance to check what's available, especially as some restaurants do not include a vegetarian option on the menu but are happy to prepare one on request. Thai, Vietnamese and Indian restaurants are usually good options.

A QUICK GUIDE TO TRADITIONAL BRITISH FOOD

BREAKFAST

Traditional British breakfasts are filling, fatty and enormously comforting. A 'fry up' is based on fried egg and bacon, usually accompanied by fried bread, sausages, mushrooms, grilled tomatoes,

A full English breakfast

toast, baked beans and sometimes black pudding (made from barley, oats and pigs' blood).

In hotels a cooked breakfast will usually be preceded by orange juice and cereals, and followed by toast.

MEAT

The British have always made a good roast. Key components are meat (usually turkey, chicken, beef, lamb or pork), gravy (made from the roasting juices), roast potatoes and boiled vegetables. On Christmas day it is usual to eat roast turkey, though in the past roast goose was preferred.

Pigs form an important part of the British diet, providing black pudding, bacon and, of course, sausages. London's 18th-century eating houses sold 'toad in the hole', and this is still available in some of the city's pubs.

Pub menus usually have a choice of meat pies. Rabbit pie, steak and ale pie and steak and kidney pie often come as small bowls filled with meat and gravy, and topped with puff pastry.

PIE AND MASH SHOPS

London has its own pie traditions, and the East End's eel, pie and mash shops are still a popular fast-food option. Steak or steak and kidney pies are cooked in the back of the shop then served up with mashed potatoes. Connoisseurs always turn the pie upside down before eating it.

Pie and mash shops also sell eel, either cooked or jellied. Cooked eels are served with mash and a thin green parsley sauce; jellied eels are cooked in large, white basins, then left to cool, so that the liquor sets, and served cold.

FISH

Another traditional London catch is whitebait, but these days very small quantities are actually caught in the River Thames. These tiny, crunchy fish are deep fried and eaten whole. They were once thought to be a separate species but are in fact the mixed fry of fish such as herring and sprat. Whitebait dinners originated in Dagenham in Kent, and were customarily eaten in the Houses of Parliament at the end of the parliamentary season.

One of Britain's favourite dishes is fish and chips: white fish—usually cod or haddock—coated in batter then deep fried and served with chips. Fish and chip shops can be found throughout the country; some say they

originated in London in the early 19th century.

SANDWICHES

Probably the most typical English sandwich is the dainty cucumber version that sometimes forms part of afternoon tea in some of the most upmarket hotels. Elsewhere you're more likely to encounter deep-filled baguettes, subs or rustic slices of bread around cheese, meat or salad. There's a huge selection of sandwich places and cafés in the city, where you can choose your filling, but avoid the lunch hour, when there's likely to be a long wait behind office-workers.

DRINKS

Traditional British wine is usually made from fruit or even flowers such as elderflower, but there is a growing number of vineyards in southern England and occasionally a wine list might offer a native white wine. Cider remains a popular British drink, and is available in most pubs. It's made from cider apples (not eating apples). Most common are the clear, commercial varieties but it's well worth tracking down ciders made by independent producers in counties such as Somerset and Herefordshire.

Traditional British ale (beer) is more strongly flavoured and less fizzy than lagers and European beers in Britain, each one producing a distinctive style of beer, and a tour of a few London pubs should provide the opportunity to sample several very different varieties. These include the Black bitter of Yorkshire (which was originally produced as a medicinal drink against scurvy) and Newcastle Brown Ale, which is sweeter than 'bitter'. Other well-established brewers include Shepherd Neame at Faversham in Kent (the country's oldest brewery), which produces a hoppy, tawny coloured bitter, and Marston's Pedigree, which comes from the famous brewing town of Burton on Trent.

AFTERNOON TEA

This great British institution remains popular and is widely available in hotels and tea rooms from about 2 or 3pm. There are many variations, but it always includes a pot of tea and something to eat. In the smartest hotels it's an impressive spread, including cucumber and other sandwiches, and cakes; cream teas include a scone (small, doughy, unsweetened bun) with cream, butter and jam.

Tea arrived in Britain in the 17th century and by the 19th century it was a very fashionable drink, with the upper classes creating their own secret tea blends, made for them by tea merchants.

Traditional afternoon tea

CAFÉS, BRASSERIES AND BISTROS

These days the word 'café' refers to the stylish Continental-style establishments found in cities such as London. These bridge the gap between pubs, restaurants and coffee bars by selling hot drinks, snacks, wine and meals. Like brasseries and bistros, they often stay open all day—in fact it can can be difficult to distinguish between the three. The 'greasy spoon' is a cheap-and-cheerful version of the café, usually serving simple traditional British meals such as sausage and mash, tea, coffee and hot drinks.

FAST FOOD

It's possible to buy a (briefly) filling take-away meal for under £5. Chains of fast food outlets have reached every corner of Britain, so you won't have to look far for a KFC, McDonald's or Pizza Hut (see page 272). Other fast food outlets include pie and mash shops, sandwich bars, fish and chip shops and a wide variety of multicultural takeaways, particularly in areas such as Brick Lane in east London.

PUBS

Within the city bounds you'll find Irish bars, sports bars, traditional street corner pubs and slick futuristic bars. Bare stone walls, open fires and wooden beams typify older establishments, often imitated in modern chains, though many London pubs feature trendy modern styling or themed décor.

One of the newest trends is the gastro pub—a fusion of pub and restaurant that promises not only a place to drink, but also good quality food. Pub menus have traditionally included bar snacks —lighter, cheaper meals such as sandwiches, baked potatoes with a variety of fillings and savoury dishes—but these days most also serve substantial meals (see above).

In addition to the restaurants on pages 252–265, the restaurants in the hotels below (all described on pages 279–291) have been inspected by the Automobile Association and awarded rosettes. All are open to non-residents.

Athenaeum: Bullochs at 116 Restaurant ❀
The Cadogan Hotel ❀ ❀
Capital ❀ ❀ ❀ ❀
The Carlton Tower Hotel: Grissini-London ❀ ❀
Claridge's: Gordon Ramsay at Claridge's ❀ ❀ ❀
Connaught ❀ ❀ ❀
The Dorchester: The Grill Room ❀ ❀;
　The Oriental ❀ ❀ ❀
The Goring ❀ ❀ ❀
Great Eastern Hotel:
　Aurora ❀ ❀ ❀; Fishmarket ❀
The Halkin Hotel: Nahm ❀ ❀ ❀
Kingsway Hall ❀
The Landmark London ❀
The Lanesborough ❀ ❀ ❀
Mandarin Oriental Hyde Park:
　Foliage Restaurant ❀ ❀ ❀ ❀
Mercure London City Bankside: Loft Restaurant ❀
The Montague on the Gardens ❀
One Aldwych: Axis ❀ ❀
Radisson Edwardian Kenilworth ❀
Raffles Brown's: Restaurant 1837 ❀ ❀ ❀
The Ritz: ❀ ❀ ❀
Royal Garden Hotel:
　Tenth Floor Restaurant ❀ ❀ ❀
Royal Lancaster: Nipa Thai ❀ ❀
The Savoy: River Restaurant ❀ ❀; Savoy Grill ❀ ❀
The Westbury ❀

> **TIP**
> Many restaurants serve a good-value set lunch menu. Look for pre-theatre menus or cheaper meals for early dining (before, say, 7.30pm). They can be a useful way of avoiding the rush and keeping to budget.

EATING

ROSETTE AWARDS

The Automobile Association's restaurant inspectors award rosettes to restaurants annually on a rising scale from one to five. The following gives an indication of the different levels of quality you can expect:

❀ **Rosette** Excellent local restaurants serving food prepared with care, understanding and skill, using good-quality ingredients.

❀ ❀ **Rosettes** The best local restaurants, which aim for and achieve higher standards, better consistency and greater precision in the cooking.

❀ ❀ ❀ **Rosettes** Outstanding restaurants that demand recognition well beyond their local area. The cooking will be underpinned by the selection and sympathetic treatment of the highest-quality ingredients. Timing, seasoning and the judgement of flavour combinations will be consistently excellent. Intelligent service and a well-chosen wine list.

❀ ❀ ❀ ❀ **Rosettes** Among the very best restaurants in Britain. These restaurants exhibit ambition, excellence, superb technical skills and remarkable consistency. They combine an appreciation of culinary traditions with a desire for further exploration and improvement.

❀ ❀ ❀ ❀ ❀ **Rosettes** Some of the finest restaurants in Britain, where the cooking stands comparison with the best in the world. These restaurants are highly individual, show exceptional culinary skills and set the standards to which other restaurants aspire.

SAVOURY DISHES

Bangers and Mash:
Sausages and mashed potato

Bubble and Squeak:
Pre-cooked cabbage and potato fried up together

Cottage Pie:
Minced beef and vegetables
topped with mashed potato

Kedgeree:
Smoked haddock, eggs and
rice with curry powder

Lancashire Hotpot:
Casserole of lamb and onions
topped with sliced potato

Scotch Egg:
Hard-boiled egg covered with
sausage meat; eaten cold,
often as a snack

Shepherd's Pie:
Minced lamb and vegetables
topped with mashed potato
and baked

Toad in the Hole:
Sausages baked in batter

Fruity red summer pudding

Welsh Rarebit:
Thick cheese sauce spread on
toast, then grilled

Yorkshire Pudding:
Batter cooked in the meat
juices of roast beef, with
which it is served

PUDDINGS

Bakewell Tart:
Almond-flavoured flan, with
jam and a pastry base

Bread and Butter Pudding:
Slices of bread and butter
baked with dried fruit, milk
and eggs

Fruit Crumble:
Stewed fruit with a topping of
crumbled flour and butter

Fruit Fool:
Cooked soft fruit blended with
cream or cold custard

Queen of Puddings:
Baked pudding of milk, sugar
and eggs, topped with jam
and meringue

Spotted Dick:
Hot pudding made with suet
pastry and raisins

Summer Pudding:
Cooked soft fruit in a shell of
white bread; served cold with
custard

Trifle:
Layers of sponge cake, fruit,
jelly, custard and cream;
served cold

RESTAURANTS BY CUISINE

The restaurants listed alphabetically on pages 252 to 265 are grouped here by cuisine.

EATING

Restaurants

The prices given are for a two-course set lunch (L) for two people and a three-course à la carte dinner (D) for two people. The wine price is for a bottle of house wine.

ADAM STREET RESTAURANT ❀
Map 246 K5
9 Adam Street WC2N 6AA
Tel 020 7379 8000

The restaurant, with its polished wood tables and white-painted walls, is in the cellars of a Robert Adam building. Club lunches include sausage and mash, steak and kidney pie and other traditional British fare. Set-price meals include Caesar salad, crispy duck salad and fish pie au gratin. Just off The Strand; entrance is gained by intercom.

🕐 12–2.15, 6–11.15, D members only. Closed Sat, Sun, 24 Dec–2 Jan
🍽 L from £29, D from £42, Wine from £14.50
🚇 Charing Cross

THE ADMIRALTY RESTAURANT ❀
Map 246 K4
Somerset House, The Strand WC2R 1LA
Tel 020 7845 4646

Set within historic Somerset House (see pages 130–131), this colourful and modern restaurant has a French-inspired menu and a nautical theme. So you'd expect to find fish here, and you won't be disappointed. Try seared fillet of red mullet with tapenade, crab beignet, ratatouille, confit fennel and lobster nage. Other dishes include ravioli of snails with artichokes, poached garlic and lemon butter, and leg of French farm rabbit with young vegetables.

🕐 12–2.45, 6–10.45. Closed D Sun, 24–26 Dec, public hols
🍽 L from £50, D from £70, Wine from £13
🚭 Section, no pipes or cigars
🚇 Charing Cross

ALBA ❀
Map 247 M3
107 Whitecross Street EC1Y 8JD
Tel 020 7588 1798

This contemporary restaurant a short stroll from the Barbican offers a taste of Piedmont and northern Italy. Like the olive green walls and brightly hued prints, the menu is modern and has such daily specials as Piedmont ravioli and tagliolini

with butter, sage and white truffles. Desserts include chocolate mousse cake on a base of amaretto-soaked panettone.

🕐 12–3, 6–11. Closed Sat, Sun, public hols
🍽 L from £31, D from £42, Wine from £11.50
🚭 No cigars
🚇 Barbican

AL DUCA ❀
Map 245 H5
4–5 Duke of York Street SW1Y 6LA
Tel 020 7839 3090

Reasonably priced but classy Italian restaurant with banquette seating and wooden tables. First-rate pasta and fish; check out the roasted cod with lentils and parsley sauce; flat spaghetti with clams, sweet chilli and parsley; and ravioli with woodpigeon and rosemary jus. The 60 or so wines are all Italian. On warm summer days the windows can be removed.

🕐 12.30–3, 6–11. Closed Sun, L public hols
🍽 L from £35, D from £48, Wine from £16
🚭 No pipes or cigars
🚇 Piccadilly

ALLORO ❀
Map 245 H5
20 Dover Street W1S 4LU
Tel 020 7495 4768

A chic traditional Italian restaurant with an adept staff. The interconnecting bar and restaurant are long and narrow with a glass front and leather banquette seating. The selection of *antipasti*, fresh pasta and risotti precedes desserts such as *tortino tiepido di aranca* (an

ALASTAIR LITTLE SOHO
❀❀❀
Map 245 J4
49 Frith Street W1V 5TE
Tel 020 7734 5183

The daily changing fixed-price menu runs on Mediterranean

lines with an unmistakable nod to Italy. Superb breads precede starters such as pappardelle with game sauce or potato pancake with smoked eel. Follow with fillet of red mullet with Umbrian lentils, or perhaps bacon braised in red wine. Don't miss the roasted black figs with honey and mascarpone. Make reservations well in advance.

🕐 12–3, 6–11.30. Closed L Sat, Sun, public hols
🍽 L from £58, D from £73, Wine from £15
🚭 No cigars
🚇 Tottenham Court Road

orange sponge cake made with olive oil) and home-made ice cream. Main courses include fresh egg tagliatelli with fresh tomato and basil sauce—a classic.

🕐 12–2.30, 7–10.30. Closed L Sat, Sun, 25–26 Dec, 1 Jan, public hols
🍽 L from £44, D from £62, Wine from £26
🚭 No pipes or cigars
🚇 Green Park

EATING

ARCHIPELAGO & BAR ❀❀
Map 245 H3
110 Whitfield Street S1T 5ED
Tel 020 7383 3346

A visual assault from the bold colour schemes is the aim of Archipelago, who dares to be different. The international dishes on the menu are inspiring and adventurous, transporting diners to the four corners of the globe. It's not perhaps the best place for the timid (although there are several tamer dishes), with crocodile steak seared in vine leaves with yellow plum sauce, Vietnamese green chicken curry, a confit of rabbit with cep mushrooms and, to follow, Italian rhubarb Alaska.

🕐 12–2.30, 6–10.45. Closed L Sat, Sun, 24–25 Dec, public hols

🍽 L from £32, D from £77, Wine from £13

🚭 Section, no pipes or cigars

🚇 Warren Street

ASSAGGI ❀❀
Map 244 C4
39 Chepstow Place W2 4TS
Tel 020 7792 5501

A relaxed and traditional Italian restaurant with bare floorboards, wooden tables and plenty of yellow and terracotta, set above the Chepstow pub. Starters may include buffalo mozzarella, *fregola con arselle* (fregula pasta with clams) and *calamari ripieni* (stuffed squid). Main courses *quaglia ripiena* (stuffed roasted quail) and *filetto di vitello al rosmarino* (panroasted fillet of white veal, rosemary and glazed baby onions). Perfectly accompanied by a selection of Sardinian wines.

🕐 12.30–2.30, 7.30–11. Closed Sun, public hols

🍽 L/D from £50, Wine from £13.95

🚭 No pipes or cigars

🚇 Notting Hill Gate, Bayswater

AUBERGINE ❀❀❀❀
Map 244 off E7
11 Park Walk SW10 0AJ
Tel 020 7352 3449

In a quiet side street off Fulham Road, Aubergine has the feel of a chic neighbourhood restaurant with a calm and unpretentious atmosphere. The cooking is accomplished and refined and very French. Try the seven-course

tasting menu, or choose a variety of faultless dishes from the à la carte one, such as seared scallops, assiette of corn-fed duck, and banana parfait with banana ice cream. The serious wine list offers few bargains but superb quality.

🕐 12–2.30, 7–11. Closed L Sat, Sun, 24 Dec–3 Jan, public hols

🍽 L from £64, D from £100, Wine from £15

🚭 No pipes or cigars

🚇 South Kensington, Fulham Broadway

BABYLON ❀❀
Map 244 C6
The Roof Gardens, 99 Kensington High Street W8 5SA
Tel 020 7368 3993

Superb roof-garden restaurant. Proceed through the cavernous marble foyer, hop into the lift and then walk past the fishtanks that form a wall of the small bar area. A generous and varied menu offers tender baby squid bursting with king prawns and Cornish bourride perfumed with ginger and spring onions. Desserts might well include an iced-coffee soufflé.

🕐 12–3, 7–11

🍽 L from £25, D from £60, Wine from £17.50

🚇 High Street Kensington

BALTIC ❀
Map 246 L6
74 Blackfriars Road SE1 8HA
Tel 020 7928 1111

The vodka bar is trendy, the restaurant even trendier. White walls, steel chairs and abstract paintings provide a modern setting for predominantly traditional Polish cuisine. You might start with *kopytka* (potato dumplings) with tomato sauce, and follow with a leek and wild mushroom risotto made from *kasza*, a type of barley with a nutty taste.

🕐 12–3, 6.30–11. Closed Sat, 25–26 Dec, 1 Jan, public hols

🍽 L from £23, D from £60, Wine from £11.50

🚇 Southwark

BANK WESTMINSTER & ZANDER BAR ❀
Map 245 H6
45 Buckingham Gate SW1E 6BS
Tel 020 7379 9797

A buzzy brasserie in the heart of Westminster, and just round the corner from Buckingham

Palace and St. James's Park. It's stylish and ultra modern, with a semicircular glass frontage and a glass ceiling. In contrast, some of the tables overlook a tranquil courtyard with a fountain and flowerbeds. An extensive menu covers Modern European flavours such as *moules marinières*, roast lamb with oyster mushrooms and rösti, and nougat ice cream. Popular with workers in the area for their seven-days-a-week breakfasts and the good-value set lunches.

🕐 12–3, 5.30–11.30. Closed L Sat, Sun, 25 Dec, 1 Jan, public hols

🍽 L from £40, D from £50, Wine from £13

🚭 Section

🚇 St. James's Park

BENTLEY'S ❀
Map 245 H5
11–15 Swallow Street W1B 4DG
Tel 020 7734 4756

Bentley's is a classically styled seafood restaurant, with its booths around the walls and oyster bar downstairs. Typical starters include smoked eel with horseradish cream and bacon or smoked salmon with capers and shallots. Follow with skate wing in black batter and capers or whole roasted red mullet, stuffed with chorizo and herbs. Desserts are comforting British classics such as bread-and-butter pudding.

🕐 12–11.30. Closed 25–26 Dec, 1 Jan

🍽 L from £44, D from £62, Wine from £22

🚭 No pipes

🚇 Piccadilly Circus

BIBENDUM ❀❀
Map 244 F7
Michelin House, 81 Fulham Road SW3 6RD
Tel 020 7581 5817

Housed in the large and remarkable Michelin building, this restaurant is light and airy with fabulous stained-glass windows depicting Bibendum, the Michelin Man, riding his bicycle, kick-boxing and drinking champagne. The Bibendum motif is also picked up on the glasses, decanters, vases, tables and even the chair legs. Great emphasis is placed on wine service, with guidance from the *sommeliers* through the list of some 600 wines. The less formal Oyster Bar opens all day (from 12pm) serving all manner of crustacea, plus salads and daily specials.

🕐 12–2.30, 7–11.30, Sat 12.30–3, 7–11.30, Sun 12.30–3, 7–10.30. Closed 25–26 Dec
🍴 L from £50, D from £61, Wine from £15.95
🚭 No pipes
Ⓜ South Kensington

BLANDFORD STREET—THE BRASSERIE ✤ ✤
Map 245 G3
5–7 Blandford Street W1U 3DB
Tel 020 7486 9696
Here you'll find accomplished Modern European cooking. Try the twice-baked Parmesan and artichoke soufflé, roasted sea bass on scallion mash with caramelized vegetable and coriander jus, or rump of Welsh lamb with the intriguingly named red pepper essence.
🕐 12–2.30, 6–10.30. Closed L Sat, Sun, 25–26 Dec, 1 Jan, Easter, public hols
🍴 L from £30, D from £43, Wine from £14
🚭 Section, no pipes
Ⓜ Bond Street

BLUEPRINT CAFÉ ✤
Map 247 P6
The Design Museum, 28 Shad Thames SE1 2YD
Tel 020 7378 7031
A bustling, stylish restaurant in the Design Museum (see page 87) with unrivalled views over the River Thames to Tower Bridge and the City. The décor

BLUES BISTRO & BAR ✤
Map 245 J4
42–43 Dean Street W1V 5AP
Tel 020 7494 1966
A jazzy bar/brasserie right in the heart of Soho bringing unpretentious international flavours to a young, lively crowd. The menu features straightforward and tasty dishes such as smoked haddock and pea risotto with shaved Parmesan, roast snapper with coriander noodles, and chocolate and walnut torte with caraway ice cream.
🕐 12–12. Closed L Sat–Sun, public hols
🍴 L from £20, D from £20, Wine from £11
🚭 No pipes or cigars
Ⓜ Piccadilly Circus

is sophisticated and simple, as is the menu, which changes twice daily. Modern British dishes with Middle Eastern and Asian influences are presented in a straightforward manner—for example, rabbit cooked with peppers, black olives and basil. A splendid place for summer dining.
🕐 12–3, 6–11. Closed Sun D, 25–28 Dec, 1 Jan
🍴 L from £30, D from £44, Wine from £12.50
Ⓜ Tower Hill, London Bridge

BOISDALE ✤
Map 245 G7
15 Eccleston Street SW1W 9LX
Tel 020 7730 6922
More than 150 malts, 100 Cuban cigars and live jazz explain the popularity of this Scottish whisky bar/restaurant. Caledonian cuisine does the rest, with favourites such as Islay-smoked salmon, haggis and Aberdeen Angus beef. You can eat in the courtyard or the atmospheric, clubhouse-style restaurant.
🕐 12–3, 7–11.15. Closed Sun, L Sat, 25–26 Dec, public hols
🍴 L from £28, D from £52, Wine from £14
Ⓜ Victoria

BUTLERS WHARF CHOP HOUSE ✤
Map 247 P5
The Butlers Wharf Building, 36e Shad Thames SE1 2YE
Tel 020 7403 3403

A traditional British restaurant on the River Thames, close to the Tower of London. Doors that run the length of the whole restaurant are opened during fine weather, and tables are set outside. Typical dishes are crab soup with sour cream and sippets (small pieces of toast), slow-roasted pork with prunes, and steamed chocolate pudding. The bar area by the entrance has its own menu and requires no booking. Check out the bargain New World wines.
🕐 12–3, 6–11. Closed D Sun, Good Fri
🍴 L from £40, D from £46, Wine from £14.50
Ⓜ Tower Hill, London Bridge

CAMBIO DE TERCIO ✤
Map 244 D8
163 Old Brompton Road SW5 0LJ
Tel 020 7244 8970
Right down to the bullfighting paraphernalia and the sunset-yellow and claret-red interior, this place is clearly proud of its Spanish roots. Service is relaxed and the wine list loaded with Spanish wines. The menu balances classics with contemporary Spanish dishes (sweetbreads sautéed with vegetables and sherry sauce). Desserts are a major draw—check out the lemon jelly, and the lemon or Rioja sorbet.
🕐 12–2.15, 7–11.30, Sun 12–2.15, 7–11. Closed 25–26 Dec, 1 Jan
🍴 L from £60, D from £70, Wine from £15
🚭 No pipes
Ⓜ Gloucester Road

CANTINA VINOPOLIS ✤ ✤
Map 247 M5
1 Bankside SE1 9BU
Tel 020 7940 8333
This vivacious, wine-themed restaurant with understated furnishings, bare brick walls, terracotta floor tiles and high ceilings has a relaxed, brasserie style. Simple dishes with a strong Mediterranean influence are prepared in the open-view kitchen, and might include terrine of smoked salmon and anchovy with crème fraîche and country bread, or sea bass in crispy skin served on couscous with tomato butter sauce. There's an expansive and inspiring international wine list and about 100 choices are available by the glass.

EATING

🕐 12–2.45, 6–10.15. Closed D Sun, 25–26 Dec, 1 Jan
🍴 L from £46, D from £52, Wine from £16.95
Ⓢ Section, no pipes or cigars
Ⓜ London Bridge

LE CAPRICE RESTAURANT ❀❀
Map 244 H5
Arlington House, Arlington Street
SW1A 1RT
Tel 020 7629 2239

Tucked away behind the Ritz, but sleek and glamorous in black, white and chrome, Le Caprice is decorated with portraits of the rich and famous by renowned British photographer David Bailey. The food is uncomplicated and international, with dishes such as Thai baked sea bass, Mexican griddled chicken salad and steak Americaine. Sunday brunch ranges from eggs Benedict to caviar and *blinis*. You may well spot someone famous as it's popular with the media set.
🕐 12–3, 5.30–12, Sun 12–4, 6–12. Closed D 24 Dec, 25–26 Dec, L 27 Dec, 1 Jan, Aug public hols
🍴 L from £70, D from £90, Wine from £12.75
Ⓢ No pipes
Ⓜ Green Park

CARAFFINI ❀
Map 245 G8
61–63 Lower Sloane Street
SW1W 8DH
Tel 020 7259 0235

Friendly service greets you at this popular neighbourhood Italian restaurant. The pale yellow painted walls are hung with mirrors and prints and the pale wood floors contrast with Venetian blinds, rattan-style chairs, banquettes and plants. The lengthy menu includes a typically generous porcini mushroom risotto, chargrilled monkfish with saffron and lemon zest, and an excellent *tiramisu*. There's a good selection of vegetarian dishes and a range of Italian wines.
🕐 12.15–2.30, 6.30–11.30. Closed Sun, public hols
🍴 L from £36, D from £44, Wine from £11.50
Ⓢ No pipes
Ⓜ Sloane Square

CHAMPOR CHAMPOR ❀
Map 247 N6
62 Weston Street SE1 3QJ
Tel 020 7403 4600
A small, wonderfully bohemian southeast Asian restaurant. The name, which can be roughly translated from Malay as 'mix and match', is the key to the menu, which reflects Asian cuisines with roots in Malaysia. A two-course, fixed-price meal might include tofu, courgette (zucchini) and lychee satay followed by spicy stingray baked in banana leaf with kukur mushroom curry. Opening times vary, so be sure to telephone in advance.
🕐 12.30–2, 6.30–10.30. Closed Sat, L Mon, Sun, Easter, 24 Dec–2 Jan
🍴 L from £36, D from £49, Wine from £12.50
Ⓢ No pipes or cigars
Ⓜ London Bridge

CHEZ MAX ❀❀❀
Map 244 F7
3 Yeoman's Row, Brompton Road
SW3 2AL
Tel 020 7590 9999
A contemporary Gallic atmosphere pervades in a brasserie-style basement room, with tables set close together and Francophile posters on the walls. A long menu of classic French dishes includes snails with garlic butter, five versions of rib-eye steak, calf's liver with sauce *diable* (the devil's sauce) and, of course their trademark *pot au chocolat*.
🕐 12–3, 5.30–11
🍴 L from £27, D from £50, Wine from £11

Ⓢ Section
Ⓜ South Kensington, Knightsbridge

CHRISTOPHERS ❀
Map 246 K4
18 Wellington Street WC2E 7DD
Tel 020 7240 4222
This self-styled American grill is actually much grander than the phrase might imply. It has a curving staircase, crisp tablecloths and high ceilings. The simpler dishes on the menu are particularly successful, with plenty of flavour in the Maryland crab cake and a really succulent Aberdeen Angus steak. Desserts include fresh fruity sorbets and light, moist chocolate cake. The modern wine list includes a very good selection by the glass.

🕐 12–3, 5–11.45. Closed D Sun, Easter, 25–26 Dec
🍴 L from £33, D from £48, Wine from £13.50
Ⓢ No pipes or cigars
Ⓜ Embankment

CHUTNEY MARY ❀❀
Map 245 off F7
535 King's Road SW10 0SZ
Tel 020 7351 3113

This popular Indian restaurant at one end of King's Road has a sophisticated, contemporary look and a menu that combines established dishes with exciting new specialities, such as buttered crab (currently popular in Bombay) and the restaurant's own *foie gras* dish

EATING

A–Z OF RESTAURANTS 255

cooked with seared mango and mild chilli marsala jelly. Don't miss one of the interesting and unusual desserts, such as the crème brûlée with strawberries and masala spice.

⏱ 12.30–3, 6.30–11.30. Closed L Mon–Fri, D 25 Dec
🍽 L from £33, D from £90, Wine from £15
🚭 Section, no pipes or cigars
Ⓜ Fulham Broadway

CIBO ❀❀
Map 244 off C6
3 Russell Gardens W14 8EZ
Tel 020 7371 2085
Cibo is at once exciting and relaxing. The cooking is straightforward and concentrates mainly on seafood; you might be treated to a fine selection of grilled fish and shellfish (spaghetti with fresh lobster, for example)—though with a choice of 15 main courses you're unlikely to be disappointed. Also modern Italian classics such as roast quail with figs. The wine list is interesting, with some hidden classics from overlooked regions. Set lunches are reasonably priced and the atmosphere quieter than in the evening. Friendly staff.

⏱ 12.15–2.30, 7–11. Closed L Sat, D Sun, 25–26 Dec
🍽 L from £29, D from £42, Wine from £12
🚭 No pipes
Ⓜ Kensington Olympia, Shepherd's Bush

CIGALA ❀
Map 246 K3
54 Lamb's Conduit Street WC1N 3LW
Tel 020 7405 1717
Tucked away around the back streets of Holborn, this popular Spanish restaurant is regularly crowded with local customers in both the light, understated upstairs restaurant and the basement tapas bar. The open-plan kitchen keeps things slightly steamy and turns out dishes such as *ternera à la plancha* (veal with broccoli, tomatoes and anchovy). The tapas are of uniformly high quality—the calamari make a good choice. A good range of Spanish wines.

⏱ 12–3, 6–10.45. Closed 25–26 Dec, 1 Jan, Easter, public hols
🍽 L from £30, D from £43, Wine from £12.50
Ⓜ Holborn

THE CINNAMON CLUB ❀❀
Map 246 J6
The Old Westminster Library, 13 Great Smith Street SW1P 3BU
Tel 020 7222 2555

Set in the former Westminster Library, the Cinnamon Club has a sophisticated look with its shelves of old books, brown leather armchairs, crisp white linen and parquet floor. Traditional Indian cooking gets surprising twists here—you've only to taste the prawns with a coconut curry sauce or the duck with green Thai spices and sweet basil as the proof. Try the above-average desserts. Impressive wine list.

⏱ 12–2.45, 6–10.45. Closed L Sat, Sun, 25–26 Dec, Easter
🍽 L from £34, D from £47, Wine from £15
Ⓜ Westminster

CLUB GASCON ❀❀❀
Map 247 M3
57 West Smithfield EC1A 9DS
Tel 020 7796 0600
Here, each of the menu's six sections focuses on a different regional cuisine in southwest France. For example, a *Foie Gras* section pays homage to the classic pâté, with 10 variations, including a magnificent carpaccio of goose *foie gras* with spicy cherries. Tapas-sized portions. Each course has a glass of wine to match.

⏱ 12–2, 7–10. Closed L Sat, Sun, 25–26 Dec, 1 Jan, public hols
🍽 L from £70, D from £44, Wine from £11
🚭 No pipes
Ⓜ Barbican, Farringdon

THE COLLECTION ❀
Map 244 E7
264 Brompton Road SW3 2AS
Tel 020 7225 1212

Take the long neon-lit catwalk from the Brompton Road entrance to this former fashion warehouse and you will find a bustling ground-floor bar and balcony restaurant. Black-clad staff, crisp linen, brick walls and high-backed contemporary seating set the tone for the modern menu, which includes seared tuna sashimi with shiitake mushroom and cucumber salad; traditional roast lamb with minted peas and beans; and mango carpaccio with coconut sorbet. Good selection of wines to compliment the courses.

⏱ 6–11, Sat–Sun brunch only. Closed 25–26 Dec, 1 Jan
🍽 L from £30, D from £50, Wine from £14
Ⓜ South Kensington

IL CONVIVIO ❀❀
Map 245 G7
143 Ebury Street SW1W 9QN
Tel 020 7730 4099
Deep red, cream and brickwork walls combine stylishly with light wooden flooring to create a chic setting for this bustling, friendly Italian restaurant. The menu offers pasta, fish and meat, such as spaghetti with tiger prawns and rocket, grilled swordfish with radicchio and borlotti beans, and lamb with pumpkin purée and thyme sauce. Desserts include nougat parfait pyramid, and there's a range of Italian organic cheese. The Italian waiters are professional and helpful.

⏱ 12–3, 7–11. Closed Sun
🍽 L from £31, D from £65, Wine from £12
Ⓜ Victoria

THE DON ❀
Map 247 N4
20 St. Swithin's Lane EC4 8AD
Tel 020 7626 2606
This restaurant is in the building that the Sandeman port

EATING

company occupied for more than 170 years and it has a bistro in the former madeira cellars. Upstairs is the strikingly chic City restaurant with stark white walls and brilliantly hued blinds. The menu has a Modern European theme, with robust dishes such as maize-fed chicken with wild mushrooms, and calves' liver with braised chicory. Reserve well in advance, especially for lunch.

🕐 12–3, 6.30–10. Closed Sat, Sun, 24 Dec–2 Jan
🍴 L from £36, D from £50, Wine from £15.95
🚭 No pipes
🚇 Bank, Cannon Street

DRONES OF PONT STREET ❀ ❀ ❀

Map 245 G7
1 Pont Street SW1X 9EJ
Tel 020 7235 9555

This restaurant tucked away off Sloane Street is owned by famous chef Marco Pierre White and bears the MPW trademark—extravagant floral displays against a background of subdued earth shades. The potted shrimps, gratinée Normande, roast *poulet noir*, calves' liver Lyonnaise, rib-eye steak au poivre, crème caramel and lemon tart all demonstrate the master's influence.

🕐 12–2.30, 6–11, Sun 12–4. Closed L Sat, D Sun, 26 Dec
🍴 L from £30, D from £40, Wine from £15.50
🚭 No pipes
🚇 Knightsbridge, Sloane Square

ENGLISH GARDEN RESTAURANT ❀ ❀

Map 245 G7
10 Lincoln Street SW3 2TS
Tel 020 7584 7272

In this stylish conversion of a Chelsea townhouse tucked away off the King's Road, clean, cool lines and pale colours cut a contemporary edge, while the designer chairs, white table linen, wooden floor and a glass-vaulted conservatory roof add polish and texture. Daily fixed-priced menus include rocket and artichokes with truffles and almonds, cod with potato gratin and warm ginger madeleines with pear and vanilla cream. Modern British cuisine with an Irish angle.

🕐 12–2.45, 6.30–10.45. Closed L Mon, 2 weeks in Aug
🍴 L from £39, D from £44, Wine from £15
🚭 No pipes
🚇 Sloane Square

L'ESCARGOT—THE GROUND FLOOR RESTAURANT ❀ ❀

Map 246 J4
48 Greek Street W1D 4EF
Tel 020 7439 7474

A Soho landmark, L'Escargot has been serving classy French cuisine since 1927. This was the first restaurant to offer fresh snails in Britain and they're still a speciality. Alongside starters such as lobster *velouté* or oxtail *bouillon*, you might find snail ravioli accompanied by parsley purée. Fine art decorates the walls—the collection includes original works by Joan Miró, Henri Matisse, David Hockney and Andy Warhol.

🕐 12.15–2.15, 6–11.30. Closed L Sat, Sun, 25–26 Dec, 1 Jan
🍴 L from £30, D from £34, Wine from £14
🚭 No pipes
🚇 Tottenham Court Road, Leicester Square

THE FIFTH FLOOR RESTAURANT ❀ ❀

Map 245 F6
Harvey Nichols, Knightsbridge SW1X 7RJ
Tel 020 7235 5250

There are fabulous views over Knightsbridge from this excellent chic department store restaurant. The lighting system mimics the outside conditions, thus creating the atmosphere of the time of day. The menu is Modern European and sprinkled with luxury dishes, with prices to match, although it is supplemented by lower-priced set menus. Roast lamb with roasted tomatoes and an olive and potato jus, or roast salmon with sautéed potatoes and truffle cabbage sauce are two possible combinations. The heavyweight international wine list is supplemented by a less daunting smaller list.

🕐 12–3, 6–11. Closed D Sun, 25–26 Dec
🍴 L from £44, D from £50, Wine from £13.50
🚭 Section, no pipes
🚇 Knightsbridge

FIRE STATION ❀

Map 246 G7
150 Waterloo Road SE1 8SB
Tel 020 7620 2226

A converted Edwardian fire station that retains many of its trappings. The interesting menu from the open kitchen includes dishes such as avocado Caesar salad, baked cod with cheese polenta, roast pork with sticky rice and *pak choi*. There are also imaginative midweek and Sunday set-price lunches and you can eat out on the patio. The bar is noisy at the front but has a good selection of real ales.

🕐 Mon–Fri 11–11, Sat 12–11, Sun 12–10.30
🍴 L from £22, D from £27, Wine from £10.95
🚭 No pipes or cigars
🚇 Waterloo

FISH HOEK ❀

Map 244 off C7
8 Elliott Road W4 1PE
Tel 020 8742 0766

If you've always had a hankering to try white steenbras or Transkei musselcracker, now's your chance. This laid-back South African restaurant specializes in seafood, and imports fish from around the world. Chatty staff are happy to guide you through the more exotic choices, but there are plenty of familiar names: seared organic Irish salmon with tomato chutney, for example, or Shetland Island black mussels steamed in Chenin Blanc, lime leaves and chives. Not to be missed are the huge prawns in garlic

HAKKASAN ❀❀❀
Map 246 J4
8 Hanway Place W1T 1HD
Tel 020 7927 7000
One of the most stylish restaurants in London, with exceptional Chinese cuisine. A winding marble staircase leads to a lobby lined with pink orchids and incense bowls; the spacious dining area is partitioned with dark wood lattice screens. The *dim sum* platter is a highlight at lunch; fried rice with dried shrimp, Chinese sausage and shiitake mushrooms served in a lotus leaf is also worth a try. Nice cocktails.

🕐 12–3, 6–12. Closed 25–26 Dec
🍴 L from £60, D from £120, Wine from £22
🚇 Tottenham Court Road

butter. The wine list is full of South African specials.

🕐 12–2.30, 6–10.30. Closed Mon, 24 Dec–2 Jan
🍴 L from £20, D from £35, Wine from £13.50
🚭 Section, no pipes or cigars
🚇 Turnham Green

LE GAVROCHE RESTAURANT ❀❀❀❀
Map 245 G5
43 Upper Brook Street W1K 7QR
Tel 020 7408 0881
No other restaurant in Britain is as faithful to classic French tradition as the long-established Le Gavroche, the name now synonymous with the French Roux brothers. Tables are set with crystal and silver and the staff are professional and well informed. Dishes include scallops baked in their shells and perfumed with truffles; lobster mousse with caviar and champagne sauce; belly, loin, feet and ears of organic pork on a cheese mash; and whole baked sea bass stuffed with fennel and wild rice. Desserts include a choice of soufflées and the famous Roux brothers' ice creams and sorbets. One of the most comprehensive wine lists in London.

🕐 12–2, 7–11. Closed Sun, L Sat, 25–26 Dec, 1 Jan, public hols
🍴 L from £90, D from £110, Wine from £20
🚭 No pipes or cigars
🚇 Marble Arch

GREEN OLIVE ❀❀
Map 244 D3
5 Warwick Place W9 2PX
Tel 020 7289 2469
Hidden away down a quiet side street in the smart district of Maida Vale, the Green Olive offers a great value set-price menu of fine modern Italian dishes. A simple starter of ricotta ravioli with wild mushrooms is wonderfully robust, and the main dishes are impeccably presented. Your choice might include succulent roast lamb with an aubergine (eggplant) and mozzarella timbale, or monkfish wrapped in Parma ham and sautéed mushrooms and baby carrots. No children under five.

🕐 12–3, 6.30–11. Closed 24–26 Dec, Good Fri, public hols
🍴 L from £20, D from £35, Wine from £13.50
🚭 No pipes or cigars
🚇 Warwick Avenue

THE IVY ❀
Map 246 J4
1 West Street, Covent Garden WC2H 9NQ
Tel 020 7836 4751

There's still a buzz at the Ivy; people clearly want to be heard as well as seen here. In the heart of theatreland, the V-shaped building opens into a small bar, which leads on to the main room with leaded windows and coloured glass. The menu offers simple dishes, from a snack to a main meal, with international influences.

🕐 12–3, 5.30–12. Closed L 27 Dec, D 24 Dec, 25–26 Dec, 1 Jan, Aug public hol
🍴 L from £37, D from £48, Wine from £17
🚇 Leicester Square, Covent Garden

J. SHEEKEY ❀❀
Map 246 J4
St. Martin's Court WC2N 4AL
Tel 020 7240 2565

This much-loved establishment, off the beaten track in theatreland, is in a class of its own when it comes to fish. The freshness of the catch is second to none. Look for seaweed risotto, seared tuna with fennel and Sicilian tomato salad, and smoked anchovy with slow-

baked beetroot and horseradish cream. Oak panelling, portraits of theatre stars and bench seating set the scene. Reserve well in advance.

🕐 12–3, 5.30–12. Closed D 24 Dec, 25–26 Dec, 1 Jan, public hols
🍴 L from £28, D from £40, Wine from £12.75
🚭 No pipes or cigars
🚇 Leicester Square

JUST ST. JAMES ❀❀
Map 245 H5
12 St. James's Street SW1A 1ER
Tel 020 7976 2222
In this former bank, whose customers have included Napoleon III and William Pitt the Younger, the ground floor now houses an airy restaurant with suede seating and cushions in bright, earthy tones. Lit by large storm lanterns, tables are surrounded by swathes of open space. The food is simple and eye-catching, with modern British dishes including duck with raspberries, tarragon and celeriac (celery root) mash or venison with red cabbage, apples and elderberries with game jus.

🕐 12–3, 6–11. Closed D Sun, 25–26 Dec
🍴 L from £33, D from £50, Wine from £13.50
🚭 No pipes or cigars
🚇 Green Park

KAI MAYFAIR ❀
Map 245 G5
65 South Audley Street W1K 2QU
Tel 020 7493 8988
An elegant restaurant with plenty of marble and luxurious

EATING

furnishings. There's a touch of poetry to the whimsical, finely detailed menu at this Chinese restaurant. Worth noting are the crispy strips of smoked chicken listed as 'Flavours of the Smoking Phoenix' and a luxurious broth of abalone and shark's fin known as 'Buddha Jumps Over the Wall', which requires five day's notice and costs around £100.

🕐 12–2.15, 6.30–11. Closed 25–26 Dec, 1 Jan
🍽 L from £40, D from £60, Wine from £19
🚇 Marble Arch

KEN LO'S MEMORIES OF CHINA ❀❀
Map 245 G7
67 Ebury Street SW1W 0NZ
Tel 020 7730 7734
Bamboo wallpaper and flooring contrast with red seating and grey slate screens. The cooking is Pekinese and Szechuan—some of the best in London—and speciality dishes are all beautifully prepared. Try fragrant braised aubergine (eggplant), sautéed salt and pepper prawns and fresh scallops steamed in their shells with black bean sauce, or the more well-known Imperial Peking duck. Best of all is the tender tasty lobster or handmade noodles with stir-fried lobster, ginger and spring onion—with chopsticks or your fingers.
🕐 12–2.15, 7–11. Closed L Sun, 25 Dec, public hols
🍽 L from £48, D from £50, Wine from £20
🚭 No pipes or cigars
🚇 Sloane Square, Victoria

LEVANT ❀❀
Map 245 G4
Jason Court, 76 Wigmore Street W1H 9DQ
Tel 020 7224 1111
The perfume of roses drifts up the stairs to greet you at this

KENSINGTON PLACE ❀❀
Map 244 C5
201–209 Kensington Church Street W8 7LX
Tel 020 7727 3184
This 1980s innovator rightly retains many fans, most in the media and showbiz world. The open-plan seating creates quite a buzz, though the retro furniture is too compactly arranged. The menu is global and unpretentious and includes well-made pig's feet terrine with piccalilli, and wild salmon with a gooseberry sabayon. The wine list offers plenty of depth and service is congenial.
🕐 12–3, 6.30–10.15. Closed 24–27 Dec
🍽 L from £33, D from £49, Wine from £13.50
🚇 Notting Hill Gate

Lebanese restaurant. Downstairs it is modern with polished stone floors and subtle lighting. Mezze selections include spicy Armenian sausages, fried eggplant with pomegranate dressing, and of course hummus and falafel. Made to share, they're eaten with warm pita bread. Staff are happy to guide newcomers, and a belly dancer or tarot card reader occasionally pops in.
🕐 12–11.30. Closed 25–26 Dec, 1 Jan
🍽 L from £37, D from £39, Wine from £14
🚇 Bond Street

MATSURI ❀
Map 245 H5
15 Bury Street SW1Y 6AL
Tel 020 7839 1101

This sophisticated Japanese restaurant occupies a basement divided into small dining areas, a sushi bar (some of the best in London), and teppan yaki

tables, where chefs cook to order before you raw slivers of tuna, salmon, sea bass, lobster tail and sirloin steak. Clear soup with chicken, prawn, tofu, lemongrass and coriander, and prawn and vegetable tempura all use fresh quality ingredients. Finish off your meal with a pot of green tea.
🕐 12–2.30, 6–10.30. Closed public hols
🍽 L from £30, D from £70, Wine from £14
🚇 Green Park

MELA ❀
Map 246 J4
152–156 Shaftesbury Avenue WC2H 8HL
Tel 020 7836 8635

An unusual Indian restaurant that uses traditional Indian cooking methods and spices and combines them with Western ingredients—for example, the *burra champ madiri*, made with lamb soaked overnight in rum and then spiced with garlic, *byadgi* chillies, fenugreek leaves and mustard. All dishes are freshly prepared, and service is friendly and prompt. Simple, minimalist décor.
🕐 12–5.30, Sat and Sun 12–11.45. Closed L 25 Dec, 26 Dec
🍽 L from £25, D from £50, Wine from £12
🚬 Section
🚇 Leicester Square

MITSUKOSHI ❀
Map 245 J5
Dorland House, 14–20 Lower Regent Street SW1Y 4PH
Tel 020 7930 0317
Established in 1985 in the basement of its namesake Japanese department store, this is an elegant restaurant with a separate sushi bar and two private dining rooms with minimal décor and classical music. Lunchtimes offer value in the form of *bento* boxes

EATING

with compartments containing several different dishes. The tempura here is light and fresh, as is the sashimi of raw tuna and salmon. Service is polite and efficient from a uniformed all-female team.

🕐 12–3, 6–9.30. Closed 25–26 Dec, 1 Jan, Easter Sun
🍴 L from £70, D from £70, Wine from £12
🚭 Section, no pipes or cigars
🚇 Piccadilly Circus

MON PLAISIR ✽ ✽

Map 246 J4
21 Monmouth Street WC2H 9DD
Tel 020 7836 7243

At this restaurant run by the same family for 50 years, an unassuming entrance leads to a maze of comfortable rooms, including a mezzanine-style loft, brightly decked with modern abstract paintings. The menu mixes classics such as *cassoulet d'escargots* and *coquilles St.-Jacques* with more contemporary fare such as steamed sea bass on a pea and mint risotto with *foie gras* sauce. Bustling, resolutely French service with its closely packed tables creating a Gallic atmosphere.

🕐 12–2.15, 5.45–11.15. Closed Sun, L Sat, 25–26 Dec, 1 Jan, public hols
🍴 L from £28, D from £50, Wine from £16
🚭 No pipes or cigars
🚇 Covent Garden, Leicester Square

MOSAICO ✽

Map 245 H5
13 Albermarle Street W1X 3HA
Tel 020 7409 1011

Mosaico is a stylish traditional Italian restaurant with a bar area, huge flower arrangements, green leather seating and lots of pale wood. The menu is in Italian with English translations and is dotted with some of the most popular Italian dishes: veal Milanese

MORO ✽ ✽

Map 246 L2
34–36 Exmouth Market EC1R 4QE
Tel 020 7833 8336

Value for money is the key at this lively and always busy Spanish/North African restaurant. Many of the dishes are

inspired by the wood-fired oven, from simple grilled chicory with ham and sherry vinegar to roasted turbot with roast beetroot lentils and *churrasco* sauce. A warm goat's cheese with pine nuts, raisins and orange blossom water in filo pastry provides an unusual end to the meal. The wine list is largely Spanish and reasonably priced.

🕐 12.30–2.30, 7–10.30. Closed L Sat, Sun, 25–26 Dec, 1 Jan, public hols
🍴 L from £44, D from £53, Wine from £11
🚭 No pipes or cigars
🚇 Farringdon, Angel

with fresh tomato and rocket, linguine with clams in white wine and olives, and saffron risotto with asparagus tips. The wines are all Italian.

mosaico
RISTORANTE

🕐 12–2.30, 6.30–10.45. Closed Sun
🍴 L from £40, D from £70, Wine from £14
🚇 Bond Street

NEW WORLD ✽

Map 246 J4
1 Gerrard Place W1D 5PA
Tel 020 7434 2508

This cavernous, three-floor, Hong Kong-style restaurant in the heart of Chinatown draws crowds to its popular daily *dim sum* ritual (*11–6*). Décor of traditional reds and golds, Chinese-style lanterns and speedy service from a posse of waitresses circulating the floor with steaming carts full of delicious morsels of food set the tone. You may have to wait for a table as the pace is non-stop. It's noisy, unpretentious and fun.

🕐 11–11.45. Closed 25–26 Dec
🍴 L from £14, D from £30, Wine from £10.50
🚭 Section
🚇 Leicester Square, Piccadilly Circus

NOBLE ROT ✽ ✽

Map 245 H4
3–5 Mill Street W1S 2AU
Tel 020 7629 8877

This contemporary restaurant takes its name from the mould which forms on over-ripe grapes and produces the richness of certain sweet wines. Not surprising, then, that it claims to feature one of the largest selection of sweet wines in Britain. Modern British and Modern European dishes include halibut with lobster, smoked eel risotto, or Pinot Noir and wild mushroom lasagne.

🕐 12–3, 6–11. Closed L Sat, Sun, 25 Dec, 1 Jan, public hols
🍴 L from £32, D from £68, Wine from £16
🚇 Oxford Circus

1 LOMBARD STREET—THE BRASSERIE ✽ ✽

Map 247 N4
1 Lombard Street EC3V 9AA
Tel 020 7929 6611

This glass-domed brasserie in the heart of the City buzzes with life. The cooking takes the best from an eclectic sweep of European traditions: roast loin of suckling pig, rolled and stuffed with a mushroom and bread stuffing on a bed of warm cabbage salad. Try the

EATING

classic crème caramel, spiced up with roasted peaches and glazed pistachios.

🕐 11.30–3, 6–10. Closed Sat, Sun, 25–26 Dec, 1 Jan, public hols
🍴 L/D from £40, Wine from £14
🚭 No pipes
Ⓜ Bank

1 LOMBARD STREET—THE FINE DINING RESTAURANT ❀❀

Map 247 N4
1 Lombard Street EC3V 9AA
Tel 020 7929 6611

A typical City building with large-scale windows, opposite the Bank of England. Inside there's a busy, informal brasserie, where City workers drink wine, relax and network. There is a fine dining area in the quiet back room, with formal service. The cooking is primarily French, with dishes such as seared *foie gras* with muscatel grapes in Armagnac; roasted turbot on the bone with woodland mushroom and herb ragoût, and *feuillantine* of caramelized Granny Smith apples with Guinness ice cream and glazed hazelnuts.

🕐 11.30–3, 6–10. Closed Sat, Sun, 25–26 Dec, 1 Jan, public hols
🍴 L from £64, D from £102, Wine from £14
🚭 No pipes
Ⓜ Bank

L'ORANGER ❀❀

Map 245 H5
5 St. James's Street SW1A 1EF
Tel 020 7839 3774

Here natural light spills on to the modern furnishings from a large skylight, and there's a courtyard in summer. Fish, prepared and presented simply, is the focus, and desserts are of a high standard. The wine list is predominantly French but can be considered rather pricey. No children under six.

🕐 12–2.30, 6.30–10.45. Closed L Sat,

ORRERY ❀❀❀

Map 245 G3
55–57 Marylebone High Street
W1M 3AE
Tel 020 7616 8000

Orrery is in the heart of Marylebone and one of the most beautiful and romantic restaurants in London, with huge, round windows and long rows of tables attended by professional French staff. The French menu has all the wealth of the dishes but is accessibly priced. Robust dishes are best, such as the terrine of *foie gras* with Sauternes *gelée*, or the delicate fillet of bream with roast artichokes and truffles. Saddle of venison with black pudding and tagine of pigeon are consistently good.

🕐 12–2.45, 7–10.45. Closed 25–26 Dec, 1 Jan, Good Fri
🍴 L from £46, D from £67, Wine from £12
🚭 No pipes
Ⓜ Baker Street, Regents Park

Sun, 25–26 Dec, public hols, one week in Aug
🍴 L from £44, D from £90, Wine from £26
🚭 No pipes or cigars
Ⓜ Green Park

ORSINO ❀

Map 244 off C5
119 Portland Road W11 4LN
Tel 020 7221 3299

Orsino is a slice of Italy in Holland Park, with terracotta walls and chic wooden blinds. The pizza and pasta dishes complete the experience. Entrées might include calves' liver with artichokes or spinach polenta with mushrooms and cream, while the wine list is mostly Italian. The special menus are good value for money.

🕐 12–11.30. Closed 24–25 Dec
🍴 L from £29, D from £38, Wine from £14
🚭 Section, no pipes or cigars
Ⓜ Holland Park

ORSO RESTAURANT ❀

Map 246 K4
27 Wellington Street WC2E 7DB
Tel 020 7240 5269

Covent Garden cellar restaurant with designer-free interior. A bilingual menu, broadly

Tuscan, offers seasonal cooking (and there are also low-priced pre-theatre and Saturday and Sunday lunch menus). Small pizzas (perhaps with wild mushrooms, goat's cheese and garlic), penne with courgettes (zucchini), basil and pecorino cheese, calves' liver with endive and pancetta and sardines dusted with Parmesan are all simply presented on colourful Italian pottery.

🕐 12–11.45. Closed 24–25 Dec
🍴 L from £28, D from £40, Wine from £14
🚭 Section, no pipes or cigars
Ⓜ Covent Garden
🚌 6, 9, 13, 23, 77A

THE OXO TOWER RESTAURANT ❀❀

Map 246 L5
8th Floor, Oxo Tower Wharf, Barge House Street SE1 9PH
Tel 020 7803 3888

With its amazing views through floor-to-ceiling windows overlooking the River Thames and the City, this cubed tower tends to impress all those who visit. Cuisine is modern and British in style, but not outlandish, with dishes such as lobster, tomato and basil jelly with Sevruga caviar and pan-fried veal sweetbreads with a sauce of cep mushrooms, parsley and lemon oil. Desserts might include unusual coconut rice pudding with rosewater ice cream.

EATING

ⓒ 12–3, 6–11.30. Closed 25–26 Dec
Ⓛ L from £60, D from £64, Wine from £14
Ⓢ No pipes
Ⓜ Blackfriars

OZER ❀❀
Map 245 H3
5 Langham Place W1N 7DD
Tel 020 7323 0505

Huseyin Ozer's restaurant is stylish and contemporary, with a rich bold interior tempered with neutral linens, cool tiles and intricate lighting. Dishes are Mediterranean, but with strong North African and Middle Eastern accents. A wide choice of menus and dishes makes selecting tricky as they cover grills, seafood, casseroles, vegetarian, set menus, hot or cold mezzes as either starters or main courses.
ⓒ 12–12
Ⓛ L from £20, D from £40, Wine from £12.50
Ⓢ Section
Ⓜ Oxford Circus

THE PEOPLE'S PALACE ❀
Map 246 K5
Royal Festival Hall, Belvedere Road
SE1 8XX
Tel 020 7928 9999

With a floor-to-ceiling window overlooking the River Thames from the South Bank, this spacious, minimalist restaurant is a great place to spend the evening. There's a fusion of

contemporary and traditional British cooking in dishes such as warm Stilton and red onion tart or roast venison loin and chicken mousse in fig wine jus.
ⓒ 12–3, 5.30–11
Ⓛ L from £25, D from £49, Wine from £14.50
Ⓢ Section
Ⓜ Waterloo

THE PORTRAIT RESTAURANT ❀
Map 246 J5
National Portrait Gallery, St. Martins Place WC2H 0HE
Tel 020 7312 2490
This unique restaurant at the top of the National Portrait Gallery (see pages 110–111) offers chic British cuisine along with some of the best views in London. Staple British classics are given a modern interpretation and prepared with skill and precision. The menu changes frequently but may include ham hock and flat parsley terrine, pot roast lamb shank with lentils and mashed potato, and prune and Armagnac tart.
ⓒ 11.45–2.45, 5.30–8.30. Closed D Fri–Wed, 25–26 Dec
Ⓛ L from £50, D from £35, Wine from £11
Ⓢ
Ⓜ Leicester Square, Trafalgar Square

QUAGLINO'S ❀
Map 245 H5
16 Bury Street SW1Y 6AJ
Tel 020 7930 6767

Quaglino's may no longer be at the cutting edge of British cuisine, but it still has its sexy cigarette girls and a regularly changing menu, offering Parisian-style brasserie food with some new innovations. Fixed-price menus include squid and *chorizo* salad, and main dishes such as chicken bourgignon served with garlic mashed potatoes.

ⓒ 12–3, 5.30–12. Closed L 26 and 31 Dec, 25 Dec, 1 Jan
Ⓛ L from £33, D from £42, Wine from £14
Ⓜ Green Park

RASA SUMUDRA ❀❀
Map 246 J3
5 Charlotte Street W1P 1HD
Tel 020 7637 0222
The name means 'a taste of the ocean', and this authentic Indian restaurant specializes in the cuisine of the home cooking of the coastal state of Kerala in southwest India, particularly fish and seafood. The exterior is hard to miss, with its bold pink, and the interior is decorated with bright silks and vibrant oil paintings. Try a crab *varuthathu* cooked dry with ginger, curry leaves, chilli and mustard seeds accompanied by rice tossed in lemon juice, curry leaves and mustard seeds.
ⓒ 12–3, 6–10.30. Closed L Sun, 2 weeks Dec
Ⓛ L from £45, D from £27, Wine from £10.50
Ⓢ
Ⓜ Tottenham Court Road, Goodge Street

THE RED CUBE ❀
Map 246 J4
1 Leicester Place, Leicester Square WC2H 7BP
Tel 020 7287 0101
Bold, red chequered walls and natural wooden floors set the scene for a modern, eclectic brand of cooking. Dishes might include wild mushroom lasagne with truffle oil and scallops with spicy red lentils and cucumber mint sauce.
ⓒ 6–1. Closed L all week, Sun, Mon
Ⓛ D from £58, Wine from £11.50
Ⓜ Leicester Square

RESTAURANT GORDON RAMSAY ❀❀❀❀❀
Map 245 off F8
68 Royal Hospital Road SW3 4HP
Tel 020 7352 4441
Attention to detail characterizes the whole of the slick operation here. There's an abundance of staff plus plenty of stylish features, such as salted and unsalted butter served on silver and marble plates, with a sprinkling of pepper on the salted. This is the mothership of famous British chef Gordon Ramsay's growing empire. Try a warm salad of caramelized calves'

ST. JOHN ✤✤
Map 246 M3
26 St. John Street EC1M 4AY
Tel 020 7251 0848

Approached through an arch-way and big iron gates, with a café/bakery below, this restaurant has a menu that nods to traditional British meat cuisine and has a pig motif with butchery markings. Don't come anywhere near it if you're vegetarian or have leanings in that direction. There's plenty of offal—salted kid's liver, rabbit's heart, kid-neys and liver—and unusual ingredients such as smoked eel with bacon and mash, roast bone marrow and tripe, sausage and chickpeas. If the meat-fest gets too much, you could go for langoustine with mayonnaise, or standard cod and chips.

⏰ 12–3, 6–11. Closed L Sat, Sun, 25–26 Dec, 1 Jan, Easter
🍽 L from £40, D from £50, Wine from £14
Ⓢ Farringdon, Barbican, Chancery Lane

sweetbreads with sautéed artichokes, grilled asparagus, mustard and honey vinaigrette. Desserts include a melt-in-the-mouth, liquid-centred choco-late fondant with milk mousse and ice cream.

⏰ 12–2.15, 6.30–11. Closed Sat, Sun, 2 weeks Christmas and New Year, public hols
🍽 L from £70, D from £130, Wine from £18
Ⓢ No pipes or cigars
Ⓢ Sloane Square

RESTAURANT TWENTYFOUR ✤✤
Map 247 N4
Tower 42, Old Broad Street EC2N 1HQ
Tel 020 7877 2424

Surrounded, but not over-looked by offices, banks and Liverpool Street railway station, this modern restaurant on the 24th floor of the NatWest Tower (once the tallest build-ing in London) has panoramic views across the City. Friendly, casually dressed staff serve starters such as sweetbread and asparagus millefeuille, and main courses such as pan-fried sea bass with crushed potato, fennel and green beans.

⏰ 11.45–2.30, 6–9. Closed Sat, Sun, 24 Dec–2 Jan
🍽 L from £60, D from £78, Wine from £14
Ⓢ No pipes or cigars
Ⓢ Bank, Liverpool Street

THE RIVER CAFÉ ✤✤✤
Map 244 off C7
Thames Wharf, Rainville Road
W6 9HA
Tel 020 7386 4200

At the River Café you will be served some of the most authentic Italian food in London by staff selected for their personality above every-thing else. The twice-daily changing menu might include spaghetti with crabmeat, olive oil and lemon, or squid char-grilled with chilli and served on rocket. Whole pigeon is cooked in the wood oven and accom-panied by roasted pumpkin, fennel, celeriac (celery root) and carrots. Desserts are typi-cally Italian, such as panacotta or tiramisu.

⏰ 12.30–2.30, 7–9.15. Closed D Sun, 22 Dec–3 Jan, Easter, public hols
🍽 L from £40, D from £66, Wine from £10.50
Ⓢ No pipes or cigars
Ⓢ Hammersmith (10-minute walk)

SALLOOS RESTAURANT ✤
Map 245 G6
62–64 Kinnerton Street SW1X 8ER
Tel 020 7235 4444

Salloos is a long-established, family-run Pakistani restaurant tucked away in a secluded Belgravia mews. The food is prepared to order, so expect up to a 30-minute wait. The exquisite *aloo paratha* is a spinach-based dish, a blend of the subtle and the spicy, and could be followed by melt-in-the-mouth charcoal grilled kebabs. House specialities such as the king prawn *karahi* come with very good basmati rice cooked with a mildly

SMITHS OF SMITHFIELD ✤✤
Map 246 L3
Top Floor, 66–67 Charterhouse Street EC1M 6HJ
Tel 020 7251 7950

This sizeable building started life as a warehouse in around 1886 before the completion of the Smithfield Meat Market that lies next door. The upper floors have panoramic views that take in the City, St. Paul's Cathedral and the Old Bailey (see pages 118 and 102). The food is organic and additive-free and includes pumpkin tortellini with oregano and Parmesan crisps and Welsh chicken with mushroom ravioli, tarragon and mustard sauce.

⏰ 12–3, 6.30–11, Sun 12–4, 7–10. Closed L Sat, 25–26 Dec, 1 Jan
🍽 L from £40, D from £52, Wine from £13
Ⓢ Farringdon, Barbican, Chancery Lane

spiced stock. No children under six.

⏰ 12–2.30, 7–11.15. Closed Sun, 25–26 Dec, public hols
🍽 L from £32, D from £46, Wine from £14.50
Ⓢ No pipes or cigars
Ⓢ Knightsbridge

SANTINI ✤✤
Map 245 G7
29 Ebury Street SW1W 0NZ
Tel 020 7730 4094

A chic and elegant Italian restaurant, with light marble floors and slatted blinds, where service matches the sophistication of the surround-ings. Start with porcini mush-room risotto, then tuck in to fresh tuna marinated in lemon, capers and herbs, and finish up with *sfogliatelle di mele* (flaky apple pastry).

⏰ 12.30–2.30, 6.30–11. Closed L Sat–Sun, 25–26 Dec, 1 Jan, Easter Sun
🍽 L from £52, D from £66, Wine from £13
Ⓢ No pipes
Ⓢ Victoria

SIMPLY NICO ✤
Map 245 H7
48a Rochester Row SW1P 1JU
Tel 020 7630 8061

Among this famous restau-rant's strengths are a romantic

Parisian atmosphere and furnishings to match. *Terrine de campagne*, salmon and crab fishcakes, and pear and almond tart all pass muster without the forceful rustic flavours that you might expect of a true French bistro.

🕐 12–2.30, 6–10.30. Closed L Sat, Sun, 25–26 Dec, Easter
🍴 L from £34, D from £44, Wine from £13
🚭 No pipes or cigars
🚇 Victoria

SIX-13 ❀
Map 245 G4
19 Wigmore Street W1H 9LA
Tel 020 7629 6133
Named after the 613 Jewish disciplines, this popular restaurant balances well-known and kosher specialities. The interior has antique marble, solid Mocassar ebony and plush velvet seating. Main courses encompass roast duck with cherry jus, rib of veal with sage risotto and courgette (zucchini) purée, salt beef sauerkraut and paprika-spiked bean broth. The desserts are equally intriguing concoctions.
🕐 12–2.30, 5.30–10.30. Closed Fri (Sat summer), L Sat winter, 25 Dec, 1 Jan, Jewish holidays
🍴 L from £40, D from £60, Wine from £16
🚇 Oxford Circus, Bond Street

LA SPIGHETTA ❀
Map 245 G3
43 Blandford Street W1H 3AE
Tel 020 7486 7340
An informal Italian restaurant, La Spighetta offers the usual mix of pizza and pasta, but the cooking is a cut above the rest. The wood-burning pizza oven churns out a selection of tasty pizzas, while the extensive pasta section and a choice of risotto dishes complete the menu. Terracotta-tiled flooring and white walls.

🕐 12–2.30, 6.30–10.30. Closed L Sun, 25–26 Dec, 1 Jan, Easter, public hols
🍴 L from £36, D from £40, Wine from £13
🚭 Section, no pipes or cigars
🚇 Baker Street

STRATFORDS ❀
Map 244 C7
7 Stratford Road W8 6RF
Tel 020 7937 6388
The restaurant and shop next door to the restaurant used to be a dairy farm until the late 1920s. Today's venue has soft candlelight at night, discreet table service and French cooking prepared to your choice, majoring in fish. This may be presented grilled or poached with roast garlic, butter sauce or tomato and fresh basil sauce. Dishes of the day can include monkfish or skate with capers and butter.

🕐 12–3, 6–11. Closed 25–26 Dec, 1 Jan
🍴 L from £23, D from £41, Wine from £11
🚭 No pipes
🚇 High Street Kensington

TAJINE ❀
Map 245 G3
7a Dorset Street W1H 3FE
Tel 020 7935 1545
As you would expect from the name, this Moroccan restaurant serves the eponymous dish among its main courses. Other main dishes include slow-cooked chicken and lamb with garlic, cumin and coriander. Friendly staff and a warm, welcoming atmosphere. The charcoal grill is visible through a glass wall.
🕐 12–3, 6–11. Closed L Sat, Sun
🍴 L from £14, D from £30, Wine from £10.50
🚇 Baker Street

TAMARIND ❀ ❀
Map 245 G5
20 Queen Street W1J 5PR
Tel 020 7629 3561

The gold pillars, copper place settings and solid leather chairs at Tamarind make a stylish basement venue for exquisite Indian food at affordable prices. Dishes might include tandoori prawns and scallops on a salad of sour grapes. The braised lamb with onions, spinach and five-spice sauce is the best in London. The choices of dessert are a

little bizarre, with dumplings of milk and semolina and *gajar ka halwa*, which can best be described as a type of exotic carrot cake. No children under 10.
🕐 12–2.45, 6–11.15. Closed L Sat, 25–26 Dec, 1 Jan
🍴 L from £29, D from £64, Wine from £14
🚭 No pipes or cigars
🚇 Green Park

TATSUSO RESTAURANT ❀
Map 247 N3
32 Broadgate Circle EC2M 2QS
Tel 020 7638 5863
On the basement floor of the Broadgate Circle, next to Liverpool Street Underground station, Tatsuso serves authentic Japanese food. Upstairs is the teppan-yaki dining room, with chefs cooking at the table in front of the customers, and downstairs is the more traditional Japanese à la carte and separate sushi bar—which has become very popular in recent years. An appetizer here might be lightly breaded scallops marinated in vinegar with a seaweed salad and thin strips of beef with a main course of *yakitori*—skewered pieces of grilled chicken with a soy-based sauce.
🕐 11.30–2.30, 6–10. Closed Sat, Sun, 25–26 Dec, 1 Jan, public hols
🍴 L from £76, D from £100, Wine from £15
🚭 No pipes
🚇 Liverpool Street

EATING

LA TROUVAILLE ✽✽
Map 245 H4
12a Newburgh Street W1F 3RR
Tel 020 7287 8488
A busy, bustling French bistro offering good value and rustic French cooking with intense flavours. Dishes range from poached ox tongue with a leek and truffle salad to squid *cassoulet* (a type of stew) to leg of rabbit confit with coffee sauce and parsnip purée. For dessert you might be able to enjoy *pot au chocolat* or traditional French *crème caramel*.
🕐 12–3, 6–11. Closed Sun, 25–26 Dec, public hols
🍽 L from £42, D from £50, Wine from £12
🚫 No pipes or cigars
🚇 Oxford Circus

VAMA ✽
Map 245 F8
438 King's Road SW10 0LJ
Tel 020 7351 4118

At Vama the cuisine is Northwest Frontier—a specialized style from the country regions of the Himalayas, with most dishes finished in the clay oven to give an authentic taste of charcoal cooking. It's a chic and authentic Indian restaurant, where the staff are charming and the food spicy and vibrant. It's also a good place for star-spotting as TV and media types are often seen here.
🕐 12–3, 6.30–11. Closed 25–26 Dec, 1 Jan
🍽 L from £14, D from £48, Wine from £13
🚇 Sloane Square

VEERASWAMY RESTAURANT ✽
Map 245 H5
Victory House, 99 Regent Street W1B 4RS
Tel 020 7734 1401
The oldest Indian restaurant in London has been given a

contemporary spin. Multi-hued lacquered walls with a creative use of glass, chrome and gold leaf add to the smart, yet informal surroundings. The menu picks up on southern and northern Indian specialities. A starter of mussels in coconut and ginger might be followed by apple *dopiaza*, a tender lamb dish of caramelized onion and apples.
🕐 12–2.30, 5.30–11.30. Closed D 25 Dec
🍽 L from £25, D from £48, Wine from £15
🚫 No pipes or cigars
🚇 Piccadilly Circus

WILTONS ✽✽
Map 245 H5
55 Jermyn Street SW1Y 6LX
Tel 020 7629 9955
Wiltons is an old-established British conservative gem with thoroughly professional service. Interconnecting rooms offer a mix of secluded booths and tables, plush upholstery, dark wood panelling and walls covered in prints and photographs. Beluga caviar, pâté de *foie gras* Strasbourg, lobster Thermidor, grills and traditional British sherry trifle are all available, as well as lighter, more up to the minute dishes. British visitors should note that Switch cards are not accepted.
🕐 12–2.30, 6.30–10.30. Closed Sat, 25 Dec–1 Jan
🍽 L from £34, D from £48, Wine from £21
🚫 No pipes
🚇 Green Park

YMING ✽✽
Map 246 J4
35–36 Greek Street W1D 5DL
Tel 020 7734 2721
A simple, elegant and home-from-home Chinese restaurant that creates both traditional and classic dishes with style and flavour. The

menu covers Mongolian, Szechuan and Hunan dishes.
🕐 12–11.45. Closed Sun (except Chinese New Year; check in advance for dates), 25–26 Dec, 1 Jan
🍽 L from £30, D from £21, Wine from £10
🚫 Section
🚇 Piccadilly Circus

YUMI RESTAURANT ✽✽
Map 245 G4
110 George Street W1V 8NX
Tel 020 7935 8320
Yumi is typically Japanese in its use of minimalist surroundings, with a sushi bar and the usual private rooms in both the main restaurant and the basement. The food is mostly along the familiar Japanese lines of sushi, sashimi, tempura and grilled beef or chicken with *teriyaki* sauce, although the chef's recommendations often offer something more unusual.
🕐 5.30–10.30. Closed L
🍽 L from £40, D from £70, Wine from £13
🚇 Marble Arch

ZAFFERANO ✽✽✽
Map 245 F6
15 Lowndes Street SW1X 9EY
Tel 020 7235 5800

Hidden away behind fashionable Sloane Street, this chic Italian restaurant attracts a well-heeled crowd of tourists and shoppers. Starters might include skate salad and thinly sliced cured venison with celeriac (celery root). For the main course there are unusual pasta options typified by pheasant ravioli with rosemary, as well as plenty of meat and fish dishes.
🕐 12–2.30, 7–11. Closed 25–26 Dec, 1 Jan, public hols
🍽 L from £42, D from £74, Wine from £14
🚫 No pipes or cigars
🚇 Knightsbridge

EATING

Pubs

Many pubs now have separate restaurants, as well as bar areas, where food is served. The prices given are for bar meals (available at lunchtimes and evenings) and dinner (D) in the restaurant; both are for two people.

THE ADMIRAL CODRINGTON
Map 244 F7
17 Mossop Street SW3 2LY
Tel 020 7581 0005
Affectionately known as The Cod, this old Chelsea pub now incorporates a smart but homelike restaurant. Starters might include wild mushroom tartlet, *foie gras* and chicken liver parfait, and main choices such as confit rabbit terrine or crispy salmon fishcake. In the separate bar, which has its own distinct identity, you can have a meal such as home-made linguini with fresh salmon or just a sandwich or filled ciabatta bread. Garden with food served outside.
🕐 11.30–11 (Sun 12–10.30).
Restaurant: 12–2.30, 7–10.30
🍽 Bar meals from £24, D from £60
🚇 South Kensington

THE ANCHOR
Map 247 M5
Bankside, 34 Park Street SE1 9EF
Tel 020 7407 1577

This historic pub lies in the shadow of the Globe Theatre (see page 126). Diarist Samuel Pepys supposedly watched the Great Fire of London from here in 1666, and regulars over the years have included writer Oliver Goldsmith and painter Sir Joshua Reynolds. There are excellent river views, black beams, faded plasterwork and a maze of tiny rooms. A varied menu includes pan-fried halibut with olives and cod in crispy bacon served on wilted spinach. Garden and patio overlooking the River Thames.
🕐 11–11 (Sun 12–10.30). Restaurant: 12–2.30, 6–10

🍽 Bar meals from £11, D from £44
🚇 London Bridge, Mansion House

THE ARGYLL ARMS
Map 245 H4
18 Argyll Street W1F 7TP
Tel 020 7734 6117

A tavern has stood on this site since 1740, but the present building is mid-Victorian and notable for its stunning floral displays. There's a range of sandwiches and the hot food menu might offer vegetarian moussaka, beef and Guinness pie and lasagne. Children are not allowed in the bar area.
🕐 11–11 (Sun 12–10.30). Meals: 11–3, D Mon–Sat only. Closed 25 Dec
🍽 Bar meals from £12
🚇 Oxford Circus

THE ATLAS
Map 244 D8
16 Seagrave Road SW6 1RX
Tel 020 7385 9129
This Victorian pub has a contemprorary twist, offering traditional ales along with quality restaurant food and business facilities. Food is mainly Mediterranean, with a daily changing menu of 12 dishes ranging from soup, antipasti, risotto and pasta to grilled and roasted fish and meat dishes. Some of the most popular are wild rocket and salmon risotto and Moroccan lamb tagine. Ten wines are offered by the glass each month. Children are welcome, and food is also served in the walled garden.
🕐 12–11 (Sun 12–10.30). Meals: Mon–Fri 12.30–3, 7–10.30. Closed 24 Dec–1 Jan, Easter
🍽 Bar meals from £12, D from £20
🚇 West Brompton

THE BLEEDING HEART TAVERN ✿
Map 246 L3
19 Greville Street EC1N 8SQ
Tel 020 7404 0333

The original tavern opened in 1746 and was named in memory of Elizabeth Hatton, murdered in nearby Hatton Garden 100 years earlier. The rustic scrubbed tables sit well with the wooden flooring. Ales are from Adnam's Brewery, there's an impressive wine list and a menu of traditional pub food with a contemporary flavour, such as spit-roast game and Suffolk pork, ale-battered haddock with fat chips and rib-eye steak with béarnaise sauce. No children.
🕐 11–11. Restaurant: 12–3, 6–10.30. Closed Sat, Sun, 24 Dec–2 Jan, public hols
🍽 Bar meals from £4.95, D from £34
🚇 Farringdon

THE BUCKINGHAM ARMS
Map 245 H6
62 Petty France SW1H 9EU
Tel 020 7222 3386
This elegant, busy pub near Buckingham Palace (see page 79) offers a good range of simple pub food in its long bar with etched mirrors. Try the mighty Buckingham burger, nachos with chilli, ciabatta breads or well-loved meals such as ham, egg and chips. No children under 16.
🕐 11–11 (Sat, Sun 12–5.30). Bar meals: 12–3, restaurant: 12–4 (Sun only), 6–11
🍽 Bar meals from £10, D from £34
🚇 St. James's Park

THE CHAPEL
Map 244 F3
48 Chapel Street NW1 5DP
Tel 020 7402 9220

A modern, open-plan pub with stripped floors and pine furniture. Menus posted daily on the chalkboards have a trendy Anglo-Mediterranean feel. Starters might include chilled watercress soup or fish croquette salad with roast vegetables, followed with pan-fried bison. Garden in which meals are served.

🕐 12–11 (Sun 12–10.30). Restaurant: 12–2.30, 7–10. Closed 24 Dec–2 Jan
🍴 Bar meals from £23, D from £30
Ⓔ Edgware Road

THE CHELSEA RAM
Map 244 off E8
32 Burnaby Street SW10 0PL
Tel 020 7351 4008
A busy neighbourhood pub near Chelsea Harbour, offering fresh produce including fish and meat from Smithfield's Market. Monthly changing menus have eclectic starters like crispy Thai duck salad or ballotine of chicken with pancetta and artichokes, and main dishes include special market selections from the blackboard, ranging from braised lamb shanks with olive oil mash to bangers and mash with roasted field mushrooms and spinach. No children after 8.30pm unless they are eating.
🕐 11–11 (Sun 12–10.30). Restaurant: 12–3, 7–10
🍴 Bar meals from £18, D from £34
Ⓔ Earl's Court

THE CHURCHILL ARMS
Map 244 C5
119 Kensington Church Street W8 7LN
Tel 020 7727 4242
Thai food is the speciality at this traditional 200-year-old pub, with strong emphasis on exotic chicken, beef and pork dishes. Try Thai rice noodles with ground peanuts, spicy sauce and a choice of pork, chicken or prawns. Oak beams,

CITTIE OF YORKE
Map 246 L3
22 High Holborn WC1V 6BN
Tel 020 7242 7670
A pub has stood on this site since 1430. In 1695 it was rebuilt as the Gray's Inn Coffee House and the large cellar bar dates from this time. The panelled front bar has an

original chandelier and portraits of illustrious locals, including Charles Dickens and Sir Thomas More. Bar food involves sandwiches, salads and soups, plus a handful of hot dishes.
🕐 11.30–11. Meals: 12–9. Closed Sun, 25–26 Dec
🍴 Bar meals from £5
Ⓔ Holborn

log fires and a conservatory. Children are not allowed at the bar.
🕐 11–11 (Sun 12–10.30). Restaurant: 12–4, Mon–Sat 12–9.30
🍴 Bar meals from £11, D from £12
Ⓔ Notting Hill Gate

THE COOPERS OF FLOOD STREET
Map 245 off F8
87 Flood Street SW3 5TB
Tel 020 7376 3120
This is a quiet backstreet Chelsea pub near the King's

Road and the River Thames, where a stuffed brown bear, Canadian moose and boar bring character to the bar. Food is served in both the bar and the quieter upstairs dining room. The adventurous menu also offers traditional dishes: from a secret recipe there's Aberdeen Angus 'steak les Hooches', seared king scallops with salad, crème frâiche and sweet chilli sauce, and garlic and chilli prawn linguine in a white wine and cream sauce. No children under 16 allowed after 6pm.
🕐 11–11. Meals: 12.30–3, Mon–Sat 6.30–9.30. Closed 25 Dec
🍴 Bar meals from £16, D from £34
Ⓔ South Kensington, Sloane Square

THE COW SALOON BAR & DINING ROOMS
Map 244 C3
89 Westbourne Park Road W2 5QH
Tel 020 7221 5400
Once known as the Railway Tavern but reputedly renamed after a former landlady of dubious personality, this pub is near the 500-year-old drovers' trail leading to Smithfield Market (possibly a more plausible source for its title). Native and rock oysters are on the menu, along with fish stew, grilled mackerel fillet, mussels in Thai yellow sauce, seafood platter and whole crab. Meat-lovers can try delicate grilled calves' liver, and the ubiquitous sausage and mash.
🕐 12–11. Bar meals: 12–3, 6–10.30. Restaurant: Sat–Sun 12.30–3.30, all week 6.30–10.30. Closed 25 Dec
🍴 Bar meals from £10, D from £70
Ⓔ Royal Oak, Westbourne Park

THE CROSS KEYS
Map 245 off F8
1 Lawrence Street SW3 5NB
Tel 020 7349 9111
This pub, dating from 1765, which has attracted the rich and famous since the 1960s, includes a banqueting room and open-plan conservatory—complete with tree growing in the middle—plus a restaurant and modern art gallery. The menu leans towards the Modern European school, with smoked duck terrine, Toulouse sausages with mashed potatoes and date and pecan sponge dessert. Evening meals have more choice. Children are not allowed in the bar area.

EATING

THE EAGLE ❀

Map 246 L3

159 Farringdon Road EC1R 3AL

Tel 020 7837 1353

On the fringe of Clerkenwell, London's focus on cool, The Eagle was one of Britain's first pubs to concentrate on the

quality of its food. The pub has even published its own cookbook, *Big Flavours and Rough Edges*. The straightforward, rustic blackboard menu favours a Mediterranean style, and Italy in particular, with bruschetta, pecorino cheese and Tuscan stews. The postwork City buzz can be truly intoxicating.

🕐 12–1am (Sun 12–5). Closed 25 Dec–1 Jan, public hols

🍴 Bar meals from £8.50

🚇 Angel, Farringdon

🕐 12–11 (Sun 12–10). Restaurant: Mon–Sat 12–3, 7–11. Closed 25–26 Dec, 1 Jan, Easter Mon

🍴 Bar meals from £12, D from £56

🚇 Sloane Square

THE CROWN

Map 247 off P4

223 Grove Road E3 5SN

Tel 020 8981 9998

In this carefully restored 1860s building, everything from the reclaimed building materials used in the restoration and the second-hand furniture to the organic menu and wine list is green–based on sound environmental practices. The menu changes with the seasons, and is a mix of European dishes, such as leek and parsnip soup, shoulder of lamb stuffed with anchovies, garlic and rosemary, and pan-fried chicken livers with sage, walnuts and noodles. The bitter chocolate mousse is delicious. Garden in which food is served.

🕐 12–11 (Mon 5–11, Sat–Sun phone for times). Restaurant: Tue–Sun 12.30–3.30, Mon–Sun 6.30–10.30. Closed 25 Dec

🍴 Bar meals from £12, D from £40

🚇 Mile End

THE DUKE OF CAMBRIDGE

Map 246 off L2

30 St. Peter's Street N1 8JT

Tel 020 7359 3066

This stylishly modernized building in a residential street in trendy Islington was one of London's first pubs to specialize in organic food, wine and beer. Blackboard menus feature seasonal Modern European dishes such as pumpkin and sage soup or grilled asparagus with anchovy. Leave space for desserts such as rhubarb fool with shortbread and pear and chocolate soufflé cake. Garden and patio.

🕐 12–11 (Mon 5–11). Restaurant: 12.30–3, 6.30–10.30. Closed 25–26 Dec, 1 Jan

🍴 Bar meals from £20, D from £42

🚇 Angel

FREEDOM BREWING COMPANY

Map 246 J4

41 Earlham Street WC2H 9LD

Tel 020 7240 0606

Launched in 1995, the Freedom Brewing Company is Britain's first micro-brewery dedicated to lager. Restaurant and bar menus offer grilled chicken, rocket (arugula) salad and bacon, seafood stew and calves' liver with bacon and mash, and a daily changing risotto. Children allowed to 7pm.

🕐 12–11. Restaurant: 12–9. Closed 25–26 Dec, 1 Jan

🍴 Bar meals from £14, D from £24

🚇 Leicester Square, Covent Garden

THE FRENCH HOUSE

Map 246 J4

49 Dean Street W1D 5BG

Tel 020 7437 2799

Notable for its custom of serving only half pints of beer, this small Soho bar holds an annual Pint Day dedicated to the long-established British charity, the National Society for the Prevention of Cruelty to Children (NSPCC). The bar remains much as it was in the 1950s, when it was popular with writers, artists and actors – Brendan Behan, Dylan Thomas and Francis Bacon, to name but a few. Weekly changing menus might feature navarin of lamb or roasted monkfish with ham. No children under 18.

🕐 12–11 (Sun 12–9). Restaurant: 11–3, Mon–Sat 5.30–11.30. Closed 25 Dec

🍴 Bar meals from £10, D from £36

🚇 Tottenham Court Road

THE GEORGE

Map 247 N5

77 Borough High Street SE1 1NH

Tel 020 7407 2056

This former coaching inn that dates to 1542 at least, when one William Shakespeare drank here, is now owned by the National Trust. It has breathtaking river views and fading plasterwork, black beams and a warren of tiny rooms inside. Food is along the lines of steak, ale-and-Guinness pie and traditional fish and chips, and they also serve some decent real ales (beers made in the barrel by the traditional method).

🕐 11–11 (Sun 12–10.30). Meals: Mon–Fri 12–4, Mon–Sat 5–10. Closed 25 Dec

🍴 Bar meals from £14, D from £40

🚇 London Bridge

THE GLOBE

Map 245 F3

43–47 Marylebone Road NW1 5JY

Tel 020 7935 6368

An 18th-century pub consisting of wine bar, main bar and restaurant. A typical menu includes steak and Stilton pie,

SPECIAL

THE GRAPES

Map 247 off P4
76 Narrow Street E14 8BP
Tel 020 7987 4396

This 1720 pub set on a narrow riverside site was used by Charles Dickens as the model for The Six Jolly Fellowship Porters in his novel Our Mutual Friend. He might still recognize many of its features. They adopt a traditional approach all round, with cask-conditioned real ales and wholesome food. Meals include home-made soups, salads and sausage and mash; while the tiny upstairs restaurant offers a wide selection of seafood.

🕐 12–3, 5.30–11 (Sat 12–11, Sun 12–10.30). Restaurant: Mon–Fri 12–2.15, Mon–Sat 7.30–9.15. Closed public hols

🍴 Bar meals from £7, D from £40
🚇 DLR Limehouse, West Ferry

pork with wild mushroom sauce and the Globe's speciality: fish and chips. Scheduled for refurbishment at time of this writing, so call ahead. Close to the Planetarium and Madame Tussaud's (see page 101). No children allowed in the bar area.

🕐 11–11 (Sun 12–10.30). Restaurant: 11–10
🍴 Bar meals from £8
🚇 Baker Street

THE GRENADIER

Map 245 G6
18 Wilton Row SW1X 7NR
Tel 020 7235 3074

Regularly used for films and television series, once the Duke of Wellington's officers' mess and much frequented by King George IV in the 1820s, the ivy-clad Grenadier stands in a cobbled mews behind Hyde Park Corner. Food ranges from solid traditional fish and chips and beef Wellington to Belgravia salmon—a dish named after a fashionable district of London.

🕐 12–11 (Sun 12–10.30). Restaurant: 12–2, 6–9.30
🍴 Bar meals from £10, D from £48
🚇 Hyde Park Corner

THE JERUSALEM TAVERN

Map 246 L3
55 Britton Street EC1M 5NA
Tel 020 7490 4281

This dimly lit bar dates from 1720, when it was a merchant's house, and has often been used as a film set. It derives its name from the Priory of St. John, originally on the site. It has bare wooden floorboards, rustic wooden tables, and a selection of magazines and daily papers. Bar food is simple—speciality sandwiches, sausage baguettes and beef casserole.

🕐 11–11. Meals: 12–3. Closed Sat, Sun, 25 Dec, Good Fri, Easter Mon
🍴 Bar meals from £9
🚇 Farringdon

THE LADBROKE ARMS

Map 244 off C5
54 Ladbroke Road W11 3NW
Tel 020 7727 6648

The Ladbroke is on busy Ladbroke Road, with a front courtyard and split-level dining area to the rear. The menu changes daily and offers imaginative but not scary choices. Why not try confit tuna with garlic lentils or soft-boiled egg and bottarga among the starters, then linguini with sweet tomato and basil, or pan-fried salmon with prosciutto, pea and mint risotto.

🕐 11–11. Restaurant: 12–7. Closed 25 Dec
🍴 Bar meals from £20, D from £48
🚇 Holland Park

THE LAMB

Map 246 K3
94 Lamb's Conduit Street WC1N 3LZ
Tel 020 7405 0713

This traditional watering hole, with a distinctive green-tiled façade, was built around 1729 and sends you back in time the minute you walk in the door, with its dark polished wood, original sepia photographs of music hall stars, rare glass snob screens, and an old phonograph in the bar that can

be wound up to play discs by request. Home-cooked bar food includes a vegetarian corner, a fish choice, light bites,

and from the 'stove' lambs' liver and bacon or traditional shepherd's pie. No children allowed in the bar area. Patio on which meals are served.

🕐 11–11 (Sun 12–4, 7–10.30). Meals: 12–2.30, Mon–Sat 6–9
🍴 Bar meals from £12
🚇 Holborn, Russell Square

THE LANSDOWNE

Map 245 off H2
90 Gloucester Avenue NW1 8HX
Tel 020 7483 0409

The Lansdowne has a light, spacious bar and outdoor seating area as well as a slightly more formal upper floor dining room, where there's waiter service (it's best to reserve a table). Organic or free-range ingredients are used wherever possible. The seasonal menu has home-made pizzas and sausages or chicken and chorizo stew, roast cod with Seville orange sauce, grilled sea bass with purple-sprouting broccoli, and spicy pan-fried scallops.

🕐 12–11 (Sun 12–4, 7–10.30). Restaurant: Sun 1–3, Tue–Sat 7–10
🍴 Bar meals from £22, D from £36
🚇 Chalk Farm

NAG'S HEAD

Map 245 G6
53 Kinnerton Street SW1X 8ED
Tel 020 7235 1135

In a quiet mews near Harrods, this old pub once claimed to be the smallest pub in London. Enjoy looking through the What the Butler Saw kinescope; donations for its use go to Queen Charlotte's Hospital in London. The menu gives a good choice of home-cooked food such as chicken and ham pie, vegetable quiche and chilli con carne. British visitors should note that Switch cards are not accepted.

🕐 11–11 (Sun 12–11). Meals: 11–9.30
🍽 Bar meals from £12
🚇 Knightsbridge

THE OLD BANK OF ENGLAND
Map 246 L4
194 Fleet Street EC4A 2LT
Tel 020 7430 2255

London's grandest pub, with tall ornate ceilings, this magnificent building, formerly the Law Courts branch of the Bank of England, lies between the site of Sweeney Todd's barbershop and his mistress's pie shop; it was in the tunnels and vaults below the present building that his victims were butchered before being cooked and sold in Mrs Lovett's pies. Don't let that put you off. The bar menu ranges from light snacks to lamb casserole with dumplings. No children under 18 allowed.

🕐 11–11. Meals: Mon–Thu 12–8. Closed Sat, Sun, public hols
🍽 Bar meals from £12
🚇 Blackfriars, Aldwych, Chancery Lane

THE OLD THAMESIDE
Map 247 N5
Pickford's Wharf, Clink Street
SE1 9DG
Tel 020 7403 4243

This former spice warehouse sits near the site of England's first prison, the Clink (see page 86). It is also only two minutes' walk from the artworks of Tate Modern, the Millennium Bridge and a show at Shakespeare's Globe (see pages 134–135, 100 and 126). A large outdoor seating area overhangs the River Thames. Food comes in the form of fish and chips, sausage and mash, different curries and vegetarian pies.

🕐 12–11. Meals: 10–5. Closed 25 Dec
🍽 Bar meals from £10
🚇 Cannon Street, London Bridge

THE PEASANT
Map 246 off L2
240 St. John Street EC1V 4PH
Tel 020 7336 7736

Here, the original Victorian features have been restored, including an inlaid mosaic floor, horseshoe bar and conservatory. The peasant-style food with a Mediterranean leaning includes chorizo with sherry, pears and walnuts, fried calamari with sweet chilli sauce, roast monkfish with spring greens and mussels. Children are not allowed in the bar area. Terrace.

🕐 12.30–12.30. Restaurant: Mon–Fri 12.30–3.30, Mon–Sat 6.30–11. Closed Sun
🍽 Bar meals from £10, D from £50
🚇 Angel, Farringdon

THE PERSEVERANCE
Map 246 K3
63 Lamb's Conduit Street WC1N 3NB
Tel 020 7405 8278

A central London haven of good food, fine wine and conviviality. The elegant, candlelit dining room upstairs offers starters such as home-made gnocchi, courgettes (zucchini) and mussels, mackerel with sweet pepper relish, and main dishes such as sea bream with artichokes, confit potatoes and red wine sauce, and pork with mushroom casserole. Good but small wine list. Book in advance if you're coming for Sunday lunch.

🕐 12–11. Restaurant: Sun–Fri 12.30–3, Mon–Sat 7–10. Closed 25–26 Dec
🍽 Bar meals from £20, D from £50
🚇 Holborn, Russell Square

THE PHENE ARMS
Map 245 off F8
Phene Street, Chelsea SW3 5NY
Tel 020 7352 3294

Hidden away down a quiet Chelsea cul-de-sac, a short stroll from the Embankment, this neighbourhood pub has a roof terrace and large garden for summer eating. The menu includes burgers, Cumberland sausages, Jerusalem salad, oven-baked cod and steaks.

🕐 11–11 (Sun 12–10.30). Restaurant: 12–3, 6–10
🍽 Bar meals from £12, D from £30
🚇 Sloane Square, South Kensington

THE SEVEN STARS
Map 246 K4
53 Carey Street WC2A 2JB
Tel 020 7242 8521

William Shakespeare was living in London when the Seven Stars was built in 1602. These days, the pub's clientele is drawn from the Law Courts close by. This highly individual free house serves fresh, home-made dishes, which arrive in a glass-panelled hoist. Try Welsh rarebit, penne in garlic sauce, or Portuguese pork with clams. Adnam's ales. No children under 18 allowed.

🕐 11–11. Meals: 12–9. Closed 25–26 Dec, 1 Jan, Easter Mon
🍽 Bar meals from £16, D from £20
🚇 Chancery Lane

THE STONEMASON'S ARMS
Map 244 off C7
54 Cambridge Grove W6 0LA
Tel 020 8748 1397

This is a trendy yet informal London gastro-pub with wooden floors and trestle tables. The food is Modern British: coriander and corn pancakes, Cumberland sausages with mashed potato and onion gravy, blackened tuna with sweet potato and roast garlic ragout, and spinach and duck spring roll with *bok choi* (Chinese white cabbage). Food is served in the garden.

🕐 12–11. Restaurant: 12–4, 6–10. Closed 25 Dec, 1 Jan

SWAG AND TAILS

Map 244 F6

10–11 Fairholt Street SW7 1EG

Tel 020 7584 6926

In a quiet street in the busy shopping and residential area of Knightsbridge, this flower-festooned pub restaurant is a real gem. Stripped wooden floorboards, comfortable wooden furniture, swagged and tailed curtains (hence the name) and a convivial atmosphere set the scene for rustic but contemporary cooking such as rocket (arugula) salad with glazed figs, chump of lamb with sweet fondant potato and a piquant Morello cherry sorbet.

🕐 11–11. Restaurant: Mon–Fri 12–3, 6–10. Closed Sat, Sun, public hols

🍴 Bar meals from £10.95, D from £44

🚇 Knightsbridge

🍴 Bar meals from £16, D from £30

🚇 Ravenscourt Park, Hammersmith

THE SUN AND DOVES

Map Off 247 M8

61–63 Coldharbour Lane SE5 9NS

Tel 020 7924 9950

The Sun and Doves is a pub known for its food, drink and art in the up-and-coming area of Camberwell. Free-range produce is used at all times, and the focus is food on skewers—haloumi (Cypriot cheese) and roast vegetables, swordfish tikka, prepared on beech skewers, marinated and grilled to order—and other interesting dishes, such as *moules marinières*. There's a comprehensive wine list and range of cocktails and food is served in the garden.

🕐 11–11. Restaurant: 11–11. Closed 25–26 Dec

🍴 Bar meals from £16, D from £35

🚇 Brixton

THE THATCHED HOUSE

Map Off 244 C7

115 Dalling Road W6 0ET

Tel 020 8746 6174

This is the trendy sister restaurant to the Chelsea Ram (see page 267). It is on a quiet street in popular Hammersmith, and is neither thatched nor a house. The cosmopolitan pub food is covered by a monthly changing menu

of freshly prepared dishes such as roasted red pepper soup, seared scallops with ginger and to follow American-style doughnuts with coffee cream and chocolate sauce. The popular English breakfast salad is a recipe from famous British TV chef Gary Rhodes. The pub acts as an art gallery, as the paintings on the walls are all by local artists and are for sale.

🕐 11–3, 5.30–11 (Sun 12–10.30).

Restaurant: 12–2.30, 7–10

🍴 Bar meals from £12, D from £40

🚇 Hammersmith

THE WESTBOURNE

Map 244 C3

101 Westbourne Park Villas W2 5ED

Tel 020 7221 1332

A classic Notting Hill pub and restaurant favoured by a bohemian, arty clientele, often residents of the area, including a few celebrities (this is a very smart place to live in London). The sunny terrace is popular in summer. The menu, which changes twice daily, might include skate with capers, duck breast salad and rabbit with mustard.

🕐 11–11 (Mon 5.30–11, Sun 12–10.30). Restaurant: 12.30–3.30, 7–9.30. Closed 24 Dec–5 Jan

🍴 Bar meals from £22, D from £30

🚇 Westbourne Park, Royal Oak

THE WHITE HORSE

Map Off 245 F8

1–3 Parson's Green SW6 4UL

Tel 020 7736 2115

There's been a coaching inn here since at least 1688. Today the pub has an imaginative Sunday brunch menu, summer barbecues and beer festivals; the Coach House restaurant serves well-priced evening meals. Dishes such as cheese soufflé, fillet of beef with béarnaise sauce and peppered smoked salmon are well prepared. Menu choices include drink suggestions: for example Highgate Mild beer to accompany traditional English breakfast, or Schlenkerla Rauchbier with smoked salmon and scrambled eggs. Food is served in the garden and the (well-heeled) clientele spill out on to Parson's Green opposite in the summer.

🕐 11–11 (Sun 12–10.30). Restaurant: 12–3.30, 6–11

🍴 Bar meals from £14, D from £50

🚇 Parson's Green

YE OLD CHESHIRE CHEESE

Map 246 L4

Wine Office Court, 145 Fleet Street EC4 2BU

Tel 020 7353 6170

This rambling institution is full of nooks and crannies and has a long history of entertaining literary greats such as novelists Sir Arthur Conan Doyle and Charles Dickens. It was the haunt of journalists when Fleet Street was the hub of Britain's newspaper world and is still one of the few remaining chop houses rebuilt after the Great Fire in 1666. Come here for traditional pub food.

🕐 11–11 (Sun 12–3). Restaurant: 12–9. Closed 25–26 Dec, public hols

🍴 Bar meals from £10, D from £30

🚇 Blackfriars, Aldwych, Chancery Lane

ZEBRANO

Map 245 H4

14–16 Gantan Street W1V 1LB

Tel 020 7287 5267

This popular pub opened in 1999, the second of the Freedom Brewing Company's micro-brew bars to take advantage of the growing demand for fresh, hand-crafted beer. The bar sells six ales made on the premises, as well as salads, sandwiches, fish and chips, and main meals such as lamb steak with grilled vegetables.

🕐 11–11 (Thu–Sat 11am–12am). Meals: Mon–Sat 12–5, 6–10. Closed 25–26 Dec, 1 Jan

🍴 Bar meals from £13

🚇 Oxford Circus

EATING

MAJOR RESTAURANT CHAINS

London is a good place for eclectic and unusual eating, but there are also plenty of tried and tested chains, where you know exactly what you're getting and how much you'll have to pay.

RESTAURANTS	Price range (£–£££)	Alcohol	Child Menu	Takeaway	Phone Number	Website
Ask Pizza and Pasta	£££	✔	✔	✔	01727 735800	www.askcentral.co.uk
Beefeater	£££	✔	✔	✗	01582 424200	www.beefeater.co.uk
Belgo	£££	✔	–	–	020 7557 6333	www.belgo-restaurant.co.uk
Bella Pasta	££	✔	✔	✔	020 7121 3200	www.bellapasta.co.uk
Browns	£££	✔	✔	✗	020 7239 9070	www.browns-restaurants.com
Café Rouge	£££	✔	✔	✗	020 7121 3200	www.caferouge.co.uk
Caffe Uno	££	✔	✔	✗	020 7747 5100	www.caffeuno.co.uk
Carluccio's Caffé	££	✔	–	–	020 7580 3050	www.carluccios.com
Chez Gérard	£££	✔	✗	✔	020 7257 8440	www.chezgerard.com
Corney and Barrow	£££	✔	✗	✗	020 7265 2500	www.corney-barrow.co.uk
Garfunkels	£££	✔	✔	✔	020 7440 5503	www.garfunkels.co.uk
Loch Fyne	£££	✔	–	✔	020 8404 6686	www.loch-fyne.com
Nando's	££	✔	✔	✔	020 8394 6730	www.nandos.co.uk
Pizza Express	£££	✔	✗	✔	01895 618618	www.pizzaexpress.com
Pizza Hut	££	✔	✔	✔	020 8732 9000	www.pizzahut.co.uk
TGI Friday's	££	✔	✔	✔	01582 844300	www.tgifridays.com
Wagamama	££	✔	✔	✔	020 7631 3140	www.wagamama.com

SANDWICHES AND FAST FOOD	Price range (£–£££)	Alcohol	Child Menu	Takeaway	Phone Number	Website
Burger King	£	✗	✔	✔	01895 206000	www.burgerking.co.uk
Domino's Pizza	££	✗	✔	✔	01908 580000	www.dominos.com.uk
Gourmet Burger Kitchen	££	✗	✔	✔	020 7585 1372	www.gbkinfo.co.uk
Kentucky Fried Chicken	£	✗	✔	✔	01483 717000	www.kfc.co.uk
McDonald's	£	✗	✔	✔	0870 241 3300	www.mcdonalds.com
Pret à Manger	£	✗	✔	✔	020 7827 8888	www.pret-a-manger.com
Subway	£	✗	✔	✔	020 7240 1400	www.subway.com
Yo Sushi	£	✔	✔	✔	020 7841 0700	www.yosushi.co.uk

COFFEE SHOPS	Price range (£–£££)	Alcohol	Child Menu	Takeaway	Phone Number	Website
Caffé Nero	£	✗	✔	✔	020 7520 5150	www.caffenero.co.uk
Coffee Republic	£	✗	–	✔	020 7033 0600	No website
Costa Coffee	£	✗	✗	✔	01582 424200	www.costa.co.uk
Starbucks	££	✗	✗	✔	020 7721 4599	www.burgerking.co.uk

Staying

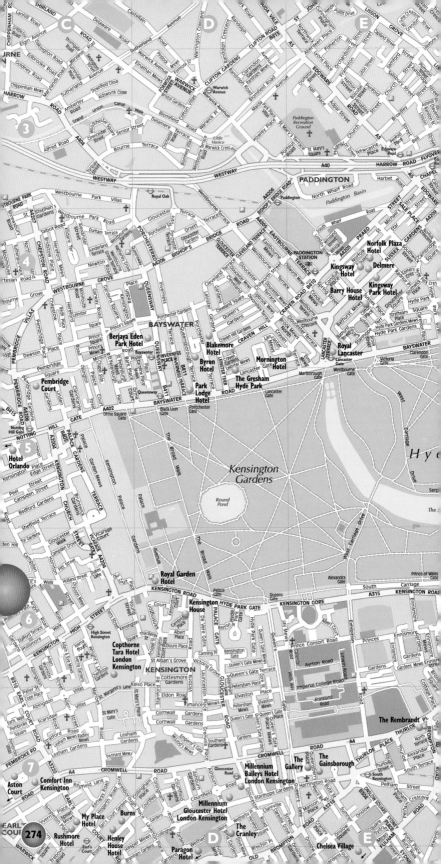

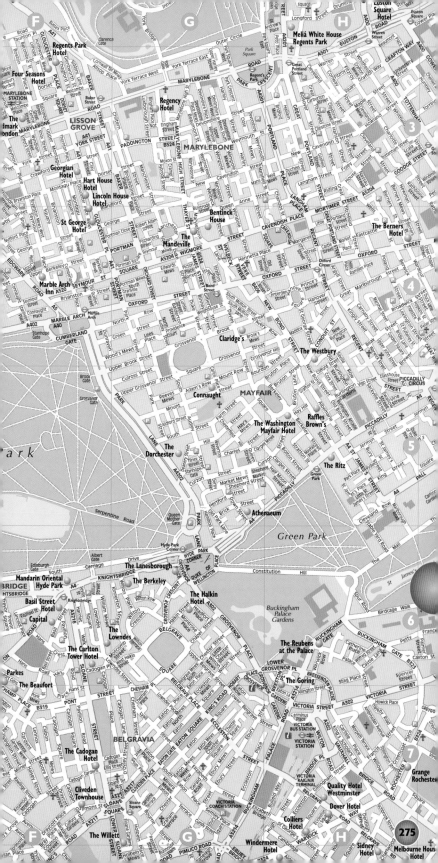

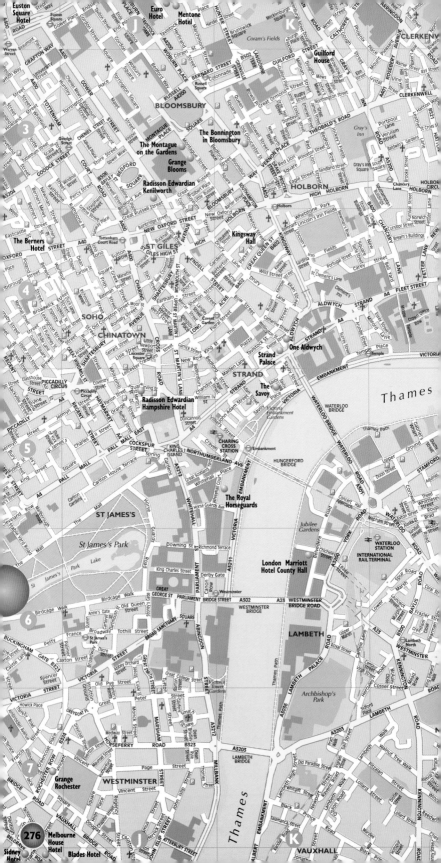

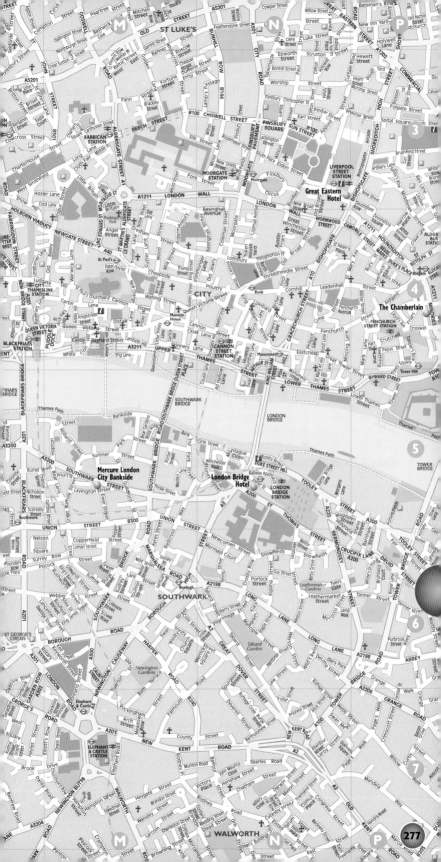

STAYING IN LONDON

London has some of the best hotels in the world, but the cost of accommodation is high. You can expect to pay £150 a night for a reasonable room, and the rates begin to soar if you stay at one of the grand old hotels such as Claridge's, the Dorchester or the Savoy.

Good value hotels and guest houses do exist (look for the diamond symbol in the following listings), but these rooms are very much in demand and you must book in advance. Many hotels will ask you to confirm your reservation and will charge a fee if you cancel at short notice or fail to turn up. You may lose your deposit and some hotels will charge the cost of the room to your credit card.

CHEAPER ACCOMMODATION
Consider alternatives to hotels, such as renting apartments or staying with a London family. The London Tourist Board has leaflets on these and other options.

Youth hostels run by the Youth Hostel Association (YHA) are a good option for visitors on a tight budget. You need to be a member of the association; either join in advance or in person at any hostel. Annual membership for British residents is £13.50 (under 18s £6.75); £12 for all ages for those from outside Britain; or £2 per night.

HOTEL FACILITIES
The biggest problem with London hotels is noise, as many are located on busy streets. Some have double glazing, but that can make rooms unbearably stuffy, especially since air-conditioning is not standard. If you value peace and quiet, look for hotels on side streets in residential areas; or request a room at the rear of or higher up in the building. Most hotels also have rooms of different sizes, so always ask whether there is a choice. You will not necessarily automatically be allocated the best room available.

For facilities such as parking, 24-hour room service, gyms and swimming pools, expect to pay a high premium in central London.

HOTEL CLASSIFICATIONS

The Automobile Association (AA) is Britain's leading organization for the classification of hotels. All hotels recognized by the AA should have the highest standards of cleanliness, keep proper records of booking, give professional service, assist with luggage on request, accept and deliver messages, provide a designated area for dinner (if available) and breakfast with drinks available in a bar or lounge, and provide an early morning call on request. A guide to some of the general expectations for each classification is below.

1 star ★ Informal yet competent style of service and an adequate range of facilities, including a television in the lounge or bedroom. Most bedrooms have a private bathroom, but a bath or shower room is always available. At least one designated eating area for breakfast and dinner (if available).

2 stars ★★ As above plus professional management, with at least one restaurant or dining room for breakfast and dinner. Last orders for dinner no earlier than 7pm.

3 stars ★★★ As above plus direct dial telephones, remote control television, ensuite bath or shower and WC, a wide selection of drinks in the bar and last orders for dinner no earlier than 8pm.

4 stars ★★★★ As above plus a range of high-quality toiletries, private bath with fixed overhead shower and a

WC. Uniformed, well-trained staff with additional services, a night porter and a serious approach to cuisine. Well-appointed public areas. Last orders for dinner no earlier than 9pm.

5 stars ★★★★★ The most luxurious hotels, offering many extra facilities and services, top-quality rooms and a full concierge service. A wide selection of drinks, including cocktails, is available in the bar and a menu complementing the hotel's own style of cooking. Last orders for dinner no earlier than 10pm.

The AA Top 200 Hotels ☆☆
These hotels, identified by open stars, stand out as the very best hotels in Britain and range from large luxury hotels to small country inns.

AA Diamond Rating ◆◆◆◆
Bed and breakfast and guesthouse accommodation is rated for the quality

of operation. This quality is rated with a diamond symbol on a rising scale from one to five. The criteria for a higher rating is guest care and quality rather than the choice of extra facilities. Evening meals may or may not be available.

At all grades, guests can expect:
- a prompt and professional check in and out
- comfortable accommodation equipped to modern standards
- regularly changed bedding and towels
- sufficient hot water at all times
- adequate storage, heating, lighting and comfortable seating
- a full English or Continental breakfast

AA Open Diamond Rating ◇◇◇◇
The best establishments in each of the top three quality ratings (five, four and three diamonds) are identified with open diamonds.

STAYING

TIPS

- Many hotels offer cheaper rates on Saturdays and Sundays. Sometimes big chains (see page 292) offer Saturday and Sunday discounts. Some hotels also offer lower rates for stays of a week or more.
- Rates can be cheaper during February and March, and October and November.

PRICES

Prices are for a double room for one night, including breakfast and VAT. All the hotels listed accept credit cards unless otherwise stated.

ASTON COURT ◆◆◆

Map 274 off C7
25–27 Matheson Road W14 8SN
Tel 020 7602 9954

This large bed-and-breakfast place is a corner property in a peaceful residential area, not far from the Olympia exhibition halls. Public areas include a small lounge bar and a conservatory where English breakfasts are served.

🛏 Double from £95
☊ 29 (13 non-smoking)
🚇 West Kensington
🚌 28, 391

ATHENAEUM ☆☆☆☆☆

Map 275 G5
116 Piccadilly W1J 7BJ
Tel 020 7499 3464
www.athenaeum.com

A well-loved hotel in the heart of Mayfair with excellent hospitality. Some bedrooms have views over Green Park (see page 90). A row of Edwardian houses next to the hotel has several spacious apartments. Public spaces include Bullochs at 116 Restaurant, the Windsor Lounge and a cocktail bar specializing in malt whisky. Sauna, massage room and spa.

🛏 Double from £285
☊ 157 (58 non-smoking)
🛗

🚇 Green Park
🚌 8, 9, 14, 19, 22, 38

BARRY HOUSE HOTEL ◆◆◆

Map 274 E4
12 Sussex Place, Hyde Park W2 2TP
Tel 020 7723 7340
www.barryhouse.co.uk

A smart, family-run property that offers bed and breakfast near Hyde Park (see page 93).

🛏 Double from £73
☊ 18 (3 non-smoking)
🚭 In dining room or lounges
🚇 Paddington, Lancaster Gate
🚌 705

BASIL STREET HOTEL ★★★

Map 275 F6
Basil Street SW3 1AH
Tel 020 7581 3311

A friendly understated hotel behind Harrods (see page 178) in Knightsbridge. Public rooms feature parquet flooring and are decorated with antiques, paintings and tapestries. There's a bar/tea room upstairs.

🛏 Double from £240
☊ 80 (40 non-smoking)
🅿 2
🚇 Knightsbridge
🚌 19, 22, 137, C1

THE BEAUFORT ★★★★

Map 275 F7
33 Beaufort Gardens SW3 1PP
Tel 020 7584 5252
www.thebeaufort.co.uk

An attractive townhouse in a tree-lined cul-de-sac just minutes' walk from Knightsbridge. Air-conditioned bedrooms are well furnished and equipped with chocolates, fruit, fresh flowers, videos, CD players and free internet and movie channel access. Drinks and afternoon tea, served in the attractive drawing room, are complimentary. There is also free entry to a health club in the vicinity.

🛏 Double from £229
☊ 29 (9 non-smoking)

🚇 South Kensington, Knightsbridge
🚌 14, 74, C1

BENTINCK HOUSE ◆◆

Map 275 G4
20 Bentinck Street W1U 2EU
Tel 020 7935 9141

A bed-and-breakfast set on a quiet street in the heart of the West End, a short walk from Oxford Street, Regent Street and Bond Street. Some rooms have private bathrooms and shower rooms. Hairdryer and trouser press on request.

🛏 Double from £95
☊ 21 (15 non-smoking)
🚭 In dining room
🚇 Oxford Circus
🚌 113, 137, 189

BERJAYA EDEN PARK HOTEL ★★★

Map 274 D4
35–39 Inverness Terrace W2 3JS
Tel 020 7221 2220
www.berjayaresorts.com

An elegant 1860 Bayswater townhouse, on a tree-lined terrace a few minutes' tube ride from Oxford Street and the West End. Rooms are simply furnished. Public rooms include a restaurant and bar. Suites have private entrance and adjoining family living room or private patio and sitting room area, including sofa bed. Breakfast extra.

🛏 Double from £125
☊ 135 (40 non-smoking)
🚇 Bayswater, Queensway
🚌 12, 70, 94

THE BERKELEY ☆☆☆☆☆

Map 275 G6
Wilton Place SW1X 7RL
Tel 020 7235 6000
www.savoygroup.co.uk

The Knightsbridge Berkeley never fails to impress. Ongoing refurbishment ensures an excellent range of bedrooms, each one furnished with perfect attention to detail. The public spaces are decorated

STAYING

with magnificent flower arrangements and the Blue Bar is strikingly furnished, its blue tones and white ceiling, complete with opulent chandelier, setting the scene for a relaxed pre-dinner drink. The health spa offers a range of treatments and there's an open-air rooftop pool. Two restaurants provide a contrast of styles: modern, influenced by Southeast Asia, at Vong, and French cuisine at La Tante Claire. Has a sauna, solarium and gym.

🛏 Double from £435
🛈 214 (34 non-smoking)
♨ 🈲
🅿 50
🚇 Hyde Park Corner
🚌 9, 10, 14, 19, 22, 52, 74, 137

THE BERNERS HOTEL ★★★★
Map 275 H4
Berners Street W1A 3BE
Tel 020 7666 2000
www.berners.co.uk
In the heart of the West End, this traditional hotel has an elegant feel, with a marble-columned lobby and ornately carved ceilings. The luxurious lounge is a popular venue for afternoon tea, and rooms are all equipped with modern facilities. In the restaurant the imaginative menu includes such dishes as crab and ginger salad, spicy lamb sausage and lightly curried monkfish.

🛏 Double from £215
🛈 216 (100 non-smoking)
🚇 Goodge Street, Tottenham Court Road, Oxford Circus

BLADES HOTEL ◇◇◇
Map 276 J8
122 Belgrave Road SW1V 2BL
Tel 020 7976 5552
Friendly, family-run bed-and-breakfast near Victoria main-line train station. There is a first-floor conservatory-style lounge; Continental breakfast is served in the attractive dining room.

🛏 Double from £75
🛈 18
🍽 In dining room
🚇 Victoria
🚌 24

BLAKEMORE HOTEL ◇◇◇
Map 274 D4
30 Leinster Gardens W2 3AN
Tel 020 7262 4591
www.starcrown.com
This bed-and-breakfast enjoys a quiet yet central position just a few minutes' walk from Hyde Park (see page 93). The bedrooms are neatly decorated and the executive rooms have been refurbished to a high standard. Spacious public areas include the Rossetti bar lounge, smart lobby and attractive Wellington restaurant.

🛏 Double from £116
🛈 164 (28 non-smoking)
🚇 Bayswater
🚌 12, 70, 94

BURNS ★★★
Map 274 C7
18–26 Barkston Gardens SW5 0EN
Tel 020 7373 3151
www.vienna-group.co.uk
Housed in a listed landmark in a quiet, residential, tree-lined garden square in Kensington and near Knightsbridge shops. There is a private walled garden; public areas include a patio restaurant and the Ellen Terry Bar, named after the famous English actress, who lived here between 1889 and 1902. One of the Best Western chain of hotels.

🛏 Double from £75
🛈 105 (38 non-smoking)
🍽 In restaurant
🚇 Russell Square, Holborn
🚌 7

BYRON HOTEL ◇◇◇
Map 274 D4
36–38 Queensborough Terrace W2 3SH
Tel 020 7243 0987
This hotel in a row of Georgian houses has been thoughtfully restored to provide comfortable accommodation, and to retain a number of original features. Bedrooms vary in size, but all are tastefully furnished and equipped with modern facilities. There's a dining room where you can have breakfast, and a guest lounge.

🛏 Double from £75
🛈 45
🍽 In dining room
🚇 Bayswater

THE BONNINGTON IN BLOOMSBURY ★★★
Map 276 K3
92 Southampton Row WC1B 4BH
Tel 020 7242 2828
www.bonnington.com
A smart hotel central to the city, the British Museum (see pages 80–85) and Covent Garden (see page 88). The public areas, all with plenty of space, include the Malt Bar, Waterfalls Restaurant and a comfortable lobby lounge. Bedrooms include a number of superb new executive rooms and suites. A good range of conference and meeting rooms is available.

🛏 Double from £159
🛈 215 (87 non-smoking)
🚇 Russell Square, Holborn
🚌 7

THE CADOGAN HOTEL ★★★★
Map 275 F7
75 Sloane Street SW1X 9SG
Tel 020 7235 7141
www.cadogan.com
This Victorian hotel in Chelsea overlooks the gardens in Cadogan Place and lists British actress Lillie Langtry and writer Oscar Wilde as two of its most celebrated visitors. Bedrooms are mostly air-conditioned and stylishly furnished. The elegant drawing room is a popular venue for afternoon tea, and the Edwardian restaurant, with its leaded windows and intricate plasterwork, serves essentially British food with a strong classical French base. Tennis courts.

🛏 Double from £195
🛈 65 (31 non-smoking)
🚇 Sloane Square
🚌 19, 22, 137, C1

CAPITAL ☆☆☆☆☆
Map 275 F6
Basil Street SW3 1AT
Tel 020 7589 5171
www.capitalhotel.co.uk
This small, family-owned hotel is in Knightsbridge, near Harrods (see page 178). The individually designed bedrooms are fresh and light with antique furniture and marble bathrooms. A highlight of any visit to this hotel is dinner in the main restaurant, where the cuisine is based on the rustic

STAYING

and earthy style of Aquitaine in southwest France, and you are assured of a warm welcome.

🛏 Double from £205
🛏 48 rooms (24 non-smoking)
🅿 15
🚇 Knightsbridge
🚌 19, 22, 137, C1

THE CARLTON TOWER HOTEL ★★★★★

Map 275 F6
Cadogan Place SW1X 9PY
Tel 020 7235 1234
www.carltontower.com
In the heart of Knightsbridge and with the Cadogan Place gardens on its doorstep. Rooms are smooth and sleek, and one of the hotel's restaurants (the Grissini—noted for its northern Italian cooking) has views over the Cadogan Place gardens through the large conservatory windows. There's also the Rib Room and the Oyster Bar. The swimming pool has a glass roof, and there are treatment rooms, gym, sauna, spa and Jacuzzi, and tennis courts, too.

🛏 Double from £235
🛏 220 (116 non-smoking)
🏊 Indoor 🛗
🚇 Sloane Square
🚌 19, 22, 137, C1

THE CHAMBERLAIN ★★★★

Map 277 P4
130–135 Minories EC3N 1NU
Tel 020 7680 1500
www.thechamberlainhotel.com
Lavishly converted from early 20th-century offices, this hotel is ideally situated for the City and Tower Bridge (see page 137). The bedrooms are stylish and the bathrooms modern and fitted with TV. A popular pub is on the premises, along with an unusual split-level dining room. Parking and discounted sports facilities for hotel guests are close by.

🛏 Double from £105
🛏 64 (30 non-smoking)
🚇 Fenchurch Street, Aldgate, Tower Hill
🚌 15, 25, 42, 78, 100

CHELSEA VILLAGE ★★★★

Map 274 off E8
Stamford Bridge, Fulham Road SW6 1HS
Tel 020 7565 1400
www.chelseavillage.co.uk
This stylish, eye-catching hotel, a bold, modern structure, forms part of an ambitious new development at Chelsea Football Club (see page 211). Bedrooms are generally large and the range of public spaces includes four eateries offering menus to cover the international spectrum. The Chelsea Club is one of London's premier gym and health clubs. Also on the premises are a half Olympic-size swimming pool and a secure outdoor jogging track.

🛏 Double from £168
🛏 291 (138 non-smoking)
🅿 250
🏊
🚇 Fulham Broadway
🚌 11, 14, 28, 211, 295, 391, 414, 424

CLARIDGE'S ☆☆☆☆☆

Map 275 G4
Brook Street W1A 2JQ
Tel 020 7629 8860
www.claridgeshotel.com

Impressive standards of luxury, style and service are upheld at this iconic bastion of British hospitality. The sumptuously decorated, air-conditioned rooms have Victorian or art-deco themes to reflect the architecture of the building. Gordon Ramsay at Claridge's, the hotel restaurant, is run by a famous British chef; the food and service are superb. The sleek cocktail bar is a popular meeting place, and the lobby is a stylish place to have afternoon tea.

🛏 Double from £233
🛏 203 (34 non-smoking)
🛗
🚇 Bond Street
🚌 8

CLIVEDEN TOWNHOUSE ★★★★★

Map 275 F7
26 Cadogan Gardens SW3 2RP
Tel 020 7730 6466
www.draycotthotel.com
Within easy reach of chic Sloane Square and the shops of the King's Road, this townhouse has luxurious, beautifully furnished bedrooms and two lounges, one with access to a delightful sheltered garden, where refreshments are served. A complimentary executive car chauffeurs guests to the City twice each morning. Beauty treatments and massage are on offer to guests.

🛏 Double from £190
🛏 35 (30 non-smoking)
🛗
🚇 Sloane Square
🚌 19, 22, 137, C1

COLLIERS HOTEL ♦

Map 275 H7
97 Warwick Way SW1V 1QL
Tel 020 7828 0210, 020 7834 6931
www.collershotel.co.uk
This small hotel offers basic but comfortable accommodation at very reasonable prices, in a pleasant row of houses not far from Buckingham Palace (see page 79).

🛏 Double from £40
🛏 19
🚭 In dining room or lounges
🚇 Victoria
🚌 24

COMFORT INN KENSINGTON ★★

Map 274 C7
22–32 West Cromwell Road SW5 9QJ
Tel 020 7373 3300
www.choicehotelseurope.com
This modern hotel is in a convenient spot for reaching lively Earl's Court. The neatly kept bedrooms all have a wide range of amenities. The welcoming public spaces are both bright and comfortable.

🛏 Double from £136
🛏 125 (48 non-smoking)
🚭 In restaurant
🚇 West Kensington, Earls Court
🚌 74, 328, C1, C3

CONNAUGHT ☆☆☆☆☆

Map 275 G5
Carlos Place W1K 6AL
Tel 020 7499 7070
www.savoy-group.com
Smaller than some of the major London hotels, the intimate, long-established Connaught

has exemplary standards of service—it's easy to see why guests return time after time. Butlers and valets will respond to guest summons at the touch of a button and nothing is too much trouble. Dining is now in the hands of Angela Hartnett, a protégé of celebrated British chef Gordon Ramsay; the menu has more than a hint of Italian about it and its standards are uncompromisingly high. The hotel has its own health club, with varied body and beauty treatments and an excellent fitness studio, complete with personal trainers.

🛏 Double from £390
ℹ️ 92
🚇 Bond Street, Marble Arch
🚌 30, 159, 274

COPTHORNE TARA HOTEL LONDON KENSINGTON ★★★★

Map 274 C6
Scarsdale Place, Wrights Lane W8 5SR
Tel 020 7937 7211
www.mill-cop.com

One of the city's larger hotels, popular with Continental tours and conferences. The public areas have a bustling atmosphere, including the relaxing Café Mozart and the Brasserie. Bedrooms fall into two grades: Classic and Connoisseur; there are also several very well-equipped rooms for guests with disabilities. All bedrooms are comfort cooled. Switch cards not accepted.

🛏 Double from £237
ℹ️ 834 (265 non-smoking)
🅿️ 86
🚇 High Street Kensington
🚌 9, 10, 27, 28, 49, 328

THE CRANLEY ★★★★

Map 274 D7
10 Bina Gardens SW5 0LA
Tel 020 7373 0123
www.thecranley.com

An elegant Victorian townhouse in a quiet residential part of South Kensington. The bedrooms, which include a number of suites, are well furnished, with many antiques and some thoughtful extras. Complimentary afternoon tea is available, along with aperitifs and canapés served in the evening.

🛏 Double from £125
ℹ️ 39
🚇 Gloucester Road
🚌 49, 74

THE DORCHESTER

☆☆☆☆☆
Map 275 G5
Park Lane W1A 2HJ
Tel 020 7629 8888
www.dorchesterhotel.com

One of London's finest hotels, the Dorchester is sumptuous. The bedrooms all have individual design schemes, are beautifully furnished and have huge, luxurious bathrooms. Leading off from the lobby, The Promenade is perfect for afternoon tea or drinks. In the evening you can catch the sound of live jazz in the bar, and enjoy a cocktail or an Italian meal. Other dining options include the traditional Grill Restaurant, which looks almost exactly as it did in 1931 when the hotel first opened, and The Oriental, which serves Cantonese cuisine in a dining room decorated with oriental objets d'art, rich silk antique robes and fragile vases. Set

SPECIAL

DELMERE ★★

Map 274 E4
130 Sussex Gardens, Hyde Park
W2 1UB
Tel 020 7706 3344
www.delmerehotels.com

The Delmere is a friendly, privately owned hotel located within easy reach of the West End. Public rooms include a jazz-theme bar and a comfortable lounge.

🛏 Double from £96
ℹ️ 35 (10 non-smoking)
🅿️ 2
🚇 Paddington
🚌 7, 15, 23, 27, 36, 205

menus with names such as Forbidden City, Imperial Phoenix and Mandarin's Tale offer an alluring but restrained range of dishes. Alternatively, you can order straight from the main menu. Other facilities include spa, health club, solarium, sauna and Jacuzzi.

🛏 Double from £387
ℹ️ 250 (34 non-smoking)
🅿️ 21
🚇 Hyde Park Corner, Marble Arch
🚌 2, 10, 16, 36, 73, 74, 82, 137, 148

DOVER HOTEL ♦♦

Map 275 H7
42–44 Belgrave Road SW1V 1RG
Tel 020 7821 9085
www.dover-hotel.co.uk
A modern, home-from-home hotel with a 24-hour reception desk. Bedrooms have private showers and WCs with cribs for babies up to 12 months old. Tea- and coffee-making facilities, TV, a hairdryer, safety deposit box and luggage storage space are all provided in the bedrooms.

🛏 Double from £85
ℹ️ 33
🚇 Victoria
🚌 24

EURO HOTEL ♦♦♦

Map 276 J2
51–53 Cartwright Gardens, Russell
Square WC1H 9IL
Tel 020 7387 4321
www.eurohotel.co.uk

This friendly bed-and-breakfast enjoys an ideal location in a leafy Georgian crescent. Russell Square Underground station, which links direct to Heathrow Airport, is only a few minutes' walk away. Many bedrooms have private bathrooms. Breakfast is served in the attractive dining room, but note that there are no meals in the evening. Tennis courts.

🛏 Double from £69
🛈 34
🍽 In dining room
Ⓜ Russell Square
🚌 7, 59, 68, 91, 168, 188

EUSTON SQUARE HOTEL ♦♦♦

Map 275 H2
152–156 North Gower Street NW1 2ND
Tel 020 7388 0099
www.euston-square-hotel.com
Not far from Euston mainline train station, this hotel has bedrooms that are compact and well equipped with facilities. Public spaces include conference rooms and a modern reception area. Also on the premises is Java Joe's, where breakfast and light snacks are offered during the day.

🛏 Double from £90
🛈 75 (40 non-smoking)
Ⓜ Euston Square
🚌 10, 24, 29, 73, 134

FOUR SEASONS HOTEL ♦♦♦♦

Map 275 F3
173 Gloucester Place, Regent's Park NW1 6DX
Tel 020 7724 3461
Right in the heart of central London, the Four Seasons is on the edge of Regent's Park (see page 115) and within easy walking distance of London Zoo

(see page 160), Madame Tussaud's and the London Planetarium (see page 101). Breakfast is served in the pretty conservatory.

🛏 Double from £95
🛈 28 (6 non-smoking)
🍽 In dining room
Ⓜ Baker Street
🚌 2, 13, 30, 74, 82, 113, 139, 189, 274

THE GAINSBOROUGH ♦♦♦♦

Map 274 E7
7–11 Queensberry Place SW7 2DL
Tel 020 7957 0000
www.eeh.co.uk

This Georgian townhouse is located in a quiet street in South Kensington, near the Natural History Museum (see pages 112–113). The bedrooms have been individually designed and are decorated with fine fabrics and quality furnishings. Breakfast is served in the dining room. There is a small public lounge and 24-hour room service is available.

🛏 Double from £141
🛈 49
🍽 In dining room
Ⓜ South Kensington
🚌 14, 49, 70, 74, 345, 360, 414

THE GALLERY ◊◊◊◊

Map 274 E7
8–10 Queensberry Place SW7 2EA
Tel 020 7915 0000
www.eeh.co.uk
This stylish property, close to Kensington and Knightsbridge, offers friendly hospitality, attentive service and sumptuously furnished bedrooms, some with a private terrace. Public areas including several lounges (one with internet access) and an elegant bar. Room service is available 24 hours a day. There are no evening meals.

🛏 Double from £141
🛈 36
🍽 In dining room
Ⓜ South Kensington
🚌 14, 49, 70, 74, 345, 360, 414

GEORGIAN HOTEL ♦♦♦

Map 275 F3
87 Gloucester Place, Baker Street W1U 6JF
Tel 020 7486 7535
www.georgianhouse.com
A traditional, privately owned hotel just a few minutes' walk from the Underground and well placed for some of London's major sights. Bedrooms vary in size but all are well equipped and there are some family rooms. Breakfast is served in the ground floor breakfast room.

🛏 Double from £85
🛈 19
🍽 In dining room or lounge
Ⓜ Marble Arch

THE GORING ☆☆☆☆☆

Map 275 H6
Beeston Place, Grosvenor Gardens SW1W 0JW
Tel 020 7396 9000
www.goringhotel.co.uk

The centrally situated Goring is within walking distance of the city's royal parks and principal shopping areas. It has the largest private garden of any of the central London hotels. Bedrooms are traditionally furnished, each to an individual design and decoration. The garden bar and drawing room are both popular for afternoon tea and cocktails. The restaurant menu has a well-deserved reputation for its contemporary British cuisine. Membership

STAYING

close by is included in the room rate.

🛏 Double from £230
ⓘ 74
🄿 8
Ⓥ Victoria
🚌 8, 16, 38, 52, 73, 82

GRANGE BLOOMS ★★★★
Map 276 J3
7 Montague Street WC1B 5BP
Tel 020 7323 1717
www.bloomshotel.com
The Grange Blooms is part of an 18th-century row of town-houses in Bloomsbury, just round the corner from the British Museum (see pages 80–85). Bedrooms are fur-nished in Regency style, and there are several day rooms: a lobby lounge, a garden ter-race, a breakfast room and a cocktail bar, all decorated with antiques, paintings and adorned with huge arrange-ments of flowers. The lounge menu is also available as room service, and unusually, meals can be delivered to your room from restaurants in the vicinity.

🛏 Double from £120
ⓘ 26
Ⓢ In restaurant
Ⓠ Holborn, Russell Square
🚌 7

GRANGE ROCHESTER ★★★
Map 275 H7
69 Vincent Square SW1P 2PA
Tel 020 7828 6611
www.grangehotels.co.uk
Overlooking leafy Vincent Square, this small hotel is not far from some of London's finest shops, theatres and attractions. Bedrooms are stylishly furnished and quiet. Some have views (and bal-conies) overlooking the square. Public spaces are relatively small, but one advantage is that you can get something to eat at any time of the day.

🛏 Double from £135
ⓘ 76 (30 non-smoking)
Ⓥ Victoria
🚌 2, 36, 185

GREAT EASTERN HOTEL
☆☆☆☆
Map 277 N3
Liverpool Street EC2M 7QN
Tel 020 7618 5000
www.great-eastern-hotel.co.uk
A minimalist hotel with a prime location in the heart of the City of London. Bedrooms have air-conditioning and are simple yet stylish, equipped with DVD and CD players. The array of restaurants includes the elegant Aurora, the Fish Market, with a champagne bar, a Japanese restaurant and another that serves meals and snacks all day. There is also a gym with treatment rooms, a steam room and personal trainers on request.

🛏 Double from £329
ⓘ 267 (74 non-smoking)
Ⓨ
Ⓠ Liverpool Street
🚌 35, 47 78, 344

THE GRESHAM HYDE PARK ★★★
Map 274 D5
66 Lancaster Gate W2 3NZ
Tel 020 7262 5090
www.gresham-hotels.com

Centrally located in Lancaster Gate, this landmark building, with its stucco façade, has been a hotel since 1817 and retains an air of gentility. It offers modern, air-conditioned bedrooms and public spaces. A fitness centre is also available.

🛏 Double from £195
ⓘ 188 (77 non-smoking)
Ⓨ
Ⓠ Lancaster Gate
🚌 705

GUILFORD HOUSE ◆◆
Map 276 K3
6 Guilford Street WC1N 1DR
Tel 020 7430 2504
www.guilfordhotel.activehotels.com
Within walking distance of the British Museum (see pages 80–85), Guilford House has single, double, triple and

THE HALKIN HOTEL
☆☆☆☆
Map 275 G6
Halkin Street, Belgravia SW1X 7DJ
Tel 020 7333 1000

www.halkin.co.uk
This one-of-a-kind contempo-rary hotel is in a peaceful area just a stroll away from Hyde Park. The stylish, air-conditioned bedrooms com-bine comfort with practicality and many include state-of-the-art facilities including TV, video and CD player, voice mail/internet access and in-room fax. You'd expect impressive food from this chic hotel, and it delivers. The restaurant, Nahm, is run by chef David Thompson, whose way with Thai cuisine has earned him a role as an advi-sor to one of Thailand's lead-ing cooking institutes.

🛏 Double from £360
ⓘ 41 (9 non-smoking)
Ⓠ Hyde Park Corner
🚌 9, 10, 14, 19, 22, 52, 74, 137

family rooms, all with private shower. Continental breakfast.

🛏 Double from £58
ⓘ 16 (4 non-smoking)
Ⓢ In dining room or lounges
Ⓠ Russell Square, King's Cross
🚌 17, 45, 46

HART HOUSE HOTEL ◆◆◆◆
Map 275 F3
51 Gloucester Place W1U 8JF
Tel 020 7935 2288
www.harthouse.co.uk
This elegant Georgian house, occupied by French nobility during the French Revolution of 1789, enjoys a prime loca-tion, a few minutes' walk from Oxford Street's shops and Madame Tussaud's (see page 101). Both bedrooms and pub-lic areas are well furnished and stylishly decorated and have

been carefully restored to retain much of the original character of the house. Excellent service and a warm welcome. English breakfast; no evening meals are served.

🛏 Double from £89
🛈 16 (all non-smoking)
🚭 No smoking anywhere
🚇 Baker Street, Marble Arch
🚌 2, 13, 30, 74, 82, 113, 139, 189, 274

HENLEY HOUSE HOTEL ◆◆◆
Map 274 C7
30 Barkston Gardens SW5 0EN
Tel 020 7370 4111
www.henleyhousehotel.com
Close to busy Earl's Court, but in a peaceful location, the Henley is a Victorian townhouse that has been tastefully modernized. There is a pleasant lobby lounge to relax in and a conservatory-style dining room. Bedrooms are neat, well equipped and welcoming.

🛏 Double from £69
🛈 21
🚭 In dining room
🚇 Earl's Court

HOTEL ORLANDO ◆◆
Map 274 off C5
83 Shepherd's Bush Road W6 7LR
Tel 020 76034890
www.hotelorlando.co.uk
A small hotel in a row of Victorian houses, with a variety of bedroom styles. Breakfast is served in the basement dining room. No evening meals.

🛏 Double from £52
🛈 14
🚭 In dining room or lounge
🚇 Hammersmith
🚌 266, 267, H91

KENSINGTON HOUSE ★★★★
Map 274 D6
15–16 Prince of Wales Terrace W8 5PQ
Tel 020 7937 2345
www.kenhouse.com
This beautiful 19th-century property has been elegantly restored to provide contemporary accommodation in the heart of Kensington. The Tiger Bar provides an airy, informal setting for light snacks and meals all day. Bedrooms are light and stylish. Guests have access to a health club close by for a small charge.

🛏 Double from £195
🛈 41 (30 non-smoking)
🚇 High Street Kensington
🚌 9, 10, 27, 28, 49, 328

KINGSWAY HALL ★★★★
Map 276 K4
Great Queen Street WC2B 5BZ
Tel 020 7309 0909
www.kingswayhall.co.uk
Close to Covent Garden, this is a modern, stylish and comfortable hotel. Air-conditioned bedrooms have such extra facilities as an in-room safe deposit box and your own private iron. The compact lounge bar serves drinks and light

snacks and the Harlequin Restaurant provides more formal dining on the premises. There's a gym in the basement.

🛏 Double from £255
🛈 170 (125 non-smoking)
🍽
🚇 Holborn
🚌 1, 59, 68, 91, 168, 171, 188

KINGSWAY HOTEL ◆◆
Map 274 E4
27 Norfolk Square, Hyde Park W2 1RX
Tel 020 7723 7784
www.kingswayhotel.net
In a square of townhouses close to Hyde Park, this bed-and-breakfast provides comfortable, reasonably priced accommodation. A traditional breakfast is served in the dining room. No evening meals.

🛏 Double from £60
🛈 33
🚭 In dining room
🚇 Paddington
🚌 705

KINGSWAY PARK HOTEL ◆◆◆
Map 274 E4
139 Sussex Gardens W2 2RX
Tel 020 77235677
www.kingswayparkhotel.com
Central bed-and-breakfast offering good value for money. Interesting modern artwork features in all the public spaces, including the basement dining room. British visitors should note that Switch cards are not accepted.

THE LANDMARK LONDON
☆☆☆☆☆
Map 275 F3
222 Marylebone Road NW1 6JQ
Tel 020 7631 8000
www.landmarklondon.co.uk

Said to be one of the last truly grand railway hotels, the Landmark is close to Hyde Park and Regent's Park. It has a number of stunning features, the most spectacular of which is the central eight-storey atrium, complete with palm trees, that forms the focal point of the hotel. There is a huge choice of bars and restaurants. The Cellars serves sophisticated bar meals; the Winter Gardens serves a varied menu all day, and the formal restaurant benefits from the talents of renowned chef John Burton-Race. Bedrooms are stylish, spacious and air-conditioned, with luxurious marble bathrooms offering deep tubs and separate showers. Guests have access to a sauna, spa and Jacuzzi.

🛏 Double from £258
🛈 299 (179 non-smoking)
🅿 90
🏊 Indoor 🍽
🚇 Marylebone, Baker Street
🚌 18

🛏 Double from £76
🛈 22 (8 non-smoking)
🅿 3
🚭 In dining room
🚇 Paddington
🚌 705

THE LANESBOROUGH
☆☆☆☆☆
Map 275 G6
Hyde Park Corner SW1X 7TA
Tel 020 7259 5599
www.lanesborough.com
Occupying an enviable position right on Hyde Park Corner,

LINCOLN HOUSE HOTEL
◆◆

Map 275 F3
33 Gloucester Place W1U 8HY
Tel 020 7486 7630
www.lincoln-house-hotel.co.uk

This friendly, family-owned

and run Georgian bed-and-breakfast is set in a townhouse near Oxford Street and has been impressively renovated. A full English breakfast is served in the cottage-style basement dining room, and Continental breakfast can be served in bedrooms. No evening meals.

🛏 Double from £85
ⓘ 24
🅿 6
Ⓜ Marble Arch
🚌 2, 13, 30, 74, 82, 113, 139, 189

this elegant hotel has an age-less charm, much appreciated by a loyal clientele. Bedrooms and public rooms reflect the highest levels of comfort. The public areas are lavishly furnished and have magnificent flower arrangements. Service is equally impressive; a personal butler attends to guests' every need 24 hours a day. The conservatory restaurant is a popular venue for accomplished international cuisine with hints of Asia and north Africa. Live music and dinner-dances add to the experience. Spa.

🛏 Double from £472
ⓘ 95 (24 non-smoking)
🅿 38
🚻
Ⓜ Hyde Park Corner
🚌 9, 10, 14, 19, 22, 52, 74, 137

LONDON BRIDGE HOTEL
★★★★

Map 277 N5
8–18 London Bridge Street SE1 9SG
Tel 020 7855 2200
www.london-bridge-hotel.co.uk

Elegant, independently owned hotel enjoying a prime location on the edge of the City, next to London Bridge train station. Bedrooms include a number of spacious deluxe rooms and suites. The public areas are small yet sophisticated. The Georgetown Asian restaurant offers upscale Malaysian cuisine in a swanky setting. There's a well-equipped gymnasium and access to a nearby gym club.

🛏 Double from £191
ⓘ 141 (82 non-smoking)
🚻
Ⓜ London Bridge
🚌 47, 343, RV1

LONDON MARRIOTT HOTEL COUNTY HALL ★★★★★

Map 276 K6
Westminster Bridge Road, County Hall SE1 7PB
Tel 020 7928 5200
www.marriott.com

Luxury hotel occupying the riverside building that formerly housed the Greater London Council, the city's governing body. Bedrooms have excellent facilities and can enjoy superb London views. Public areas include the library lounge and a restaurant that serves contemporary cuisine. Residents have access to the extensive spa and health complex.

🛏 Double from £245
ⓘ 200 (147 non-smoking)
🅿 120
🏊 Indoor 🚻

Ⓜ Westminster
🚌 77, RV1

THE LOWNDES ★★★★

Map 275 F6
21 Lowndes Street SW1X 9ES
Tel 020 7823 1234
www.lowndeshotel.com

Small hotel within walking distance of Harrods and Harvey Nichols (see page 178). The bedrooms have a modern feel with good facilities including data ports. The public areas

are small but attractive and include a brasserie restaurant. Guests may use the Peak Health Club & Spa and the pool at the Carlton Tower Hotel across the street. British visitors should note that Switch cards are not accepted.

🛏 Double from £320
ⓘ 78 (31 non-smoking)
Ⓜ Knightsbridge
🚌 19, 22, 137, C1

MANDARIN ORIENTAL HYDE PARK ☆☆☆☆☆

Map 275 F6
66 Knightsbridge SW1X 7LA
Tel 020 7235 2000
www.mandarinoriental.com

A stylish hotel in the heart of Knightsbridge, between Harvey Nichols and Hyde Park (see pages 178 and 93). Bedrooms and suites are decorated to a high standard, and many have superb views. There's a choice of dining options, among them the Park Restaurant, offering light brasserie-style dishes; the

STAYING

sophisticated Foliage, with a menu of ambitious cuisine; and the fashionable Mandarin Bar, serving light snacks and exotic cocktails. The spa has an impressive range of treatments. British visitors should note that Switch cards are not accepted.

🛏 Double from £305
ⓘ 200 (72 non-smoking)
🌿
🚇 Knightsbridge
🚌 9, 10, 14, 19, 22, 52, 74, 137

THE MANDEVILLE ★★★

Map 275 G4
Mandeville Place W1U 2BE
Tel 020 7935 5599
www.mandeville.co.uk

This elegant Edwardian building is only a short stroll from Oxford Street. There are several eating and drinking options, and 24-hour room service is also available. Popular with foreign guests as the staff speak several languages.

🛏 Double from £115
ⓘ 166 (30 non-smoking)
🚇 Bond Street
🚌 3, 25, 53, 55, 176

MARBLE ARCH INN ◆◆

Map 275 F4
49–50 Upper Berkeley Street, Marble Arch W1H 5QR
Tel 020 7723 7888
www.marblearch-inn.co.uk

Modern bed-and-breakfast a few minutes' walk from Hyde Park and Oxford Street. All rooms have remote-control TV, hairdryer, tea and coffee bar, wash basin and fridge, and most have a private shower and WC. The reception is open 24 hours.

🛏 Double from £45
ⓘ 29
🚇 Marble Arch
🚌 6, 7, 15, 16, 23, 36, 98

MELBOURNE HOUSE HOTEL ◆◆◆

Map 275 H8
79 Belgrave Road SW1V 2BG
Tel 020 7828 3516
www.melbournehousehotel.co.uk

Family-run bed-and-breakfast an easy walk from Victoria mainline train station. Bedrooms are modern and some are suitable for families. Continental breakfast is served in the basement dining room. No evening meals are served.

🛏 Double from £75
ⓘ 17
🚭 No smoking anywhere

🚇 Pimlico
🚌 24

MELIÁ WHITE HOUSE REGENTS PARK ★★★★

Map 275 H2
Albany Street NW1 3UP
Tel 020 7391 3000
www.solmelia.com

An impressive art-deco building, which was built as an apartment block in 1936. Public areas are very comfortable and the bedrooms are elegant. Fine dining is to be had in the restaurant, with soft lighting, chandeliers and lots of dark wood. Also an informal brasserie. Sauna.

🛏 Double from £271
ⓘ 582 (166 non-smoking)
🅿 7
🌿
🚇 Great Portland Street, Regent's Park, Warren Street
🚌 C2

MENTONE HOTEL ◆◆◆

Map 276 J2
54–56 Cartwright Gardens WC1H 9EL
Tel 020 7387 3927

This impressive bed-and-breakfast in a row of Victorian houses overlooking pleasant gardens in Bloomsbury is close to many central London attractions and a few minutes' walk from Russell Square Undergound station. Most of the bedrooms have private bathrooms, five of which provided facilities for visitors with disabilities. Breakfast is taken in the downstairs dining room and free internet access is available. Tennis courts. No evening meals.

🛏 Double from £80
ⓘ 45
🍽 In dining room
🚇 King's Cross, Russell Square, Euston
🚌 10, 30, 73, 91, 205

MERCURE LONDON CITY BANKSIDE ★★★

Map 277 M5
71–79 Southwark Street SE1 0JA
Tel 020 7902 0800
www.mercure.com

A contemporary hotel forming part of the South Bank rejuvenation. The air-conditioned bedrooms are spacious and there's modern dining in the stylish restaurant.

🛏 Double from £173
ⓘ 144 (88 non-smoking)
🌿

🚇 Waterloo, Blackfriars, London Bridge
🚌 381, 705

MILLENNIUM BAILEYS HOTEL LONDON KENSINGTON ★★★★

Map 274 D7
140 Gloucester Road SW7 4QH
Tel 020 7373 6000
www.millenniumhotels.co

An elegant hotel that feels like a townhouse, in a prime location opposite Gloucester Road Underground station. The air-conditioned bedrooms are well decorated and thoughtfully equipped, particularly the club rooms, which have DVD players. Public areas include a contemporary restaurant and bar. Guests may also use the facilities at a hotel close by, the Millennium Gloucester (see below).

🛏 Double from £244
ⓘ 212 (120 non-smoking)
🅿 70
🌿
🚇 Gloucester Road
🚌 49, 74

MILLENNIUM GLOUCESTER HOTEL LONDON KENSINGTON ★★★★

Map 274 D7
4–18 Harrington Gardens SW7 4LH
Tel 020 7373 6030
www.millenniumhotels.com

Popular choice among international visitors for its proximity to the Underground station, its easy access from Heathrow

STAYING

Airport and pleasant surroundings. Air-conditioned bedrooms are furnished in contemporary style. The club rooms have a dedicated lounge. Eating options include Singaporean cuisine and more formal Italian dining.

🛏 Double from £244
ℹ 610 (458 non-smoking)
🅿 110
🍽
🚇 Gloucester Road
🚌 49, 74

THE MONTAGUE ON THE GARDENS ★★★★
Map 276 J3
15 Montague Street WC1B 5BJ
Tel 020 7637 1001
www.redcarnationshotels.com
A chic hotel next to the British Museum (see page 80) with an alfresco terrace overlooking the garden. Other public areas include the restaurant, a bar lounge and conservatory, where traditional afternoon teas are served. The luxurious accommodation ranges from compact bedrooms to spacious split-level suites. There's a sauna and Jacuzzi.

🛏 Double from £302
ℹ 104 (40 non-smoking)
🍽
🚇 Russell Square
🚌 7, 59, 68, 91, 168, 188

MORNINGTON HOTEL ◆◆◆◆
Map 274 E4
12 Lancaster Gate W2 3LG
Tel 020 7262 7361
www.mornington.com

Fine Victorian building on a quiet road with direct Underground service to the West End and close to Hyde Park. Bedrooms provide comfortable, up-to-date accommodation. There are two lounges and an attractive dining room where an extensive Scandinavian-style breakfast is served. No evening meals.

🛏 Double from £140

ℹ 66 (27 non-smoking)
🍽 In dining room
🚇 Lancaster Gate
🚌 705

MY PLACE HOTEL ◊◊◊
Map 274 C7
1–3 Trebvoir Road SW5 9LS
Tel 020 7373 0833
www.myplacehotel.co.uk
Refurbished Victorian house in a peaceful residential street conveniently close to Earl's Court train station. Breakfast and light snacks are served in the restaurant. The bedrooms

are well presented and have an extremely good range of modern facilities. Night club.

🛏 Double from £69
ℹ 50 (9 non-smoking)
🍽 In area of dining room
🚇 Earl's Court
🚌 74, 328, C1, C3

NORFOLK PLAZA HOTEL ◆◆◆◆
Map 274 E4
29–33 Norfolk Square W2 1RX
Tel 020 7723 0792
www.norfolkplazahotel.co.uk
This popular hotel in the heart of Paddington is within easy walking distance of the West End. Bedrooms provide good facilities and include a number of split-level suites. The public areas include a smartly decorated bar and lounge and an attractive restaurant where breakfast is served. No dinner.

🛏 Double from £136
ℹ 87
🍽 In dining room or lounge
🚇 Paddington
🚌 705

ONE ALDWYCH ☆☆☆☆☆
Map 276 K4
1 Aldwych WC2B 4RH
Tel 020 7300 1000
www.onealdwych.com
Still relatively new on the scene, One Aldwych is already well known for its chic and contemporary style set in an Edwardian

building. There's a host of interesting features: a swimming pool with underwater music in the health club, the dramatic amber city mural in the modern and lofty Axis Restaurant, where Mediterranean cooking meets Asian, and the contemporary lobby bar where American martini cocktails are the thing to drink. Live jazz on Tuesday and Wednesday evenings. Bedrooms are no less stylish, with giant pillows, down duvets and granite bathroom surfaces.

🛏 Double from £195
ℹ 105 (60 non-smoking)
🏊 Indoor 🍽
🚇 Charing Cross, Covent Garden
🚌 521

PARAGON HOTEL ★★★
Map 274 off D8
47 Lillie Road SW6 1UD
Tel 020 7610 0880
www.paragonhotel.net
Modern hotel opposite the Earl's Court Exhibition Centre. Two restaurants offer a choice of light meals or a more formal traditional menu and carvery. Extensive conference facilities and the added bonus of an underground car park.

🛏 Double from £65
ℹ 503 (240 non-smoking)
🅿 120
🚇 West Brompton
🚌 74, 190, 430

PARK LODGE HOTEL ◆◆◆
Map 274 D5
73 Queensborough Terrace W2 3SU
Tel 020 7229 6424
Within a few minutes' walk of Kensington Gardens and fashionable Queensway, this former townhouse has been sympathetically converted to provide practical bedrooms with power showers in the bathrooms. English breakfast is served in an intimate basement dining room.

🛏 Double from £85
ℹ 29
🍽 In dining room or lounge
🚇 Paddington, Queensway, Bayswater
🚌 705

PARKES ★★★★
Map 275 F6
41 Beaufort Gardens SW3 1PW
Tel 020 7581 9944
www.parkeshotel.com
A sophisticated but intimate hotel in a tree-lined square in the heart of the borough of

Knightsbridge, catering for a maximum of just 50 guests. It's a few minutes' walk from Harrods and only 40 minutes from Heathrow Airport. The bedrooms and spacious suites with kitchens have every extra, including UK/US-compatible modems and sockets, Broadband and mini bars with 81 varieties of spirits. There's no hotel restaurant, but a wide range of dishes can be delivered from local restaurants and cafés. There is an arrangement with a nearby gym—each guest pays £15 for a one-day pass.

🛏 Double from £299
🚪 33
📺 Facilities available for guests
🚇 South Kensington, Knightsbridge
🚌 14, 74, C1

PEMBRIDGE COURT ★★★★
Map 274 C5
34 Pembridge Gardens W2 4DX
Tel 020 7229 9977
www.pemct.co.uk

This is an attractive Victorian townhouse in a residential street near the Portobello Market (see page 183). Most bedrooms are a good size and air-conditioned, and framed Victoriana and a collection of headwear feature throughout the hotel. There's a stylish lounge, and guests are given temporary membership to a local health club.

🛏 Double from £190
🚪 20
🅿 2
🚇 Notting Hill Gate
🚌 12, 27, 28, 31, 52, 70, 94, 148, 328

QUALITY HOTEL WESTMINSTER ★★★
Map 275 H7
82–83 Eccleston Square SW1V 1PS
Tel 020 7834 8042
Close to Victoria and a good base from which to explore London. Bedrooms vary in size but all have private bathrooms. The Connaughts Brasserie pro-

RAFFLES BROWN'S ★★★★
Map 275 H5
Albemarle Street W1S 4BP
Tel 020 7493 6020
www.brownshotel.com
Brown's is famous for its English country-house style, traditional furnishings and quality fixtures and fittings. Accommodation is excellent and rooms are particularly spacious for Mayfair. The elegant Restaurant 1837, claiming to be the oldest hotel restaurant in London, offers traditional luxury and individual cooking, creating an intriguing mix. The lounges prove a popular venue for afternoon tea.

🛏 Double from £220
🚪 118
📺
🚇 Green Park
🚌 8

vides a good range of meals.
🛏 Double from £130
🚪 107 (62 non-smoking)
🍽 In restaurant
🚇 Victoria

RADISSON EDWARDIAN HAMPSHIRE HOTEL ★★★★★
Map 276 J5
31 Leicester Square WC2H 7LH
Tel 020 7839 9399
www.radissonedwardian.com
This popular hotel is in central Leicester Square. The public areas have all been elegantly refurbished, with wood-panelled lounges and sitting rooms. Bedrooms and suites are air-conditioned. Excellent restaurant. You can have drinks in the vaulted alcoves of the Crescent Bar.

🛏 Double from £165
🚪 124 (93 non-smoking)
📺
🚇 Leicester Square
🚌 24, 29, 176

RADISSON EDWARDIAN KENILWORTH ★★★★
Map 276 J3
Great Russell Street WC1B 3LB
Tel 020 7637 3477
www.radissonedwardian.com
Following extensive refurbishment, the hotel has been completely transformed and now features a stylish, contemporary bar and restaurant with

an open kitchen, as well as a range of meeting rooms and a small gym and steam room. Of note are the sculptural displays of tropical flowers and the specially commissioned paintings and photographs. Bedrooms are air-conditioned and modern, and great attention has been paid to fabrics and furnishings. Each room has a seating area and work space and comes equipped with data ports and a voice mail service.

🛏 Double from £278
🚪 187 (139 non-smoking)
🚇 Tottenham Court Road
🚌 7

REGENCY HOTEL ◆◆◆
Map 275 G3
19 Nottingham Place W1U 5LQ
Tel 020 7486 5347
www.regencyhotelwestend.co.uk
The Regency Hotel is close to Madame Tussaud's (see page 101) and the West End. The bedrooms are well furnished and include some suitable for families. Breakfast is served in a light and friendly basement breakfast room.

🛏 Double from £89
🚪 20 (2 non-smoking)
🍽 In dining room or lounge
🚇 Euston, King's Cross, Baker Street
🚌 2, 13, 30, 74, 82, 113, 139, 189, 27

REGENTS PARK HOTEL ★★
Map 275 F3
156 Gloucester Place NW1 6DT
Tel 020 7258 1911
www.regentsparkhotel.com
A privately owned hotel in the heart of London, near Madame Tussaud's (see page 101). Bedrooms have private bathrooms and good facilities. A conservatory-style restaurant serves cuisine from Singapore.

🛏 Double from £89
🚪 29
🚇 King's Cross, Baker Street
🚌 2, 13, 30, 74, 82, 113, 139, 189, 274

STAYING

THE REMBRANDT ★★★★
Map 274 E7
11 Thurloe Place SW7 2RS
Tel 020 7589 8100
www.sarova.com
This attractive, ornate hotel opposite the Victoria & Albert Museum (see pages 144–149), very close to Harrods, has well-furnished bedrooms, a carvery restaurant and an attractive bar and conservatory. Guests also benefit from concessions at the adjacent Roman-styled health spa. Sauna, solarium, Jacuzzi.
🛏 Double from £215
ℹ 194 (110 non-smoking)
🏊 Indoor 🧖
🚇 South Kensington
🚌 14, 49, 70, 74, 345, 360, 414, C1

THE RITZ ☆☆☆☆☆
Map 275 H5
150 Piccadilly W1J 9BP
Tel 020 7493 8181
www.theritzlondon.com

Synonymous with style, sophistication and attention to detail, the Ritz continues its stately progress into the third millennium, having recaptured much of its former glory. All bedrooms are furnished in Louis XVI style, with marble bathrooms and every imaginable comfort and facility. A choice of elegant reception rooms includes the Palm Court, with its legendary afternoon tea, the beautifully refurbished Rivoli Bar and the sumptuous Ritz Restaurant, complete with delicate gold chandeliers and extraordinary *trompe-l'oeil* decoration.
🛏 Double from £372
ℹ 133 (20 non-smoking)
🧖
🚇 Green Park
🚌 8, 9, 14, 19, 22, 38

ROYAL GARDEN HOTEL
☆☆☆☆☆
Map 274 D6
2–24 Kensington High Street W8 4PT
Tel 020 7937 8000
www.royalgardenhotel.co.uk
A well-known landmark on the edge of Hyde Park, within walking distance of the concerts in the Royal Albert Hall (see page 194) and the shops in Kensington, this modern hotel provides guests with excellent levels of comfort and service, and a number of drinking and eating options. Rooms are generally spacious and overlook either Hyde Park or the Kensington rooftops. The showcase Tenth Floor Restaurant is contemporary in style with great views and offers classical cooking with modern and oriental influences. Sauna and solarium.
🛏 Double from £372
ℹ 396 (164 non-smoking)
🅿 160
🧖
🚇 Kensington High Street
🚌 9. 10, 27, 28, 49, 328

THE ROYAL HORSEGUARDS
★★★★
Map 276 K5
Whitehall Court SW1A 2EJ
Tel 020 7839 3400
www.thistlehotels.com
Set in the heart of Whitehall, this impressive hotel is just a short walk from Trafalgar Square (see page 136). the bedrooms offer high standards, with some overlooking the River Thames. The restaurant blends a traditional feel with modern décor.
🛏 Double from £379
ℹ 280 (180 non-smoking)
🧖
🚇 Charing Cross, Embankment
🚌 3, 11, 12, 24, 53, 77A, 88, 159

ROYAL LANCASTER ★★★★
Map 274 E4
Lancaster Terrace W2 2TY
Tel 020 7262 6737
www.royallancaster.com
Overlooking Hyde Park and Kensington Gardens, this is a smart, well-established hotel with an excellent range of public facilities, including impressive conference rooms with a theatre to seat 1,500, a 24-hour business centre and car parking. The authentic and well-known Nipa Thai is among a good choice of drinking and

eating options; more developments to the interior are planned for completion by 2004. Bedrooms are modern, with upper floors providing views across London.
🛏 Double from £303
ℹ 416 (111 non-smoking)
🅿 100
🚇 Lancaster Gate, Paddington
🚌 705

THE RUBENS AT THE PALACE
★★★★
Map 275 H6
39 Buckingham Palace Road
SW1W 0PS
Tel 020 7834 6600
If you want to stay near Buckingham Palace, this is the hotel for you. Right opposite the Royal Mews, it has stylish, air-conditioned bedrooms, including the pinstripe-walled Savile Row rooms, which follow a tailoring theme, and the opulent royal rooms, which are named after different monarchs. Two dining rooms and a plush cocktail bar complete the facilities.
🛏 Double from £150
ℹ 173 (80 non-smoking)
🚭 In dining rooms
🚇 Victoria

RUSHMORE HOTEL ◆◆◆
Map 274 C7
11 Trebovir Road SW5 9LS
Tel 020 7370 3839
www.rushmore-hotel.co.uk

This private hotel is conveniently close to the exhibition halls of Earl's Court. Bedrooms are individually themed and include some rooms suitable for families. A Continental buffet breakfast is served in the modern conservatory. No evening meals.
🛏 Double from £79
ℹ 22 (4 non-smoking)
🚭 In dining room
🚇 Earl's Court
🚌 74, 328, C1, C3

STAYING

ST. GEORGE HOTEL ♦♦♦♦

Map 275 F4
49 Gloucester Place W1U 8JE
Tel 020 7486 8586
www.stgeorge-hotel.net

A Grade II-listed house (that means it is protected from development) in the West End. Bedrooms are well furnished and feature an excellent range of facilities, including modem points, safes and mini fridges. Breakfast is served in a chic breakfast room and the friendly staff offer a warm welcome. No evening meals.

🛏 Double from £135
🛉 19 (6 non-smoking)
🍴 In dining room
🚇 Baker Street
🚌 2, 13, 30, 74, 82, 113, 139, 189, 274

THE SAVOY ☆☆☆☆☆

Map 276 K5
Strand WC2R 0EU
Tel 020 7836 4343
www.savoygroup.co.uk

The Savoy is internationally renowned and lives up to its reputation. Service flows smoothly and there's a high level of comfort in all the bedrooms, many of which have fine views along the River Thames. A choice of dining areas includes The Grill and a new restaurant run by Marcus Wareing that opened in 2003. No visit would be complete without experiencing afternoon tea in the Thames Foyer; or try the regular Sunday afternoon tea dance. Health and beauty treatments and a sauna.

🛏 Double from £395
🛉 263 (55 non-smoking)
🅿 65
🏊 Indoor 📺
🚇 Charing Cross, Covent Garden
🚌 6, 9, 11, 13, 15, 23, 77A, 91, 176

SIDNEY HOTEL ♦♦♦

Map 275 H8
68–76 Belgrave Road SW1V 2BP
Tel 020 7834 2738
www.sidneyhotel.com

A pleasant hotel conveniently located close to Victoria train station. Several bedrooms are suitable for family use. The public areas include a bar lounge and an airy breakfast room. No evening meals.

🛏 Double from £98
🛉 81 (30 non-smoking)
🍴 In dining room or lounge
🚇 Victoria, Pimlico
🚌 24

STRAND PALACE ★★★

Map 276 K4
372 The Strand WC2R 0JJ
Tel 020 7836 8080
www.strandpalacehotel.co.uk

At the heart of theatreland, the Strand Palace is a vast hotel, with rooms that vary in style, including Club rooms with enhanced facilities and exclusive use of the Club lounge. The extensive public areas include four places in which to eat and a popular cocktail bar.

🛏 Double from £138
🛉 785 (400 non-smoking)
🚇 Charing Cross

THE WASHINGTON MAYFAIR HOTEL ★★★★

Map 275 H5
5–7 Curzon Street W1J 5HE
Tel 020 7499 7000
www.washington-mayfair.co.uk

A modern hotel in stylish Mayfair, with a high standard of accommodation. Bedrooms are all very comfortable. A popular venue for light refreshments, which are served in the marbled and wood-panelled public areas.

🛏 Double from £188
🛉 171 (94 non-smoking)
📺
🚇 Green Park
🚌 8

THE WESTBURY ★★★★

Map 275 H4
Bond Street W1S 2YF
Tel 020 7629 7755
www.westbury-london.co.uk

THE WILLETT ♦♦♦♦

Map 275 G7
32 Sloane Gardens, Sloane Square SW1W 8DJ
Tel 020 7824 8415
www.eeh.co.uk

Part of a terracotta row of Victorian townhouses in Chelsea. This friendly hotel, with 24-hour room service, prides itself on retaining a quiet and dignified atmosphere. Interesting features include the reception area's ornately carved Dutch bed and handsome gilt ormolu clock, a stained-glass mosaic, paintings and chandeliers.

🛏 Double from £106
🛉 19
🍴 In dining room
🚇 Sloane Square
🚌 319

The Westbury is right in the heart of London's finest shopping area. Standards of accommodation are high throughout. The public spaces offer a variety of eating and drinking options, including the Polo Bar for cocktails.

🛏 Double from £282
🛉 249 (150 non-smoking)
📺
🚇 Bond Street
🚌 8

WINDERMERE HOTEL ♦♦♦♦

Map 275 H8
142–144 Warwick Way SW1V 4JE
Tel 020 7834 5163
www.windermere-hotel.co.uk

A relaxed and informal family-run hotel within easy reach of Victoria mainline train station. The Pimlico Restaurant serves renowned evening meals and good breakfasts.

🛏 Double from £109
🛉 22 (7 non-smoking)
🍴 In dining room or lounges
🚇 Victoria 🚌 24

STAYING

MAJOR HOTEL CHAINS

Company Logo	Company statement	Number of Hotels	Contact Number and Website
Best Western	Britain's largest group has around 350 independently owned and managed, modern and traditional, two-, three- and four-star hotels. Many with leisure facilities and rosette awards.	16	08457 737373 www.bestwestern.co.uk
DAYS INN	Good quality, modern, budget accommodation at motorway services.	4	0800 0280400 www.daysinn.com
Express by Holiday Inn	Express by Holiday Inn offers superior budget accommodation with complimentary breakfast at more than 70 modern hotels in the UK.	15	0800 434040 www.ichotelsgroup.com
GRANGE HOTELS	A collection of privately owned hotels, 10 located in central London and one in Bracknell, Berkshire.	11	020 7233 7888 www.grangehotels
Holiday Inn HOTELS · RESORTS	The internationally known group offers a wide range of hotels throughout the UK.	34	0800 405060 www.ichotelsgroup.com
ibis Accor	Ibis is a fast-growing chain of modern travel accommodation with properties across the UK.	10	020 8283 4550 www.ibishotel.com
INTER-CONTINENTAL. HOTELS AND RESORTS	An internationally renowned group primarily represented in the UK with three five-star hotels in central London.	3	0800 0289 387 www.ichotelsgroup.com
JURYS DOYLE HOTELS	This Irish company has a range of three- and four-star hotels in the UK and the Republic of Ireland.	6	00 353 1607 0050 ww.jurysdoyle.com
Marriott HOTELS · RESORTS · SUITES	This international brand offers four-star hotels in prime locations. Most are modern and have leisure facilities; some have a focus on golf.	8	0800 221 222 0800 699 996 www.marriott.com
MERIDIEN HOTELS & RESORTS	An international brand of four- and five-star hotels, with good representation in and around London.	10	08000 28 28 40 www.lemeridien.com
MILLENNIUM HOTELS AND RESORTS	Part of the Millennium and Copthorne group, comprising six high-quality four-star hotels, mainly in central London.	4	0800 41 47 41 www.millennium.com
NOVOTEL	Part of the French group Accor, Novotel provides modern three-star hotels in key locations throughout the UK.	2	020 8283 4500 www.novotel.com
Radisson EDWARDIAN	This high-quality London-based group offers mainly four-star hotels in key locations throughout the capital.	10	0800 374411 www.radissonedwardian.com
Red Carnation HOTELS	A collection of prestigious four- and five-star central London hotels, providing luxurious surroundings and attentive service.	5	020 7514 5633 www.redcarnationhotels.com
RENAISSANCE HOTELS	One of the Marriott brands, Renaissance is a collection of individual hotels offering comfortable rooms, quality cuisine and good service.	2	0800 221 222 0800 699 996 www.marriott.com
The Savoy Group	A prestigious group of four five-star hotels in central London and a four-star hotel in the Cotswolds.	5	00800 7671 7671 www.savoy-group.com
Sheraton HOTELS & RESORTS	Sheraton is represented in the UK by a small number of four- and five-star hotels in London and Scotland.	6	0800 35 35 35 www.sheraton.com
THISTLE HOTELS	A large group of mainly four-star hotels across the UK, with many in London, and some country-house properties.	24	0800 18 17 16 www.thistlehotels.com
Travelodge	Good quality, modern, budget accommodation. Almost every lodge has an adjacent family restaurant, often a Little Chef, Harry Ramsden's (fish) or Burger King.	11	08700 850950 www.travelodge.co.uk

TASTING & STAYING

Planning

BEFORE YOU GO

CLIMATE AND WHEN TO GO

● London's sprawl of heated buildings has created its own microclimate, so frost and lingering snow are very rare. The temperature seldom falls below freezing, although northerly winds can make it feel very chilly in the winter. On average, January remains the coldest month. The temperature in London is generally two degrees above that of the rest of Britain.

● Be prepared for rain at any time of year. Officially, the wettest weeks are from late September to the end of November, but it can be just as wet in the middle of summer.

● The period between June and August is the warmest and busiest (school holidays run from late July to early September). Spring and September are appreciably quieter, but the weather is less reliable. May and June have the bonus of long daylight hours (see table above).

● The winter months can be a good time for visiting London, as sights are far less crowded and accommodation is often cheaper.

WEATHER REPORTS

● Daily forecasts are given at the end of television and radio news shows. They are also available by phone, fax, text or on the internet. Telephone 09003 444 900 for regional forecasts over the phone or fax 09060 100 400 for a list of regions covered by faxed forecasts.

● For forecasts texted to a mobile (cell) phone type wthr4 followed by a UK town or city. Send this message to 82222 (available on all networks except Virgin).

WHAT TO TAKE

You may find the following check-list useful, but if you forget or need to replace any items, there's every chance that you'll be able to find its equivalent in London.

● A selection of clothing for a wide range of weather conditions. Rainwear is essential all year. Umbrellas can be more trouble than they're worth, especially on windy days; a lightweight water-proof jacket is a better option.

● Addresses and phone numbers of emergency contacts.

● Compass (useful for finding your way).

● Driver's licence (if you hold a licence or permit from Australia, Canada, Ireland, New Zealand or the USA, this will suffice) or International Driver's Licence (if your licence is in a language other than English).

● Photocopies of passport and travel insurance (or send scanned versions of these to an e-mail account that you can access while you are away).

● Credit cards (preferably more than one credit card), and/or travellers' cheques, and a small amount of cash in sterling.

● Numbers of credit/debit cards, registration numbers of mobile (cell) phones, cameras and other expensive equipment (in case you need to report loss to the police). Keep these separately from the items.

DAYLIGHT HOURS	
January	8
February	9
March	11
April	13
May	15
June	17
July	16
August	15
September	13
October	11
November	10
December	8

TIMES ZONES

Britain is on GMT (Greenwich Mean Time—also known as Universal Time or UTC) during winter. In summer (late March to late October) clocks go forward one hour to British Summer Time (BST). The world is divided into 24 time zones. The chart shows time differences from GMT.

City	Time difference	Time at 12 noon GMT
Amsterdam	+1	1pm
Chicago	-6	6am
Auckland	+10	10pm
Berlin	+1	1pm
Brussels	+1	1pm
Chicago	-6	6am
Dublin	0	noon
Johannesburg	+2	2pm
Madrid	+1	1pm
Montréal	-6	6am
New York	-5	7am
Paris	+1	1pm
Perth, Australia	+8	8pm
Rome	+1	1pm
San Francisco	-8	4am
Sydney	+10	10pm
Tokyo	+9	9pm

TEMPERATURE

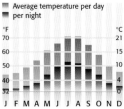

■ Average temperature per day
■ per night

°F / °C
70 / 21
60 / 15
50 / 10
40 / 4
32 / 0

J F M A M J J A S O N D

■ Average no. of days above 70°F
■ below 32°F

30 / 30
20 / 20
10 / 10
0 / 0

J F M A M J J A S O N D

RAINFALL

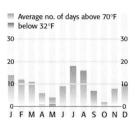

Average rainfall

in / mm
5 / 127
4 / 102
3 / 76
2 / 51
1 / 25
0 / 0

J F M A M J J A S O N D

WEATHER WEBSITES		
Organization	Notes	Website
BBC	London, UK and world weather reports and forecasts, plus many related topics. Includes satellite imagery	www.bbc.co.uk/weather/
The Met Office (UK)	Clear, professional site with good specialist links	www.metoffice.com

- Spare passport photos for travel cards (see page 48).

PASSPORTS

- Visitors from outside the UK must have a passport valid for at least six months from the date of entry into the country.
- The United Kingdom (England, Wales, Scotland and Northern Ireland), the Channel Islands, the Isle of Man and the Republic of

Ireland form a common travel area. Once you have entered any part of it through immigration control, you do not need further clearance with customs to travel within it.
- You must show photographic ID, such as a passport or driver's licence with a photo for all internal flights.

VISAS

- Before travelling you should double check visa requirements: see www.ukvisas.gov.uk.
- Citizens of countries in the European Economic Area (EEA)—the European Union (EU), Switzerland, Norway, Finland and Iceland—can enter the UK for purposes of holiday or work for any length of stay, without requiring a visa.
- If you are a citizen of the United States, Australia, Canada or New Zealand, you do not require a visa for stays of up to six months. However, you must have enough money to support yourself without needing to work or receiving any money from public funds.

Goods you buy in EU countries

If you bring back to the UK large quantities of alcohol or tobacco, a Customs Officer is likely to ask about the purposes for which you hold the goods. This particularly applies if you have with you more than the amounts listed below:

- 3,200 cigarettes
- 400 cigarillos
- 200 cigars
- 3kg of smoking tobacco

- 110 litres of beer
- 10 litres of spirits
- 90 litres of wine (of which only 60 litres can be sparkling wine)
- 20 litres of fortified wine (such as port or sherry)

The European Union countries are: Austria, Belgium, Denmark, Finland, France, Germany, Greece, Republic of Ireland, Italy, Luxembourg, Netherlands, Portugal, Spain (but not the Canary Islands), Sweden and the United Kingdom (but not the Channel Islands).

Bringing goods to the UK from outside the EU

You are entitled to the allowances shown below only if you travel with the goods and do not plan to sell them. For further information see the HM Customs and Excise website: www.hmce.gov.uk.

- 200 cigarettes; or
- 100 cigarillos; or
- 50 cigars; or
- 250g of tobacco

- 60cc/ml of perfume
- 250cc/ml of toilet water

- 2 litres of still table wine
- 1 litre of spirits or strong liqueurs over 22% volume; or
- 2 litres of fortified wine, sparkling wine or other liqueurs

- £145 worth of all other goods including gifts and souvenirs

- Those wishing to stay longer, and nationals of certain countries require a visa—check with the embassy or consulate in your own country.
- You are usually allowed to enter and leave the UK as many times as you like while your visa is valid. On arrival in the UK, you must be able to produce documentation establishing your identity and nationality.

TRAVEL INSURANCE

- Recommended for insuring your possessions and legal liability, but not always needed to cover medical expenses, as some visitors (including citizens of European Union countries,

Australia and New Zealand) receive free treatment under the National Health Service (see page 300). However, visitors from countries not included in this arrangement, such as the United States and Canada, must make provision for their own medical insurance.
- An annual travel insurance policy may be the best value for those who make several trips away from home in any 12-month period. Be aware, however, that long trips abroad may not be covered.

OTHER HEALTH DOCUMENTS

- E111 form (see page 300).

PLANNING

BRITISH EMBASSIES AND CONSULATES ABROAD		
Country	Address	Website
Australia	High Commission, Commonwealth Avenue, Yarralumla, Canberra ACT 2600, tel 02 62706666	www.uk.emb.gov.au
Canada	High Commission, 80 Elgin Street, Ottowa 5K7, tel 613 237-1530	
Ireland	29 Merrion Road, Ballsbridge, Dublin 4, tel 01 203700	www.britishembassy.ie
New Zealand	High Commission, 44 Hill Street, Wellington 1, tel 04 4726049	www.britain.org.nz
South Africa	High Commission, 91 Parliament Street, Cape Town 8001, tel 21 461 7220	
USA	3100 Massachusetts Avenue NW, Washington DC 20008, tel 202 588-6500	www.britainusa.com

PRACTICALITIES

ELECTRICITY
● Britain is on 240-volts AC, and plugs have three square pins. If you are bringing an electrical appliance from another country where the voltage is the same, a plug adaptor will work. If the voltage is different, as in the United States—110 volts—you need a converter.
● Small appliances such as razors and laptops can run on a 50-watt converter, while heating appliances, irons and hairdryers require a 1,600-watt converter. Combination converters cover both types.
● Telephone sockets are also different and will require an adaptor.

LAUNDRY
● When you book your hotel or bed-and-breakfast, check whether there are laundry facilities.
● Telephone directories list launderettes and dry-cleaning companies.
● Some launderettes offer service washes, where the washing and drying is done for you (typical cost £5–£6 for a small bag), either within a day or with a 2- to 4-day turnaround.
● Dry cleaning is expensive, but widely available: A jacket or skirt individually cleaned might cost around £4. Some dry-cleaning companies also offer clothes-mending services or small repairs such as zipper replacement.

MEASUREMENTS
● Britain officially uses the metric system. Fuel is sold by the litre, and food in grams and kilograms. However, imperial measurements are still used widely in everyday speech (pounds, ounces and stones, to measure the weight of a person), and road distances and speed limits are in miles and miles per hour respectively.
● Beer in pubs is sold in pints (one pint is slightly less than 0.5 litres).
● Note that the British gallon (4.5460 litres) is larger than the US gallon (3.7854 litres).

PUBLIC LAVATORIES
● Generally these are well located, plentiful and free of charge in built-up areas. In some city locations neat, self-cleaning stainless steel cubicles are available (usual cost 20p), and there is a small charge to use lavatories at large rail stations. Some unpleasant facilities still survive, but most are modern and well maintained.
● All major road service stations and filling stations have free lavatories. In rural areas lavatories can be found at some roadside pull-ins and parking areas.

SMOKING
● Most restaurants have no-smoking areas, and an increasing number forbid smoking altogether.
● In pubs you can generally smoke, but there are sometimes dedicated no-smoking zones within dining areas.

CLOTHING SIZES			

The chart below shows how British, European and US clothes sizes differ

UK	Europe	USA	
36	46	36	SUITS
38	48	38	
40	50	40	
42	52	42	
44	54	44	
46	56	46	
48	58	48	
7	41	8	SHOES
7.5	42	8.5	
8.5	43	9.5	
9.5	44	10.5	
10.5	45	11.5	
11	46	12	
14.5	37	14.5	SHIRTS
15	38	15	
15.5	39/40	15.5	
16	41	16	
16.5	42	16.5	
17	43	17	
8	36	6	DRESSES
10	38	8	
12	40	10	
14	42	12	
16	44	14	
18	46	16	
20	48	18	
4.5	37.5	6	SHOES
5	38	6.5	
5.5	38.5	7	
6	39	7.5	
6.5	40	8	
7	41	8.5	

CONVERSION CHART		
From	To	Multiply by
Inches	Centimetres	2.54
Centimetres	Inches	0.3937
Feet	Metres	0.3048
Metres	Feet	3.2810
Yards	Metres	0.9144
Metres	Yards	1.0940
Miles	Kilometres	1.6090
Kilometres	Miles	0.6214
Acres	Hectares	0.4047
Hectares	Acres	2.4710
Gallons	Litres	4.5460
Litres	Gallons	0.2200
Ounces	Grams	28.35
Grams	Ounces	0.0353
Pounds	Grams	453.6
Grams	Pounds	0.0022
Pounds	Kilograms	0.4536
Kilograms	Pounds	2.205
Tons	Tonnes	1.0160
Tonnes	Tons	0.9842

● Smoking is banned on nearly all trains and buses, although long-distance rail services have designated smokers' carriages. Smoking is not permitted anywhere on the London Underground nor on London buses.
● For an online guide to smoke-free pubs, restaurants and hotels go to www.ash.org.uk.

DOGS
● London is not an ideal place to bring dogs; few hotels accept them and the enforcement of bylaws is strict.
● There are no restrictions for taking dogs on London Underground, but all dogs must be carried on escalators.
● Dogs are accepted on buses at the discretion of the driver.

CHILDREN
● Some hotels, restaurants and pubs have a strict no-children policy or serve only those over a certain age. However, there are places to stay with excellent facilities for children, including babysitting services and baby monitors.
● Many tourist attractions offer reduced admission fees or are free for children, and some sell family tickets.
● In pubs, children must be accompanied by an adult (if they are allowed in at all). Children under 14 are not allowed in the bar area and it is illegal for

anyone under 18 to purchase alcohol. Some restaurants and pubs provide high chairs, especially the larger chains (see page 272).

● Most major department stores, shopping malls and public venues such as theatres have changing tables for babies, but these tend to be located in the women's toilet areas.

VISITORS WITH DISABILITIES

● Most tourist attractions and public places have facilities for visitors with disabilities, but it is always wise to check in advance in case your particular need is not catered for.

● Any special needs should be mentioned when you are booking accommodation, as many places may not be accessible to wheel-chairs or for visitors with visual impairments. The Holiday Care Service *(tel 08451 249971)* provides information on accom-modation suitable for visitors with disabilities, classing hotels as Category 1—for independent wheelchair-users, Category 2—for wheelchair-users with a helper, and Category 3—for wheelchair-users who can take a few steps.

● The national organization for people with disabilities is RADAR (Royal Association for Disability and Rehabilitation), 12 City Forum, 250 City Road EC1V 8AF, tel 020 7250 3222, www.radar.org.uk.

● The best places for accessible public toilets for those with disabilities are in the major department stores, such as John Lewis and Selfridge's (Oxford Street), Harrods (Knightsbridge) and Peter Jones (Sloane Square).

● Artsline *(tel 020 7388 2227, www.dircon.co.uk/artsline)* has

detailed information on arts, attractions and entertainment for those with disabilities.

● The Royal National Institute for the Blind *(tel 020 7388 1266)* publishes a hotel guide book.

● For information on public transport services for visitors with disabilities, see page 64.

CAR RENTAL

● Arranging a rental car through your travel agent before arriving saves money and allows you to find out in advance about deposits, drop-off charges, cancellation penalties and insurance costs. There are several established car rental companies in London. Large firms have offices around the city and at the main airports.

● The majority of rental cars in London have manual rather than automatic transmission. Automatic cars are available but are usually more expensive.

Costs

● You must have a driver's licence. An international driver's licence is not required unless your licence is in a language other than English.

● Most rental firms require the driver to be at least 23 years old with at least 12 months' driving experience. If you are under 25 you will probably be charged a higher rate.

● Rental rates usually include unlimited mileage. A cheaper option may be to opt for a limited mileage allowance, which makes an extra charge for additional mileage thereafter.

● It is important to ensure that you have some form of personal insurance along with Collision Damage Waiver (CDW). Many companies also offer Damage

Excess Reduction (DER) and Theft Protection, for an additional charge. You will also have to pay more for any additional drivers.

● Make sure you find out what equipment comes as standard (air-conditioning and automatic transmission are not always available) and check that the price quoted includes VAT (Value Added Tax), the sales tax levied on most goods and services.

● Ask about optional extras such as roof racks and child seats before collecting the car.

● Budget for about £40 per day for an economy car (such as a Ford Fiesta), £50 per day for a mid-range vehicle (such as a Rover 4 series) and £60 or more for a premium car.

● Most cars use unleaded fuel; make sure you know what's required (normal, unleaded or diesel) before filling the tank.

● When the car is returned, fuel should be topped up to the level shown when you first picked it up—otherwise you will be charged at the rental company's own tariff per litre, which is much higher than you would pay elsewhere.

Before Driving Off

Although reputable companies operate new cars and service them to a high standard, make your own checks before you accept a rental car.

● Check for minor bodywork damage.

● Check for tyre wear (insist on a different vehicle if the tread appears low or uneven or if there are cuts or bulges in any sidewalls).

● Arrange for a car seat if you have small children.

CAR RENTAL COMPANIES		
Name	**Details**	**Website**
Alamo	Gatwick Airport, South Terminal, Lower Forecourt Road, tel 01293 567790	
	Heathrow Airport, Northern Perimeter Road, tel 020 8750 2800	
	Open daily 24 hours (airports); Mon 8–7,	
	Sat 8–6, Sun 9–4 (central information office)	www.alamo.co.uk
Avis	Gatwick Airport, South Terminal	
	Heathrow Airport, Northrop Road, tel 08700 100 287	
	Open daily 24 hours (airports); 6am–midnight (central information office)	www.avis.co.uk
Europcar BCR	Gatwick Airport, International Arrivals, tel 01293 531062	
	Heathrow Airport, Northern Perimeter Road West, tel 020 8897 0811	www.europecar.com
Hertz	Gatwick Airport, International Arrivals Halls	
	Heathrow Airport, Northern Perimeter Road West, tel 08705 996 699	
	Open daily 24 hours	www.hertz.co.uk

MONEY

- Britain is an expensive country to travel in, so it's a good idea to explore your options for carrying and changing money.
- Expect to spend a minimum of about £40 per day, if you're touring independently.
- The best idea is to carry money in a range of forms—cash, at least one credit card, bank card/charge card/Switch card and travellers' cheques.

CASH
- Britain's currency is the pound sterling (see below).
- Scotland has its own notes, which are legal tender through-out the UK.
- There is no limit to the amount of cash you may import or export.
- It is worth keeping a few 10p, 20p, 50p and £1 coins handy for pay-and-display parking machines and parking meters.

CREDIT CARDS
- Credit cards are widely accepted throughout London

and Britain; Visa and MasterCard are the most popular, followed by American Express, Diners Club and JCB.

There are ATMs all over the city

- Credit cards can also be used for withdrawing currency at cashpoints (ATMs) at any bank displaying the appropriate sign. If your credit cards or travellers' cheques are stolen or lost, call the issuer immediately, then report the loss to the police; you'll need a reference number for insurance purposes.

CASHPOINTS (ATMs)
- ATMs are at most banks across the country. Check with your bank if you are uncertain whether you will be charged for using another bank's ATM.
- LINK is the UK's only branded network of self-service cash machines. Use of LINK machines is free, except for credit, charge and store cards, for which you pay a cash advance fee.
- You will be charged for using the convenience machines at certain private locations (such as fuel garages); fees are displayed, and are usually £1.25–£1.50.

CASH

There are 100 pence (p) to the pound (£).
Coins are in denominations of **1p, 2p, 5p, 10p, 20p, 50p, £1** and **£2**.
Banknotes are in denominations of **£5, £10, £20** and **£50**.

2 pounds—£2   1 pound—£1   50 pence—50p   20 pence—20p

10 pence—10p   5 pence—5p   2 pence—2p   1 penny—1p

PLANNING

CHEQUEP☉INT
CHANGECAMBIO

Chequepoint
548 Oxford Street W1N 9HJ
Tel 020 7723 1005
Marble Arch Underground

71 Gloucester Road SW7 5BW
Tel 020 7373 9682
Gloucester Road Underground

2 Queensway W2 4RH
Tel 020 7229 0093
Queensway Underground

TRAVELLERS' CHEQUES
● These are the safest way to carry money, as you will be refunded in the event of loss usually within 24 hours (keep the counterfoil separate from the cheques themselves).

BANKS
● Most banks open Monday to Friday 9.30 to 4.30. Some branches also open on Saturday morning.
● It pays to shop around for the best exchange and commission rates on currency. You do not pay commission on sterling travellers' cheques, provided you cash them at a bank affiliated with the issuing bank.
● You need to present ID (usually a passport) when cashing travellers' cheques.

POST OFFICES
● Most post offices are open Monday–Friday 9–5.30 and Saturday 9–12.
● Apart from the main post offices offering full postal services, there are sub-post offices, often forming part of a newsagent.
● Many post offices offer commission-free bureaux de change services (tel 08458 500900), with an online ordering service available through www.postoffice.co.uk. Payment can be made in cash, or by cheque, banker's draft, Visa, MasterCard, Switch, Delta, Solo or Electron.

BUREAUX DE CHANGE
● These money-changing operations can be found at most major rail and Underground stations in central London, as well as at airports and at on-street locations, and are mostly

Name	Head Office Address	Telephone
Barclays	54 Lombard Street EC3 P3AA	020 7699 5000
Lloyds/TSB	25 Gresham Street EC2V 7HN	020 7626 1500
NatWest	135 Bishopsgate EC2M 3UR	0870 240 1155
HSBC	8 Canada Square E14 5HQ	020 7991 8888

MAJOR BANKS
There are four main banks in the UK and they have branches all over London. All have foreign exchange facilities.

open 8am to 10pm. Rates of exchange may be higher than at banks; it pays to shop around. Commission rates for currency and travellers' cheques should be clearly displayed.
● Beware of commission-free bureaux as they often charge very poor rates of exchange, and should generally be used only for changing small amounts.

DISCOUNTS
● Reduced fares on buses, Underground services and trains are available for children under 16.
● Over 60s and 16- to 25-year-olds can purchase railcards for £20 and £18 respectively, giving a one-third reduction on off-peak national rail services. See also page 59.

THE EURO
● Britain may not yet have committed itself to the euro currency, but it is possible to spend euros in Britain.
● One euro is made up of 100 cents. Euro notes come in denominations of 5, 10, 20, 50, 100, 200 and 500 euros. Coins come in denominations of 1 and 2 euros, and 1, 2, 5, 10, 20 and 50 cents.
● It is not always clear where you might be able to spend euros, but many major high-street chain stores accept them in some or all of their branches: for example the Body Shop, Clarks, Debenhams, Habitat, HMV, Marks and Spencer, Miss

Selfridge, Topshop, Virgin, WH Smith and the bookstore Waterstone's.
● Some pubs owned by JD Wetherspoon, Scottish and Newcastle and Shepherd Neame take euros, as do some BP fuel stations.
● Train tickets on the Stansted Express, the Gatwick Express and Virgin trains can be paid for in euros.
● Outside London, in general the bigger the city, the more places will accept euros.

WIRING MONEY
● Having money wired from your home country can be expensive (agents charge fees for the service) and time-consuming.
● Money can be wired from bank to bank, which takes up to two working days, or to agents such as Travelex (tel 01733 318922, www.travelex.co.uk) and Western Union (tel 0800 833 833, www.westernunion. com).

VAT REFUNDS
See page 170.

TIPPING	
Restaurants (where service is not included)	10%
Tour guides	£1–£2
Hairdressers	10%
Taxis	10%
Chambermaids	50p–£1 per day
Porters	50p–£1 per bag

10 EVERYDAY ITEMS AND HOW MUCH THEY COST	
Takeaway sandwich	£2.50
Bottle of water	£1
Cup of tea or coffee	90p–£1.75
Pint of beer	£2.40
Glass of house wine	£2.50
British national daily newspaper	40p–£1.30
Roll of camera film	£5
20 cigarettes	£4.80
Ice cream	£1
Litre of unleaded petrol	78p

PLANNING

HEALTH

- Britain's National Health Service (the NHS) was set up in 1948 to provide healthcare for the country's citizens based on need rather than the ability to pay. It is funded by the taxpayer and managed by a government department.
- While NHS care for British citizens is free, private health care can also be bought from organizations such as BUPA.
- Visitors from the European Union (EU) are entitled to free NHS treatment (see below).

BEFORE YOU DEPART

- Consult your doctor at least six to eight weeks before leaving.
- Free medical treatment is available through the NHS for visitors from EU countries, who should pick up a free E111 form from their local post office and have it stamped and signed before they leave. The same E111 can be re-used, unless your personal details have changed.
- Several countries have reciprocal healthcare agreements with the United Kingdom (see below). In most cases a passport is sufficient identification for hospital treatment. Most countries, however, including the United States and Canada, do not have agreements with the UK, and a comprehensive travel insurance policy is advised.
- No inoculations are required to enter Britain. However, it is advisable to have an anti-tetanus booster before leaving. Check with your doctor whether you need immunization or health advice for: meningococcal meningitis; hepatitis B; diphtheria booster; or measles/MMR.

COUNTRIES WITH RECIPROCAL HEALTH AGREEMENTS WITH THE UNITED KINGDOM

Anguilla
Australia
Barbados
British Virgin Islands
Bulgaria
Channel Islands
Czech Republic
Falkland Islands
Hungary
Malta
Montserrat
New Zealand
Poland

Romania
Russia
Slovak Republic
St. Helena
Turks and Caicos Islands
Republics of the former USSR except Latvia, Lithuania and Estonia
Yugoslavia (i.e., Serbia and Montenegro) and successor states (Croatia, Bosnia, Slovenia and Macedonia)

HEALTHY FLYING

- Visitors from the United States, Australia or New Zealand may be concerned about the effect of a long flight on their health. The most widely publicized concern is Deep Vein Thrombosis (DVT). Misleadingly labelled 'economy class syndrome', DVT is when a blood clot forms in the body's deep veins, particularly in the legs. The clot can move around the bloodstream and can be fatal.
- You are most at risk if you are elderly, pregnant, using the contraceptive pill, smoke or are overweight. If you think you are at increased risk of DVT, see your doctor before departing. Flying increases the likelihood of DVT because passengers are often seated in a cramped position for long periods of time and may become dehydrated.
- Other health hazards for flyers are airborne diseases and bugs spread by the air-conditioning system on board. These hazards are largely unavoidable but if you have a serious medical condition seek advice from a doctor before flying.

To minimize risk:
- drink water (not alcohol)
- don't stay immobile for hours at a time
- stretch and exercise your legs periodically
- wear elastic flight socks, which support veins and reduce the chances of a clot forming
- a small dose of aspirin, which thins the blood, may be recommended.

EXERCISES

1 ANKLE ROTATIONS   2 CALF STRETCHES   3 KNEE LIFTS

Lift feet off the floor. Draw a circle with the toes, moving one foot clockwise and the other counter-clockwise.

With heel on the floor, point foot upward as high as you can. Then lift heel, keeping ball of foot on the floor.

Lift leg with knee bent while contracting your thigh muscle. Straighten leg, pressing foot flat to the floor.

WHAT TO TAKE WITH YOU

- Visitors from the EU should bring a stamped E111 form and a photocopy, which should be kept in a safe place.
- Those from outside the European Union should bring their travel insurance policy and a photocopy.
- Visitors with existing medical conditions and allergies, for example to commonly used drugs, should wear a warning bracelet or tag.

MAJOR PHARMACIES

Name	Telephone	Website
Co-op Pharmacy	0161 834 1212	www.co-oppharmacy.co.uk
Boots the Chemist	0115 950 6111	www.wellbeing.com
Lloyds Pharmacy	024 7643 2400	www.lloydspharmacy.com
Moss Pharmacy	020 8890 9333	www.mosspharmacy.co.uk
Superdrug	020 8684 7000	www.superdrug.com
Sainsbury Pharmacy	020 7695 6000	www.sainsbury.com
Tesco Pharmacy	01992 632222	www.tesco.com

HOSPITALS WITH EMERGENCY DEPARTMENTS

Name	Address	Telephone
Charing Cross Hospital	Fulham Palace Road W6 8RF	020 8846 1234
Chelsea Royal Hospital	Royal Hospital Road SW3	020 7730 0161
Guy's Hospital	St. Thomas Street SE1 9RT	020 7955 5000
Royal Free Hospital	Pond Street, Hampstead NW3 2QG	020 7794 0500
St. Thomas's Hospital	Lambeth Palace Road SE1 7EH	020 7928 9292

Call 999 for an ambulance

IF YOU NEED TREATMENT
● If you are injured or in an accident, go immediately to a hospital casualty department (emergency room).
● Dial 999 for an ambulance.
● If you are staying at a hotel or bed-and-breakfast, members of staff should be able to help you contact a doctor. Emergency telephone numbers are often on a noticeboard in a central area or in your room.
● Another option is to contact NHS Direct *(tel 0845 4647* or *www.nhsdirect.nhs.uk)* and explain the problem. Free medical advice from a qualified nurse is available to everyone through this government-funded service. You do not have to give personal details.
● Non-urgent appointments can be made with any doctor listed in the *Yellow Pages*. There are also eight NHS walk-in centres in London, with three–Soho, Fulham and Whitechapel—giving fast access to health advice and treatment; these are open seven days a week. Initial advice, such as if you need to go to hospital, will be given, but those visitors without a reciprocal arrangement with the UK, such as the Unites States and Canada, will be charged to speak to a nurse (£25) or doctor (£55) and for any prescription drugs required. You will be issued with a receipt for your insurance company.
● To find the nearest doctor, dentist or pharmacy, ask at your hotel, or search the website www.nhs.uk/localnhsservices.

● Major pharmacies and large supermarkets have a wide range of medicines that you can buy over the counter, although items such as antibiotics will require a prescription from a doctor.
● Pharmacists operate a roster system of out-of-hours opening times in many areas, with times of the duty pharmacist displayed in the shop window and in the local newspaper.

WATER
● Tap water is safe to drink everywhere, but bottled water is readily available.

SUMMER HAZARDS
● Between May and September the sun can be strong and a high-factor sunscreen of factor 15 or above is recommended.
● Insect bites are irritating rather than dangerous, but it is advisable to take insect repellents in hot weather, especially if you are going near water.

DENTAL TREATMENT
● You will have to pay for dental treatment, either as a private patient or (slightly cheaper) as an NHS patient. However, costs can be lower than many other countries.
● In the UK, dentists are listed in telephone directories or you can use the British Dental Association's online service at www.bda-findadentist.org.uk.

OPTICIANS
● Bring your own prescription or a spare pair of spectacles in case of loss or breakage.

OPTICIANS

Name	Telephone	Website
Boots Opticians	0845 070 8090	www.wellbeing.com/bootsopticians
David Clulow (London)	020 8515 6700	www.davidclulow.com
Dollond & Aitchison	0121 7066133	www.danda.co.uk
Specsavers	01481 236000	www.specsavers.co.uk
Vision Express	0115 986 5225	www.visionexpress.com

ALTERNATIVE MEDICAL TREATMENTS
A wide range of alternative treatments is available in the UK.
These treatments are chargeable for visitors. The listings below are a starting point; local telephone directories will have more details.

Name	Telephone	Website
British Osteopathic Association	01582 488455	www.osteopathy.org enquiries@osteopathy.org
British Chiropractic Association	0118 950 5950	www.chiropractic-uk.co.uk enquiries@chiropractic-uk.co.uk
The Society of Homeopaths	01604 621400	www.homeopathy-soh.org info@homeopathy-soh.org

PLANNING

COMMUNICATION

With technology rapidly changing the way we communicate, the humble postcard is in danger of looking old-fashioned. But however you want to keep in touch with friends and family, there is a multitude of generally swift, convenient and reliable options in Britain.

TELEPHONES
The main public telephone company, British Telecom (BT), operates 10,000 payphones throughout the UK.

Area Codes, Country Codes and Telephone Directories
● Most area codes are four- or five-digit numbers beginning with 01.
● For London the code is 020. Telephone directories (phone books) and *Yellow Pages* show the code in brackets for each telephone number.
● There is a full list of area codes and country codes in every phone book.
● When making a local call, omit the area code.
● When making an international call, dial the international code followed by the phone number minus the 0 of the area code.

Public Phones
● Phone boxes (booths) are generally silver or red and are found at all major rail stations, Underground stations and on the streets throughout the city.
● You can use credit and debit cards to make calls from 60,000 BT payphones (50p minimum charge; 20p per minute for all inland calls).
● Payphones accept 10p, 20p, 50p and £1 coins; some also accept £2 coins. Only wholly unused coins are returned, so avoid using high denomination coins for short calls.
● Some establishments, such as hotels and pubs, have their own payphones, for which they set their own profit margin. These can be exorbitant and are recommended only in an emergency. Telephone calls made from hotel rooms will also be very expensive.

USING A MOBILE (CELL) PHONE
Britain has embraced mobile phone technology, although mobile phones are sometimes discouraged in some pubs and other public places (some rail carriages are dedicated quiet areas). There's a proliferation of mobile phone shops in almost every shopping area.
● Single band GSM (Global System for Mobile Communications) phones, which work on 900MHz freqency, can be used in more than 100 countries, but not in the USA or Canada.
● Most mobile phones sold in the USA work on 1900MHz and require an interchangeable sim card—this temporarily replaces your existing card, which slots into the phone and transfers it

COUNTRY CODES FROM THE UK	
Australia	00 61
Belgium	00 32
Canada	00 1
Germany	00 49
Ireland	00 353
Italy	00 39
Netherlands	00 31
New Zealand	00 64
Spain	00 34
Sweden	00 46
UK	00 44
USA	00 1

DIALLING CODE PREFIXES	
00	international codes
01	area codes
02	area codes
07	calls charged at mobile rates
080	freephone calls
084	calls charged at local rates
087	calls charged at national rates
09	calls charged at premium rates

For details of charges, call the operator on 100.

When calling Britain from abroad, dial +44 and omit the first 0 of the area code.

USEFUL TELEPHONE NUMBERS

Directory inquiries: competing services from several companies: try **118500** (BT) and **118111** (One.Tel).

International directory inquiries: competing services from several companies: try **118505** (BT) and **118211** (One.Tel).

International operator: 155

Operator: 100

Time: 123

PRICES	
Minimum charge	20p
All UK calls	11p a minute
Calls to mobile phones	63p Mon–Fri 8–6, 38p per minute Mon–Fri after 6pm and before 8am, and 19p per minute all other times
Italy, US and Canada	75p per minute at all times
Belgium, France, Germany, Netherlands and Sweden	67p per minute at all times
Australia and New Zealand	£1 per minute at all times
Call Charges	These are lower after 6pm on weekdays and all day Saturday and Sunday. Local calls are cheaper than long-distance calls within Britain, and calls to mobile phones are generally more expensive than other calls.

PLANNING

to the local network. You can purchase a sim card for between £10 and £20, and this will give you access to one of the main networks such as BT, Orange or Vodafone.

● Dual- (900 and 1900MHz) and tri-band phones can be used in most countries around the world without alteration.

● A pay-as-you-go option means you don't pay a subscription charge, but just pay for the calls you make. You can top up your account at supermarkets and other shops when necessary. You are usually given a choice of accounts, depending how much and when you are likely to make calls. A subscription-type account is more useful if you are staying in the country for a long period.

● It is also possible to use your own phone and sim card, depending on what sort of phone you have.

● Note that there are still areas in London and around the country where you cannot get a mobile phone signal, and that these vary for each network.

● Remember to pack a plug adaptor for the charger.

INTERNET ACCESS

● Multimedia web phones (blue boxes) are being installed by British Telecom in shopping areas, rail stations, airports and road service stations across the country. These enable users to surf the internet and send e-mails and text messages. Internet access costs 50p for five minutes, and 10p per minute thereafter. E-mails and text messages cost 20p a message. Web phones may threaten the future of internet cafés (charges typically £1–£2 per hour) in major cities and towns.

● Additionally about 2,000 payphones allow you to send text messages and e-mail—look for the sign that indicates this.

● Thousands of libraries have free internet access; for details go to www.peoplesnetwork.gov.uk.

● In addition to internet cafés and web phones, BT has introduced more than 400 wireless hotspots in locations such as airports, hotels and service stations. These hubs allow laptop- and pocket PC-users broadband access to the internet, using wireless technology known as Wi-Fi. You need a laptop or pocket PC PDA running Microsoft Windows XP, 2000 or Microsoft Pocket PC 2002, and a wireless LAN card. You need to be within a radius of 100m (330ft) of the hub.

● Any Wi-Fi approved card should work with BT Openzone.

● Note that the service remains an expensive, if convenient, way of surfing the internet.

USING A LAPTOP

● If you intend to use your own laptop in the UK, remember to bring a power converter to recharge it and a plug adaptor (see Electricity page 296). A surge protector is also useful.

● To connect to the internet you need an adaptor for the phone socket, available (in the UK) from companies such as Teleadapt (*www.teleadapt.com*). If you use an international service provider, such as Compuserve or AOL, it's cheaper to dial up a local node rather than the number in your home country.

● Wireless technology, such as Bluetooth, allows you to connect to the internet using a mobile phone; check beforehand what the charges will be. Dial tone frequencies vary from country to country, so set your modem to ignore dial tones.

POST

● For all post office information, call Customer Services (*tel 0845 7740 740*).

● Post boxes are painted bright red (except some in post offices) and are either set into walls or are stand-alone pillar boxes. Collection times are shown on each post box.

● Stamps are available from newsagents, supermarkets and some other shops in addition to post offices. Look for the sign.

● Generally, airmail is preferable for mail sent outside Europe; for bulky items surface mail is substantially cheaper, but typically takes around eight weeks outside Europe. Airmail to Europe takes around three days, and to the rest of the world from five days.

● Large post offices have poste restante services. Mail addressed to the recipient and inscribed with the words Poste Restante will be kept at the specified post office until collected by the addressee, who will need a form of identification to collect it.

● To send items within the UK for guaranteed next-day delivery, use special delivery. This service also enables you to insure the items in case of loss.

POSTAGE RATES		
First class within UK	Up to 60g (2oz)	28p
	(usually arrives next day, but not guaranteed)	
Second class within UK	Up to 60g (2oz)	20p
	(usually two days)	
Proof of posting	Free	
Airmail Rates		
Americas, Middle East, Africa,	Letter (100g/3.5oz)	£2.16
India, Southeast Asia	Postcard	42p
Europe	Letter (100g/3.5oz)	£1.01
	Postcard	38p
Australasia	Letter (100g/3.5oz)	£2.44
	Postcard	42p

FINDING HELP

PERSONAL SECURITY

Levels of violent crime remain relatively low, but there are hotspots to avoid in London. In most tourist areas, however, the main danger is petty theft.

● Be particularly wary of thieves on the London Underground, and in crowded public places.

● Avoid unlit urban areas at night, and carry bags close to you. If someone tries to grab your bag don't fight back; let go.

● If you are going out late, arrange a lift home or take a taxi, and use only reputable or licensed minicab firms, or black cabs.

● If you are driving alone, take a mobile phone.

● Lock the doors when the car is stationary, particularly at night.

● Don't pick up hitchhikers.

● Sit near the driver or conductor on buses and avoid empty carriages on trains and the Underground.

LOST PROPERTY

● If you lose an item, contact the nearest police station and complete a lost property form. Give as much detail as possible, such as identifying marks, registration numbers and credit card numbers.

● www.lostandfound.co.uk and www.virtualbumblebee.co.uk are free to use lost and found services, where you can log a loss or search a database of lost and found items throughout the country.

● At airports, dedicated offices deal with lost property within terminal buildings, but you will need to contact the individual airline if you lose belongings on board the aircraft.

● In London, items found on buses and Underground trains and in taxis are usually handed in to the local police station. They are then forwarded to the

Transport for London Lost Property Office, 200 Baker Street, London NW1 5RZ, tel 020 7918 2000, fax 020 7918 1028. Open Monday–Friday 9–4. You may go in person to the office Monday–Friday 9–2. A small charge (from £3) is payable on collection.

LOST PASSPORT

● If you lose your passport, contact your embassy in the UK (see below). It will help if you have your passport number. Either carry a photocopy of the opening pages or e-mail the details to yourself at an account that you can access anywhere (such as www.hotmail.com).

SEEKING HELP

● Telephone 999 or 112 in an emergency. The operator will ask you which service you require. State where you are, the number of the phone you are using, what

the problem is and where it has occurred.

● If your police enquiry is not an emergency, contact the nearest police station. Call directory enquiries on 118 888.

● If you have non-urgent health concerns, contact NHS Direct on 0845 4647 or www.nhsdirect.nhs.uk, where trained medical staff listen to your problem, give advice and tell you where to find the nearest non-emergency doctor. This free service is available to all.

● Policemen who patrol the streets on foot will give information and directions if asked.

● The British Transport Police work on Britain's railways. Report any non-emergency crimes experienced while travelling on the railways to them on 0800 40 50 40.

● If you are the victim of a crime, call Victim Support on 0845 30 30 900 for support and advice.

ARREST, FINES AND THE LAW

● You cannot be arrested for minor offences such as speeding unless you compound this with another action, such as behaving violently or failing to give satisfactory proof of identity.

● If you are involved in a motoring incident you are obliged to give your name and address.

● Police have the power to give on-the-spot fines for a few offences involving antisocial behaviour or wasting police time.

● You can be fined if you are found to be excessively drunk, or drunk and disorderly, in a public place, in licensed premises or on a highway.

● On-the-spot fixed penalty notices (traffic tickets) are also given out for speeding, driving in a bus lane, driving through a red light and other motoring offences.

EMBASSIES IN LONDON		
Country	**Details**	**Website**
Australian High Commission	Australia House, Strand WC2B 4LA, tel 020 7379 4334	www.australia.org.uk
Canadian High Commission	Canada House, Trafalgar Square, Pall Mall East SW1Y 5BJ, tel 020 7258 6600	www.dfait-maeci.gc.ca www.canada.org.uk
New Zealand High Commission	Haymarket, Westminster, SW1Y 4TQ, tel 020 7930 8422	www.nzembassy.com/uk
South African High Commission	South Africa House, Trafalgar Square, WC2N 5DP, tel 020 7451 729	www.southafricahouse.com
American Embassy	24 Grosvenor Square, W1A 1AE, tel 020 7499 9000	www.usembassy.org.uk

MEDIA

Britain has a vibrant media culture, with some of the world's oldest newspapers; publicly funded TV channels; and the global media presence of the BBC (British Broadcasting Corporation).

TELEVISION

● Excluding satellite, cable and digital, there are five main national terrestrial channels in Britain (see opposite).
● There is no advertising on the BBC channels, which are funded by a licence fee from all owners of a TV.
● BBC1 and 2 are available on terrestrial television and BBC News 24 is broadcast on BBC1 throughout the night.
● BBC4, featuring cultural programming, BBC News 24, BBC Parliament and BBC Choice, which transmits extended coverage of shows featured on BBC1 and 2, are all available on cable networks and via digital television.

Cable and Digital

● Not many homes in Britain have cable, although this is increasing, and there are few cable-specific channels, although it is possible to get a greater variety of free channels via cable.
● Digital satellite receivers are free and allow viewers to receive a skeleton service of free digital channels.
● A monthly subscription must be paid to view all sports and film channels.
● Digital terrestrial television receivers can be purchased with one payment of around £100, allowing viewers to watch more channels than on normal terrestrial services.
● Digital television has many interactive services offering shopping, e-mail, games and information through the TV remote control.

RADIO

Analogue Radio
● Analogue FM and AM receivers are used all over the world because they are relatively cheap and free to use. Analogue radios are widely available and come in many

shapes and sizes, but analogue FM and AM stations are now also available digitally.

Digital Radio
● There is an increasing number of digital radio stations broadcasting throughout the UK. Digital technology allows for more stations and choice while offering better sound quality with no interference. It is not necessary to retune on the move and the receiver automatically identifies all available stations. There are no frequencies to worry about as you can just flick through station names until you find the one you want.
● Digital radio is free, but the radios themselves are scarce and expensive. It is also possible to listen to digital radio through digital television.
● Information about current digital radio stations can be found at www.digitalradionow. com, or tel 08707 747474.

National Radio Stations
The television licence funds the BBC's national and regional radio stations. There are also several independent and commercial stations nationwide.

Radio 1 A diverse selection of the latest music from mainstream dance, rock and pop to indie and R&B. There are regular national, international and entertainment news bulletins and every Sunday from 4 to 7pm the UK singles chart, a run-down of the best-selling music. www.bbc.co.uk/radio1

Radio 2 New and old classic rock, pop, country, folk, reggae and soul interspersed with chat, regular news and travel bulletins and music documentaries. www.bbc.co.uk/radio2

Radio 3 Classical and jazz to new and world music along with culture and drama. The BBC Proms, a classical music festival held every summer in the Royal Albert Hall, is broadcast live every summer on Radio 3. www.bbc.co.uk/radio3

Radio 4 Topical and political news, comedy, art, drama and quiz shows, along with radio plays and documentaries. There are also in-depth national and international news bulletins. www.bbc.co.uk/radio4

TERRESTRIAL CHANNELS

BBC1 Broadcasts soaps, chat shows, lifestyle programmes, films, children's shows, documentaries and drama.
News and weather: 6am–9am, 1pm, 6pm, 10pm weekdays and BBC News 24 4.15am–6am. Regional news is shown after national news broadcasts.

BBC2 Specializes in cultural programmes, comedy, natural history and history.
News: Newsnight 10.30pm weekdays

ITV 1 Shows a variety of programmes including soaps, quiz shows, children's programmes, drama and films.
News and weather: 12.30pm, 6.30pm, 10pm weekdays. Regional news updates are shown after the national news broadcasts. ITV is split into different regional companies, which take national programmes at peak times and broadcast their own programmes and regional news broadcasts at other times.

Channel 4 Broadcasts quality films, documentaries, comedy and quiz shows, science and natural history programmes. In Wales, Channel 4 is replaced by Welsh-language Channel S4C, which occasionally shows Channel 4 programmes at off-peak times.
News and weather: 7pm weekdays

Channel 5 Shows children's programmes, game shows, popular films and reruns of soaps and well-known series. Not every area of the country can receive Channel 5 owing to the lack of available terrestrial frequencies, but Channel 5, along with the other terrestrial channels, is available through digital television and satellite.
News and weather: 6am, 12pm, 5pm, 7.30pm weekdays

STATIONS AND FREQUENCIES	
Radio 1	97–99 FM
Radio 2	88–91 FM
Radio 3	90–93 FM
Radio 4	92–95FM or 198 LW
Radio Five Live	909/693 AM
Classic FM	100–102 FM
talkSPORT	1089/1053 AM
Virgin Radio	105.8 FM in London, 1215 AM/MW in the rest of the UK

Radio Five Live A 24-hour news and sports station with chat and current affairs debates. www.bbc.co.uk/fivelive

Classic FM An advertising-funded independent station broadcasting classical music and regular national, international and classical music news. www.classicfm.com

talkSPORT A national commercial talk show broadcasting sport and current affairs. www.talksport.net

Virgin Radio A national commercial radio station transmitting rock and new music along with sports and music news. www.virginradio.co.uk

NEWSPAPERS

● National newspapers in Britain are divided into quality papers in a broadsheet format and the smaller papers known as the tabloids. Broadsheets focus on relatively objective news reporting while most tabloids cover sensational human-interest stories and celebrity gossip.
● The Sunday newspapers are slightly more expensive and bigger than their daily counterparts. They have special sections on travel, property, finance, the arts and media, and contain supplements with listings, reviews and articles.

Evening Standard

● Founded in 1827, the *Evening Standard* is London's only evening newspaper, tabloid in size, and covering national, international and regional news for London and the southeast.
● It also has city and entertainment news, sport reports, lifestyle and travel articles, and guides to London.
● The first edition is on the streets at 9am, and four days a week the paper is sold with a supplement.

International Newspapers

● Newspapers from around the world, including foreign-language papers, can be purchased at airports and larger train stations.
● The bookstore and newsagents WH Smith also stocks major international newspapers, including the *International Herald Tribune*, as do Borders bookstores and independent City newsagents.

MAGAZINES

● Newsagents, fuel garages, supermarkets and some of the larger bookstores stock magazines. There are many lifestyle special interest magazines available in the UK.
● There are also several current affairs magazines such as *The Week*, *The Spectator*, *The New Statesman* and *Private Eye* (the most satirical and controversial), offering opinion, analysis and discussion of the week's events.
● *Time Out* is issued monthly and contains articles and features detailing what's on in London from concerts and musicals to exhibitions and films, and with information and reviews on restaurants, pubs, shopping and accommodation.

PLANNING

NATIONAL NEWSPAPERS				
Type	Name	Political perspective	Focus	Online
Broadsheets	Daily Telegraph (1855) and Sunday Telegraph	Right wing	In-depth national and international news, property, arts, politics, business	www.telegraph.co.uk
	The Times (1785) and The Sunday Times (1822)	Centre right	In-depth national and international news, law, politics, finance, travel, education, media and arts	www.thetimes.co.uk
	Financial Times (1888)	Centre right	In-depth national and international news, finance, business, analysis of the markets	www.ft.com
	Guardian (1821) and Observer (1791)	Left wing/ Liberal	In-depth national and international news, politics, finance, travel, social issues, media and arts	www.guardian.co.uk
	Independent (1986) and Independent on Sunday (1990)	Centre left/ liberal	In-depth national and international news, politics, finance, travel, education, media and arts	www.independent.co.uk
Tabloids	Daily Mail (1896) and Mail on Sunday (1982)	Right wing	National and international news, celebrity gossip, general interest stories, sport	www.dailymail.co.uk
	Daily Express and Sunday Express	Right wing	National news, entertainment, gossip, sport	www.express.co.uk
	Sun (1969)	Right wing	Sensationalism, celebrity gossip, general interest stories, sport	www.the-sun.co.uk
	Daily Mirror (1903) and Sunday Mirror (1988)	Left wing	News, campaigning, celebrity gossip, entertainment, sport	www.mirror.co.uk
	Daily Star (1978)	None	Sensationalism, gossip, entertainment	www.dailystar.co.uk

OPENING TIMES AND TICKETS

ENTRANCE FEES

Most museums, houses, galleries, gardens, cinemas, theatres and other attractions have reduced entrance fees for children under 16, holders of student cards, those on unemployment benefit and those aged 60 and over. Family tickets, generally for two adults and two children, are available at most sights in London.

HERITAGE ORGANIZATIONS

● National Trust (NT) membership is excellent value if you wish to visit more than one or two properties owned by the National Trust (there are 13 in London and many more within easy reach of the city).

● You can join at any NT property. Membership gives free admission to all properties. Alternatively, the NT Touring Pass gives free entry to all NT properties for 7 or 14 days for one or two persons or a family. Buy in advance on tel 0870 240 4197 or online.

● For further information contact the National Trust, PO Box 39, Bromley, Kent BR1 3XL, tel 0870 458 4000; fax 020 8466 6824, www.nationaltrust.org.uk.

● English Heritage (EH), CADW in Wales and Historic Scotland (HS) in Scotland manage hundreds of historic properties, statues and monuments in Britain. EH membership gives free entry to all EH properties plus half-price admission to CADW and HS properties for one year, and free entry thereafter.

● You can join at any EH, CADW or HS staffed property: English Heritage, Overseas Membership Department, PO Box 570, Swindon SN2 2YR, tel 0870 333 1181, www.english-heritage. org.uk.

DISCOUNT PASSES

● If you are planning extensive sightseeing, buy a discount card. The following are all available from the Britain and London Visitor Centre in Regent's Street (see page 308), major tourist offices and airports.

London Pass

This gives admission to 60 attractions in and around London, free travel on all London public transport and a pocket guide. Passes are for one, two, three or six days and cost £27 for a one-day adult pass to £94 for six days; www.londonpass.com

Great British Heritage Pass

Allows free entry to 600 historic properties and gardens, including those not run by EH or NT. Passes for four, seven or fifteen days or one month. Passes range from £22 for a four-day adult pass to £60 for one month.

NATIONAL HOLIDAYS

Although banks and businesses close on public (bank) holidays, the trend in London is for tourist attractions and shops to remain open, except on 25 and 26 December and 1 January, when almost everything closes. If any of these days falls on a Saturday or Sunday, the next week day is a holiday.

New Year's Day (1 January)
Good Friday
Easter Monday
First Monday in May
Last Monday in May
Last Monday in August
Christmas Day (25 December)
Boxing Day (26 December)

OPENING TIMES

Opening hours can vary so check in advance with individual sights.

Banks	Monday–Friday 9.30–4.30	Some large branches also open Saturday morning.
Doctors and Pharmacies	Most pharmacies open Monday–Saturday 9–5–5.30 Many open only Monday–Friday, typically 8.30–6.30 and on Saturday morning	Notices in the window and in local newspapers indicate extended-hour rosters of local pharmacies (usually for a few extra hours in the evening and for short periods on Sunday). Doctors and dentists are usually closed on Sunday.
Museums, Houses and Galleries	Many open Monday–Saturday 10–5, Sunday 12–5, but hours vary	Some do not admit visitors who arrive less than 30 minutes before closing time.
Post Offices	Monday–Friday 9–5.30, Saturday 9–12	
Pubs	Changes in licensing laws mean that pubs now negotiate their own individual opening hours	Most pubs, however, still maintain the traditional hours, which are from about 11–11. Some close between 3 and 6pm. In England and Wales pubs open on Sunday 12–10.30pm. Many stay open all afternoon, although food may not be available from 2/2.30pm until around 6.30–8.30pm.
Restaurants	No hard-and-fast opening hours, but typically around 12–2.30pm and 6–9pm or 6–11pm (slightly earlier on Sundays)	Takeaway restaurants stay open until around 11pm or later. Many places in the City are closed on Saturday and Sunday.
Shops	Usual open Monday–Saturday 9–5/5.30 but London shop hours vary. See page 170	Newsagents open on Sunday morning as well. Some corner shops and convenience stores open longer hours—8am–10pm or 11pm, seven days a week.
Supermarkets	Usually 8am–9pm or later and for six hours (usually 10–4) on Sunday.	Some are open 24 hours.

PLANNING

TOURIST INFORMATION

TOURIST INFORMATION CENTRES (TIC)

● TICs are a useful source of maps, brochures and information on places to stay, where to eat out and local events in London. Many will also supply free street maps and sometimes guidebooks.

● Most tourist information centres will book accommodation free of charge (the hotelier pays a commission); for bookings outside London, you may be charged a small fee (about £2.50).

● After office hours, some tourist information centres display lists of accommodation in their office windows.

TOURIST INFORMATION CENTRES

LONDON AND AROUND

Britain and London Visitor Centre
1 Lower Regent Street
SW1Y 4XT
www.visitlondon.com
No phone—visit the office in person.
Open daily 8–5
This is the official London tourist office and website.

Local Tourist Information

Greenwich (Town) TIC
Pepys House
2 Cutty Sark Gardens
Greenwich SE10 9LW
Tel 0870 608 2000
Fax 020 8853 4607
Open daily 10–5

Heathrow Airport TIC
Underground Station Concourse
Middlesex TW6 2JA
No phone—visit the office in person.
Open daily 8–5

Kingston TIC
The Market House, Market Place
Kingston upon Thames, Surrey KT1 1JS
Tel 020 8547 5592
Fax 020 8547 5594
Open Mon–Sat 10–5

Richmond TIC
Old Town Hall
Whittaker Avenue
Richmond, Surrey TW9 1TP
Tel 020 8940 9125
Fax 020 8940 6899
Open Mon–Sat 10–5, Sun 10.30–1.30

Twickenham TIC
Civic Centre
44 York Street
Twickenham, Middlesex TW1 3BZ
Tel 020 8891 7272
Fax 020 8891 7738
Open Mon–Fri 9–5

Waterloo International TIC
London Visitor Centre
Waterloo International Terminal
Waterloo SE1 7LT
No phone—visit the office in person.
Open daily 8.30am–10.30pm

OUTSIDE LONDON

Visit Britain
Thames Tower
Black's Road W6 9EL
Tel 020 8846 9000
Fax 020 8563 0302
www.visitbritain.com
The website has a search facility for tourist information centres across Britain, giving addresses, telephone numbers and opening hours. This information is also available on tel 0900 2192192 (calls cost 50p per minute, billed per second).

Tourism South East
The Old Brew House, Warwick Park
Tunbridge Wells
Kent TN2 5TU
Tel 01892 540766
Fax 01892 511008
www.southeastengland.uk.com
Open Mon–Thu 9–5, Fri 9–4.30

Tourism South
40 Chamberlayne Road
Eastleigh, Hampshire SO50 5JH
Tel 02380 625400
Fax 02380 602210
www.southernengland.com

West Country Holiday Information Line
Tel 0870 442 0880
Fax 0870 442 0881
www.westcountrynow.com

VISIT BRITAIN OFFICES OVERSEAS

Australia
1 Macquarie Place
Sydney
NSW 2000
Tel 02 9377 4400
Fax 02 9377 4499

Canada
Suite 120
5915 Airport Road
Mississauga
Ontario L4V 1T1
Tel 1 888 VISIT UK (847 4885)
Fax 0905 405 1835

Republic of Ireland
18–19 College Green
Dublin 2
Tel 01 670 8000
Fax 01 670 8244

New Zealand
151 Queen Street
Auckland
Tel 09 303 1446
Fax 09 377 6965

South Africa
Lancaster Gate, Hyde Park Lane

Hyde Park
Johannesburg 2196 (visitors)
PO Box 41896
Craighall 2024 (mail)
Tel 011 325 0343; Fax 011 325 0344

USA
551 Fifth Avenue at 45th Street
New York
NY 10176-0799
Tel 1 212 986 2200, 1 800 GO 2 BRITAIN

Website for Americans visiting Britain:
www.travelbritain.org

BOOKS AND FILMS

London's vitality, variety, glamour and squalor have always provided rich pickings for writers and film-makers. Many have sung the city's praises; for some it's been a love-hate affair.

LITERATURE
Eminent historian Peter Ackroyd's biography of the great city, *London: The Biography* (Vintage, 2000), has been meticulously researched and presented and is essential reading for those wishing to understand the capital that defines the country.

The London Encyclopedia, by Ben Weinreb and Christopher Hibbert (Macmillan, 1983), is a vast undertaking, and provides succinct and comprehensive information about London's buildings past and present.

Perhaps the most famous book about London is *The Diary of Samuel Pepys*, in which the observer, Pepys, recorded events in Britain from 1600 to 1669.

Jeremy Paxman's *The English: a Portrait of a People* (Penguin, 1999) makes delightful reading. A galloping overview of the English as a whole, the book covers topics such as their attitude to private property, and astutely perceives what defines the English character.

Several of Charles Dickens' novels were set in London—*Oliver Twist* (1837), *Bleak House* (1853) and *Little Dorrit* (1857). *Oliver Twist*, which was made into the film of the same name, tells the story of an orphan born into a workhouse who runs away to London, only to fall in with thieves. The story does have a happy ending, however, when Oliver discovers his birthright and the gang is exposed. Dickens' social conscience shines through this tale of hardship and reward.

William Blake (1757–1827), born in London, was another writer to express a keen awareness of cruelty and injustice, notably in his poem '**London**', in the *Songs of Experience* collection.

In 1887, Sir Arthur Conan Doyle first introduced his creation, Sherlock Holmes, perhaps the most famous fictional detective of all, in the novel *A Study in Scarlet*. Holmes lived at 221b Baker Street and the Sherlock Holmes Museum is now at No. 239 (see page 127).

The highly amusing *Bridget Jones's Diary*, by Helen Fielding (Picador, 1997), defined a generation of 30-something single women living in London in the late 1990s. It was made into a hugely successful film.

Zadie Smith's *White Teeth* (Penguin, 2001) is the perceptive story of three generations of families—one white, one Indian and one mixed—living in north London in the 1990s.

Monica Ali has written sharply on a similar subject—multinational, multidenominational London, in her 2003 novel *Brick Lane* (Doubleday).

Nick Hornby's three highly successful novels, *Fever Pitch* (Cassell, 1992), *High Fidelity* (Cassell, 1995) and *About a Boy* (Cassell, 1998), have all been set in London, in the varying worlds of football (Arsenal in particular), record shops and single mothers. All of them have been made into films.

FILMS
In the opening sequences of *The World Is Not Enough* (1999), James Bond hurtled from the MI6 building by Vauxhall Bridge, pursued (as usual) by a beautiful assassin, and provided a fantastic high-speed river chase all the way to the Greenwich Dome.

Lock, Stock and Two Smoking Barrels (1998), directed by Guy Ritchie, is a pastiche of the old gangster movies.

Classic Ealing comedies such as *Passport to Pimlico* (1948), starring Stanley Holloway, were all made in the Ealing studios, founded in 1929 and the first British sound-film studios.

In 1998, playwright Tom Stoppard wrote the screenplay for *Shakespeare in Love*, with Joseph Fiennes as the eponymous hero and Gwyneth Paltrow as the lady with whom he falls in love, plus just about every other notable actor in England and the United States at the time.

My Beautiful Launderette caused something of a stir in 1985 when Daniel Day-Lewis starred as one of two men (one Asian) in this well-observed story of the relationship between two young men in the intolerant London of the time.

In 2002 came *28 Days Later*, a chilling tale of a young man who wakes after a cycling accident to discover a desolate London, populated by a brave few and the 'infected'.

Other classic films that might transport you to your favourite part of London are *Blow-Up* (1966), in which David Hemmings has some strange adventures in Maryon Park, *Alfie* (1966), which sees Michael Caine ducking and diving around town, *An American Werewolf in London* (1981), a comedy horror movie about a visiting American who gets bitten, and *A Fish Called Wanda* (1988), starring John Cleese, Jamie Lee Curtis and Michael Palin.

GUIDEBOOKS

AA City Pack *London*
Pocket book and map. £6.99

London: A City Revealed
A visual tribute to London, with more than 350 large colour photographs. £30

The AA Days Out Guide
More than 2,000 places to visit. £11.99

The AA Hotel Guide
£16.99

The AA Restaurant Guide
£16.99

MAPS
AA *Street by Street London*
17 maps and atlases in a variety of sizes, scales and bindings. £3.99 to £30

Street by Street A–Z Maps
£1.50

WEBSITES

A vast amount of information can be found on the internet, from booking rail tickets to renting a car. The websites listed below are a good place to start.

GENERAL TOURIST INFORMATION
www.visitbritain.com—the official website for the Britain and London Tourist Information Centre
www.southeastengland.com
www.southerntb.co.uk
www.westcountrynow.com
www.fco.gov.uk—Foreign and Commonwealth Office

ABOUT LONDON
www.visitlondon.com
www.londontown.com
www.netlondon.com—a directory covering sights, events and accommodation
www.londoneverything.co.uk—an online shopping site offering everything you can imagine in London
www.dolke.co.uk—information on all aspects of London
www.a-london-guide.co.uk
www.see-london.com
www.visiting-london.com
www.tripadvisor.com
www.gingerbeer.co.uk—the London gay scene
www.english-heritage.org.uk
www.cadw.wales.gov.uk
www.historic-scotland.gov.uk
www.nationaltrust.org.uk
www.hrp.org.uk—historic royal palaces
www.royal.gov.uk—royal residences/royal collection
www.royalparks.gov.uk

NEWS AND REVIEWS
www.bbc.co.uk/london—news as it happens from the BBC, plus weather, sport and TV listings
www.guardian.co.uk
www.timesonline.co.uk

CHILDREN'S LONDON
www.travelbritain.com/london/kids.html—what to do and see with the children
www.londonnet.co.uk/In/out/ent/kids.html

THEATRE/MUSIC
www.londontheatre.co.uk—the latest news, what's on, reviews
www.ticketmaster.co.uk—where to get cheap tickets

www.theambassadors.com—information on what's on, what's coming up and where to get tickets
www.rutheatres.com—the official website for the Really Useful Theatre group
www.sbc.org.uk—the website for the South Bank Centre, including the Royal Festival Hall, Purcell Room and Queen Elizabeth Hall
www.royalalberthall.com
www.royalopera.org

CINEMA
www.bfi.org.uk/imax—British Film Institute
www.ugicinemas.co.uk
www.odeon.co.uk

TRAVEL
Airports
www.baa.co.uk/gatwick
www.baa.co.uk/heathrow
www.baa.co.uk/stansted
www.london-luton.co.uk
www.londoncityairport.com

Bus/Coach
www.greenline.co.uk
www.nationalexpress.com—timetables and general information on routes
www.coachtourismcouncil.co.uk

Rail
www.thameslink.co.uk
www.heathrowexpress.co.uk
www.gatwickexpress.co.uk
www.stanstedexpress.co.uk

www.eurostar.com
www.thetrainline.com—book tickets and find out fares and journey times
www.nationalrail.co.uk—general information on rail travel and train times

London Transport
www.transportforlondon.gov.uk
www.thetube.com
www.thetube.com/content/visit—Underground information in German, Spanish, French, Italian, Portuguese
www.dlr.co.uk—information on the Docklands Light Railway

Car Rental
www.alamo.co.uk
www.avis.co.uk
www.europcar.com
www.hertz.co.uk

CAR BREAKDOWN
www.theaa.com
www.rac.co.uk

WEATHER REPORTS
www.bbc.co.uk/weather
www.metoffice.com

EMBASSIES
www.australia.org.uk
www.canada.org.uk
www.newzealand.org.uk
www.southafricahouse.com
www.usembassy.org.uk

HEALTH
www.nhsdirect.nhs.uk

MAJOR SIGHTS		
Sight	Website	Page
British Museum	www.thebritishmuseum.ac.uk	80
HMS *Belfast*	www.iwm.org.uk/belfast	91
Houses of Parliament	www.parliament.uk	92
Imperial War Museum	www.iwm.org.uk;	96
London Eye	www.ba-londoneye.com	99
Madame Tussaud's	www.madame-tussauds.com	101
Museum of London	www.museumoflondon.org.uk	103
National Gallery	www.nationalgallery.org.uk	104
National Portrait Gallery	www.npg.org.uk	110
Natural History Museum	www.nhm.ac.uk	112
St. Paul's Cathedral	www.stpauls.co.uk	118
Science Museum	www.sciencemuseum.org.uk	124
Shakespeare's Globe	www.shakespeares-globe.org	126
Sir John Soane's Museum	www.soane.org	128
Somerset House	www.somerset-house.org.uk	130
Tate Galleries	www.tate.org.uk	132
Tower Bridge	www.towerbridge.org.uk	137
Tower of London	www.hrp.org.uk	139
Victoria & Albert Museum	www.vam.ac.uk	144
Westminster Abbey	www.westminster-abbey.org	152

PLANNING

GLOSSARY FOR THE US VISITOR

anticlockwise	counterclockwise
aubergine	eggplant
bank holiday	a public holiday that falls on a Monday; there are two in May and one in August
bill	check (at restaurant)
biscuit	cookie
bonnet	hood (car)
boot	trunk (car)
busker	street musician
caravan	house trailer or RV
car park	parking lot
carriage	car (on a train)
cashpoint	ATM or cash machine
casualty	emergency room (hospital department)
chemist	pharmacy
chips	french fries
coach	long-distance bus
concessions	reduced entrance fees or fares
coriander	cilantro
courgette	zucchini
crèche	day care
crisps	potato chips
directory enquiries	directory assistance
dual carriageway	two-lane highway
en suite	a bedroom with its own private bathroom; may also just refer to the bathroom
football	soccer
full board	a hotel tariff that includes all meals
garage	gas station
garden	yard (residential)
GP	doctor
half board	hotel tariff that includes breakfast and either lunch or dinner
high street	main street
hire	rent
inland	within the UK
jelly	Jello™
jumper, jersey	sweater
junction	intersection
layby	pull-off
level crossing	grade crossing
lorry	truck
licensed	a café or restaurant that has a license to serve alcohol (beer and wine only unless it's 'fully' licensed)
lift	elevator
listed building	protected building

main line station	a train station as opposed to an underground or subway station (although it may be served by the underground/subway)
nappy	diaper
newsagent	newsstand, newspaper shop
note	paper money
off-licence	liquor store
pants	underpants (men's)
pavement	sidewalk
petrol	gas
phone box	phone booth
plaster	Band-Aid or bandage
post	mail
public school	private school
pudding	dessert
purse	change purse
pushchair	stroller
quay	wharf/pier
return ticket	roundtrip ticket
rocket	arugula
roundabout	traffic circle or rotary
self-catering	accommodation including a kitchen
single ticket	one-way ticket
solicitor	lawyer
stalls	orchestra seats (in theatre)
subway	underpass
surgery	doctor's office
swede	American turnip
tailback, traffic jam	stalled line of traffic
takeaway	takeout
taxi rank	taxi stand
terrace	row houses
tights	panty-hose
T-junction	an intersection where one road meets another at right angles (making a T shape)
toilets	restrooms
torch	flashlight
trolley	cart
trousers	pants
vest	undershirt
waistcoat	vest
way out	exit
zebra crossing	crosswalk

BRITISH FLOOR NUMBERING

In Britain the first floor of a building is called the ground floor, and the floor above it is the first floor. So a British second floor is a US third floor, and so on. This is something to watch for in museums and galleries in particular.

A BRIEF GUIDE TO ARCHITECTURAL PERIODS

Roman
London's growth as a city began when the invading Romans founded their base of Londinium, occupying roughly the same area as today's City. A well-preserved remnant of the thick stone wall built around the city after its sacking by Queen Boudica in AD61 stands next to Tower Hill Underground station and Cooper's Row. The unearthed Temple to Mithras is now adjacent to the Bucklersbury House office block on Queen Victoria Street.

Anglo-Saxon
Churches were built of stone and characterized by their simple arched windows with thick central supports. The first St. Paul's Cathedral was founded in AD604 and Edward the Confessor had Westminster Abbey (see pages 152–153) completed in 1066.

Norman
In the late 11th and 12th centuries the Norman conquerors brought new styles and craftsmen from Normandy. Massive fortified buildings and churches were thrown up in the wake of the Norman invasion, recognizable by their round arches, heavy masonry and decorated walls and doorways.
Examples: Westminster Hall, the oldest remaining part of the medieval Westminster Palace, erected in 1097 (but renovated in the 14th century).
The White Tower, at the heart of the Tower of London (see pages 138–143), built in 1078.

Early English and Decorated
Architecture of the late 12th and 13th centuries became lighter, using pointed rather than rounded arches, especially in lancet windows. This period marked the move towards the long, vertical lines of the Gothic style and an increasing focus on window space. As windows became bigger, buttresses were added to transfer the outward thrust of the roof to the ground. Increasingly elaborate tracery and decoration were employed on arches, doorways and especially windows in buildings of the later 13th and 14th centuries.

Examples: Southwark Cathedral's choir and retrochoir (see page 127); Westminster Abbey.

Perpendicular Gothic
Evolving from the Decorated style, simpler lines and more uniform tracery on windows and walls emerged during the late 14th and 15th centuries, with much use of fan-vaulting and four-centred arches. Designs became lighter, using greater areas of glass.
Examples: Henry VII Chapel, Westminster Abbey.

Tudor and Early Stuart
The late 15th and 16th centuries marked a shift from the Gothic to the Renaissance styles, with the emphasis on domestic architecture for the expanding aristocracy and gentry. Brick and wood-panelling became popular.
Examples: Hampton Court Palace (see page 159), Kingston upon Thames; Shakespeare's Globe Theatre (see page 126), Southwark—a reconstruction of the 16th-century original.

Late Stuart
The Palladian style, recalling the work of 16th-century Italian architect Andrea Palladio, reflected Roman classical influences in porticoes and restrained symmetrical façades. Classical styles merged in the 18th century with baroque ornamentation and rich detail.

Major Architects: **Inigo Jones** (1573–1652): designed Queen's House (see page 157), Greenwich, and Banqueting House (see page 77). Brought the Palladian style into fashion, as well as the use of movable scenery and the proscenium arch.
Sir Christopher Wren (1632–1723): designed St. Paul's Cathedral (see pages 118–123), Greenwich Hospital and many of the City churches following the Great Fire of 1666. Professor of Astronomy at London and Oxford.
Nicholas Hawksmoor (1661–1736): Wren's assistant, who favoured monumental classicism. Designed many churches, including St. George's Bloomsbury, St. Mary Woolnoth, Christchurch Spitalfields.

James Gibbs (1682–1754): Scottish architect who designed St. Martin-in-the-Fields (see page 117), St. Mary-le-Strand and St. Clement Danes (see page 116).

Georgian and Regency
During the Georgian period architects turned back to the Palladian style, and in the late 18th and early 19th centuries Greek classical influences came to the fore, prompting an emphasis on simplicity and symmetry, especially in the new terraced townhouses. The Regency period saw the introduction of floor-to-roof bow windows and wrought-ironwork in staircases and balconies.
Major Architects: **Robert Adam** (1728–92): designed Osterley House (see page 162) and Syon House (see page 162) and took care in designing decoration and furniture as well as exteriors.
William Kent (1675–1748): a Yorkshireman who advocated the return to Palladianism. Designed Chiswick House (see page 154) and Kensington Palace (see page 95).
John Nash (1752–1835): known for his Regency houses and responsible for the Regent's Park (see page 115) terraces.
Sir John Soane (1753–1837): favoured austere classical designs. Responsible for the Bank of England (see page 76), Dulwich Picture Gallery (see page 155).
Decimus Burton (1800–81): a leader in the Regency style, who designed the Athenaeum Club.
Sir William Chambers (1723–96): a Swedish-born architect and first treasurer of the Royal Academy; designed Somerset House (see pages 130–131).

Victorian
Architecture of the period 1837–1901 called on a mish-mash of influences as new public buildings such as railway stations and municipal offices sprang up. These were notable for their neo-Gothic designs, florid and romanticized medieval motifs, rich details and extensive use of steel, iron and glass. In contrast, mass housing was built to accommodate industrial workers.
Examples: Houses of Parliament;

Natural History Museum; Albert Memorial; St. Pancras station; Tower Bridge.

Major Architects: **Sir Charles Barry** (1795–1860): designed the Houses of Parliament (see page 92) after their destruction by fire in 1834. An exponent of classicism.

Sir George Gilbert Scott (1811–78): designed St. Pancras station; compelled to tone down his neo-Gothic design for the Foreign Office.

Augustus Welby Northmore Pugin (1812–52): led the neo-Gothic movement and worked with Barry on the Houses of Parliament, as well as designing several churches.

Alfred Waterhouse (1830–1905): designed the Natural History Museum (see pages 112–113) and many churches.

William Butterfield (1814–1900): leading exponent of the Gothic Revival. Used red brick and a wooden spire in All Saints' Church (see page 76).

Sir Aston Webb (1849–1930): a President of the Royal Academy, who designed Admiralty Arch, the façade of Buckingham Palace's east front (see page 79), and the Victoria & Albert Museum (see pages 144–149).

Late Victorian and Edwardian
In the late 19th century the Arts and Crafts movement was promoted by William Morris as a reaction against mass production, with the aim of making hand-made objects and fine art an integral part of daily life. Its influence extended to architecture as suburban brick houses, with terracotta panelling, balconies and large gardens. The organic motifs of art nouveau were popular until about 1914.
Examples: Red House, Bexley Heath; Holy Trinity Church, Chelsea.

Major Architects: **Philip Webb** (1831–1915): an exponent of simple domestic architecture who designed furniture, metalwork and jewellery with Morris as well as buildings such as the Red House, Bexley Heath.

Sir Edwin Lutyens (1869–1944): designed the Cenotaph in Whitehall (see page 151), as well as many characterful country houses outside London.

Sir Herbert Baker (1862–1946): worked with Lutyens. Best known in Britain for his controversial reconstruction of the Bank of England. Designed India House, on Aldwych, and South Africa House, overlooking Trafalgar Square, in Cape Dutch style.

Inter-War
Public and domestic buildings made full use of art deco's geometric lines, bold colours and exotic motifs, often using Egyptian themes, marking the huge public interest in archaeologist Howard Carter's discovery of the tomb of Tutankhamun. Traditional materials such as coloured tiles and stained glass were combined with modern chromium plating.
Examples: BBC Broadcasting House, Langham Place; Odeon Cinema, Islington; Hoover Building, Perivale; Daily Express Building, Fleet Street.

Major Architects: **Berthold Lubetkin** (1901–90): Russian architect who was prolific in the 1930s, designing the Gorilla House and Penguin Pool in London Zoo (see page 160).

Post World War II
After 1945 designs became increasingly stark and massive, using materials such as concrete, especially in the tower blocks of the 1960s and the rough, unfinished designs of Brutalism. In contrast, the high-tech style of the 1970s and 1980s exposed the inner workings of public buildings. Stainless steel and glass were popular materials and bright colours and lights were favoured means of decoration.
Examples: National Theatre and South Bank Centre (see page 127); Lloyds Building (see page 232); Millennium Bridge (see page 100).

Major Architects: **Richard Rogers** (1933–): designed the Lloyds Building.

Norman Foster (1935–): responsible for the Millennium Bridge (see page 100).

THE REIGNS OF ENGLAND'S KINGS AND QUEENS
Anglo-Saxons
Early Saxon kings 886–1042
Edward the Confessor 1042–66
Harold II 1066
Normans
William I 1066–87
William II 1087–1100
Henry I 1100–35
Stephen 1135–54
Angevins
Henry II 1154–89
Richard I 1189–99
John 1199–1216
Plantagenets
Henry III 1216–72
Edward I 1272–1307
Edward II 1307–27
Edward III 1327–77
Richard II 1377–99
Lancaster
Henry IV 1399–1413
Henry V 1413–22
Henry VI 1422–61 and 1470–71
York
Edward IV 1461–1470 and 1471–83
Richard III 1483–85
Tudor
Henry VII 1485–1509
Henry VIII 1509–47
Edward VI 1547–53
Mary I 1553–58
Elizabeth I 1558–1603
Stuart
James I (James VI of Scotland) 1603–25
Charles I 1625–49
Interregnum
Commonwealth 1649–53
Protectorate 1653–59
Stuart
Charles II 1660–85
James II 1685–88
William III (of Orange) 1688–1702 and Mary II 1688–94
Anne 1702–14
Hanover
George I 1714–27
George II 1727–60
George III 1760–1820
George IV 1820–30
William IV 1830–37
Victoria 1837–1901
Saxe-Coburg Gotha
Edward VII 1901–10
Windsor
George V 1910–36
Edward VIII 1936
George VI 1936–1952
Elizabeth II 1952–

A CHRONOLOGY OF LONDON'S HISTORY

AD43
Emperor Claudius invades Britain and a deep-water port, Londinium, is soon established.

200
The Romans finish erecting a wall around Londinium, now capital of Britannia Superior.

400
The Romans withdraw from Britain.

886
Saxon king Alfred captures the town, now called Lundenberg, from the Vikings.

1042
King Edward the Confessor makes London capital of England and establishes his court in Westminster.

1066
Norman invader William the Conqueror defeats King Harold at Hastings. Starts building Tower of London.

1176
Peter de Colechurch builds London Bridge, the city's first stone crossing.

1477
William Caxton published the first book printed in England on his Westminster press.

1485
As Tudor rule begins, London is Europe's fastest growing city.

1529
Cardinal Thomas Wolsey fails to win Henry VIII a divorce and falls from favour.

1531
Inigo Jones designs London's first square, Covent Garden Piazza.

1533
Henry VIII breaks with Rome to marry Anne Boleyn and becomes head of the Church of England.

1649
Charles I is executed in Whitehall after years of civil war. The Commonwealth (1649–53) and Protectorate (1653–59) govern until Charles II is restored to the throne in 1660.

1666
The Great Fire of London.

1675
Sir Christopher Wren begins St. Paul's Cathedral.

1694
William Paterson founds the Bank of England to fund William and Mary's war with France.

1700
London is Europe's biggest and wealthiest city: population 700,000.

1759
The British Museum, London's first public museum, opens.

1800–1900
London's population grows from 1 to 6.5 million; 14 Thames bridges built 1811–17 and 15 railway stations 1846–74.

1802
London becomes the world's biggest port.

1816–28
John Nash lays out Regent Street, Regent's Park and Regent's Canal.

1829
Sir Robert Peel establishes the Metropolitan Police Force; a horse-drawn bus services begins.

1834
The Palace of Westminster burns down; its replacement is almost complete by 1847.

1851
The Great Exhibition is held in Hyde Park.

1863
The world's first urban underground train service opens. In 1890 the first tube train runs on the Northern Line.

1922
First daily wireless (radio) programme broadcast from Savoy Hill; BBC established in 1927; first TV broadcasts from Alexandra Palace in 1936.

1939–45
Bombs destroy a third of the City of London and much of the docks.

1951
Festival of Britain held on the site of the South Bank Centre.

1960S
Carnaby Street and the King's Road become the focus of 'Swinging London'.

1974
Covent Garden's fruit and veg market moves to south London and site is redeveloped.

1981
Redevelopment of the docklands as a commercial and residential area begins.

1985
London's local authority, the Greater London Council, is abolished.

1994
First Eurostar trains travel from Waterloo to Paris through the Channel Tunnel.

2000
London Eye opens to celebrate new millennium. New mayor of London elected and Greater London Authority established.

2003
Controversial system of congestion charging introduced to cut traffic in central London.

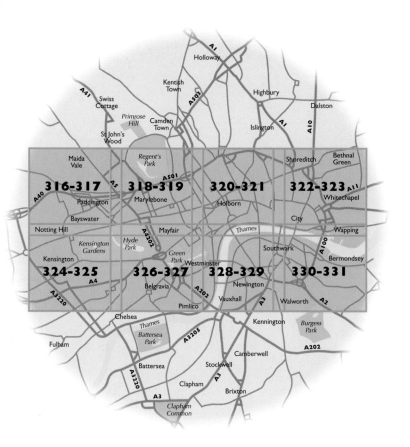

A road single / dual

B road single / dual

Other road

Footpath

Central London Congestion
Charging Zone boundary

Railway station

Park

Building

Featured place of interest

Monument / statue

Tourist information office

Church

Underground station

Parking

316-331

| 0 | | 500 metres |
| 0 | | 500 yards |

Maps

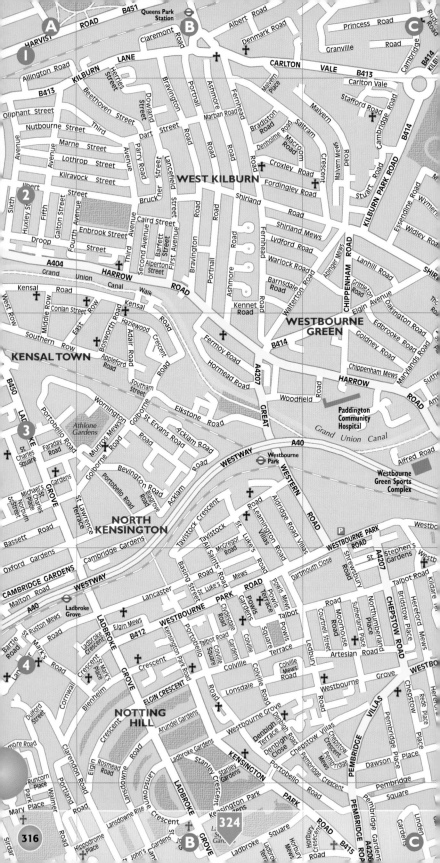

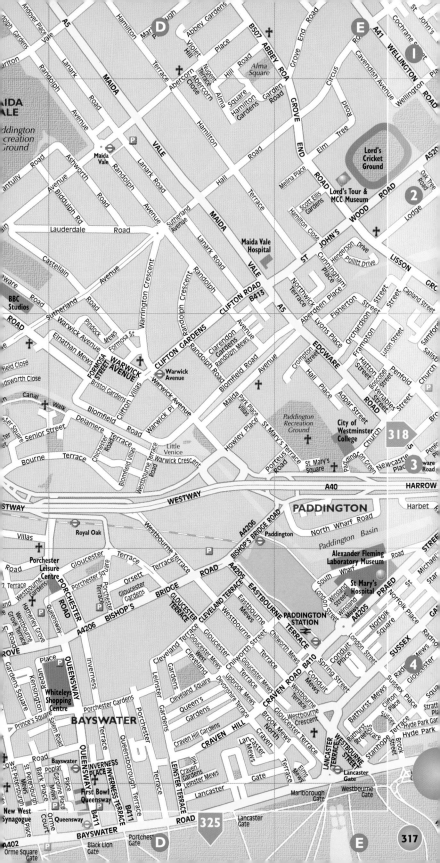

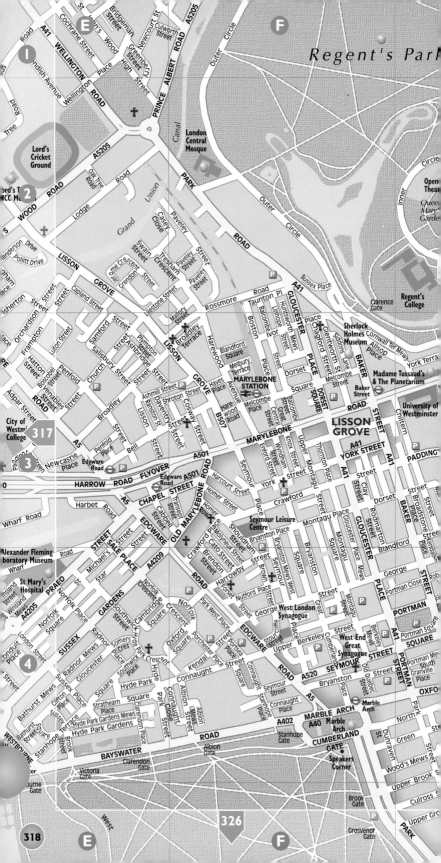

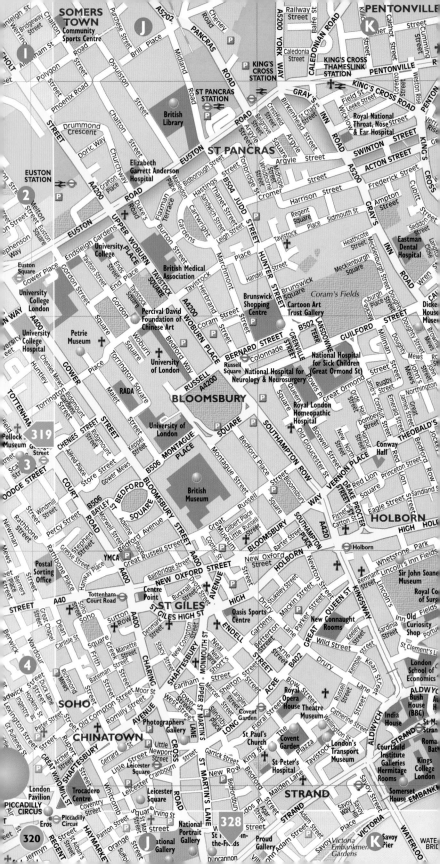

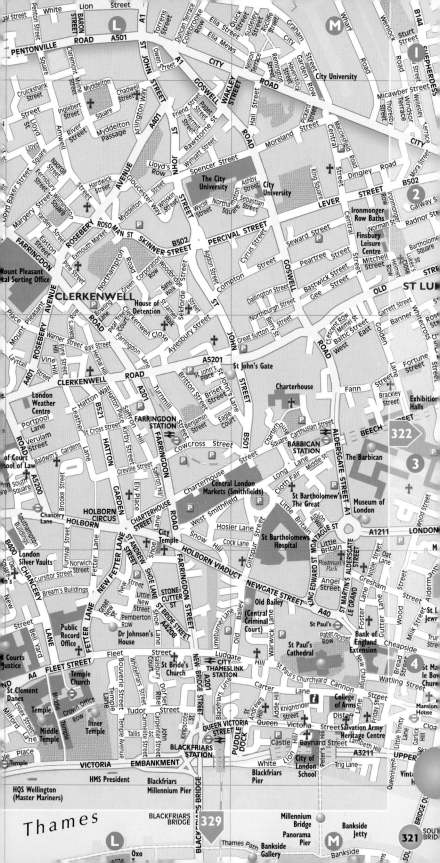

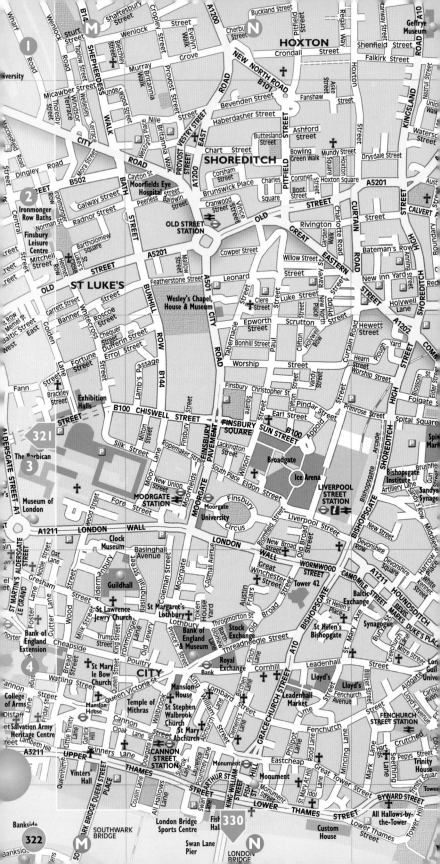

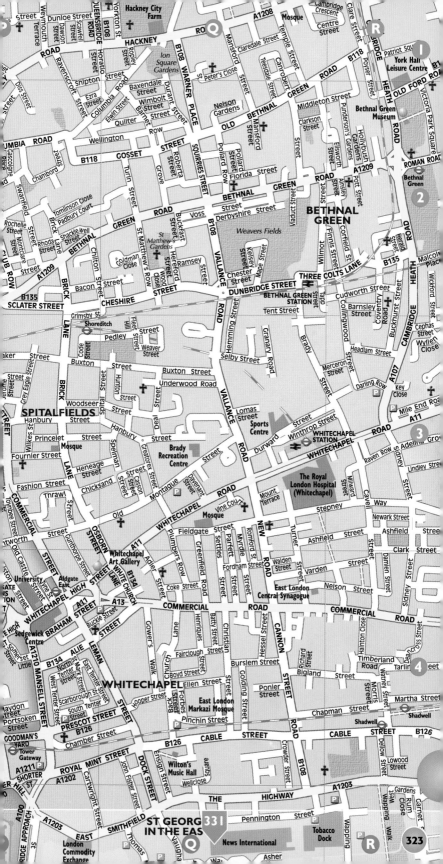

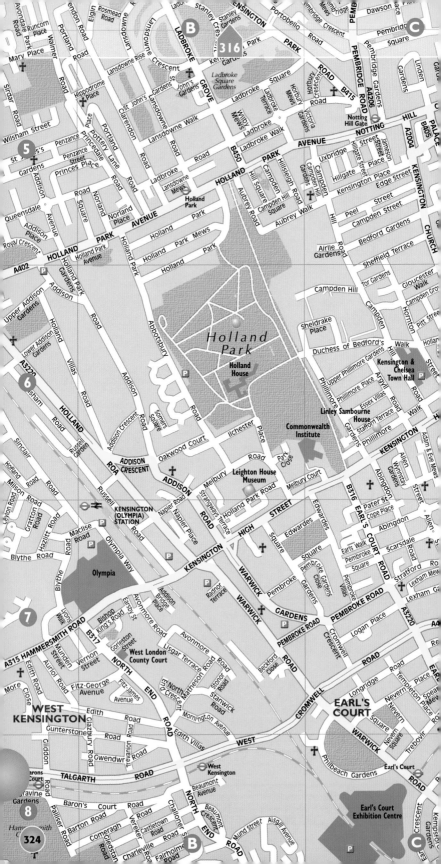

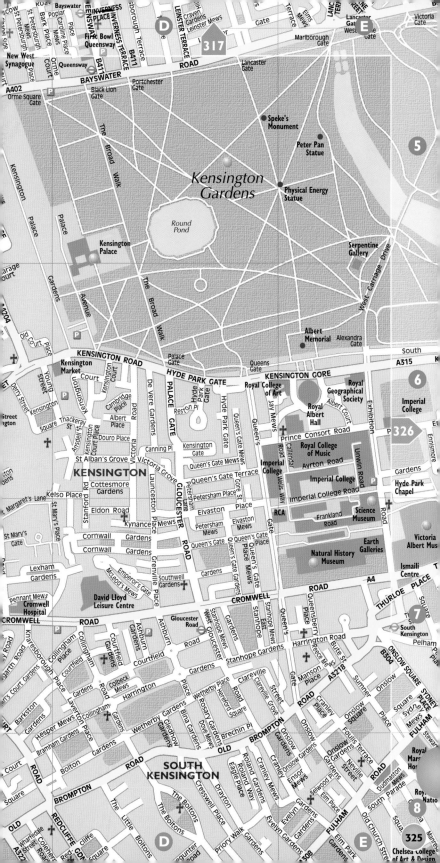

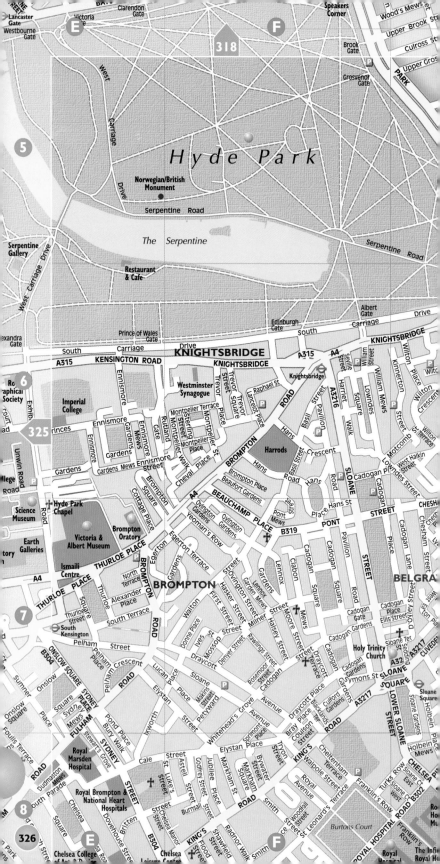

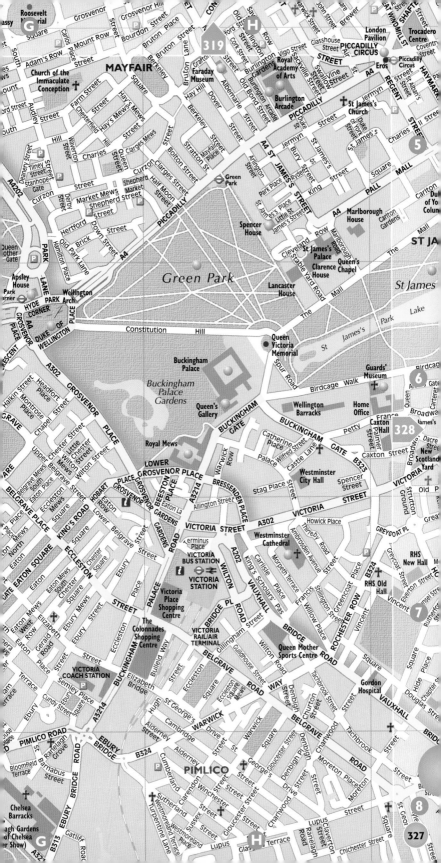

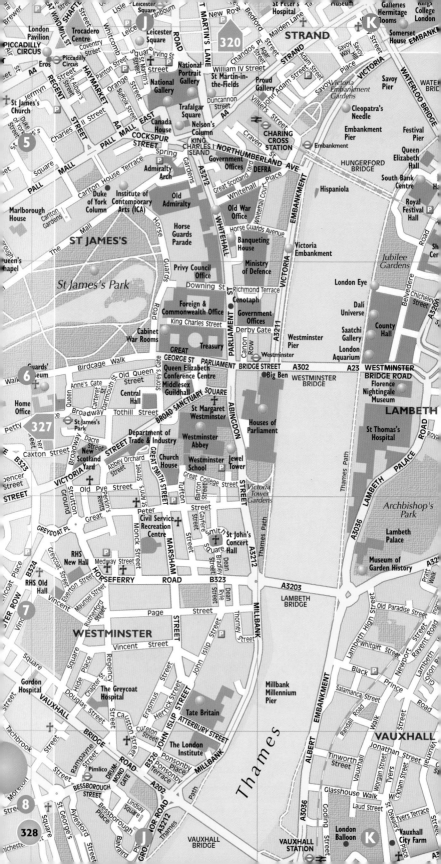

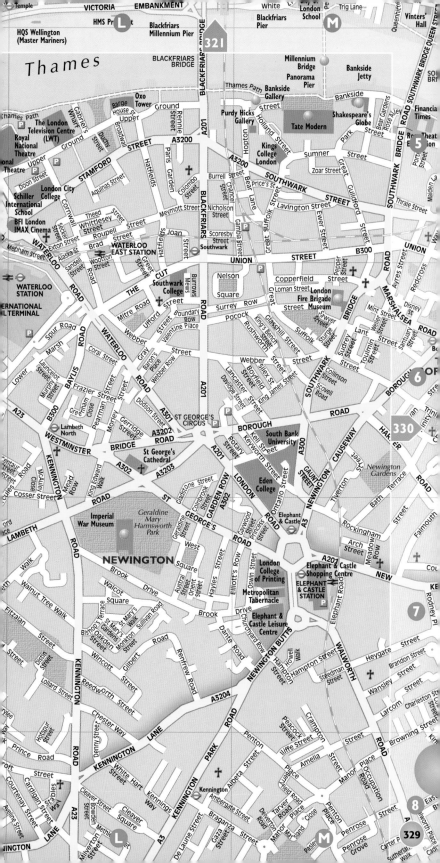

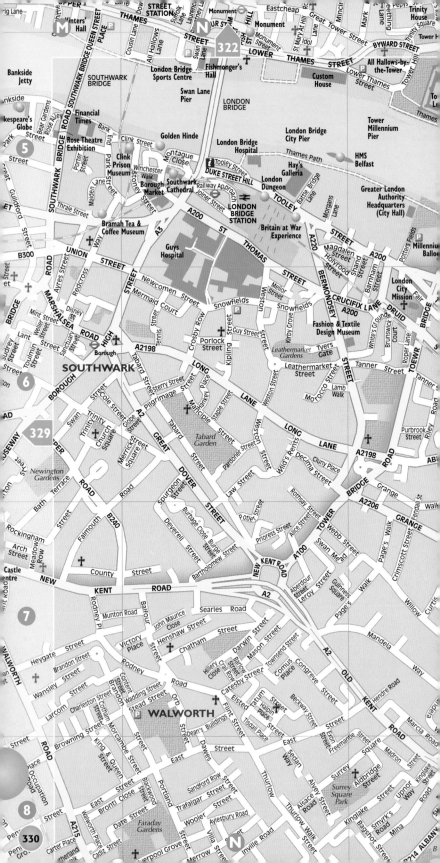

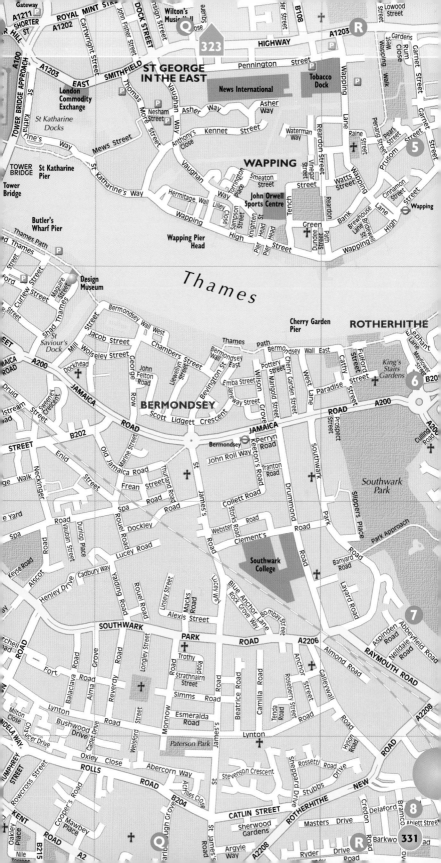

A

Street	Ref
Abbey Orchard Street	328 J6
Abbey Road	317 D1
Abbey Street	330 P6
Abbotsbury Road	324 B6
Abchurch Lane	322 N4
Abercorn Close	317 D2
Abercorn Place	317 D2
Aberdeen Place	317 E3
Abingdon Road	324 C6
Abingdon Street	328 J6
Abingdon Villas	324 C7
Acklam Road	316 B3
Acton Street	320 K2
Adam Street	328 K5
Adam's Row	327 G5
Addison Avenue	324 A5
Addison Crescent	324 B6
Addison Road	325 A6
Addle Hill	321 M4
Adler Street	323 Q4
Adpar Street	317 E3
Agar Street	320 K5
Agdon Street	321 L2
Air Street	319 H5
Albany Road	330 P8
Albany Street	319 H1
Albemarle Street	327 H5
Albert Court	325 E7
Albert Embankment	328 K8
Albion Street	318 F4
Albion Way	321 M3
Aldenham Street	319 H1
Aldermanbury	322 M4
Alderney Street	327 H7
Aldersgate Street	321 M3
Aldford Street	327 G5
Aldgate	322 P4
Aldgate High Street	323 P4
Aldridge Road Villas	316 B3
Aldwych	320 K4
Alexander Place	327 E7
Alexander Street	316 C4
Alexis Street	331 Q7
Alfred Place	320 J3
Alie Street	323 P4
All Hallows Lane	322 N5
All Saints' Road	316 A3
Allen Street	324 C6
Allington Street	327 H7
Allsop Place	318 F3
Alma Grove	331 P7
Alscot Road	331 P7
Alscot Way	331 P7
Alvey Street	330 N8
Amberley Road	316 C3
Ambrosden Avenue	327 H7
Amelia Street	329 M8
Amwell Street	321 L2
Anchor Street	331 Q7
Angel Street	321 M4
Appold Street	322 N3
Aquinas Street	329 L5
Argyle Square	320 K2
Argyle Street	320 J2
Argyll Road	324 C6
Argyll Street	319 H4
Arlington Street	327 H5
Arlington Way	321 L2

Street	Ref
Arne Street	320 K4
Artesian Road	316 C4
Arthur Street	322 N5
Artillery Lane	322 P3
Arundel Gardens	316 B4
Arundel Street	321 K4
Ashbridge Street	318 E3
Ashburn Gardens	325 D7
Ashburn Place	325 D7
Ashby Street	321 M2
Asher Way	331 Q5
Ashfield Street	323 Q3
Ashmill Street	318 E3
Ashmore Road	316 B2
Ashworth Road	317 D2
Aske Street	322 N2
Astell Street	26 F8
Atterbury Street	328 J7
Aubrey Road	324 B5
Aubrey Walk	324 B5
Augustus Street	319 H1
Auriol Road	324 A7
Austin Friars	322 N4
Austin Street	322 P2
Austral Street	329 L7
Avery Row	319 G4
Avonmore Road	324 B7
Aybrook Street	319 G3
Aylesbury Street	321 L3
Ayres Street	330 M6
Ayrton Road	325 E6

B

Street	Ref
Back Church Lane	323 Q4
Bacon Street	323 P2
Bainbridge Street	320 J4
Baker Street	318 F3
Baker's Row	321 L3
Balaclava Road	331 P7
Balcombe Street	318 F3
Balderton Street	319 G4
Baldwin's Gardens	321 L3
Balfour Street	330 N7
Bank End	330 M5
Bankside	329 M5
Banner Street	322 M3
Barge House Street	329 L5
Bark Place	317 C4
Barkston Gardens	325 C7
Barnby Street	319 H1
Barnet Grove	323 Q2
Barnham Street	330 P6
Baron's Court Road	324 A8
Bartholomew Lane	322 N4
Bartholomew Square	322 M2
Bartholomew Street	330 N7
Basil Street	326 F6
Basing Street	316 A4
Basinghall Avenue	322 N3
Basinghall Street	322 N4
Bastwick Street	321 M2
Bateman Street	320 J4
Bateman's Row	322 P2
Bath Street	322 M2
Bath Terrace	329 M7
Bathurst Mews	317 E4
Battle Bridge Lane	330 N5
Batty Street	323 Q4
Baxendale Street	323 Q2

Street	Ref
Bayley Street	320 J3
Baylis Road	329 L6
Beak Street	319 H4
Bear Gardens	329 M5
Bear Lane	329 M5
Beatrice Road	331 Q7
Beauchamp Place	326 F6
Beaufort Gardens	326 F6
Beaumont Street	319 G3
Beckway Street	330 N7
Bedford Avenue	320 J3
Bedford Gardens	324 C5
Bedford Place	320 J3
Bedford Row	320 K3
Bedford Square	320 J3
Bedford Street	320 J4
Bedford Way	320 J3
Bedfordbury	320 J4
Beech Street	321 M3
Beeston Place	327 H7
Beethoven Street	316 B2
Belgrave Road	327 H7
Belgrave Square	327 G6
Bell Lane	322 P3
Bell Street	318 E3
Bell Yard	321 L4
Belvedere Road	328 K6
Bentinck Street	318 G4
Berkeley Square	327 H5
Berkeley Street	327 H5
Bermondsey Street	330 N6
Bermondsey Wall East	331 Q6
Bermondsey Wall West	331 Q6
Bernard Street	320 J3
Berners Mews	319 H3
Berners Street	319 H3
Berry Street	321 M3
Berryfield Road	329 M8
Berwick Street	319 H4
Bessborough Street	328 J8
Bessborough Place	328 J8
Bethnal Green Road	323 P2
Betterton Stree	320 J4
Bevenden Street	322 N2
Bevington Road	316 B3
Bevington Street	331 Q6
Bevis Marks	322 P4
Bidborough Street	320 J2
Biddulph Road	317 D2
Bigland Street	323 Q4
Billiter Street	322 P4
Bina Gardens	325 D7
Binney Street	319 G4
Birchen Lane	322 N4
Birdcage Walk	327 H6
Birkenhead Street	320 K2
Bishop King's Road	324 B7
Bishop's Bridge Road	317 D4
Bishop's Terrace	329 L7
Bishopsgate	322 N4
Black Prince Road	328 K7
Blackfriars Bridge	329 L5
Blackfriars Lane	321 L4
Blackfriars Road	329 L5
Blandford Square	318 F3
Blandford Street	318 F4
Blenheim Crescent	317 B4
Blomfield Road	317 D3
Blomfield Street	322 N3

Street	Ref
Bloomsbury Square	320 K3
Bloomsbury Street	320 J3
Bloomsbury Way	320 J3
Blue Anchor Lane	331 Q7
Blythe Road	324 A7
Bolsover Street	319 H3
Bolton Gardens	325 D8
Bolton Gardens	327 H5
Bolton Street	327 H5
Borough High Street	329 M6
Borough Road	329 M6
Boscobel Street	317 E3
Boston Place	318 F3
Boswell Street	320 K3
Bosworth Road	316 B3
Boundary Street	322 P2
Bourdon Street	319 G5
Bourne Street	326 G7
Bourne Terrace	317 C3
Bouverie Street	321 L4
Bowling Green Lane	321 L2
Bow Street	320 K4
Boyfield Street	329 M6
Brackley Street	321 M3
Brady Street	323 Q3
Braganza Street	329 L8
Braham Street	323 P4
Bravington Road	316 B2
Bray Place	326 F7
Bread Street	322 M4
Bream's Buildings	321 L4
Bressenden Place	327 H6
Brewer Street	319 H4
Brick Lane	323 P2
Brick Street	327 G5
Bridge Place	327 H7
Bridge Street	328 J6
Brill Place	320 J1
Bristol Gardens	317 D3
Britten Street	326 E8
Britton Street	321 L3
Broad Sanctuary	328 J6
Broadley Street	318 E3
Broadley Terrace	318 F3
Broadwall	329 L5
Broadway	328 J6
Broadwick Street	319 H4
Brompton Road	326 F6
Brompton Square	326 E6
Brook Drive	329 L7
Brook Street	318 E4
Brook Street	319 G4
Brooke Street	321 L3
Browning Street	330 M8
Brownlow Street	320 K3
Brunswick Gardens	324 C5
Brunswick Place	322 N2
Brushfield Street	322 P3
Bruton Lane	327 H5
Bruton Place	319 H5
Bruton Street	319 H5
Bryanston Place	318 F3
Bryanston Square	318 F3
Bryanston Street	318 F4
Buckfast Street	323 Q2
Buckhurst Street	323 R3
Buckingham Gate	327 H6
Buckingham Palace Road	327 G7
Bucknall Street	320 J4
Bulleid Way	327 H7

Street	Ref
Great Eastern Street	322 N2
Great George Street	329 J6
Great Guildford Street	329 M5
Great James Street	320 K3
Great Marlborough Street	319 H4
Great New Street	321 L4
Great Ormond Street	320 K3
Great Percy Street	320 K2
Great Peter Street	328 J7
Great Portland Street	319 H3
Great Pulteney Street	319 H4
Great Queen Street	320 K4
Great Russell Street	320 J4
Great Scotland Yard	328 J5
Great Smith Street	328 J6
Great Suffolk Street	329 M5
Great Sutton Street	321 M3
Great Titchfield Street	319 H3
Great Tower Street	322 N4
Great Western Road	316 B3
Great Winchester Street	322 N4
Great Windmill Street	319 J4
Greatorex Street	323 Q3
Greek Street	320 J4
Green Bank	331 Q5
Green Street	318 G4
Greencoat Place	327 H7
Greenfield Road	323 Q3
Grendon Street	318 E2
Grenville Place	325 D7
Grenville Street	320 K3
Gresham Street	321 M4
Gresse Street	320 J3
Greville Street	321 L3
Grey Eagle Street	323 P3
Greycoat Place	327 J7
Greycoat Street	327 J7
Grosvenor Crescent	327 G6
Grosvenor Gardens	327 G6
Grosvenor Place	327 G6
Grosvenor Road	328 J8
Grosvenor Square	319 G4
Grosvenor Street	319 G4
Guildhouse Street	327 H7
Guilford Street	320 K3
Gunterstone Road	324 A7
Gunthorpe Street	323 P3
Gutter Lane	321 M4
Guy Street	330 N6

H

Street	Ref
Haberdasher Street	322 N2
Hackney Road	323 P2
Hainton Close	323 R4
Half Moon Street	327 H5
Halkin Street	327 G6
Hall Place	317 E3
Hall Road	317 D2
Hall Street	321 M2
Hallam Street	319 H3
Halsey Street	326 F7
Hamilton Place	327 G5
Hamilton Terrace	317 D1
Hammersmith Road	324 A7
Hampstead Road	319 H1
Hampton Street	329 M7
Hanbury Street	323 P3
Hanover Square	319 H4
Hanover Street	319 H4
Hans Crescent	326 F6
Hans Place	326 F6
Hans Road	326 F6
Hans Street	326 F7
Hanson Street	319 H3
Harbet Road	318 E3
Harcourt Street	318 F3
Hardwick Street	321 L2
Harewood Avenue	318 F3
Harley Street	319 G3
Harper Road	329 M6
Harriet Walk	326 F6
Harrington Gardens	325 D7
Harrington Road	325 F7
Harrison Street	320 K2
Harrow Road	316 B2
Harrowby Street	318 F4
Hart Street	322 P4
Hasker Street	326 F7
Hastings Street	320 J2
Hatfields	329 L5
Hatton Garden	321 L3
Hatton Place	321 L3
Hatton Wall	321 L3
Hay Hill	327 H5
Hayles Street	329 L7
Haymarket	328 M5
Hay's Mews	327 G5
Hazlitt Road	324 A7
Headfort Place	327 G6
Headlam Street	323 R3
Hemming Street	323 Q3
Heneage Street	323 P3
Henley Drive	331 P7
Henrietta Place	319 G4
Henriques Street	323 Q4
Henshaw Street	330 N7
Herald Street	323 R2
Herbal Hill	321 L3
Herbrand Street	320 J2
Hercules Road	328 L7
Hereford Mews	316 C4
Hereford Road	316 C4
Hereford Street	323 Q2
Herrick Street	327 G5
Hertford Street	327 G5
Hessel Street	323 Q4
Heygate Street	329 M7
Hide Place	328 J7
High Holborn	320 J4
Hill Road	317 D1
Hill Square	324 C5
Hill Street	327 G5
Hillgate Place	324 C5
Hillgate Street	324 C5
Hillsleigh Road	324 B5
Hippodrome Place	324 A5
Hobart Place	327 G7
Hogarth Road	325 C7
Holbein Place	326 G7
Holborn	321 L3
Holborn Circus	321 L3
Holborn Viaduct	321 L3
Holland Park	324 B5
Holland Park Gardens	324 A5
Holland Park Mews	324 B5
Holland Park Road	324 B7
Holland Road	324 A6
Holland Street	324 C6
Holland Street	329 M5
Holland Villas Road	324 A6
Holles Street	319 H4
Holyrood Street	330 N5
Holywell Lane	322 P2
Holywell Row	322 N3
Homer Street	318 F3
Hooper Street	323 P4
Hopton Street	329 M5
Horatio Street	323 P1
Hormead Road	316 B3
Hornton Street	324 C7
Horse Guards Avenue	328 J5
Horse Guards Road	328 J5
Horseferry Road	328 J7
Horseferry Road	328 J7
Horselydown Lane	330 P6
Hosier Lane	321 L3
Houndsditch	322 P4
Howick Place	327 H7
Howland Street	319 H3
Howley Place	317 D3
Hoxton Square	322 N2
Hoxton Street	322 P1
Hugh Street	327 G7
Humphrey Street	331 P8
Hunter Street	320 K2
Huntley Street	319 J3
Hunton Street	323 Q3
Hyde Park Corner	327 G6
Hyde Park Crescent	318 E4
Hyde Park Gardens	318 E4
Hyde Park Gate	325 D6
Hyde Park Square	318 E4
Hyde Park Street	318 E4

I

Street	Ref
Ilbert Street	316 A2
Ilchester Place	324 B6
Iliffe Street	329 M8
Imperial College Road	325 E7
Inglebert Street	321 L2
Ingram Close	328 K7
Inner Circle	318 G2
Inverness Place	317 D4
Inverness Terrace	317 D4
Ironmonger Lane	322 M4
Ironmonger Row	322 M2
Irving Street	328 J5
Iverna Court	324 C6
Iverna Gardens	324 C6
Ivor Place	318 F3
Ixworth Place	326 E7

J

Street	Ref
Jacob Street	331 P6
Jamaica Road	331 P6
James Street	319 G4
Jay Mews	325 D6
Jermyn Street	327 H5
Jerome Street	323 P3
Joan Street	329 L5
Jockey's Fields	320 K3
John Adam Street	328 K5
John Carpenter Street	321 L4
John Fisher Street	323 P4
John Islip Street	328 J8
John Princes Street	319 H4
John Street	320 K3
John's Mews	320 K3
Joiner Street	330 N5
Jonathan Street	328 K8
Jubilee Place	326 F8
Judd Street	320 J2

K

Street	Ref
Kean Street	320 K4
Keeton's Road	331 Q6
Kelso Place	325 C7
Kemble Street	320 K4
Kendal Street	318 F4
Kennings Way	329 L8
Kennington Lane	328 L8
Kennington Park Road	329 L8
Kennington Road	329 L6
Kensal Road	316 A2
Kensington Church Street	324 C5
Kensington Court	325 D6
Kensington Court Place	325 D6
Kensington Gardens Square	317 C4
Kensington Gate	325 D6
Kensington Gore	325 D6
Kensington High Street	324 B7
Kensington Palace Gardens	325 C5
Kensington Park Gardens	324 B5
Kensington Park Road	316 A4
Kensington Place	324 C5
Kensington Road	325 D6
Kensington Square	325 C6
Kenway Road	325 C7
Keyworth Street	329 K6
Kilburn Lane	316 A2
Kilburn Park Road	316 C2
Kildare Terrace	316 C4
Kilravock Street	316 A2
King & Queen Street	330 M8
King Charles Street	328 J6
King Edward Street	321 M4
King Edward Walk	329 L6
King James Street	329 M6
King Square	321 M2
King's Road	326 F8
King Street	320 J4
King Street	322 M4
King Street	327 H5
King William Street	322 N5
Kingly Street	319 H4
King's Cross Road	320 K2
Kingsland Road	322 P2
Kingsway	320 K4
Kinnerton Street	326 G6
Kipling Street	330 N6
Kirby Grove	330 N6
Kirby Street	321 L3
Knaresborough Place	325 C7
Knightrider Street	321 M4
Knightsbridge	326 F6
Kynance Mews	325 D7

L

Street	Ref
Lackington Street	322 N3
Ladbroke Gardens	316 B4
Ladbroke Grove	316 A3
Ladbroke Road	324 B5
Ladbroke Square	324 B5
Ladbroke Terrace	324 B5
Lafone Street	331 P6
Lamb Street	322 P3
Lambeth High Street	328 K7
Lambeth Hill	321 M4
Lambeth Palace Road	328 K7
Lambeth Road	329 L7
Lambeth Walk	328 K7

Norman Street	321 M2
North Audley Street	319 G4
North End Road	324 B7
North Gower Street	319 H2
North Row	318 G4
North Wharf Road	317 E3
Northampton Road	321 L2
Northampton Square	321 L2
Northburgh Street	321 M3
Northington Street	320 K3
Northumberland Avenue	328 J5
Northumberland Place	316 C4
Northwick Terrace	317 E2
Norwich Street	321 L4
Nottingham Street	318 G3
Notting Hill Gate	324 C5
Nutbourne Street	316 A2
Nutford Place	318 F4

O

Oakden Street	329 L7
Oakington Road	316 C2
Oakley Square	319 H1
Oakwood Court	324 B6
Old Bailey	321 L4
Old Bethnal Green Road	323 Q2
Old Bond Street	327 H5
Old Broad Street	322 N4
Old Brompton Road	324 C8
Old Burlington Street	319 H4
Old Castle Street	323 P3
Old Cavendish Street	319 H4
Old Compton Street	320 J4
Old Court Place	325 C6
Old Gloucester Street	320 K3
Old Jamaica Road	331 Q6
Old Jewry	322 N4
Old Kent Road	330 N7
Old Marylebone Road	318 F3
Old Montague Street	323 Q3
Old Paradise Street	328 K7
Old Park Lane	327 G5
Old Pye Street	328 J6
Old Queen Street	328 J6
Old Square	321 L4
Old Street	321 M2
Oldbury Place	319 G3
Olympia Way	324 B7
Onslow Gardens	325 E7
Onslow Square	325 E7
Ontario Street	329 M7
Orange Street	328 J5
Orb Street	330 N7
Orchard Street	318 G4
Orchardson Street	317 E3
Orde Hall Street	320 K3
Orme Court	325 C5
Orsett Street	328 K8
Orsett Terrace	317 D4
Osborn Street	323 P3
Osnaburgh Street	319 H3
Ossington Street	316 C5
Ossulston Street	320 J1
Oswin Street	329 M7
Outer Circle	318 F2
Ovington Gardens	326 F7
Ovington Street	326 F7
Oxford Square	318 F4
Oxford Street	318 G4

P

Paddington Green	317 E3
Paddington Street	318 G3
Page Street	328 J7
Page's Walk	330 N7
Pakenham Street	320 K2
Palace Gardens Terrace	324 C5
Palace Gate	325 D6
Palace Street	327 H6
Pall Mall	327 H5
Pall Mall East	328 J5
Palliser Road	324 A8
Pancras Road	320 J1
Panton Street	328 J5
Paradise Street	331 Q6
Pardoner Street	330 N6
Parfett Street	323 Q3
Paris Garden	329 L5
Park Crescent	319 G3
Park Lane	326 G5
Park Road	318 F2
Park Square East	319 G2
Park Square West	319 G3
Park Street	318 G4
Park Street	329 M5
Parker Street	320 K4
Parliament Square	328 J6
Parliament Street	328 J6
Paternoster Row	321 M4
Paul Street	322 N3
Paveley Street	318 F2
Pavilion Road	326 F6
Pearman Street	329 L6
Peartree Street	321 M2
Pedley Street	323 Q3
Peel Street	324 C5
Peerless Street	322 N2
Pelham Crescent	326 E7
Pelham Street	326 E7
Pelter Street	323 P2
Pemberton Row	321 L4
Pembridge Crescent	316 C4
Pembridge Gardens	316 C5
Pembridge Place	316 C4
Pembridge Road	316 C5
Pembridge Square	316 C5
Pembridge Villas	316 C4
Pembroke Gardens	324 B7
Pembroke Gardens Close	324 B7
Pembroke Road	324 B7
Pembroke Square	324 C7
Pembroke Villas	324 C7
Penang Street	331 R5
Penfold Street	318 E3
Pennington Street	331 Q5
Penton Place	329 M8
Penton Rise	320 K1
Pentonville Road	320 K2
Penywern Road	324 C8
Penzance Place	324 A5
Pepys Street	322 P4
Percival Street	321 L2
Percy Street	319 J3
Perkin's Rents	328 J6
Peter Street	319 H4
Peter's Hill	321 M4
Petersham Place	325 D6
Petty France	327 H6
Petyward	326 F7
Philbeach Gardens	324 C8
Phillimore Gardens	324 C6

Phillimore Place	324 C6
Phillimore Walk	324 C6
Philpot Lane	322 N4
Phipp Street	322 N2
Phoenix Place	321 K2
Phoenix Road	320 J2
Piccadilly	327 H5
Piccadilly Circus	319 H5
Pilgrimage Street	330 N6
Pimlico Road	326 G8
Pinchin Street	323 Q4
Pindar Street	322 N3
Pitt Street	324 C6
Plough Yard	322 P3
Plumbers Row	323 Q3
Pocock Street	329 L6
Poland Street	319 H4
Pollard Row	323 Q2
Pollard Street	323 Q2
Polygon Road	319 J1
Pond Place	326 E7
Ponsonby Place	328 J8
Pont Street	326 F7
Pont Street Mews	326 F7
Porchester Gardens	317 D4
Porchester Place	318 F4
Porchester Road	317 D4
Porlock Street	330 N6
Porter Street	330 M5
Portland Place	319 H3
Portland Street	330 N8
Portman Close	318 F4
Portman Square	318 G4
Portman Street	318 G4
Portnall Road	316 B2
Portobello Road	316 A3
Portsoken Street	323 P4
Portugal Street	320 K4
Potters Fields	330 P5
Poultry	322 N4
Powis Gardens	316 B4
Powis Place	320 K3
Powis Square	316 B4
Powis Terrace	316 B4
Poyser Street	323 R1
Praed Street	317 E4
Pratt Walk	328 K7
Prescot Street	323 P4
Prideaux Place	321 K2
Primrose Street	322 N3
Prince Albert Road	318 E2
Prince Consort Road	325 E6
Princedale Road	324 B5
Princelet Street	323 P3
Princes Gardens	325 F6
Princes Place	324 A5
Prince's Street	319 H4
Prince's Street	322 N4
Princeton Street	320 K3
Prioress Street	330 N7
Procter Street	320 K3
Provost Street	322 N1
Prusom Street	331 R5
Puddle Dock	321 M4
Punderson's Gardens	323 R2

Q

Quaker Street	323 P3
Queen Anne Street	319 G4
Queen Anne's Gate	328 J6
Queen Elizabeth Street	330 P6

Queen Square	320 K3
Queen Street Place	323 M5
Queen Street	322 M4
Queen Street	327 G5
Queen Victoria Street	321 L4
Queenhithe	322 M5
Queen's Gardens	317 D4
Queen's Gate Gardens	325 D7
Queen's Gate Place	325 D7
Queen's Gate Terrace	325 D6
Queen's Gat	325 D6
Queensberry Place	325 F7
Queensborough Terrace	317 D4
Queensbridge Road	323 P1
Queensdale Road	324 A5
Queensway	317 D4
Quilter Street	323 Q2

R

Radnor Mews	318 E4
Radnor Place	318 E4
Radnor Street	322 M2
Railway Approach	330 N5
Ramilles Place	319 H4
Rampayne Street	328 J8
Ramsey Street	323 Q2
Randolph Avenue	317 C1
Randolph Crescent	317 D3
Randolph Road	317 D3
Raphael Street	326 F6
Rathbone Place	319 J3
Rathbone Street	319 H3
Raven Row	323 R3
Ravenscroft Street	323 P1
Ravey Street	322 N2
Rawlings Street	326 F7
Rawstorne Street	321 L2
Ray Street	321 L3
Raymouth Road	331 R7
Reardon Path	331 R5
Reardon Street	331 Q5
Red Lion Square	320 K3
Red Lion Street	320 K3
Redan Place	317 C4
Redchurch Street	322 P2
Redcross Way	330 M6
Redfield Lane	324 C7
Redhill Street	319 H1
Reece Mews	325 E7
Reedworth Street	329 L7
Reeves Mews	327 G5
Regency Street	328 J7
Regent Square	20 K2
Regent Street	319 H4
Renfrew Road	329 L7
Rennie Street	329 L5
Reverdy Road	331 Q7
Richmond Terrace	328 J6
Ridgmount Street	320 J2
Riding House Street	319 H3
Riley Road	330 P6
River Street	321 L2
Rivington Street	322 N2
Robert Adam Street	318 G4
Robert Street	319 H2
Roberta Street	323 Q2
Rochester Row	327 H7
Rockingham Street	329 M7
Rodney Place	330 M7
Rodney Road	330 N7
Roger Street	320 K3

ACKNOWLEDGMENTS

Abbreviations for the credits are as follows:
AA = AA World Travel Library, t (top), b (bottom), c (centre), l (left), r (right)

UNDERSTANDING LONDON

5cl AA/S McBride; 5c AA/P Kenward; 5cr AA/R Mort; 6cl AA/R Mort; 6c AA/P Kenward; 6cr AA/M Jourdan; 7cl AA/G Wrona; 7c AA/J A Tims; 7cr AA/J A Tims; 10tl AA/P Kenward; 10tc AA/R Strange; 10tr AA; 10ct AA/M Jourdan; 10c AA; 10cr AA/M Jourdan; 10bl Digital Vision; 10bc AA; 11tl AA/W Voysey; 11tc Britain On View; 11clt AA; 11clb Britain On View; 11cr Britain On View; 11bl Lincoln House Hotel; 11bc Britain On View; 12tl Britain On View; 12tr Britain On View; 12cl AA/M Jourdan; 12crt AA/M Jourdan; 12crb AA/M Jourdan; 12b Britain On View.

LIVING LONDON

13 AA/S McBride; 14/15 bg AA/S McBride; 14tl AA/M Jourdan; 14tr AA/M Jourdan; 14c AA/S McBride; 14cr AA/M Jourdan; 14clb AA/M Jourdan; 14b Clive Totman/Corporation of London; 15t AA/M Jourdan; 15ct AA/M Jourdan; 15cl Patak's Spices; 15c AA/M Jourdan; 15cr Rex Features Ltd; 16/17bg Empics Ltd; 16t Empics Ltd; 16cl Empics Ltd; 16cr AA/M Jourdan; 16b AA/A Kouprianoff; 17t WSDL; 17cl London Marathon Ltd; 17cr AA; 17b Empics Ltd; 18/19bg AA/S McBride; 18t AA/M Jourdan; 18cl AA/M Jourdan; 18cr Rex Features Ltd; 18b Rex Features Ltd; 19tl Guards Polo Club; 19tr Rex Features Ltd; 19cl AA/R Victor; 19c AA/L Allen; 19cr The Royal Collection © 2003 Her Majesty Queen Elizabeth II; 20/21bg AA/M Jourdan; 20tc AA/S McBride; 20tr AA/M Jourdan; 20cl Britain On View; 20cr Rex Features Ltd; 20cb AA/M Jourdan; 20b AA/M Jourdan; 21tc AA/M Jourdan; 21tr AA/M Jourdan; 21cl AA/S McBride; 21cb Skyline view from south of the river, Photomontage by Smoothe; 22/23bg AA/S & O Mathews; 22t AA; 22cl Number 10 Downing Street; 22c Houses of Parliament Information Service; 22cr Britain On View; 23tl AA/T Woodcock; 23tr Britain On View; 23c Clive Totman/Corporation of London; 23c Greater London Authority/Melanie Cox; 23b Rex Features Ltd; 24bg Britain On View; 24tl AA/J Miller; 24tr Britain On View/Doug McKinlay; 24cl Photodisc; 24c Photodisc; 24cr AA.

THE STORY OF LONDON

25 Illustrated London News; 26/27bg AA/P Kenward; 26cl AA/T Woodcock; 26c AA/T Woodcock; 26cr AA/T Woodcock; 26bl AA; 26/27 AA/P Kenward; 27cl AA; 27cr AA 27b AA/S & O Mathews; 28/29bg AA; 28tl AA; 28tr AA; 28bl AA; 28/29 AA; 29tl AA; 29tc AA/J Welsh; 29tr AA; 29bc AA/P Kenward; 29br AA; 30/31bg AA/R Strange; 30cl AA 30cr AA; 30bl AA; 30/31 AA/R Strange; 31cl AA; 31cr AA; 31bc AA/S & O Mathews; 31br AA; 32/33bg AA; 32cl AA; 32cr AA/P Wilson; 32bl AA; 32/33 AA; 33cl AA; 33c AA; 33cr AA; 33bl AA/P Wilson; 33br AA/P Kenward; 34/35bg AA/ M Trelawney; 34cl Britain On View; 34cr AA; 34bl AA/G Wrona; 34/35 AA/M Trelawney; 35cl AA; 35c Illustrated London News; 35cr AA; 35bl AA/P Kenward; 35bc Illustrated London News; 35br AA; 36/37bg Mary Evans Picture Library; 36cl AA; 36c AA; 36bl AA/M Trelawney; 36/37 AA; 37cl AA/P Kenward; 37c Illustrated London News; 37cr Illustrated London News; 37bl AA/M Jourdan; 37br Illustrated London News; 38/39bg AA/S Gibson; 38cl Illustrated London News; 38c Illustrated London News; 38cr Illustrated London News; 38bl Hulton Archive/Getty Images; 38/39 Hulton Archive/Getty Images; 39cl Illustrated London News; 39c Hulton Archive/Getty Images; 39bl Rex Features Ltd; 39bc Rex Features Ltd; 39br AA/R Strange; 40bg AA/M Jourdan; 40cl Britain On View; 40cr Rex Features Ltd; 40b Rex Features Ltd.

ON THE MOVE

41 AA/M Jourdan; 42 Digital Vision; 43 Digital Vision; 44 Digital Vision; 45t AA/M Jourdan; 45c AA/S McBride; 46 Digital Vision; 47 Digital Vision; 48 AA/B Smith; 49t AA/B Smith; 49c AA/M Jourdan; 50t AA/B Smith; 50c Britain On View; 51 AA/B Smith; 52 AA/M Jourdan; 53t AA/M Jourdan; 53c AA/M Jourdan; 54t AA/M Jourdan; 54cl AA/M Jourdan; 54cr AA/W Voysey; 55t AA/M Jourdan; 55b AA/W Voysey; 56t Britain On View; 56cl AA/B Smith; 56cr Britain On View; 57t AA/M Jourdan; 57cr AA/M Jourdan; 57cl AA; 58 Digital Vision; 59 Digital Vision; 60 Digital Vision; 61 Digital Vision; 62 Digital Vision; 63 Digital Vision; 64 AA/S McBride.

THE SIGHTS

65 AA/R Victor; 70cl Britain On View; 70cr AA/J A Tims; 71cl AA/T Woodcock; 71cr Britain On View; 72cl AA/R Victor; 72cr AA/J A Tims; 73cl AA/J McMillan; 73cr AA/R Mort; 74cl AA/R Turpin; 74cr AA/S McBride; 75cl AA/R Victor; 75cr AA/S Gibson; 76t Britain On View; 76tc AA/P Kenward; 76tr AA; 77tl AA/J A Tims; 77tc AA/J A Tims; 77tr Bramah Tea and Coffee Museum; 77b Britain On View; 78tl Hulton Archive/Getty Images; 78tc AA/J A Tims; 78tr AA/T Woodcock; 79t AA/M Jourdan; 79tr AA/J McMillan; 79c The Royal Collection © 2003 Her Majesty Queen Elizabeth II; 80 © British Museum; 81t AA/R Strange; 81cl AA/G Wrona; 81c AA; 81cr AA/M Jourdan; 82cl AA; 82c AA; 82cr AA; 83 AA; 84 main © British Museum; 84t Britain On View; 84c AA; 84b AA/M Trelawney; 85 © British Museum; 86tl Britain On View; 86tc Imperial War Museum; 86tr AA/P Kenward; 87tl Dali Universe © Richard Price; 87tc AA/J A Tims; 87tr Design Museum © Jefferson Hack; 87b Britain On View/Doug McKinlay; 88t AA/M Jourdan; 88c Britain On View; 88b AA; 89tl AA; 89tc AA/P Kenward; 89tr AA/P Wilson; 90tl AA/J McMillan; 90tr The Handel House Trust Ltd; 91t AA/S McBride; 91c AA/S McBride; 92t Houses of Parliament Information Service; 92cl Britain On View; 92cr AA/W Voysey; 93tl AA/R Strange; 93tr AA/M Trelawney; 94t AA/R Strange; 94c AA/J A Tims; 95t AA/P Kenward; 95c AA/P Kenward; 96t AA/B Strange; 96cl AA/B Strange; 96c AA/M Trelawney; 97tl AA/M Jourdan; 97tc AA/R Mort; 97tr AA/P Kenward; 97b AA/M Jourdan; 98tc London Aquarium; 98tc AA/P Kenward; 98tr London Dungeon (Merlin Entertainments Group Ltd) 99 AA/M Moody; 100tl Britain On View; 100tc AA/P Kenward; 100tr AA/M Jourdan; 101t Madame Tussauds; 101tr AA/P Kenward; 101cr AA/P Kenward; 102tl AA/R Strange; 102tc AA/M Trelawney; 102tr Britain On View; 102b Britain On View; 103t Britain On View; 103c AA/T Woodcock; 104 AA/J A Tims; 105t AA; 105cl Britain On View; 105c AA/M Jourdan; 105cr AA/R Strange; 105b The Portrait of Giovanni Arnolfini and his Wife Giovanna Cenami (The Arnolfini Marriage) 1434 by Jan van Eyck (c1390–1441) National Gallery, London, UK/Bridgeman Art Library; 106 Venus and Mars, c. 1485 by Sandro Botticellin (1444/5-1510) National Gallery, London, UK/Bridgeman Art Library; 107 The National Gallery, London; 108tl AA/J A Tims; 108tr Sunflowers, 1888 by Vincent van Gogh (1853–90) National Gallery, London, UK/Bridgeman Art Library; 108b The Beach at Trouville, 1870 by Claude Monet (1840–1926) National Gallery, London UK/Bridgeman Art Library; 109 The 'Fighting Termeraire' Tugged to her Last Berth to be Broken up, before 1839 by Joseph Mallord William Turner (1775–1851) National Gallery, London UK/Bridgeman Art Library; 110t National Portrait Gallery/©Dennis Gilbert/View; 110l AA/R Turpin; 110/111 Andrew Putland/National Portrait Gallery; 111c © National Portrait Gallery; 111r Andrew Putland/National Portrait Gallery; 112t AA/B Smith; 112l AA/M Jourdan; 113t AA/M Jourdan; 113cld AA/M Jourdan; 113cl AA/M Jourdan; 113cr AA/R Strange; 113rcr AA/R Strange; 114tl Petrie Museum of Egyptian Archaeology; 114tc AA/M Jourdan; 114tr AA/R Strange; 114b AA/P Baker; 115tl AA/S McBride; 115tr AA/M Jourdan; 116tl AA/P Wilson; 116tc AA/R Strange; 116tr AA/P Kenward; 117tl AA/P Wilson; 117tc AA/R Victor; 117tr AA/R Strange; 117b AA/P Enticknap; 118 AA/J A Tims; 119t AA/M Jourdan; 119cl AA/S McBride; 119c AA/R Strange; 119cr AA/R Strange; 120cl AA/R Strange; 120c AA/R Strange; 120cr AA/J A Tims; 121 AA/B Smith; 122tl AA/R Strange; 122tr AA/P Baker; 122b AA/R Strange; 123 AA/R Strange; 124t AA/J A Tims; 124cl Science Museum; 124cr Science Museum; 125t Science Museum; 125r Science Museum; 126l Globe Theatre/Richard Kalina; 126r AA/R Turpin; 127tl AA/R Strange; 127tc AA/M Jourdan; 127tr AA/R Turpin; 128t Sir John Soane's Museum; 128cl AA/ JA Tims; 128cr Sir John Soane's Museum; 128b Sir John Soane's Museum/Martin Charles; 129 AA/J A Tims; 130t AA/M Jourdan; 130cr AA/M Jourdan; 131t AA/M Jourdan; 131cl The

Courtauld Institute Gallery, Somerset House, London; 131c AA/M Jourdan; 132t Tate. Presented anonymously 1955; 132l Britain On View; 133t Tate. Bequeathed by Miss Isabel Constable as the gift of Maria Louisa, Isabel and Lionel Bicknell Constable 1888; 133cr Tate. Bequeathed by the Artist 1856; 133c Tate. Purchased with assistance from the National Lottery through the Heritage Lottery Fund, and from the National Arts Collections Fund 1996 © Estate of J Epstein; 134t AA/M Jourdan; 134l AA/M Jourdan; 134r AA/S McBride; 135cl AA/S McBride; 135c AA/M Jourdan; 135cr AA/S McBride; 135b AA/M Jourdan; 136tl AA; 136tc AA/P Kenward; 136tr AA/J McMillan; 136b AA/R Strange; 137 AA/M Jourdan; 138 Britain On View; 139t AA/S McBride; 139cl Britain On View; 139c Britain On View; 139r AA/S McBride; 140/141 AA/S McBride; 140c AA/S McBride; 140b Britain On View; 142cl Britain On View; 142c AA/W Voysey; 142cr AA/S McBride; 143l Britain On View; 143r AA/S McBride; 144t Victoria & Albert Museum; 144cl AA/G Wrona; 144c AA/R Strange; 144cr AA/J A Tims; 145 Victoria & Albert Museum; 146t Britain On View; 146b Victoria & Albert Museum; 148/149 Victoria & Albert Museum; 148b Victoria & Albert Museum; 149t Britain On View; 149b Victoria & Albert Museum; 150l By kind permission of the Trustees of the Wallace Collection; 150r AA/P Kenward; 151tl AA/S McBride; 151tc AA/R Elliott; 151tr AA/M Jourdan; 152t AA; 152cl AA/R Strange; 152cr Britain On View; 152b AA/R Strange; 153c AA/J A Tims; 153r Britain On View; 154tl AA/R Turpin; 154tc AA/M Trelawney; 154tr AA/M Trelawney; 155tl AA/R Mort; 155tc Dulwich Picture Gallery; 155tr AA/S & O Mathews; 155b Dulwich Picture Gallery; 156t AA; 156cl AA/R Turpin; 156cr AA/T Woodcock; 157t Britain On View; 157c AA/M Jourdan; 157b AA/S & O Mathews; 158tl AA/M Trelawney; 158tc AA/M Trelawney; 158tr AA/M Trelawney; 159t AA/R Turpin; 159c AA/R Turpin; 160tl AA/M Trelawney; 160tc Britain On View; 160tr Britain On View; 161tl AA/P Kenward; 161tc AA/R Strange; 161tr AA/R Strange; 162tl AA/M Trelawney; 162tc Britain On View; 162tr AA/P Kenward; 163t AA/R Mort; 163c AA/R Mort; 163b AA/W Voysey; 164tl AA/M Trelawney; 164tc AA/B Smith.

WHAT TO DO

165 Photodisc; 170t Britain On View; 170ct Britain On View; 170cl Britain On View; 170cr Britain On View; 171cl Cologne and Cotton; 171cr Britain On View; 172cl Jo Malone; 172cr VV Rouleaux; 173cl Harvey Nichols; 173c Jimmy Choo; 173cr Jimmy Choo; 174cl Selfridges; 174cr AA; 175cl Neals Yard Remedies; 175cr Ted Baker; 176t Selfridges; 176c Wills Art Warehouse; 176cr AA/J A Tims; 176br Books for Cooks; 177t Selfridges; 177cr Britain On View; 178t Selfridges; 178cl Young England; 178c Britain On View; 178b Selfridges; 179t Selfridges; 179cl AA/P Kenward; 179cr Britain On View; 180t Selfridges; 180tr AA/R Strange; 180cl Britain On View; 180c AA/M Trelawney; 180br Halcyon Days; 181t Selfridges; 181c Christopher Wray Lighting – www.christopherwray.com; 182t Selfridges; 182tr AA; 182c Janet Reger; 182br Britain On View; 183t Selfridges; 183c Footes; 183cr AA/R Strange; 184t Selfridges; 184c AA/C Sawyer; 185t Selfridge's; 185c AA/C Sawyer186t Selfridges; 186cl AA/M Trelawney; 186c Paperchase Ltd; 187t Digital Vision; 187cl Digital Vision; 187cr Digital Vision; 192t AA/M Jourdan; 192c AA/M Jourdan; 193t AA/M Jourdan; 193c Odeon; 194t Digital Vision; 194c Royal Academy of Music; 194b AA/P Kenward; 195t Digital Vision; 195tl Royal Albert Hall; 195bl Sadlers Wells Theatre; 195tc Royal Festival Hall; 196t Digital Vision; 196tr Earls Court and Olympia Group; 197t Digital Vision; 197tl Ocean Rock Venue; 197tc Digital Vision; 198t Britain On View; 198b Britain On View; 199t Britain On View; 199tc Britain On View; 199ct AA/M Jourdan; 199c Britain On View; 200t Britain On View; 200c AA/M Jourdan; 201t Britain On View; 201cl AA/R Strange; 201cr AA/M Jourdan; 202t The Red Rooms; 202c Brand X Pictures; 202b The Comedy Store; 203t The Red Rooms; 203tl Britain On View; 203b Britain On View; 204t The Red Rooms; 204cl Britain On View; 204c Brand X Pictures; 204cr Brand X Pictures; 204b Notting Hill Arts Club/Jorn G. Tomter; 205t The Red Rooms; 205bl Canal Café Theatre; 205bc The Comedy Store; 105br Jongleurs; 206t The Red Rooms; 206tr Fluid Bar; 206c Brand X Pictures; 206b Britain On View; 207t The Red Rooms; 207tc Fridge Nightclub; 207bl Britain On View; 207bc Brand X Pictures; 208t The Red Rooms; 208cl Fridge Nightclub; 208c

Britain On View; 209t AA/C Jones; 209cl Britain On View; 209cr The All England Lawn Tennis Club; 210t AA/C Jones; 210tl Photodisc; 210cl Photodisc; 210c Photodisc; 211t AA/C Jones; 211bc AA/C Jones; 211br AA/S McBride; 212t AA/C Jones; 212tc Kempton Park Racecourse; 212bl Britain On View; 212bc Photodisc; 213t AA/C Jones; 213c Photodisc; 213b The All England Lawn Tennis Club; 214t Photodisc; 214tl Britain On View; 214tr AA/C Jones; 214c Lee Valley Regional Park Authority; 214cr AA/M Trelawney; 215t Photodisc; 215c AA/M Jourdan; 216t Photodisc; 216b Photodisc; 217t Image 100; 217c Image 100; 217b Bliss London; 218t Image 100; 218c Berkeley Health Club and Spa/The Savoy Group; 219t Digital Vision; 219tr AA/M Jourdan; 219b Namco; 220t Digital Vision; 220c AA/B Smith; 221t Digital Vision ; 221tl AA/W Voysey; 221tr AA/P Kenward; 222t Britain On View; 222c Britain On View; 222cr Britain On View; 222b Britain On View; 223t Britain On View; 223c AA/L Allen; 223b Britain On View; 224t Britain On View; 224c Britain On View.

OUT AND ABOUT

225 AA/R Strange; 226t Britain On View; 227tl AA/P Baker; 227tr AA/R Turpin; 227cl AA/M Jourdan; 227cr AA/R Turpin; 227b AA/B Smith; 228 AA/R Mort; 229tl AA/B Smith; 229tr AA/W Voysey; 229cr AA/R Turpin; 229cr AA/R Turpin; 229b AA/S McBride; 231tl AA/R Victor; 231tr AA/T Woodcock; 231c AA/M Jourdan; 231cb AA/R Turpin; 231t AA/R Turpin; 232 AA/R Strange; 233tl AA/T Woodcock; 233tr AA/P Kenward; 233cb AA/R Turpin; 233b AA/R Turpin; 234 Britain On View; 235t Britain On View; 235cr Britain On View; 235cb Britain On View; 235b Britain On View; 236c AA/R Strange; 236b AA/J Miller; 237tl AA/R Strange; 237tr AA/W Voysey, by permission of the Dean and Canons of Windsor; 237c AA/W Voysey; 237b AA/J Miller; 238 AA/C Jones; 239t AA/S & O Mathews; 239cl AA/A Lawson; 239cr AA/C Jones; 239b AA/A Lawson; 240 AA/E Meacher; 241t AA/E Meacher; 241cl AA/E Meacher; 241cr AA/S Day; 241b AA/C Jones; 242cl AA/W Voysey; 242c AA/M Jourdan; 242cr AA.

EATING

243 AA/C Sawyer; 248lcl AA/C Sawyer; 248cl Britain On View; 248cr Britain On View; 248rcr AA/C Sawyer; 249t AA; 249b AA; 250 AA/M Jourdan; 251 Britain On View; 252tr AA/W Voysey; 252c AA/W Voysey; 253 AA/W Voysey; 255tl AA/W Voysey; 255cr AA/W Voysey; 255br AA/W Voysey; 258cr AA/W Voysey; 258cb AA/W Voysey; 260cr AA/W Voysey; 260bc AA/W Voysey; 261tr AA/W Voysey; 262bc AA/W Voysey; 263 AA/W Voysey; 266tr AA/W Voysey; 266c AA/W Voysey; 266bl Britain On View; 267tl AA/W Voysey; 267tc AA/W Voysey; 267b AA/W Voysey; 268tl AA/W Voysey; 268tc AA; 268b AA/W Voysey; 269tr AA/W Voysey; 269b AA/R Victor; 270tl AA/W Voysey; 270tr AA/W Voysey; 270b AA/W Voysey; 271tr AA/P Wilson; 271cb Britain On View.

STAYING

273 AA/C Sawyer; 278cl AA/C Sawyer; 278cr AA/C Sawyer.

PLANNING

293 AA/C Sawyer; 295 AA; 298c AA/R Strange; 299 AA/R Strange; 301 AA/JA Tims; 302 AA/A Kouprianoff; 303c AA/R Strange; 303b AA/JA Tims; 304 AA/JA Tims.

Project editor
Rebecca Snelling

Interior Design
David Austin, Glyn Barlow, Alan Gooch, Kate Harling, Bob Johnson,
Nick Otway, Carole Philp, Keith Russell

Picture research
Vivien Little

Cover design
Tigist Getachew

Internal repro work
Michael Moody, Ian Little, Susan Crowhurst

Production
Lyn Kirby, Caroline Nyman

Mapping
Maps produced by the Cartography Department of AA Publishing

Main contributors
Judith Bamber, Richard Cavendish, Colin Follett, Stephen Frost, Tim Locke, John Mabbett,
Heather Morley, Michael Nation, Nia Williams

Copy editor
Nia Williams

ISBN 1-4000-1389-5

Published in the United States by Fodor's Travel Publications and simultaneously in Canada by
Random House of Canada Limited, Toronto.
Published in the United Kingdom by AA Publishing.

Fodor's is a registered trademark of Random House, Inc., and Fodor's See It
is a trademark of Random House, Inc.
Fodor's Travel Publications is a division of Fodor's LLC.

Color separation by Keenes
Printed and bound by Leo, China
10 9 8 7 6 5 4 3 2

Special Sales: Fodor's Travel Publications are available at special discounts for bulk purchases for
sales promotions or premiums. Special editions, including personalized covers, excerpts of existing
guides, and corporate imprints, can be created in large quantities for special needs. For more
information, contact your local bookseller or write to Special Marketing, Fodor's Travel Publications,
1745 Broadway, New York, NY 10019. Inquiries from Canada should be directed to your local
Canadian bookseller or sent to Random House of Canada, Ltd., Marketing Department,
2775 Matheson Blvd. East, Mississauga, Ontario L4W 4P7.

A02293

Ordnance Survey This product includes mapping data licensed from Ordnance Survey® with the
permission of the Controller of Her Majesty's Stationery Office. © Crown copyright
2004. All rights reserved. Licence number 399221.
Traffic signs © Crown copyright. Reproduced with the permission of the Controller of
Her Majesty's Stationery Office.
Weathercharts © Copyright 2004 Canty and Associates, LLC.

Important Note: Time inevitably brings changes, so always confirm prices, travel facts, and
other perishable information when it matters. Although Fodor's cannot accept responsibility
for errors, you can use this guide in the confidence that we have taken every care to ensure
its accuracy.

Fodor's Key to the Guides

AMERICA'S **GUIDEBOOK LEADER** PUBLISHES GUIDES FOR **EVERY KIND OF TRAVELER**. CHECK OUT OUR MANY SERIES AND FIND YOUR **PERFECT MATCH**.

FODOR'S GOLD GUIDES
America's favorite travel-guide series offers the most detailed insider reviews of hotels, restaurants, and attractions in all price ranges, plus great background information, smart tips, and useful maps.

COMPASS AMERICAN GUIDES
Stunning guides from top local writers and photographers, with gorgeous photos, literary excerpts, and colorful anecdotes. A must-have for culture mavens, history buffs, and new residents.

FODOR'S CITYPACKS
Concise city coverage in a guide plus a foldout map. The right choice for urban travelers who want everything under one cover.

FODOR'S WHERE TO WEEKEND
A fresh take on weekending, this series identifies the best places to escape outside the city and details loads of rejuvenating activities as well as cool places to stay, great restaurants, and practical information.

FODOR'S AROUND THE CITY WITH KIDS
Up to 68 great ideas for family days, recommended by resident parents. Perfect for exploring in your own backyard or on the road.

FODOR'S TRAVEL HISTORIC AMERICA
For travelers who want to experience history firsthand, this series gives in-depth coverage of historic sights, plus nearby restaurants and hotels. Themes include the Thirteen Colonies, the Old West, and the Lewis and Clark Trail.

FODOR'S FLASHMAPS
Every resident's map guide, with 60 easy-to-follow maps of public transit, parks, museums, zip codes, and more.

FODOR'S LANGUAGES FOR TRAVELERS
Practice the local language before you hit the road. Available in phrase books, cassette sets, and CD sets.

THE COLLECTED TRAVELER
These collections of the best published essays and articles on various European destinations will give you a feel for the culture, cuisine, and way of life.

FODOR'S HOW TO GUIDES
Get tips from the pros on planning the perfect trip. Learn how to pack, fly hassle-free, plan a honeymoon or cruise, stay healthy on the road, and travel with your baby.

KAREN BROWN'S GUIDES
Engaging guides—many with easy-to-follow inn-to-inn itineraries—to the most charming inns and B&Bs in the U.S.A. and Europe.

BAEDEKER'S GUIDES
Comprehensive guides, trusted since 1829, packed with A–Z reviews and star ratings.

OTHER GREAT TITLES FROM FODOR'S
Baseball Vacations, The Complete Guide to the National Parks, Family Vacations, Golf Digest's Places to Play, Great American Drives of the East, Great American Drives of the West, Great American Vacations, Healthy Escapes, National Parks of the West, Skiing USA.

Dear Traveler

From buying a plane ticket to booking a room and seeing the sights, a trip goes much more smoothly when you have a good travel guide. Dozens of writers, editors, designers, and cartographers have worked hard to make the book you hold in your hands a good one. Was it everything you expected? Were our descriptions accurate? Were our recommendations on target? And did you find our tips and practical advice helpful? Your ideas and experiences matter to us. If we have missed or misstated something, we'd love to hear about it. Fill out our survey at www.fodors.com/books/feedback/, or e-mail us at seeit@fodors.com. Or you can snail mail to the See It Editor at Fodor's, 1745 Broadway, New York, New York 10019. We'll look forward to hearing from you.

Karen Cure
Editorial Director